INTRODUCTION

This book has been compiled for the purpose of serving as a research tool for locating the men and women of St. Mary's and Calvert Counties, Maryland, who served in the military, rendered material aid to the army or navy, took the Oath of Allegiance and Fidelity, served in an office or on a committee at the town, county or state level, or in some fashion contributed and supported the fight for freedom by the American colonies from the rule of Great Britain during the Revolutionary War, 1775-1783.

Information has been gleaned from many primary and secondary sources, making this book far more than just a listing of names and ranks. Most of the approximately 4,000 persons named herein also have genealogical data included with their respective entries, such as places of residence and dates of birth, death, and marriage, names of wives, husbands, children, and other relatives, physical descriptions, occupations, and information gleaned from military, pension, probate, and other court records. It is hoped that this source book, which is the eighth in a series on the Revolutionary Patriots of Maryland, will encourage and enable interested persons to become members of patriotic organizations like The Sons of the American Revolution, The Daughters of the American Revolution, The Sons of the Revolution, and The Society of the Cincinnati.

Each entry in this book has been documented and a key to that documentation has been implemented within the text to enable the reader to review the cited source. A letter followed by a number is the code used for a source and the page within that source. For example, "Ref: D-555" indicates that the information can be found in "Archives of Maryland, Volume 18, page 555." Coded sources cited in this book are as follows:

A = *Archives of Maryland, Volume XI*. "Journal of the Maryland Convention, July 26, 1775 - August 14, 1775, and Journal and Correspondence of the Maryland Council of Safety, August 29, 1775 - July 6, 1776" (Baltimore: Maryland Historical Society, 1892)

B = *Archives of Maryland, Volume XII*. "Journal and Correspondence of the Maryland Council of Safety, July 7, 1776 - December 31, 1776" (Baltimore: Maryland Historical Society, 1893)

C = *Archives of Maryland, Volume XVI*. "Journal and Correspondence of the Council of Safety, January 1, 1777 - March 20, 1777" and "Journal and Correspondence of the State Council, March 20, 1777 - March 28, 1778" (Baltimore: Maryland Historical Society, 1897)

D = *Archives of Maryland, Volume XVIII*. "Muster Rolls and Other Records of Service of Maryland Troops in the American Revolution, 1775-1783" (Baltimore: Maryland Historical Society, 1900)

E = *Archives of Maryland, Volume XXI*. "Journal and Correspondence of the Council of Maryland, April 1, 1778 - October 26, 1779" (Baltimore: Maryland Historical Society, 1901)

F = *Archives of Maryland, Volume XLIII*. "Journal and Correspondence of the State Council of Maryland, 1779-1780" (Baltimore: Maryland Historical Society, 1924)

G = *Archives of Maryland, Volume XLV*. "Journal and Correspondence of the State Council of Maryland, 1780-1781" (Baltimore: Maryland Historical Society, 1927)

H = *Archives of Maryland, Volume XLVIII*. "Journal and Correspondence of the State Council of Maryland, 1781-1784" (Baltimore: Maryland Historical Society, 1931)

HG = Ridgely, Helen W. *Historic Graves of Maryland and the District of Columbia* (Westminster: Family Line Publications, 1992, reprint)

I = Brumbaugh, Gaius M. *Maryland Records: Colonial, Revolutionary, County and Church From Original Sources, Volume II* (Baltimore: Genealogical Publishing Company, Inc., 1985, reprint)

J = *Revolutionary War Military Collection, Manuscript MS.1146* (Baltimore: Maryland Historical Society, Manuscript Division)

K = Carothers, Bettie. *9000 Men Who Took the Oath of Allegiance and Fidelity to Maryland During the Revolution* (Lutherville, Maryland: Compiled by the Author, 1978, 2 volumes)

L = Carothers, Bettie. *Maryland Source Records, Volume I* (Lutherville, Maryland: Compiled by the Author, 1975)

M = Clements, S. Eugene and Wright, F. Edward. *The Maryland Militia in the Revolutionary War* (Silver Spring, Maryland: Family Line Publications, 1987)

MB = "Register of St. Andrew's (Anglican) Church of St. Mary's County," *Maryland Genealogical Society Bulletin*, Volume 35, No. 3 (Summer, 1994), pp. 379-387

MC = Peden, Henry C. Jr. *Marylanders to Carolina: Migration of Marylanders to North Carolina and South Carolina Prior to 1800* (Westminster, Maryland: Family Line Publications, 1994)

MK = Peden, Henry C. Jr. *Marylanders to Kentucky, 1775-1825* (Westminster, Maryland: Family Line Publications, 1991)

MM = Barnes, Robert W. *Maryland Marriages, 1778-1800* (Baltimore: Genealogical Publishing Company, Inc., 1979)

MR = Richardson, Albert Levin, ed. *The Maryland Original Research Society of Baltimore*. "Revolutionary Committees of Importance in St. Mary's County," by Hester Dorsey Richardson, Bulletin No. 3, 1913 (Baltimore: Genealogical Publishing Company, 1973, reprint)

N = Papenfuse, Edward, et al. *A Biographical Dictionary of the Maryland Legislature, 1635-1789* (Baltimore: Johns Hopkins Press, 1979)

O = O'Brien, Mildred B. *Calvert County, Maryland Family Records, 1670-1929*, "Christ Church Register" (Privately published by the Calvert County Genealogy Newsletter, Sunderland, Maryland, 1978)

P = White, Virgil D. *Genealogical Abstracts of Revolutionary War Pension Files* (Waynesboro, Tennessee: The National Historical Publishing Company, 1990, 4 volumes)

Q = "Some Little Known Data Regarding Maryland Signers of the Oath of Fidelity," by Richard B. Miller, *Maryland Genealogical Society Bulletin*, Volume 27, No. 1 (Winter, 1986), pp. 101-124

R = Fresco, Margaret E. *Marriages and Deaths of St. Mary's County, Maryland, 1634-1900* (Ridge, Maryland: Published by Author, 1982)

S = Beitzell, Edwin W. *Calendar of Events in St. Mary's County in the American Revolution* (Leonardtown, Maryland: St. Mary's County, Maryland Bicentennial Commission, 1975)

SC = O'Rourke, Timothy J. *Catholic Families of Southern Maryland* (Baltimore: Genealogical Publishing Company, Inc., 1985)

SM = *Chronicles of St. Mary's: Monthly Bulletin of the St. Mary's County Historical Society*, Volume 24, Nos. 1, 4, 5, and 9 (1976)

SO = St. Mary's County Orphans Court Proceedings, 1777-1801 (Also published in the *Chronicles of St. Mary's*, Volumes 34, 35, and 36)

T = *Revolutionary War Military Collection, Manuscript MS.1814* (Baltimore: Maryland Historical Society, Manuscript Division)

U = *Maryland Pension Rolls of 1835: Report from the Secretary of War in Relation to the Pension Establishment of the United States* (Baltimore: Genealogical Publishing Company, Inc., 1968, reprint)

V = Papenfuse, Edward, et al. *An Inventory of Maryland State Papers, Volume I*, "The Era of the American Revolution, 1775-1789" (Annapolis: Hall of Records Commission, 1977)

W = Burns, Annie W. *Maryland Soldiers of the Revolutionary War Who Settled in Kentucky* (Baltimore: Compiled by the Author, 1939)

X = Hammett, Regina C. *History of St. Mary's County, Maryland* (Ridge, Maryland: Published by the Author, 1977)

Y = *DAR Patriot Index, Volume I* (Washington, D. C.: National Society of the Daughters of the American Revolution, 1966)

Z = Newman, Harry W. *Maryland Revolutionary Records* (Baltimore: Genealogical Publishing Company, Inc., 1980, reprint)

It must be noted that it is not possible to know who all of the patriots and soldiers were who served in or from Calvert and St. Mary's Counties during the entire Revolutionary War. This is especially true for those who joined the Maryland Line and served in the Continental Army. Due to the constant reorganization of the Maryland troops during the war, it is not easily determinable which soldier served from which county. Apparently, many from St. Mary's County served in the 1st and 2nd Maryland Regiments and many from Calvert County served in the 3rd and 4th Maryland Regiments.

It is possible that some patriots may have been inadvertently omitted from this book. Therefore, one should check the many lists found in the *Archives of Maryland, Volume 18*, for perhaps even more names.

Henry C. Peden, Jr.
Bel Air, Maryland
September 1, 1996

CALVERT AND ST. MARY'S COUNTIES

1795

REVOLUTIONARY PATRIOTS OF CALVERT
AND ST. MARY'S COUNTIES, MARYLAND 1775-1783

ABBOTT, John. Private, St. Mary's County, who served in the 5th Maryland Line until discharged in 1781 [Ref: D-273, D-406].

ABELL, Aaron. Private, Calvert County, enlisted by Lt. Nathaniel Wilson on Aug. 23, 1776 [Ref: D-34, S-146]. Private, St. Mary's County Militia, 1777 [Ref: M-213, SM-110].

ABELL, Alethia. See "Benedict Spalding," q.v.

ABELL, Ann Draden. See "William Russell," q.v.

ABELL, Arthur. Private, St. Mary's County Militia, 1777 [Ref: M-211]. Took the Oath of Allegiance before the Hon. Richard Barnes in St. Mary's County in 1778 [Ref: J-1146, K-66]. The Register of St. Andrew's Episcopal Church states Arthur Abell and Henrietta Raily were married (by license) on Jan. 12, 1784 [Ref: MB-385].

ABELL, Barton. Private, St. Mary's County Militia, 1777 [Ref: M-211]. Second Lieutenant, Lower Bn., Aug. 28, 1777, and Captain, June 22, 1780 [Ref: M-47, C-346, F-201]. Took the Oath of Allegiance before the Hon. Henry Reeder in St. Mary's County in 1778 [Ref: J-1146, K-64]. Barton Abell and family moved to Kentucky prior to 1800 [Ref: MK-1].

ABELL, Clark (Clarke). Private, St. Mary's County Militia, 1777 [Ref: M-211]. Took the Oath of Allegiance before the Hon. Robert Watts in St. Mary's County in 1778 [Ref: J-1146, K-62]. The Register of St. Andrew's Episcopal Church states Clarke Abell and Catharine Hutchins were married on June 3, 1779 [Ref: MB-383].

ABELL, Cuthbert. (1) Private, St. Mary's County Militia, 1777 [Ref: M-211]. One Cuthbert Abell died by Oct., 1795, and the court appointed Mary Milburn Abell as guardian of her children, Matthew Abell, Francis Abell and Mary Simmonds Abell [Ref: SO-232, SO-250]. (2) Private, Calvert County, enlisted by Lt. Nathaniel Wilson on Aug. 23, 1776 [Ref: D-34]. (3) Sergeant, 1st Maryland Regiment, 1780-1781 [Ref: D-34, S-146]. This name appeared three times on the list of those men who took the Oath of Allegiance before the Hon. Robert Watts in St. Mary's County in 1778 [Ref: J-1146, K-62]. See "Cuthbert Abell, Jr.," q.v., as there appears to be some confusion in the records as to which service data applied to which Cuthbert Abell.

ABELL, Cuthbert Jr. Private, St. Mary's County Militia, 1777 [Ref: M-211]. Cuthbert Abell (Feb. 1, 1759 - Dec. 2, 1824) served as a sergeant in the 7th Maryland Line in 1780 and married Mary M. Simmonds [Ref: Y-2, D-184]. The Register of St. Andrew's Episcopal Church states that Cuthbert Abell and Mary Simmons were married (by license) Feb. 1, 1785 [Ref: MB-386]. See "Cuthbert Abell," q.v., and Source S-139 for further information indicating that one Cuthbert Abell was the son of Capt. Robert Abell.

ABELL, Dorothy. See "Robert Wimsatt," q.v.

ABELL, Edmond (Edmund). Private, St. Mary's County Militia, 1777 [Ref: M-211]. Took the Oath of Allegiance before the Hon. Henry Reeder in St. Mary's County in 1778 [Ref: J-1146, K-64].

ABELL, Edward. (1) "Edward Abell, Jr." was elected to a General Committee in St. Mary's County in accordance with the resolves of the Continental Congress in 1775 [Ref: MR-127]. "Capt. Edward Abell" served on the Committee of Observation in 1776 [Ref: S-16, B-100]. Captain, St. Mary's County Militia, 1776 [Ref: S-146]. (2) Another Edward Abell was a private, St. Mary's County Militia, 1777 [Ref: M-212]. The Register of St. Andrew's Episcopal Church states that one Edward Abell and Statia Taylor were married on Nov. 7, 1778 [Ref: MB-382].

ABELL, Elizabeth. See "John Sanner, Jr." and "John Jarboe" and "Henry Jarboe" and "Enoch Abell," q.v.

ABELL, Enoch (1745 - March, 1784). Private, St. Mary's County Militia, 1777 [Ref: M-211]. First Lieutenant, Lower Bn., Aug. 26, 1777 [Ref: M-47, C-346]. "Enoch Abell, Jr." took the Oath of Allegiance before the Hon. Richard Barnes in St. Mary's County in 1778 [Ref: J-1146, K-66]. Enoch was a son of John and Elizabeth Abell and he married Judith ---- [Ref: Y-2, S-139].

ABELL, Francis. See "Cuthbert Abell," q.v.

ABELL, George. Private, St. Mary's County Militia, 1777 [Ref: M-211]. Took the Oath of Allegiance before the Hon. Henry Reeder in St. Mary's County in 1778 [Ref: J-1146, K-64]. Supplied provisions (wheat, mutton, or bacon) for the Army in 1780 [Ref: S-77].

ABELL, Henrietta. See "Thomas Thompson," q.v.

ABELL, Henry. Private, St. Mary's County Militia, 1777 [Ref: M-211]. Ensign, Lower Bn., July 5, 1781 [Ref: M-47, G-426]. Took the Oath of Allegiance before the Hon. Richard Barnes in St. Mary's County in 1778 [Ref: J-1146, K-66].

ABELL, Ignatius. (1) Private, St. Mary's County Militia, 1777 [Ref: M-211]. Ensign, Lower Bn., July 5, 1781 [Ref: M-47]. (2) Captain, Lower Bn., St. Mary's County, from Aug. 26, 1777 through June 22, 1780 [Ref: M-47, C-346, F-201]. The Register of St. Francis Xavier Catholic Church states one Ignatius Abell and Mary Abell were married Nov. 8, 1773 [Ref: SC-35].

ABELL, Jane. See "Thomas Thomas," q.v.

ABELL, John, Jr. (1746-1794). First Lieutenant, Lower Bn., St. Mary's County, Aug. 28, 1777 [Ref: M-47, C-346]. The Register of St. Andrew's Episcopal Church states that one John Abell and Elizabeth Abell were married June 4, 1780 [Ref: MB-383, Y-2, S-139]. "John Abell, J. P." moved to Washington County, Maryland in 1793 [Ref: X-85]. "John Abell, the youngest" took the Oath of Allegiance before the Hon. Robert Watts in St. Mary's County in 1778 [Ref: J-1146, K-62]. "John Abel, younger" and "John Abell, Sr." were elected to serve on a General

Committee in St. Mary's County in accordance with the resolves of the Continental Congress in 1775 [Ref: MR-127]. See "Enoch Abell," q.v.

ABELL, John Sr. Paid bounty by the State for making salt in 1782 [Ref: S-117, S-126]. See "John Abell, Jr.," q.v.

ABELL, John (of Samuel). Took the Oath of Allegiance before the Hon. Jeremiah Jordan in St. Mary's County in 1778 [Ref: J-1146, K-67].

ABELL, John Barton. Second Lieutenant, St. Mary's County, Lower Bn., Aug. 26, 1777. Captain, April 22, 1780 [Ref: S-146].

ABELL, John Booth. Took the Oath of Allegiance before the Hon. Robert Watts in St. Mary's County in 1778 [Ref: J-1146, K-62]. Private, St. Mary's County Militia, 1777 [Ref: M-211].

ABELL, John Horn (Horne). Private, St. Mary's County Militia, 1777 [Ref: M-215]. Captain, Lower Bn., Aug. 26, 1777 [Ref: M-47, C-346]. Took the Oath of Allegiance before the Hon. Bennett Biscoe in St. Mary's County in 1778 [Ref: J-1146, K-63]. "John H. Abell, Revolutionary patriot," died on Feb. 8, 1801, and is buried in the St. George Episcopal Church Cemetery (no marker) at Poplar Hill [Ref: S-128].

ABELL, Joseph (1752 - July 22, 1846). Private, St. Mary's County Militia, 1777 [Ref: M-215]. Joseph Abell married Catherine Hartley [Ref: Y-2].

ABELL, Joshua (c1760 - April 10, 1814). Private, St. Mary's County Militia, 1777 [Ref: M-211]. Took the Oath of Allegiance before the Hon. John Ireland in St. Mary's County in 1778 [Ref: J-1146, K-65]. Joshua Abell married Susannah Mills [Ref: Y-2].

ABELL, Margaret, and children. See "Robert Abell," q.v.

ABELL, Mary. See "John Henning" and "Ignatius Abell," q.v.

ABELL, Matthew and Mary Simmonds. See "Cuthbert Abell," q.v.

ABELL, Philip. Private, St. Mary's County Militia, 1777 [Ref: M-213]. Took the Oath of Allegiance before the Hon. Robert Watts in St. Mary's County in 1778 [Ref: J-1146, K-62]. One Philip Abell died by June, 1778 [Ref: SO-10].

ABELL, Robert. Son of Samuel Abell and Ellen or Elinore O'Brien. Private, St. Mary's County Militia, 1777 [Ref: M-211]. Took the Oath of Allegiance before the Hon. Jeremiah Jordan in St. Mary's County in 1778 [Ref: J-1146, K-67]. Supplied provisions (wheat, mutton, or bacon) for the Army in 1780 [Ref: S-77, S-146]. Robert Abell married Margaret Mills on Nov. 3, 1777, at St. Francis Xavier Catholic Church, and had ten children: Samuel, Jesse, James, Robert A., Ignatius, Benjamin, John, Mary, Ellen, and Janet. They moved to Nelson County, Kentucky in 1788 and settled in the Catholic settlement of Rolling Fork. In 1802 Robert returned to Maryland for a visit, became ill and died [Ref: MK-1, SC-36]. See "Benedict Spalding" and "Cuthbert Abell," q.v.

ABELL, Samuel, "youngest" (c1738/9 - June 4, 1795). Private, St. Mary's County Militia, 1777 [Ref: M-214]. Took the Oath of Allegiance before the Hon. Richard Barnes in St. Mary's County in 1778 [Ref: J-1146, K-66]. He married Ann ---- [Ref: Y-2]. "Samuel Abell, Jun." was elected to a General Committee in St. Mary's County in accordance with the resolves of the Continental Congress in 1775 [Ref: MR-127]. See "Robert Abell," q.v.

ABELL, Samuel (c1716-1777). Elected to a General Committee in St. Mary's County in accordance with the resolves of the Continental Congress in 1775 [Ref: MR-127]. See "Robert Abell," q.v.

ABELL, Samuel Jr. Second Major, 21st Bn., St. Mary's County, Dec. 1, 1776 [Ref: M-47]. Took the Oath of Allegiance before the Hon. Richard Barnes in St. Mary's County [Ref: J-1146, K-66]. Samuel Abell married Elinore O'Brien [Ref: Y-2]. Served on the Committee of Observation in 1776 [Ref: S-16, B-100]. Sheriff of St. Mary's County in 1776 [Ref: S-146]. See "Robert Abell," q.v.

ABELL, Susan. See "William Heard," q.v.

ABELL, Thomas. Private, St. Mary's County Militia, 1777 [Ref: M-211]. Took the Oath of Allegiance before the Hon. Jeremiah Jordan in St. Mary's County in 1778 [Ref: J-1146, K-67].

ABELL, Zachariah (Zacharias). Private, St. Mary's County Militia, 1777 [Ref: M-211]. Took the Oath of Allegiance before the Hon. Ignatius Fenwick, Jr. in St. Mary's County in 1778 [Ref: J-1146, K-68]. The Register of St. Francis Xavier Catholic Church states that Zachariah Abell (NC) and Mary Strong were married Oct. 18, 1772 [Ref: SC-34, which noted that "NC" meant "non-Catholic"].

ADAMS, Abraham. Private, St. Mary's County Militia, 1777 [Ref: M-215, which listed the name as "Abm.(?) Addams"]. Took the Oath of Allegiance in St. Mary's County in 1780 [Ref: Q-104]. The Register of St. Andrew's Episcopal Church states that Abraham Adams and Sabra Silance were married (by license) Sep. 14, 1784 [Ref: MB-385].

ADAMS, David Jenifer. Third Lieutenant, 1st Independent Maryland Co., Charles and Calvert Counties, 1776 [Ref: D-20].

ADAMS, Enoch. Private, Capt. Uriah Forrest's Co., Flying Camp, St. Mary's County, July 28, 1776 [Ref: D-30, SM-110].

ADAMS, Ignatius. Private, 1st Maryland Line, 1779-1780 [Ref: S-146]. Private (substitute), St. Mary's County, July 23, 1781 [Ref: D-384]. Private, Continental Army, 1781-1783 [Ref: D-406, S-121].

ADAMS, James (1737-1795). Private, enlisted April 6, 1776 [Ref: S-146]. Private (substitute), St. Mary's County, July 28, 1781 [Ref: D-384, S-101]. He married Jane Brinam in 1756 [Ref: S-139].

ADAMS, Jo. (Jr.?). Private, Capt. Uriah Forrest's Co., Flying Camp, St. Mary's County, July 28, 1776 [Ref: D-30, S-146, SM-110].

ADAMS, John. (1) Took the Oath of Allegiance before the Hon. Jeremiah Jordan in St. Mary's County in 1778 [Ref: J-1146, K-67]. Private, St. Mary's County, 3rd Maryland Line, Capt. Armstrong's Co., 1778-1781 [Ref: D-406, D-298, S-146]. (2) Took the Oath of Allegiance in Calvert County in 1778 [Ref: L-35].

ADAMS, Moses. Private, Capt. Uriah Forrest's Co., Flying Camp, St. Mary's County, July 28, 1776 [Ref: D-30]. Private (substitute), St. Mary's County, July 31, 1781. Private, Continental Army, 1781 [Ref: D-384, D-406, S-146].
ADAMS, Nathan. Private, St. Mary's County Militia, 1777 [Ref: M-215]. Private, St. Mary's County, enlisted May 22, 1778, for 9 months [Ref: D-330, SM-110].
ADAMS, Sarah. See "William Cissell," q.v.
ADAMS, Solomon. Private, St. Mary's County Militia, 1777 [Ref: M-214]. Took the Oath of Allegiance in St. Mary's County in 1780 [Ref: Q-104].
ADAMS, Stephen. Private, St. Mary's County Militia, 1777 [Ref: M-214, which listed the name as "Stephen Addams"]. The Register of St. Francis Xavier Catholic Church states that Stephen Adams and Henrietta Low were married Nov. 29, 1778 [Ref: SC-36].
ADAMS, Thomas. Private, St. Mary's County Militia, 1777 [Ref: M-215]. Took the Oath of Allegiance in St. Mary's County in 1780 [Ref: Q-104].
ADAMS, William. Private, Capt. Uriah Forrest's Co., Flying Camp, St. Mary's County, July 28, 1776 [Ref: D-30]. Private, St. Mary's County, drafted on July 27, 1781 [Ref: D-384]. Private, Continental Army, 1781 [Ref: D-406, S-146].
ADDERTON, Ann. See "James Adderton," q.v.
ADDERTON, Henry. Private, Capt. Thomas Truman Greenfield's Co., Calvert County Militia, 1778 [Ref: J-1146, M-150].
ADDERTON, James. Elected to serve on a General Committee in St. Mary's County in accordance with the resolves of the Continental Congress in 1775 [Ref: MR-127]. Captured by the British on April 24, 1781 [Ref: S-147]. One "James Aderton" died testate by Aug., 1788, leaving a daughter Ann [Ref: SO-125, SO-131, SO-136, SO-168, SO-225].
ADDERTON, Rebecca Mrs. She loaned money in St. Mary's County for the war effort in 1781, and her property was destroyed by the British that same year [Ref: S-147, SM-187].
ADDISON, Rebecca. See "George Plater," q.v.
AISQUITH, George. Private, St. Mary's County Militia, 1777 [Ref: M-213]. Ensign, Lower Bn., Aug. 26, 1777 [Ref: M-49, C-346, which listed the name as "George Asquith"]. Took the Oath of Allegiance before the Hon. Robert Watts in St. Mary's County in 1778 [Ref: J-1146, K-62]. The Register of St. Andrew's Episcopal Church states that George Aisquith and Elizabeth Guider were married (by license) March 3, 1784 [Ref: MB-385]. He was dead by Oct., 1790, and Elizabeth was his administratrix [Ref: SO-158].
AISQUITH, John. Private, St. Mary's County Militia, 1777 [Ref: M-215, which listed the name as "John Asquith"]. First Lieutenant, Lower Bn., Aug. 26, 1777 [Ref: M-49, C-346]. Mentioned as a captain on Oct. 20, 1780 [Ref: S-147]. Took the Oath of Allegiance before the Hon. Robert Watts in St. Mary's County in 1778 [Ref: J-1146, K-62]. The Register of

St. Andrew's Episcopal Church states that John Aisquith and Mary Chisley (Chesley) were married June 3, 1779 [Ref: MB-383].
AISQUITH, Sarah. See "John Avis," q.v.
ALEXANDER, John. Private, St. Mary's County, who served in the Maryland Line until 1781 when discharged [Ref: D-406].
ALLEIN, Richard. See "Richard Allen," q.v.
ALLEIN, William (c1742-c1802). Son of Benjamin and Mary Allein, of Anne Arundel County, who died when he was a young boy. He married by 1771 to Sarah Weems (died 1804), daughter of Roger Weems, of Calvert County, and had children: William Jr., George W., Mary D., and Priscilla H. Allein. Served in the Lower House, Calvert County, 1775-1782, and was a Delegate to the Maryland Convention in 1776. Justice of Calvert County, 1773, 1777, and 1782. County Sheriff, 1785-1788. Patuxent Association (State officer), 1781 [Ref: N-72, N-76, N-86, N-104]. Also see "William Allen," q.v.
ALLEN, Anne. See "William Thomas," q.v.
ALLEN, Charles. Private, Capt. Richard Parran's Co., Calvert County Militia, 1778 [Ref: J-1146, M-149]. Took the Oath of Allegiance in Calvert County in 1780 [Ref: Q-104].
ALLEN, Elizabeth. See "John Allen Thomas," q.v.
ALLEN, John. Private, Capt. Richard Parran's Co., Calvert County Militia, 1778 [Ref: J-1146, M-149].
ALLEN (ALLEIN), Richard. Private, Calvert County, enlisted by Lt. Nathaniel Wilson on Aug. 23, 1776 [Ref: D-34]. Private, Capt. Richard Parran's Co., Calvert County Militia, 1778 [Ref: J-1146, M-149]. Took the Oath of Allegiance in Calvert County in 1780 [Ref: Q-104]. "Richard Allein" and Phebe Dixon were married on Jan. 23, 1780, by Rev. Francis Lauder, of Christ Church Parish [Ref: K-35].
ALLEN, Thomas. Private, 3rd Maryland Line, 1782 [Ref: S-118].
ALLEN (ALLEIN), William. (1) Quartermaster, 15th Bn., Calvert County, June 1, 1776 [Ref: M-48]. (2) Private, Capt. Richard Parran's Co., Calvert County Militia, 1778 [Ref: J-1146, M-149]. (3) Private, Capt. Richard Lane's Co., Calvert County Militia, 1778 [Ref: J-1146, M-150, which listed the name as "William Allien"]. "William Allin" took the Oath of Allegiance in Calvert County in 1778 [Ref: L-35]. "William Allein" married Elizabeth Cowen on Dec. 1, 1778, by Rev. Francis Lauder, of Christ Church Parish [Ref: K-34]. Also see "William Allein," q.v.
ALLENDER, John. Private, 2nd Maryland Line, 1777-1780; probably from St. Mary's County [Ref: D-78].
ALLENDER, Perry. Private, St. Mary's County, who served in the Maryland Line until 1781 when discharged [Ref: D-406].
ALLINGHAM, Stephen. Private, Capt. James Grahame's Co., Calvert County Militia, 1778 [Ref: J-1146, M-148]. Took the Oath of Allegiance in Calvert County in 1778 [Ref: L-35].

ALLISON, Henry. Private, St. Mary's County Militia, 1777 [Ref: M-214]. Took the Oath of Allegiance in St. Mary's County in 1780 [Ref: Q-104]. The Register of St. Andrew's Episcopal Church states that Henry Allison and Margaret Dillion (Dillian) were married May 25, 1779 [Ref: MB-383].
ALLISON, James. Private, St. Mary's County Militia, 1777 [Ref: M-215]. Took the Oath of Allegiance in St. Mary's County in 1780 [Ref: Q-104].
ALLISON, John. This name appeared twice as a private, St. Mary's County Militia, 1777 [Ref: M-214, M-215]. Took the Oath of Allegiance in St. Mary's County in 1780 [Ref: Q-104].
ALLNUTT, Elizabeth. See "William Allnutt," q.v.
ALLNUTT, James Jr. (1752-1838). Private, Capt. Frisby Freeland's Co., Calvert County Militia, 1778 [Ref: Y-2, J-1146, M-148, which listed the name as "James Aulnutt"]. See "William Allnutt," q.v.
ALLNUTT, James Sr. (1713-1786). Took the Oath of Allegiance in Calvert County in 1778 [Ref: L-35, Y-2].
ALLNUTT, Mary. See "William Allnutt," q.v.
ALLNUTT, Sarah. See "Samuel Hance, Jr.," q.v.
ALLNUTT, William (c1711-c1781). Served on a committee in Calvert County in 1774 formed to carry out the mandates of the Continental Congress. As one of three Judges of Elections, he reported to the Council of Safety on Dec. 21, 1776, regarding the election returns for Sheriff of Calvert County and the representatives to the General Assembly. He was appointed one of five Justices of the Orphans Court in 1777, and also served as a Justice of the Peace in 1777 and a Judge of the Orphans Court in 1778 and 1779. He administered and took the Oath of Allegiance in Calvert County in 1778. He was married twice: (1) Mary Talbot circa 1736; and, (2) name unknown, and had these children: Mary, James Jr., Elizabeth, Zacheus, and William Jr. (and possibly others). [Ref: V-74, E-242, F-22, L-35, Y-12, and "William Allnutt and Wife Sarah (Mears) Talbott, Widow of John Talbott, of Calvert County, Maryland: The Progenitors of the American Colonial Family of Allnutt With One Line of Their Descendants in Montgomery County, Maryland," by Ernest C. Allnutt, Jr., Lt.Col., AUS (Ret.), *Maryland Genealogical Society Bulletin*, Volume 33, No. 4, pp. 712-766 (Fall, 1992), which is a very well documented accounting of this prominent Maryland family and should be consulted for more information].
ALLNUTT, William Jr. Private, Capt. Thomas Cleland's Co., Calvert County Militia, 1778 [Ref: J-1146, M-147]. Took the Oath of Allegiance in Calvert County in 1778 [Ref: L-35]. See "William Allnutt," q.v.
ALLNUTT, Zaccheus. Private, Capt. Frisby Freeland's Co., Calvert County Militia, 1778 [Ref: J-1146, M-148]. Took the Oath of Allegiance in Calvert County in 1778 [Ref: L-35]. See "William Allnutt," q.v.
ALLSOP, John. Private from St. Mary's County who served in the Continental Army in 1781 [Ref: D-406].

ALLSOP, Joseph (1743-1783). Private, St. Mary's County, who served in the 7th Maryland Line, June 8, 1778 to March 30, 1779, and again served in the Continental Army in 1781 [Ref: D-184, D-406]. One Joseph Allsop married Mary Freeman in Frederick County in 1778 and died in 1783. She married second to Peter Casey who died in 1794. Mary applied for and received pension W3129 on Aug. 28, 1843, in Franklin County, Pennsylvania, aged 86 [Ref: P-47, Y-12].

ALLSOP, Richard. Private, Capt. Frederick Skinner's Co., Calvert County Militia, 1778 [Ref: J-1146, M-150, which listed the name as "Richard Alsops"]. Private, Capt. John Mackall's Co., Calvert County Militia, 15th Bn., June 12, 1778 [Ref: M-146]. Took the Oath of Allegiance in Calvert County in 1778 [Ref: L-35]. "Richard Allsup" and Keziah Howse were married on Sep. 28, 1780, by Rev. Francis Lauder, of Christ Church Parish [Ref: K-35].

ALLSTAN (ALLSTONE), Jeremiah. Private, Capt. Uriah Forrest's Co., Flying Camp, St. Mary's County, July 28, 1776 [Ref: D-30, SM-110].

ALLSTAN, Thomas. Took the Oath of Allegiance before the Hon. Jeremiah Jordan in St. Mary's County in 1778 [Ref: J-1146, K-67]. One Thomas Allstan died intestate by Dec., 1794 [Ref: SO-218].

ALLSTAN, Thomas Jr. Took the Oath of Allegiance before the Hon. John Shanks in St. Mary's County in 1778 [Ref: J-1146, K-69].

ALSEY, William. Private, St. Mary's County, who served in the Maryland Line until 1781 when discharged [Ref: D-406].

ALVEY, James. Took the Oath of Allegiance before the Hon. John Ireland in St. Mary's County in 1778 [Ref: J-1146, K-65]. Supplied provisions (wheat, mutton, or bacon) for the Army in 1780 [Ref: S-77].

ALVEY, Jesse. Private, St. Mary's County Militia, 1777 [Ref: M-212]. Took the Oath of Allegiance before the Hon. John Ireland in St. Mary's County in 1778 [Ref: J-1146, K-65].

ALVEY, John. Private, St. Mary's County Militia, 1777 [Ref: M-213]. Private, 1st and 2nd Maryland Lines, June 10, 1779 to 1783 [Ref: D-78, S-147]. "John Alvy" moved to Washington County, Kentucky in 1797 [Ref: X-85]. "John Alvey" and Thomas S. Alvey migrated to Kentucky and settled in the Catholic settlement on Hardin's Creek [Ref: MK-3].

ALVEY, Joseph. Private, Capt. Uriah Forrest's Co., Flying Camp, St. Mary's County, July 28, 1776 [Ref: D-30, SM-110]. This name appeared twice as a private, St. Mary's County Militia, 1777 [Ref: M-210, M-212].

ALVEY, Josias (Josiah). Private, 1st and 2nd Maryland Lines, enlisted May 24, 1779, discharged May 24, 1782. The Treasurer of Maryland was directed in 1815 to pay him "half pay of a private, quarterly, during life, as a further remuneration for those services by which his country has been so essentially benefitted." [Ref: I-315]. He applied for and received pension S34625 in St. Mary's County on April 21, 1818, aged 63. In 1820 he had a wife and two children, but no names were given. Still on the pension rolls in 1835, aged 78 [Ref: P-49, D-78, D-441, S-147, U-40].

ALVEY, Mary. See "Bennett Dailey," q.v.
ALVEY, Thomas. Corporal, 3rd Maryland Line, 1778 [Ref: D-298].
ALVEY, Thomas Green. Private, St. Mary's County Militia, 1777 [Ref: M-214, which listed the name as "Thomas Green Abby"]. Private, St. Mary's County, enlisted on April 21 or 24, 1778, for 3 years [Ref: D-329]. Private, 3rd Maryland Line, 1778; wounded (no date given); promoted to corporal on Feb. 1, 1779 [Ref: D-79]. The Court allowed him one-fourth of the pay of a corporal from 1785 to 1789 as he was "rendered incapable of serving in the army though not totally disabled from getting a livelihood" [Ref: SO-83, SO-133].
ALVEY, Thomas S. See "John Alvey," q.v.
ALVEY, Travers. Private, St. Mary's County, enlisted April 28, 1778, for 3 years [Ref: D-329]. Private, 3rd Maryland Line, Capt. Armstrong's Co., 1778-1780 [Ref: D-79, D-298].
ALVEY(?), William. See "William Alsey," q.v.
ANDERSON, Alexander. Private, St. Mary's County Militia, 1777 [Ref: M-212].
ANDERSON, Archibald. Major, 3rd Maryland Line, and commander of troops from St. Mary's County, 1779 [Ref: D-298].
ANDERSON, Bennett. Private, St. Mary's County, drafted July 27, 1781 [Ref: D-384]. Private, Continental Army, 1781 [Ref: D-406].
ANDERSON, Jonathan. Private, St. Mary's County Militia, 1777 [Ref: M-209].
ANDERSON, Joseph. Took the Oath of Allegiance before the Hon. Vernon Hebb in St. Mary's County in 1778 [Ref: J-1146, K-67].
ANDERSON, Mary Ann. See "Joshua Gibson," q.v.
ANDERSON, Thomas. Private, St. Mary's County Militia, 1777 [Ref: M-210].
ANSELL, Edward. Private, Capt. Frederick Skinner's Co., Calvert County Militia, 1778 [Ref: J-1146, M-150]. Took the Oath of Allegiance in Calvert County in 1778 [Ref: L-35].
ANTHONY, John. Private, St. Mary's County, who served in the Maryland Line until 1781 when he was discharged [Ref: D-406].
APRICE, Bennett. See "Bennett Price," q.v.
ARBOR (AUBURGH), John. Private, St. Mary's County, who served in the Maryland Line until 1781 when he was discharged [Ref: D-406].
ARDINGTON, John. Took the Oath of Allegiance in Calvert County in 1778 [Ref: L-35].
ARIS, Richard. Private, St. Mary's County, 3rd Maryland Line, Capt. Armstrong's Co., 1778-1780 [Ref: D-298].
ARMOND, Abell. Private, 7th Maryland Line, June 7, 1778 to July 1, 1780, when deserted; probably from St. Mary's County [Ref: D-184].
ARMSTRONG, George. Brother of "Lieutenant Robert Armstrong," q.v. Private, Capt. Uriah Forrest's Co., Flying Camp, St. Mary's County, July 28, 1776 [Ref: D-30]. Lieutenant, 3rd Maryland Line, Dec. 10, 1776,

and Captain-Lieutenant, 1777, serving in many battles in New York, New Jersey, and Pennsylvania until 1779 when he became involved in recruiting. Promoted to Captain, 1st Maryland Line, Feb. 11, 1780, and was killed at the Battle of Ninety Six in South Carolina; death was reported on June 18, 1781 [Ref: SM-147, SM-110, D-79, D-298, S-147].

ARMSTRONG, James. Took the Oath of Allegiance before the Hon. Vernon Hebb in St. Mary's County in 1778 [Ref: J-1146, K-67]. One James Armstrong was a drummer in the 3rd Maryland Line and was reported missing at the Battle of Camden in South Carolina on Aug. 16, 1780 [Ref: D-79]. Another James, or perhaps this same one, was a private in the marines aboard the State ship *Defence* in 1776 and 1777 [Ref: S-25, S-147, D-606].

ARMSTRONG, John. (1) Private, St. Mary's County Militia, 1777 [Ref: M-214]. (2) Captain, Lower Bn., St. Mary's County, Aug. 28, 1777 [Ref: M-48, C-346]. Took the Oath of Allegiance before the Hon. Vernon Hebb in St. Mary's County in 1778 [Ref: J-1146, K-67]. Loaned money in St. Mary's County for the war effort in 1781 [Ref: X-78, H-479]. Major in 1794 [Ref: S-147].

ARMSTRONG, R. Private, St. Mary's County Militia, 1777 [Ref: M-215].

ARMSTRONG, Robert. Elected to serve on a General Committee in St. Mary's County in accordance with the resolves of the Continental Congress in 1775 [Ref: MR-127]. First Lieutenant, Lower Bn., Aug. 26, 1777, and First Lieutenant, Upper Bn., April 16, 1778 [Ref: M-48, C-346]. Justice who administered the Oath of Allegiance in St. Mary's County in 1778 [Ref: J-1146, K-62]. He notified Col. Barnes of the approach of enemy ships on Sep. 9, 1781 [Ref: V-436], and loaned money in St. Mary's County for the war effort in 1781 [Ref: X-78, H-479]. Commissioned to establish a chain of "Expresses" from Point Lookout to Annapolis in 1781 [Ref: S-147]. Brother of "Capt. George Armstrong," q.v.

ARMSWORTHY, Abraham. Private, St. Mary's County Militia, 1777 [Ref: M-214]. Took the Oath of Allegiance in St. Mary's County in 1780 [Ref: Q-104].

ARMSWORTHY, Baptist. Private, St. Mary's County, 3rd Maryland Line, Capt. Armstrong's Co., 1777-1780 [Ref: D-298, which listed the name as "Baptis Armesworthy"]. He enlisted on April 22, 1777, and was reported missing at the Battle of Camden in South Carolina in Aug. 16, 1780 [Ref: D-79].

ARMSWORTHY, Bent. Private, St. Mary's County Militia, 1777 [Ref: M-215].

ARMSWORTHY, George. Private, St. Mary's County Militia, 1777 [Ref: M-214]. Took the Oath of Allegiance in St. Mary's County in 1780 [Ref: Q-104].

ARMSWORTHY, James. Took the Oath of Allegiance in St. Mary's County in 1780 [Ref: Q-104].

ARMSWORTHY, John. Private, St. Mary's County Militia, 1777 [Ref: M-214]. Took the Oath of Allegiance in St. Mary's County in 1780 [Ref: Q-104]. The Register of St. Andrew's Episcopal Church states that John Armsworthy and Mary Armsworthy were married Jan. 16, 1780 [Ref: MB-383].
ARMSWORTHY, Mary. See "John Armsworthy," q.v.
ARMSWORTHY, William. Took the Oath of Allegiance in St. Mary's County in 1780 [Ref: Q-104].
ARNOLD, David. Private, Capt. Thomas Truman Greenfield's Co., Calvert County Militia, 1778 [Ref: J-1146, M-150]. Took the Oath of Allegiance in Calvert County in 1778 [Ref: L-35]. Also see "Edward Johnson," q.v.
ARTERBURY, Thomas. Private, Capt. Henry Skinner's Foot Co. of Hunting Hundred, Calvert County, 1777 [Ref: T-1814, O-125].
ARTHURS (ARTERS), Joseph. Took the Oath of Allegiance before the Hon. Bennett Biscoe in St. Mary's County in 1778 [Ref: J-1146, K-63]. Property destroyed by the British in 1781 [Ref: S-147].
ARTIS, Matthias. Private, St. Mary's County Militia, 1777 [Ref: M-215].
ASGRUE, John. Private, Capt. Benjamin Bond's Co., Calvert County Militia, 1778 [Ref: J-1146, M-149].
ASHCOM, Samuel. Private, Calvert County, enlisted by Lt. Nathaniel Wilson on Aug. 23, 1776 [Ref: D-34].
ASKEW, Abraham. Private, Capt. Thomas Truman Greenfield's Co., Calvert County Militia, 1778 [Ref: J-1146, M-150, which listed the name as "Abraham Osque"]. Took the Oath of Allegiance in Calvert County in 1778 [Ref: L-35].
ASKEW, Benjamin. Private, Capt. Frederick Skinner's Co., Calvert County Militia, 1778 [Ref: J-1146, M-150, which listed the name as "Benjamin Asque"]. Private, Capt. John Mackall's Co., Calvert County Militia, 15th Bn., June 12, 1778 [Ref: M-146].
ASKEW, Henry. Took the Oath of Allegiance in Calvert County in 1778 [Ref: L-35]. The Christ Church Register in Calvert County records the birth of James Askew, son of Henry and Dinah, on Jan. 14, 1790 [Ref: O-1].
ASKEW, William. Took the Oath of Allegiance in Calvert County in 1778 [Ref: L-35, which listed the name as "William Asque"].
ASKEY, Henry. Private, Capt. James Patterson's Co., Calvert County Militia, Aug. 10, 1777 [Ref: M-146].
ASKEY, Mary. See "Richard Wilkinson," q.v.
ASKUM, Nathaniel. Took the Oath of Allegiance before the Hon. Henry G. Sothoron in St. Mary's County in 1778 [Ref: J-1146, K-68].
ATKINSON, James. Private, St. Mary's County Militia, 1777 [Ref: M-212]. Took the Oath of Allegiance before the Hon. Robert Watts in St. Mary's County in 1778 [Ref: J-1146, K-62].
ATKINSON, William. Private, St. Mary's County Militia, 1777 [Ref: M-215].

ATTAWAY, Elizabeth. See "Thomas Bond," q.v.
ATTWOOD (ATWOOD), Charles. Private, St. Mary's County, drafted on July 27, 1781 [Ref: D-384]. Took an oath on July 27, 1782, concerning the manufacture and sale of salt [Ref: V-532].
ATTWOOD (ATWOOD), James. Took the Oath of Allegiance before the Hon. Bennett Biscoe in St. Mary's County in 1778 [Ref: J-1146, K-63]. First Lieutenant, Lower Bn., April 5, 1780 [Ref: M-49, G-426]. Took an oath on Aug. 1, 1782, concerning the manufacture and sale of salt [Ref: V-534]. The Register of St. Inigoes Catholic Church states that James Atwood and Henrietta Jarboe were married Jan. 19, 1768, and James Atwood and Ann Jenkins were married Aug. 1, 1784 [Ref: SC-33, SC-36].
ATWELL, Joseph. Private, St. Mary's County, who served in the Maryland Line until 1781 when discharged [Ref: D-406].
AUD, John. Private, St. Mary's County Militia, 1777 [Ref: M-214]. Took the Oath of Allegiance before the Hon. Richard Barnes in St. Mary's County in 1778 [Ref: J-1146, K-66].
AUD, Joseph. Private, St. Mary's County Militia, 1777 [Ref: M-214]. Took the Oath of Allegiance before the Hon. Richard Barnes in St. Mary's County in 1778 [Ref: J-1146, K-66, which source listed the name as "Joseph Aug"].
AUD, Robert. Private, St. Mary's County Militia, 1777 [Ref: M-214].
AUD, Thomas. Private, St. Mary's County Militia, 1777 [Ref: M-211].
AUD, William. Private, St. Mary's County Militia, 1777 [Ref: M-214]. Took the Oath of Allegiance before the Hon. Richard Barnes in St. Mary's County in 1778 [Ref: J-1146, K-66, which source listed the name as "William Aug"].
AUSTIN, James. Private, Capt. Charles Williamson's Co., Calvert County Militia, 1778 [Ref: J-1146, M-148]. Took the Oath of Allegiance in Calvert County in 1778 [Ref: L-35].
AUSTIN, Samuel. Private, Capt. Charles Williamson's Co., Calvert County Militia, 1778 [Ref: J-1146, M-148]. Took the Oath of Allegiance in Calvert County in 1778 [Ref: L-35].
AUSTIN, William. Private, Capt. Charles Williamson's Co., Calvert County Militia, 1778 [Ref: J-1146, M-148]. Took the Oath of Allegiance in Calvert County in 1778 [Ref: L-35].
AUSTON, John. Private, Capt. Henry Skinner's Foot Co. of Hunting Hundred, Calvert County, 1777 [Ref: T-1814, O-125].
AUSTON, Thomas. Private, St. Mary's County Militia, 1777 [Ref: M-213].
AVERY, John. Private, St. Mary's County Militia, 1777 [Ref: M-212]. Took the Oath of Allegiance before the Hon. John Shanks in St. Mary's County in 1778 [Ref: J-1146, K-69].
AVIS, David. Private, Capt. Richard Parran's Co., Calvert County Militia, 1778 [Ref: J-1146, M-149]. Took the Oath of Allegiance in Calvert County in 1778 [Ref: L-35].

AVIS, Henry. Took the Oath of Allegiance in Calvert County in 1778 [Ref: L-35].
AVIS, James. Took the Oath of Allegiance in Calvert County in 1778 [Ref: L-35].
AVIS, James Greaves. Private, Calvert County, enlisted by Ensign James Somervill on July 25, 1776 [Ref: D-34].
AVIS, Jarvis (Jervis). Private, Capt. Benjamin Bond's Co., Calvert County Militia, 1778 [Ref: J-1146, M-149]. Took the Oath of Allegiance in Calvert County in 1778 [Ref: L-35].
AVIS, John. Private, Capt. Benjamin Bond's Co., Calvert County Militia, 1778 [Ref: J-1146, M-149]. Private, Capt. Richard Parran's Co., Calvert County Militia, 1778 [Ref: J-1146, M-149]. Took the Oath of Allegiance in Calvert County in 1778 [Ref: L-35]. One John Avis and Sarah Asquith (Aisquith) were married on Nov. 23, 1780, by Rev. Francis Lauder, of Christ Church Parish [Ref: K-36].
AVIS, John (of Henry). Took the Oath of Allegiance in Calvert County in 1778 [Ref: L-35].
BACCUS, James. Took the Oath of Allegiance before the Hon. Henry G. Sothoron in St. Mary's County in 1778 [Ref: J-1146, K-68].
BADEN, Thomas. Took the Oath of Allegiance in Calvert County in 1778 [Ref: L-35].
BAILEY, Elias. Private, Capt. Uriah Forrest's Co., Flying Camp, St. Mary's County, July 28, 1776 [Ref: D-30, SM-110].
BAILEY, John. Lieutenant, 3rd Maryland Line on March 27, 1777, and was in the New York, New Jersey and Pennsylvania campaigns from 1777 to 1779. In 1779 he was assigned to recruiting service in St. Mary's County. Resigned in the summer of 1779 [Ref: SM-149, D-85]. Took the Oath of Allegiance before the Hon. John Shanks in St. Mary's County in 1778 [Ref: J-1146, K-69]. One "John Baily" moved from St. Mary's County to Nelson County, Kentucky in 1795 [Ref: X-85].
BAILEY, John Baptist. Private, Continental Army, enlisted May 18, 1778; served from St. Mary's County [Ref: S-51, S-149].
BAILEY, Thomas. Took the Oath of Allegiance before the Hon. Bennett Biscoe in St. Mary's County in 1778 [Ref: J-1146, K-63]. The Register of St. Inigoes Catholic Church states that "Thomas Baily" and Mary Smith were married July 5, 1784 [Ref: SC-36].
BAILEY, William (Esquire). Paid for services rendered to the State on Nov. 24, 1781; St. Mary's County [Ref: S-108, S-149, H-2].
BAKER, Christopher. Took the Oath of Allegiance in Calvert County in 1780 [Ref: Q-104].
BAKER, Isaac. Private, Capt. Richard Parran's Co., Calvert County Militia, 1778 [Ref: J-1146, M-149]. Took the Oath of Allegiance in Calvert County in 1778 [Ref: L-35].
BAKER, Isaac Jr. Private, Capt. Richard Parran's Co., Calvert County Militia, 1778 [Ref: J-1146, M-149].

BAKER, Isaac Oystin. Private, Capt. Richard Parran's Co., Calvert County Militia, 1778 [Ref: J-1146, M-149].
BAKER, John. Private, Calvert County, enlisted by Capt. John Brooke on July 25, 1776 [Ref: D-33, SM-110]. Private, Capt. Richard Parran's Co., Calvert County Militia, 1778 [Ref: J-1146, M-149]. Took the Oath of Allegiance in Calvert County in 1780 [Ref: Q-105].
BAKER, Nathan Jr. Private, Capt. Richard Parran's Co., Calvert County Militia, 1778 [Ref: J-1146, M-149].
BAKER, Nathan Sr. Private, Capt. Richard Parran's Co., Calvert County Militia, 1778 [Ref: J-1146, M-149].
BAKER, Nathaniel. Took the Oath of Allegiance in Calvert County in 1778 [Ref: L-35]. Nathaniel Baker and Anne Grover were married on April 30, 1778, by Rev. Francis Lauder, of Christ Church Parish [Ref: K-34].
BAKER, Raston. Took the Oath of Allegiance in Calvert County in 1778 [Ref: L-35].
BAKER, Raston Jr. Took the Oath of Allegiance in Calvert County in 1778 [Ref: L-35].
BAKER, Rebecca. See "Isaac Gardiner," q.v.
BAKER, William. There were several men with this name: (1) Private, Calvert County, enlisted by Ensign James Somervill on July 25, 1776 [Ref: D-34]. (2) Private, Capt. Richard Parran's Co., Calvert County Militia, 1778 [Ref: J-1146, M-149]. (3) Private, Capt. Henry Skinner's Foot Co. of Hunting Hundred, Calvert County, 1777 [Ref: T-1814, O-125]. (4) William Baker took the Oath of Allegiance in Calvert County in 1780 [Ref: Q-105]. (5) William Baker appeared twice as a private in the St. Mary's County Militia in 1777 [Ref: M-213, M-215]. (6) "William Baker, physician" moved to Washington, D. C. in 1792 [Ref: X-85]. The Register of St. Andrew's Episcopal Church states that William Baker and Jane Davis were married (by license) Jan. 1, 1782 [Ref: MB-384].
BALCH, Stephen B. Private, Capt. Charles Williamson's Co., Calvert County Militia, 1778 [Ref: J-1146, M-147]. Took the Oath of Allegiance in Calvert County in 1778 [Ref: L-35].
BALDWIN, Lydia. See "Bennett Clocker," q.v.
BALLARD, Levin. Private, Capt. James Grahame's Co., Calvert County Militia, 1778 [Ref: J-1146, M-149]. Took the Oath of Allegiance in Calvert County in 1778 [Ref: L-35].
BARBER, Ann. See "Archibald Barber" and "Baptist Barber," q.v.
BARBER, Archibald. "Archibald D. Barber" took the Oath of Allegiance before the Hon. John Reeder in St. Mary's County in 1778 [Ref: J-1146, K-69]. "Archibald Barber" died by June, 1786 when his administratrix Ann Barber was appointed guardian to her children Elizabeth, Rebecca, Mary, and George Barber [Ref: SO-99, SO-147].
BARBER, Baptist. "Baptist Barber" was a private, St. Mary's County Militia, 1777 [Ref: M-210]. "Babtist Barber" died by Oct., 1789, when

Ann Barber was appointed guardian to his son George [Ref: SO-146, SO-243].

BARBER, Barnet White (c1748 - May 21, 1802). Private, St. Mary's County Militia, 1777 [Ref: M-210]. Supplied provisions (wheat, mutton, or bacon) for the Army in 1780, and served as a Juror at the General Court in Annapolis in 1781 [Ref: S-77, S-149]. Barnet White Barber married Elizabeth Story Briscoe, daughter of Philip Briscoe and Chloe Hanson, and drowned in the Wicomica River in 1802. Elizabeth Barber died June 17, 1820, at "Luckland" in Chaptico, St. Mary's County [Ref: R-334, Y-34, S-139].

BARBER, Clement. Private, 1st Maryland Line, from Dec. 10, 1776 until Dec. 27, 1779, when discharged [Ref: D-82].

BARBER, Cornelius. Elected to a General Committee in St. Mary's County in accordance with the resolves of the Continental Congress in 1775 [Ref: S-77, MR-126, which incorrectly listed the name as "Cornelius Barbe"]. Took the Oath of Allegiance before the Hon. Henry Tubman in St. Mary's County in 1778 [Ref: J-1146, K-70]. Supplied provisions (wheat, mutton, or bacon) for the Army in 1780 [Ref: S-77, S-126, S-149].

BARBER, Edward. Supplied provisions (wheat, mutton, or bacon) for the Army in St. Mary's County in 1780 [Ref: S-149].

BARBER, Elias. Son of Luke Barber (died 1793). Private, St. Mary's County Militia, 1777 [Ref: M-210]. He married Elizabeth Wainwright on Dec. 14, 1777, by Rev. George Goldie, All Saints Episcopal Church. About 1794 a number of Episcopal families moved to the western part of Rowan County, North Carolina with Rev. Hatch Dent, an Episcopal clergyman and an uncle of the Barbers, and purchased the "Dent Tract." Elias Barber died testate by Feb., 1843. His brother Jonathan (1765-1839) also moved to North Carolina and their brother Luke migrated to Missouri [Ref: R-3343, I-535, MC-15]. An "Elias Barber, farmer" moved from Chaptico in St. Mary's County to Washington County, Maryland in 1797 [Ref: X-85].

BARBER, Elizabeth and George. See "Archibald Barber," q.v.

BARBER, Hezekiah. Private, St. Mary's County Militia, 1777 [Ref: M-210].

BARBER, John Myvert. Private, St. Mary's County Militia, 1777 [Ref: M-211].

BARBER, Joseph. Private, St. Mary's County Militia, 1777 [Ref: M-210].

BARBER, Luke Jr. Private, St. Mary's County Militia, 1777 [Ref: M-210]. Luke Barber migrated to Missouri and was a brother of "Elias Barber," q.v. [Ref: R-334].

BARBER, Mary and Rebecca. See "Archibald Barber," q.v.

BARBER, Samuel. Adjutant, 1st Maryland Line, from May 5, 1777 until July 6, 1778, when he resigned [Ref: D-82].

BARBER, William. Private, Capt. Walter Smith's Co., Calvert County Militia, 1778 [Ref: J-1146, M-148]. Took the Oath of Allegiance in Calvert County in 1778 [Ref: L-35].

BARBER, William (of George). Private, Capt. John Mackall's Co., Calvert County Militia, 15th Bn., June 12, 1778 [Ref: M-146].

BAREFOOT (BARFORD), William. "William Barefoot" was a private in Capt. Walter Smith's Co., Calvert County Militia, 1778 [Ref: J-1146]. "William Barford" took the Oath of Allegiance in Calvert County in 1778 [Ref: L-35]. "William Barefoot" and Eleanor Margun [Morgan?] were married on Sep. 2(?), 1786, by Rev. William Gill, of All Saint's Parish [Ref: K-33].

BARKER, John Baptist. Supplied provisions (wheat, mutton, or bacon) to the Army in 1780 in St. Mary's County [Ref: S-80, S-149].

BARNECLOW, Charles. Private, St. Mary's County, who served in the Maryland Line until 1781 when discharged [Ref: D-406].

BARNECLOW, John. Private, St. Mary's County, who served in the Maryland Line until 1781 when discharged [Ref: D-406].

BARNES, Abraham. "Col. Abraham Barnes" was elected to a General Committee in St. Mary's County in accordance with the resolves of the Continental Congress in 1775. He served on the Committee of Correspondence and was chairman of the Committee of Observation in 1776 [Ref: MR-127, S-16, B-100]. Judge of Elections in 1776 [Ref: S-150]. "Abraham Barnes, Revolutionary patriot" is buried in the yard of Tudor Hall (no marker) in Leonardtown [Ref: S-128]. See "John Barnes" and "Richard Barnes," q.v.

BARNES, Catherine Redmond. See "John Jarboe," q.v.

BARNES, Henry. Seaman from St. Mary's County who served aboard the State ship *Defence* in 1777 [Ref: S-150].

BARNES, James. Private, St. Mary's County Militia, 1777 [Ref: M-213]. Private, St. Mary's County, enlisted on May 31, 1778, for 9 months [Ref: D-330, SM-110]. James Barnes married Anne Grimes on Jan. 18, 1784, St. Mary's County, by Rev. John Stephen, Rector of All Faith's Parish [Ref: I-535].

BARNES, John. (1) c1743-1800. Son of Abraham Barnes and Elizabeth Rousby. Elected a delegate from St. Mary's County to the Maryland Convention in 1775, but did not attend. Moved to Washington County, Maryland in 1777 and served in these capacities: Lower House, 1777-1783, Court Justice, 1777-1800, Chief Justice, 1791-1800, Orphans Court Justice, 1778-1785, and was called Colonel at time of death. His father died circa 1778 and left nothing to John in his will. He had lost all that his father had given him and had bound his father in debt as his security. His father also called him "careless and obstinate." [Ref: N-70, N-115, N-116]. (2) Private, Capt. Frisby Freeland's Co., Calvert County Militia, 1778 [Ref: J-1146, M-148, which listed the name as "John Barns"]. One John Barnes was elected to a General Committee in St.

Mary's County in accordance with the resolves of the Continental Congress in 1775 [Ref: MR-127, S-150].

BARNES, Leonard. Private, Capt. Thomas Cleland's Co., Calvert County Militia, 1778 [Ref: J-1146, M-147, which listed the name as "Leonard Barns"].

BARNES, Richard (c1740-1804). Son of Abraham Barnes and Elizabeth Rousby, of St. Mary's County. Richard served in many official capacities, including: Maryland Lower House, 1773-1774; Member of the Committee of Correspondence, 1775; Delegate to the Maryland Convention, 1775-1777; Member of the House of Delegates, 1777-1778; Member of the Senate, 1779-1783; Constitution Ratification Committee, 1788; County Justice, 1772-1778; Orphans Court Justice, 1777-1778 [Ref: N-70, N-72, N-74, N-78, N-82, N-84, N-86, N-87, N-116, MR-127]. Colonel, 21st Bn., St. Mary's County Militia, Jan. 12, 1776 [Ref: M-50]. County Lieutenant, 1777-1781 [Ref: D-593, C-303, V-373, S-36]. Justice who administered the Oath of Allegiance in St. Mary's County in 1778 [Ref: J-1146, K-66]. He wrote to the Governor on Jan. 18, 1778, about the appointment of Zachariah Forrest as Sheriff of Calvert County [Ref: V-141]. Loaned money in St. Mary's County for the war effort in 1781 [Ref: X-78, H-412]. "Richard Barnes, Revolutionary patriot," is buried in the yard at Tudor Hall (no marker) in Leonardtown [Ref: S-128].

BARNES, Thomas. Private, St. Mary's County, who served in the Maryland Line until 1781 when discharged [Ref: D-406].

BARNES, Timothy. Elected to serve on a General Committee in St. Mary's County in accordance with the resolves of the Continental Congress in 1775 [Ref: MR-127].

BARNES, Zachariah. Private, St. Mary's County Militia, 1777 [Ref: M-211]. Took the Oath of Allegiance before the Hon. John Reeder in St. Mary's County in 1778 [Ref: J-1146, K-69].

BARNHOUSE, George. Private, St. Mary's County Militia, 1777 [Ref: M-212].

BARNHOUSE, Richard. Private, St. Mary's County Militia, 1777 [Ref: M-215, which listed the name twice]. Took the Oath of Allegiance before the Hon. Robert Armstrong in St. Mary's County in 1778 [Ref: J-1146, K-62]. Paid for manufacturing salt in 1782 [Ref: S-150].

BARNHOUSE, Rudolph. Private, St. Mary's County, enlisted on June 1 or 10, 1778, for 9 months [Ref: D-330, which listed the name as "Rudolph Barnchouse (Barnhouse)"]. Took the Oath of Allegiance before the Hon. Bennett Biscoe in St. Mary's County in 1778 [Ref: J-1146, K-63]. "Rodolph Barnhouse" was a private, 3rd Maryland Line, from June 1, 1778 to Aug. 4, 1779, when discharged [Ref: D-86, S-150].

BARRETT, William. Private, 7th Maryland line, enlisted on March 17, 1777, promoted to corporal on Sep. 30, 1778, and discharged on March 17, 1780 [Ref: D-188, which listed the name as "Williams Barrett"]. The Register of St. Andrew's Episcopal Church states that William Barrett

and Margaret Malley were married (by license) Feb. 23, 1783 [Ref: MB-385].
BARRS, Joseph. Private, Capt. Thomas Cleland's Co., Calvert County Militia, 1778 [Ref: J-1146, M-147].
BARTCLY, Thomas. Private, Capt. Uriah Forrest's Co., Flying Camp, St. Mary's County, July 28, 1776 [Ref: D-30, SM-110].
BARTLET, John. Private, St. Mary's County Militia, 1777 [Ref: M-212].
BARTON, Betty. See "Charles Owens," q.v.
BASSEY, Edmund. Took the Oath of Allegiance before the Hon. Bennett Biscoe in St. Mary's County in 1778 [Ref: J-1146, K-63]. Private, St. Mary's County Militia, 1777 [Ref: M-215, which listed the name as "Edmund Basey"]. Paid for services in 1782 [Ref: S-150].
BATS, John. Private, St. Mary's County Militia, 1777 [Ref: M-215].
BATTIN, Stanley. Private, St. Mary's County, enlisted May 31, 1778, for 9 months [Ref: D-330, SM-110].
BAXTER, Anthony. Private, St. Mary's County Militia, 1777 [Ref: M-214]. Took an oath on July 24, 1782, concerning the manufacture and sale of salt [Ref: V-531].
BAXTER, Joseph. Private, St. Mary's County Militia, 1777 [Ref: M-214]. Took the Oath of Allegiance before the Hon. Bennett Biscoe in St. Mary's County in 1778 [Ref: J-1146, K-63].
BAYARD, William. Elected to serve on a General Committee in St. Mary's County in accordance with the resolves of the Continental Congress in 1775 [Ref: MR-127]. Took the Oath of Allegiance before the Hon. John Shanks in St. Mary's County in 1778 [Ref: J-1146, K-69]. Second Lieutenant, Upper Bn., Nov. 18, 1779 [Ref: M-51, F-18].
BAYFIELD, George. Private, Capt. Richard Lane's Co., Calvert County Militia, 1778 [Ref: J-1146, M-150].
BAYLEY, John. Private, St. Mary's County Militia, 1777 [Ref: M-213].
BEALE, Thomas. Second Lieutenant, 1st Independent Maryland Co., Charles and Calvert Counties, 1776 [Ref: D-20].
BEALL, Margaret. See "Benjamin Edwards," q.v.
BEALL, Rezin. Captain, 1st Independent Maryland Co., Charles and Calvert Counties, 1776 [Ref: D-20].
BEAN, Alexander. Private, St. Mary's County Militia, 1777 [Ref: M-214].
BEAN, Benjamin Sr. (1758 - April 17, 1828). Private, St. Mary's County Militia, 1777 [Ref: M-214]. Took the Oath of Allegiance before the Hon. Vernon Hebb in St. Mary's County in 1778 [Ref: J-1146, K-67]. He married Rebecca Evans [Ref: Y-46].
BEAN, Charlotte, Edna, and Frances. See "Leonard Bean," q.v.
BEAN, Gabriel. Private, St. Mary's County Militia, 1777 [Ref: M-215].
BEAN, George (1723-c1797). Private, St. Mary's County Militia, 1777 [Ref: M-214]. Paid for making salt in 1782 [Ref: S-150]. The Register of St. Andrew's Episcopal Church states that "George Beane" and Anne Dillion were married Oct. 14, 1778 [Ref: MB-382, Y-46].

BEAN, John. Took the Oath of Allegiance in St. Mary's County in 1780 [Ref: Q-105, which listed the name as "John Beane"]. Private, 3rd Maryland Line, from June 5, 1778 to at least Nov. 1, 1780 [Ref: SM-110, D-86]. The Register of St. Andrew's Episcopal Church states that John Bean and Anne Henning were married (by license) June 26, 1781 [Ref: MB-384]. One John Bean died by Oct., 1789 [Ref: SO-147].
BEAN, John Albert. See "Leonard Bean," q.v.
BEAN, John (of Benjamin). Private, St. Mary's County Militia, 1777 [Ref: M-214].
BEAN, John (of Robert). Private, St. Mary's County Militia, 1777 [Ref: M-214].
BEAN, Leonard. Private, 3rd Maryland Line, enlisted May 29, 1778. Corporal, Jan. 1, 1780. Applied for an received pension S35189 in Mason County, Kentucky, on May 5, 1818. In 1820 he was aged 62 with a wife aged about 60 (not named) and five children: John Albert Bean (aged 28), Leonard Harrison Bean (aged 23), Matilda Bean (aged 18, who married Frank McClure), Frances or Fanny Bean (aged 16), and William Gallenous Bean (aged 13). Leonard died on May 29, 1851 [Ref: P-200, W-63, D-86]. Other children were Letitia Bean (who married John Crutcher) and Charlotte Bean (who married Joseph Tolle). Leonard's wife was Edna Kellow and she was the widow of William Kilgour [Ref: MK-8].
BEAN, Leonard, Letitia, and Matilda. See "Leonard Bean," q.v.
BEAN, Robert. Private, St. Mary's County Militia, 1777 [Ref: M-214]. Took the Oath of Allegiance before the Hon. Vernon Hebb in St. Mary's County in 1778 [Ref: J-1146, K-67]. One Robert Bean died by Oct., 1789 [Ref: SO-147, SO-157]. "Robert Beane" was paid for manufacturing salt in 1782 [Ref: S-150].
BEAN, Thomas (1755-c1805). Private, St. Mary's County Militia, 1777 [Ref: M-214]. Thomas Bean married Mary Gwynne [Ref: Y-47].
BEAN, William. Paid for manufacturing salt in 1782 in St. Mary's County [Ref: S-150, which listed the name as "William Beane"].
BEAN, William Gallenous. See "Leonard Bean," q.v.
BEARD, Thomas. Private, St. Mary's County, who served in the Maryland Line until 1781 when discharged [Ref: D-406].
BECKETT, Humphrey. Took the Oath of Allegiance in Calvert County in 1778 [Ref: L-35]. "Humphry Beckett" married Lydia Sunderland on Oct. 31, 1777, by Rev. Thomas John Clagett, All Saint's Parish [Ref: K-33].
BELLWOOD, Benjamin. Ensign, Lower Bn., St. Mary's County, July 5, 1781 [Ref: M-52].
BELLWOOD, Henry. Took the Oath of Allegiance before the Hon. Robert Watts in St. Mary's County in 1778 [Ref: J-1146, K-62].
BELLWOOD, William. Private, St. Mary's County Militia, 1777 [Ref: M-215, which listed the name as "William Belwad(?)"]. Took the Oath of Allegiance before the Hon. Robert Watts in St. Mary's County in 1778

[Ref: J-1146, K-62]. Ensign, Lower Bn., on July 5, 1781 [Ref: M-52, G-426]. Capt. William Bellwood captured a British sloop on Sep. 8, 1781 [Ref: S-150]. One William Bellwood died by 1791 [Ref: SO-160]. See "Philip Fenwick," q.v.

BENDING, John. Took the Oath of Allegiance before the Hon. Bennett Biscoe in St. Mary's County in 1778 [Ref: J-1146, K-63].

BENFIELD, Samuel. Private, St. Mary's County Militia, 1777 [Ref: M-211]. Took the Oath of Allegiance before the Hon. Ignatius Fenwick, Jr. in St. Mary's County in 1778 [Ref: J-1146, K-68].

BENNETT, Ann Sophia. See "Bennett Shirley," q.v.

BENNETT, George. Seaman from St. Mary's County who served aboard the State ship *Defence* in 1777 [Ref: S-150].

BENNETT, Joseph (1753 - Aug. 19, 1815). Private in the St. Mary's County Militia in 1777 [Ref: M-215]. He is buried with his wife Susanna (1757-1806) at "Fresh Pond Neck" near Scotland in St. Mary's County [Ref: HG-43]. This name appeared twice on the list of those men who took the Oath of Allegiance before the Hon. Robert Armstrong in St. Mary's County in 1778 [Ref: J-1146, K-62]. One had property destroyed by the British in 1781 [Ref: S-150].

BENNETT, Joshua. Private, Continental Army, 1781 [Ref: S-150].

BENNETT, Margaret. See "Thomas Biscoe," q.v.

BENNETT, Richard. Private, St. Mary's County Militia, 1777 [Ref: M-215]. Took the Oath of Allegiance before the Hon. Robert Armstrong in St. Mary's County in 1778 [Ref: J-1146, K-62].

BENNETT, Robert. Private, St. Mary's County Militia, 1777 [Ref: M-215]. Took the Oath of Allegiance before the Hon. Robert Armstrong in St. Mary's County in 1778 [Ref: J-1146, K-62].

BENNETT, Stephen. Private, St. Mary's County Militia, 1777 [Ref: M-215].

BENNETT, Susannah. See "Joseph Bennett," q.v.

BENNETT, William. Private, St. Mary's County Militia, 1777 [Ref: M-215]. Second Lieutenant, Lower Bn., Aug. 26, 1777. First Lieutenant, 21st Bn., April 16, 1778 [Ref: C-346, E-37, M-52].

BENTLEY, Nancy. See "Thomas Wooton," q.v.

BENTLEY, William. Private, St. Mary's County, who served in the Maryland Line until 1781 when discharged [Ref: D-407].

BENTON, Jacob. Private, Capt. John Mackall's Co., Calvert County Militia, 15th Bn., June 12, 1778 [Ref: M-146].

BENYON (BINYON), Alexander. Private, St. Mary's County, who served in the Maryland Line until 1781 when discharged [Ref: D-406].

BENYON (BINYON), Benjamin. Private, Capt. Richard Parran's Co., Calvert County Militia, 1778 [Ref: J-1146, M-149]. Took the Oath of Allegiance in Calvert County in 1778 [Ref: L-35].

BENYON (BINYON), John. Took the Oath of Allegiance in Calvert County in 1778 [Ref: L-35].

BENYON (BINYON), Thomas. Private, Capt. Richard Parran's Co., Calvert County Militia, 1778 [Ref: J-1146, M-149]. Took the Oath of Allegiance in Calvert County in 1778 [Ref: L-35].
BEVERLY, Adam. Private, St. Mary's County Militia, 1777 [Ref: M-215].
BEVERLY, Michael. Private, St. Mary's County Militia, 1777 [Ref: M-215, which listed the name as "Michael Beaverly"]. Took the Oath of Allegiance in St. Mary's County in 1780 [Ref: Q-105].
BEVERLY, Rhode. Private, St. Mary's County Militia, 1777 [Ref: M-214].
BIAL (BEAL), John. Took the Oath of Allegiance before the Hon. Bennett Biscoe in St. Mary's County in 1778 [Ref: J-1146, K-63].
BIGGS, Thomas. Private, Capt. Uriah Forrest's Co., Flying Camp, St. Mary's County, July 28, 1776 [Ref: D-30]. Private, St. Mary's County Militia, 1777 [Ref: M-212, which listed the name as "Thomas Bigges"]. Private, St. Mary's County, enlisted April 4, 1778, for 9 months [Ref: D-329].
BILES, Benson. Private, Calvert County, enlisted by Lt. Nathaniel Wilson on Aug. 23, 1776 [Ref: D-34].
BILLINGSLEY, Allen. Private, St. Mary's County Militia, 1777 [Ref: M-213]. Took the Oath of Allegiance before the Hon. John Reeder in St. Mary's County in 1778 [Ref: J-1146, K-69].
BILLINGSLEY, Ann. See "William Shemwell," q.v.
BILLINGSLEY, Clement. Private, St. Mary's County Militia, 1777 [Ref: M-210, which listed the name as "Clement Bittlingsley"].
BILLINGSLEY, James. Private, St. Mary's County Militia, 1777 [Ref: M-209]. Took the Oath of Allegiance before the Hon. Henry Tubman in St. Mary's County in 1778 [Ref: J-1146, K-70]. There was also a James Billingsley, son of James and Elizabeth, who was born in St. Mary's County in Oct., 1749, and moved with his family first to Baltimore County and then to Guilford County, North Carolina prior to the Revolutionary War. He was a captain and served with his brothers. Their father James was harassed and hanged by Tories in his own yard in April, 1776. Their mother Elizabeth moved to Tennessee with her son and died in 1839 at the very advanced age of 113 [Ref: MC-19, MC-20, which contains more family information. Also see *Baltimore County Families, 1659-1759*, by Robert W. Barnes, page 43, and *For King and Country, Volume I*, by the Orange County Genealogical Society, in Orange, California, page 28 (1975)]. See "John Billingsley," q.v.
BILLINGSLEY, Jane and Jessie. See "John Billingsley," q.v.
BILLINGSLEY, John (Aug. 17, 1754 - Sep., 1844). Son of James Billingsley and Elizabeth Crabtree, of St. Mary's County. Moved in 1758 to Baltimore County with his parents and siblings, and then to Guilford County, North Carolina prior to the Revolutionary War. John married Jean Milsap in June, 1772, and their children were Sarah, Jessie, James, Thomas, Mary, Samuel, and Jane. John served as a private in the militia in 1776 and 1777, as did his brothers James and Walter Billinglsey.

About 1794 they moved to Sullivan County, Tennessee, and in 1833 John applied for and received pension S30862 in Warren County, Kentucky. Jean Billingsley died in 1842 and John in 1844 [Ref: MC-20, P-263, which sources both contain more family information]. See "James Billingsley," q.v.

BILLINGSLEY, Mary. See "John Billingsley," q.v.

BILLINGSLEY, Nancy. See "Joseph Shamwell," q.v.

BILLINGSLEY, Samuel, Sarah and Thomas. See "John Billingsley," q.v.

BILLINGSLEY, Walter. Private, St. Mary's County Militia, 1777 [Ref: M-212, Y-59]. Took the Oath of Allegiance in St. Mary's County in 1780 [Ref: Q-105].

BILLINGSLEY, Zachariah. Private, St. Mary's County Militia, 1777 [Ref: M-213, which listed the name as "Zacharia Billinsley"]. Took the Oath of Allegiance before the Hon. Henry Tubman in St. Mary's County in 1778 [Ref: J-1146, K-70].

BINYON, Alexander. See "Alexander Benyon," q.v.

BIRCHMORE, Ann. See "Francis Wheeler," q.v.

BIRKETT, Edward. Took the Oath of Allegiance in Calvert County in 1778 [Ref: L-35].

BIRKHEAD, John. Private, Capt. Thomas Truman Greenfield's Co., Calvert County Militia, 1778 [Ref: J-1146, M-150, which listed the name as "John Burkhead"].

BIRKHEAD, Nehemiah. Private, Capt. Frisby Freeland's Co., Calvert County Militia, 1778 [Ref: J-1146, M-148, which listed the name as "Nemiah Birkhead"]. Took the Oath of Allegiance in Calvert County in 1778 [Ref: L-35, which listed the name as "Nehemiah Birckhead"].

BISCOE, Araminta. See "Henry Carroll," q.v.

BISCOE, Bennett. Justice who administered the Oath of Allegiance in St. Mary's County in 1778 [Ref: J-1146, K-63]. Elected to a General Committee in St. Mary's County in accordance with the resolves of the Continental Congress in 1775 [Ref: MR-127, which listed the name as "Benne Biscoe"]. Justice of the Peace, 1778-1779 [Ref: S-150].

BISCOE, Elizabeth. See "Thomas Biscoe" and "Seneca Nelson Cheseldine," q.v.

BISCOE, George. Private, St. Mary's County Militia, 1777 [Ref: M-213]. Took the Oath of Allegiance before the Hon. Robert Watts in St. Mary's County in 1778 [Ref: J-1146, K-62]. Naval Officer for Patuxent River in 1783 [Ref: S-150]. "George Biscoe, elite" moved from Harvey to Prince George's County, Maryland, in 1799 [Ref: X-85]. Served as Collector of Customs for the Port of Nottingham and died there on April 1, 1817 [Ref: R-337]. See "James Biscoe, Sr." and Henry Carroll," q.v.

BISCOE, Ignatius Jr. Took the Oath of Allegiance before the Hon. Robert Watts in St. Mary's County in 1778 [Ref: J-1146, K-62].

BISCOE, Ignatius Sr. Private, St. Mary's County Militia, 1777 [Ref: M-215]. Took the Oath of Allegiance before the Hon. Robert Armstrong in

St. Mary's County in 1778 [Ref: J-1146, K-62]. One Ignatius Biscoe died intestate by Aug., 1786 [Ref: SO-103].

BISCOE, James Jr. Private, St. Mary's County, Militia, 1777 [Ref: M-210, M-215, S-150]. Took the Oath of Allegiance before the Hon. Bennett Biscoe in St. Mary's County in 1778 [Ref: J-1146, K-63].

BISCOE, James Sr. Private, St. Mary's County Militia, 1777 [Ref: M-210, M-215, S-150]. Took the Oath of Allegiance before the Hon. Bennett Biscoe in St. Mary's County in 1778 [Ref: J-1146, K-63, Y-61]. One James Biscoe died by Aug., 1790, leaving orphans James, Jonathan, and Mary Bond Biscoe [Ref: SO-157, SO-290]. However, Source S-139 indicates James Biscoe, Sr. was born in 1730 and died in 1796, and was a son of George Biscoe.

BISCOE, John. See "Mackay or Mackey Biscoe," q.v.

BISCOE, Jonathan. Private, St. Mary's County Militia, 1777 [Ref: M-215]. Took the Oath of Allegiance before the Hon. Robert Armstrong in St. Mary's County in 1778 [Ref: J-1146, K-62]. See "James Biscoe," q.v.

BISCOE, Joseph. Private, St. Mary's County Militia, 1777 [Ref: M-215]. Took the Oath of Allegiance before the Hon. Robert Armstrong in St. Mary's County in 1778 [Ref: J-1146, K-62]. Also see "Josiah Biscoe," q.v.

BISCOE, Josiah (March 30, 1760 - May 29, 1845). Private, Maryland Line, and Privateer Service. Captured off the Capes by the British on June 14, 1782 [Ref: S-151]. Born in St. Mary's County on March 30, 1760, he applied for a pension (R859) on Aug. 10, 1832, aged 73, stating he enlisted there and his father's name was Joseph. His pension application was rejected, however [Ref: P-268, R-339].

BISCOE, Mackay, Mackey or Mackie (1754 - March 2, 1829). Took the Oath of Allegiance before the Hon. Robert Armstrong in St. Mary's County in 1778. Served on the State ship *Defence* from May 19, 1777 to June 1, 1777 [Ref: D-654, J-1146, K-62, R-339, S-151]. Mackey Biscoe was executor of John Biscoe in 1778 [Ref: SO-17].

BISCOE, Margaret. See "Thomas Biscoe," q.v.

BISCOE, Mary Bond. See "James Biscoe," q.v.

BISCOE, Nancy. See "Richard Hammett," q.v.

BISCOE, Stephen. Took the Oath of Allegiance before the Hon. Robert Armstrong in St. Mary's County in 1778 [Ref: J-1146, K-62].

BISCOE, Thomas. This name appeared twice on the list of those men who took the Oath of Allegiance before the Hon. Robert Armstrong in St. Mary's County in 1778 [Ref: J-1146, K-62]. The Register of St. Andrew's Episcopal Church states that Thomas Biscoe and Margaret Bennett were married (by license) Nov. 27, 1782 [Ref: MB-384]. Thomas Biscoe (May 8, 1756 - April 29, 1816) is buried beside his wife Margaret (April 14, 1764 - July 20, 1833) at "Long Neck" near Scotland in St. Mary's County. Another Thomas Biscoe is also buried there (unmarked grave) beside his wife Elizabeth (1733-1804) whose grave is marked [Ref: R-339, HG-43, HG-44].

BISCOE, Thomas (of John). Took the Oath of Allegiance before the Hon. Bennett Biscoe in St. Mary's County in 1778 [Ref: J-1146, K-63].
BISHOP, Ann. See "William Bowling," q.v.
BLACK, John. Elected to a General Committee in St. Mary's County in accordance with the resolves of the Continental Congress in 1775, and also served on the Committee of Correspondence [Ref: MR-127].
BLACK, Moses. Private from St. Mary's County who served in the Continental Army in 1781 [Ref: D-407, S-151].
BLACKBURN, Benjamin. Private, Capt. Walter Smith's Co., Calvert County Militia, 1778 [Ref: J-1146, M-148]. Took the Oath of Allegiance in Calvert County in 1778 [Ref: L-35]. The Christ Church Register in Calvert County records the birth of Sarah Blackburn, daughter of Benjamin and Barbara Blackburn, on Nov. 9, 1786 [Ref: O-3].
BLACKBURN, Charles. Private, Capt. Walter Smith's Co., Calvert County Militia, 1778 [Ref: J-1146, M-148]. Took the Oath of Allegiance in Calvert County in 1778 [Ref: L-35].
BLACKBURN, David. Private, Capt. Walter Smith's Co., Calvert County Militia, 1778 [Ref: J-1146, M-148]. Took the Oath of Allegiance in Calvert County in 1778 [Ref: L-35].
BLACKBURN, Edward. Private, Capt. Edward Wood's Co., Calvert County Militia, 1778 [Ref: J-1146, M-147]. Took the Oath of Allegiance in Calvert County in 1778 [Ref: L-35].
BLACKBURN, Lydia. See "James Hellen (Hillen)," q.v.
BLACKBURN, Nathan (Nathaniel). Private, Capt. Walter Smith's Co., Calvert County Militia, 1778 [Ref: J-1146, M-148]. Took the Oath of Allegiance in Calvert County in 1778 [Ref: L-35].
BLACKBURN, Sarah. See "Benjamin Blackburn," q.v.
BLACKBURN, Thomas. Private, Capt. Walter Smith's Co., Calvert County Militia, 1778 [Ref: J-1146, M-148]. Took the Oath of Allegiance in Calvert County in 1778 [Ref: L-35].
BLACKBURN, Zachariah. Private, Capt. Walter Smith's Co., Calvert County Militia, 1778 [Ref: J-1146, M-148]. Took the Oath of Allegiance in Calvert County in 1778 [Ref: L-35].
BLACKISTONE, John. Private, St. Mary's County Militia. Sergeant, 5th Independent Co., 1776. Participated in the Battle of Brooklyn on Aug. 27, 1776. Promoted to Ensign, 2nd Maryland Line, in March, 1777, and commissioned First Lieutenant, Upper Bn., St. Mary's County Militia, on Nov. 18, 1779 [Ref: M-213, SM-149]. "John Blakistone" died on Nov. 11, 1806 [Ref: R-340]. See "Nehemiah Herbert Blackistone," q.v.
BLACKISTONE, Nehemiah Herbert (1740 - June 2, 1816). Son of John Blackistone and Eleanor Dent. "Herbert Blackston" was a private, St. Mary's County Militia, 1777 [Ref: M-212]. "Herbert Blackistone" took the Oath of Allegiance before the Hon. John Shanks in St. Mary's County in 1778 [Ref: J-1146, K-69]. "Herbert Blakiston" was elected to a General Committee in St. Mary's County in accordance with the

resolves of the Continental Congress in 1775 [Ref: MR-127]. "Herbert Blakistone" died on June 2, 1816 [Ref: R-340]. "Nehemiah Herbert Blackistone" served on the Committee of Safety in 1774. He was captured by the British and his home burned on June 16, 1781 because of his rebellious sympathies [Ref: S-139, S-151].

BLAIR, John. (1) Private, St. Mary's County Militia, 1777 [Ref: M-213]. Private, St. Mary's County, enlisted on May 23, 1778, for 9 months [Ref: D-329]. (2) Private, enlisted on Jan. 15, 1777, St. Mary's County, 3rd Maryland Line, Capt. Armstrong's Co., 1778-1780. Discharged from 7th Maryland Line on April 2, 1780. Appears to have served again in the 1st Maryland Line and was invalided (disabled) on June 10, 1782 [Ref: D-298, S-151]. One John Blair died by Feb., 1797, leaving a daughter Elizabeth [Ref: SO-256].

BLAKE, Joseph. Private, Capt. Frederick Skinner's Co., Calvert County Militia, 1777, and Ensign, 15th Bn., April 16, 1778 [Ref: J-1146, M-53, M-150, E-37]. Took the Oath of Allegiance in Calvert County in 1778 [Ref: L-35].

BLAKE, Joseph Jr. Private, Capt. James Patterson's Co., Calvert County Militia, Aug. 10, 1777 [Ref: M-146]. Took the Oath of Allegiance in Calvert County in 1778 [Ref: L-35]. Accounted and paid for collecting cattle for the State in 1781 [Ref: V-469].

BLAKE, Sarah. Paid by the State for making salt in St. Mary's County in 1782 [Ref: S-151].

BLAKE, Thomas. Took the Oath of Allegiance in Calvert County in 1778 [Ref: L-35].

BLAKE, Thomas Jr. Private, Capt. Frederick Skinner's Co., Calvert County Militia, 1778 [Ref: J-1146, M-150]. Took the Oath of Allegiance in Calvert County in 1778 [Ref: L-35].

BLANDFORD (BLANFORD), Ignatius. Private, Calvert County, enlisted by Lt. Frederick Skinner on Aug. 23, 1776 [Ref: D-33]. Migrated to Cartwright's Creek in now Washington County, Kentucky in 1788 [Ref: MK-12].

BLANDFORD (BLANFORD), Joseph. Private, Calvert County, enlisted by Lt. Frederick Skinner on Aug. 23, 1776 [Ref: D-33].

BLANDFORD (BLANFORD), Richard. Private, 2nd Maryland Line, June 12, 1779; taken prisoner of war at the Battle of Camden on Aug. 16, 1780; and, paid for his services in the 1st Maryland Line in 1781 [Ref: D-84, D-357, D-398].

BLITHIN, Samuel. Private, St. Mary's County Militia, 1777 [Ref: M-210].

BLUNDELL, John. Private, St. Mary's County, enlisted April 30, 1778, for 3 years [Ref: S-151, D-329, which listed the name as "John Blundull"]. Took the Oath of Allegiance before the Hon. Bennett Biscoe in St. Mary's County in 1778 [Ref: J-1146, K-63].

BOARMAN, Catherine. See "William Thomas," q.v.

BOARMAN, John. Took the Oath of Allegiance before the Hon. John Shanks in St. Mary's County in 1778 [Ref: J-1146, K-69].

BOARMAN, Richard. Took the Oath of Allegiance before the Hon. John Reeder in St. Mary's County in 1778 [Ref: J-1146, K-69].

BOARMAN, Sylvester (Catholic Priest). Took the Oath of Allegiance before the Hon. John Shanks in St. Mary's County in 1778 [Ref: J-1146, K-69, SM-185]. "Sylvester Boarman, clergy" moved from St. Inigoes to Charles County, Maryland, in 1807 and died on Jan. 18, 1812 [Ref: X-85, R-341]. One Sylvester Boarman, born 1801 in Charles County, died in 1854 in Hardin County, Kentucky [Ref: MK-13].

BOHANON, George. Private, St. Mary's County Militia, 1777 [Ref: M-212]. Took the Oath of Allegiance in St. Mary's County in 1780 [Ref: Q-105].

BOHANON, John. Private, St. Mary's County Militia, 1777 [Ref: M-212]. Took the Oath of Allegiance in St. Mary's County in 1780 [Ref: Q-105].

BOHANON, Moses. Private, St. Mary's County Militia, 1777 [Ref: M-212]. Took the Oath of Allegiance in St. Mary's County in 1780 [Ref: Q-105].

BOIQUET (BOQUET), James. "James Boiquet" took the Oath of Allegiance in Calvert County in 1778 [Ref: L-35]. "James Boquet" and Elizabeth Saxe were married on Jan. 17, 1779, by Rev. Francis Lauder, of Christ Church Parish [Ref: MM-21, K-35, which latter source listed the name as "James Bognet"].

BOND, Benjamin. Captain, Calvert County Militia, 1777, and Captain, 15th Bn., April 16, 1778 [Ref: J-1146, M-54, M-149, E-37]. Took the Oath of Allegiance in Calvert County in 1778 [Ref: L-35].

BOND, Cecelia. See "Thomas Bond," q.v.

BOND, Charles. Private, Capt. Uriah Forrest's Co., Flying Camp, St. Mary's County, July 28, 1776 [Ref: D-30, SM-110].

BOND, Eleanor. See "Thomas Flower," q.v.

BOND, Elizabeth. See "Barton Tabbs" and "John Hanson Briscoe" and "Justinian Jordan" and "Thomas Bond," q.v.

BOND, Francis. Took the Oath of Allegiance in Calvert County in 1778 [Ref: L-35].

BOND, Gerrard (Gerard). Private, St. Mary's County Militia, 1777 [Ref: M-212]. Captain, Upper Bn., Aug. 26, 1777 through Nov. 18, 1779, when he resigned [Ref: M-54, C-345, F-18, S-147]. "Mr. Gerard Bond" was elected to a General Committee in St. Mary's County in accordance with the resolves of the Continental Congress in 1775 [Ref: MR-126, MR-127]. "Capt. Gerrard Bond" served on the Committee of Observation in 1776 [Ref: S-16, B-100]. One Gerard Bond died testate by 1790 [Ref: SO-148].

BOND, Jeremiah. Took the Oath of Allegiance before the Hon. John Shanks in St. Mary's County in 1778 [Ref: J-1146, K-69].

BOND, John. (1) Private, Capt. Walter Smith's Co., Calvert County Militia, 1778 [Ref: J-1146, M-148]. (2) Took the Oath of Allegiance before the Hon. John Shanks in St. Mary's County in 1778 [Ref: J-1146, K-69]. (3) Private, 2nd Maryland Line, May 1, 1782 [Ref: S-147]. One John Bond died intestate by 1800 and John Bond was his administrator [Ref: SO-305]. See "Thomas Bond," q.v.

BOND, John Jr. Took the Oath of Allegiance before the Hon. John Shanks in St. Mary's County in 1778 [Ref: J-1146, K-69]. Private, Capt. Uriah Forrest's Co., Flying Camp, St. Mary's County, July 28, 1776 [Ref: D-30, SM-110]. See "John Bond," q.v.

BOND, Nathaniel. Midshipman and Purser from St. Mary's County who served aboard the State ship *Defence* on April 15, 1777 [Ref: S-148].

BOND, Peregrine. See "Thomas Bond," q.v.

BOND, Rebecca. See "William Ramsey (Ramsay)," q.v.

BOND, Richard. Elected to serve on a General Committee in St. Mary's County in accordance with the resolves of the Continental Congress in 1775 [Ref: MR-127]. Supplier of horses in 1781 [Ref: S-148].

BOND, Thomas (c1740-1797). Son of Capt. John Bond and Elizabeth Attaway, of St. Mary's County. He married Cecelia Brown, daughter of Dr. Gustavus Brown and widow of Dr. John Key, by 1757 and their children were Peregrine, Thomas, John, Cecelia, and Elizabeth, and his stepchildren were Philip Key and Susannah Gardiner Key. Thomas served in several official capacities, including the following: Member of Lower House, 1773-1774, 1782-1785, 1790-1792; County Justice, 1764-1773, 1778-1792; Justice of the Court of Oyer and Terminer and Goal Delivery, 1768-1772; Orphans Court Justice, 1778-1786; Tax Commissioner, 1779-1785; Member of the House of Delegates in 1783 [Ref: N-87, N-142]. Took the Oath of Allegiance before the Hon. Jeremiah Jordan in St. Mary's County in 1778 [Ref: J-1146, K-67]. Thomas was also called Major (period of his service not known). [Ref: N-142]. (2) Private, St. Mary's County Militia, 1777; Private, Pulaski's Legion, May 12, 1778 [Ref: M-210, SM-110, S-148]. Supplied provisions (wheat, mutton, or bacon) to the Army in 1780 [Ref: S-77].

BOND, William. (1) First Lieutenant, Flying Camp, St. Mary's County, July 12, 1776. Captain, Upper Bn., Aug. 26, 1777 to Nov. 18, 1779 [Ref: D-30, M-54, C-346]. (2) Private, St. Mary's County Militia, 1777 [Ref: M-213]. One took the Oath of Allegiance before the Hon. Henry G. Sothoron in St. Mary's County in 1778 [Ref: J-1146, K-68]. (3) Private, Capt. Henry Skinner's Foot Co. of Hunting Hundred, Calvert County, 1777 [Ref: T-1814, O-125]. One William Bond married Mary Nevison on Feb. 28, 1777 in St. Mary's County, by Rev. George Goldie [Ref: I-535]. "W. William Bond" was elected to a General Committee in St. Mary's County in accordance with the resolves of the Continental Congress in 1775 [Ref: MR-127].

BOND, Zachariah. "Major Zacharia Bond" was elected to a General Committee in St. Mary's County in accordance with the resolves of the

Continental Congress in 1775 [Ref: MR-126]. "Zachariah Bond" died testate by Dec., 1777 [Ref: SO-6].

BONEY, Thomas. Took the Oath of Allegiance in Calvert County in 1778 [Ref: L-35]. The Register of St. Andrew's Episcopal Church in St. Mary's County records that Thomas Boney and Jean Davidson were married Oct. 20, 1771 [Ref: MB-383]. One Thomas Boney and Sarah Fleet were married on Oct. 31, 1780, by Rev. Francis Lauder, of Christ Church Parish [Ref: K-36].

BOOKER, James. Private, St. Mary's County Militia, 1777 [Ref: M-213]. Took the Oath of Allegiance in St. Mary's County in 1780 [Ref: Q-105].

BOOKER, Joseph. Private, St. Mary's County Militia, 1777 [Ref: M-213]. Took the Oath of Allegiance before the Hon. Henry G. Sothoron in St. Mary's County in 1778 [Ref: J-1146, K-68]. Joseph Booker married Eleanor Plummer on Jan. 3, 1778, St. Mary's County, by Rev. John Stephen, Rector of All Faith's Parish [Ref: I-535].

BOON, John. Private, Calvert County, enlisted by Lt. Frederick Skinner on Aug. 23, 1776 [Ref: D-33].

BOOTH, Basil. Private, St. Mary's County Militia, 1777 [Ref: M-210]. Took the Oath of Allegiance before the Hon. Richard Barnes in St. Mary's County in 1778 [Ref: J-1146, K-66]. The Register of St. Francis Xavier Catholic Church states that Basil Booth and Elizabeth Henry were married March 9, 1780 [Ref: SC-36].

BOOTH, George. Took the Oath of Allegiance before the Hon. John Ireland in St. Mary's County in 1778 [Ref: J-1146, K-65]. One George Booth died intestate by March, 1795 [Ref: SO-224].

BOOTH, Henry. Private, St. Mary's County Militia, 1777 [Ref: M-213].

BOOTH, James. Private, St. Mary's County Militia, 1777 [Ref: M-210]. Took the Oath of Allegiance before the Hon. Richard Barnes in St. Mary's County in 1778 [Ref: J-1146, K-66].

BOOTH, John. Private, St. Mary's County Militia, 1777 [Ref: M-214]. Took the Oath of Allegiance before the Hon. Vernon Hebb in St. Mary's County in 1778 [Ref: J-1146, K-67]. "John Booth, Sr." took the Oath of Allegiance before the Hon. Richard Barnes in St. Mary's County in 1778 [Ref: J-1146, K-66]. One John Booth died testate by Aug., 1792, leavings orphans William, Ignatius, and Matthias Booth, all above the age of 14 [Ref: SO-178, SO-182, SO-222].

BOOTH, Joseph. Took the Oath of Allegiance before the Hon. Richard Barnes in St. Mary's County in 1778 [Ref: J-1146, K-66].

BOOTH, Joshua. Private, St. Mary's County Militia, 1777 [Ref: M-214].

BOOTH, Leonard. Took the Oath of Allegiance before the Hon. Richard Barnes in St. Mary's County in 1778 [Ref: J-1146, K-66]. One "Leo Booth" was born on May 4, 1758, died on May 18, 1810 and was buried at St. Xavier Roman Catholic Church [Ref: R-342].

BOOTH, Richard. This name appeared twice as a private in the St. Mary's County Militia in 1777 [Ref: M-210, M-214]. Took the Oath of

Allegiance before the Hon. Richard Barnes in St. Mary's County in 1778 [Ref: J-1146, K-66].

BOTHICK, John. Took the Oath of Allegiance before the Hon. John Ireland in St. Mary's County in 1778 [Ref: J-1146, K-65].

BOUCHER, John Thomas. Lieutenant aboard the State ship *Defence* on March 28, 1776; from St. Mary's County [Ref: S-148].

BOULDS, James. Private, St. Mary's County Militia, 1777 [Ref: M-214, which listed the name as "James Bould"].

BOULDS, John. Took the Oath of Allegiance before the Hon. Richard Barnes in St. Mary's County in 1778 [Ref: J-1146, K-66, which listed the name as "John Bolds"].

BOULDS, William. Took the Oath of Allegiance before the Hon. John Ireland in St. Mary's County in 1778 [Ref: J-1146, K-65].

BOULT (BOLT), Thomas. Private, St. Mary's County Militia, 1777 [Ref: M-212, which listed the name as "Thomas Bolt"]. Took the Oath of Allegiance before the Hon. Vernon Hebb in St. Mary's County in 1778 [Ref: J-1146, K-67]. Loaned money in St. Mary's County for the war effort in 1781 [Ref: X-78, H-479].

BOURNE, Cassandra. See "Nathaniel Cullumber (Cullember)," q.v.

BOURNE, Jesse. Private, Capt. Richard Parran's Co., Calvert County Militia, 1778 [Ref: J-1146, M-149]. Took the Oath of Allegiance in Calvert County in 1778 [Ref: L-35].

BOURNE, Jesse Jacob. Ensign, Capt. Richard Parran's Co., Calvert County Militia, 1778 [Ref: J-1146, M-55, M-149, E-37]. Took the Oath of Allegiance in Calvert County in 1778 [Ref: L-35]. The Christ Church Register in Calvert County records the birth of James E. Bourne, son of Jesse Jacob and Ann Bourne, on Aug. 19, 1781 [Ref: O-4].

BOURNE, Mark. Took the Oath of Allegiance before the Hon. John Shanks in St. Mary's County in 1778 [Ref: J-1146, K-69].

BOURNE, Thomas. Private, Capt. Edward Wood's Co., Calvert County Militia, 1778 [Ref: J-1146, M-147].

BOWEN, Abraham. Private, Capt. Edward Wood's Co., Calvert County Militia, 1778 [Ref: J-1146, M-147]. Took the Oath of Allegiance in Calvert County in 1778 [Ref: L-35].

BOWEN, Ann (Anne). See "Robert Games" and "Thomas Gray," q.v.

BOWEN, Barbara. See "John Bowen, of Basil," q.v.

BOWEN, Basil. Private, Capt. Edward Wood's Co., Calvert County Militia, 1778 [Ref: J-1146, M-147]. Took the Oath of Allegiance in Calvert County in 1778 [Ref: L-35, which listed the name as "Basis Bowen"].

BOWEN, Basil (of Basil). Private, Capt. Edward Wood's Co., Calvert County Militia, 1778 [Ref: J-1146, M-147, which listed the name as "Bazil Bowen, for Bazl."].

BOWEN, Benjamin. See "John Bowen, of Basil," q.v.

BOWEN, Charles. Private, Capt. Edward Wood's Co., Calvert County Militia, 1778 [Ref: J-1146, M-147]. Private, Capt. Henry Skinner's Foot Co. of Hunting Hundred, Calvert County, 1777 [Ref: T-1814, O-125]. Took the Oath of Allegiance in Calvert County in 1778 [Ref: L-35]. Charles Bowen and Martha Gray were married on April 16, 1779, by Rev. Francis Lauder, of Christ Church Parish [Ref: K-35].

BOWEN, David. Private, Capt. Edward Wood's Co., Calvert County Militia, 1778 [Ref: J-1146, M-147]. Took the Oath of Allegiance in Calvert County in 1778 [Ref: L-35].

BOWEN, Dinah and Elenor. See "John Bowen, of Basil," q.v.

BOWEN, Elizabeth. See "Jesse Bowen," q.v.

BOWEN, Isaac. Private, Capt. Henry Skinner's Foot Co. of Hunting Hundred, Calvert County, 1777 [Ref: T-1814, O-125]. This name appeared twice as a private in Capt. Edward Wood's Co., Calvert County Militia, 1778 [Ref: J-1146, M-147]. Took the Oath of Allegiance in Calvert County in 1778 [Ref: L-35].

BOWEN, Jacob. Private, Capt. Thomas Truman Greenfield's Co., Calvert County Militia, 1778 [Ref: J-1146, M-150]. Private, Capt. Henry Skinner's Foot Co. of Hunting Hundred, Calvert County, 1777 [Ref: T-1814, O-125]. Took the Oath of Allegiance in Calvert County in 1778 [Ref: L-35].

BOWEN, Jacob Jr. Took the Oath of Allegiance in Calvert County in 1778 [Ref: L-35].

BOWEN, James. Private, Capt. Edward Wood's Co., Calvert County Militia, 1778 [Ref: J-1146, M-147].

BOWEN, Jesse. Took the Oath of Allegiance in Calvert County in 1778 [Ref: L-35]. The Christ Church Register in Calvert County records the birth of Jesse Bowen, son of Jesse and Elizabeth Bowen, on Dec. 1, 1742 [Ref: O-4].

BOWEN, John. Private, Capt. Edward Wood's Co., Calvert County Militia, 1778 [Ref: J-1146, M-147]. This name appeared twice on the list of those who took the Oath of Allegiance in Calvert County in 1778 [Ref: L-35]. John Bowen and Sarah Tucker were married on Nov. 5, 1778, by Rev. Francis Lauder, of Christ Church Parish [Ref: K-34].

BOWEN, John (of Basil). Private, Capt. Edward Wood's Co., Calvert County Militia, 1778 [Ref: J-1146, M-147, which listed the name as "John Bowen, for Bazl."]. "John Bowen, of Basil" married twice: (1) Martha ----, and had twins Benjamin and Elenor born on Dec. 22, 1781; and, (2) Dinah ----, and had these children: Barbara (born Oct. 22, 1796); Rebeccah (born May 28, 1798); and, John (born June 19, 1802). [Ref: O-32].

BOWEN, Mark. Private, St. Mary's County Militia, 1777 [Ref: M-212].

BOWEN, Martha. See "John Bowen, of Basil," q.v.

BOWEN, Parker. Private, Capt. Edward Wood's Co., Calvert County Militia, 1778 [Ref: J-1146, M-147]. Took the Oath of Allegiance in Calvert County in 1778 [Ref: L-35].
BOWEN, Thomas. Took the Oath of Allegiance in Calvert County in 1778 [Ref: L-35].
BOWEN, Walter. Private, Calvert County, enlisted by Capt. John Brooke on July 25, 1776 [Ref: D-33, which listed the name as "Walter Bowen (Bawen)"]. Private, Capt. Edward Wood's Co., Calvert County Militia, 1778 [Ref: J-1146, M-147]. Took the Oath of Allegiance in Calvert County in 1778 [Ref: L-35].
BOWEN, Young. Private, Capt. Edward Wood's Co., Calvert County Militia, 1778 [Ref: J-1146, M-147]. Took the Oath of Allegiance in Calvert County in 1778 [Ref: L-35].
BOWES, Timothy. "Tim. Bowes" was a private in the St. Mary's County Militia, 1777 [Ref: M-214]. "Timothy Bowes" was selected to served on the Committee of Correspondence in 1775, and was clerk of the General Committee in St. Mary's County that had been elected in accordance with the resolves of the Continental Congress [Ref: MR-127]. Served as clerk on the Committee of Observation in 1776 [Ref: S-16, B-100]. "Timothy Bowes, Revolutionary patriot," is buried in Old St. Aloysius Cemetery (no marker) at the north end of Leonardtown [Ref: S-128].
BOWIE, Allen. See "Frisby Freeland," q.v.
BOWIE, Barbara. See "Ignatius Taylor," q.v.
BOWIE, Matthew. Private, St. Mary's County, 3rd Maryland Line, Capt. Armstrong's Co., 1778-1780 [Ref: D-299].
BOWIE, Sarah. See "Frisby Freeland," q.v.
BOWLES, Henrietta. See "John Bowles," q.v.
BOWLES, Ignatius. Took the Oath of Allegiance before the Hon. Henry Reeder in St. Mary's County in 1778 [Ref: J-1146, K-64]. The Register of St. Francis Xavier Catholic Church states that Ignatius Bowles and Catherine Gough were married Jan. 21, 1777 [Ref: SC-36]. See "John Bowles," q.v.
BOWLES, James. Private, St. Mary's County Militia, 1777 [Ref: M-210]. See "John Bowles," q.v.
BOWLES, John. This name appeared twice as a private in the St. Mary's County Militia in 1777 [Ref: M-210]. The Register of St. Francis Xavier Catholic Church states one "John Bowls and Elizabeth Payn" were married Jan. 11, 1776 [Ref: SC-35]. One John Bowles had the following children in 1774: William, John Baptist, Joseph, James J., Jane, Susan, Henrietta, and Mary [Ref: MK-14]. John Bowles and his brothers Ignatius and William were among the early Catholic settlers who migrated from St. Mary's County to Pottinger's Creek in now Washington County, Kentucky, in 1785 [Ref: MK-15].
BOWLES, Joseph. See "John Bowles," q.v.
BOWLES, Mary. See "Joshua Clarke" and "John Bowles," q.v.

BOWLES, Susan. See "John Bowles," q.v.
BOWLES, Timothy. See "Timothy Bowes," q.v.
BOWLES, William. Private, St. Mary's County Militia, 1777 [Ref: M-210]. Sergeant, 2nd Maryland Line, 1779. Supplied provisions (wheat, mutton, or bacon) to the Army in 1780 [Ref: S-77, S-148]. See "John Bowles," q.v.
BOWLING, William. Private, St. Mary's County Militia, 1777 [Ref: M-212]. Took the Oath of Allegiance before the Hon. John Shanks in St. Mary's County in 1778 [Ref: J-1146, K-69]. "William Ignatius Bowling," private, 5th Maryland Line, applied for and received pensions S34655 on May 11, 1818, in St. Mary's County, aged 58, stating he had enlisted on March 1, 1782 in St. Mary's County and was discharged on June 5, 1783 at Frederick Town, Maryland. His daughters Teresia Stirling and Ann Bishop were named in a letter from Baltimore on Feb. 6, 1838, and it appears that William died on March 4, 1820 [Ref: P-343, P-344, *National Genealogical Society Quarterly*, Volume 24, No. 2 (1936), p. 51]. A pensioner named "William I. Bowling" died on Aug. 8, 1820, aged 60, St. Mary's County [Ref: U-40]. "William Bowling, farmer" moved from Lower Newtown in St. Mary's County to Jefferson County, Kentucky in 1802 [Ref: X-85].
BOYCE, Rebecca and Roger. See "Edward Johnson," q.v.
BOYD, James. Manufacturer of muskets and bayonets in 1776 [Ref: S-148]. Took the Oath of Allegiance before the Hon. Jeremiah Jordan in St. Mary's County in 1778 [Ref: J-1146, K-67]. Colonel Jeremiah Jordan was paid "for the use of James Boyd" in 1777 [Ref: S-33]. One James Boyd died intestate by April, 1800 [Ref: SO-155].
BOYD, John Jr. Private, St. Mary's County Militia, 1777 [Ref: M-212].
BOYD, Robert. Took the Oath of Allegiance in Calvert County in 1778 [Ref: L-35].
BRACCO, Bennett. First Lieutenant, later Captain, 1st Independent Maryland Co., Charles and Calvert Counties, 1776 [Ref: D-20].
BRADBURN, James. Private, St. Mary's County Militia, 1777 [Ref: M-210]. Took the Oath of Allegiance before the Hon. Richard Barnes in St. Mary's County in 1778 [Ref: J-1146, K-66].
BRADBURN, John. Took the Oath of Allegiance before the Hon. John Ireland in St. Mary's County in 1778 [Ref: J-1146, K-65].
BRADBURN, John Jr. Took the Oath of Allegiance before the Hon. John Ireland in St. Mary's County in 1778 [Ref: J-1146, K-65].
BRADBURN, Notley. Private, St. Mary's County Militia, 1777 [Ref: M-210].
BRADBURN, William. Took the Oath of Allegiance before the Hon. Henry Reeder in St. Mary's County in 1778 [Ref: J-1146, K-64]. The Register of St. Francis Xavier Catholic Church states that William Bradburn and Elizabeth Edley were married Dec. 22, 1778 [Ref: SC-36].
BRADFORD, Mary. See "Charles McGee," q.v.

BRADSHAW, Jo. Private, Capt. Uriah Forrest's Co., Flying Camp, St. Mary's County, July 28, 1776 [Ref: D-30, SM-111].

BRADY, Basil. Took the Oath of Allegiance in St. Mary's County in 1780 [Ref: Q-106]. Private, St. Mary's County Militia, 1777 [Ref: M-211, which listed the name as "Basil Bradey"].

BRADY, Benjamin. Took the Oath of Allegiance in Calvert County in 1780 [Ref: Q-106].

BRADY, Edward. Private, Capt. Benjamin Bond's Co., Calvert County Militia, 1778 [Ref: J-1146, M-149, which listed the name as "Edward Bradie"]. Took the Oath of Allegiance in Calvert County in 1778 [Ref: L-35].

BRADY, Henry. Private, St. Mary's County Militia, 1777 [Ref: M-210]. Took the Oath of Allegiance in St. Mary's County in 1780 [Ref: Q-106].

BRADY, James. "James Bradey" was a private, St. Mary's County Militia, 1777 [Ref: M-210]. "James Bready" was a private, St. Mary's County Militia, 1777 [Ref: M-209]. "John Brady" took the Oath of Allegiance in St. Mary's County in 1780 [Ref: Q-106].

BRADY, John. "John Brady" took the Oath of Allegiance in St. Mary's County in 1780 [Ref: Q-106]. "John Brawdy" married Elizabeth Davis on April 8, 1778, St. Mary's County, by Rev. John Stephen, Rector of All Faith's Parish [Ref: I-535].

BRADY, John Jr. (1) "John Bready, Jr." was a private, St. Mary's County Militia, 1777 [Ref: M-210]. (2) "John Braddy, Jr." was a private, Capt. Henry Skinner's Foot Co. of Hunting Hundred, Calvert County, 1777 [Ref: T-1814, O-125].

BRADY, Joseph. Private, Capt. Henry Skinner's Foot Co. of Hunting Hundred, Calvert County, 1777 [Ref: T-1814, O-125, which listed the name as "Joseph Braddy"].

BRAMHALL, James. Private, Capt. Uriah Forrest's Co., Flying Camp, St. Mary's County, July 28, 1776 [Ref: D-30, SM-111].

BRAMHALL, John. Private, Capt. Uriah Forrest's Co., Flying Camp, St. Mary's County, July 28, 1776 [Ref: D-30, SM-111].

BRAMHALL, Joseph. Private, St. Mary's County Militia, 1777 [Ref: M-210].

BRANSON, James. Private, St. Mary's County Militia, 1777 [Ref: M-210].

BRANSON, John B. (1756-c1839). Private, 1st Maryland Line, 1781-1782. Treasurer of Maryland was directed in 1812 to pay him "the half pay of a private, quarterly, as a provision to him in his indigent situation and advanced life, for those services to which his country has been so essentially benefitted." [Ref: I-322]. Applied for and received pension S34662 on April 21, 1818, in St. Mary's County, aged 62. In 1820 he had a wife (aged 44) and two female children aged 4 and 2 years, but no names were given [Ref: P-368, D-355, D-441]. He was on the pension rolls in 1835, aged 79 [Ref: U-40, which source listed the name as "John Brunson"]. On March 3, 1840, the Treasurer of Maryland was directed "to pay Mary Branson, of St. Mary's County, or her order, $12.11, the amount of arrears due her late husband at the time of his death. Treasurer was also directed to pay Mary Branson, widow of John B. Branson, late a soldier of the revolution, quarterly, during life, the half pay of a private commencing Jan. 1, 1840, in consideration of the services rendered by her husband during the war." [Ref: I-322].

BRANSON, Leonard. Private, St. Mary's County, enlisted May 25, 1778, for 9 months [Ref: D-329, SM-111].

BRANSON, Leonard Jr. Private, St. Mary's County Militia, 1777 [Ref: M-211].

BRANSON, Mary. See "John B. Branson," q.v.

BRANSON, Michael. Took the Oath of Allegiance in St. Mary's County in 1780 [Ref: Q-106].

BRANSON, Thomas. Private, St. Mary's County, enlisted May 25, 1778, for 9 months [Ref: D-329]. Took the Oath of Allegiance before the Hon. Ignatius Fenwick, Jr. in St. Mary's County in 1778 [Ref: J-1146, K-68]. One Thomas Branson died intestate by April, 1779 [Ref: SO-20].

BRASHEAR, Elizabeth. See "Basil Brown," q.v.

BRASHEARS, John. Private, St. Mary's County, who served in the Maryland Line until 1781 when discharged [Ref: D-406].

BRASSAU, John. Took the Oath of Allegiance in Calvert County in 1778 [Ref: L-35].

BRASSAU, John Jr. Private, Capt. Charles Williamson's Co., Calvert County Militia, 1778 [Ref: J-1146, M-147]. Took the Oath of Allegiance in Calvert County in 1778 [Ref: L-35].

BRAWDY, John. See "John Brady," q.v.

BREEDEN, Angelica. See "Matthias Breeden," q.v.

BREEDEN, Enoch. Private, St. Mary's County Militia, 1777 [Ref: M-213]. Took the Oath of Allegiance before the Hon. Robert Watts in St. Mary's County in 1778 [Ref: J-1146, K-62].

BREEDEN, Joseph. Private, Calvert County, enlisted by Ensign James Somervill on July 25, 1776 [Ref: D-34, which listed the name as "Joseph Bruden"]. Private, Capt. Richard Parran's Co., Calvert County Militia, 1778 [Ref: J-1146, M-149, which listed the name as "Jos. Breden"]. Took the Oath of Allegiance in Calvert County in 1778 [Ref: L-35]. "Joseph Breedin" and Susanna Stallions were married on Jan. 21, 1779, by Rev. Francis Lauder, of Christ Church Parish [Ref: K-35].

BREEDEN, Josiah. See "Matthias Breeden," q.v.

BREEDEN, Matthias. Private, St. Mary's County Militia, 1777 [Ref: M-215]. One Mathias Breeden died by April, 1789, leaving orphaned children Josiah, Morris and Angelica [Ref: SO-10, S0-189, SO-200].

BREEDEN, Morris. See "Matthias Breeden," q.v.

BREEM, John. First Lieutenant, Upper Bn., St. Mary's County, Aug. 26, 1777 [Ref: M-56, C-346, SM-111].

BREEZE, John. Private, Capt. Thomas Truman Greenfield's Co., Calvert County Militia, 1778 [Ref: J-1146, M-150]. Took the Oath of Allegiance in Calvert County in 1778 [Ref: L-35].

BREHON, James G. (Doctor). Native of Ireland who came to America prior to the Revolution and was surgeon in the Navy during that war. In 1776 Dr. Brehon may have been reluctant in giving up books on physic which he had recovered from the wrecks of the British fleet off St. George's Island, St. Mary's County. He died on April 8, 1819, at an advanced age, in Warrenton, South Carolina [Ref: R-344, B-388, B-389].

BREWER, Bennett. Private, St. Mary's County Militia, 1777 [Ref: M-214].

BREWER, George. Private, St. Mary's County Militia, 1777 [Ref: M-214]. Took the Oath of Allegiance before the Hon. Vernon Hebb in St. Mary's County in 1778 [Ref: J-1146, K-67].

BREWER, James. Private, St. Mary's County Militia, 1777 [Ref: M-211]. Took the Oath of Allegiance before the Hon. John Reeder in St. Mary's County in 1778 [Ref: J-1146, K-69]. One James Brewer married Mary Yates and migrated to Washington County, Kentucky, where he died in 1810 [Ref: MK-17].

BREWER, John. Took the Oath of Allegiance in St. Mary's County in 1778 before the Hon. Henry Reeder [Ref: J-1146, K-64] Private, 2nd Bn., 4th Co., died on July 7, 1782 [Ref: SM-111, R-345].

BREWER, John Sr. Took the Oath of Allegiance before the Hon. John Ireland in St. Mary's County in 1778 [Ref: J-1146, K-65]. Loaned money in St. Mary's County for the war effort in 1781 [Ref: X-78, H-436].

BREWER, John Baptist. Took the Oath of Allegiance before the Hon. Henry G. Sothoron in St. Mary's County in 1778 [Ref: J-1146, K-68]. Private, St. Mary's County Militia, 1777 [Ref: M-213].

BREWER, Mark. Took the Oath of Allegiance before the Hon. John Reeder in St. Mary's County in 1778 [Ref: J-1146, K-69].

BREWER, Mary. See "John Tompkins," q.v.

BREWER, Thomas. Private, St. Mary's County Militia, 1777 [Ref: M-211]. Took the Oath of Allegiance before the Hon. Henry Reeder in St. Mary's County in 1778 [Ref: J-1146, K-64]. Sergeant, 2nd Maryland Line, from Aug. 7, 1777 until discharged June 1, 1780 [Ref: D-82, S-37]. The Register of St. Francis Xavier Catholic Church states Thomas Brewer and Minta Dawsey were married Sep. 27, 1773 [Ref: SC-35]. See "William Brewer," q.v.

BREWER, William. Private, St. Mary's County Militia, 1777 [Ref: M-212]. Took the Oath of Allegiance before the Hon. Henry Reeder in St. Mary's County in 1778 [Ref: J-1146, K-64]. One William Brewer was an early Catholic settler in Nelson County, Kentucky in 1785, and Thomas Brewer had settled on Cox's Creek by 1800 [Ref: MK-17].

BREWER, Zachariah (Zacharias). Private, St. Mary's County Militia, 1777 [Ref: M-212]. Took the Oath of Allegiance before the Hon. Henry Reeder in St. Mary's County in 1778 [Ref: J-1146, K-64]. The Register of St. Francis Xavier Catholic Church states that Zachariah Brewer and Dorothy Cecil were married Jan. 26, 1778 [Ref: SC-36]. Zachariah Brewer died intestate before 1786 and his wife Dorothy married John McGill [Ref: SO-102, SO-106, SO-123].

BRIANT, Joseph. Private, Calvert County, enlisted by Lt. Frederick Skinner on Aug. 23, 1776 [Ref: D-33].

BRIANT, William. Took the Oath of Allegiance in St. Mary's County in 1780 [Ref: Q-106].

BRIDGET (BRIDGETT), Charles. Private, St. Mary's County Militia, 1777 [Ref: M-213].

BRIDGET (BRIDGETT), Thomas. (1) Private, St. Mary's County Militia, 1777 [Ref: M-213]. Took the Oath of Allegiance before the Hon. Jeremiah Jordan in St. Mary's County in 1778 [Ref: J-1146, K-67]. (2) Private, Capt. Uriah Forrest's Co., Flying Camp, St. Mary's County, July 28, 1776 [Ref: D-30, SM-111]. Took the Oath of Allegiance before the Hon. Henry G. Sothoron in St. Mary's County in 1778 [Ref: J-1146, K-68].

BRIGHT, Basil. Private, St. Mary's County Militia, 1777 [Ref: M-211].

BRIGHT, James. Took the Oath of Allegiance before the Hon. Jeremiah Jordan in St. Mary's County in 1778 [Ref: J-1146, K-67]. Private, 5th Maryland Line, discharged on May 14, 1780 [Ref: S-36, D-184].

BRIGHT, John. Took the Oath of Allegiance before the Hon. Richard Barnes in St. Mary's County in 1778 [Ref: J-1146, K-66].

BRIGHT, John B. Took the Oath of Allegiance before the Hon. Richard Barnes in St. Mary's County in 1778 [Ref: J-1146, K-66].

BRINAM, Jane. See "James Adams," q.v.

BRINGLE, Catharine. See "John Wood," q.v.

BRINKLEY, James. Private, Capt. Henry Skinner's Foot Co. of Hunting Hundred, Calvert County, 1777 [Ref: T-1814, O-125]. Private, Capt. Edward Wood's Co., Calvert County Militia, 1778 [Ref: J-1146, M-147]. Took the Oath of Allegiance in Calvert County in 1778 [Ref: L-35].

BRINKLEY, William. Private, Calvert County, enlisted by Capt. John Brooke on July 25, 1776 [Ref: D-33]. Private, Capt. Benjamin Bond's Co., Calvert County Militia, 1778 [Ref: J-1146, M-149]. Private, Capt. Henry Skinner's Foot Co. of Hunting Hundred, Calvert County, 1777 [Ref: T-1814, O-125]. Took the Oath of Allegiance in Calvert County in 1778 [Ref: L-35].

BRISCOE, Bennett. Private, St. Mary's County Militia, 1777 [Ref: M-215].

BRISCOE, Clement. Private, St. Mary's County Militia, 1777 [Ref: M-210]. Collector of the Tax in 1780 [Ref: S-148]. "Clem Briscoe and wife died on June 3, 1816." [Ref: R-345].

BRISCOE, Elizabeth. See "Seneca Chiseldine," q.v.

BRISCOE, Elizabeth Attaway. See "John Hanson Briscoe," q.v.

BRISCOE, Elizabeth Story. See "Barnet White Barber," q.v.

BRISCOE, Hanson. See "John Hanson Briscoe," q.v.
BRISCOE, Henrietta. See "William Thomas," q.v.
BRISCOE, Henry. Private, St. Mary's County, drafted July 27, 1781, at Leonardtown, for six months. Private, Maryland Line, discharged at Annapolis, Dec. 10, 1781. Applied for and received pension S30888 on Dec. 3, 1832 in Jefferson County, Kentucky, aged 70, stating he was born in St. Mary's County on Feb. 3, 1763 and moved to Jefferson County, Kentucky in 1802. He purchased a farm in Clark County, Illinois in Oct., 1835, and moved there in 1837. He died on Sep. 26, 1839, leaving a child (no name given). Affidavit given by Joseph Briscoe, but no relationship was stated [Ref: D-384, D-406, P-390, S-148, W-51, MK-18].
BRISCOE, Ignatius Jr. Private, St. Mary's County Militia, 1777 [Ref: M-215].
BRISCOE, John. See "Philip Briscoe," q.v.
BRISCOE, John Hanson. There was more than one man with this name. One John Hanson Briscoe (1752-1796) was a doctor and Second Major, 6th Bn., St. Mary's County, Jan. 12, 1776; Surgeon, 2nd Maryland Line, Jan. 1, 1777; Major, Upper Bn., Nov. 18, 1779 [Ref: M-56, F-18, S-140]. He was appointed by the State to collect gold and silver in St. Mary's County and was also appointed surgeon to the seven Independent Companies of Maryland in 1776. Justice of the Peace, 1778-1782. He furnished vessels in 1781 to transport wheat collected for taxes in the county to Georgetown and Baltimore and served as Judge of the Orphans Court in 1782-1783. On Jan. 7, 1782, at Chaptico, St. Mary's County, "Hanson Briscoe" wrote to Col. John Allen Thomas and requested a replacement for the confiscated sail on the State ship *Plater* [Ref: V-469]. "John Hanson Briscoe" was commissioned Brigadier General of the St. Mary's County Militia in 1794 [Ref: SM-149, SM-150]. He died intestate by Oct., 1796, and Elizabeth Attaway Briscoe was his administratrix [Ref: SO-249]. Elizabeth Attaway Briscoe (nee Bond), relict of Dr. John Hanson Briscoe, of St. Mary's County, died on June 5, 1816, at Chaptico, aged 48 [Ref: R-345]. A "Hanson Briscoe, elite" moved from Chaptico to Allegany County, Maryland, in 1792 [Ref: X-85]. "Major Hanson Briscoe, Clerk of the County Court at Cumberland, Maryland, died on Sep. 12, 1816, aged 68. He was a native of St. Mary's County and held a commission during the Revolutionary War." [Ref: R-345]. However, there appears to be a discrepancy in the records for in addition to the aforementioned Briscoes, another source notes that "Dr. John Hanson Briscoe, Revolutionary patriot," died on May 29, 1822, aged 81, and his stone in Christ Church Cemetery at Chaptico reads "Sacred to the memory of John Briscoe who died May 20, 1822, aged 81 years, emphatically it may be said that his life was a life of scrupulous integrity, rigid justice and temperance with great moderation and self denial." This same source also indicates that "Sergt. John Hanson

Briscoe, 2nd Maryland Line, is likely buried at Christ Church Cemetery (no marker) at Chaptico [Ref: S-128].

BRISCOE, Joseph. Private, St. Mary's County Militia, 1777 [Ref: M-215]. See "Henry Briscoe," q.v.

BRISCOE, McKay or Mackay. Private, St. Mary's County Militia, 1777 [Ref: M-215, which listed the name as "McHay Briscoe"].

BRISCOE, Philip Jr. "Philip Briscoe, Jr." was a private, St. Mary's County Militia, 1777 [Ref: M-210]. "Philip Briscoe" was a private, 1st Maryland Line, from June 1, 1778 until April 5, 1779, when he was discharged [Ref: D-82, S-149]. He was born in 1729, son of John Briscoe (1678-1734), and married Chloe Hanson circa 1750 [Ref: S-140]. See "Barnet White Barber," q.v.

BRISCOE, Robert. Private, St. Mary's County Militia, 1777 [Ref: M-210]. Ensign, Upper Bn., Nov. 18, 1779 [Ref: M-56, F-18]. Loaned money in St. Mary's County for the war effort in 1781 [Ref: X-78, H-412].

BRISCOE, Samuel H. Private, Capt. Uriah Forrest's Co., Flying Camp, St. Mary's County, July 28, 1776 [Ref: D-30, SM-111].

BRISCOE, Stephen. Private, St. Mary's County Militia, 1777 [Ref: M-215].

BRISCOE, Thomas. Paid by the State for riding "Express" on June 25, 1776, and for making salt on July 8, 1782 [Ref: S-149].

BRISCOE, Thomas Jr. Private, St. Mary's County Militia, 1777 [Ref: M-215].

BRITAIN, Slater. Private, Capt. Charles Williamson's Co., Calvert County Militia, 1778 [Ref: J-1146, M-148]. Took the Oath of Allegiance in Calvert County in 1778 [Ref: L-35, which listed the name as "States Britain"].

BRODOC, John. Private, St. Mary's County Militia, 1777 [Ref: M-213].

BROME, Anne. See "Nathaniel Wilson," q.v.

BROME (BROOME), Hooper. "Hooper Brome" was a private in St. Mary's County Militia, 1777 [Ref: M-213]. "Hooper Broome" took the Oath of Allegiance before the Hon. Henry G. Sothoron in St. Mary's County in 1778 [Ref: J-1146, K-68]. "Hooper Broom" married Catherine ----- and was still living in 1797 [Ref: SO-265].

BROME, James Mackall. See "John Brome," q.v.

BROME (BROOME), John (1749-1778). Son of Col. John Brome and Mary Mackall. Captain John Brome was a vestryman of Christ Church in Calvert County in 1774 and took the vestryman's oath to support the colonies against Great Britain. He served in several official capacities, including: Member of the Committee of Observation, 1774-1775; Council of Safety; Member of the Provincial Convention held in Annapolis; and, commissioned Colonel in 1776. He married Elizabeth (Betty) Heigh Gantt (1757-1789), daughter of Thomas Gantt, Jr. and Susanna Mackall, and had these children: John Brome (born 1775, married Ann Wilson (cousin) in 1805; was an officer in the War of 1812); James Mackall

Brome (born 1777, died young); and Mary Mackall Brome (born 1778, married Dr. Alexander Duke, and moved to Kentucky). [Re: *Colonial Families of the United States of America*, Vol. I, by George Norbury Mackenzie (1907), pp. 37, 187]. Took the Oath of Allegiance in Calvert County in 1778 [Ref: L-35].

BROME (BROOME, BROOM), John Jr. "John Brome, Jr." took the Oath of Allegiance in Calvert County in 1778 [Ref: L-35]. "John Broom, Jr." was a private in Capt. Walter Smith's Co., Calvert County Militia, 1778 [Ref: J-1146, M-148].

BROME (BROOME), John Hooper. Private, St. Mary's County Militia, 1777 [Ref: M-212]. "John Hooper Brome" took the Oath of Allegiance before the Hon. John Reeder in St. Mary's County in 1778 [Ref: J-1146, K-69]. "John Hooper Broome" was a Captain, Upper Bn., Nov. 18, 1779 [Ref: M-56, F-18]. "John H. Brome" was elected to a General Committee in St. Mary's County in accordance with the resolves of the Continental Congress in 1775 [Ref: MR-127]. "John H. Brome" died testate by Aug., 1799, and his name was listed as "John Hooper Broome" in the probate records [Ref: SO-289, SO-299].

BROME, Mary Mackall. See "John Brome," q.v.

BROME (BROOME), Thomas. Private, Capt. Walter Smith's Co., Calvert County Militia, 1778 [Ref: J-1146, M-148].

BROME (BROOME), William. "William D. Broome" was a private, Capt. Walter Smith's Co., Calvert County Militia, 1778 [Ref: J-1146, M-148]. "William Brome" took the Oath of Allegiance in Calvert County in 1778 [Ref: L-35].

BROOKBANK, James. Private, St. Mary's County Militia, 1777 [Ref: M-210]. Private, 1st Maryland Line, enlisted on July 5, 1779, and later reported "dead or deserted" (no date given). [Ref: D-82].

BROOKBANK, John Sr. Private, St. Mary's County Militia, 1777 [Ref: M-210]. "Jno. Brookbank" was a private, 1st Maryland Line, from July 31, 1779 to at least Nov. 1, 1780 [Ref: D-82]. "John Brookbank, farmer" moved from Chaptico to Washington County, Maryland after 1790 [Ref: X-85].

BROOKE, Basil. (1) Private, St. Mary's County Militia, 1777 [Ref: M-213]. (2) Private, Capt. Benjamin Bond's Co., Calvert County Militia, 1778 [Ref: J-1146, M-149].

BROOKE, Basil Jr. Took the Oath of Allegiance in Calvert County in 1778 [Ref: L-35].

BROOKE, Francis. Took the Oath of Allegiance before the Hon. Ignatius Fenwick, Jr. in St. Mary's County in 1778 [Ref: J-1146, K-68]. Ensign, Lower Bn., June 22, 1780 [Ref: S-23, S-149]. See "Francis Brookes," q.v.

BROOKE, John. Captain, Calvert County, July, 1776 [Ref: D-33]. Took the Oath of Allegiance in Calvert County in 1778 [Ref: L-35]. Major, 15th Bn., April 16, 1778 [Ref: M-56, E-37].

BROOKE, Michael. Took the Oath of Allegiance before the Hon. John Ireland in St. Mary's County in 1778 [Ref: J-1146, K-65].
BROOKE, Monica. See "Michael Taney," q.v.
BROOKE, Priscilla. See "Edward Gantt," q.v.
BROOKE, Roger. See "Michael Taney," q.v.
BROOKEN (BROOKN?), John Jr. Private, St. Mary's County Militia, 1777 [Ref: M-210].
BROOKES, Francis. Private, St. Mary's County Militia, 1777 [Ref: M-211]. Ensign, Lower Bn., June 22, 1780 [Ref: M-56, F-201].
BROOME, John. See "John Brome," q.v.
BROTHERS, Cornelius. Private, St. Mary's County Militia, 1777 [Ref: M-212]. Took the Oath of Allegiance before the Hon. Richard Barnes in St. Mary's County in 1778 [Ref: J-1146, K-66].
BROWN, Basil (Oct. 25, 1732 - Feb. 10, 1807). Private, St. Mary's County Militia, 1777 [Ref: M-211]. Private, 3rd and 1st Maryland Lines, 1778-1780 and 1781-1783 [Ref: S-149]. He married Elizabeth Brashear [Ref: Y-91]. The Register of St. Francis Xavier Catholic Church states that one Basil Brown and Ann Mattingly were married on June 20, 1777 [Ref: SC-36]. "John Basil Brown, elite" moved from Lower Newtown to Nelson County, Kentucky after 1790 [Ref: X-85].
BROWN, Cecelia. See "Thomas Bond" and "Philip Key," q.v.
BROWN, Cloe. See "Basil Thompson," q.v.
BROWN, George Jr. Took the Oath of Allegiance in Calvert County in 1778 [Ref: L-35].
BROWN, George Thomas. Took the Oath of Allegiance before the Hon. Jeremiah Jordan in St. Mary's County in 1778 [Ref: J-1146, K-67].
BROWN, Gustavus (1751 - July 3, 1801). Son of Rev. Richard Brown, M. D., and grandson of Gustavus Brown, M. D., of Charles County (not to be confused with Dr. Gustavus Richard Brown, 1748-1804). Dr. Brown was a private in the St. Mary's County Militia in 1777. He married by 1788 to Susannah (Reeder) Ireland, widow of "John Ireland," q.v., and died in 1801, with burial in a private cemetery of the Reeder family at "Westfield" in St. Mary's County [Ref: M-212, N-675, R-346, SO-127]. See "Thomas Bond" and "John Reeder, Jr.," q.v.
BROWN, Ignatius. Private, St. Mary's County Militia, 1777 [Ref: M-212]. Took the Oath of Allegiance before the Hon. Richard Barnes in St. Mary's County in 1778 [Ref: J-1146, K-66].
BROWN, James. (1) Private, Capt. James Patterson's Co., Calvert County Militia, Aug. 10, 1777 [Ref: M-146]. Private, Capt. James Grahame's Co., Calvert County Militia, 1778 [Ref: J-1146, M-149]. Took the Oath of Allegiance in Calvert County in 1778 [Ref: L-35]. (2) Private, St. Mary's County Militia, 1777 [Ref: M-212]. (3) Cabin Boy aboard the State ship *Defence* in 1776 [Ref: S-25, D-607]. Three men with this name took the Oath of Allegiance in St. Mary's County in 1778: one before the Hon.

Richard Barnes, one before the Hon. John Shanks, and one before the Hon. John Reeder [Ref: J-1146, K-66, K-69].

BROWN, John Basil. See "Basil Brown," q.v.

BROWN, Joseph. Private (substitute), St. Mary's County, Aug. 2, 1781 [Ref: D-384]. Private, Continental Army, 1781 [Ref: D-406].

BROWN, Lydia. See "Richard Hill," q.v.

BROWN, Mary Ann. See "Cuthbert Clarke," q.v.

BROWN, Monica. See "John Horrell," q.v.

BROWN, Nicholas. Private, St. Mary's County Militia, 1777 [Ref: M-213]. Took the Oath of Allegiance before the Hon. Henry Reeder in St. Mary's County in 1778 [Ref: J-1146, K-64]. Supplied provisions (wheat, mutton, or bacon) to the Army in 1780 [Ref: S-77, S-149].

BROWN, Peter. Took the Oath of Allegiance before the Hon. Henry Reeder in St. Mary's County in 1778 [Ref: J-1146, K-64]. The Register of St. Francis Xavier Catholic Church states one Peter Brown and Susan Low were married Dec. 21, 1773 [Ref: SC-35].

BROWN, Peter Jr. Private, St. Mary's County Militia, 1777 [Ref: M-213]. Took the Oath of Allegiance before the Hon. Henry Reeder in St. Mary's County in 1778 [Ref: J-1146, K-64].

BROWN, Richard. See "Gustavus Brown." q.v.

BROWN, Robert. Private, 4th Maryland Line, 1778-1780 [Ref: D-415]. He married Mary Ireland on Dec. 26, 1777, in St. Mary's County, by Rev. George Goldie [Ref: I-535].

BROWN, William. Took the Oath of Allegiance in Calvert County in 1778 [Ref: L-35]. William Brown and Dorcas Woodward were married on April 26, 1778, by Rev. Francis Lauder, of Christ Church Parish [Ref: K-34, MM-27].

BROWN, William Jr. Took the Oath of Allegiance before the Hon. Jeremiah Jordan in St. Mary's County in 1778 [Ref: J-1146, K-67].

BRUCE, Henrietta. See "Samuel Sothoron," q.v.

BRUCE, Sarah. See "Jesse Locke (Lock)," q.v.

BRUCE, William. Elected to serve on a General Committee in St. Mary's County in accordance with the resolves of the Continental Congress in 1775 [Ref: MR-127].

BRUNSON, John. See "John Branson," q.v.

BRYAN, Francis. Private, St. Mary's County Militia, 1777 [Ref: M-212].

BRYAN, Henry. Private, Continental Army, 1781 [Ref: S-149].

BRYAN, Ignatius. Private, St. Mary's County, drafted July 27, 1781 [Ref: D-384, which listed the name as "Ignatius Brion"]. Private, Continental Army, 1781 [Ref: D-406, which listed the name as "Ignatius Bryan"]. Took the Oath of Allegiance before the Hon. Robert Watts in St. Mary's County in 1778 [Ref: J-1146, K-62].

BRYAN, Philip. Sergeant, St. Mary's County Militia, 1777 [Ref: M-213]. Took the Oath of Allegiance before the Hon. John Reeder in St. Mary's County in 1778 [Ref: J-1146, K-69].

BRYAN, Susannah. See "Adam Wise," q.v.
BRYAN, William. Private, St. Mary's County Militia, 1777 [Ref: M-213]. Took the Oath of Allegiance before the Hon. Henry G. Sothoron in St. Mary's County in 1778 [Ref: J-1146, K-68].
BUCKINGHAM, John. Private, Capt. Edward Wood's Co., Calvert County Militia, 1778 [Ref: J-1146, M-147]. Took the Oath of Allegiance in Calvert County in 1778 [Ref: L-35]. The Christ Church Register in Calvert County records the birth of the children of John and Sarah Buckingham as follows: Mary (born Oct. 2, 1776); Anne (born Dec. 8, 1778, died Nov. 8, 1781); Rebeccah (born Feb. 16, 1781); Martha (born Jan. 8, 1783); Catherine (born Sep. 11, 1784); Thomas (born Sep. 28, 1786); and, Sarah (born Sep. 28, 1788). [Ref: O-4, O-5].
BUCKINGHAM, Sarah, and children. See "John Buckingham," q.v.
BUCKLER, Benjamin. Private, St. Mary's County Militia, 1777 [Ref: M-213]. Took the Oath of Allegiance in St. Mary's County in 1780 [Ref: Q-106].
BUCKLER, Robert. Took the Oath of Allegiance before the Hon. Jeremiah Jordan in St. Mary's County in 1778 [Ref: J-1146, K-67]. He married Anna Bullock on Jan. 10, 1778, St. Mary's County, by Rev. George Goldie [Ref: I-535].
BUCKLER, Walter. Private (substitute), St. Mary's County, Aug. 5, 1781 [Ref: D-384].
BUCKMAN, Charles. Took the Oath of Allegiance before the Hon. Jeremiah Jordan in St. Mary's County in 1778 [Ref: J-1146, K-67].
BUCKMAN, Ignatius. Took the Oath of Allegiance before the Hon. Jeremiah Jordan in St. Mary's County in 1778 [Ref: J-1146, K-67]. Migrated to Washington County, Kentucky before 1800 [Ref: MK-20].
BUCKMASTER, Benjamin. Private, Capt. Henry Skinner's Foot Co. of Hunting Hundred, Calvert County, 1777 [Ref: T-1814, O-125]. Took the Oath of Allegiance in Calvert County in 1778 [Ref: L-35]. Private, Capt. Thomas Truman Greenfield's Co., Calvert County Militia, 1778 [Ref: J-1146, M-150].
BUCKMASTER, Henry. Private, Capt. Thomas Truman Greenfield's Co., Calvert County Militia, 1778 [Ref: J-1146, M-150]. Took the Oath of Allegiance in Calvert County in 1778 [Ref: L-35].
BUCKMASTER, N. Took the Oath of Allegiance in Calvert County in 1778 [Ref: L-35].
BUCKMASTER, Thomas. Private, Capt. Henry Skinner's Foot Co. of Hunting Hundred, Calvert County, 1777 [Ref: T-1814, O-125]. Took the Oath of Allegiance in Calvert County in 1778 [Ref: L-35].
BUDD, John. Private, St. Mary's County Militia, 1777 [Ref: M-210].
BUDD, Joseph. Took the Oath of Allegiance before the Hon. John Ireland in St. Mary's County in 1778 [Ref: J-1146, K-65].
BULL, Miss. See "William Evans," q.v.
BULLOCK, Anna. See "Robert Buckler," q.v.

BULLOCK, George. Took the Oath of Allegiance before the Hon. John Shanks in St. Mary's County in 1778 [Ref: J-1146, K-69].
BULLOCK, James. Private, St. Mary's County Militia, 1777 [Ref: M-212].
BULLOCK, Jesse. Private, St. Mary's County Militia, 1777 [Ref: M-213].
BULLOCK, John. Private, 3rd Maryland Line, 1780 [Ref: D-87, S-149].
BULLOCK, Joseph. Seaman from St. Mary's County who served aboard the sloop "Molly" from March 5, 1777 until discharged on May 10, 1777 [Ref: S-149, S-32].
BULLOCK, Joseph Lee. Private, St. Mary's County, served in Colonel Grayson's Regiment, from March 17, 1777 [Ref: SM-111, S-32, D-602].
BULLOCK, Justinian. Private, St. Mary's County, enlisted on April 24, 1778, for 3 years, and served in the 3rd Maryland Line [Ref: D-329, D-86]. Captured, escaped, and re-enlisted, but could not march due to swollen legs and was discharged [Ref: S-149]. Colonel John Allen Thomas wrote to the Governor on June 30, 1778, and requested disability pay for him, but he died later in 1778 [Ref: SM-111, R-348, D-86, S-149, V-178].
BULLOCK, Richard. Private, Capt. Uriah Forrest's Co., Flying Camp, St. Mary's County, July 28, 1776 [Ref: D-30, SM-111, S-149].
BULLOCK, William. Private, St. Mary's County Militia, 1777 [Ref: M-212].
BURKETT, Edward. Private, Capt. Edward Wood's Co., Calvert County Militia, 1778 [Ref: J-1146, M-147].
BURKETT, John. Private, Calvert County, enlisted by Ensign James Somervill on July 26, 1776 [Ref: D-34].
BURN, James Kent. Private, Capt. Edward Wood's Co., Calvert County Militia, 1778 [Ref: J-1146, M-147].
BURN, William. Private, St. Mary's County Militia, 1777 [Ref: M-213].
BURNETT, William. Private, Capt. Uriah Forrest's Co., Flying Camp, St. Mary's County, July 28, 1776 [Ref: D-30, SM-111, which latter source mistakenly listed the name as "Tom Burnett"].
BURNS, Timothy. Private, St. Mary's County, who served in the Maryland Line until 1781 when discharged [Ref: D-407].
BURRAGE, Edward Jr. Private, St. Mary's County Militia, 1777 [Ref: M-210].
BURRAGE, Thomas. Private, St. Mary's County Militia, 1777 [Ref: M-213].
BURRIS, Robert. Private, St. Mary's County, who served in the Maryland Line until 1781 when discharged [Ref: D-406].
BURROUGHS, Benjamin. Took the Oath of Allegiance before the Hon. Henry Tubman in St. Mary's County in 1778 [Ref: J-1146, K-70].
BURROUGHS, Benjamin Jr. Private, St. Mary's County Militia, 1777 [Ref: M-209]. Took the Oath of Allegiance before the Hon. Henry Tubman in St. Mary's County in 1778 [Ref: J-1146, K-70]. Private, 2nd Maryland Line, March 10, 1776 [Ref: SM-111, S-149].

BURROUGHS, Charles. Private, 2nd Maryland Line, March 11, 1777 [Ref: SM-111].
BURROUGHS, Elisha. Private (substitute), St. Mary's County, July 30, 1781 [Ref: D-384, which listed the name as "Elisha Burrowes"]. Private, Continental Army, discharged Dec. 3, 1781 [Ref: H-11 and S-109, which listed the name as "Elisha Burroughs," and D-406, which listed the name as "Elisha Burris"].
BURROUGHS, Eliza T. See "George Dent," q.v.
BURROUGHS, George. Private, St. Mary's County Militia, 1777 [Ref: M-209]. Took the Oath of Allegiance before the Hon. Henry Tubman in St. Mary's County in 1778 [Ref: J-1146, K-70].
BURROUGHS, Henry. Private, St. Mary's County Militia, 1777 [Ref: M-210].
BURROUGHS, Hezekiah (1747-1806). Son of Richard Burroughs. Hezekiah married Ann Sothoron in 1768 [Ref: S-140]. Private, St. Mary's County Militia, 1777 [Ref: M-209]. Took the Oath of Allegiance before the Hon. Henry Tubman in St. Mary's County in 1778 [Ref: J-1146, K-70]. Private, 1st Maryland Line, enlisted on June 3, 1778, fought at the Battle of White Plains on Sep. 2, 1778, and was discharged on April 5, 1779 [Ref: S-140]. "Hezikiah Burroughs" was appointed guardian of his two children Margaret Cartwright Burroughs and Mary Willson Burroughs in March, 1795 [Ref: SO-223]. "Hezekiah Burroughs, Jr., taylor" moved from Chaptico to Bourbon County, Kentucky, in 1799 [Ref: X-86].
BURROUGHS, James (of John). Sergeant, St. Mary's County Militia, 1777 [Ref: M-212]. Took the Oath of Allegiance in St. Mary's County in 1780 [Ref: Q-106].
BURROUGHS, James Sr. Private, St. Mary's County Militia, 1777 [Ref: M-209]. Took the Oath of Allegiance before the Hon. Henry Tubman in St. Mary's County in 1778 [Ref: J-1146, K-70, SM-111]. Ensign, Upper Bn., from Aug. 26, 1777 through Nov. 18, 1779 [Ref M-54, M-56, F-18, which listed the name both as "James Boroughs" and "James Burroughs"].
BURROUGHS, John Jr. Private, St. Mary's County Militia, 1777 [Ref: M-209]. Took the Oath of Allegiance before the Hon. Henry Tubman in St. Mary's County in 1778 [Ref: J-1146, K-70].
BURROUGHS, John Sr. Took the Oath of Allegiance before the Hon. Henry Tubman in St. Mary's County in 1778 [Ref: J-1146, K-70].
BURROUGHS, John C. See "Norman Burroughs," q.v.
BURROUGHS, Joseph. Took the Oath of Allegiance before the Hon. Henry Tubman in St. Mary's County in 1778 [Ref: J-1146, K-70].
BURROUGHS, Margaret and Mary. See "Hezekiah Burroughs," q.v.
BURROUGHS, Matthew. Private, St. Mary's County Militia, 1777 [Ref: M-210]. Took the Oath of Allegiance before the Hon. Henry Tubman in St. Mary's County in 1778 [Ref: J-1146, K-70].

BURROUGHS, Norman (Normand). Private, St. Mary's County Militia, 1777. Private, St. Mary's County, enlisted May 30, 1778, for 9 months, Maryland Line, Continental Army [Ref: M-210, SM-111, D-329, which listed the name as "Norman Bouroughs"]. He died in 1812 and his widow Esther Turner applied for and received pension W3935 on March 30, 1842, in Charles County, Maryland, stating she was born in St. Mary's County and they were married in King & Queen Parish in 1784. Also mentioned in 1842 was John C. Burroughs (no relation stated) who lived in St. Mary's County [Ref: P-487].

BURROUGHS, Richard. Private, St. Mary's County Militia, 1777 [Ref: M-209]. Took the Oath of Allegiance before the Hon. Henry Tubman in St. Mary's County in 1778 [Ref: J-1146, K-70]. Richard Burroughs married Barbara Wilson on Nov. 9, 1783, St. Mary's County, by Rev. John Stephen, Rector of All Faith's Parish [Ref: I-535]. See "Hezekiah Burroughs," q.v.

BURROUGHS, Samuel. "Samuel Burroughs" was a private in St. Mary's County Militia, 1777 [Ref: M-209]. "Samuel Burroughs, Sr." was a private in St. Mary's County Militia, 1777 [Ref: M-213]. One Samuel Burroughs died testate by Dec., 1796 [Ref: SO-254].

BURROUGHS, Samuel Jr. Took the Oath of Allegiance before the Hon. Henry Tubman in St. Mary's County in 1778 [Ref: J-1146, K-70].

BURROUGHS, William. Private, St. Mary's County Militia, 1777 [Ref: M-209]. Took the Oath of Allegiance before the Hon. Henry Tubman in St. Mary's County in 1778 [Ref: J-1146, K-70]. William Burroughs married Susanna Dent on Feb. 9, 1778, St. Mary's County, by Rev. John Stephen, Rector of All Faith's Parish [Ref: I-535].

BURROUGHS, Williamson. Took the Oath of Allegiance before the Hon. Henry Tubman in St. Mary's County in 1778 [Ref: J-1146, K-70].

BUSSEY, Charles. Took the Oath of Allegiance in Calvert County in 1780 [Ref: Q-106, which listed the name as "Charles Busy"].

BUSSEY, Charles Jr. Private, Capt. Richard Lane's Co., Calvert County Militia, 1778 [Ref: J-1146, M-150, which listed the name as "Charles Beausey, Jr."]. Took the Oath of Allegiance in Calvert County in 1780 [Ref: Q-106, which listed the name as "Charles Busy, Jr."].

BUSSEY, Daniel. Private, Capt. Richard Lane's Co., Calvert County Militia, 1778 [Ref: J-1146, M-149]. Took the Oath of Allegiance in Calvert County in 1780 [Ref: Q-106, which listed the name as "Daniel Busy"].

BUSSEY, Samuel. Took the Oath of Allegiance in Calvert County in 1780 [Ref: Q-107, which listed the name as "Samuel Busy"]. There was also a Samuel Bussey who served in the Maryland Line in 1781 [Ref: D-406].

BUSSEY, William. Private, Capt. Richard Lane's Co., Calvert County Militia, 1778 [Ref: J-1146, M-150, which listed the name as "William Beausey"]. Took the Oath of Allegiance in Calvert County in 1780 [Ref: Q-107, which listed the name as "William Busy"].

BYAL (RYAL), Elizabeth. See "Charles Mills," q.v.
BYRN, Eleanor. See "Joseph Vansweringen, Jr.," q.v.
BYRN, Michael. Private, St. Mary's County Militia, 1777 [Ref: M-215].Took the Oath of Allegiance before the Hon. Bennett Biscoe in St. Mary's County in 1778 [Ref: J-1146, K-63, which listed the name as "Michael Byrne"].
BYRN, Nicholas. Private, St. Mary's County Militia, 1777 [Ref: M-215]. Took the Oath of Allegiance before the Hon. Robert Armstrong in St. Mary's County in 1778 [Ref: J-1146, K-62].
CAHILL, Nathaniel. Private, St. Mary's County, drafted July 27, 1781 [Ref: D-384, which listed the name as "Nathaniel Kahil"]. Private, Continental Army, 1781 [Ref: D-409, which listed the name as "Nathaniel Kahill"].
CAHILL, Peregrine. Private, St. Mary's County Militia, 1777 [Ref: M-213]. Took the Oath of Allegiance in St. Mary's County in 1780 [Ref: Q-107].
CAHILL, Thomas. Private, Capt. Uriah Forrest's Co., Flying Camp, St. Mary's County, July 28, 1776 [Ref: D-30, SM-111].
CAIN, Marshak. Private, St. Mary's County Militia, 1777 [Ref: M-214].
CAIN, Michael. Took the Oath of Allegiance in Calvert County in 1778 [Ref: L-35].
CAIN, Thomas. Took the Oath of Allegiance before the Hon. Bennett Biscoe in St. Mary's County in 1778 [Ref: J-1146, K-63].
CAMDEN, Joseph. Private, Capt. Richard Lane's Co., Calvert County Militia, 1778 [Ref: J-1146, M-149]. Took the Oath of Allegiance in Calvert County in 1778 [Ref: L-35].
CAMPBELL, Allen. Private, St. Mary's County, who served in the Maryland Line until 1781 when discharged [Ref: D-407].
CAMPBELL, Archibald. Took the Oath of Allegiance before the Hon. Henry Reeder in St. Mary's County in 1778 [Ref: J-1146, K-64].
CAMPBELL, Edward. Private, St. Mary's County Militia, 1777 [Ref: M-212]. Took the Oath of Allegiance before the Hon. John Ireland in St. Mary's County in 1778 [Ref: J-1146, K-65].
CAMPBELL, Enoch. Private, St. Mary's County Militia, 1777 [Ref: M-211]. Took the Oath of Allegiance before the Hon. John Reeder in St. Mary's County in 1778 [Ref: J-1146, K-69]. The Register of St. Francis Xavier Catholic Church states that Enoch Campbell and Elizabeth Hall were married Dec. 30, 1771 [Ref: SC-34].
CAMPBELL, Ignatius. Private, St. Mary's County Militia, 1777 [Ref: M-213].
CANFIELD, Thomas. Private, St. Mary's County, who served in the Maryland Line until 1781 when discharged [Ref: D-407].
CARBERRY, Henry. Cadet, St. Mary's County, March 19, 1776. Applied for sea service and was an Able Seaman who served aboard the State ship *Defence* in 1776 [Ref: S-25, S-151, D-606].

CARBERRY, Joseph. Private, St. Mary's County Militia, 1777 [Ref: M-210]. Took the Oath of Allegiance before the Hon. Henry Reeder in St. Mary's County in 1778 [Ref: J-1146, K-64].
CARBERRY, Patrick. Private, St. Mary's County Militia, 1777 [Ref: M-212]. Took the Oath of Allegiance before the Hon. John Ireland in St. Mary's County in 1778 [Ref: J-1146, K-65].
CARBERRY, Peter. Private, St. Mary's County, Capt. Moore's Co., March 10, 1777. Took the Oath of Allegiance before the Hon. John Ireland in St. Mary's County in 1778. Private, 3rd Maryland Line, 1781-1782; Capt. Lynn's Co., Northern Detachment, 1783, and invalided (disabled) on Nov. 15, 1783 [Ref: J-1146, K-65, S-32, D-345, D-394, D-453, D-509, D-529, D-601, D-603, S-32, S-151].
CARBERRY, Richard. Private, 4th Maryland Line, Jan. 29, 1776 [Ref: SM-111].
CARBERRY, Thomas. See "William McGee," q.v.
CARD, Benson. Private, St. Mary's County Militia, 1777 [Ref: M-209].
CARD, Justinian. Took the Oath of Allegiance before the Hon. Jeremiah Jordan in St. Mary's County in 1778 [Ref: J-1146, K-67].
CARD, Sabret. Took the Oath of Allegiance in Calvert County in 1778 [Ref: L-35]. Private, Capt. Frisby Freeland's Co., Calvert County Militia, 1778 [Ref: J-1146, M-148].
CARD, Thomas. Took the Oath of Allegiance before the Hon. Jeremiah Jordan in St. Mary's County in 1778 [Ref: J-1146, K-67].
CARD, William. (1) Private, Capt. Benjamin Bond's Co., Calvert County Militia, 1778 [Ref: J-1146, M-149]. Took the Oath of Allegiance in Calvert County in 1778 [Ref: L-35]. (2) Private, St. Mary's County Militia, 1777 [Ref: M-210]. Took the Oath of Allegiance before the Hon. Henry Tubman in St. Mary's County in 1778 [Ref: J-1146, K-70].
CARLILE, Basil. Private, St. Mary's County, who served in the Maryland Line until 1781 when discharged [Ref: D-407].
CARPENTER, George. Two men with this name took the Oath of Allegiance in St. Mary's County in 1778: one before the Hon. Jeremiah Jordan and one before the Hon. Richard Barnes [Ref: J-1146, K-66, K-67]. One married Catharine Maddox on July 14, 1777, St. Mary's County, by Rev. George Goldie [Ref: I-535].
CARPENTER, John. This name appeared twice as a private, St. Mary's County Militia, 1777 [Ref: M-212]. One was a private, St. Mary's County, who enlisted May 23, 1778, for 9 months [Ref: D-329, which listed the name as "John Carpentor"]. Took the Oath of Allegiance before the Hon. Jeremiah Jordan in St. Mary's County in 1778 [Ref: J-1146, K-67]. "John Carpenter, Sr." took the Oath of Allegiance before the Hon. John Ireland in St. Mary's County in 1778 [Ref: J-1146, K-65]. One John Carpenter died on Feb. 25, 1803, aged 68, and was buried with his wife Susannah Turner (1749-1805), daughter of Edward Turner, at Christ Church, Chaptico, St. Mary's County [Ref: R-352, HG-

37, S-128, S-140, which latter source states that John Carpenter (1735-1803) was a son of Joseph and Susanna Carpenter, married Susannah Turner, served as a private in 1778 and 1779, and was promoted to captain in the militia in 1780, as noted "in DAR Scrapbook"].
CARPENTER, Joseph and Susannah. See "John Carpenter," q.v.
CARPENTER, William. Private, St. Mary's County Militia, 1777 [Ref: M-210]. Two men with this name took the Oath of Allegiance in St. Mary's County in 1778: one before the Hon. Richard Barnes and one before the Hon. Bennett Biscoe [Ref: J-1146, K-63, K-66].
CARPENTER, William Jr. Private, Capt. Uriah Forrest's Co., Flying Camp, St. Mary's County, July 28, 1776 [Ref: D-30, SM-111].
CARPENTER, William Freeman. Private, Capt. Henry Skinner's Foot Co. of Hunting Hundred, Calvert County, 1777 [Ref: T-1814, O-125].
CARR, Ambrose. Private, St. Mary's County Militia, 1777 [Ref: M-211]. Took the Oath of Allegiance before the Hon. John Reeder in St. Mary's County in 1778 [Ref: J-1146, K-69].
CARR, Jacob. Private, Capt. Richard Lane's Co., Calvert County Militia, 1778 [Ref: J-1146, M-149]. Took the Oath of Allegiance in Calvert County in 1778 [Ref: L-35].
CARR, Samuel. Private, Capt. Richard Lane's Co., Calvert County Militia, 1778 [Ref: J-1146, M-150].
CARR, Seaborn. Private, Capt. Richard Lane's Co., Calvert County Militia, 1778 [Ref: J-1146, M-149]. Took the Oath of Allegiance in Calvert County in 1778 [Ref: L-35].
CARRIER, Thomas. Private, St. Mary's County, 3rd Maryland Line, Capt. Armstrong's Co., 1778-1780 [Ref: D-298].
CARROLL, Araminta and Harriot. See "Henry Carroll," q.v.
CARROLL, Henry. Elected to serve on a General Committee in St. Mary's County in accordance with the resolves of the Continental Congress in 1775 [Ref: MR-127]. One Henry Carroll died testate by April 16, 1776, and named his daughters Julian, Margaret, Harriot, and wife (no name given in his will, but she was his executrix). In Oct., 1777, George Biscoe and Araminta his wife were named executors of Henry Carroll [Ref: SO-4, and *Maryland Calendar of Wills, Volume 16, 1774-1777*, page 117].
CARROLL, Julian and Margaret. See "Henry Carroll," q.v.
CARROLL, William. Private, St. Mary's County Militia, 1777 [Ref: M-212].
CARTER, Edward. Private, St. Mary's County, who served in the Maryland Line until 1781 when discharged [Ref: D-407].
CARTER, Henry Horn. Private, Capt. Uriah Forrest's Co., Flying Camp, St. Mary's County, July 28, 1776 [Ref: D-30, SM-111]. The Register of St. Andrew's Episcopal Church states that Henry Carter and Elizabeth Hogan were married Feb. 7, 1779 [Ref: MB-382].

CARTER, James. Private, St. Mary's County Militia, 1777 [Ref: M-210]. Took the Oath of Allegiance before the Hon. Jeremiah Jordan in St. Mary's County in 1778 [Ref: J-1146, K-67]. Private, Count Pulaski's Legion, May 16, 1778 [Ref: SM-111].
CARTER, Jesse. Private, St. Mary's County, enlisted May 25, 1778, for 9 months [Ref: D-330]. Listed as deserted in June, 1778, he enlisted in the Maryland Line on Feb. 25, 1782 [Ref: S-151].
CARTER, John. Private, Capt. Walter Smith's Co., Calvert County Militia, 1778 [Ref: J-1146, M-148].
CARTER, Justinian. Private, St. Mary's County, enlisted May 14, 1778, for 3 years [Ref: D-329]. Private, 3rd Maryland Line; died Aug. 11, 1778 [Ref: SM-111].
CARTER, Luke. Private, St. Mary's County, enlisted May 19, 1778, for the duration of the war [Ref: D-329]. Private, St. Mary's County, 3rd Maryland Line, Capt. Armstrong's Co., 1778-1780 [Ref: D-298].
CARTWRIGHT, John. Private, St. Mary's County Militia, 1777 [Ref: M-212]. Took the Oath of Allegiance before the Hon. John Reeder in St. Mary's County in 1778 [Ref: J-1146, K-69]. Second Lieutenant, Upper Bn., Aug. 16, 1777, and First Lieutenant, from Sep. 12, 1777 through Nov. 18, 1779 [Ref: M-60, C-346, C-373, F-18]. One John Cartwright died intestate by April, 1794, and Elizabeth Keech Cartwright was his administratrix. He left orphans Henry Greenfield Cartwright and Julian Cartwright [Ref: SO-210, SO-211, SO-312].
CARTWRIGHT, Justinian. Private, St. Mary's County Militia, 1777 [Ref: M-210].
CARTWRIGHT, William. Private, St. Mary's County Militia, 1777 [Ref: M-210]. Ensign, Upper Bn., Aug. 29, 1777, and Second Lieutenant, Nov. 18, 1779 [Ref: M-60, C-346, F-18]. William Cartwright died intestate by Jan., 1801 [Ref: SO-313].
CASEY, Robert. Took the Oath of Allegiance in Calvert County in 1778 [Ref: L-35].
CASSADY, James. Private, St. Mary's County, who served in the Maryland Line until 1781 when discharged [Ref: D-407].
CATTERTON, Michael. Private, Capt. Frederick Skinner's Co., Calvert County Militia, 1778 [Ref: J-1146, M-150]. Took the Oath of Allegiance in Calvert County in 1778 [Ref: L-35].
CAUSEY, Henry. Private, St. Mary's County, enlisted May 16, 1778, for 3 years, Continental Army [Ref: D-329, SM-111].
CAVENOUGH, William. Elected to serve on a General Committee in St. Mary's County in accordance with the resolves of the Continental Congress in 1775 [Ref: MR-127].
CAWOOD, Benjamin. Private, St. Mary's County Militia, 1777 [Ref: M-210].

CAWOOD, Stephen. Private, St. Mary's County Militia, 1777 [Ref: M-210]. Supplied provisions (wheat, mutton, or bacon) for the Army in 1780 [Ref: S-77, S-151].
CAWOOD, Thomas. Took the Oath of Allegiance before the Hon. Bennett Biscoe in St. Mary's County in 1778 [Ref: J-1146, K-63, which listed the name as "Thomas Kaywood"].
CECIL, Dorothy. See "Zachariah Brewer," q.v.
CECIL, Nicholas. Private, 3rd Maryland Line, 1780 [Ref: S-151]. Also see "Cissell" for other persons possibly named "Cecil."
CHAMBERLAIN, Ignatius. Took the Oath of Allegiance before the Hon. Henry Reeder in St. Mary's County in 1778 [Ref: J-1146, K-64].
CHAMBERS, Orton. Private, Capt. James Patterson's Co., Calvert County Militia, Aug. 10, 1777 [Ref: M-146].
CHANEY, Lewis. Took the Oath of Allegiance in Calvert County in 1778 [Ref: L-35].
CHANEY, Thomas. Took the Oath of Allegiance in Calvert County in 1778 [Ref: L-35].
CHANEY, Thomas Jr. Took the Oath of Allegiance in Calvert County in 1778 [Ref: L-35].
CHAPELAIR, Elias. Private, St. Mary's County Militia, 1777 [Ref: M-210].
CHAPELAIR, James. Private, St. Mary's County Militia, 1777 [Ref: M-210].
CHARAM, Ann. See "Elijah Vessels," q.v.
CHARD, William. Private, St. Mary's County, who served in the 1st Maryland Line from Jan. 26, 1777 until 1781 when discharged [Ref: D-93, D-407].
CHARLTON, Edward. Private, Capt. Edward Wood's Co., Calvert County Militia, 1778 [Ref: J-1146, M-147].
CHARLTON, James. Private, Capt. Edward Wood's Co., Calvert County Militia, 1778 [Ref: J-1146, M-147]. Took the Oath of Allegiance in Calvert County in 1778 [Ref: L-35].
CHARLTON, Jean. See "Joseph Younger," q.v.
CHARLTON, Thomas. Private, Capt. Henry Skinner's Foot Co. of Hunting Hundred, Calvert County, 1777 [Ref: T-1814, O-125]. Private, Capt. James Grahame's Co., Calvert County Militia, 1778 [Ref: J-1146, M-148]. This name appeared twice on the list of those who took the Oath of Allegiance in Calvert County in 1778 [Ref: l-35].
CHENEY, Lewis. Private, Capt. Charles Williamson's Co., Calvert County Militia, 1778 [Ref: J-1146, M-147].
CHENEY, Thomas. Private, Capt. Charles Williamson's Co., Calvert County Militia, 1778 [Ref: J-1146, M-147].
CHESELDINE, Gerard. (1) Adjutant, Flying Camp, who reviewed and passed new recruits in St. Mary's County in July, 1776 [Ref: D-30, SM-111]. Took the Oath of Allegiance before the Hon. John Shanks in St.

Mary's County in 1778 [Ref: J-1146, K-69]. (2) Private, St. Mary's County Militia, 1777 [Ref: M-212]. In June, 1799, the Court appointed Stephen Tarlton as guardian of his two grandchildren, Richard Cheseldine and John Cheseldine, the orphan sons of Gerard Cheseldine, deceased [Ref: SO-286].

CHESELDINE, John. See "Gerard Cheseldine," q.v.

CHESELDINE, Kenelm. Private, St. Mary's County Militia, 1777 [Ref: Maryland Society of the Sons of the American Revolution, Approved Supplemental Membership Application No. 2528-B, which stated he was born circa 1758 and died circa 1805. Ref: M-212 which listed the name as "Kenelin Cheseldine"]. Took the Oath of Allegiance before the Hon. John Shanks in St. Mary's County in 1778 [Ref: J-1146, K-69]. One Kenelm Cheseldine died by Nov., 1778, leaving an orphan daughter Mary Neal Cheseldine who was above the age of 14 in April, 1785 [Ref: SO-15, SO-73].

CHESELDINE, Mary Neal. See "Kenelm Cheseldine," q.v.

CHESELDINE, Richard. See "Gerard Cheseldine," q.v.

CHESELDINE, Seneca Nelson. Took the Oath of Allegiance before the Hon. Robert Watts in St. Mary's County in 1778 [Ref: J-1146, K-62]. Private, St. Mary's County Militia, 1777 [Ref: M-215, which listed the name as "Senica(?) Chezaldine"]. The Register of St. Andrew's Episcopal Church states that Seneca Chiseldine and Elizabeth Briscoe were married Nov. 4, 1779 [Ref: MB-383]. Seneca Nelson Cheseldine (c1750-1816) was a private in the militia in 1780. He married (1) Elizabeth Biscoe *[sic]* in 1779 and (2) Elizabeth Turner in 1798 [Ref: S-140, S-152].

CHESELDINE, William. Private, Capt. Uriah Forrest's Co., Flying Camp, St. Mary's County, July 28, 1776 [Ref: D-30, SM-111]. Private, St. Mary's County Militia, 1777 [Ref: M-212]. Took the Oath of Allegiance before the Hon. John Shanks in St. Mary's County in 1778 [Ref: J-1146, K-69].

CHESHIRE, Benjamin. Private, St. Mary's County Militia, 1777 [Ref: M-211]. Served on the State ship *Defence* from May 25 to Dec. 31, 1777 [Ref: D-655]. Private, 3rd Maryland Line, enlisted April 26, 1778, for the duration of the war, but reportedly "run off" in June, 1778. However, he was transferred to the Invalids Corps on Feb. 7, 1780 [Ref: S-35, D-623, D-655, D-329, which latter source listed the name as "Benj. Chesher"]. One "Benjamin Burch Cheshire, farmer" moved from Chaptico in St. Mary's County to Cumberland County, Virginia in 1791 [Ref: X-86].

CHESHIRE (CHESSER), Bennett. Private, St. Mary's County, 3rd Maryland Line, Capt. Armstrong's Co., 1778-1780 [Ref: D-298]. Transferred to invalids corps in 1780 and "discharged on pension" in July, 1783 [Ref: D-96, S-152].

CHESHIRE, John. Sergeant, 2nd Maryland Line, reported killed on June 18, 1781 [Ref: D-514, D-528].

CHESHIRE, Thomas. Private, Capt. Henry Skinner's Foot Co. of Hunting Hundred, Calvert County, 1777 [Ref: T-1814, O-125]. Private, 2nd Maryland Line, until Dec., 1777 [Ref: D-92].
CHESLEY (CHISLEY), Elizabeth. See "William Somerville," q.v.
CHESLEY, John. Private, St. Mary's County Militia, 1777 [Ref: M-215]. Took the Oath of Allegiance before the Hon. Henry Tubman in St. Mary's County in 1778 [Ref: J-1146, K-70]. Second Lieutenant, Lower Bn., Aug. 26, 1777, and Captain, May 7, 1781 [Ref: M-62, C-346, G-426]. John Chesley married Mary Ashcum Parran on Jan. 5, 1779, by Rev. Francis Lauder, of Christ Church Parish [Ref: K-34]. See "Robert Chesley," q.v.
CHESLEY (CHISLEY), Mary. See "John Aisquith," q.v.
CHESLEY, Robert. Applied for sea service in 1776 in St. Mary's County and was recommended by Capt. John Allen Thomas as a cadet on March 8, 1776. Commissioned a Third Lieutenant, 5th Independent Co., on Aug. 7, 1776, and fought in the Battle of Brooklyn. Saw action in both the northern and southern campaigns. Captain, 2nd Maryland Line, from June 10, 1777 to Oct. 25, 1781, when he retired [Ref: SM-151, D-94, D-363, D-379, D-407, D-480, D-519, SM-111]. One Robert Chesley died by Aug., 1779, leaving an orphan son John, and another Robert Chesley died intestate by Jan., 1800, with Matia and Robert Chesley as administrators [Ref: SO-223, SO-96].
CHEW, John Hamilton. See "Samuel Chew" and "Edward Reynolds," q.v.
CHEW, Samuel (1737 - Feb. 20, 1790). Son of Samuel Chew (who died in London in 1749) and Sarah Loch (1721-1791), daughter of Dr. William Loch. Samuel married twice: (1) Sarah Weems, daughter of James Weems, in 1763, and (2) Priscilla Clagett, daughter of Rev. Samuel Clagett. Children: Samuel Chew (1763-1800, who died in Kentucky), John Hamilton Chew (1771-1830), and Thomas John Chew (died by 1794). Samuel served as a Justice of Calvert County, 1761-1790, Delegate to the Maryland Convention in 1775, and Member of the House of Delegates in 1777, 1778, 1779, 1782 and 1783. Justice of the Orphans Court of Calvert County, 1777-1789. Commissioner of Tax, 1777-1779. Took the Oath of Allegiance in Calvert County in 1778 [Ref: L-35, N-71, N-78, N-80, N-86, N-87, N-219]. There was also a Samuel Chew who was prominent in Queen Anne's County during the American Revolution [Ref: N-218].
CHEW, Sarah. See "Frisby Freeland" and "Samuel Chew," q.v.
CHEW, Thomas John. See "Samuel Chew," q.v.
CHEW, William. Took the Oath of Allegiance in Calvert County in 1778 [Ref: L-35]. Also see "Frisby Freeland," q.v.
CHILDREN, William. Private, enlisted in May, 1777, St. Mary's County, 3rd Maryland Line, Capt. Armstrong's Co., 1778-1780 [Ref: D-298].
CHILDS, Cud (Cudbert). Served on the State ship *Defence* from June 1, 1777 to at least Dec. 31, 1777 [Ref: D-655].

CHILDS, Gabriel. Ensign, Capt. Thomas Cleland's Co., Calvert County Militia, 15th Bn., April 16, 1778 [Ref: J-1146, M-62, M-147, E-37]. Took the Oath of Allegiance in Calvert County in 1778 [Ref: L-35].

CHILTON, Charles. Applied for marine service in 1776. Property was destroyed by the British in 1781. Member of the Convention that ratified the Constitution in 1788 [Ref: S-152, which source noted "this may be two persons of same name"]. Charles Chilton died at his residence in St. Mary's County on April 10, 1824, in his 69th year, "a patriot of the Revolutionary War." [Ref: *Baltimore Patriot and Merchants Advertiser*, June 24, 1824, and *Maryland Genealogical Society Bulletin*, Volume 6, No. 4 (1965), p. 96, but not listed in *Archives of Maryland, Volume 18*. Also, Reference R-355 states he died on April 9, 1824]. See "George Chilton," q.v.

CHILTON, George. Took the Oath of Allegiance before the Hon. Vernon Hebb in St. Mary's County in 1778 [Ref: J-1146, K-67]. One George Chilton, orphan of George Chilton, deceased, chose Charles Chilton as his guardian in Oct., 1785 [Ref: SO-84].

CHILTON, Henry. This name appeared twice as a private in the St. Mary's County Militia in 1777 [Ref: M-214]. Took the Oath of Allegiance before the Hon. Vernon Hebb in St. Mary's County in 1778 [Ref: J-1146, K-67].

CHILTON, Littleton. Private, Capt. Charles Williamson's Co., Calvert County Militia, 1778 [Ref: J-1146, M-147].

CHILTON, Thomas (1740-c1807). Private (later Ensign), St. Mary's County Militia, 1777 [Ref: M-214]. He married Sapphira Pierce [Ref: Y-129].

CHITTAM (CHITTIM), James. Private, St. Mary's County Militia, 1777 [Ref: M-212]. Took the Oath of Allegiance before the Hon. John Shanks in St. Mary's County in 1778 [Ref: J-1146, K-69].

CHIVERALL, Jesse. Private, St. Mary's County Militia, 1777 [Ref: M-214]. Private, St. Mary's County, enlisted on May 30, 1778, for 9 months, Continental Army [Ref: D-330, SM-111]. Took the Oath of Allegiance before the Hon. Bennett Biscoe in St. Mary's County in 1778 [Ref: J-1146, K-63, which listed the name as "Jessey Cheverill (Cheserill)"]. He married Catherine Guither, daughter of George Guither, on Feb. 12, 1780 and had a daughter (name not stated) baptized on June 27, 1799 [Ref: SM-151, MB-383, which listed the name as "Jesse Cheverlin"].

CHIVERALL, John. Private, Maryland Line, Continental Army, who was paid on Oct. 25, 1781 as an exchanged prisoner of war, and died in Sep., 1783 [Ref: SM-111, S-152, D-617, which latter source listed the name as "John Chivel"].

CHRISTMAN, Luke. Private, St. Mary's County Militia, 1777 [Ref: M-214, which listed the name as "Luke Crisman"]. Took the Oath of Allegiance in St. Mary's County in 1780 [Ref: Q-107].

CHRISTOPHER, John. Private, Capt. Uriah Forrest's Co., Flying Camp, St. Mary's County, July 28, 1776 [Ref: D-30]. Private, 2nd Maryland Line; prisoner of war at the Battle of Camden on Aug. 16, 1780 until Nov. 1, 1780 [Ref: D-92, S-36].

CHUNN, Jonathan. Private, 1st Maryland Line, from Dec. 10, 1776 until March 6, 1777, when reported dead. He probably served from either St. Mary's County or Charles County, as a number of Chunns migrated from this region of Maryland to the western part of Rowan County, North Carolina with other Episcopal families around 1794 [Ref: D-91, MC-34].

CISSELL (CECIL), Anastatia. See "Francis Wheatley," q.v.

CISSELL, Barton. Took the Oath of Allegiance before the Hon. John Ireland in St. Mary's County in 1778 [Ref: J-1146, K-65]. Private, 3rd Maryland Line, April 27, 1778, and corporal, Jan. 15, 1779; served to at least Nov. 1, 1780 [Ref: D-96].

CISSELL, Bennett. Private, St. Mary's County Militia, 1777 [Ref: M-210, which listed the name as "Bennit Cissill"]. Took the Oath of Allegiance before the Hon. John Ireland in St. Mary's County in 1778 [Ref: J-1146, K-65]. "Bennet Cissel, farmer" moved from Upper Newtown to Washington County, Kentucky, after 1790 [Ref: X-86].

CISSELL, Bernard. Private, St. Mary's County Militia, 1777 [Ref: M-210, which listed the name as "Bernard Cissill"]. Took the Oath of Allegiance before the Hon. Richard Barnes in St. Mary's County in 1778 [Ref: J-1146, K-66].

CISSELL (CECIL), Dorothy. See "Zachariah Brewer," q.v.

CISSELL, Edmund Barton. Private, St. Mary's County Militia, 1777 [Ref: M-210, which listed the name as "Edmond Barton Cissill"]. Private, St. Mary's County, enlisted April 27, 1778, for 9 months [Ref: D-329]. Private, 3rd Maryland Line; died Jan. 13, 1782 [Ref: R-353, SM-111, which listed the name as "Ed. Barton Cecil"].

CISSELL, Francis. Private, St. Mary's County Militia, 1777 [Ref: M-210, which listed the name as "Francis Cissill"]. Took the Oath of Allegiance before the Hon. Richard Barnes in St. Mary's County in 1778 [Ref: J-1146, K-66].

CISSELL, Gerrard. Private, St. Mary's County Militia, 1777 [Ref: M-210, which listed the name as "Gerrard Cissill"].

CISSELL, James Jr. Took the Oath of Allegiance before the Hon. Richard Barnes in St. Mary's County in 1778 [Ref: J-1146, K-66].

CISSELL, John. This name appeared three times as a private, St. Mary's County Militia, 1777 [Ref: M-210, M-211, M-212, which listed the name as "John Cissill"]. Two men with this name took the Oath of Allegiance: one before the Hon. Henry Reeder and one before the Hon. Richard Barnes in 1778 [Ref: J-1146, K-64, K-66]. One "John Sissill" married Eleanor Combs on Aug. 26, 1777, St. Mary's County, by Rev. Joseph Messenger, Rector of St. Andrew's Parish [Ref: I-535]. One "John

Cissell" settled on Hardin's Creek in now Washington County, Kentucky, by 1786 [Ref: MK-27]. Another "John Cissel" died intestate in St. Mary's County by Dec., 1791, and Susanna Cissel was his administratrix [Ref: SO-173].

CISSELL, John B. Private, St. Mary's County Militia, 1777 [Ref: M-210, which listed the name as "John B. Cissill"]. Took the Oath of Allegiance before the Hon. Henry Reeder in St. Mary's County in 1778 [Ref: J-1146, K-64]. Private and later corporal, 3rd Maryland Line, enlisted on Jan. 15, 1779 [Ref: D-97, D-298, SM-111].

CISSELL, John Baptist. Took the Oath of Allegiance before the Hon. John Ireland in St. Mary's County in 1778 [Ref: J-1146, K-65].

CISSELL, Nicholas. See "Nicholas Cecil," q.v.

CISSELL, Ralph. Private, St. Mary's County Militia, 1777 [Ref: M-214, which listed the name as "Ralph Sissill"].

CISSELL, Raphael. Took the Oath of Allegiance before the Hon. John Ireland in St. Mary's County in 1778 [Ref: J-1146, K-65].

CISSELL, Susannah. See "Raphael Wimsatt" and "John Cissell," q.v.

CISSELL, William. Took the Oath of Allegiance before the Hon. Richard Barnes in St. Mary's County in 1778 [Ref: J-1146, K-66]. The Register of St. Andrew's Episcopal Church states that "William Sissel" and Sarah Adams were married (by license) April 27, 1784 [Ref: MB-385].

CLAGETT, Priscilla and Samuel. See "Samuel Chew," q.v.

CLAGETT, Thomas John (Bishop). See "Edward Gantt," q.v.

CLARE, Ann. See "Isaac Clare," q.v.

CLARE, Edmund. Second Lieutenant, Capt. Richard Parran's Co., Calvert County Militia, 15th Bn., July 5, 1776 through April 16, 1778 [Ref: J-1146, M-62, M-149, E-37]. Took the Oath of Allegiance in Calvert County in 1778 [Ref: L-35].

CLARE, Elizabeth. See "Isaac Clare," q.v.

CLARE, Isaac. Took the Oath of Allegiance in Calvert County in 1778 [Ref: L-35]. The Christ Church Register in Calvert County records the births of the children of Isaac and Elizabeth Clare as follows: "John Clare," q.v. (born Feb. 13, 1747, died April 12, 1804); Rebecca (born Jan. 9, 1749); William (born Dec. 6, 1750); Elizabeth (born June 11, 1753); and Ann (born Feb. 10, 1757). [Ref: O-5].

CLARE, John (Feb. 13, 1747 - April 12, 1804). Son of Isaac and Elizabeth Clare. Second Lieutenant, Capt. Walter Smith's Co., Calvert County Militia, 15th Bn., April 10, 1776 to April 16, 1778 [Ref: Maryland Society, Sons of the American Revolution, Approved Membership Application No. 2806; M-62, A-320, E-37, J-1146, M-148, which latter source listed the name as "John Clara"]. Took the Oath of Allegiance in Calvert County in 1778 [Ref: L-35].

CLARE, John Jr. Private, Capt. Richard Parran's Co., Calvert County Militia, 1778 [Ref: J-1146, M-149, which listed the name as "John Clara, Jr."]. Took the Oath of Allegiance in Calvert County in 1778 [Ref: L-35].

CLARE, Rebecca and William. See "Isaac Clare," q.v.
CLARK, Ann. See "Ignatius Fenwick, Sr.," q.v.
CLARK, Edward. See "Ignatius Clarke," q.v.
CLARKE, Abraham. Took the Oath of Allegiance before the Hon. Henry Reeder in St. Mary's County in 1778 [Ref: J-1146, K-64].
CLARKE, Charles. Private, St. Mary's County, enlisted May 30, 1778, for 9 months [Ref: D-330]. Private, 2nd Maryland Line, 1778-1779 [Ref: S-152].
CLARKE, Cuthbert. Private, St. Mary's County Militia, 1777 [Ref: M-211]. Took the Oath of Allegiance before the Hon. Richard Barnes in St. Mary's County in 1778 [Ref: J-1146, K-66]. Took the Oath of Allegiance in St. Mary's County in 1780 [Ref: Q-107]. The Register of St. Francis Xavier Catholic Church states that "Cuthbert Clark" and Mary Ann Brown were married June 19, 1774 [Ref: SC-35].
CLARKE, Elizabeth. See "William Mattingly," q.v.
CLARKE, George. Private, St. Mary's County Militia, 1777 [Ref: M-211]. Private, Continental Army, 1781 [Ref: S-152]. "George Clarke, pilot" moved from St. Inigoes to Baltimore in 1811 [Ref: X-86].
CLARKE, George McCaul. Private, St. Mary's County Militia, 1777 [Ref: M-211].
CLARKE, Henry. Private, St. Mary's County Militia, 1777 [Ref: M-210]. "Henry Clark, farmer" moved to Lincoln County, Kentucky, in 1793 [Ref: X-86].
CLARKE, Ignatius. Private, St. Mary's County Militia, 1777 [Ref: M-210]. Private, 2nd Maryland Line, enlisted on May 30, 1778, for 9 months; discharged on April 3, 1779 [Ref: D-330, which listed the name as "Ignatius Clark"]. Ignatius Clark was an early Catholic settler on Hardin's Creek in now Washington County, Kentucky circa 1786. He married Aloysia Hill, daughter of Thomas Hill, and had a son, Rev. Edward Clark [Ref: MK-27]. Yet, another source indicates that Ignatius Clarke (1750-1789), son of Thomas and Julia Clarke, married Frances Leigh in 1772, but mistakenly indicates Frances was born in 1752 and died in 1770 [Ref: S-140].
CLARKE, Isaac. Private, St. Mary's County Militia, 1777 [Ref: M-211]. "Isaac Clark, farmer" moved to Christian County, Kentucky, in 1793 [Ref: X-86].
CLARKE, James. Marine from St. Mary's County who served aboard the State ship *Defence* in 1777 [Ref: S-152]. Also see "James Clerke," q.v.
CLARKE, John. Took the Oath of Allegiance before the Hon. John Ireland in St. Mary's County in 1778 [Ref: J-1146, K-65]. It must also be mentioned that one "John Clark" of the 3rd Maryland Line (county of residence not stated) was charged with desertion and attempting to go to the enemy in 1779. He was sentenced to death [Ref: *Summer Soldiers: A Survey & Index of Revolutionary War Courts-Martial*, by James C. Neagles (1986), page 105].

CLARKE, John Attaway. "John A. Clarke" took the Oath of Allegiance before the Hon. Vernon Hebb in St. Mary's County in 1778 [Ref: J-1146, K-67]. "John Attaway Clark" was coroner of St. Mary's County in 1777 and "John Attaway Clarke" died testate by Aug., 1785 [Ref: SO-78, S-152].

CLARKE, Joshua. Private, St. Mary's County Militia, 1777 [Ref: M-210]. The Register of St. Francis Xavier Catholic Church states that "Josua Clark" and Mary Bowles were married Oct. 11, 1772 [Ref: SC-34]. Another source indicates Joshua Clarke (1750-1823) married Mary Thompson (born 1753), daughter of Thomas Thompson (died 1777), and he served in the militia in 1780 [Ref: S-141].

CLARKE, Julia. See "Ignatius Clarke," q.v.

CLARKE, Kenelm. Private, St. Mary's County Militia, 1777 [Ref: M-212, which listed the name as "Kenelin Clark"]. Took the Oath of Allegiance before the Hon. Robert Watts in St. Mary's County in 1778 [Ref: J-1146, K-62, which listed the name as "Kenelm Clarke"].

CLARKE, Lavinia. See "William Taylor," q.v.

CLARKE, Leonard. Private, St. Mary's County Militia, 1777 [Ref: M-210].

CLARKE, Matthew. Took the Oath of Allegiance before the Hon. John Reeder in St. Mary's County in 1778 [Ref: J-1146, K-69].

CLARKE, Philip. Took the Oath of Allegiance before the Hon. Robert Watts in St. Mary's County in 1778 [Ref: J-1146, K-62].

CLARKE, Richard. (1) Private, St. Mary's County Militia, 1777 [Ref: M-214]. Took the Oath of Allegiance before the Hon. Richard Barnes in St. Mary's County in 1778 [Ref: J-1146, K-66]. (2) Private, St. Mary's County Militia, 1777 [Ref: M-211]. "Richard Clarke" took the Oath of Allegiance before the Hon. Richard Barnes in St. Mary's County in 1778 [Ref: J-1146, K-66]. "Richard Clark" was elected to a General Committee in St. Mary's County in accordance with the resolves of the Continental Congress in 1775 [Ref: MR-127]. One "Richard Clarke" died testate by Aug., 1792, leaving orphans George Clarke and Peregrine Clarke [Ref: SO-177, SO-255].

CLARKE, Robert. (1) Private, St. Mary's County Militia, 1777 [Ref: M-213]. Took the Oath of Allegiance before the Hon. John Reeder in St. Mary's County in 1778 [Ref: J-1146, K-69]. (2) Private, St. Mary's County Militia, 1777 [Ref: M-212]. Took the Oath of Allegiance before the Hon. Robert Armstrong in St. Mary's County in 1778 [Ref: J-1146, K-62]. (3) Took the Oath of Allegiance before the Hon. Henry Reeder in St. Mary's County in 1778 [Ref: J-1146, K-64]. Supplied provisions (wheat, mutton, or bacon) for the Army in 1780 [Ref: S-77, S-152]. One Richard Clarke was buried on Dec. 31, 1806 [Ref: R-356].

CLARKE, Roger. This name appeared twice as a private in the St. Mary's County Militia in 1777 [Ref: M-211, M-213]. One took the Oath of Allegiance before the Hon. Robert Watts in St. Mary's County in 1778 [Ref: J-1146, K-62].

CLARKE, Susannah. See "William Somerville" and "John Somerville" and "George Clarke Somerville," q.v.

CLARKE, Thomas. Private, St. Mary's County Militia, 1777 [Ref: M-210]. Two men with this name took the Oath of Allegiance in 1778: one before the Hon. John Shanks and one before the Hon. Bennett Biscoe [Ref: J-1146, K-63, K-69]. See "Ignatius Clarke," q.v.

CLARKE, William. Private, St. Mary's County Militia, 1777 [Ref: M-212]. Took the Oath of Allegiance before the Hon. Ignatius Fenwick, Jr. in St. Mary's County in 1778 [Ref: J-1146, K-68]. The Register of St. Andrew's Episcopal Church states that William Clarke and Monica Woodward were married (by license) Oct. 18, 1781 [Ref: MB-384]. The Register of St. Francis Xavier Catholic Church states that "William Clark" and Mary Hopewell were married April 19, 1778 [Ref: SC-36]. One "William Clarke" died by June, 1779, leaving a minor son Zachariah Clarke [Ref: SO-23]. Another William Clarke was born in St. Mary's County on Dec. 18, 1758, and he applied for and received pension S8213 on Sep. 15, 1832, He indicated that he enlisted at Hagerstown in 1775 and lived in Washington County, Maryland. He had served one year as a sergeant and one year as a lieutenant under Capt. Basil Williams in 1776. "William Clark or Clarke" lived in Berkeley County, Virginia at the time of his application in 1832 and he moved to Allegany County in 1833. He was still there in 1854 [Ref: P-664, and *National Genealogical Society Quarterly*, Volume 33, No. 2 (1945), p. 57].

CLAYTON, Thomas. Took the Oath of Allegiance before the Hon. Jeremiah Jordan in St. Mary's County in 1778 [Ref: J-1146, K-67]. One Thomas Clayton died intestate by Nov., 1793 [Ref: SO-202].

CLELAND, Thomas. Captain, 15th Bn., Calvert County Militia, April 16, 1778 [Ref: J-1146, M-63, M-147, E-37]. Took the Oath of Allegiance in Calvert County in 1778 [Ref: L-35]. Captain, Select Militia, Sep. 1, 1781 [Ref: G-596].

CLEMENTS, Henry. Private, St. Mary's County, who served in the 1st Maryland Line from April 16, 1777 until 1781 when discharged [Ref: D-91, D-407]. There was also a Henry Clements in the 3rd Maryland Line who enlisted on Feb. 28, 1777, was promoted to corporal on Aug. 1, 1777, to sergeant on June 1, 1779, and subsequently was an ensign [Ref: D-94].

CLEMENTS, James. Private, 1st Maryland Line, 1777-1780 [Ref: D-91].

CLEMENTS, John. Private, 1st Maryland Line, 1777-1780 [Ref: D-91].

CLEMENTS, Mark. Private, 3rd Maryland Line, enlisted March 16, 1778 and reported missing at the Battle of Camden in South Carolina on Aug. 16, 1780 [Ref: D-97].

CLEMENTS, William. Private, 1st Maryland Line, 1779-1780 [Ref: D-92].

CLERKE, James. Private, Calvert County, enlisted by Lt. Frederick Skinner on Aug. 23, 1776 [Ref: D-33].

CLOCKER, Bennett. "Bennett Clocker" took the Oath of Allegiance before the Hon. Bennett Biscoe in St. Mary's County in 1778 [Ref: J-1146, K-63]. The Register of St. Andrew's Episcopal Church states that "Benjamin Clocker" and Lydia Baldwin were married (by license) May 19, 1784 [Ref: MB-385].

CLOCKER, Elizabeth. See "William Wise," q.v.

COACHMAN, James. Private, St. Mary's County, enlisted May 31, 1778, for 9 months, Continental Army [Ref: D-330, SM-112].

COAD, James. Took the Oath of Allegiance before the Hon. Bennett Biscoe in St. Mary's County in 1778 [Ref: J-1146, K-63].

COAD, John. Private, St. Mary's County Militia, 1777 [Ref: M-215]. Took the Oath of Allegiance before the Hon. Bennett Biscoe in St. Mary's County in 1778 [Ref: J-1146, K-63].

COAD, Joseph. Took the Oath of Allegiance before the Hon. Bennett Biscoe in St. Mary's County in 1778 [Ref: J-1146, K-63].

COCKS (COAKS), George. Took the Oath of Allegiance in St. Mary's County in 1780 [Ref: Q-107].

COCKS (COAKS), James. Took the Oath of Allegiance in St. Mary's County in 1780 [Ref: Q-107].

COE, Alexander Benson. See "William Coe," q.v.

COE, Ann. See "Samuel Coe," q.v.

COE, Elizabeth. See "William Coe," q.v.

COE, Samuel. Took the Oath of Allegiance in Calvert County in 1778 [Ref: L-35]. The Christ Church Register in Calvert County records the births of the children of Samuel and Elizabeth Coe as "William Coe," q.v. (born Nov. 9, 1757) and Ann (born March 25, 1760). [Ref: O-5]. See "William Coe," q.v.

COE, William (Nov. 9, 1757 - Dec. 30, 1833). Son of Samuel and Elizabeth Coe, of Calvert County. Private in Capt. John Allen Thomas' 5th Independent Co., Continental Army, Feb. 1, 1776. Saw action in New Jersey and participated in the Battle of Long Island. Became a corporal in 1777 and served as a gunner in a matross (artillery) co. under Capt. William Campbell. Took the Oath of Allegiance in Calvert County in 1780 [Ref: Q-107]. He was discharged from the service on March 19, 1779. A tailor by trade, William was paid for making clothes for soldiers in 1779. He married twice: (1) Eleanor Devonish on July 16, 1780; she died on Jan. 6, 1793; (2) Mary Sears on June 29, 1793. By 1783 he had moved to Annapolis and operated a tailor shop on Main Street, where he made clothing for Thomas Jefferson when he attended a session of Congress in 1783-1784. William was commissioned a Second Lieutenant in the Maryland militia in 1794 and promoted to First Lieutenant in 1797. He was still in Annapolis in 1821 when he received a pension equal to the half pay of a matross during the Revolutionary War. About 1830 he moved to Baltimore and operated a tailor shop on South Charles Street. On April 25, 1818 (and apparently again in 1832) he applied for a pension (S8227) and had some difficulty being accepted on the rolls. He died in 1833 and was buried in St. Ann's Episcopal Church in Annapolis. His widow received a pension without protest in 1834. She died on June 29, 1835. This William Coe was the father of Alexander Benson Coe, Clerk of the Courts of Baltimore County, and Dr. William Gwynn Coe, Bishop in the Baltimore Conference of the Methodist Episcopal Church [Ref: P-692, "William Coe of Calvert County," by Carl Robert Coe (Summer, 1992), *Maryland Genealogical Society Bulletin*, Volume 33, No. 3, pp. 577-583, which includes much more information then is written here and also clarifies the confusion between William Coe of Calvert County and William Coe of Baltimore County, both of whom served].

COE, William Gwynn. See "William Coe," q.v.

COFFEY, Henry. Private, St. Mary's County Militia, 1777 [Ref: M-215].

COLE, Charles. Private, St. Mary's County, drafted July 27, 1781 [Ref: D-384]. Private, Continental Army, 1781 [Ref: D-407].

COLE, Edmond. Private, St. Mary's County Militia, 1777 [Ref: M-214].

COLE, Edward. Took the Oath of Allegiance before the Hon. Henry Reeder in St. Mary's County in 1778 [Ref: J-1146, K-64].

COLE, Francis. This name appeared twice as a private in the St. Mary's County Militia in 1777 [Ref: M-212, M-213]. One took the Oath of Allegiance in St. Mary's County in 1780 [Ref: Q-107].

COLE, George. Private, St. Mary's County Militia, 1777 [Ref: M-214]. Took the Oath of Allegiance before the Hon. Vernon Hebb in St. Mary's County in 1778 [Ref: J-1146, K-67]. Second Lieutenant, Lower Bn., St. Mary's County, July 5, 1781 [Ref: M-63, G-426].

COLE, Hoshier. Seaman from St. Mary's County who served aboard the State ship *Defence* in 1776 [Ref: S-25, D-606].

COLE, Isaac. Took the Oath of Allegiance before the Hon. Bennett Biscoe in St. Mary's County in 1778 [Ref: J-1146, K-63].

COLE, Jeremiah. Private, St. Mary's County Militia, 1777 [Ref: M-212].

COLE, John. (1) Private, St. Mary's County Militia, 1777 [Ref: M-212]. Took the Oath of Allegiance in St. Mary's County in 1780 [Ref: Q-107]. (2) Private, St. Mary's County Militia, 1777 [Ref: M-213]. Took the Oath of Allegiance before the Hon. Vernon Hebb in St. Mary's County in 1778 [Ref: J-1146, K-67]. One John Cole died testate by Dec., 1793, leaving a minor son John Cole [Ref: SO-204, SO-219].

COLE, John (of Valentine). Private, St. Mary's County Militia, 1777 [Ref: M-214].

COLE, Mary. See "Joseph Hebb" and Ignatius Fenwick, Jr.," q.v.

COLE, Patrick. Seaman from St. Mary's County who served aboard the State ship *Defence* in 1776 [Ref: S-25, D-606].

COLE, Robert. Private, St. Mary's County Militia, 1777 [Ref: M-214]. Took the Oath of Allegiance before the Hon. Henry Reeder in St. Mary's County in 1778 [Ref: J-1146, K-64].

COLE, Valentine. Took the Oath of Allegiance before the Hon. Vernon Hebb in St. Mary's County in 1778 [Ref: J-1146, K-67].
COLLINS, George. Private, St. Mary's County, enlisted April 25 or 26, 1778, for 3 years [Ref: D-298, D-329, which listed the name as "George Collings"]. Private, St. Mary's County, 3rd Maryland Line, Capt. Armstrong's Co., 1778-1780 [Ref: D-298].
COLLINS, John. Private, enlisted May 3, 1777, St. Mary's County, 3rd Maryland Line, Capt. Armstrong's Co., 1778-1780 [Ref: D-298].
COLLINS, William. Took the Oath of Allegiance before the Hon. Jeremiah Jordan in St. Mary's County in 1778 [Ref: J-1146, K-67].
COLLOSON, Anne. See "Nicholas Fielder," q.v.
COLLOSON, John. See "John Cullison," q.v.
COLLOSON, Mary. See "Thomas Sanner," q.v.
COLLWELL, Samuel. Private, St. Mary's County Militia, 1777 [Ref: M-215].
COMBS, Bennett. Ensign, Leonardtown Co., St. Mary's County Militia, Feb. 23, 1776. Second Lieutenant, March 7, 1776 [Ref: A-181, A-205, C-346, M-64, M-214]. Took the Oath of Allegiance before the Hon. Henry Reeder in St. Mary's County in 1778 [Ref: J-1146, K-64]. Captain, Lower Bn., June 22, 1780 [Ref: M-64, F-201]. Bennett Combs died on July 2, 1815 [Ref: R358].
COMBS, Eleanor. See "John Cissell," q.v.
COMBS, Enoch. See "Ignatius Combs," q.v.
COMBS, George. Private, St. Mary's County Militia, 1777 [Ref: M-214]. Took the Oath of Allegiance before the Hon. Bennett Biscoe in St. Mary's County in 1778 [Ref: J-1146, K-63]. Second Lieutenant, 21st Bn., April 16, 1778 [Ref: M-64, E-37, SM-112]. Also see "John Greenwell," q.v.
COMBS, Ignatius (1740-1790). Son of Enoch Combs and Mary Manning. He married Mary Fenwick in 1761 [Ref: S-141]. Second Lieutenant, Lower Bn., St. Mary's County Militia, Aug. 26, 1777 [Ref: M-64, C-346, M-214]. Took the Oath of Allegiance before the Hon. Bennett Biscoe in St. Mary's County in 1778 [Ref: J-1146, K-63, which listed the name as "Ignatius Coombs"]. Elected to a General Committee in St. Mary's County in accordance with the resolves of the Continental Congress, 1774-1775 [Ref: MR-127]. Member of the Council of Safety and the Association of Freemen [Ref: S-141].
COMBS, Philip. Private, St. Mary's County Militia, 1777 [Ref: M-214]. Took the Oath of Allegiance before the Hon. Henry Reeder in St. Mary's County in 1778 [Ref: J-1146, K-64].
COMBS, Ralph. Private, St. Mary's County Militia, 1777 [Ref: M-214].
COMBS, William. Private, St. Mary's County Militia, 1777 [Ref: M-215]. One William Combs died testate by Sep., 1778, leaving a son William Combs who was above the age of 14 in June, 1780, when he chose Stephen Greenwell as his guardian [Ref: SO-13, SO-32].

COMPTON, Ann. See "John Weems," q.v.
COMPTON, Edmund H. Ensign, 1st Maryland Line, April 12, 1779, and Lieutenant, Aug. 1, 1780 [Ref: D-356, D-92, which listed the name as "Edmund Campton" and "Edmund Compton"]. He applied for pension on June 30, 1828, aged 67, in Washington County, Kentucky, stating he served in the 1st Maryland Line in 1780 and received five year's full pay instead of half pay for life under the Act of 1783. Also, bounty land warrant 1266-200 was issued in 1828 to Edmund Compton alias Edmund H. Compton (who applied on Dec. 6, 1827, aged 68). In 1835 James H. Compton wrote that his uncle Edmund Compton died without issue, leaving himself (James), brothers and sisters, as his heirs, and that he (Edmund) served as a lieutenant in the Maryland Line to the end of the war [Ref: P-725, and *National Genealogical Society Quarterly*, Volume 32, No. 1 (1944), p. 32].
COMPTON, James. Private, St. Mary's County Militia, 1777 [Ref: M-213]. Also see "Edmund H. Compton," q.v.
COMPTON, John. Private, St. Mary's County Militia, 1777 [Ref: M-210]. Private, Capt. Uriah Forrest's Co., Flying Camp, St. Mary's County, July 28, 1776 [Ref: D-30, SM-112].
COMPTON, Matthew. Private, St. Mary's County Militia, 1777 [Ref: M-211].
COMPTON, William. See "Charles Hazeltine," q.v.
CONNELLY, Joshua. Took the Oath of Allegiance in St. Mary's County in 1780 [Ref: Q-108]. Private, St. Mary's County Militia, 1777 [Ref: M-212, which listed the name as "Joshua Connoly"].
CONNER, John. Private, Capt. Thomas Cleland's Co., Calvert County Militia, 1778 [Ref: J-1146, M-147]. Took the Oath of Allegiance in Calvert County in 1778 [Ref: L-35].
CONWELL, Arthur. Took the Oath of Allegiance in Calvert County in 1778 [Ref: L-35, which listed the name as "Author Conwill"]. Private, Capt. Walter Smith's Co., Calvert County Militia, 1778 [Ref: J-1146, M-148, which listed the name as "Arthur Conwill"].
CONWELL, John. Private, Capt. Walter Smith's Co., Calvert County Militia, 1778 [Ref: J-1146, M-148, which listed the name as "John Conwill"].
CONWELL, Joseph. Took the Oath of Allegiance in Calvert County in 1778 [Ref: L-35].
CONWELL, Richard. Private, Capt. Richard Parran's Co., Calvert County Militia, 1778 [Ref: J-1146, M-149]. Took the Oath of Allegiance in Calvert County in 1778 [Ref: L-35].
CONWELL, William. Private, Capt. Benjamin Bond's Co., Calvert County Militia, 1778 [Ref: J-1146, M-149]. Took the Oath of Allegiance in Calvert County in 1778 [Ref: L-35].
CONWELL, Yeates. Took the Oath of Allegiance in Calvert County in 1778 [Ref: L-35].

COODE, John. Private, St. Mary's County Militia, 1777 [Ref: M-212]. Served on the State ship *Defence* in 1777 [Ref: S-152]. One John Coode died intestate in 1794, and a John Coode was his administrator [Ref: SO-217].

COODE, Joshua. Private, St. Mary's County, who served in a co. of matrosses (artillery) on Feb. 3, 1777 [Ref: SM-112].

COODE, Mary. See "James Jordan" and "Jeremiah Jordan," q.v.

COODE, William. Private, Capt. Uriah Forrest's Co., Flying Camp, St. Mary's County, July 28, 1776 [Ref: D-30]. Private, 2nd Maryland Line, 1778-1779 [Ref: S-153].

COOK, Elizabeth Louder. See "John Sedwick," q.v.

COOK, George. Elected to serve on a General Committee in St. Mary's County in accordance with the resolves of the Continental Congress in 1775 [Ref: MR-127]. Lieutenant, Sep. 12, 1776 to Nov. 15, 1776. Captain of the State ship *Defence* from Nov. 15 to Dec. 31, 1777 [Ref: D-606, D-655, S-25, SM-149]. Commissioned as the principal officer of the Maryland galleys *Baltimore* and *Conqueror* and *Independence*. He loaned $1000 to the State for the war effort in 1780 [Ref: SM-149, SM-187, S-153].

COOK, Thomas Jr. Private, Capt. Uriah Forrest's Co., Flying Camp, St. Mary's County, July 28, 1776 [Ref: D-30].

COOK, Thomas Sr. Private, St. Mary's County Militia, 1777 [Ref: M-214, SM-112]. Took the Oath of Allegiance in St. Mary's County in 1780 [Ref: Q-108].

COOKE, Alexander. Took the Oath of Allegiance before the Hon. Henry G. Sothoron in St. Mary's County in 1778 [Ref: J-1146, K-68].

COOKE, John Sr. Took the Oath of Allegiance before the Hon. John Ireland in St. Mary's County in 1778 [Ref: J-1146, K-65].

COPELAND, Samuel. Private, St. Mary's County Militia, 1777 [Ref: M-212].

CORAM, John. See "Richard Greenwell," q.v.

COSTER, John. Took the Oath of Allegiance in Calvert County in 1778 [Ref: L-35].

COTTON, George. Took the Oath of Allegiance in Calvert County in 1778 [Ref: L-36].

COTTON, Jeremiah. Private, Capt. Richard Parran's Co., Calvert County Militia, 1778 [Ref: J-1146, M-149].

COTTON, John. Took the Oath of Allegiance in Calvert County in 1778 [Ref: L-36].

COTTON, Sarah. See "David Platford," q.v.

COTTREAL, Samuel. Took the Oath of Allegiance before the Hon. Robert Armstrong in St. Mary's County in 1778 [Ref: J-1146, K-62].

COURT, Christopher. See "Athanasius Ford," q.v.

COURTS, Elizabeth and William. See "William Thomas," q.v.

COVES, William. Private, St. Mary's County, who served in the Maryland Line until 1781 when discharged [Ref: D-407].
COVINGTON, Rebecca. See "Levin Covington Mackall," q.v.
COWEN, Elizabeth. See "William Allen," q.v.
COWEN, Mary. See "John Hungerford," q.v.
COWMAN, Jeremiah. Took the Oath of Allegiance in Calvert County in 1778 [Ref: L-36].
COWMAN, Jeremiah Jr. Took the Oath of Allegiance in Calvert County in 1778 [Ref: L-36].
COWMAN, John. Took the Oath of Allegiance in Calvert County in 1778 [Ref: L-36].
COWMAN, Joseph. Private, Capt. James Grahame's Co., Calvert County Militia, 1778 [Ref: J-1146, M-148]. Took the Oath of Allegiance in Calvert County in 1778 [Ref: L-36].
COX, Bennett. Private, St. Mary's County Militia, 1777 [Ref: M-212]. Private, St. Mary's County, enlisted on May 4, 1778, for 9 months in the Maryland Line, but reported as "vagrant, deserted" in June, 1778 [Ref: D-329]. Took the Oath of Allegiance before the Hon. John Shanks in St. Mary's County in 1778 [Ref: J-1146, K-69].
COX, George. Private, St. Mary's County Militia, 1777 [Ref: M-215].
COX, James. Private, St. Mary's County Militia, 1777 [Ref: M-215].
COX, Jane. See "Lazarus Ross," q.v.
COX, Jeremiah. Private, Capt. Henry Skinner's Foot Co. of Hunting Hundred, Calvert County, 1777 [Ref: T-1814, O-125]. Private, Capt. Edward Wood's Co., Calvert County Militia, 1778 [Ref: J-1146, M-147].
COX, John. Private, Capt. Charles Williamson's Co., Calvert County Militia, 1778 [Ref: J-1146, M-148].
COX, John Jr. "John Cox, Jr."was a private in the St. Mary's County Militia, 1777 [Ref: M-214]. The Register of St. Andrew's Episcopal Church states that "John Cox" and Anne Shermintine were married (by license) Sep. 2, 1782 [Ref: MB-384].
COX, Joseph. Private, St. Mary's County Militia, 1777 [Ref: M-214].
COX, Young. Private, Capt. Frisby Freeland's Co., Calvert County Militia, 1778 [Ref: J-1146, M-148]. Took the Oath of Allegiance in Calvert County in 1778 [Ref: L-36].
CRABTREE, Elizabeth. See "James and John Billingsley," q.v.
CRAGHILL, Elizabeth. See "William Holton," q.v.
CRAGHILL, Grace. See "Baptist Peake," q.v.
CRAIG, Michael. Seaman and Sergeant of Marines from St. Mary's County who served aboard the State ship *Defence* in 1776 [Ref: S-25, S-153, D-606].
CRAIG, Peter. Took the Oath of Allegiance before the Hon. John Ireland in St. Mary's County in 1778 [Ref: J-1146, K-65].
CRAIG, Rachel. See "Jeremiah Graves," q.v.

CRAIG, Reubin. Private, Capt. Uriah Forrest's Co., Flying Camp, St. Mary's County, July 28, 1776 [Ref: D-30, SM-112]. Took the Oath of Allegiance before the Hon. John Ireland in St. Mary's County in 1778 [Ref: J-1146, K-65, which listed the name as "Rubin Craige"]. See "Meveral Locke (Lock)," q.v.
CRAIN, Thomas. Took the Oath of Allegiance before the Hon. Vernon Hebb in St. Mary's County in 1778 [Ref: J-1146, K-67].
CRAMPFOOT, Fielder. Took the Oath of Allegiance before the Hon. Ignatius Fenwick, Jr. in St. Mary's County in 1778 [Ref: J-1146, K-68].
CRAMPHER, Danmund. Private, Capt. Charles Williamson's Co., Calvert County Militia, 1778 [Ref: J-1146, M-148].
CRANCE, James. Private, St. Mary's County Militia, 1777 [Ref: M-214].
CRANE, Sampson. Private, Capt. Frisby Freeland's Co., Calvert County Militia, 1778 [Ref: J-1146, M-148]. Took the Oath of Allegiance in Calvert County in 1778 [Ref: L-36].
CRANE, William. (1) Private, St. Mary's County Militia, 1777 [Ref: M-215]. Took the Oath of Allegiance before the Hon. Bennett Biscoe in St. Mary's County in 1778 [Ref: J-1146, K-63, which listed the name as "William Crain"]. (2) Private, Capt. Richard Parran's Co., Calvert County Militia, 1778 [Ref: J-1146, M-149]. Took the Oath of Allegiance in Calvert County in 1778 [Ref: L-36].
CRANFORD, James. Private, Capt. Thomas Cleland's Co., Calvert County Militia, 1778 [Ref: J-1146, M-147]. Took the Oath of Allegiance in Calvert County in 1778 [Ref: L-36].
CRANFORD, Lemuel Jr. Private, Capt. Thomas Cleland's Co., Calvert County Militia, 1778 [Ref: J-1146, M-147].
CRANFORD, Nathan. Private, Capt. Thomas Cleland's Co., Calvert County Militia, 1778 [Ref: J-1146, M-147].
CRANFORD, William Jr. Private, Capt. Thomas Cleland's Co., Calvert County Militia, 1778 [Ref: J-1146, M-147].
CRAWLEY, James. Private, St. Mary's County Militia, 1777 [Ref: M-215]. Took the Oath of Allegiance before the Hon. Bennett Biscoe in St. Mary's County in 1778 [Ref: J-1146, K-63].
CRAWLEY, William. Took the Oath of Allegiance in St. Mary's County in 1780 [Ref: Q-108].
CRAYCROFT, Bladen. Loaned money in St. Mary's County for the war effort in 1781 [Ref: X-78, H-409].
CRAYCROFT, Edward. Took the Oath of Allegiance before the Hon. Ignatius Fenwick, Jr. in St. Mary's County in 1778 [Ref: J-1146, K-68].
CRAYCROFT, Ignatius. Took the Oath of Allegiance before the Hon. Henry Reeder in St. Mary's County in 1778 [Ref: J-1146, K-64]. Loaned money in St. Mary's County for the war effort in 1781 [Ref: X-78, H-397].
CREEDY, Peter. Private, Capt. James Grahame's Co., Calvert County Militia, 1778 [Ref: J-1146, M-148].

CREGAR, Michael. Private, St. Mary's County, who served in the Maryland Line until 1781 when discharged [Ref: D-407].
CROCKER, John. Took the Oath of Allegiance before the Hon. Bennett Biscoe in St. Mary's County in 1778 [Ref: J-1146, K-63].
CROMWELL, James. Private, St. Mary's County, who served in the Maryland Line until 1781 when discharged [Ref: D-407].
CRONEY, William. Private, St. Mary's County, who served in the Maryland Line until 1781 when discharged [Ref: D-407].
CROOK, Jesse. Private, St. Mary's County Militia, 1777 [Ref: M-213].
CROOK, Absalom and Mary. See "Zachariah Crook," q.v.
CROOK, Joseph. (1) Private, St. Mary's County Militia, 1777 [Ref: M-212]. Private, St. Mary's County, enlisted May 28, 1778, for 9 months [Ref: D-329]. Private, 2nd Maryland Line, who may have died in Feb., 1779 [Ref: SM-112]. (3) Private, Calvert County, enlisted by Lt. Nathaniel Wilson on Aug. 23, 1776 [Ref: D-34].
CROOK, Justinian. Private, St. Mary's County Militia, 1777 [Ref: M-213]. Took the Oath of Allegiance in St. Mary's County in 1780 [Ref: Q-108, which listed the name as "Justinian Crooke"].
CROOK (CROOKE), Zachariah. Son of Absalom Crooke and Mary Ann Poffer. Born in St. Mary's County circa 1760 and served in the Revolutionary War. He died in Madison County, Kentucky, after 1800 [Ref: MK-34, but not listed in *Archives of Maryland, Volume 18*].
CROSBY, Burdin. Private, Capt. Richard Lane's Co., Calvert County Militia, 1778 [Ref: J-1146, M-149].
CROSBY, John (c1760-1789). Took the Oath of Allegiance in Calvert County in 1778 [Ref: L-36]. Private, Capt. Richard Lane's Co., Calvert County Militia, 1778 [Ref: Maryland Society, Sons of the American Revolution, Approved Membership Application No. 3083; J-1146; M-150, which listed the name as "John Crosbey"].
CROSBY, Joseph. Took the Oath of Allegiance in Calvert County in 1778 [Ref: L-36]. Private, Capt. Richard Lane's Co., Calvert County Militia, 1778 [Ref: J-1146, M-150, which listed the name as "Joseph Crosbey"].
CROSBY, Josias. Took the Oath of Allegiance in Calvert County in 1778 [Ref: L-36].
CROWED, Joseph Smith. Took the Oath of Allegiance in Calvert County in 1778 [Ref: L-36].
CROWLEY, Elizabeth. See "Peregrine Fitzhugh," q.v.
CRUCKLEY, Benjamin. Private, St. Mary's County, who served in the Maryland Line until 1781 when discharged [Ref: D-407].
CRUTCHER, John. See "Leonard Bean," q.v.
CRUTCHLY, Thomas. Took the Oath of Allegiance in Calvert County in 1780 [Ref: Q-108].
CULLISON (COLLOSON), Anne. See "Nicholas Fielder," q.v.

CULLISON, John. Private, St. Mary's County Militia, 1777 [Ref: M-214, which listed the name as "John Coloson"]. Took the Oath of Allegiance in St. Mary's County in 1780 [Ref: Q-108].
CULLISON (COLLASON), Mary. See "Thomas Sanner," q.v.
CULLISON, Peter. Took the Oath of Allegiance in St. Mary's County in 1780 [Ref: Q-108].
CULLISON, Thomas. Private, St. Mary's County Militia, 1777 [Ref: M-215, which listed the name as "Thos. Calloson"].
CULLUMBER (CULLEMBER), Benjamin. Private, Capt. Benjamin Bond's Co., Calvert County Militia, 1778 [Ref: J-1146, M-149]. Took the Oath of Allegiance in Calvert County in 1778 [Ref: L-36].
CULLUMBER (CULLEMBER), Charles. Private, Capt. Benjamin Bond's Co., Calvert County Militia, 1778 [Ref: J-1146, M-149]. Took the Oath of Allegiance in Calvert County in 1778 [Ref: L-36].
CULLUMBER (CULLEMBER), Henry. Took the Oath of Allegiance in Calvert County in 1778 [Ref: L-36].
CULLUMBER (CULLEMBER), Jerre. Took the Oath of Allegiance in Calvert County in 1778 [Ref: L-36].
CULLUMBER (CULLEMBER), Jesse. Took the Oath of Allegiance in Calvert County in 1778 [Ref: L-36]. Private, Capt. Benjamin Bond's Co., Calvert County Militia, 1778 [Ref: J-1146, M-149].
CULLUMBER (CULLEMBER), John. (1) Private, Calvert County, enlisted by Lt. Nathaniel Wilson on Aug. 23, 1776 [Ref: D-34, which listed the name as "John Cullenber"]. Private, Capt. Walter Smith's Co., Calvert County Militia, 1778 [Ref: J-1146, M-148]. (2) Private, Capt. Edward Wood's Co., Calvert County Militia, 1778 [Ref: J-1146, M-147]. This name appeared twice on the list of those who took the Oath of Allegiance in Calvert County in 1778, one as "John Cullumber" and the other as "John Cullenber" [Ref: L-36]. The Christ Church Register in Calvert County records the birth of "John Collembre," son of Thomas and Alice Collembre, on Jan. 9, 1723 [Ref: O-6].
CULLUMBER (CULLEMBER), Nathaniel. Private, Calvert County, enlisted by Capt. John Brooke on July 26, 1776 [Ref: D-33]. Took the Oath of Allegiance in Calvert County in 1778 [Ref: L-36]. Private, Capt. Benjamin Bond's Co., Calvert County Militia, 1778 [Ref: J-1146, M-149]. Nathaniel Cullember and Cassandra Bourn were married on Nov. 8, 1778, by Rev. Francis Lauder, of Christ Church Parish [Ref: K-34].
CULLUMBER (CULLEMBER), Richard. Private, Capt. Benjamin Bond's Co., Calvert County Militia, 1778 [Ref: J-1146, M-149]. Took the Oath of Allegiance in Calvert County in 1778 [Ref: L-36].
CULLUMBER (CULLEMBER), William. Took the Oath of Allegiance in Calvert County in 1778 [Ref: L-36]. Private, Capt. Edward Wood's Co., Calvert County Militia, 1778 [Ref: J-1146, M-147].
CULPEPPER, John. Took the Oath of Allegiance in Calvert County in 1778 [Ref: L-36].

CULPEPPER, Michael. Private, Capt. Walter Smith's Co., Calvert County Militia, 1778 [Ref: J-1146, M-148]. Took the Oath of Allegiance in Calvert County in 1778 [Ref: L-36].
CURRENT, Matthew. Private, Capt. Benjamin Bond's Co., Calvert County Militia, 1778 [Ref: J-1146, M-149]. Took the Oath of Allegiance in Calvert County in 1778 [Ref: L-36].
CURRY, McGolds. Private, St. Mary's County Militia, 1777 [Ref: M-210].
CURTIS, James. Took the Oath of Allegiance before the Hon. Jeremiah Jordan in St. Mary's County in 1778 [Ref: J-1146, K-67].
CURTIS, Joseph. Took the Oath of Allegiance before the Hon. Jeremiah Jordan in St. Mary's County in 1778 [Ref: J-1146, K-67].
CURTIS, Michael. Took the Oath of Allegiance in St. Mary's County in 1780 [Ref: Q-108].
CURTIS, Robert. Took the Oath of Allegiance in St. Mary's County in 1780 [Ref: Q-108].
CURTIS, Thomas. Private, St. Mary's County, enlisted April 22, 1778, for the duration of the war [Ref: D-329]. Private (substitute), St. Mary's County, July 26, 1781 [Ref: D-384]. Private, Continental Army, 1781 [Ref: D-407].
CUSACK (CUSICK), Ignatius. Private, St. Mary's County Militia, 1777 [Ref: M-213].
CUSACK (CUSICK), Luke. Private, Capt. Uriah Forrest's Co., Flying Camp, St. Mary's County, July 28, 1776 [Ref: D-30, SM-112].
CUSACK (CUSICK), Michael. Private, St. Mary's County Militia, 1777 [Ref: M-210 which listed the name as "Michael Cusack"]. Private, 2nd Maryland Line, who reportedly "deserted" on Dec. 18, 1778 [Ref: D-93].
DAFFIN, James. Took the Oath of Allegiance before the Hon. Robert Watts in St. Mary's County in 1778 [Ref: J-1146, K-62]. Corporal, 4th Maryland Line, April 5, 1778 - April 5, 1781; Sergeant, April 27, 1781 [Ref: S-153]. See "Robert Daffin," q.v.
DAFFIN, Robert. Private, St. Mary's County Militia, 1777 [Ref: M-215]. Took the Oath of Allegiance before the Hon. Robert Watts in St. Mary's County in 1778 [Ref: J-1146, K-62]. Second Lieutenant, Lower Bn., May 7, 1781 [Ref: M-67, G-426, which listed the name as "Robert Daffon"]. The Register of St. Andrew's Episcopal Church states that Robert Daffin and Elizabeth Simmonds were married (by license) Jan. 16, 1781 [Ref: MB-383]. One Robert Daffin died by Feb., 1797, leaving a son James Daffin whose guardian was Elizabeth Daffin [Ref: SO-255].
DAFFIN, William. Private, St. Mary's County Militia, 1777 [Ref: M-215]. Took the Oath of Allegiance before the Hon. Robert Watts in St. Mary's County in 1778 [Ref: J-1146, K-62].
DAFT, Ignatius. Private, St. Mary's County Militia, 1777 [Ref: M-210]. Took the Oath of Allegiance before the Hon. John Ireland in St. Mary's County in 1778 [Ref: J-1146, K-65].

DAFT, Matthew. Private, St. Mary's County Militia, 1777 [Ref: M-213]. Took the Oath of Allegiance before the Hon. John Ireland in St. Mary's County in 1778 [Ref: J-1146, K-65].
DAFT, Thomas. Private, St. Mary's County Militia, 1777 [Ref: M-213].
DAFT, William. Took the Oath of Allegiance before the Hon. Richard Barnes in St. Mary's County in 1778 [Ref: J-1146, K-66].
DAILEY, Benjamin. Private, St. Mary's County, enlisted May 28, 1778, for 9 months, Continental Army [Ref: D-329, SM-112].
DAILEY, Bennett. Applied for and received pension S30980 on Aug. 27, 1832, aged 75, in Washington County, Kentucky, stating that he had enlisted in St. Mary's County in April, 1777, and served in Pennsylvania. After the war he returned to Maryland for 10 or 12 years and then went to Kentucky (stating he had been there for 45 years in 1832). Mary Alvey, aged 70, made affidavit on Nov. 13, 1833 in Washington County and stated she knew Bennett Dailey in 1776 or 1777 and that he was raised about a mile from where she lived in St. Mary's County. She moved to Kentucky about 2 years after he did. Randall Hoskins also made affidavit on Nov. 14, 1833 that he lived in Charles County, Maryland within 5 or 6 miles of Bennett Dailey and they had enlisted in the same co. during the war [Ref: P-867, W-57, MK-34, MK-35].
DAILEY, Joseph. Private, Capt. Uriah Forrest's Co., Flying Camp, St. Mary's County, July 28, 1776 [Ref: D-30, SM-112].
DALRYMPLE, William. Took the Oath of Allegiance in Calvert County in 1778 [Ref: L-36].
DANT, Charles. Private, St. Mary's County Militia, 1777 [Ref: M-215, which listed the name as "Charles Dantt"].
DANT, John Baptist. Took the Oath of Allegiance before the Hon. John Ireland in St. Mary's County in 1778 [Ref: J-1146, K-65]. Along with Joseph Dant and James Dant he migrated with the early Catholics who settled on Pottinger's Creek in Washington County, Kentucky in 1785 [Ref: MK-35, MK-36].
DANT, Mary. See "Abram Rhodes" and "Justinian Mills," q.v.
DARE, Anne. See "James Sollers," q.v.
DARE, Elizabeth. See "Isaac Kent," q.v.
DARE, Gideon. Private, Capt. Benjamin Bond's Co., Calvert County Militia, 1778 [Ref: J-1146, M-149, which listed the name as "Guideon Dare"]. Private, Capt. Frisby Freeland's Co., Calvert County Militia, 1778 [Ref: J-1146, M-148]. There was also a Gideon Dare who was a First Lieutenant in the Anne Arundel County Militia, 1776-1778 [Ref: M-67, A-336, C-525].
DARE, Gideon Jr. Took the Oath of Allegiance in Calvert County in 1778 [Ref: L-36].
DARE, John. Private, Capt. Benjamin Bond's Co., Calvert County Militia, 1778 [Ref: J-1146, M-149]. Took the Oath of Allegiance in Calvert County in 1778 [Ref: L-36].

DARE, Mary. See "George Ireland," q.v.
DARE, Nathaniel. Private, Capt. Walter Smith's Co., Calvert County Militia, 1778 [Ref: J-1146, M-148]. Took the Oath of Allegiance in Calvert County in 1778 [Ref: L-36]. Nathaniel Dare and Jean Gray were married on Jan. 22, 1778, by Rev. Francis Lauder, of Christ Church Parish [Ref: K-33].
DARE, Rebecca. See "Alexander Somerville," q.v.
DARE, Samuel. Private, Capt. John Mackall's Co., Calvert County Militia, 15th Bn., June 12, 1778 [Ref: M-146]. Private, Capt. Frederick Skinner's Co., Calvert County Militia, 1778 [Ref: J-1146, M-150]. Took the Oath of Allegiance in Calvert County in 1778 [Ref: L-36].
DARE, Sarah. See "Benjamin Hance," q.v.
DARE, Thomas Cleverly. Took the Oath of Allegiance in Calvert County in 1778 [Ref: L-36].
DARE, William Jr. First Lieutenant, Capt. Frederick Skinner's Co., Calvert County Militia, June 16, 1778 [Ref: J-1146, M-67, M-150, E-137]. Lieutenant, Capt. John Mackall's Co., Calvert County Militia, 15th Bn., June 12, 1778 [Ref: M-146]. Also, on June 12, 1778, a petition was sent to the House of Delegates to appoint him a captain [Ref: V-175]. Took the Oath of Allegiance in Calvert County in 1778 [Ref: L-36].
DARE, William Sr. Took the Oath of Allegiance in Calvert County in 1778 [Ref: L-36].
DARLEY, Benjamin. Private, St. Mary's County Militia, 1777 [Ref: M-213].
DART, John. Took the Oath of Allegiance before the Hon. Bennett Biscoe in St. Mary's County in 1778 [Ref: J-1146, K-63].
DART, Thomas. Took the Oath of Allegiance in St. Mary's County in 1780 [Ref: Q-108].
DASHEAL (DASHEEL), Benjamin. "Benjamin Dasheal" was a private in Capt. Thomas Truman Greenfield's Co., Calvert County Militia, 1778 [Ref: J-1146, M-150]. "Benjamin Dasheel" and Ann Yoe were married on Dec. 25, 1777, by Rev. Thomas John Clagett, All Saint's Parish [Ref: K-33].
DAVID, John. Captain of the rows *Galley* and *Conqueror* and hauled State troops in 1776-1777; from St. Mary's County [Ref: S-153].
DAVID, Joseph. Private, Capt. Charles Williamson's Co., Calvert County Militia, 1778 [Ref: J-1146, M-147].
DAVIDSON, Jean. See "Thomas Boney," q.v.
DAVIDSON, John. Second Lieutenant, 5th Independent Maryland Co., St. Mary's County, Jan. 2, 1776 [Ref: D-25]. Saw action during the Dunmore invasion of St. Mary's County in July, 1776, and was promoted to First Lieutenant on Aug. 7, 1776, to Captain on Dec. 10, 1776, and later a Major in the 2nd Maryland Line [Ref: SM-147]. Reported to the Governor on Aug. 26, 1777, that a "relapse of fever prevented his arrival at camp." [Ref: V-118]. Took the Oath of Allegiance in St. Mary's

County in 1780 [Ref: Q-108]. Participated in the Battle of Brooklyn and served in the Northern and Southern Campaigns. Served as a Major, 5th Maryland Line, from Jan. 1, 1781 until Jan. 21, 1783, when he was appointed Intendant (Comptroller) of the State of Maryland by Gov. William Paca [Ref: SM-147, SM-148, S-153]. "John Davieson" took the Oath of Allegiance in St. Mary's County in 1780 [Ref: Q-108].

DAVIES, Joseph. See "Joseph Davis," q.v.

DAVIS, Acquilla. Private, St. Mary's County Militia, 1777 [Ref: M-215].

DAVIS, Ann. See "James Davis," q.v.

DAVIS, Anthony. Private, St. Mary's County, Maryland Line. Applied for and received pension S34729 on May 11, 1818, aged about 63, in St. Mary's County [Ref: P-890, but is not listed in *Archives of Maryland, Volume 18*]. The pension rolls of 1835 listed him as aged 79, but also noted he had been dropped from the rolls under the Act of May 1, 1820 [Ref: U-40].

DAVIS, Briscoe. Private, St. Mary's County Militia, 1777 [Ref: M-210].

DAVIS, Eliazer. Supplied provisions (wheat, mutton, or bacon) to the Army in 1780 in St. Mary's County [Ref: S-153].

DAVIS, Elizabeth. See "John Brady," q.v.

DAVIS, George. "George Davis" was a private in St. Mary's County Militia, 1777 [Ref: M-209]. "George Davis, Jr., farmer" moved from Upper Resurrection to Charles County after 1810 [Ref: X-86].

DAVIS, Gerrard. Private, St. Mary's County Militia, 1777 [Ref: M-210].

DAVIS, Gray. Took the Oath of Allegiance in St. Mary's County in 1780 [Ref: Q-108].

DAVIS, Hezekiah. Took the Oath of Allegiance in St. Mary's County in 1780 [Ref: Q-108].

DAVIS, James. (1) Private, St. Mary's County Militia, 1777 [Ref: M-210]. Took the Oath of Allegiance before the Hon. John Reeder in St. Mary's County in 1778 [Ref: J-1146, K-69]. (2) Private, Capt. Richard Parran's Co., Calvert County Militia, 1778 [Ref: J-1146, M-149]. One James Davis, of St. Mary's County, died intestate by April, 1786, and his administratrix Ann Perce Davis by that time had left Maryland without administering on his estate [Ref: SO-96].

DAVIS, Jane. See "William Baker," q.v.

DAVIS, John. (1) Private, St. Mary's County Militia, 1777 [Ref: M-213]. Took the Oath of Allegiance before the Hon. John Ireland in St. Mary's County in 1778 [Ref: J-1146, K-65]. One John Davis died intestate by March, 1787 [Ref: SO-111]. (2) There was also a John Davis who was born in St. Mary's County on June 9, 1764 and lived in Edgecombe County, North Carolina at the time of his enlistment in the Revolutionary War. He applied for and received pension S6787 in 1832 in Duplin County, North Carolina [Ref: MC-41, P-899]. (3) Seaman from St. Mary's County who served aboard the State ship *Defence* in 1776 and Corporal of Marines in 1777 [Ref: S-25, S-153, D-606].

DAVIS, Joseph. (1) Private, Calvert County, enlisted by Ensign James Somervill on July 25, 1776 [Ref: D-34]. Took the Oath of Allegiance in Calvert County in 1778 [Ref: L-36]. (2) Private, St. Mary's County Militia, 1777 [Ref: M-211]. Took the Oath of Allegiance before the Hon. Henry G. Sothoron in St. Mary's County in 1778 [Ref: J-1146, K-68]. One "Joseph Daviss" supplied provisions (wheat, mutton, or bacon) to the Army in St. Mary's County in 1780 [Ref: S-77]. The Register of St. Francis Xavier Catholic Church states that one Joseph Davis and Jemima Wimsatt were married on Oct. 11, 1772 [Ref: SC-34]. A "Joseph Davies" and Sarah Miller were married on Oct. 21, 1780, by Rev. Francis Lauder, of Christ Church Parish [Ref: K-35].

DAVIS, Lawson. Private, St. Mary's County Militia, 1777 [Ref: M-209].

DAVIS, Mary. See "Aquila Hall," q.v.

DAVIS, Moses. Took the Oath of Allegiance before the Hon. Richard Barnes in St. Mary's County in 1778 [Ref: J-1146, K-66]. Private, St. Mary's County Militia, 1777 [Ref: M-215, which listed the name as "Moses Daress(?)"]. Paid for making salt in 1782 [Ref: S-153]. The Register of St. Andrew's Episcopal Church states that Moses Davis and Anne Evans married on May 18, 1779 [Ref: MB-382].

DAVIS, Owen. Private, St. Mary's County Militia, 1777 [Ref: M-210]. Supplied provisions (wheat, mutton, or bacon) for the Army in 1780 [Ref: S-153, S-77, which listed the name as "Owen Daviss"].

DAVIS, Philip. (1) Private, St. Mary's County Militia, 1777 [Ref: M-209]. (2) Private, Capt. Richard Lane's Co., Calvert County Militia, 1778 [Ref: J-1146, M-149].

DAVIS, Stephen. Took the Oath of Allegiance before the Hon. John Ireland in St. Mary's County in 1778 [Ref: J-1146, K-65].

DAVIS (DAVIE, DAVIES), Thomas. Private, Capt. Uriah Forrest's Co., Flying Camp, St. Mary's County, July 28, 1776 [Ref: D-30, SM-112, S-153].

DAVIS, Tilgh. Private, St. Mary's County Militia, 1777 [Ref: M-215].

DAVIS, Walter. Took the Oath of Allegiance before the Hon. John Ireland in St. Mary's County in 1778 [Ref: J-1146, K-65].

DAVIS, William. Private from St. Mary's County who served in the marines aboard the State ship *Defence* in 1776-1777 [Ref: S-25, D-606].

DAWKINS, Alexander. Private, Capt. Walter Smith's Co., Calvert County Militia, 1778 [Ref: J-1146, M-148]. Took the Oath of Allegiance in Calvert County in 1778 [Ref: L-36].

DAWKINS, Ann. See "Charles Dawkins," q.v.

DAWKINS, Barbara. See "Brian Taylor," q.v.

DAWKINS, Charles. (1) Private, Capt. Walter Smith's Co., Calvert County Militia, 1778 [Ref: J-1146, M-148]. (2) Private, Capt. Benjamin Bond's Co., Calvert County Militia, 1778 [Ref: J-1146, M-149]. Charles Dawkins and Charles Dawkins, Jr. both took the Oath of Allegiance in Calvert County in 1778 [Ref: L-36]. The Christ Church Register in

Calvert County records the births of the children of Charles Dawkins (born Aug. 22, 1736, son of William and Mary Dawkins) and his wife Rebecca as follows: Ann (born May 13, 1775); Rebecca (born March 23, 1777); Dorcas (born Feb. 1, 1779); and, William (born Dec. 31, 1781). [Ref: O-7].

DAWKINS, Dorcas. See "Charles Dawkins," q.v.

DAWKINS, James. Private, Capt. Benjamin Bond's Co., Calvert County Militia, 1778 [Ref: J-1146, M-149]. Took the Oath of Allegiance in Calvert County in 1778 [Ref: L-36]. The Christ Church Register in Calvert County records the birth of James Dawkins, son of William and Mary Dawkins, on Jan. 15, 1726 [Ref: O-7].

DAWKINS, Jesse. Private, Capt. Walter Smith's Co., Calvert County Militia, 1778 [Ref: J-1146, M-148]. Took the Oath of Allegiance in Calvert County in 1778 [Ref: L-36]. The Christ Church Register in Calvert County records the birth of Jesse Dawkins, son of William and Mary Dawkins, on July 31, 1742 [Ref: O-7].

DAWKINS, Joseph. Private, Capt. Walter Smith's Co., Calvert County Militia, 1778 [Ref: J-1146, M-148]. The Christ Church Register in Calvert County records the birth of Joseph Dawkins, son of William and Mary Dawkins, on Jan. 22, 1728 [Ref: O-7].

DAWKINS, Rebecca. See "Charles Dawkins" and "Alexander Somerville," q.v.

DAWKINS, William. Private, Capt. Walter Smith's Co., Calvert County Militia, 1778 [Ref: J-1146, M-148]. Took the Oath of Allegiance in Calvert County in 1778 [Ref: L-36]. The Christ Church Register in Calvert County records the birth of William Dawkins, son of William and Mary Dawkins, on Aug. 3, 1734 [Ref: O-7]. Also see "Charles Dawkins," q.v.

DAWKINS, William Jr. Private, Capt. Walter Smith's Co., Calvert County Militia, 1778 [Ref: J-1146, M-148]. Took the Oath of Allegiance in Calvert County in 1778 [Ref: L-36].

DAWSEY, Minta. See "Thomas Brewer," q.v.

DAY, Daniel. Private, Capt. Richard Parran's Co., Calvert County Militia, 1778 [Ref: J-1146, M-149]. Took the Oath of Allegiance in Calvert County in 1780 [Ref: Q-108].

DAY, Jesse. Private, Calvert County, enlisted by Ensign James Somervill on July 26, 1776 [Ref: D-34]. Private, Capt. Richard Parran's Co., Calvert County Militia, 1778 [Ref: J-1146, M-149]. Took the Oath of Allegiance in Calvert County in 1780 [Ref: Q-108].

DAY, Nathan. Private, Capt. Richard Parran's Co., Calvert County Militia, 1778 [Ref: J-1146, M-149]. Nathaniel Day took the Oath of Allegiance in Calvert County in 1780 [Ref: Q-109].

DAY, Richard. Private, Capt. Walter Smith's Co., Calvert County Militia, 1778 [Ref: J-1146, M-148]. Took the Oath of Allegiance in Calvert County in 1780 [Ref: Q-109].

DAY, Robert. Private, Capt. Richard Parran's Co., Calvert County Militia, 1778 [Ref: J-1146, M-149].
DAY, Robert Jr. Private, Capt. Richard Parran's Co., Calvert County Militia, 1778 [Ref: J-1146, M-149]. Took the Oath of Allegiance in Calvert County in 1780 [Ref: Q-109].
DAY, Samuel. Private, Calvert County, enlisted by Lt. Nathaniel Wilson on Aug. 31, 1776 [Ref: D-34].
DEADMAN (DEDMAN), Nancy. See "Thomas Lowry," q.v.
DEALE, Henry. Private, Capt. James Grahame's Co., Calvert County Militia, 1778 [Ref: J-1146, M-149].
DEALE, Jacob Jr. Private, Capt. Thomas Cleland's Co., Calvert County Militia, 1778 [Ref: J-1146, M-147].
DEALE, James. Private, Capt. James Grahame's Co., Calvert County Militia, 1778 [Ref: J-1146, M-149].
DEALE, Joseph. Private, Calvert County, enlisted by Ensign James Somervill on July 26, 1776 [Ref: D-34].
DEALE, Richard. Private, Capt. James Grahame's Co., Calvert County Militia, 1778 [Ref: J-1146, M-148].
DEALE, Richard Jr. Took the Oath of Allegiance in Calvert County in 1778 [Ref: L-36].
DEALE, Samuel. Private, Capt. Frederick Skinner's Co., Calvert County Militia, 1778 [Ref: J-1146, M-150]. Private, Capt. John Mackall's Co., Calvert County Militia, 15th Bn., June 12, 1778 [Ref: M-146].
DEALE, William. Private, Capt. James Patterson's Co., Calvert County Militia, Aug. 10, 1777 [Ref: M-146]. Private, Capt. Frederick Skinner's Co., Calvert County Militia, 1778 [Ref: J-1146, M-150]. Private, Capt. John Mackall's Co., Calvert County Militia, 15th Bn., June 12, 1778 [Ref: M-146]. Took the Oath of Allegiance in Calvert County in 1778 [Ref: L-36].
DEAN, Ann. See "John Dean," q.v.
DEAN, James. Private, St. Mary's County Militia, 1777 [Ref: M-211, which listed the name as "James Deane"]. Took the Oath of Allegiance before the Hon. Ignatius Fenwick, Jr. in St. Mary's County in 1778 [Ref: J-1146, K-68].
DEAN, John. Private, St. Mary's County Militia, 1777 [Ref: M-211, which listed the name as "John Deane"]. Took the Oath of Allegiance before the Hon. Ignatius Fenwick, Jr. in St. Mary's County in 1778 [Ref: J-1146, K-68]. The Register of St. Francis Xavier Catholic Church states that "John Dean, widower" and Mary Moore were married on Sep. 12, 1774 [Ref: SC-35, which noted "either they or their descendants eventually settled at The Barrens in Perry County, Missouri"]. One John Dean died intestate by Dec., 1793, and his administratrix was Ann Dean [Ref: SO-204].
DEAN, Thomas. Took the Oath of Allegiance before the Hon. Ignatius Fenwick, Jr. in St. Mary's County in 1778 [Ref: J-1146, K-68].

DEAN, William. Private, St. Mary's County Militia, 1777 [Ref: M-211]. Took the Oath of Allegiance before the Hon. Ignatius Fenwick, Jr. in St. Mary's County in 1778 [Ref: J-1146, K-68].
DEAVER, James. Private, Capt. Henry Skinner's Foot Co. of Hunting Hundred, Calvert County, 1777 [Ref: T-1814, O-125].
DEAVER, John. Private, Capt. Henry Skinner's Foot Co. of Hunting Hundred, Calvert County, 1777 [Ref: T-1814, O-125].
DEAVER, John Jr. Private, Capt. Henry Skinner's Foot Co. of Hunting Hundred, Calvert County, 1777 [Ref: T-1814, O-125].
DEAVER, Peter. Took the Oath of Allegiance in Calvert County in 1780 [Ref: Q-109].
DEAVER, William. Private, Capt. Henry Skinner's Foot Co. of Hunting Hundred, Calvert County, 1777 [Ref: T-1814, O-125].
DEBUTTS, John (c1740-1796). Born in County Sligo, Ireland, and immigrated to St. Mary's County, probably a son of Richard DeButts. John married Margaret Truman (died 1798), daughter of Margaret Somerville, and died without progeny. Served as a Delegate to the Maryland Convention, 1774-1775, County Justice, 1772-1774, Orphans Court Justice, 1779-1789, Tax Commissioner, 1782-1783, and Member of the House of Delegates in 1783 [Ref: N-70, N-88, N-258, N-259]. "John DeButts" was elected to a General Committee in St. Mary's County in accordance with the resolves of the Continental Congress in 1775, and served on the Committee of Correspondence [Ref: MR-127]. John DeButts died testate by Dec., 1796, and his executor was Samuel DeButts. In 1797 George Ralph petitioned the Court that his wife Catherine Ralph had not received her distributive part of the estate of John DeButts. In 1798 Margaret Truman DeButts, widow of John, died intestate [Ref: SO-254, SO-257, SO-264, SO-279].
DEBUTTS, Margaret, Richard, and Samuel. See "John DeButts," q.v.
DELAFRANY, John Baptist. Private, Calvert County, enlisted by Capt. John Brooke on July 26, 1776 [Ref: D-33]. Took the Oath of Allegiance in Calvert County in 1778 [Ref: L-36, which listed the name as "John Baptest Delapany"]. Private, Capt. Richard Lane's Co., Calvert County Militia, 1778 [Ref: J-1146, M-150, which listed the name as "John Baptist Delifrany"].
DEMAR, Joshua. Took the Oath of Allegiance in Calvert County in 1778 [Ref: L-36].
DEMENT, Thomas. Took the Oath of Allegiance in St. Mary's County in 1780 [Ref: Q-109, which also listed the name as "Thomas Demond"].
DENNIS, Abram. Private, St. Mary's County Militia, 1777 [Ref: M-214].
DENNIS, Jesse. Private, Capt. Uriah Forrest's Co., Flying Camp, St. Mary's County, July 28, 1776 [Ref: D-30, SM-112].
DENNISON, Thomas. Took the Oath of Allegiance before the Hon. Robert Armstrong in St. Mary's County in 1778 [Ref: J-1146, K-62].

DENT, Charles. Took the Oath of Allegiance before the Hon. Robert Watts in St. Mary's County in 1778 [Ref: J-1146, K-62].

DENT, Eleanor. See "Nehemiah Herbert Blackistone," q.v.

DENT, George (Dec. 21, 1756 - Oct. 15, 1842). Private, St. Mary's County Militia, 1777. Private, St. Mary's County, enlisted May 25, 1778, for 9 months in the 2nd Maryland Line [Ref: M-210, D-329]. Took the Oath of Allegiance before the Hon. Henry Tubman in St. Mary's County in 1778 [Ref: J-1146, K-70]. George applied for and received pension S12755 on April 21, 1818, in St. Mary's County and died there in 1842. In 1853 his surviving children were William Dent, Hezekiah Dent, Mary A. Dukes, and Eliza T. Burroughs [Ref: P-952]. He married Elizabeth Temperance Mills [Ref: Y-188]. Pension rolls of 1835 listed him as age 74, but noted he had been dropped from the rolls under the Act of May 1, 1820 [Ref: U-40]. Another source states George Dent was 83 in 1840 and lived in the Second District in the household of William Dent [Ref: R-367]. Also, the Treasurer of Maryland was directed in 1829 to "pay George Dent, of St. Mary's County, during life, half yearly, half pay of a private, for his services during the war." [Ref: I-336]. Source S-141 states that George Dent (1756/7-1845) was a son of Thomas Dent and Elizabeth Edwards, and he married Elizabeth Mills in 1790. This same source indicates George Dent was Captain of the Home Guard in the War of 1812 and served in the United States Congress from 1793 to 1801, and was U. S. Marshall for the Potomac District in 1801. He is buried in St. Andrews Episcopal Church near Leonardtown [Ref: S-128, S-141]. It should be noted that there was also a George Dent who was a lieutenant in the 2nd Maryland Line, but he was from Charles County.

DENT, Hatch (1757 - Dec. 30, 1799). Reverend Hatch Dent was a son of Hatch Dent and grandson of John Dent of Yorkshire, England. One of the early settlers of Maryland, he was a captain in the 2nd Maryland Line in 1777, and an eminent teacher and minister of the Trinity Parish Church. His wife was Judith Poston (1758-1814) and they (among others) were removed from the Glebe of Trinity Parish and reinterred at the Dent Memorial at Charlotte Hall in St. Mary's County in 1883 [Ref: HG-40, HG-41, D-18, D-101]. Also see "Elias Barber," q.v.

DENT, Hezekiah. See "George Dent," q.v.

DENT, John. Took the Oath of Allegiance before the Hon. Henry Tubman in St. Mary's County in 1778 [Ref: J-1146, K-70].

DENT, Joseph. Private, St. Mary's County Militia, 1777 [Ref: M-215].

DENT, Sarah. See "George Harrison," q.v.

DENT, Susanna. See "William Burroughs," q.v.

DENT, Thomas and William. See "George Dent," q.v.

DENTON, Edward. Private, Calvert County, enlisted by Capt. John Brooke on July 25, 1776 [Ref: D-33]. Private, Capt. Benjamin Bond's Co., Calvert County Militia, 1778 [Ref: J-1146, M-149]. Edward Denton

and Mary Games were married on Oct. 20, 1778, by Rev. Francis Lauder, of Christ Church Parish [Ref: K-34].
DENTON, George. Private, Capt. Walter Smith's Co., Calvert County Militia, 1778 [Ref: J-1146, M-14]. Took the Oath of Allegiance in Calvert County in 1778 [Ref: L-36].
DENTON, John. (1) Private, Capt. Walter Smith's Co., Calvert County Militia, 1778 [Ref: J-1146, M-148]. Took the Oath of Allegiance in Calvert County in 1778 [Ref: L-36]. (2) Private, Capt. Edward Wood's Co., Calvert County Militia, 1778 [Ref: J-1146, M-147]. Took the Oath of Allegiance in Calvert County in 1778 [Ref: L-36].
DENTON, Rennes. See "Henry Sax," q.v.
DENTON, Thomas. (1) Private, Capt. Benjamin Bond's Co., Calvert County Militia, 1778 [Ref: J-1146, M-149]. (2) Private, Capt. Edward Wood's Co., Calvert County Militia, 1778 [Ref: J-1146, M-147]. One took the Oath of Allegiance in Calvert County in 1778 [Ref: L-36].
DEVAUX, Michael. Private, Capt. Henry Skinner's Foot Co. of Hunting Hundred, Calvert County, 1777 [Ref: T-1814, O-125].
DEVEAUX, Thomas. Private, Capt. Henry Skinner's Foot Co. of Hunting Hundred, Calvert County, 1777 [Ref: T-1814, O-125].
DEVONISH, Eleanor. See "William Coe," q.v.
DEW (DUE), John. Took the Oath of Allegiance in Calvert County in 1778 [Ref: L-36]. "John Due" was a private, Capt. Richard Lane's Co., Calvert County Militia, 1778 [Ref: J-1146, M-149].
DICKS, John. Private, Capt. Richard Lane's Co., Calvert County Militia, 1778 [Ref: J-1146, M-149]. Took the Oath of Allegiance in Calvert County in 1778 [Ref: L-36].
DIDDLE, Francis. Took the Oath of Allegiance before the Hon. Henry G. Sothoron in St. Mary's County in 1778 [Ref: J-1146, K-68].
DILLAHAY, Arthur. Private, St. Mary's County Militia, 1777 [Ref: M-214, which listed the name as "Arthur Dillihay"].
DILLAHAY, John. Took the Oath of Allegiance before the Hon. Henry G. Sothoron in St. Mary's County in 1778 [Ref: J-1146, K-68].
DILLAHAY, Road. Took the Oath of Allegiance before the Hon. Henry G. Sothoron in St. Mary's County in 1778 [Ref: J-1146, K-68].
DILLEHAY, Thomas. Took the Oath of Allegiance before the Hon. John Ireland in St. Mary's County in 1778 [Ref: J-1146, K-65].
DILLEN, Thomas. Private, St. Mary's County Militia, 1777 [Ref: M-212]. Although recorded on the list of the Hon. Robert Watts in St. Mary's County in 1778, it was noted that Thomas Dillen took the Oath of Allegiance "at Baltimore" [Ref: J-1146, K-62]. Paid for making salt in 1782 [Ref: S-153].
DILLIN, William. Corporal, St. Mary's County, 3rd Maryland Line, Capt. Armstrong's Co., 1778-1780 [Ref: D-298].
DILLION, Anne. See "George Bean," q.v.
DILLION, Margaret. See "Henry Allison," q.v.

DILMAN, John. Private, St. Mary's County, who served in the Maryland Line until 1781 when discharged [Ref: D-407].
DISNEY, Ezekiel Jr. Marine from Calvert County who served on the State ship *Defence* in 1777 [Ref: D-656].
DISNEY, Ezekiel Sr. Ordinary Seaman from Calvert County who served on the State ship *Defence* in 1777 [Ref: D-656].
DISNEY, William. Private, Capt. Frederick Skinner's Co., Calvert County Militia, 1778 [Ref: J-1146, M-150]. Private, Capt. John Mackall's Co., Calvert County Militia, 15th Bn., June 12, 1778 [Ref: M-146].
DIXON, Abraham. Took the Oath of Allegiance in St. Mary's County in 1780 [Ref: Q-109].
DIXON, Absolom. Private, St. Mary's County Militia, 1777 [Ref: M-212]. One Absalom Dixon died testate by April, 1797, leaving a wife Elizabeth Dixon and a son (name not stated here). [Ref: SO-260].
DIXON, Ellis. Private, Calvert County, enlisted by Capt. John Brooke on July 25, 1776 [Ref: D-33].
DIXON, George. Took the Oath of Allegiance in St. Mary's County in 1780 [Ref: Q-109].
DIXON, Henry. Took the Oath of Allegiance before the Hon. Bennett Biscoe in St. Mary's County in 1778 [Ref: J-1146, K-63].
DIXON, James. Private, Capt. Richard Parran's Co., Calvert County Militia, 1778 [Ref: J-1146, M-149]. Took the Oath of Allegiance in Calvert County in 1780 [Ref: Q-109].
DIXON, Jeremiah. Took the Oath of Allegiance in St. Mary's County in 1780 [Ref: Q-109].
DIXON, Jesse. Private, Capt. Benjamin Bond's Co., Calvert County Militia, 1778 [Ref: J-1146, M-149].
DIXON, Mary. See "Obed Dixon," q.v.
DIXON, Obed. Took the Oath of Allegiance in Calvert County in 1778 [Ref: L-36]. Private, Capt. Richard Parran's Co., Calvert County Militia, 1778 [Ref: J-1146, M-149]. The Christ Church Register in Calvert County records the birth of one Obed Dixon, son of Robert Dixon and Ruth Manning, on May 20, 1709. He married Sarah ---- and they had these children: Mary (born Aug. 2, 1741), Robert (born Sep. 17, 1743), Ruth (born Jan. 7, 1748), and Benjamin (born Feb. 6, 1750). [Ref: O-7].
DIXON, Peter. Private, St. Mary's County Militia, 1777 [Ref: M-212]. Took the Oath of Allegiance before the Hon. Henry G. Sothoron in St. Mary's County in 1778 [Ref: J-1146, K-68].
DIXON, Phebe. See "Richard Allen (Allein)," q.v.
DIXON, Robert, Ruth, and Sarah. See "Obed Dixon," q.v.
DIXON, Solomon. Private, St. Mary's County, drafted July 27, 1781 [Ref: D-384]. Private, Continental Army; discharged "not fit for duty" by Dr. Murray on Oct. 18, 1781 [Ref: D-407, S-107, S-153, G-646].
DIXON, Thomas. (1) Private, St. Mary's County Militia, 1777 [Ref: M-212]. Took the Oath of Allegiance in St. Mary's County in 1780 [Ref: Q-

109]. (2) Took the Oath of Allegiance in Calvert County in 1778 [Ref: L-36].

DIXON, William Rooke. Took the Oath of Allegiance before the Hon. Bennett Biscoe in St. Mary's County in 1778 [Ref: J-1146, K-63].

DOBSON, Benjamin. Took the Oath of Allegiance in Calvert County in 1778 [Ref: L-36].

DOBSON, John Jr. Took the Oath of Allegiance in Calvert County in 1778 [Ref: L-36].

DOCKETT, John. Private, Capt. Charles Williamson's Co., Calvert County Militia, 1778 [Ref: J-1146, M-148]. Took the Oath of Allegiance in Calvert County in 1778 [Ref: L-36].

DODSON, Benjamin. Private, Capt. Henry Skinner's Foot Co. of Hunting Hundred, Calvert County, 1777 [Ref: T-1814, O-125].

DODSON, Elias. Private, Capt. Henry Skinner's Foot Co. of Hunting Hundred, Calvert County, 1777 [Ref: T-1814, O-125].

DODSON, John. Private, Capt. Henry Skinner's Foot Co. of Hunting Hundred, Calvert County, 1777 [Ref: T-1814, O-125].

DONALDSON, George. Private, Capt. James Grahame's Co., Calvert County Militia, 1778 [Ref: J-1146, M-148]. Took the Oath of Allegiance in Calvert County in 1778 [Ref: L-36].

DORING, Charles. Took the Oath of Allegiance in Calvert County in 1778 [Ref: L-36].

DORNABY, Thomas. Private, Capt. Henry Skinner's Foot Co. of Hunting Hundred, Calvert County, 1777 [Ref: T-1814, O-125].

DORRUMPLE, Jesse. Private, Capt. Walter Smith's Co., Calvert County Militia, 1778 [Ref: J-1146, M-148, which listed the name as "Jesse Dorremple"].

DORRUMPLE, John. Private, Capt. James Grahame's Co., Calvert County Militia, 1778 [Ref: J-1146, M-148, which listed the name as "John Durumple"]. The Christ Church Register in Calvert County records the birth of John Dorrumple, son of John and Grace Dorrumple, on March 2, 1720 [Ref: O-9].

DORRUMPLE, William. Private, Capt. Walter Smith's Co., Calvert County Militia, 1778 [Ref: J-1146, M-148, which listed the name as "William Dorremple"]. The Christ Church Register in Calvert County records the birth of William Dorrumple, son of John and Grace Dorrumple, on Feb. 12, 1723 [Ref: O-9].

DORSETT, Henry. Private, Capt. James Patterson's Co., Calvert County Militia, Aug. 10, 1777 [Ref: M-146].

DORSEY, Ann. See "James Moore," q.v.

DORSEY, Benjamin. Private, Capt. Thomas Cleland's Co., Calvert County Militia, 1778 [Ref: J-1146, M-147]. Took the Oath of Allegiance in Calvert County in 1780 [Ref: Q-109].

DORSEY, Daniel. Private, Capt. Thomas Cleland's Co., Calvert County Militia, 1778 [Ref: J-1146, M-147]. Took the Oath of Allegiance in Calvert County in 1780 [Ref: Q-109].

DORSEY, Francis. Private, Capt. Thomas Cleland's Co., Calvert County Militia, 1778 [Ref: J-1146, M-147].

DORSEY (DOSSEY), James. "James Dossey" was a private, St. Mary's County Militia, 1777 [Ref: M-215]. "James Dorsey" took the Oath of Allegiance before the Hon. Bennett Biscoe in St. Mary's County in 1778 [Ref: J-1146, K-63]. There was also a "James Dossey" who took the Oath of Allegiance in Calvert County in 1778 [Ref: L-36]. The Christ Church Register in Calvert County records the birth of James Dorsey, son of Philip and Anne Dorsey, on Sep. 18, 1735 [Ref: O-10].

DORSEY, James Jr. Private, Capt. Thomas Cleland's Co., Calvert County Militia, 1778 [Ref: J-1146, M-147].

DORSEY (DOSSEY), John. "John Dorsey" was a private, Capt. Frisby Freeland's Co., Calvert County Militia, 1778 [Ref: J-1146, M-148]. "John Dossey" was a private, St. Mary's County Militia, 1777 [Ref: M-215]. One "John Dossey" took the Oath of Allegiance before the Hon. Richard Barnes in St. Mary's County in 1778, and a "John Dorsey" took the Oath of Allegiance before the Hon. Bennett Biscoe in St. Mary's County in 1778 [Ref: J-1146, K-63, K-66].

DORSEY, John Jr. Private, Capt. Thomas Cleland's Co., Calvert County Militia, 1778 [Ref: J-1146, M-147].

DORSEY, Joseph. (1) Private, Capt. Thomas Cleland's Co., Calvert County Militia, 1778 [Ref: J-1146, M-147]. (2) Private, St. Mary's County Militia, 1777 [Ref: M-212]. Marine aboard the State ship *Defence* on Oct. 23, 1777 [Ref: S-154].

DORSEY (DOSSEY), Lanford. Private, St. Mary's County Militia, 1777 [Ref: M-215].

DORSEY (DOSSEY, DAWSEY), Minta. See "Thomas Brewer," q.v.

DORSEY (DOSSEY), Philip. "Philip Dorsey" was a private in Capt. Thomas Cleland's Co., Calvert County Militia, 1778 [Ref: J-1146, M-147]. "Philip Dossey" was a private, Capt. Thomas Truman Greenfield's Co., Calvert County Militia, 1778 [Ref: J-1146, M-150]. Also see "James Dorsey," q.v.

DORSEY (DOSSEY), Philip Jr. "Philip Dorsey, Jr." was a private in Capt. Frisby Freeland's Co., Calvert County Militia, 1778 [Ref: J-1146, M-148]. "Phillip Dossey, Jr." took the Oath of Allegiance in Calvert County in 1778 [Ref: L-36]. The Christ Church Register in Calvert County records the birth of Philip Dorsey, son of Philip and Martha Dorsey, on Aug. 11, 1759 [Ref: O-9].

DORSEY, Richard. Midshipman from St. Mary's County who served aboard the State ship *Defence* in 1777 [Ref: S-154].

DORSEY, Samuel. Private, Capt. Thomas Cleland's Co., Calvert County Militia, 1778 [Ref: J-1146, M-147].

DORSEY (DOSSEY), William. Private, St. Mary's County Militia, 1777 [Ref: M-215]. Also see "William Doxey," q.v.
DOTSON, Benjamin. Private, Capt. Edward Wood's Co., Calvert County Militia, 1778 [Ref: J-1146, M-147].
DOTSON, Elias. Took the Oath of Allegiance in Calvert County in 1778 [Ref: L-36].
DOTSON, James. Private, Capt. Edward Wood's Co., Calvert County Militia, 1778 [Ref: J-1146, M-147]. Took the Oath of Allegiance in Calvert County in 1778 [Ref: L-36].
DOTSON, John. Private, Capt. Thomas Truman Greenfield's Co., Calvert County Militia, 1778 [Ref: J-1146, M-150]. Took the Oath of Allegiance in Calvert County in 1778 [Ref: L-36].
DOUGLAS, Elizabeth. See "Robert Harrison," q.v.
DOVE, Marmaduke. Private, Capt. Richard Lane's Co., Calvert County Militia, 1778 [Ref: J-1146, M-149].
DOWELL, Henry. Private, Capt. Frederick Skinner's Co., Calvert County Militia, 1778 [Ref: J-1146, M-150]. Private, Capt. John Mackall's Co., Calvert County Militia, 15th Bn., June 12, 1778 [Ref: M-146].
DOWELL, John. Private, Capt. Charles Williamson's Co., Calvert County Militia, 1778 [Ref: J-1146, M-147]. Took the Oath of Allegiance in Calvert County in 1778 [Ref: L-36].
DOWELL, Thomas. Private, Capt. Thomas Cleland's Co., Calvert County Militia, 1778 [Ref: J-1146, M-147].
DOWNING, Charles. Private, Capt. Frisby Freeland's Co., Calvert County Militia, 1778 [Ref: J-1146, M-148].
DOWNING, Richard. Private, Capt. Frisby Freeland's Co., Calvert County Militia, 1778 [Ref: J-1146, M-148].
DOWNS, Ignatius. Private, St. Mary's County, enlisted May 14, 1778, for 3 years, Continental Army [Ref: D-329, SM-112].
DOWNS, Joseph. Took the Oath of Allegiance before the Hon. Bennett Biscoe in St. Mary's County in 1778 [Ref: J-1146, K-63].
DOXEY, Austin Lanford. Took the Oath of Allegiance before the Hon. Robert Armstrong in St. Mary's County in 1778 [Ref: J-1146, K-62, which listed the name as "Austin S. Doxey"]. Austin Lanford Doxey died by Dec., 1795, at which time his orphan son Thomas Doxey was bound out to learn to be a house carpenter [Ref: SO-234].
DOXEY, Thomas. See "Austin Lanford Doxey," q.v.
DOXEY, William. Took the Oath of Allegiance before the Hon. Bennett Biscoe in St. Mary's County in 1778 [Ref: J-1146, K-63].
DOYNE, Jane. See "Michael Taney," q.v.
DRUDGE, John. Took the Oath of Allegiance before the Hon. John Ireland in St. Mary's County in 1778 [Ref: J-1146, K-65]. The Register of St. Francis Xavier Catholic Church states John Drudge and Ann Howard were married July 12, 1774 [Ref: SC-35].

DRUDGE, Thomas. Private, 3rd Maryland Line, 1780 [Ref: D-104, which listed the name as "Thomas Drudges"].
DRURY, Barton. Private, St. Mary's County Militia, 1777 [Ref: M-210]. Took the Oath of Allegiance in St. Mary's County in 1780 [Ref: Q-109].
DRURY, Enoch Jr. Private, St. Mary's County Militia, 1777 [Ref: M-212]. Took the Oath of Allegiance before the Hon. John Ireland in St. Mary's County in 1778 [Ref: J-1146, K-65].
DRURY, Enoch Sr. Took the Oath of Allegiance before the Hon. John Ireland in St. Mary's County in 1778 [Ref: J-1146, K-65].
DRURY, Francis. Property destroyed by the British in St. Mary's County in 1781 [Ref: S-154].
DRURY, Ignatius. Private, St. Mary's County Militia, 1777 [Ref: M-212]. Took the Oath of Allegiance before the Hon. John Ireland in St. Mary's County in 1778 [Ref: J-1146, K-65]. Migrated to Kentucky by 1800 [Ref: MK-42].
DRURY, James. Took the Oath of Allegiance before the Hon. Ignatius Fenwick, Jr. in St. Mary's County in 1778 [Ref: J-1146, K-68].
DRURY, John. Private, St. Mary's County Militia, 1777 [Ref: M-213]. Private, 3rd Maryland Line, missing in action May 31, 1778 [Ref: D-112]. Private, 3rd Maryland Line, 1780, missing in action after the Battle of Camden on Aug. 16, 1780 [Ref: S-154].
DRURY, John Sr. Took the Oath of Allegiance before the Hon. Jeremiah Jordan in St. Mary's County in 1778 [Ref: J-1146, K-67]. Property destroyed by the British in 1781 [Ref: S-154].
DRURY, John Barton. Private, St. Mary's County, enlisted June 1, 1778, for 9 months, Continental Army [Ref: D-330, SM-112]. Took the Oath of Allegiance before the Hon. Ignatius Fenwick, Jr. in St. Mary's County in 1778 [Ref: J-1146, K-68].
DRURY, Joseph. Private, 2nd Maryland Line, from May 24, 1778 until discharged on April 3, 1779; from St. Mary's County [Ref: D-102].
DRURY, Leonard. Private, St. Mary's County Militia, 1777 [Ref: M-210].
DRURY, Michael. This name appeared three times as a private, St. Mary's County Militia, 1777 [Ref: M-211, M-212]. Took the Oath of Allegiance before the Hon. Ignatius Fenwick, Jr. in St. Mary's County in 1778 [Ref: J-1146, K-68].
DRURY, Nicholas. Private, St. Mary's County Militia, 1777 [Ref: M-213].
DRURY, Peter. Private, St. Mary's County Militia, 1777 [Ref: M-212].
DRURY, Philip. Private, St. Mary's County Militia, 1777 [Ref: M-211]. Took the Oath of Allegiance before the Hon. Ignatius Fenwick, Jr. in St. Mary's County in 1778 [Ref: J-1146, K-68].
DRURY, Robert. Took the Oath of Allegiance before the Hon. John Reeder in St. Mary's County in 1778 [Ref: J-1146, K-69, which listed the name as "Robert Drewry"].
DRURY, Robert B. Private, 2nd Maryland Line, until discharged on April 3, 1779; from St. Mary's County [Ref: D-102, S-154].

DRURY, Susannah. See "Bennett Riley," q.v.
DRURY, Thomas. Took the Oath of Allegiance before the Hon. John Reeder in St. Mary's County in 1778 [Ref: J-1146, K-69, which listed the name as "Thomas Drewry"]. Private, 3rd Maryland Line, May 24, 1780 to Feb. 10, 1781, when discharged [Ref: S-154].
DUGAN, John. Took the Oath of Allegiance in St. Mary's County in 1780 [Ref: Q-109].
DUKE, Alexander. See "John Brome (Broome)," q.v.
DUKE, Andrew. Private, Capt. Richard Parran's Co., Calvert County Militia, 1778 [Ref: J-1146, M-149]. Took the Oath of Allegiance in Calvert County in 1780 [Ref: Q-109]. Andrew Duke, a son of James Duke (c1680-1754, a Justice of Calvert County), moved to Harpers Ferry, Virginia (no date or family information given). [Ref: *Colonial Families of the United States of America*, Volume I, by George Norbury Mackenzie (1907), p. 140].
DUKE, Ann P. See "Francis Kirshaw," q.v.
DUKE, James. See "Andrew Duke" and "Alexander Somerville," q.v.
DUKE, Jonathan. Private, St. Mary's County Militia, 1777 [Ref: M-215].
DUKE, Moses P. (Moses R.?). "Moses P. Duke" was a private, Capt. Walter Smith's Co., Calvert County Militia, 1778 [Ref: J-1146, M-148]. "Moses R. Duke" took the Oath of Allegiance in Calvert County in 1778 [Ref: L-36].
DUKES, Mary A. See "George Dent," q.v.
DUNBAR, Henrietta. See "Joseph Dunbar," q.v.
DUNBAR, John. Private, St. Mary's County Militia, 1777 [Ref: M-215, which listed the name as "John Dunbars"]. Took the Oath of Allegiance before the Hon. Bennett Biscoe in St. Mary's County in 1778 [Ref: J-1146, K-63].
DUNBAR, Joseph (1718/9 - Feb. 27, 1801). Son of William and Elizabeth Dunbar. He married Henrietta ----, served as Ship Steward aboard the State ship *Defence* in 1776 and as cooper in 1777 [Ref: S-25, S-141, S-154, D-607, D-656]. Took the Oath of Allegiance before the Hon. John Ireland in St. Mary's County in 1778 [Ref: J-1146, K-65]. Supplied provisions (wheat, mutton, or bacon) to the Army in 1780 [Ref: S-77]. He is buried at Christ Church Cemetery, Chaptico, St. Mary's County [Ref: R-371, HG-37].
DUNBAR, William. See "Joseph Dunbar," q.v.
DUNCASTER, John. Private, St. Mary's County, enlisted April 24, 1778, for 9 months, Continental Army [Ref: D-329, SM-112]. Took the Oath of Allegiance before the Hon. Richard Barnes in St. Mary's County in 1778 [Ref: J-1146, K-66].
DUNKINSON, Robert. Private, St. Mary's County Militia, 1777 [Ref: M-215].
DUNNARD, John. Took the Oath of Allegiance before the Hon. Ignatius Fenwick, Jr. in St. Mary's County in 1778 [Ref: J-1146, K-68].

a General Committee in St. Mary's County in accordance with the resolves of the Continental Congress in 1775 [Ref: MR-127]. One John Eden died testate and Townshend Eden was named his executor in Nov., 1778, but his estate had not yet been properly administered by Feb., 1787, resulting in a Court action to do so. Townshend Eden died intestate by Aug., 1790 [Ref: SO-15, SO-108].

EDEN, Rebecca. See "Francis Gibbons," q.v.

EDEN, Townshend. See "John Eden," q.v.

EDLEY, Elizabeth. See "William Bradburn," q.v.

EDLEY, John. Private, St. Mary's County Militia, 1777 [Ref: M-212]. Took the Oath of Allegiance before the Hon. Henry Reeder in St. Mary's County in 1778 [Ref: J-1146, K-64].

EDMONDS, Easom. Took the Oath of Allegiance in Calvert County in 1778 [Ref: L-36]. Private, Capt. Benjamin Bond's Co., Calvert County Militia, 1778 [Ref: J-1146, M-149].

EDMONDS, Francis. Took the Oath of Allegiance in Calvert County in 1778 [Ref: L-36].

EDMONDS, William. Private, Capt. Frisby Freeland's Co., Calvert County Militia, 1778 [Ref: J-1146, M-148]. This name appeared three times on the list of those who took the Oath of Allegiance in Calvert County in 1778 [Ref: L-36].

EDMONDSON, Archibald. Private, Calvert County, enlisted by Lt. Frederick Skinner on Aug. 23, 1776 [Ref: D-33]. Took the Oath of Allegiance in Calvert County in 1778 [Ref: L-36, which listed the name as "Archibald Edmonston"].

EDMONDSON, William. Private, Capt. Frisby Freeland's Co., Calvert County Militia, 1778 [Ref: J-1146, M-148].

EDWARDS, Anne. See "Zachariah Forrest," q.v.

EDWARDS, Benjamin (Aug. 12, 1752 - Nov. 13, 1826). Second Lieutenant, Upper Bn., St. Mary's County Militia, Aug. 26, 1777 [Ref: M-73, M-209, C-346, SM-112]. Took the Oath of Allegiance before the Hon. Henry Tubman in St. Mary's County in 1778 [Ref: J-1146, K-70]. He married Margaret Beall [Ref: Y-215].

EDWARDS, Elizabeth. See "George Dent," q.v.

EDWARDS, Henry. See "John Edwards, of John," q.v.

EDWARDS, Hezekiah. Private, St. Mary's County Militia, 1777 [Ref: M-209]. Took the Oath of Allegiance before the Hon. Henry Tubman in St. Mary's County in 1778 [Ref: J-1146, K-70].

EDWARDS, Ignatius. Took the Oath of Allegiance before the Hon. Henry Tubman in St. Mary's County in 1778 [Ref: J-1146, K-70].

EDWARDS, Jeremiah. Took the Oath of Allegiance before the Hon. Richard Barnes in St. Mary's County in 1778 [Ref: J-1146, K-66].

EDWARDS, Jesse. Private, St. Mary's County Militia, 1777 [Ref: M-213]. Took the Oath of Allegiance before the Hon. Henry Tubman in St. Mary's County in 1778 [Ref: J-1146, K-70]. "Jesse Edwards, farmer" moved from Upper Resurrection to Charles County, Maryland, in 1807 [Ref: X-86].

EDWARDS, John. Private, St. Mary's County Militia, 1777 [Ref: M-214]. First Lieutenant, Upper Bn., Aug. 26, 1777 [Ref: M-73, M-209, C-346, which latter source listed the name as "John Edwards, Sr."]. Source S-141 indicates that John Dent (1735-1830), a Brigadier General from Charles County, married Violette Winnert in 1753, was a member of the First Provincial Congress in 1775, and declined command of the Maryland Troops. However, in July, 1776, he was in command of the Maryland Militia in St. Mary's County during the attempted invasion by Lord Dunmore [Ref: S-141].

EDWARDS, John (of John). Private, St. Mary's County Militia, 1777 [Ref: M-209]. Took the Oath of Allegiance before the Hon. Henry Tubman in St. Mary's County in 1778 [Ref: J-1146, K-70]. The Register of St. Andrew's Episcopal Church states that one John Edwards and Mary Morgan were married (by license) Aug. 8, 1784 [Ref: MB-385]. One John Edwards died intestate by April, 1786, leaving orphan sons John and Henry Edwards [Ref: SO-95, SO-139, SO-160, SO-190]. See "John Edwards," q.v.

EDWARDS, John (of Robert). Took the Oath of Allegiance before the Hon. Henry Tubman in St. Mary's County in 1778 [Ref: J-1146, K-70].

EDWARDS, Jonathan. Second Lieutenant, Upper Bn., St. Mary's County Militia, Aug. 26, 1777, and First Lieutenant, Nov. 18, 1779 [Ref: C-346, F-18, M-73, M-209, S-154].

EDWARDS, Joseph. Private, St. Mary's County Militia, 1777 [Ref: M-212].

EDWARDS, Peggy. See "James Scott," q.v.

EDWARDS, Stourton (Stratton). Took the Oath of Allegiance before the Hon. Henry G. Sothoron in St. Mary's County in 1778 [Ref: J-1146, K-68]. Private, St. Mary's County Militia, 1777 [Ref: M-213, which listed the name as "Stouston Edwards(?)"]. Private, St. Mary's County, drafted July 27, 1781 [Ref: D-384, which listed the name as "Struton Edwards"]. Private, Continental Army, 1781 [Ref: D-408, which listed the name as "Stratton Edwards"]. "Stourton Edwards, of John, farmer" moved from St. Clements to Jefferson County, Kentucky in 1806 [Ref: X-86].

EDWARDS, Thomas. Private, St. Mary's County Militia, 1777 [Ref: M-209].

EGAN, Barnaby (1734 - Nov. 5, 1781). Took the Oath of Allegiance in Calvert County in 1778 [Ref: L-36, which listed the name only as "B. Egan"]. Barnaby Egan (1734 - Nov. 5, 1781) and John R. Egan (1759 - July 5, 1786) are buried in a private cemetery at "Westfield" [Ref: R-373]. The Christ Church Register in Calvert County records the births of the children of Barnaby and Henrietta Egan as follows: Henrietta Reeder (born March 13, 1764); Thomas Henry (born Feb. 10, 1767); and, Susanna (born Aug. 26, 1770). [Ref: O-11].

EGAN, Henrietta Reeder. See "Barnaby Egan," q.v.
EGAN, John R. (1759 - July 5, 1786). Private, Capt. Benjamin Bond's Co., Calvert County Militia, 1778 [Ref: J-1146, M-149, which listed the name as "John R. Eagan"]. See "Barnaby Egan," q.v.
EGAN, R. Took the Oath of Allegiance in Calvert County in 1778 [Ref: L-36].
EGAN, Susanna and Thomas Henry. See "Barnaby Egan," q.v.
EGERTON, James. Private, St. Mary's County Militia, 1777 [Ref: M-215]. One "James Egerton died Dec. 4, 1810, and Mrs. Egerton died Jan. 26, 1810." [Ref: R-373].
EGERTON, John. Private, St. Mary's County Militia, 1777 [Ref: M-215]. Took the Oath of Allegiance before the Hon. Bennett Biscoe in St. Mary's County in 1778 [Ref: J-1146, K-63].
EGERTON, Mary. Loaned money in St. Mary's County for the war effort in 1781 [Ref: SM-187]. Property destroyed by the British in 1781 [Ref: S-154].
EGERTON, Thomas. Private, St. Mary's County Militia, 1777 [Ref: M-215]. Took the Oath of Allegiance before the Hon. Bennett Biscoe in St. Mary's County in 1778 [Ref: J-1146, K-63].
ELISHA, John. Private, Capt. Richard Lane's Co., Calvert County Militia, 1778 [Ref: J-1146, M-149].
ELLET, Susan. See "Thomas Fitzgerald," q.v.
ELLIOT, Benjamin. See "Benjamin Ellt," q.v.
ELLIOT, James and Mary. See "Matthew Ellt," q.v.
ELLIOT, John. Private, Capt. Frisby Freeland's Co., Calvert County Militia, 1778 [Ref: J-1146, M-148]. Took the Oath of Allegiance in Calvert County in 1778 [Ref: L-36].
ELLIOT, Matthew. See "Matthew Ellt (Ellet)," q.v.
ELLIOT, Richard. Took the Oath of Allegiance before the Hon. Ignatius Fenwick, Jr. in St. Mary's County in 1778 [Ref: J-1146, K-68]. Private, 1st Maryland Line, April 17, 1779 [Ref: SM-112].
ELLIS, James. Took the Oath of Allegiance before the Hon. Jeremiah Jordan in St. Mary's County in 1778 [Ref: J-1146, K-67].
ELLIS, John. (1) Private, Capt. Henry Skinner's Foot Co. of Hunting Hundred, Calvert County, 1777 [Ref: T-1814, O-125]. (2) Took the Oath of Allegiance before the Hon. Jeremiah Jordan in St. Mary's County in 1778 [Ref: J-1146, K-67].
ELLIS, Joshua. Private, Capt. Uriah Forrest's Co., Flying Camp, St. Mary's County, July 28, 1776 [Ref: D-30, SM-112].
ELLIS, Thomas. Took the Oath of Allegiance before the Hon. Jeremiah Jordan in St. Mary's County in 1778 [Ref: J-1146, K-67].
ELLIS, William. Took the Oath of Allegiance before the Hon. Jeremiah Jordan in St. Mary's County in 1778 [Ref: J-1146, K-67].
ELLT (ELLET), Benjamin. Private, Capt. Richard Parran's Co., Calvert County Militia, 1778 [Ref: J-1146, M-149]. Took the Oath of Allegiance

in Calvert County in 1778 [Ref: L-36]. The Christ Church Register in Calvert County records the birth of one Benjamin Ellt, son of William and Eleanor Ellt, on March 16, 1718 [Ref: O-11].

ELLT (ELT), Rebecca. See "James Mackall Sollers," q.v.

ELLT (ELLET), Matthew. Took the Oath of Allegiance before the Hon. Bennett Biscoe in St. Mary's County in 1778 [Ref: J-1146, K-63, which listed the name as "Matthew Ellet"]. One Matthew Elliott died by Feb., 1781, leaving orphans Stephen (above age 14), James, and Mary Elliot [Ref: SO-38, SO-137].

ELMS, George. Private, Capt. Uriah Forrest's Co., Flying Camp, St. Mary's County, July 28, 1776 [Ref: D-30]. Fifer, 6th Maryland Line, discharged Nov. 1, 1780 [Ref: S-40, D-203, D-469, D-510].

ELZEY, Margaret. Loaned money to the Continental Congress on March 6, 1778 [Ref: V-149].

ENDS, John. Private, St. Mary's County Militia, 1777 [Ref: M-214].

ENDS, Vincent Jr. Private, St. Mary's County Militia, 1777 [Ref: M-214, which listed the name as "Vincen Ends Junr"].

ENNIS, William. Private, Capt. Uriah Forrest's Co., Flying Camp, St. Mary's County, July 28, 1776 [Ref: D-30, SM-112, which latter source mistakenly listed the name as "Tom Ennis"].

ESSEX, Isaac. Private, Capt. Frisby Freeland's Co., Calvert County Militia, 1778 [Ref: J-1146, M-148].

ESSEX, Isaac Jr. Took the Oath of Allegiance in Calvert County in 1778 [Ref: L-36].

ESSEX, John. Private, Capt. Thomas Truman Greenfield's Co., Calvert County Militia, 1778 [Ref: J-1146, M-150].

ESSEX, Joseph. Private, Capt. Frisby Freeland's Co., Calvert County Militia, 1778 [Ref: J-1146, M-148]. Took the Oath of Allegiance in Calvert County in 1778 [Ref: L-36].

ESTEP, Ann. See "James Keech," q.v.

ESTEP, Joshua. Private, St. Mary's County Militia, 1777 [Ref: M-209, which listed the name as "Joshua Eastep"]. Took the Oath of Allegiance before the Hon. Henry Tubman in St. Mary's County in 1778 [Ref: J-1146, K-70].

ESTEP, Philamon. Took the Oath of Allegiance before the Hon. Henry Tubman in St. Mary's County in 1778 [Ref: J-1146, K-70].

ESTEP, Rezin. See "Gilbert Ireland," q.v.

EVANS, Alice. See "William Powell," q.v.

EVANS, Anne. See "Moses Davis," q.v.

EVANS, Jeremiah. Private, St. Mary's County Militia, 1777 [Ref: M-213].

EVANS, Jona. Paid for making salt in Aug., 1782, in St. Mary's County [Ref: S-154].

EVANS, Philip. Private, St. Mary's County Militia, 1777 [Ref: M-211]. Two men with this name took the Oath of Allegiance in 1778 in St. Mary's County: one before the Hon. Ignatius Fenwick, Jr., and one before the Hon. Bennett Biscoe [Ref: J-1146, K-63, K-68]. See "John Wilkinson," q.v.

EVANS, Richard. (1) Private, St. Mary's County Militia, 1777 [Ref: M-213]. Private, 6th Maryland Line, until discharged May 1, 1780 [Ref: S-34, D-203]. Took the Oath of Allegiance before the Hon. Robert Watts in St. Mary's County in 1778 [Ref: J-1146, K-62]. (2) Private, Capt. Frisby Freeland's Co., Calvert County Militia, 1778 [Ref: J-1146, M-148].

EVANS, Robert. Seaman from St. Mary's County who served aboard the State ship *Defence* in 1777 [Ref: S-154].

EVANS, William. (1) Private, St. Mary's County Militia, 1777 [Ref: M-212]. (2) Two men with this name took the Oath of Allegiance in St. Mary's County in 1778: one before the Hon. Bennett Biscoe, and one before the Hon. John Ireland [Ref: J-1146, K-63, K-65, which latter source listed the name as "William Evens"]. One William Evans married --- Bull on Nov. 16, 1778, St. Mary's County, by Rev. George Goldie [Ref: I-535]. (3) Private, Calvert County, enlisted by Lt. Nathaniel Wilson on Aug. 23, 1776 [Ref: D-34]. Took the Oath of Allegiance in Calvert County in 1778 [Ref: L-36].

EVEREST, Richard Jr. Took the Oath of Allegiance in Calvert County in 1778 [Ref: L-36].

EVEREST, Thomas. Took the Oath of Allegiance in Calvert County in 1778 [Ref: L-36].

EVERITH, William. Took the Oath of Allegiance in Calvert County in 1778 [Ref: L-36].

EVERITT, Richard (of William). Private, Capt. Edward Wood's Co., Calvert County Militia, 1778 [Ref: J-1146, M-147, which listed the name as "Richard Everitt, for Wm."].

EVERITT, Richard. Private, Calvert County, enlisted by Capt. John Brooke on July 25, 1776 [Ref: D-33]. Private, Capt. Benjamin Bond's Co., Calvert County Militia, 1778 [Ref: J-1146, M-149].

EVERITT, Thomas. Private, Calvert County, enlisted by Capt. John Brooke on July 26, 1776 [Ref: D-33, which listed the name as "Thomas Everett"]. Private, Capt. Benjamin Bond's Co., Calvert County Militia, 1778 [Ref: J-1146, M-149].

EWING, Nathaniel. See "John Reeder, Jr.," q.v.

EWING, Thomas. See "James Eden," q.v.

FARDEN (FARDING), John. Private, St. Mary's County, enlisted April 27, 1778, for 3 years, Continental Army [Ref: D-329]. Private, 3rd Maryland Line; probably died in Nov., 1780 [Ref: SM-112].

FARDEVELL, Abraham. Took the Oath of Allegiance in St. Mary's County in 1780 [Ref: Q-110].

FARTHING, Aaron. Private, St. Mary's County Militia, 1777 [Ref: M-212].

FARTHING, Moses. Private, St. Mary's County Militia, 1777 [Ref: M-212].

FEBBINS, Daniel. (1) Private, Capt. Frederick Skinner's Co., Calvert County Militia, 1778 [Ref: J-1146, M-150]. (2) Private, Capt. James Grahame's Co., Calvert County Militia, 1778 [Ref: J-1146, M-149]. Private, Capt. John Mackall's Co., Calvert County Militia, 15th Bn., June 12, 1778 [Ref: M-146, which listed the name as "Daniel Fibbens"]. Took the Oath of Allegiance in Calvert County in 1778 [Ref: L-36].
FENWICK, Alexander. See "Edward Fenwick," q.v.
FENWICK, Benjamin. Took the Oath of Allegiance before the Hon. Ignatius Fenwick, Jr. in St. Mary's County in 1778 [Ref: J-1146, K-68].
FENWICK, Bennett. Private, St. Mary's County Militia, 1777 [Ref: M-213]. Took the Oath of Allegiance before the Hon. Robert Watts in St. Mary's County in 1778 [Ref: J-1146, K-62].
FENWICK, Charles. See "Ignatius Fenwick, Jr.," q.v.
FENWICK, Cornelius. A native of St. Mary's County, he served in the U. S. Navy as a sailor and was a prisoner of war. He migrated to Nelson County, Kentucky and settled on Cartwright's Creek circa 1785. He died in Franklin County, Kentucky at the age of 94 (no date given). A daughter Mary Fenwick (1800-1878) married Jacob Cox [Ref: MK-49]. Although he is not listed in *Archives of Maryland, Volume 18*, it is curious to note that a Cornelius Fenton *[sic]* and a Richard Fenwick, whose names are listed together, were marines on the State ship *Defence* in 1777 [Ref: D-656].
FENWICK, Cuthbert. This name appeared twice as a private in the St. Mary's County Militia in 1777 [Ref: M-211, M-212]. Took the Oath of Allegiance before the Hon. Ignatius Fenwick, Jr. in St. Mary's County in 1778 [Ref: J-1146, K-68]. See "Robert Fenwick," q.v.
FENWICK, Edward. Elected to serve on a General Committee in St. Mary's County in accordance with the resolves of the Continental Congress in 1775 [Ref: MR-127]. Took the Oath of Allegiance before the Hon. Bennett Biscoe in St. Mary's County in 1778 [Ref: J-1146, K-63]. One Edward Fenwick died by Dec., 1799, leaving orphan sons Henry and Alexander Fenwick with their guardian James Fenwick [Ref: SO-294, SO-295, SO-303]. See "Ignatius Fenwick, Jr.," q.v.
FENWICK, Elenor. See "Clement Sewall," q.v.
FENWICK, Elizabeth. See "Enoch Fenwick, Sr.," q.v.
FENWICK, Enoch Jr. Private, St. Mary's County Militia, 1777 [Ref: M-212]. Took the Oath of Allegiance before the Hon. Ignatius Fenwick, Jr. in St. Mary's County in 1778 [Ref: J-1146, K-68]. See "Philip Fenwick," q.v.
FENWICK, Enoch Sr. Recommended to the Council of Safety on Dec. 22, 1776, that he be appointed Inspector of Tobacco in St. Mary's County [Ref: V-74]. Took the Oath of Allegiance before the Hon. Henry Reeder in St. Mary's County in 1778 [Ref: J-1146, K-64]. "Enoch Fenwick" was elected to a General Committee in St. Mary's County in accordance with the resolves of the Continental Congress in 1775 [Ref: MR-127]. One

Enoch Fenwick died testate by Jan., 1788, leaving a widow Elizabeth [Ref: SO-119, SO-132, S0-163].

FENWICK, Francis Jr. Private, St. Mary's County Militia, 1777 [Ref: M-212].

FENWICK, Francis Sr. Private, St. Mary's County Militia, 1777 [Ref: M-211]. Private, 2nd Maryland Line, discharged on April 14, 1779 [Ref: S-155].

FENWICK, Francis (of Benjamin). Took the Oath of Allegiance before the Hon. Ignatius Fenwick, Jr. in St. Mary's County in 1778 [Ref: J-1146, K-68].

FENWICK, Francis (of Ignatius). Took the Oath of Allegiance before the Hon. Ignatius Fenwick, Jr. in St. Mary's County in 1778 [Ref: J-1146, K-68].

FENWICK, George. Private, St. Mary's County Militia, 1777 [Ref: M-211]. Took the Oath of Allegiance before the Hon. Ignatius Fenwick, Jr. in St. Mary's County in 1778 [Ref: J-1146, K-68]. "George Fenwick, farmer" moved from Lower Resurrection to Washington, D. C. in 1793 [Ref: X-86].

FENWICK, Helena. See "Ignatius Fenwick, Sr.," q.v.

FENWICK, Henry. See "Edward Fenwick" and "Ignatius Fenwick," q.v.

FENWICK, Ignatius. An "Ignatius Fenwick (Coles)" was elected to a General Committee in St. Mary's County in accordance with the resolves of the Continental Congress in 1775 [Ref: MR-127].

FENWICK, Ignatius Jr. (1736-c1784). Son of Ignatius Fenwick (died 1776) and Mary Cole. He married by 1761 to Sarah Taney, daughter of Michael Taney, of Calvert County, and their children were James, Edward, Michael, Thomas, Nicholas, Charles, Mary, and Sarah [Ref: N-320, Y-233, SO-100, which latter source named his orphaned sons Michael, Thomas, Nicholas and Charles in 1786 when James Fenwick, Jr. was appointed their guardian]. Ignatius served in these capacities: Delegate from St. Mary's County to the Maryland Convention, 1776; County Justice, 1777-1784; Commissioner of Tax, 1779-1784; Orphans Court Justice, 1782-1784 [Ref: N-74, N-320]. First Major, 21st Bn., St. Mary's County Militia, Jan. 12, 1776. Colonel, Lower Bn., Aug. 26, 1777 [Ref: M-75, B-232, C-346, N-319, N-320]. Justice who administered the Oath of Allegiance in St. Mary's County in 1778 [Ref: J-1146, K-68]. Took the Oath of Allegiance before the Hon. Vernon Hebb in St. Mary's County in 1778 [Ref: J-1146, K-67]. Major Ignatius Fenwick served on the Committee of Observation in 1776 [Ref: S-16, B-100]. There was also a "Capt. Ignatius Fenwick" who loaned money in St. Mary's County for the war in 1781 [Ref: X-78, H-405]. He was probably the Ignatius Fenwick who was captain of the State ship *Lydia* [Ref: SM-187]. Source S-141 indicates that "Col. Ignatius Fenwick" died in 1792. He is buried in Newtown Cemetery (stone with name, but no dates). [Ref: S-128].

FENWICK, Ignatius Sr. (c1710-1776). Served on the Committee of Correspondence for St. Mary's County in 1775 [Ref: N-319]. He died testate by Oct., 1776, leaving children Edward Fenwick, James Fenwick, Richard Fenwick, John Fenwick, Henry Fenwick, Helena Fenwick, Elizabeth Fenwick, Ann Clark, and Mary Jenkins [Ref: SO-19, and *Maryland Calendar of Wills, Volume 16, 1774-1777*, p. 175].

FENWICK, Ignatius (of Enoch). Took the Oath of Allegiance before the Hon. Ignatius Fenwick, Jr. in St. Mary's County in 1778 [Ref: J-1146, K-68]. Paid for services (unspecified) in 1782 [Ref: S-155].

FENWICK, James. (1) Private, St. Mary's County Militia, 1777 [Ref: M-212]. Took the Oath of Allegiance before the Hon. John Ireland in St. Mary's County in 1778 [Ref: J-1146, K-65]. (2) Private, St. Mary's County Militia, 1777 [Ref: M-214]. Took the Oath of Allegiance before the Hon. Vernon Hebb in St. Mary's County in 1778 [Ref: J-1146, K-67]. One James Fenwick supplied provisions (wheat, mutton, or bacon) to the Army in 1780 [Ref: S-77]. "James Fenwick, of Ign., merchant" moved from Lower Resurrection to Pomonkey, Virginia, after 1800 [Ref: X-86]. He was probably the James Fenwick, brother of "Ignatius Fenwick, Jr.," q.v., who was a mariner and ship's captain during and after the war [Ref: N-319]. "Capt. James Fenwick" was buried at St. Inigoes Roman Catholic cemetery. His stone reads "Here lies the body of James Fenwick, who died on the third day of Feb., 1806, in the 56th year of his age. He was a worthy, candid, honest and generous and truly attached to the liberties of his country. His fore-fathers were among the first settlers of this ancient country and he left a numerous connection; for all, of whom he felt like a father. May his virtues be long revered and perpetuated among them." [Ref: R-376, S-128]. The Register of St. Francis Xavier Catholic Church states James Fenwick and Henrietta Howard were married June 12, 1776. and James Fenwick and Catherine Ford were married Nov. 29, 1778 [Ref: SC-35, SC-36, which also noted "they (James and Henrietta) or their descendants eventually settled at The Barrens in Perry County, Missouri"]. See "Edward Fenwick" and "Ignatius Fenwick, Jr.," q.v.

FENWICK, John. (1) Private, St. Mary's County Militia, 1777 [Ref: M-212]. Took the Oath of Allegiance before the Hon. John Ireland in St. Mary's County in 1778 [Ref: J-1146, K-65]. (2) Private, St. Mary's County Militia, 1777 [Ref: M-212]. Took the Oath of Allegiance before the Hon. Robert Armstrong in St. Mary's County in 1778 [Ref: J-1146, K-62]. (3) Private, St. Mary's County Militia, 1777 [Ref: M-215]. Took the Oath of Allegiance before the Hon. Ignatius Fenwick, Jr. in St. Mary's County in 1778 [Ref: J-1146, K-68]. One John Fenwick supplied provisions (wheat, mutton, or bacon) to the Army in 1780 [Ref: S-77]. "John Fenwick, farmer" moved to Washington County, Kentucky, in 1793 [Ref: X-86]. John Fenwick (c1720-c1781) rendered civil service and married (1) Elizabeth Guyther and (2) Monica Ford [Ref: Y-233]. The

Register of St. Francis Xavier Catholic Church states that one John Fenwick and Mary Thompson were married Nov. 10, 1772 [Ref: SC-34]. One John Fenwick was elected to a General Committee in St. Mary's County in accordance with the resolves of the Continental Congress in 1775 [Ref: MR-127].

FENWICK, John Jr. Took the Oath of Allegiance before the Hon. Robert Armstrong in St. Mary's County in 1778 [Ref: J-1146, K-62].

FENWICK, Joseph. Private, St. Mary's County Militia, 1777 [Ref: M-215]. Took the Oath of Allegiance before the Hon. Henry Reeder in St. Mary's County in 1778 [Ref: J-1146, K-64].

FENWICK, Mary. See "Ignatius Fenwick" and "Ignatius Combs," q.v.

FENWICK, Michael and Nicholas. See "Ignatius Fenwick, Jr.," q.v.

FENWICK, Philip. First Lieutenant, Lower Bn., St. Mary's County Militia, Aug. 26, 1777 [Ref: M-75, M-211, C-346]. "Capt. Fenwick" was captured by the enemy at Leonardtown on Feb. 10, 1778 [Ref: V-145]. Supplied provisions (wheat, mutton, or bacon) to the Army in 1780 [Ref: S-77]. One Philip Fenwick died testate by Aug., 1785, leaving a son Enoch (above the age of 14) and a widow Rebecca who married William Bellwood prior to Oct., 1786 [Ref: SO-81, SO-97, SO-106, SO-116, SO-141, S0-154, SO-155]. One Philip Fenwick was the executor of Robert Fenwick in 1788 [Ref: SO-124].

FENWICK, Philip (of Philip). Took the Oath of Allegiance before the Hon. Ignatius Fenwick, Jr. in St. Mary's County in 1778 [Ref: J-1146, K-68].

FENWICK, Philip (of Enoch). Took the Oath of Allegiance before the Hon. Richard Barnes in St. Mary's County in 1778 [Ref: J-1146, K-66].

FENWICK, Rebecca. See "Philip Fenwick," q.v.

FENWICK, Richard. (1) Richard Fenwick (1747 - April 10, 1799) is buried at St. Inigoes Roman Catholic Church [Ref: R-376, HG-28, S-128]. Served as a private, St. Mary's County Militia, 1777 [Ref: M-212]. Took the Oath of Allegiance before the Hon. Bennett Biscoe in St. Mary's County in 1778 [Ref: J-1146, K-63]. (2) Richard Fenwick served as a marine on the State ship *Defence* from Oct. 23, 1777 to Dec. 31, 1777, and died in 1778 when "blown up in a barge" [Ref: D-656, SM-112]. (3) Richard Fenwick (1760-1829) was a private and married Ann Welch [Ref: Y-233, M-214]. "Richard Fenwick, Jr., mill owner" moved from Lower St. Mary's County to Washington, D. C. in 1804 [Ref: X-86]. See "Ignatius Fenwick, Sr.," q.v.

FENWICK, Robert (c1741-c1807). Private, St. Mary's County Militia, 1777 [Ref: M-214]. He married twice, first to Ann Elizabeth Manning and secondly to Belinda Miles [Ref: Y-233]. One Robert Fenwick died testate by Aug., 1786, leaving an orphan son Nicholas (above the age of 14). Cuthbert Fenwick was appointed guardian [Ref: SO-103]. See "Philip Fenwick," q.v.

FENWICK, Robert (of John). Took the Oath of Allegiance before the Hon. Richard Barnes in St. Mary's County in 1778 [Ref: J-1146, K-66].
FENWICK, Sarah. See "Ignatius Fenwick, Jr.," q.v.
FENWICK, Thomas. Private, St. Mary's County Militia, 1777 [Ref: M-211]. Took the Oath of Allegiance before the Hon. Henry Reeder in St. Mary's County in 1778 [Ref: J-1146, K-64]. The Register of St. Francis Xavier Catholic Church states Thomas Fenwick and Elizabeth Thomas, widow, were married July 3, 1774 [Ref: SC-35, which noted that "either they or their descendants eventually settled at The Barrens in Perry County, Missouri."]. "Thomas Fenwick, physician" moved from Lower Resurrection to Washington, D. C. after 1800 [Ref: X-86]. See "Ignatius Fenwick, Jr.," q.v.
FENWICK, William. Private, St. Mary's County, Capt. John Allen Thomas' Co., 1776. Applied for and received pension S16381 on Jan. 3, 1833, in Franklin County, Kentucky, stating he served six months "when at the interference of his parents he was got off from service by their procuring a man to be enlisted for life term in his place." He later served another six months in the militia. At the time of Lafayette's muster in Baltimore, he owned two vessels, one a sloop and the other a pilot boat. He was pressed into service and served with the French Fleet on the Chesapeake Bay until the surrender of Cornwallis at Yorktown in 1781. He commanded the pilot boat "Fair Maid" and transported provisions from Baltimore to the York River. He also stated that no one could testify as to his services except Catharine Holton. He was born in St. Mary's County in 1757 and moved to Kentucky in 1790 [Ref: W-38, P-1175, MK-49]. This name appeared twice as a private in the St. Mary's County Militia in 1777 [Ref: M-211, M-214]. One William Fenwick took the Oath of Allegiance before the Hon. Ignatius Fenwick, Jr., and the other before the Hon. Richard Barnes in 1778 [Ref: J-1146, K-66. K-68]. William Fenwick (1757 - June 18, 1833) was a private and a seaman and married Catherine ---- [Ref: Y-233]. One William Fenwick supplied provisions (wheat, mutton, or bacon) to the Army in St. Mary's County in 1780 [Ref: S-77].
FERREL, John. Private, 3rd Maryland Line, 1780 [Ref: S-155].
FERRILL, Thomas. Took the Oath of Allegiance before the Hon. Jeremiah Jordan in St. Mary's County in 1778 [Ref: J-1146, K-67].
FERRILL, William Jr. Took the Oath of Allegiance before the Hon. Jeremiah Jordan in St. Mary's County in 1778 [Ref: J-1146, K-67]. "William Ferrell" died intestate by Feb., 1797 [Ref: SO-265].
FERRILL, William Sr. Took the Oath of Allegiance before the Hon. Jeremiah Jordan in St. Mary's County in 1778 [Ref: J-1146, K-67].
FIELD, John. Private, St. Mary's County Militia, 1777 [Ref: M-213].
FIELDER, Nicholas. Private, St. Mary's County Militia, 1777 [Ref: M-215]. Took the Oath of Allegiance before the Hon. Robert Watts in St. Mary's County in 1778 [Ref: J-1146, K-62]. The Register of St. Andrew's

Episcopal Church states that Nicholas Fielder and Anne Colloson were married Jan. 16, 1780 [Ref: MB-382].

FIELDS, John. Private, Capt. Uriah Forrest's Co., Flying Camp, St. Mary's County, July 28, 1776 [Ref: D-30]. Private, St. Mary's County, enlisted April 23, 1778, for 9 months [Ref: D-329, S-155].

FIELDS, Joseph. Private, St. Mary's County, enlisted May 30, 1778, for 9 months [Ref: D-330]. Private, 3rd Maryland Line, 1778-1779 [Ref: S-155].

FIELDS, Leonard. Took the Oath of Allegiance before the Hon. John Reeder in St. Mary's County in 1778 [Ref: J-1146, K-69].

FIELDS, Michael. Private, St. Mary's County, enlisted June 10, 1778, for 3 years, Continental Army [Ref: D-330, SM-112].

FIELDS, Sarah. See "Thomas Joy," q.v.

FIELDS, William. Took the Oath of Allegiance before the Hon. John Ireland in St. Mary's County in 1778 [Ref: J-1146, K-65].

FILES, Thomas. Private, Capt. Uriah Forrest's Co., Flying Camp, St. Mary's County, July 28, 1776 [Ref: D-30, SM-112]. Private, St. Mary's County Militia, 1777 [Ref: M-215]. Took the Oath of Allegiance in St. Mary's County in 1780 [Ref: Q-110].

FIND, John Jr. Private, St. Mary's County Militia, 1777 [Ref: M-211].

FISH, James. Private, St. Mary's County Militia, 1777 [Ref: M-213]. The Register of St. Francis Xavier Catholic Church states that James Fish and Ann Wheatley were married Aug. 22, 1777 [Ref: SC-36].

FISH, Joseph. Private, St. Mary's County Militia, 1777 [Ref: M-213].

FISH, William. Private, St. Mary's County Militia, 1777 [Ref: M-214].

FISHER, Christopher. Took the Oath of Allegiance before the Hon. Robert Watts in St. Mary's County in 1778 [Ref: J-1146, K-62].

FITZGERALD, John. Private, St. Mary's County, who served in the Maryland Line until 1781 when discharged [Ref: D-408].

FITZGERALD, Thomas. Private, 5th Maryland Line, enlisted May 12, 1778 and served until Feb., 1779, when "not heard of." [Ref: D-205]. The Register of St. Inigoes Catholic Church states that Thomas Fitzgerald and Susan Ellet were married on March 20, 1784 [Ref: SC-36].

FITZGO, William. Took the Oath of Allegiance before the Hon. Robert Watts in St. Mary's County in 1778 [Ref: J-1146, K-62]. Private, St. Mary's County Militia, 1777 [Ref: M-213, which listed the name as "William Fitzjoeh(?)"].

FITZHUGH, Ann and Daniel. See "William Fitzhugh, Jr.," q.v.

FITZHUGH, George, John, and Mary. See "William Fitzhugh," q.v.

FITZHUGH, Henry and James. See "William Fitzhugh, Jr.," q.v.

FITZHUGH, Peregrine. Son of "Hon. William Fitzhugh," q.v. First Lieutenant, Capt. James Grahame's Co., Calvert County Militia, Sep. 24, 1777 [Ref: J-1146, M-75, M-148, C-384]. Took the Oath of Allegiance in Calvert County in 1778 [Ref: L-36]. Captain and Aide to General George Washington during the war. He married Elizabeth Crowley and resided in Queen Anne's County, Maryland in 1792, Washington County, Maryland in 1797, and Soder's Bay, Lake Ontario from 1799 until his death (no date given). [Ref: N-322].

FITZHUGH, Richard, Robert, and Samuel. See "William Fitzhugh, Jr.," q.v.

FITZHUGH, William (c1722 - Feb. 10, 1798). Son of George Fitzhugh, of Virginia, and Mary Mason, daughter of Col. George Mason, of Virginia. He immigrated to Calvert County by 1752 and married twice: (1) ---- Lee, daughter of Richard Lee and widow of George Turberville; and (2) Ann Frisby, daughter of Peregrine Frisby and widow of John Rousby, in 1752. Children: George, John, William Jr., and "Capt. Peregrine Fitzhugh," q.v. William served as a Delegate from Calvert County to the Maryland Convention in 1776, a member of the House of Delegates from 1777 to 1783, and Speaker of the House in 1777 and 1778 [Ref: N-74, N-76, N-78, N-82, N-84, N-86, N-87]. On May 15, 1781, he recommended to the Governor of Maryland that Dr. Watts be appointed Surgeon [Ref: V-394].

FITZHUGH, William Jr. (1761, Calvert County - 1839, New York). Son of "William Fitzhugh," q.v. William married Ann (or Nancy) Hughes, daughter of Col. David Hughes, of Washington County, Maryland, and they had these children: William H. (1786-1829), Daniel (physician in western New York), Samuel (a New York judge), James (moved to Kentucky), Henry (moved to New York), Richard (moved to Livingston County, New York), Robert, and two daughters (names not stated, but one married Rev. Backus and one married James Birney). William Fitzhugh, Jr. was an Ensign, Capt. James Grahame's Co., 15th Bn., St. Mary's County, April 16, 1778, and Captain by 1783; subsequently a Colonel, but period of service not stated; served in Lower House from Calvert County, 1786-1788. Moved to Washington County, Maryland, by 1790, and to Genesee, Livingston County, New York, circa 1800 [Ref: M-75, E-37, N-322, N-323].

FITZHUGH, William H. See "William Fitzhugh, Jr.," q.v.

FITZJEFFERY, Aaron. Sailor from St. Mary's County who served on the State ship *Defence* from June 21 to July 15, 1777 [Ref: D-656, which listed the name as "Aaron Fitzjeffrys"].

FITZJEFFERY, Charles. Took the Oath of Allegiance before the Hon. Bennett Biscoe in St. Mary's County in 1778 [Ref: J-1146, K-63]. "Charles FitzJerry" (also spelled "FitzJeffery") died by Oct., 1796, leaving orphans (names not stated here). [Ref: SO-248].

FITZJEFFERY, Joseph. Took the Oath of Allegiance before the Hon. Robert Armstrong in St. Mary's County in 1778 [Ref: J-1146, K-62].

FITZJEFFERY, Richard. Private, St. Mary's County Militia, 1777 [Ref: M-215, which listed the name as "Richd. Fitzgeffery"]. Took the Oath of Allegiance before the Hon. Robert Armstrong in St. Mary's County in 1778 [Ref: J-1146, K-62].

FITZJEFFERY, ---- [blank]. Private, St. Mary's County Militia, 1777 [Ref: M-215].
FLECHINGER, Michael. Private, St. Mary's County, who served in the Maryland Line until 1781 when discharged [Ref: D-408].
FLEET, Littleton. Took the Oath of Allegiance in Calvert County in 1778 [Ref: L-36].
FLEET, Sarah. See "Thomas Boney," q.v.
FLETCHER, Henry. Took the Oath of Allegiance before the Hon. Bennett Biscoe in St. Mary's County in 1778 [Ref: J-1146, K-63].
FLETCHER, John. Took the Oath of Allegiance in Calvert County in 1778 [Ref: L-36].
FLOOD, Joseph. Took the Oath of Allegiance before the Hon. John Shanks in St. Mary's County in 1778 [Ref: J-1146, K-69]. Private, St. Mary's County Militia, 1777 [Ref: M-213, which listed the name as "Joseph Fluld"].
FLOWER, Charles. Private, Capt. Walter Smith's Co., Calvert County Militia, 1778 [Ref: J-1146, M-148, which listed the name as "Charles Flowers"]. The Register of St. Andrew's Episcopal Church states that Charles Flower and Mary Hutchins were married (by publication) on Oct. 28, 1780 [Ref: MB-383].
FLOWER, Jeremiah. Private, St. Mary's County Militia, 1777 [Ref: M-213]. Took the Oath of Allegiance before the Hon. Jeremiah Jordan in St. Mary's County in 1778 [Ref: J-1146, K-67].
FLOWER, Moses. Private, St. Mary's County Militia, 1777 [Ref: M-214]. Paid for services (unspecified) in 1782 [Ref: S-155].
FLOWER, Thomas. Took the Oath of Allegiance before the Hon. Jeremiah Jordan in St. Mary's County in 1778 [Ref: J-1146, K-67]. The Register of St. Andrew's Episcopal Church states that Thomas Flower and Eleanor Bond were married (by publication) Dec. 2, 1781 [Ref: MB-384].
FLOYD, Jesse. Private, St. Mary's County Militia, 1777 [Ref: M-211]. Took the Oath of Allegiance before the Hon. Ignatius Fenwick, Jr. in St. Mary's County in 1778 [Ref: J-1146, K-68]. The Register of St. Francis Xavier Catholic Church states that Jesse Floyd and Elizabeth Swales were married Nov. 5, 1774, and "Jesse Floyd, widower, and Mary Cavey (?) Reed" were married March 18, 1777 [Ref: SC-35, SC-36]. Also, the Register of St. Andrew's Episcopal Church states that Jesse Floyd and Elizabeth Taylor were married (by license) Feb. 6, 1785 [Ref: MB-386].
FORBES, John (March 19, 1757 - Dec. 31, 1804). Lieutenant in Charles County in 1776. He is buried at "The Plains" in the upper part of St. Mary's County [Ref: R-377, D-31, D-32, HG-42].
FORD, Athanasius (c1728-c1790). Probably a son of John Ford, and grandson of Robert Ford, of St. Mary's County. "Athanasius Ford" was elected to a General Committee in St. Mary's County in accordance with the resolves of the Continental Congress in 1775, and "Mr. Ananasius

GIBSON, Richard. Private, Capt. Charles Williamson's Co., Calvert County Militia, 1778 [Ref: J-1146, M-148]. Took the Oath of Allegiance in Calvert County in 1778 [Ref: L-36].
GIBSON, Roswell. Private, St. Mary's County Militia, 1777 [Ref: M-213]. Took the Oath of Allegiance before the Hon. Jeremiah Jordan in St. Mary's County in 1778 [Ref: J-1146, K-67].
GIBSON, Samuel. See "Joshua Gibson," q.v.
GIBSON, Sarah. See "Benjamin Jones," q.v.
GIBSON, William. Took the Oath of Allegiance before the Hon. Jeremiah Jordan in St. Mary's County in 1778 [Ref: J-1146, K-67].
GILL, Henry. Private, St. Mary's County Militia, 1777 [Ref: M-215]. Took the Oath of Allegiance before the Hon. Bennett Biscoe in St. Mary's County in 1778 [Ref: J-1146, K-63].
GILLEY, Robert. Private, Capt. Henry Skinner's Foot Co. of Hunting Hundred, Calvert County, 1777 [Ref: T-1814, O-125].
GILLEY, William. Private, Capt. Henry Skinner's Foot Co. of Hunting Hundred, Calvert County, 1777 [Ref: T-1814, O-125].
GILLUM, Thomas. Private, St. Mary's County, who served in the Maryland Line until 1781 when discharged [Ref: D-408].
GILPIN, Benjamin. Private, St. Mary's County, who served in the Maryland Line until 1781 when discharged [Ref: D-408].
GILPIN, Henry. Private, St. Mary's County Militia, 1777 [Ref: M-209]. Took the Oath of Allegiance in St. Mary's County in 1780 [Ref: Q-111].
GIPSON, Alby. Private, Capt. James Patterson's Co., Calvert County Militia, Aug. 10, 1777 [Ref: M-146].
GLEBB, Caleb. Private, St. Mary's County Militia, 1777 [Ref: M-214].
GLOVER, William. Private, St. Mary's County Militia, 1777 [Ref: M-210]. William Glover married Phebe Hutchinson on Dec. 16, 1783, St. Mary's County, by Rev. John Stephen, Rector of All Faith's Parish [Ref: I-535].
GODDARD (GODDART), Barton. Private, St. Mary's County Militia, 1777 [Ref: M-211, which listed the name as "Barton Goddard"]. Took the Oath of Allegiance before the Hon. John Reeder in St. Mary's County in 1778 [Ref: J-1146, K-69].
GODDARD (GODDART), Edward Barton. Private, St. Mary's County, enlisted May 30, 1778, for 9 months, 2nd Maryland Line [Ref: D-329, S-157]. Applied for and received pension S34901 on May 5, 1818, aged 65, in St. Mary's County [Ref: P-1369]. Pension rolls of 1835 listed him as age 81, but noted he had been dropped from the rolls under the Act of May 1, 1820 [Ref: U-40].
GODDARD (GODDART), Ignatius. Took the Oath of Allegiance before the Hon. John Reeder in St. Mary's County in 1778 [Ref: J-1146, K-69]. This name appeared twice as a private in the St. Mary's County Militia in 1777; perhaps one was "Ignatius Goodart, Jr.," q.v. [Ref: M-211, M-212, which listed the name as "Ignatius Goddard"]. The Register of St. Francis Xavier Catholic Church states that Ignatius Goddard and Ann

Ford" served on the Committee of Correspondence [Ref: MR-127]. Delegate to the Maryland Convention in 1776 and a member of the House of Delegates from 1777 through 1783. A receipt of attendance order was given by him to James Vineyard from the House of Delegates on March 13, 1778 [Ref: V-151, N-72, N-76, N-78, N-80, N-87]. Supplied provisions (wheat, mutton, or bacon) to the Army in 1780 [Ref: S-77, which listed his name as "Athanias Ford"]. "According to his London creditor Christopher Court, Ford sold his property between 1785 and 1786, moved from Maryland, and died insolvent." [Ref: N-324, SO-139]. In Dec., 1791, John Smith, administrator of Athanatius Ford, advised the Court that he [Ford] had "died considerably in debt." [Ref: SO-173].

FORD, Benjamin. Private, 5th Maryland Line, 1781 [Ref: S-155].

FORD, Catherine. See "James Fenwick," q.v.

FORD, Elizabeth. See "John Smith," q.v.

FORD, Henry. Private, St. Mary's County Militia, 1777 [Ref: M-211]. Took the Oath of Allegiance before the Hon. Richard Barnes in St. Mary's County in 1778 [Ref: J-1146, K-66].

FORD, Jesse. Private, St. Mary's County Militia, 1777 [Ref: M-213].

FORD, John. This name appeared twice as a private in the St. Mary's County Militia in 1777 [Ref: M-212, M-214]. Three men with this name took the Oath of Allegiance in 1778: one before the Hon. Henry Reeder [Ref: J-1146, K-64], one before the Hon. Robert Watts [Ref: J-1146, K-62], and one before the Hon. Richard Barnes [Ref: J-1146, K-66]. See "Athanasius Ford" and "Philip Ford," q.v.

FORD, John Jr. Took the Oath of Allegiance before the Hon. Richard Barnes in St. Mary's County in 1778 [Ref: J-1146, K-66]. John Ford, Jr. died intestate by May, 1795 [Ref: SO-228].

FORD, John (of Peter). Took the Oath of Allegiance before the Hon. Henry Reeder in St. Mary's County in 1778 [Ref: J-1146, K-64].

FORD, Joseph (1752 - Jan. 23, 1812). Private, St. Mary's County, 1776. Second Lieutenant, 1st Maryland Line, March 27, 1777, and later Captain. He may have been wounded in the campaigns to the north in 1776-1777, and later resigned his commission. Appointed Commissary of Purchases in 1778 and served throughout the war. As the Commissary at Leonardtown he wrote to the Governor on June 19, 1781, regarding his problems with procuring supplies in St. Mary's County [Ref: V-405, V-457, SM-149]. The Register of St. Francis Xavier Catholic Church states that Joseph Ford and Henrietta Spink were married Nov. 29, 1778 [Ref: SC-36]. "He was a father and husband." [Ref: R-378].

FORD, Margaret. See "Henry Medley," q.v.

FORD, Mary Eleanor. See "Philip Ford," q.v.

FORD, Monica. See "John Fenwick," q.v.

FORD, Peter. Private, St. Mary's County Militia, 1777 [Ref: M-212]. Took the Oath of Allegiance before the Hon. Henry Reeder in St. Mary's County in 1778 [Ref: J-1146, K-64]. The Register of St. Francis Xavier

Catholic Church states that Peter Ford and Mary Sewall were married in 1779 [Ref: SC-36].

FORD, Philip (1748 - June 12, 1807). Private, St. Mary's County Militia, 1777 [Ref: M-210]. Took the Oath of Allegiance before the Hon. Henry Reeder in St. Mary's County in 1778 [Ref: J-1146, K-64]. He married Mary Eleanor ---- [Ref: R-379]. Another Philip Ford married Elizabeth Spalding at St. Francis Xavier Catholic Church on Sep. 30, 1775, and also served as a private in the St. Mary's County Militia in 1777 [Ref: SC-35, M-212]. Source S-142 indicates that Philip Ford (1750-1806), son of John Ford and Harriet Neale, married Mary Eleanor Thompson in 1770, lived in Leonardtown, and took the Oath of Allegiance in 1778. There was no mention of any military service although it appears from the above records that two Philip Fords were privates in the St. Mary's County militia.

FORD, Raphael. Private, St. Mary's County Militia, 1777 [Ref: M-212]. Took the Oath of Allegiance before the Hon. John Ireland in St. Mary's County in 1778 [Ref: J-1146, K-65, which listed the name as "Raphael Foard"]. The Register of St. Francis Xavier Catholic Church states that Raphael Ford and Ann Spalden were married Jan. 29, 1771 [Ref: SC-34].

FORD, Richard. Took the Oath of Allegiance before the Hon. Henry Reeder in St. Mary's County in 1778 [Ref: J-1146, K-64].

FORD, Robert Jr. Private, St. Mary's County Militia, 1777 [Ref: M-212]. Second Lieutenant, Lower Bn., St. Mary's County, June 22, 1780 [Ref: M-76, F-201]. Took the Oath of Allegiance before the Hon. Richard Barnes in St. Mary's County in 1778 [Ref: J-1146, K-66]. See "Athanasius Ford," q.v.

FORD, Robert Sr. Private, St. Mary's County Militia, 1777 [Ref: M-214]. Took the Oath of Allegiance before the Hon. John Ireland in St. Mary's County in 1778 [Ref: J-1146, K-65]. "Robert Ford" supplied provisions to the Army in 1780 [Ref: S-77].

FORD, William. Took the Oath of Allegiance before the Hon. Jeremiah Jordan in St. Mary's County in 1778 [Ref: J-1146, K-67]. Private, St. Mary's County, who served in the Maryland Line until 1781 when discharged [Ref: D-408].

FORREST, Ann. See "Zachariah Forrest" and "Uriah Forrest," q.v.

FORREST, Catherine and Elizabeth. See "Zachariah Forrest," q.v.

FORREST, Henry. See "Uriah Forrest," q.v.

FORREST, Henrietta, James and Joseph. See "Zachariah Forrest," q.v.

FORREST, Maria and Rebecca. See "Uriah Forrest," q.v.

FORREST, Richard. See "Zachariah Forrest," q.v.

FORREST, Thomas. Private, St. Mary's County Militia, 1777 [Ref: M-212]. Took the Oath of Allegiance before the Hon. Ignatius Fenwick, Jr. in St. Mary's County in 1778 [Ref: J-1146, K-68]. "Thomas Forrest, Sen." was elected to a General Committee in St. Mary's County in accordance with the resolves of the Continental Congress in 1775 [Ref: MR-127]. See "Uriah Forrest" and "Zachariah Forrest" and "Zephaniah Forrest," q.v.

FORREST, Thomas Jr. (1751 - April 1, 1829). Son of Dr. Thomas Forrest. "He taught school in London, England and in St. George's Hundred in St. Mary's County, called the Squire and considered the wanderer." He married Catherine Mattingly, widow, on June 1, 1776, at St. Francis Xavier Catholic Church. Around 1791 he moved with his brother "Zephaniah Forrest," q.v., to Kentucky and then on to Perry County, Missouri circa 1822 [Ref: R-380, SC-35]. Thomas took the Oath of Allegiance before the Hon. John Ireland in St. Mary's County in 1778 [Ref: J-1146, K-65].

FORREST, Uriah (1746 - July 6, 1805). Son of Dr. Thomas Forrest, of St. Mary's County, descendant of the Forrest family who immigrated to Jamestown, Virginia in 1607. Uriah married Rebecca Plater, daughter of Gov. George Plater, and had these children: Joseph, Henry, Uriah, Ann, and Maria. Served in Lower House from St. Mary's County, 1781-1783. Lived in London, England, 1783-1786. Settled in Georgetown, Montgomery County, circa 1786. Second Lieutenant, 2nd Independent Co., Jan. 2, 1776, and Captain, Flying Camp, St. Mary's County, July 12, 1776, when he saw his first action during the Dunmore invasion of St. Mary's County in July, 1776 and the subsequent campaigns in New York and New Jersey. Captain, 3rd Maryland Line, Dec. 10, 1776, and Major, May 3, 1777. He was wounded in the leg during the Battle of Germantown on Oct. 4, 1777, which resulted in an amputation on Nov. 20, 1778. Promoted to Lieutenant Colonel in the 7th Maryland Line on Dec. 27, 1779, appointed Auditor General of Maryland on Aug. 18, 1779, and Lieutenant Colonel in the 1st Maryland Line on Jan. 1, 1781; resigned Feb. 19, 1781, and was appointed Commissioner of Confiscated British Property on March 30, 1781. He served as a Delegate to Continental Congress, 1786-1787, Mayor of Georgetown, 1792, Representative to U. S. Congress, 1793-1794, County Court Justice, Montgomery County, 1799-1800, and Clerk of the Circuit Court, District of Columbia, 1801-1805. Died deeply in debt in 1805 and buried in Oak Hill Cemetery in Washington, D. C. [Ref: N-86, N-87, N-325, D-30, SM-147, V-420]. "Uriah Forrest was a man of substance and in 1797 when the State of Maryland made a loan to the impecunious federal government for the erection of the capitol buildings, he was one of those who signed their names as security to the bonds." [Ref: R-381]. Also see "Philip Key" and "Zachariah Forrest," q.v.

FORREST, Zachariah (Nov. 6, 1742 - Jan. 29, 1817). Son of Dr. Thomas Forrest and Henrietta Raley, and brother of "Uriah Forrest," q.v. He married twice: (1) Anne or Nancy Edwards; and (2) Ann Ford. Children: Richard (1767-1828), Joseph (1768-1845), James, Uriah, Catherine, Sarah, Ann, Elizabeth, and another daughter (name not stated). His death notice stated he had nine children by his first wife and one by the second [Ref: R-381]. First Lieutenant, Lower Bn., St. Mary's County Militia, Aug. 26, 1777, and Captain, June 22, 1780. Served as a Court Justice, St. Mary's County, 1785-1805, Tax Commissioner, 1786-1796, and County Sheriff, 1778-1782 [Ref: M-76, M-211, C-346, F-201, N-325, V-141, R-380]. Took the Oath of Allegiance before the Hon. Henry Reeder in St. Mary's County in 1778 [Ref: J-1146, K-64]. He loaned money in St. Mary's County for the war effort in 1781 [Ref: X-78, H-414]. "Ann Forrest, relict of the late Capt. Zachariah Forrest, died at an advanced age in St. Mary's County on June 5, 1823." [Ref: R-379]. It should be noted that Source S-142 states that James and Henrietta were the parents of Zachariah Forrest while Source N-325 states it was probably Thomas and Henrietta.

FORREST, Zephaniah. Son of Dr. Thomas Forrest. Second Lieutenant, Lower Bn., St. Mary's County Militia, Aug. 26, 1777, and First Lieutenant, June 22, 1780 [Ref: M-76, M-211, C-346, F-201]. Took the Oath of Allegiance before the Hon. Richard Barnes in St. Mary's County in 1778 [Ref: J-1146, K-66]. He died testate by Jan., 1812, in Washington County, Kentucky [Ref: R-381]. See "Thomas Forrest, Jr.," q.v.

FOSTER, James. Private, St. Mary's County, enlisted May 28, 1778, for 9 months, Continental Army [Ref: D-330]. Private, 3rd Maryland Line, reported dead June 30, 1781 [Ref: SM-112, D-298].

FOUTCH, John. See "Thomas Wherritt," q.v.

FOWLER, Abraham. Private, Capt. Thomas Truman Greenfield's Co., Calvert County Militia, 1778 [Ref: J-1146, M-150]. Took the Oath of Allegiance in Calvert County in 1778 [Ref: L-36].

FOWLER, Benjamin. Private, Capt. Thomas Truman Greenfield's Co., Calvert County Militia, 1778 [Ref: J-1146, M-150]. Took the Oath of Allegiance in Calvert County in 1778 [Ref: L-36].

FOWLER, Catherine. See "Joseph Parker," q.v.

FOWLER, Charles. (1) Private, St. Mary's County Militia, 1777 [Ref: M-213]. "Charles Fowler, farmer" moved to Washington County, Kentucky in 1795 [Ref: X-86]. (2) Private, Capt. Henry Skinner's Foot Co. of Hunting Hundred, Calvert County, 1777 [Ref: T-1814, O-125]. Took the Oath of Allegiance in Calvert County in 1778 [Ref: L-36].

FOWLER, George. Private, Capt. Henry Skinner's Foot Co. of Hunting Hundred, Calvert County, 1777 [Ref: T-1814, O-125]. The Christ Church Register in Calvert County records the birth of George Fowler, son of Joseph and Catherine Fowler, on March 29, 1724 [Ref: O-11].

FOWLER, Henry. Private, St. Mary's County Militia, 1777 [Ref: M-210]. Took the Oath of Allegiance in St. Mary's County in 1780 [Ref: Q-110].

FOWLER, James. Private, Capt. Henry Skinner's Foot Co. of Hunting Hundred, Calvert County, 1777 [Ref: T-1814, O-125].

FOWLER, Jesse. Private, Capt. Frisby Freeland's Co., Calvert County Militia, 1778 [Ref: J-1146, M-148]. Took the Oath of Allegiance in Calvert County in 1778 [Ref: L-36].

FOWLER, Jonathan. Private, St. Mary's County Militia, 1777 [Ref: M-210].

FOWLER, Joseph. Private, Capt. Henry Skinner's Foot Co. of Hunting Hundred, Calvert County, 1777 [Ref: T-1814, O-125]. The Christ Church Register in Calvert County records the birth of Joseph Parker, son of Joseph and Catherine Parker, on March 6, 1725 [Ref: O-111]. There was also a Joseph Fowler who served as a Cabin Boy on the State ship *Defence* in 1777 [Ref: S-156].

FOWLER, Josiah. Private, Capt. Henry Skinner's Foot Co. of Hunting Hundred, Calvert County, 1777 [Ref: T-1814, O-125].

FOWLER, Parker. Private, Capt. Henry Skinner's Foot Co. of Hunting Hundred, Calvert County, 1777 [Ref: T-1814, O-125]. The Christ Church Register in Calvert County records the birth of Parker Fowler, son of Joseph and Catherine Fowler, on June 23, 1728 [Ref: O-11].

FOWLER, Thomas. Private, St. Mary's County Militia, 1777 [Ref: M-210].

FOWLER, William. (1) Private, Capt. Richard Lane's Co., Calvert County Militia, 1778 [Ref: J-1146, M-149]. Took the Oath of Allegiance in Calvert County in 1778 [Ref: L-36]. (2) Private, St. Mary's County Militia, 1777 [Ref: M-213]. The Register of St. Francis Xavier Catholic Church states that William Fowler and Mary Mattingly were married on Feb. 19, 1776 [Ref: SC-35]. One William Fowler was a supplier of provisions (wheat, mutton, or bacon) to the Army in 1780 [Ref: S-77, S-156].

FOYLES, Catharine S. See "Clement Sewall," q.v.

FRANKLIN, John. Private, St. Mary's County, who served in the Maryland Line until 1781 when discharged [Ref: D-408].

FRAZIER, Alexander. Private, Capt. Charles Williamson's Co., Calvert County Militia, 1778 [Ref: J-1146, M-147]. Took the Oath of Allegiance in Calvert County in 1778 [Ref: L-36, which listed the name as "Alexander Fraizur"].

FRAZIER, Alexander Jr. Took the Oath of Allegiance in Calvert County in 1778 [Ref: L-36, which listed the name as "Alexander Fraizur"].

FRAZIER (FRASER), China. See "Leonard Mills," q.v.

FRAZIER (FRAISER), Elizabeth. See "Silvester Wheatley," q.v.

FRAZIER, Margaret. See "John Pardoe," q.v.

FREELAND, Frisby (c1747-c1807). Son of Robert Freeland, of Upper Clifts, Calvert County. He married Sarah Chew, daughter of William Chew and widow of Allen Bowie (died 1795), and may have had a son Frisby Freeland, Jr. Served as Coroner, 1774, 1790, and 1795, and in the Lower House, 1779-1781. Committee of Observation, 1774, and Tobacco Inspector, Lower Marlboro Warehouse, 1786-1790. Captain, 15th Bn., Calvert County Militia, from May 10, 1776 through at least

April 16, 1778. Took the Oath of Allegiance in Calvert County in 1778. Commissioner of Tax, 1798 [Ref: J-1146, M-76, M-148, A-320, E-37, L-36, N-82, N-84, N-330].

FREELAND, Jacob. Private, Capt. Frisby Freeland's Co., Calvert County Militia, 1778 [Ref: J-1146, M-148]. Took the Oath of Allegiance in Calvert County in 1778 [Ref: L-36].

FREELAND, Peregrine. Son of Robert Freeland. Private, Capt. Frisby Freeland's Co., Calvert County Militia, 1778 [Ref: J-1146, M-148]. Took the Oath of Allegiance in Calvert County in 1778 [Ref: L-36]. Served in Lower House from Calvert County, 1789-1794, and a Coroner, 1783-1789. Resided in Upper Hundred of the Clifts in the Second Tax District, may have married, and probably died between 1810 and 1820. Brother of "Frisby Freeland," q.v. [Ref: N-330].

FREELAND, Robert. Private, Capt. Thomas Truman Greenfield's Co., Calvert County Militia, 1778 [Ref: J-1146, M-150]. Also see "Frisby Freeland" and "Peregrine Freeland," q.v.

FREELAND, Robert Jr. Private, Capt. Thomas Truman Greenfield's Co., Calvert County Militia, 1778 [Ref: J-1146, M-150].

FREEMAN, Elizabeth. See "John Freeman," q.v.

FREEMAN, Ezra. Took the Oath of Allegiance in Calvert County in 1778 [Ref: L-36].

FREEMAN, George Gallimore. Private, Capt. Henry Skinner's Foot Co. of Hunting Hundred, Calvert County, 1777 [Ref: T-1814, O-125].

FREEMAN, Israel. Private, Capt. Edward Wood's Co., Calvert County Militia, 1778 [Ref: J-1146, M-147].

FREEMAN, John. Private, Capt. Henry Skinner's Foot Co. of Hunting Hundred, Calvert County, 1777 [Ref: T-1814, O-125]. Private, Capt. Walter Smith's Co., Calvert County Militia, 1778 [Ref: J-1146, M-148]. Took the Oath of Allegiance in Calvert County in 1778 [Ref: L-36]. The Christ Church Register in Calvert County records the birth of John Freeman, son of John and Elizabeth Freeman, on July 24, 1755 [Ref: O-12].

FREEMAN, Joseph. Private, Capt. Henry Skinner's Foot Co. of Hunting Hundred, Calvert County, 1777 [Ref: T-1814, O-125]. Took the Oath of Allegiance in Calvert County in 1778 [Ref: L-36].

FREEMAN, Kinsey. Private, Capt. Thomas Truman Greenfield's Co., Calvert County Militia, 1778 [Ref: J-1146, M-150]. Took the Oath of Allegiance in Calvert County in 1778 [Ref: L-36].

FREEMAN, Mary. See "Joseph Allsop," q.v.

FREEMAN, Patterson (Pattison). Took the Oath of Allegiance in Calvert County in 1778 [Ref: L-36]. Private, Capt. Benjamin Bond's Co., Calvert County Militia, 1778 [Ref: J-1146, M-149].

FREEMAN, Richard. Private, Capt. Henry Skinner's Foot Co. of Hunting Hundred, Calvert County, 1777 [Ref: T-1814, O-125].

FREEMAN, Samuel. (1) Private, Capt. James Patterson's Co., Calvert County Militia, Aug. 10, 1777 [Ref: M-146]. (2) Private, Capt. James Grahame's Co., Calvert County Militia, 1778 [Ref: J-1146, M-148].

FREEMAN, Thomas. (1) Private, Capt. Henry Skinner's Foot Co. of Hunting Hundred, Calvert County, 1777 [Ref: T-1814, O-125]. Private, Capt. Thomas Truman Greenfield's Co., Calvert County Militia, 1778 [Ref: J-1146, M-150]. (2) Private, Capt. Walter Smith's Co., Calvert County Militia, 1778 [Ref: J-1146, M-148]. One Thomas Freeman took the Oath of Allegiance in Calvert County in 1778 [Ref: L-36]. One Thomas Freeman and Sarah Mitchell were married on April 6, 1779, by Rev. Francis Lauder, of Christ Church Parish [Ref: K-35].

FREEMAN, William (carpenter). Private, Capt. Henry Skinner's Foot Co. of Hunting Hundred, Calvert County, 1777 [Ref: T-1814, O-125].

FRENCH, Ann. See "John Reynolds," q.v.

FRENCH, Benedict. Took the Oath of Allegiance before the Hon. John Ireland in St. Mary's County in 1778 [Ref: J-1146, K-65].

FRENCH, Bennett (Bennit). Private, St. Mary's County Militia, 1777 [Ref: M-210]. "Benet French" died by Feb., 1797, leaving a minor daughter Monica French [Ref: SO-257].

FRENCH, Ignatius. This name appeared twice as a private in the St. Mary's County Militia in 1777 [Ref: M-210, M-211]. One took the Oath of Allegiance before the Hon. John Ireland in St. Mary's County in 1778 [Ref: J-1146, K-65]. An Ignatius French migrated with the early Catholic settlers to Nelson County, Kentucky circa 1785 [Ref: MK-52].

FRENCH, James. Private, Maryland Line, 1781-1782 [Ref: D-398, D-535]. The Register of St. Francis Xavier Catholic Church states James French and Susan Melton were married May 25, 1773 [Ref: SC-34].

FRENCH, Jeremiah. Private, Maryland Line, 1781-1782 [Ref: D-535].

FRENCH, Monica. See "Bennett French," q.v.

FRENCH, Raphael. Private, St. Mary's County Militia, 1777 [Ref: M-210]. Took the Oath of Allegiance before the Hon. John Ireland in St. Mary's County in 1778 [Ref: J-1146, K-65].

FRENCH, Randolph. Private, 3rd Maryland Line, April 27, 1778 until discharged in Feb., 1779; from St. Mary's County [Ref: S-156].

FRENCH, Rudolph. "Rhode French" was a private, St. Mary's County Militia, 1777 [Ref: M-213]. "Rudolph French" was a private, St. Mary's County, enlisted April 27, 1778, for 9 months [Ref: D-329].

FRENCH, Stephen. This name appeared twice as a private in the St. Mary's County Militia in 1777 [Ref: M-210, M-211]. Private, St. Mary's County, enlisted May 25, 1778, for 9 months [Ref: D-329]. Private, 2nd Maryland Line, 1778-1779 [Ref: S-156].

FRIEND, Daniel. Private, St. Mary's County, drafted May 30, 1778, for 9 months, noting he was a ship carpenter [Ref: D-330, S-156]. Took the Oath of Allegiance before the Hon. John Ireland in St. Mary's County in 1778 [Ref: J-1146, K-65]. The Register of St. Francis Xavier Catholic

Church states Daniel Friend and Cloe Payne were married Aug. 8, 1775 [Ref: SC-35].

FRISBY, Ann and Peregrine. See "William Fitzhugh," q.v.

FROGGET, Richard. Private, St. Mary's County, who served in the Maryland Line until 1781 when discharged [Ref: D-408].

FRYER, Thomas. Took the Oath of Allegiance before the Hon. Henry G. Sothoron in St. Mary's County in 1778 [Ref: J-1146, K-68].

FRYER, William. Private, Capt. Edward Wood's Co., Calvert County Militia, 1778 [Ref: J-1146, M-147]. Took the Oath of Allegiance in Calvert County in 1778 [Ref: L-36, which listed the name as "William Fryar"]. The Christ Church Register in Calvert County records the birth of the children of "William Fryeir" and his wife Mary as John Edward Henry, born July 29, 1761, and Zachariah, born April 8, 1764 [Ref: O-12].

GADDEN, Edward. Took the Oath of Allegiance before the Hon. John Reeder in St. Mary's County in 1778 [Ref: J-1146, K-69].

GADDEN, Jeremiah. Took the Oath of Allegiance before the Hon. John Reeder in St. Mary's County in 1778 [Ref: J-1146, K-69].

GADDEN, Richard Ellis. Took the Oath of Allegiance before the Hon. John Reeder in St. Mary's County in 1778 [Ref: J-1146, K-69].

GAITHER, George. See "George Guither (Guyther)," q.v.

GALLOWAY, John. Private, Capt. Frederick Skinner's Co., Calvert County Militia, 1778 [Ref: J-1146, M-150]. Private, Capt. John Mackall's Co., Calvert County Militia, 15th Bn., June 12, 1778 [Ref: M-146, which listed the name as "John Gallerway"].

GALLOWAY, Samuel. Private, Capt. Charles Williamson's Co., Calvert County Militia, 1778 [Ref: J-1146, M-147].

GAMES, Absalom. Private, Calvert County, enlisted by Capt. John Brooke on July 25, 1776 [Ref: D-33]. Private, Capt. Benjamin Bond's Co., Calvert County Militia, 1778 [Ref: J-1146, M-149]. Took the Oath of Allegiance in Calvert County in 1778 [Ref: L-36].

GAMES, Francis. Took the Oath of Allegiance in Calvert County in 1778 [Ref: L-36].

GAMES, Howerton. Private, Capt. Benjamin Bond's Co., Calvert County Militia, 1778 [Ref: J-1146, M-149]. Took the Oath of Allegiance in Calvert County in 1778 [Ref: L-36].

GAMES, John. This name appeared twice on the list of those who took the Oath of Allegiance in Calvert County in 1778 [Ref: L-36].

GAMES, Martha. See "Kinsey Gardiner," q.v.

GAMES, Mary. See "Edward Denton" and "Henry Tanner," q.v.

GAMES, Robert. Private, Calvert County, enlisted by Lt. Nathaniel Wilson on Aug. 23, 1776 [Ref: D-34]. Private, Capt. Benjamin Bond's Co., Calvert County Militia, 1778 [Ref: J-1146, M-149]. Robert Games and Ann Bowen were married on Aug. 12, 1777, by Rev. Francis Lauder, of Christ Church Parish [Ref: K-33].

GANTT, Ann. See "Thomas Harwood, III," q.v.
GANTT, Benjamin, Charles, and Daniel. See "Thomas Gantt, the 4th, Jr.," q.v.
GANTT, Edward (c1725-c1783). Son of Thomas Gantt (died 1765) and Priscilla Brooke, of Prince George's County. He married by 1749 to Elizabeth Wheeler, daughter of Robert Wheeler, of Charles County, and had these children: Thomas, Edward, and Mary (who married Bishop Thomas John Clagett, 1742-1816). Edward was a captain by 1751, served in the Lower House from Calvert County, 1751-1770, and was a Delegate to the Maryland Convention, 1775-1776 [Ref: N-71, N-72, N-339, N-340].
GANTT, Edward Jr. Private, Capt. Charles Williamson's Co., Calvert County Militia, 1778 [Ref: J-1146, M-147].
GANTT, Elizabeth Heigh. See "John Brome (Broome)," q.v.
GANTT, George. See "Thomas Harwood, III," q.v.
GANTT, John Mackall. See "Thomas Gantt, the 4th, Jr.," q.v.
GANTT, Mary. See "Edward Gantt," q.v.
GANTT, Richard. See "Thomas Gantt, the 4th, Jr.," q.v.
GANTT, Thomas (Doctor). Son of "Edward Gantt," q.v. and Elizabeth Wheeler. He married Barbara ---- (who subsequently married George F. Janney, a Quaker). Thomas' sons were Edward, Thomas, and John. Served as a private, Capt. James Grahame's Co., Calvert County Militia, 1778 [Ref: J-1146, M-149]. Member of the Lower House in 1780-1781, 1785-1792. Senate Elector, 1791 and 1801. "He termed himself Dr. Thomas Gantt or Dr. Thomas Gantt, Jr...in land records...and there was no other Thomas Gantt of the appropriate age in Calvert County during his period of service in the legislature." [Ref: N-84, N-343]. Also see "Thomas Gantt, the 4th, Jr.," q.v.
GANTT, Thomas III. Took the Oath of Allegiance in Calvert County in 1778 [Ref: L-36]. See "Thomas Gantt, the 4th, Jr.," q.v.
GANTT, Thomas "the 4th, Jr." (Aug. 18, 1736, Calvert County - Dec. 12, 1800, Prince George's County). Son of Thomas Gantt and Rachel Smith. He married Susanna Mackall (1737-1777), daughter of John Mackall and Mary Hance, and had these children: Elizabeth Heigh Gantt (1757-1789, married "John Brome," q.v.); Thomas Gantt (died in 1786); John Mackall Gantt (married Mrs. Mary Sprigg Hermans and died in 1811); Benjamin Gantt (M. D., died in Georgia in 1808); Mary Gantt (married ---- Newburn); Richard Judge Gantt (married Sarah Allen and moved to South Carolina); Daniel Gantt (married Mrs. Woods); and, Charles Gantt (married Mary Parran in 1798, although *Mackenzie's Colonial Families* states that he died unmarried). Thomas was a signer of the Declaration of Freemen of Maryland in 1775, a member of the Committee of Safety from 1774 through 1777, and took the Oath of Allegiance in Prince George's County, Maryland in 1778 [Ref: Maryland Society, Sons of the American Revolution, Membership Application No. 3127,

filed by George Blunt Breeden and approved in 1991 by the National Society; *Colonial Families of the United States of America*, Volume I, by George Norbury Mackenzie (1907), p. 187].

GARBY, John. Private, St. Mary's County Militia, 1777 [Ref: M-210].

GARDINER, Clement. Marine on the State ship *Defence* from May 22, 1777 to Dec. 31, 1777 [Ref: D-656, which listed the name as "Clement Gardner (or Garner)"]. Private, St. Mary's County Militia, 1777 [Ref: M-212, which listed the name as "Clement Garner"]. Second Lieutenant, Upper Bn., St. Mary's County, Aug. 26, 1777 [Ref: M-77, SM-112, Y-259, C-345, which listed the name as "Clement Gardner"]. Took the Oath of Allegiance before the Hon. John Shanks in St. Mary's County in 1778 [Ref: J-1146, K-70]. Clement Gardiner died intestate by May, 1799 [Ref: SO-285].

GARDINER, Edward. Private, St. Mary's County Militia, 1777 [Ref: M-210].

GARDINER, Isaac. Private, Capt. Richard Parran's Co., Calvert County Militia, 1778 [Ref: J-1146, M-149]. Took the Oath of Allegiance in Calvert County in 1778 [Ref: L-36, which listed the name as "Isaac Gardner"]. The Register of St. Andrew's Episcopal Church states that "Isaac Gardner" and Ann Hollyday were married (by license) Sep. 23, 1784 [Ref: MB-386]. "Isaac Gardiner" and Rebecca Baker were married on Jan. 13, 1778, by Rev. Francis Lauder, of Christ Church Parish [Ref: K-33].

GARDINER, John. Private, 5th Maryland Independent Co., St. Mary's County, discharged Dec. 5, 1776 [Ref: S-156]. Private, St. Mary's County Militia, 1777 [Ref: M-211]. Took the Oath of Allegiance before the Hon. John Shanks in St. Mary's County in 1778 [Ref: J-1146, K-70].

GARDINER, John Jr. Private, Capt. Benjamin Bond's Co., Calvert County Militia, 1778 [Ref: J-1146, M-149]. Took the Oath of Allegiance in Calvert County in 1778 [Ref: L-36, which listed the name as "John Gardner, Jr."].

GARDINER, John Sr. Took the Oath of Allegiance in Calvert County in 1778 [Ref: L-36].

GARDINER, Joseph. Private, Capt. Walter Smith's Co., Calvert County Militia, 1778 [Ref: J-1146, M-148]. Took the Oath of Allegiance in Calvert County in 1778 [Ref: L-36, which listed the name as "Joseph Gardner"].

GARDINER, Kinsey. Private, Capt. Benjamin Bond's Co., Calvert County Militia, 1778 [Ref: J-1146, M-149]. Took the Oath of Allegiance in Calvert County in 1778 [Ref: L-36, which listed the name as "Kinsey Gardner"]. Kinsey Gardiner and Martha Games were married on Jan. 15, 1778, by Rev. Francis Lauder, of Christ Church Parish [Ref: K-33].

GARDINER, Richard. Private, Capt. Uriah Forrest's Co., Flying Camp, St. Mary's County, July 28, 1776 [Ref: D-30, SM-112]. Private, St.

Mary's County Militia, 1777 [Ref: M-212, which listed the name as "Richard Gardner"].

GARDINER, Robert. Private, Capt. Walter Smith's Co., Calvert County Militia, 1778 [Ref: J-1146, M-148]. Took the Oath of Allegiance in Calvert County in 1778 [Ref: L-36, which listed the name as "Robert Gardner"].

GARDINER, Simon. Took the Oath of Allegiance before the Hon. Bennett Biscoe in St. Mary's County in 1778 [Ref: J-1146, K-63].

GARDINER, Thomas. Served on the State ship *Defence* from May 22 to July 7, 1777 [Ref: D-656, which listed the name as "Thomas Gardner"]. Thomas Gardiner married Henrietta Goodrum on Sep. 27, 1777, St. Mary's County, by Rev. George Goldie [Ref: I-535]. Paid for making salt in 1782 [Ref: S-156].

GARDINER, William. (1) Private, Calvert County, enlisted by Capt. John Brooke on July 25, 1776 [Ref: D-33]. Took the Oath of Allegiance in Calvert County in 1778 [Ref: L-36, which listed the name as "William Gardner"]. (2) Private, St. Mary's County Militia, 1777 [Ref: M-213]. One William Gardiner and Keziah Willin (Wellin) were married on June 29, 1780, by Rev. Francis Lauder, of Christ Church Parish [Ref: K-35].

GARDINER, William Jr. Private, Capt. Benjamin Bond's Co., Calvert County Militia, 1778 [Ref: J-1146, M-149].

GARDINER, William Sr. Private, Capt. Benjamin Bond's Co., Calvert County Militia, 1778 [Ref: J-1146, M-149]. Took the Oath of Allegiance in Calvert County in 1778 [Ref: L-36, which listed the name as "William Gardner"].

GARNER, Clement. See "Clement Gardiner," q.v.

GARNER, Henry. Private, 2nd Maryland Line, discharged April 4, 1779; from St. Mary's County [Ref: S-156].

GATES, James. See "James Yates," q.v.

GATES, Joseph. Supplied provisions (wheat, mutton, or bacon) for the Army in St. Mary's County in 1780 [Ref: S-77, S-156].

GATTON, Azariah. Private, St. Mary's County, who served in the Maryland Line until discharged in 1781 [Ref: D-408, S-156].

GATTON, Richard Ellis. Private, Capt. Uriah Forrest's Co., Flying Camp, St. Mary's County, July 28, 1776 [Ref: D-30]. Private, 1st Maryland Line, June 10, 1778 to April 26, 1781 [Ref: S-156].

GATTON, Sylvester. Private, St. Mary's County Militia, 1777 [Ref: M-211]. Private, 1st Maryland Line, from Oct. 4, 1778 through at least Nov. 1, 1778, and apparently enlisted again from Charles County in 1781 [Ref: D-331, D-418, D-112, which listed the name as "Sulvester Gatton"].

GAUGH, Ignatius. See "Ignatius Gough," q.v.

GAY, Thomas. Took the Oath of Allegiance before the Hon. John Ireland in St. Mary's County in 1778 [Ref: J-1146, K-65].

GIBBONS, Edward. Marine from St. Mary's County who served on the State ship *Defence* in 1777 [Ref: D-656].

GIBBONS, Francis. Private, St. Mary's County Militia, 1777 [Ref: M-214]. Took the Oath of Allegiance before the Hon. Vernon Hebb in St. Mary's County in 1778 [Ref: J-1146, K-67]. The Register of St. Andrew's Episcopal Church states that Francis Gibbons and Rebecca Eden were married Feb. 20, 1780 [Ref: MB-383].

GIBBONS, John. Private, St. Mary's County Militia, 1777 [Ref: M-215]. Took the Oath of Allegiance before the Hon. Henry G. Sothoron in St. Mary's County in 1778 [Ref: J-1146, K-68].

GIBBONS, Thomas. Took an oath on July 27, 1782, concerning the manufacture and sale of salt in St. Mary's County [Ref: V-532].

GIBSON, Bartholomew. Private, Capt. Frederick Skinner's Co., Calvert County Militia, 1778 [Ref: J-1146, M-150]. Private, Capt. John Mackall's Co., Calvert County Militia, 15th Bn., June 12, 1778 [Ref: M-146]. Took the Oath of Allegiance in Calvert County in 1778 [Ref: L-36, which listed the name as "Bartholemy Gibson"].

GIBSON, Charles. See "Joshua Gibson," q.v.

GIBSON, James. Took the Oath of Allegiance in Calvert County in 1778 [Ref: L-36].

GIBSON, Jeremiah. Private, St. Mary's County Militia, 1777 [Ref: M-212]. Took the Oath of Allegiance before the Hon. John Shanks in St. Mary's County in 1778 [Ref: J-1146, K-70].

GIBSON, John. (1) Private, Capt. James Grahame's Co., Calvert County Militia, 1778 [Ref: J-1146, M-149]. Took the Oath of Allegiance in Calvert County in 1778 [Ref: L-36]. (2) Took the Oath of Allegiance before the Hon. Jeremiah Jordan in St. Mary's County in 1778 [Ref: J-1146, K-67].

GIBSON, John (of John). Private, Capt. James Grahame's Co., Calvert County Militia, 1778 [Ref: J-1146, M-148].

GIBSON, John (of Peter). Private, Capt. James Grahame's Co., Calvert County Militia, 1778 [Ref: J-1146, M-148].

GIBSON, John (of William). Private, St. Mary's County Militia, 1777 [Ref: M-213]. Took the Oath of Allegiance before the Hon. John Ireland in St. Mary's County in 1778 [Ref: J-1146, K-65].

GIBSON, Joshua. Marine on the State ship *Defence* from May 22, 1777 to Dec. 31, 1777 [Ref: D-656]. Took the Oath of Allegiance before the Hon. Jeremiah Jordan in St. Mary's County in 1778 [Ref: J-1146, K-67]. Joshua Gibson married Mary Ann Anderson on Feb. 10, 1778, St. Mary's County, by Rev. George Goldie [Ref: I-535]. "Joshua Gibson, Jr., farmer" moved from St. Clements to Fayette County, Pennsylvania, in 1797 [Ref: X-86]. One Joshua Gibson died by Aug., 1799, when his son Charles (aged 14 on Jan. 2, 1799) and son Samuel (aged 13 in Sep., 1799) were bound to Rhodum Gibson, guardian [Ref: SO-288, SO-289].

GIBSON, Rhodolph. Private, St. Mary's County Militia, 1777 [Ref: M-213].

GIBSON, Rhodum. See "Joshua Gibson," q.v.

DUVALL, Bennett. Took the Oath of Allegiance before the Hon. Jeremiah Jordan in St. Mary's County in 1778 [Ref: J-1146, K-67].
DUVALL, Jacob. Private, St. Mary's County Militia, 1777 [Ref: M-214].
DUVALL, John Miles. Private, St. Mary's County Militia, 1777 [Ref: M-214, which listed the name as "John M Duall"]. Took the Oath of Allegiance before the Hon. Bennett Biscoe in St. Mary's County in 1778 [Ref: J-1146, K-63, which listed the name as "John Miles Duvaul"].
DUVALL, Sennit. Private, St. Mary's County Militia, 1777 [Ref: M-212]. Private, 3rd Maryland Line, May 22, 1778 [Ref: SM-112].
DYER, James. Private, St. Mary's County Militia, 1777 [Ref: M-214]. Private, St. Mary's County, enlisted on May 22, 1778, for 9 months [Ref: D-330]. Private, 3rd Maryland Line, 1778 [Ref: S-154].
DYER, William. Private, St. Mary's County Militia, 1777 [Ref: M-210, which listed the name as "William Diar"].
DYSON, Ann. See "Henry Swann," q.v.
EADES, Isaac. Private, Capt. Thomas Truman Greenfield's Co., Calvert County Militia, 1778 [Ref: J-1146, M-150].
EADES, Jacob. (1) Private, Capt. Thomas Cleland's Co., Calvert County Militia, 1778 [Ref: J-1146, M-147]. (2) Private, Capt. James Grahame's Co., Calvert County Militia, 1778 [Ref: J-1146, M-148].
EADES, Joseph. Private, Capt. James Patterson's Co., Calvert County Militia, Aug. 10, 1777 [Ref: M-146, which listed the name as "Joseph Edes"].
EADES, Thomas. Private, Capt. Thomas Cleland's Co., Calvert County Militia, 1778 [Ref: J-1146, M-147]. Private, 4th Maryland Line, from May 6, 1778, until reported missing at the Battle of Camden in South Carolina on Aug. 16, 1780 [Ref: D-107].
EADIE, William. Took the Oath of Allegiance before the Hon. Jeremiah Jordan in St. Mary's County in 1778 [Ref: J-1146, K-67].
EDEN, Elizabeth. See "Justinian Jordan," q.v.
EDEN, James. Member of the St. Mary's County Committee of Safety and Correspondence on Dec. 23, 1774, member of a General Committee [of Safety] in 1775, and member of the Committee of Observation on July 23, 1776 [Ref: SM-147, MR-126, S-16, B-100]. First Major, 6th Bn., St. Mary's County Militia, Jan. 12, 1776 [Ref: M-73], and in the 3rd Maryland Line. Participated in battles in New York where, at Harlem, Col. Thomas Ewing stated on Oct. 13, 1776, "The first three companies have gained great honor under the command of the Major, who I believe to be a brave man..." James Eden apparently died in the campaign of 1776 as his undated will was recorded by his brother "Lieut. John Eden," q.v., on Jan. 21, 1777 [Ref: SM-147].
EDEN, John. First Lieutenant, Upper Bn., St. Mary's County Militia, Aug. 26, 1777 [Ref: M-73, C-345]. Brother of "Major James Eden," q.v. It should be noted that there was also a John Eden who died on July 1, 1775, in St. Mary's County [Ref: R-373]. "John Eden, Jr." was elected to

Pyke (NC) were married Dec. 22, 1772 [Ref: SC-34, which noted that "NC" meant "non-Catholic"].

GODDARD (GODDART), Ignatius Jr. Took the Oath of Allegiance before the Hon. Ignatius Fenwick, Jr. in St. Mary's County in 1778 [Ref: J-1146, K-68].

GODDARD (GODDART), John. Took the Oath of Allegiance before the Hon. Ignatius Fenwick, Jr. in St. Mary's County in 1778 [Ref: J-1146, K-68]. Private, 3rd Maryland Line, 1780-1783 [Ref: S-157]. Applied for and received pension S35973 on Feb. 1, 1819, aged about 65, in Prince George's County, Maryland, stating he served in the Maryland Line during the war [Ref: P-1370]. One "John Goddard, farmer" moved from Lower Resurrection to Fleming County, Kentucky, after 1790 [Ref: X-86].

GODDARD (GODDART), John Baptist. Private, St. Mary's County Militia, 1777 [Ref: M-213, which listed the name as "Jno. Bapts. Goddard"]. Took the Oath of Allegiance before the Hon. John Reeder in St. Mary's County in 1778 [Ref: J-1146, K-69].

GOINGS, John. Private, St. Mary's County Militia, 1777 [Ref: M-214]. Took the Oath of Allegiance before the Hon. Robert Watts in St. Mary's County in 1778 [Ref: J-1146, K-62, which listed the name as "John Gowing"].

GOLDIE, George (Reverend). Took the Oath of Allegiance in St. Mary's County, King and Queen Parish, in 1778 [Ref: SM-186]. He died testate by March, 1793 [Ref: SO-189, SO-291].

GOLDSBOROUGH, Ann (Anne). See "Charles Goldsbury," q.v.

GOLDSBOROUGH, Charles. "Charles Goldsberry or Goldsborough" applied for a pension on April 27, 1818, aged 56, in St. Mary's County, stating he served in the Revolutionary War and the War of 1812. In 1820 he had a wife aged 45, a son aged 10, and three daughters aged 7, 5, and 2 years (no names were given). Charles died on Jan. 5, 1834, and his widow applied for a pension (W9459) on Aug. 5, 1843, aged 68, stating that she had married Charles on Oct. 28, 1793, her maiden name was Ann Goldsborough, and Mrs. Polly Norris attended the wedding. Also received bounty land warrants #647-100 and #337-60-55 [Ref: P-1374]. The pension rolls of 1835 listed his age as 71, but it was not noted that he had died in 1834 [Ref: U-40]. The Treasurer of Maryland was directed on March 11, 1834 "to pay Ann Goldsborough, of St. Mary's County, during life, quarterly, half pay of a private, for the services contributed by her husband [his name was not stated] during the Revolutionary War." [Ref: I-347]. Private, 3rd Maryland Line, 1780 [Ref: S-157].

GOLDSBOROUGH, Henry. Private, St. Mary's County, 3rd Maryland Line, enlisted May 14, 1778, and died June 17, 1781, leaving a son Joshua (who was above the age of 14). [Ref: SM-113, R-386, SO-39, D-114, D-298, which latter source listed the name as "Henry Gouldsborou" and stated he enlisted on Nov. 18, 1778]. "Henry Goldsbury" was a private, St. Mary's County Militia, 1777 [Ref: M-215]. Private, St. Mary's County, enlisted May 14, 1778, for 9 months [Ref: D-329, which listed the name as "Henry Gouldsburry"].

GOLDSBOROUGH, John. Marine on the State ship *Defence* in 1777; from St. Mary's County [Ref: S-157].

GOLDSBOROUGH, Nicholas. Private, St. Mary's County Militia, 1777 [Ref: M-214, which listed the name as "Nicholas Goldsberry"]. Private, Maryland Line, drafted July 27, 1781; discharged "not fit for duty" by Dr. Murray on Oct. 18, 1781 [Ref: S-107, S-157, D-384, G-646].

GOLDSBOROUGH, Stephen. Private, St. Mary's County Militia, 1777 [Ref: M-214, which listed the name as "Steph. Goldsburry"]. Marine on the State ship *Defence* from Oct. 23 to Nov. 15, 1777, when he was "discharged, being unfit for duty" [Ref: D-656, S-157, which latter source listed the name as "Stephen Goldsborough"].

GOLDSBURY, James. Private, St. Mary's County Militia, 1777 [Ref: M-214, which listed the name as "James Goldsberry"]. The Register of St. Andrew's Episcopal Church states that "James Goldsburry" and Araminta Roberts were married (by license) Jan. 9, 1783 [Ref: MB-384].

GOLDSBURY, John. Private, St. Mary's County Militia, 1777 [Ref: M-215, which listed the name as "John Goldsberry"]. Marine on the State ship *Defence* from Oct. 23 to Nov. 15, 1777 [Ref: D-656].

GOLDSBURY, Jonathan. Took the Oath of Allegiance before the Hon. Ignatius Fenwick, Jr. in St. Mary's County in 1778 [Ref: J-1146, K-68].

GOLDSBURY (GOLDSBERRY), Monica. See "Enoch Stone," q.v.

GOLDSBURY, Robert. Private, St. Mary's County Militia, 1777 [Ref: M-211, which listed the name as "Robert Goldsberry"].

GOLDSBURY, William. Private, St. Mary's County Militia, 1777 [Ref: M-215]. Took the Oath of Allegiance in St. Mary's County in 1780 [Ref: Q-111].

GOLDSMITH, Bennett. See "John Goldsmith," q.v.

GOLDSMITH, Harriet. See "Thomas Goldsmith," q.v.

GOLDSMITH, John. Private, St. Mary's County Militia, 1777 [Ref: M-212]. Took the Oath of Allegiance before the Hon. Jeremiah Jordan in St. Mary's County in 1778 [Ref: J-1146, K-67]. John Goldsmith died by 1798, leaving orphan sons John and Bennett, both above the age of 14 [Ref: SO-280, SO-283]. Paid for making salt in 1782 [Ref: S-157].

GOLDSMITH, John (of Benjamin). Took the Oath of Allegiance before the Hon. Jeremiah Jordan in St. Mary's County in 1778 [Ref: J-1146, K-67].

GOLDSMITH, Michael. Took the Oath of Allegiance before the Hon. John Shanks in St. Mary's County in 1778 [Ref: J-1146, K-70].

GOLDSMITH, Notley. Private, St. Mary's County, enlisted May 28, 1778, for 9 months [Ref: D-329]. Took the Oath of Allegiance before the Hon.

Jeremiah Jordan in St. Mary's County in 1778 [Ref: J-1146, K-67]. Private, 3rd Maryland Line, 1778-1779 [Ref: S-157].
GOLDSMITH, Susanna. See "Joseph Shanks," q.v.
GOLDSMITH, Thomas. Private, St. Mary's County Militia, 1777 [Ref: M-213]. Two men with this name took the Oath of Allegiance in 1778: one before the Hon. Henry G. Sothoron and the other before the Hon. Jeremiah Jordan [Ref: J-1146, K-67, K-68]. One Thomas Goldsmith was killed early in the war and his heirs applied for and received bounty land warrant #2399-200 on June 16, 1846, in Anne Arundel County, namely Harriet Goldsmith, Elizabeth Mills, Ann Lamden, Edward C. Mills, Margaret Mills, and Thomas Mills [Ref: P-1374].
GOODIN, Susannah. See "John Sanner," q.v.
GOODIN, William. Private, St. Mary's County Militia, 1777 [Ref: M-213].
GOODLOE, Mary. See "John Somerville," q.v.
GOODMAN, John. Took the Oath of Allegiance before the Hon. Robert Watts in St. Mary's County in 1778 [Ref: J-1146, K-62].
GOODRUM, Henrietta. See "Thomas Gardiner," q.v.
GOODWIN, John. Took the Oath of Allegiance in Calvert County in 1778 [Ref: L-36].
GOODWIN, Matthew. Took the Oath of Allegiance before the Hon. Jeremiah Jordan in St. Mary's County in 1778 [Ref: J-1146, K-67].
GOODWIN, William. Took the Oath of Allegiance before the Hon. Jeremiah Jordan in St. Mary's County in 1778 [Ref: J-1146, K-67].
GOUGH, Baptist. Private (substitute), St. Mary's County, July 28, 1781 [Ref: D-384]. Private, Continental Army, until discharged on Dec. 3, 1781 [Ref: D-408, S-157, H-11].
GOUGH, Bennett. Took the Oath of Allegiance before the Hon. John Shanks in St. Mary's County in 1778 [Ref: J-1146, K-70]. Private, St. Mary's County Militia, 1777 [Ref: M-212]. See "Stephen Gough," q.v.
GOUGH, Catherine. See "Ignatius Bowles," q.v.
GOUGH, Charles. Private (substitute), St. Mary's County, July 31, 1781 [Ref: D-384]. Private, Continental Army; dicharged Dec. 3, 1781 [Ref: D-408, S-109, H-11].
GOUGH, Cornelius. See "Ignatius Gough," q.v.
GOUGH, George. Took the Oath of Allegiance before the Hon. Bennett Biscoe in St. Mary's County in 1778 [Ref: J-1146, K-63]. Property destroyed by the British in 1781 [Ref: S-157].
GOUGH, Ignatius. Private, St. Mary's County Militia, 1777 [Ref: M-214]. Applied for and received pension S1205 in Oct., 1832, aged 79, in Breckenridge County, Kentucky, stating he enlisted in Feb., 1776, in St. Mary's County and served in the Maryland Line under Capt. McAllene Thomas [John Allen Thomas]. In May, 1777, he transferred to the command of Capt. William Campbell and served in Annapolis. He was discharged on account of ill health in May, 1778, and resided in the extreme east end of the county about 20 miles from the courthouse. He

made his application in the presence of Cornelius Gough, Justice of the Peace (no relationship stated). In Nelson County, Kentucky, on Aug. 19, 1833, Anne Howard (aged 90) and Susan Montgomery (aged 80) stated they were sisters of Ignatius Gaugh and verified his service as stated [Ref: P-1393, W-16, which listed the name as "Ignatius Gaugh"]. Two men by this name took the Oath of Allegiance in St. Mary's County in 1778: one before the Hon. Henry Reeder and one before the Hon. John Shanks [Ref: J-1146, K-64, K-70, MK-54].

GOUGH, James. Private, St. Mary's County Militia, 1777 [Ref: M-214]. Took the Oath of Allegiance before the Hon. Richard Barnes in St. Mary's County in 1778 [Ref: J-1146, K-66]. One James Gough died by Feb., 1780, leaving a son John Baptist Gough (above the age of 14). [Ref: SO-30]. One "James Gough, farmer" moved from Upper Newtown to Scott County, Kentucky, after 1790 [Ref: X-86].

GOUGH, John. See "Solomon Jones," q.v.

GOUGH, John Baptist and Joseph. See "James Gough," q.v.

GOUGH, Peter. See "Stephen Gough," q.v.

GOUGH, Stephen. This name appeared twice as a private in the St. Mary's County Militia in 1777 [Ref: M-214, M-215]. Took the Oath of Allegiance before the Hon. Richard Barnes in St. Mary's County in 1778 [Ref: J-1146, K-66]. One Stephen Gough died by Feb., 1796, leaving orphan sons Peter (above the age of 14), Stephen, and Bennett Gough, with Joseph Gough as their guardian [Ref: SO-239].

GOVER, William. Private, Capt. Richard Lane's Co., Calvert County Militia, 1778 [Ref: J-1146, M-149].

GRAHAM, Alexander. Private, St. Mary's County Militia, 1777 [Ref: M-209].

GRAHAME, Ann and Asenath. See "John and Charles Grahame," q.v.

GRAHAME, Charles (1721-1779). Born in Scotland, son of John Grahame and Ann Campbell, and immigrated to Calvert County by 1751 with his brother David who settled in Queen Anne's County. He married by 1753 to Asenath Hutton and had children John, Asenath, and Ann. Charles served in several official capacities: Naval Officer, Pocomoke, 1754-1755; Surveyor General, Eastern Shore, 1754-1755; Committee to protest the Stamp Act, 1765, and to protest the Fee Bill put in by Gov. Eden in 1772; Court Justice, 1756-1779; Member of the Lower House, Calvert County, 1762-1776; Senate, 1776-1781; Delegate, Maryland Convention, 1776; and, Member, Maryland Council of Safety, 1776 and 1777 [Ref: N-74, N-369, N-370]. Took the Oath of Allegiance in Calvert County in 1778 [Ref: L-36]. Recommended to the Governor of Maryland on Dec. 27, 1777, that Francis King be appointed Calvert County Register of Wills [Ref: V-134].

GRAHAME, David. See "Charles Grahame," q.v.

GRAHAME, James. Captain, 15th Bn., Calvert County Militia, Sep. 24, 1777 [Ref: J-1146, M-79, M-148, C-384, E-37, which listed the name as

"James Graham" and as "James Grahame"]. Took the Oath of Allegiance in Calvert County in 1778 [Ref: L-36]. Member of the House of Delegates in 1783 [Ref: N-88].

GRAHAME, John (1760-1833). Son of "Charles Grahame," q.v., and Asenath Hutton. He married Anne Jennings, daughter of Thomas Johnson, in 1788, and had children Thomas J. and Ann Rebecca. Private, Capt. Charles Williamson's Co., Calvert County Militia, 1778 [Ref: J-1146, M-147]. Second Lieutenant, 15th Bn., April 16, 1778 [Ref: M-80, E-37]. Served in Lower House, 1783-1788. Court Justice, Calvert County, 1782-1787. Moved to "Rose Hill Farm" in Frederick County, Maryland in 1788. Served in Senate, 1796-1801 [Ref: N-370].

GRAIN, Thomas. Private, St. Mary's County Militia, 1777 [Ref: M-214].

GRAVES, Absolom. See "Absolom Greaves," q.v.

GRAVES, James. Private, St. Mary's County, enlisted May 13, 1778, for 9 months [Ref: D-329].

GRAVES, Jeremiah. Private, St. Mary's County Militia, 1777 [Ref: M-212]. Took the Oath of Allegiance before the Hon. John Ireland in St. Mary's County in 1778 [Ref: J-1146, K-65]. The Register of St. Andrew's Episcopal Church states that Jeremiah Graves and Rachel Craig were married (published) Oct. 3, 1780 [Ref: MB-383].

GRAVES, John. Private, Capt. Uriah Forrest's Co., Flying Camp, St. Mary's County, July 28, 1776 [Ref: D-30, SM-113]. Took the Oath of Allegiance before the Hon. John Ireland in St. Mary's County in 1778 [Ref: J-1146, K-65]. Ensign, Upper Bn., Nov. 18, 1779 [Ref: M-80, SM-113, F-18, which listed the name as "John Greaves"].

GRAVES, John Jr. Private, St. Mary's County Militia, 1777 [Ref: M-212].

GRAVES, John B. Took the Oath of Allegiance before the Hon. John Ireland in St. Mary's County in 1778 [Ref: J-1146, K-65].

GRAVES, Joshua. Private, St. Mary's County Militia, 1777 [Ref: M-212]. Took the Oath of Allegiance before the Hon. John Ireland in St. Mary's County in 1778 [Ref: J-1146, K-65]. One Joshua Graves died intestate by April, 1796 [Ref: SO-242, SO-258, SO-273].

GRAVES, Luke. Private, St. Mary's County Militia, 1777 [Ref: M-213].

GRAVES, Robert. Ensign, 21st Bn., St. Mary's County Militia, April 16, 1778 [Ref: M-80, SM-113, E-37, which listed the name as "Robert Greaves"].

GRAVES, Susannah. See "Thomas Reeder" and "John Reeder, Jr.," q.v.

GRAY, George. Private, Calvert County, enlisted by Ensign James Somervill on July 25, 1776 [Ref: D-34]. Private, Capt. Thomas Truman Greenfield's Co., Calvert County Militia, 1778 [Ref: J-1146, M-150]. Took the Oath of Allegiance in Calvert County in 1780 and apparently again in 1781 [Ref: Q-111].

GRAY, George Sr. Took the Oath of Allegiance in Calvert County in 1780 [Ref: Q-111].

GRAY, Henry. Private, Capt. Edward Wood's Co., Calvert County Militia, 1778 [Ref: J-1146, M-147]. Took the Oath of Allegiance in Calvert County in 1778 [Ref: L-36].

GRAY, Jacob. Private, St. Mary's County, served in the 2nd Maryland Line, from March 4, 1777; promoted to sergeant; lost an arm in 1780 [Ref: D-112, S-32, S-157].

GRAY, James. Private, Capt. Walter Smith's Co., Calvert County Militia, 1778 [Ref: J-1146, M-148]. The Christ Church Register in Calvert County records the birth of James Gray, a son of John and Jane Gray, on April 26, 1746 [Ref: O-13].

GRAY, Jean. See "Nathaniel Dare," q.v.

GRAY, John. (1) Private, Capt. Walter Smith's Co., Calvert County Militia, 1778 [Ref: J-1146, M-148]. Took the Oath of Allegiance in Calvert County in 1778 [Ref: L-36]. (2) Took the Oath of Allegiance before the Hon. John Reeder in St. Mary's County in 1778 [Ref: J-1146, K-69]. The Register of St. Andrew's Episcopal Church states that John Gray and Elizabeth Turner were married (by license) Nov. 27, 1783 [Ref: MB-385]. Also see "James Gray," q.v.

GRAY, Marcy (Masey?). See "John Jefferson," q.v.

GRAY, Martha. See "Charles Bowen," q.v.

GRAY, Moses. Took the Oath of Allegiance in Calvert County in 1780 [Ref: Q-111].

GRAY, Rebecca. See "Edward Wood," q.v.

GRAY, Richard. Private, Calvert County, enlisted by Capt. John Brooke on July 25, 1776 [Ref: D-33]. Private, Capt. Benjamin Bond's Co., Calvert County Militia, 1778 [Ref: J-1146, M-149].

GRAY, Thomas. (1) Private, Calvert County, enlisted by Capt. John Brooke on July 25, 1776 [Ref: D-33]. Private, Capt. Edward Wood's Co., Calvert County Militia, 1778 [Ref: J-1146, M-147]. Took the Oath of Allegiance in Calvert County in 1778 [Ref: L-36]. (2) Second Lieutenant, Capt. Charles Williamson's Co., 21st Bn., Calvert County Militia, April 10, 1776 through April 16, 1778 [Ref: J-1146, M-80, M-147, A-320, E-37]. Took the Oath of Allegiance in Calvert County in 1778 [Ref: L-36]. One Thomas Gray married Anne Bowen on Nov. 3, 1778, by Rev. Francis Lauder, of Christ Church Parish [Ref: K-34].

GRAY, William. Took the Oath of Allegiance in Calvert County in 1778 [Ref: L-36]. There was also a William Gray who was born in St. Mary's County, Maryland, on Aug. 23, 1755, and served in the Revolutionary War in Chester County, Pennsylvania, in 1776, and in Rockbridge County, Virginia, in 1781. He applied for and received pension S2253 in Montgomery County, Kentucky, in 1832, having also lived in Warren County, Ohio [Ref: MK-58].

GRAY, William, "B. C." Private, Capt. Edward Wood's Co., Calvert County Militia, 1778 [Ref: J-1146, M-147].

GRAY, William, "H. P." Private, Capt. Edward Wood's Co., Calvert County Militia, 1778 [Ref: J-1146, M-147].

GREAVES, Absolom. Private, Calvert County, enlisted by Capt. John Brooke on July 26, 1776 [Ref: D-33]. The Register of St. Andrew's Episcopal Church in St. Mary's County records that Absolom Greaves and Alathia Smith were married (by license) Jan. 16, 1781 [Ref: MB-383].

GREAVES, John. See "John Graves," q.v.

GREAVES, Robert. See "Robert Greeves" and "Robert Graves," q.v.

GREEN, Ignatius. Private, St. Mary's County Militia, 1777 [Ref: M-215].

GREENFIELD, Anne Truman. See "Patrick Sim Smith," q.v.

GREENFIELD, James Truman. Private, St. Mary's County Militia, 1777 [Ref: M-210]. Took the Oath of Allegiance before the Hon. Henry Tubman in St. Mary's County in 1778 [Ref: J-1146, K-70]. Also see "Patrick Sim Smith," q.v.

GREENFIELD, Nathaniel Truman. Private, St. Mary's County Militia, 1777 [Ref: M-209]. Took the Oath of Allegiance before the Hon. Henry Tubman in St. Mary's County in 1778 [Ref: J-1146, K-70].

GREENFIELD, Susanna. See "Thomas Truman Greenfield," q.v.

GREENFIELD, Thomas. Private, St. Mary's County Militia, 1777 [Ref: M-210]. Coroner of St. Mary's County in 1777 [Ref: S-157].

GREENFIELD, Thomas Truman. Captain, 15th Bn., Calvert County Militia, April 10, 1776 [Ref: J-1146, M-80, M-150, A-320, E-37]. Took the Oath of Allegiance in Calvert County in 1778 [Ref: L-36]. "Truman Greenfield" died testate in St. Mary's County by Dec., 1778, and Susanna Greenfield was his executrix [Ref: SO-16]. Also see "Patrick Sim Smith," q.v.

GREENWELL, Archibald. Private, St. Mary's County Militia, 1777 [Ref: M-214, which listed the name as "Archd. Greenweld"]. Took the Oath of Allegiance before the Hon. John Ireland in St. Mary's County in 1778 [Ref: J-1146, K-65].

GREENWELL, Arnold. Private, St. Mary's County Militia, 1777 [Ref: M-211].

GREENWELL, Barnaby. Took the Oath of Allegiance before the Hon. Henry G. Sothoron in St. Mary's County in 1778 [Ref: J-1146, K-69].

GREENWELL, Barton. Private, St. Mary's County Militia, 1777 [Ref: M-211].

GREENWELL, Bennett (Dec. 7, 1761 - July 12, 1838). Private, St. Mary's County, Maryland Line. Applied for and received pension S16391 on Feb. 6, 1833, in Scott County, Kentucky, stating he was born on Dec. 7, 1761 in St. Mary's County and moved to Kentucky in 1795. He had served with "William Fenwick," q.v., under Capt. John Greenwell in St. Mary's County (no relationship stated) and he also mentioned his brother Joseph Greenwell who lived in Maryland in 1810 [Ref: P-1430, W-39, MK-59]. Took the Oath of Allegiance before the Hon. Henry

Reeder in St. Mary's County in 1778 [Ref: J-1146, K-64]. See "Ignatius Greenwell," q.v.

GREENWELL, Catherine, Charles, and Claressa. See "Ignatius Greenwell," q.v.

GREENWELL, Clement. Private, St. Mary's County Militia, 1777 [Ref: M-214]. Took the Oath of Allegiance before the Hon. Henry Reeder in St. Mary's County in 1778 [Ref: J-1146, K-64].

GREENWELL, Cuthbert. Took the Oath of Allegiance before the Hon. Richard Barnes in St. Mary's County in 1778 [Ref: J-1146, K-66].

GREENWELL, Edmond Barton. Private, St. Mary's County Militia, 1777 [Ref: M-211]. Took the Oath of Allegiance before the Hon. Henry Reeder in St. Mary's County in 1778 [Ref: J-1146, K-64, which listed the name as "Edmund B. Greenwell"].

GREENWELL, Edmund. See "John Greenwell" and "John Greenwell, of George," q.v.

GREENWELL, Edward. Private, St. Mary's County Militia, 1777 [Ref: M-214]. Took the Oath of Allegiance before the Hon. Richard Barnes in St. Mary's County in 1778 [Ref: J-1146, K-66]. One Edward Greenwell died intestate by Feb., 1791 [Ref: SO-160, SO-162].

GREENWELL, Elizabeth. See "John Greenwell," q.v.

GREENWELL, Enoch. Took the Oath of Allegiance before the Hon. Henry Reeder in St. Mary's County in 1778 [Ref: J-1146, K-64].

GREENWELL, George. Took the Oath of Allegiance before the Hon. Henry Reeder in St. Mary's County in 1778 [Ref: J-1146, K-64]. One George Greenwell died intestate by Feb., 1790 [Ref: SO-151]. See "John Greenwell," q.v.

GREENWELL, Henry. Private, St. Mary's County Militia, 1777 [Ref: M-211]. Took the Oath of Allegiance before the Hon. Henry Reeder in St. Mary's County in 1778 [Ref: J-1146, K-64].

GREENWELL, Ignatius. Private, St. Mary's County Militia, 1777 [Ref: M-211]. Took the Oath of Allegiance before the Hon. Henry Reeder in St. Mary's County in 1778 [Ref: J-1146, K-64]. One Ignatius Greenwell died intestate by June, 1797, when Monica Greenwell was appointed administratrix and she was appointed as guardian of her children Claressa, Charles, and Catherine [Ref: SO-262, SO-263].

GREENWELL, Ignatius Jr. Took the Oath of Allegiance before the Hon. Ignatius Fenwick, Jr. in St. Mary's County in 1778 [Ref: J-1146, K-68]. Private, St. Mary's County Militia, 1777 [Ref: M-214]. One Ignatius Greenwell (Dec. 23, 1754 - Sep. 6, 1847) applied for and received pension S16836 on June 15, 1833, in Ralls County, Missouri, aged 83 [sic], stating he served in St. Mary's County under Capt. John Greenwell (no relationship was stated). "Bennett Greenwell," q.v., made affidavit in Scott County, Kentucky in 1833 in support of Ignatius' service [Ref: Y-284, P-1430].

GREENWELL, Ignatius (of Henry). Took the Oath of Allegiance before the Hon. Henry Reeder in St. Mary's County in 1778 [Ref: J-1146, K-64].

GREENWELL, James. This name appeared twice as a private, St. Mary's County Militia, 1777 [Ref: M-214, which listed the name as "Jas. Greenwell" and as "Jams. Greenwell"]. Took the Oath of Allegiance before the Hon. Richard Barnes in St. Mary's County in 1778 [Ref: J-1146, K-66].

GREENWELL, Jesse. This name appeared twice as a private, St. Mary's County Militia, 1777 [Ref: M-213, M-214]. One was a private in the 3rd Maryland Line and died of wounds in Feb., 1778 [Ref: SM-113].

GREENWELL, John. (1) Captain, Lower Bn., St. Mary's County, Aug. 26, 1777 through June 22, 1780 [Ref: M-80, C-346, F-201]. (2) This name appeared twice as a private in St. Mary's County Militia in 1777 [Ref: M-211, M-214], and one served as a private (substitute), Maryland Line, Continental Army, until discharged on Dec. 3, 1781 [Ref: D-384, D-408, S-109, H-11]. He saw action at Yorktown and was present at the surrender of Cornwallis [Ref: SM-149]. John Greenwell, Jr. and John Greenwell, Sr. both took the Oath of Allegiance before the Hon. Richard Barnes in St. Mary's County in 1778 [Ref: J-1146, K-66]. One John Greenwell applied for and received pension S31076 on Sep. 11, 1834, aged 74, in Green County, Kentucky, stating he was born on Oct. 2, 1760, in St. Mary's County and had lived in Green County for 32 years and in Kentucky for 36 years. He served in the 3rd Maryland Line in 1781 for a total of seven months and also served as a substitute for George Combs under Col. Barnes. An affidavit was given by his brother Richard Greenwell, aged 67, of Kentucky. It was also noted that John Greenwell was on the East Tennessee Roll of Pensions on Sep. 27, 1834, and was transferred later to Greensburg, Scott County, Kentucky [Ref: W-43, P-1430, MK-60]. A John Greenwell died by Aug., 1790, in St. Mary's County, leaving orphans George and Edmund (both above the age of 14 in 1790), John (above the age of 14 in 1791), and Elizabeth (above the age of 14 in 1794). [Ref: SO-158, SO-161, SO-215. Source S-157 states that John Greenwell was the private and John Greenwell, Jr. was the captain].

GREENWELL, John E. Took the Oath of Allegiance before the Hon. Richard Barnes in St. Mary's County in 1778 [Ref: J-1146, K-66].

GREENWELL, John (of George). Took the Oath of Allegiance before the Hon. Richard Barnes in St. Mary's County in 1778 [Ref: J-1146, K-66]. He died by Feb., 1784, leaving orphan sons Edmund and John [Ref: SO-71, SO-72].

GREENWELL, John (of Ignatius). Elected to serve on a General Committee in St. Mary's County in accordance with the resolves of the Continental Congress in 1775 [Ref: MR-127, S-157].

GREENWELL, John (of James). Private, St. Mary's County Militia, 1777 [Ref: M-211]. Took the Oath of Allegiance before the Hon. Richard Barnes in St. Mary's County in 1778 [Ref: J-1146, K-66].
GREENWELL, Joseph. (1) Private, St. Mary's County Militia, 1777 [Ref: M-214]. Took the Oath of Allegiance before the Hon. Henry Reeder in St. Mary's County in 1778 [Ref: J-1146, K-64]. (2) Private, St. Mary's County Militia, 1777 [Ref: M-214]. Took the Oath of Allegiance before the Hon. Richard Barnes in St. Mary's County in 1778 [Ref: J-1146, K-66].
GREENWELL, Joseph (of Thomas). Private, St. Mary's County Militia, 1777 [Ref: M-211].
GREENWELL, Joshua. Two men with this name took the Oath of Allegiance in St. Mary's County in 1778: one before the Hon. Henry Reeder and one before the Hon. Richard Barnes [Ref: J-1146, K-64, K-66]. The Register of St. Francis Xavier Catholic Church states one Joshua Greenwell and Elizabeth Newton were married in June, 1774 [Ref: SC-35].
GREENWELL, Justinian. Took the Oath of Allegiance before the Hon. Jeremiah Jordan in St. Mary's County in 1778 [Ref: J-1146, K-67].
GREENWELL, Leonard. Took the Oath of Allegiance before the Hon. Henry Reeder in St. Mary's County in 1778 [Ref: J-1146, K-64].
GREENWELL, Monica. See "Ignatius Greenwell" and "James Norris," q.v.
GREENWELL, Nicholas. Private, St. Mary's County Militia, 1777 [Ref: M-214]. Took the Oath of Allegiance before the Hon. Henry Reeder in St. Mary's County in 1778 [Ref: J-1146, K-64].
GREENWELL, Noah. Private, St. Mary's County Militia, 1777 [Ref: M-212].
GREENWELL, Raphael. Private, St. Mary's County Militia, 1777 [Ref: M-213]. Took the Oath of Allegiance before the Hon. Richard Barnes in St. Mary's County in 1778 [Ref: J-1146, K-66]. The Register of St. Francis Xavier Catholic Church states Raphael Greenwell and Cloa Tarlton were married April 10, 1774 [Ref: SC-35].
GREENWELL, Richard. Mariner from St. Mary's County in 1777-1778. He wrote to the Governor on Jan. 8, 1778, regarding the impressment of John Coram [Ref: V-139]. Also see "John Greenwell," q.v.
GREENWELL, Robert. Private, St. Mary's County Militia, 1777 [Ref: M-211]. Private, St. Mary's County, enlisted May 29, 1778, for 9 months [Ref: D-329]. Took the Oath of Allegiance before the Hon. Ignatius Fenwick, Jr. in St. Mary's County in 1778 [Ref: J-1146, K-68]. Second Lieutenant, Lower Bn., May 7, 1781 [Ref: M-80, G-426].
GREENWELL, Stephen. (1) Private, St. Mary's County Militia, 1777 [Ref: M-214]. Took the Oath of Allegiance before the Hon. Henry Reeder in St. Mary's County in 1778 [Ref: J-1146, K-64]. (2) Private, St. Mary's County Militia, 1777 [Ref: M-214]. Took the Oath of Allegiance before the Hon. Richard Barnes in St. Mary's County in 1778 [Ref: J-

1146, K-66]. One enlisted as a private in the Continental Army on May 29, 1778, for 9 months [Ref: D-329]. The Register of St. Andrew's Episcopal Church states that one Stephen Greenwell and Henrietta Wise were married (by license) Feb. 18, 1783 [Ref: MB-385]. See "William Combs," q.v.

GREENWELL, Thomas. (1) Private, St. Mary's County Militia, 1777 [Ref: M-214]. Took the Oath of Allegiance before the Hon. Richard Barnes in St. Mary's County in 1778 [Ref: J-1146, K-66]. (2) Private, St. Mary's County Militia, 1777 [Ref: M-211]. Took the Oath of Allegiance before the Hon. John Ireland in St. Mary's County in 1778 [Ref: J-1146, K-65].

GREENWELL, William. Private, St. Mary's County Militia, 1777 [Ref: M-214]. Took the Oath of Allegiance before the Hon. Henry Reeder in St. Mary's County in 1778 [Ref: J-1146, K-64].

GREENWELL, William (of William). Private, St. Mary's County Militia, 1777 [Ref: M-214]. Took the Oath of Allegiance before the Hon. Henry Reeder in St. Mary's County in 1778 [Ref: J-1146, K-64].

GREEVES, Absalom. See "Absolom Greaves," q.v.

GREEVES, Driver. Private, Capt. Richard Parran's Co., Calvert County Militia, 1778 [Ref: J-1146, M-149]. Took the Oath of Allegiance in Calvert County in 1778 [Ref: L-36]. Gave deposition in 1780 and again in 1781, regarding the status and questionable loyalty of some Calvert Countians [Ref: V-257, V-352].

GREEVES, Robert. (1) Private, Capt. Richard Parran's Co., Calvert County Militia, 1778 [Ref: J-1146, M-149, which listed the name as "Robert Greves"]. Took the Oath of Allegiance in Calvert County in 1778 [Ref: L-36]. (2) Took the Oath of Allegiance before the Hon. Bennett Biscoe in St. Mary's County in 1778 [Ref: J-1146, K-63]. Private, St. Mary's County Militia, 1777 [Ref: M-215, which listed the name as "Robert Grieves"]. See "Robert Graves," q.v.

GRIFFIN, Abraham. Took the Oath of Allegiance before the Hon. Bennett Biscoe in St. Mary's County in 1778 [Ref: J-1146, K-63].

GRIFFIN, Edward. Private, Capt. Frederick Skinner's Co., Calvert County Militia, 1778 [Ref: J-1146, M-150]. Private, Capt. James Patterson's Co., Calvert County Militia, Aug. 10, 1777 [Ref: M-146, which listed the name as "Edward Griffen"].

GRIFFIN, Ignatius. Private, St. Mary's County Militia, 1777 [Ref: M-210]. Private (substitute), Maryland Line, on Aug. 2, 1781; discharged unfit on Oct. 30, 1781 [Ref: D-384, S-157].

GRIFFIN, John. Private, Capt. James Patterson's Co., Calvert County Militia, Aug. 10, 1777 [Ref: M-146, which listed the name as "John Griffen"]. Private, Capt. Frederick Skinner's Co., Calvert County Militia, 1778 [Ref: J-1146, M-150, which listed the name as "John Griffen"]. Took the Oath of Allegiance in Calvert County in 1780 [Ref: Q-111].

GRIFFIN, John Jr. Private, Capt. Frederick Skinner's Co., Calvert County Militia, 1778 [Ref: J-1146, M-150].

GRIFFIN, Samuel. Private, Capt. Richard Lane's Co., Calvert County Militia, 1778 [Ref: J-1146, M-149].

GRIFFIN, Thomas. Elected to serve on a General Committee in St. Mary's County in accordance with the resolves of the Continental Congress in 1775 [Ref: MR-127]. Took the Oath of Allegiance before the Hon. Bennett Biscoe in St. Mary's County in 1778 [Ref: J-1146, K-63]. Private, 3rd Maryland Line, April 17, 1779 [Ref: SM-113, which listed the name as "Tom Griffin"]. Captured off the Capes by the British on June 14, 1782 [Ref: S-157]. The Register of St. Andrew's Episcopal Church states that Thomas Griffin and Elizabeth Jarboe were married (by license) on Jan. 29, 1784 [Ref: MB-385].

GRIFFIN, Thomas Ann. See "Matthias Jones," q.v.

GRIFFIN, William. Private, 3rd Maryland Line, re-enlisted on May 4, 1779; from St. Mary's County [Ref: S-157].

GRIFFITH, Lewis (of John). Private, Capt. Richard Lane's Co., Calvert County Militia, 1778 [Ref: J-1146, M-150].

GRIFFITH, Marshal. Private, Capt. Richard Lane's Co., Calvert County Militia, 1778 [Ref: J-1146, M-150].

GRIFFITH, Samuel. Took the Oath of Allegiance in Calvert County in 1778 [Ref: L-36].

GRIGGS, Sabbaston. Took the Oath of Allegiance before the Hon. Bennett Biscoe in St. Mary's County in 1778 [Ref: J-1146, K-63].

GRIMES, Anne. See "James Barnes," q.v.

GRIMES, John. Private, Calvert County, enlisted by Lt. Frederick Skinner on Aug. 23, 1776 [Ref: D-33].

GRINDALL, Josias. Private, St. Mary's County Militia, 1777 [Ref: M-210].

GRISTY, Clement. Took the Oath of Allegiance in St. Mary's County in 1780 [Ref: Q-111].

GRISTY, Richard. Took the Oath of Allegiance before the Hon. Henry G. Sothoron in St. Mary's County in 1778 [Ref: J-1146, K-69].

GROVER, Anne. See "Nathaniel Baker," q.v.

GROVER, John. Private, Capt. Henry Skinner's Foot Co. of Hunting Hundred, Calvert County, 1777 [Ref: T-1814, O-125].

GROVER, John Jr. Private, Capt. Richard Parran's Co., Calvert County Militia, 1778 [Ref: J-1146, M-149].

GRYAR, Thomas. Private, St. Mary's County Militia, 1777 [Ref: M-213].

GUIBERT, Thomas. Member of the Committee of Correspondence and Safety on Dec. 23, 1774. Captured off the Capes by the British on June 14, 1782 [Ref: S-157].

GUIDER, Elizabeth. See "George Aisquith," q.v.

GUITHER (GUYTHER), George. Private, St. Mary's County Militia, 1777 [Ref: M-214, which listed the name as "George Guyther"]. Took the Oath of Allegiance before the Hon. Vernon Hebb in St. Mary's County in 1778 [Ref: J-1146, K-67]. First Lieutenant, Lower Bn., St. Mary's County, Aug. 26, 1777 [Ref: M-77, C-246, SM-112, which mistakenly listed the name as "George Gaither"]. George Guither or Guyther married Sarah ---- and died testate in June, 1797 [Ref: Y-291, SM-151, SM-152, citing information from Mrs. Charles B. Grace, of Charlotte Hall, Maryland, in 1976]. "George Guyther" was elected to a General Committee in St. Mary's County in accordance with the resolves of the Continental Congress in 1775 [Ref: MR-127].

GUNBY, Ann Maria. See "Bennett Shirley," q.v.

GUNNER, John. Private, Capt. Henry Skinner's Foot Co. of Hunting Hundred, Calvert County, 1777 [Ref: T-1814, O-125].

GUY, George. Paid for making salt in St. Mary's County in 1782 [Ref: S-157].

GUYTHER, Elizabeth. See "John Fenwick," q.v.

GUYTHER, George and Sarah. See "George Guither," q.v.

GWIN, Thomas. Private, Calvert County, enlisted by Lt. Frederick Skinner on Aug. 23, 1776 [Ref: D-33].

GWYNNE, Mary. See "Thomas Bean," q.v.

HACKET, Rodolph. "Rhode Hacket" was a private, St. Mary's County Militia, 1777 [Ref: M-214]. "Rodolph Hacket" took the Oath of Allegiance before the Hon. Richard Barnes in St. Mary's County in 1778 [Ref: J-1146, K-66].

HADEN, George. See "Henry Rigby," q.v.

HAGAR, Millburn. See "Francis Kirby," q.v.

HAGER, Robert. Private, St. Mary's County Militia, 1777 [Ref: M-211, which listed the name as "Robert Hagar"]. Took the Oath of Allegiance before the Hon. Ignatius Fenwick, Jr. in St. Mary's County in 1778 [Ref: J-1146, K-68, which listed the name as "Robert Hagan"].

HAGER, William Jenkins. Private, Capt. Uriah Forrest's Co., Flying Camp, St. Mary's County, July 28, 1776 [Ref: D-30]. Private, St. Mary's County Militia, 1777 [Ref: M-212, which listed the name as "William Hagar"]. Took the Oath of Allegiance before the Hon. Robert Watts in St. Mary's County in 1778 [Ref: J-1146, K-62].

HALKERSTON, John. Second Lieutenant, later First Lieutenant, 1st Independent Maryland Co., Charles and Calvert Counties, 1776 [Ref: D-20].

HALL, Aquila (Acquilla). Private, St. Mary's County Militia, 1777 [Ref: M-213]. Took the Oath of Allegiance before the Hon. Robert Watts in St. Mary's County in 1778 [Ref: J-1146, K-62]. The Register of St. Francis Xavier Catholic Church states that Aquilla Hall (NC) and Mary Davis were married Dec. 22, 1772 [Ref: SC-34, which noted that "NC" meant "non-Catholic"]. Also see "Philip Key," q.v.

HALL, Arthur. (1) Private, St. Mary's County Militia, 1777 [Ref: M-211]. Took the Oath of Allegiance before the Hon. Robert Watts in St. Mary's County in 1778 [Ref: J-1146, K-62]. (2) Private, Calvert County, enlisted by Lt. Nathaniel Wilson on Aug. 31, 1776 [Ref: D-34].

HALL, Basil. Sergeant, St. Mary's County Militia, 1777 [Ref: M-213]. Took the Oath of Allegiance before the Hon. Henry G. Sothoron in St. Mary's County in 1778 [Ref: J-1146, K-69]. Ensign, Upper Bn., Nov. 18, 1779 [Ref: SM-113].

HALL, Benjamin. Took the Oath of Allegiance in Calvert County in 1778 [Ref: L-36].

HALL, Elisha. Private, Capt. Thomas Cleland's Co., Calvert County Militia, 1778 [Ref: J-1146, M-147]. Private, Capt. Charles Williamson's Co., Calvert County Militia, 1778 [Ref: J-1146, M-147]. Took the Oath of Allegiance in Calvert County in 1778 [Ref: L-36].

HALL, Elizabeth. See "Enoch Campbell," q.v.

HALL, Ignatius. Private, St. Mary's County Militia, 1777 [Ref: M-212]. Took the Oath of Allegiance before the Hon. Robert Watts in St. Mary's County in 1778 [Ref: J-1146, K-62].

HALL, John. Private, St. Mary's County Militia, 1777 [Ref: M-213]. Third Mate on the State ship *Defence* in 1777 [Ref: S-158]. Took the Oath of Allegiance before the Hon. Robert Watts in St. Mary's County in 1778 [Ref: J-1146, K-62].

HALL, Joseph. (1) Private, Capt. Thomas Truman Greenfield's Co., Calvert County Militia, 1778 [Ref: J-1146, M-150]. (2) Private, St. Mary's County Militia, 1777 [Ref: M-211]. Took the Oath of Allegiance before the Hon. Richard Barnes in St. Mary's County in 1778 [Ref: J-1146, K-66]. The Register of St. Andrew's Episcopal Church states that Joseph Hall and Mary McGill were married July 2, 1780 [Ref: MB-383]. One "Joseph Hall, physician" moved from St. Clements to Montgomery County, Maryland, in 1801 [Ref: X-86].

HALL, Richard. Private, St. Mary's County, 3rd Maryland Line, enlisted April 21, 1778, for 3 years [Ref: D-329, D-298, SM-113]. Took the Oath of Allegiance before the Hon. Jeremiah Jordan in St. Mary's County in 1778 [Ref: J-1146, K-67].

HALL, Sophia. See "Philip Key," q.v.

HALL, Stephen. Mate on the State ship *Defence* in 1777; from St. Mary's County [Ref: S-158].

HALL, Thomas. (1) Private, St. Mary's County Militia, 1777 [Ref: M-212]. Took the Oath of Allegiance before the Hon. John Ireland in St. Mary's County in 1778 [Ref: J-1146, K-65]. (2) Private, St. Mary's County Militia, 1777 [Ref: M-215]. Took the Oath of Allegiance before the Hon. Bennett Biscoe in St. Mary's County in 1778 [Ref: J-1146, K-63]. Private, St. Mary's County, who served in the Maryland Line until 1781 when discharged [Ref: D-408].

HALL, Thomas Henry. See "Ignatius Taylor," q.v.

HALL, William. (1) Private, Capt. Walter Smith's Co., Calvert County Militia, 1778 [Ref: J-1146, M-148]. Took the Oath of Allegiance in Calvert County in 1778 [Ref: L-36]. (2) Seaman on the State ship *Defence* in May, 1777; from St. Mary's County [Ref: S-158].

HAMILTON, James. Took the Oath of Allegiance before the Hon. John Reeder in St. Mary's County in 1778 [Ref: J-1146, K-69].
HAMILTON, John. See "Alexander Hamilton Smith," q.v. There was also a John Hamilton who served in the Maryland Line until 1781 when discharged [Ref: D-409].
HAMILTON, William. Private, St. Mary's County Militia, 1777 [Ref: M-209]. Took the Oath of Allegiance before the Hon. Henry Tubman in St. Mary's County in 1778 [Ref: J-1146, K-70]. "William Hambleton" took the Oath of Allegiance in St. Mary's County in 1780 [Ref: Q-112].
HAMMERSLY, Janet (Jane). See "Edmund Plowden," q.v.
HAMMERSLY, William. "Mr. Wm. Hamersley" was elected to a General Committee in St. Mary's County in accordance with the resolves of the Continental Congress in 1775 [Ref: MR-126]. Supplied provisions (wheat, mutton, or bacon) to the Army in 1780 [Ref: S-158]. See "Edmund Plowden," q.v.
HAMMETT, Caleb. Private, St. Mary's County Militia, 1777 [Ref: M-212]. Took the Oath of Allegiance before the Hon. Robert Watts in St. Mary's County in 1778 [Ref: J-1146, K-62].
HAMMETT, Cartwright. Private, St. Mary's County Militia, 1777 [Ref: M-212]. Took the Oath of Allegiance before the Hon. Robert Watts in St. Mary's County in 1778 [Ref: J-1146, K-62]. In June, 1796, he bound out his son Robert Hammett (aged 11 in Feb., 1797) to learn to be a bricklayer [Ref: SO-77].
HAMMETT, James M. K. See "Thomas Lynch," q.v.
HAMMETT, John. Took the Oath of Allegiance in St. Mary's County in 1780 [Ref: Q-112].
HAMMETT, John B. See "Richard Hammett," q.v.
HAMMETT, Joseph. Private, St. Mary's County Militia, 1777 [Ref: M-213].
HAMMETT, McKelvie. Private, St. Mary's County Militia, 1777 [Ref: M-212]. Coroner in St. Mary's County in 1777 [Ref: S-158, which listed the name as "Mackelery Hammett"].
HAMMETT, Richard (Jan. 12, 1754 - 1823). Private, St. Mary's County Militia, 1777 [Ref: M-212]. Took the Oath of Allegiance before the Hon. Robert Watts in St. Mary's County in 1778 [Ref: J-1146, K-62]. He married Nancy Biscoe in 1778 and a son John B. Hammett (1803-1874) married Anne B. Wilkinson in 1822 [Ref: Maryland Society, Sons of the American Revolution, Membership Applications No. 3066 and 3146, filed by David Hammett and David Hammett, Jr., approved in 1990 and 1991, respectively, by the National Society, SAR; and, Ref: Y-299, which listed the wife's name as "Nancy Briscoe"].
HAMMETT, Robert. Took the Oath of Allegiance before the Hon. Henry G. Sothoron in St. Mary's County in 1778 [Ref: J-1146, K-69]. Private, St. Mary's County Militia, 1777 [Ref: M-213]. "Robert Hammitt" was

elected to a General Committee in St. Mary's County in accordance with the resolves of the Continental Congress in 1775 [Ref: MR-127].

HAMMETT, William. Private, St. Mary's County Militia, 1777 [Ref: M-214]. Took the Oath of Allegiance before the Hon. Vernon Hebb in St. Mary's County in 1778 [Ref: J-1146, K-67].

HAMMETT, Zachariah. Private, St. Mary's County Militia, 1777 [Ref: M-212]. Took the Oath of Allegiance before the Hon. Henry G. Sothoron in St. Mary's County in 1778 [Ref: J-1146, K-69]. Ensign, Upper Bn., Aug. 26, 1777, and Second Lieutenant, Upper Bn., Nov. 18, 1779 [Ref: S-158, SM-113].

HAMMOND, Acquilla. Private, Capt. Richard Lane's Co., Calvert County Militia, 1778 [Ref: J-1146, M-150].

HAMMOND, William. Private, Capt. Richard Lane's Co., Calvert County Militia, 1778 [Ref: J-1146, M-149]. Took the Oath of Allegiance in Calvert County in 1778 [Ref: L-36].

HANCE, Benjamin. (1) Private, Capt. Frisby Freeland's Co., Calvert County Militia, 1778 [Ref: J-1146, M-148]. (2) Private, Capt. Thomas Cleland's Co., Calvert County Militia, 1778 [Ref: J-1146, M-147]. (3) Private, Capt. Thomas Truman Greenfield's Co., Calvert County Militia, 1778 [Ref: J-1146, M-150]. (4) This name appeared twice on the list of those who took the Oath of Allegiance in Calvert County in 1778 [Ref: L-36]. One Benjamin Hance and Sarah Dare were married on April 2, 1780, by Rev. Francis Lauder, of Christ Church Parish [Ref: K-35]. See "Samuel Hance," q.v.

HANCE, Benjamin (of Samuel). Took the Oath of Allegiance in Calvert County in 1778 [Ref: L-36].

HANCE, Elisha. Private, Capt. Thomas Cleland's Co., Calvert County Militia, 1778 [Ref: J-1146, M-147, which mistakenly listed the name as "Elisha Haner"]. Took the Oath of Allegiance in Calvert County in 1778 [Ref: L-36].

HANCE, John. Private, Capt. Frisby Freeland's Co., Calvert County Militia, 1778 [Ref: J-1146, M-148]. Took the Oath of Allegiance in Calvert County in 1778 [Ref: L-36].

HANCE, Joseph. Private, Capt. Walter Smith's Co., Calvert County Militia, 1778 [Ref: J-1146, M-148]. Took the Oath of Allegiance in Calvert County in 1778 [Ref: L-36].

HANCE, Kinsey. Private, Capt. Frisby Freeland's Co., Calvert County Militia, 1778 [Ref: J-1146, M-148]. Took the Oath of Allegiance in Calvert County in 1778 [Ref: L-36].

HANCE, Margaret. See "Richard Harris," q.v.

HANCE, Mary. See "John Mackall" and "Thomas Mackall" and "Benjamin Mackall IV" and "Thomas Gantt," q.v.

HANCE, Richard. Private, Capt. Thomas Cleland's Co., Calvert County Militia, 1778 [Ref: J-1146, M-147]. Took the Oath of Allegiance in Calvert County in 1778 [Ref: L-36].

HANCE, Samuel. Son of Benjamin Hance (1684-1738) and Mary Hutchins. He was "of age by 1753" and served as Ensign, 15th Bn., Capt. Frisby Freeland's Co., Calvert County Militia, from April 10, 1776 through April 21, 1780. Member of the House of Delegates in 1777 and 1778. Served on a Committee of Observation to watch for British warships in 1780 [Ref: A-320, E-37, J-1146, M-83, M-148, N-78, N-400, N-401]. Took the Oath of Allegiance in Calvert County in 1778 [Ref: L-36, which listed the name twice].

HANCE, Samuel Jr. Private, Capt. Thomas Truman Greenfield's Co., Calvert County Militia, 1778 [Ref: J-1146, M-150]. Took the Oath of Allegiance in Calvert County in 1778 [Ref: L-36]. Samuel Hance, Jr. and Sarah Allnutt were married on Dec. 6, 1778, by Rev. Francis Lauder, of Christ Church Parish [Ref: K-34].

HANCOCK, William. Private, St. Mary's County Militia, 1777 [Ref: M-213]. Took the Oath of Allegiance before the Hon. John Reeder in St. Mary's County in 1778 [Ref: J-1146, K-69].

HANEY, James. Took the Oath of Allegiance before the Hon. Henry Reeder in St. Mary's County in 1778 [Ref: J-1146, K-64].

HANSON, Chloe. See "Barnet White Barber" and "Philip Briscoe," q.v.

HANSON, Edward. Private, Capt. James Patterson's Co., Calvert County Militia, Aug. 10, 1777 [Ref: M-146, which listed the name as "Edward Hansin"].

HANSON, Robert. Took the Oath of Allegiance in Calvert County in 1778 [Ref: L-36].

HARBER, James. Private, St. Mary's County Militia, 1777 [Ref: M-212].

HARBERT, James. See "James Herbert," q.v.

HARDACER, Joseph. Private, Capt. Thomas Truman Greenfield's Co., Calvert County Militia, 1778 [Ref: J-1146, M-150]. Took the Oath of Allegiance in Calvert County in 1778 [Ref: L-36].

HARDEN, Baptist. Private, St. Mary's County Militia, 1777 [Ref: M-212].

HARDEN, John Baptist. Took the Oath of Allegiance before the Hon. John Shanks in St. Mary's County in 1778 [Ref: J-1146, K-70].

HARDESTY, Elisha. Private, Capt. James Grahame's Co., Calvert County Militia, 1778 [Ref: J-1146, M-148]. Private, Capt. James Patterson's Co., Calvert County Militia, Aug. 10, 1777 [Ref: M-146].

HARDESTY, George. Private, Capt. James Patterson's Co., Calvert County Militia, Aug. 10, 1777 [Ref: M-146, which listed the name as "Jorge Hardesty"]. Private, Capt. Frederick Skinner's Co., Calvert County Militia, 1778 [Ref: J-1146, M-150]. Private, Capt. John Mackall's Co., Calvert County Militia, 15th Bn., June 12, 1778 [Ref: M-146].

HARDESTY, Henry. Private, Capt. James Grahame's Co., Calvert County Militia, 1778 [Ref: J-1146, M-148]. Took the Oath of Allegiance in Calvert County in 1778 [Ref: L-36].

HARDESTY, John. (1) Private, Capt. Henry Skinner's Foot Co. of Hunting Hundred, Calvert County, 1777 [Ref: T-1814, O-125]. (2)

Private, St. Mary's County Militia, 1777 [Ref: M-213]. Took the Oath of Allegiance in St. Mary's County in 1780 [Ref: Q-112, which listed the name as "John Hardisley"]. The Register of St. Francis Xavier Catholic Church states one John Hardesty and Catherine Thompson were married July 25, 1775 [Ref: SC-35].

HARDESTY, John Jr. Private, Capt. James Patterson's Co., Calvert County Militia, Aug. 10, 1777 [Ref: M-146].

HARDESTY, Joseph. Private, Capt. Frederick Skinner's Co., Calvert County Militia, 1778 [Ref: J-1146, M-150]. Took the Oath of Allegiance in Calvert County in 1778 [Ref: L-36].

HARDESTY, Joseph Jr. Took the Oath of Allegiance in Calvert County in 1778 [Ref: L-36]. Private, Capt. Frisby Freeland's Co., Calvert County Militia, 1778 [Ref: J-1146, M-148].

HARDESTY, Mary. See "Joseph Hutchins," q.v.

HARDESTY, Richard. Private, Capt. Frisby Freeland's Co., Calvert County Militia, 1778 [Ref: J-1146, M-148]. Took the Oath of Allegiance in Calvert County in 1778 [Ref: L-36].

HARDESTY, Thomas. (1) Private, Calvert County, enlisted by Ensign James Somervill on July 26, 1776 [Ref: D-34]. Private, Capt. John Mackall's Co., Calvert County Militia, 15th Bn., June 12, 1778 [Ref: M-146]. (2) Private, Capt. Thomas Cleland's Co., Calvert County Militia, 1778 [Ref: J-1146, M-147]. (3) Private, Capt. James Grahame's Co., Calvert County Militia, 1778 [Ref: J-1146, M-149]. (4) Private, Capt. James Grahame's Co., Calvert County Militia, 1778 [Ref: J-1146, M-148].

HARDESTY, Thomas Jr. Took the Oath of Allegiance in Calvert County in 1778 [Ref: L-36]. Private, Capt. James Patterson's Co., Calvert County Militia, Aug. 10, 1777 [Ref: M-146].

HARDESTY, Thomas (of John). Private, Capt. James Patterson's Co., Calvert County Militia, Aug. 10, 1777 [Ref: M-146].

HARDESTY, Thomas (of Joseph). Private, Calvert County, enlisted by Capt. John Brooke on July 26, 1776 [Ref: D-33]. Private, Capt. Frederick Skinner's Co., Calvert County Militia, 1778 [Ref: J-1146, M-150, which listed the name as "Thoms. Hardesty son Jos."]. Private, Capt. James Patterson's Co., Calvert County Militia, Aug. 10, 1777 [Ref: M-146].

HARDESTY, William. Private, Capt. Frederick Skinner's Co., Calvert County Militia, 1778 [Ref: J-1146, M-150]. Private, Capt. John Mackall's Co., Calvert County Militia, 15th Bn., June 12, 1778 [Ref: M-146].

HARGIS, Joseph. Private, St. Mary's County Militia, 1777 [Ref: M-213]. Took the Oath of Allegiance before the Hon. John Ireland in St. Mary's County in 1778 [Ref: J-1146, K-65].

HARGNEY, James. Private, Capt. James Patterson's Co., Calvert County Militia, Aug. 10, 1777 [Ref: M-146].

HARLEY, Edward. Private, St. Mary's County, 3rd Maryland Line, enlisted on May 5, 1778, for 3 years [Ref: D-298, D-329]. Private (substitute), St. Mary's County, on Aug. 1, 1781 [Ref: D-384].
HARLEY, Henry. Private, St. Mary's County, enlisted April 25, 1778, for 3 years [Ref: D-329]. Private in Smallwood's Regiment, Maryland Line, reported missing in action on May 18, 1778 [Ref: SM-113].
HARPER, Ignatius. See "John Harper," q.v.
HARPER, James. Took the Oath of Allegiance before the Hon. Henry G. Sothoron in St. Mary's County in 1778 [Ref: J-1146, K-69].
HARPER, John. Private, St. Mary's County Militia, 1777 [Ref: M-211]. Took the Oath of Allegiance before the Hon. Henry Reeder in St. Mary's County in 1778 [Ref: J-1146, K-64]. One John Harper died by Feb., 1797, leaving a son Ignatius, aged 16 [Ref: SO-258].
HARRIS, Benjamin. Private, Capt. Frisby Freeland's Co., Calvert County Militia, 1778 [Ref: J-1146, M-148]. Took the Oath of Allegiance in Calvert County in 1778 [Ref: L-36].
HARRIS, Benjamin Jr. Private, Capt. Frisby Freeland's Co., Calvert County Militia, 1778 [Ref: J-1146, M-148]. Took the Oath of Allegiance in Calvert County in 1778 [Ref: L-36].
HARRIS, Benjamin "the third." Private, Capt. Thomas Cleland's Co., Calvert County Militia, 1778 [Ref: J-1146, M-147].
HARRIS, Joseph. Took the Oath of Allegiance in Calvert County in 1778 [Ref: L-36].
HARRIS, Joseph Jr. Took the Oath of Allegiance in Calvert County in 1778 [Ref: L-36]. Private, Capt. Thomas Cleland's Co., Calvert County Militia, 1778 [Ref: J-1146, M-147].
HARRIS, Josias. Took the Oath of Allegiance before the Hon. Henry Reeder in St. Mary's County in 1778 [Ref: J-1146, K-64].
HARRIS, Richard. Private, Capt. Thomas Cleland's Co., Calvert County Militia, 1778 [Ref: J-1146, M-147]. Took the Oath of Allegiance in Calvert County in 1778 [Ref: L-36]. Richard Harris and Margaret Hance were married on Dec. 19, 1779, by Rev. Francis Lauder, of Christ Church Parish [Ref: MM-79, K-35, which latter source listed her name as "Margaret Hana"].
HARRIS, Samuel. Private, St. Mary's County Militia, 1777 [Ref: M-211]. Took the Oath of Allegiance before the Hon. Richard Barnes in St. Mary's County in 1778 [Ref: J-1146, K-66].
HARRIS, Thomas. Private, St. Mary's County Militia, 1777 [Ref: M-210]. The Register of St. Francis Xavier Catholic Church states that "Thomas Bryan Harris and Mary Mattingly, widow" were married Dec. 1, 1777 [Ref: SC-36].
HARRIS, William. Took the Oath of Allegiance in Calvert County in 1778 [Ref: L-36].
HARRIS, William (of William). Private, Capt. Thomas Cleland's Co., Calvert County Militia, 1778 [Ref: J-1146, M-147, which listed the name

as "William Harris, for Wm."]. "William Harris, Jr." took the Oath of Allegiance in Calvert County in 1778 [Ref: L-36].

HARRIS, William, "the third." Private, Capt. Thomas Cleland's Co., Calvert County Militia, 1778 [Ref: J-1146, M-147]. "William Harris III" took the Oath of Allegiance in Calvert County in 1778 [Ref: L-37].

HARRIS, William, "the fifth." Private, Capt. Thomas Cleland's Co., Calvert County Militia, 1778 [Ref: J-1146, M-147]. "William Harris V" took the Oath of Allegiance in Calvert County in 1778 [Ref: L-37].

HARRISON, Benjamin. (1) Private, St. Mary's County Militia, 1777 [Ref: M-210]. (2) Private, Capt. Charles Williamson's Co., Calvert County Militia, 1778 [Ref: J-1146, M-147].

HARRISON, Elisha. Private, Capt. Charles Williamson's Co., Calvert County Militia, 1778 [Ref: J-1146, M-147].

HARRISON, George. Private, St. Mary's County Militia, 1777 [Ref: M-210]. Private, Capt. Thomas Truman Greenfield's Co., Calvert County Militia, 1778 [Ref: J-1146, M-150]. One George Harrison married Sarah Dent on Dec. 16, 1777, St. Mary's County, by Rev. John Stephen, Rector of All Faith's Parish [Ref: I-536].

HARRISON, Henry. (1) Private, Capt. John Mackall's Co., Calvert County Militia, 15th Bn., June 12, 1778 [Ref: M-146]. (2) Private, Capt. Thomas Cleland's Co., Calvert County Militia, 1778 [Ref: J-1146, M-147]. (3) Private, Capt. Frederick Skinner's Co., Calvert County Militia, 1778 [Ref: J-1146, M-150]. (4) This name appeared twice in the list of those who took the Oath of Allegiance in Calvert County in 1778 [Ref: L-37].

HARRISON, John. Private, St. Mary's County Militia, 1777 [Ref: M-210]. Private, Capt. Thomas Truman Greenfield's Co., Calvert County Militia, 1778 [Ref: J-1146, M-150].

HARRISON, Joseph. Private, St. Mary's County Militia, 1777 [Ref: M-210].

HARRISON, Richard. Private, Capt. Frederick Skinner's Co., Calvert County Militia, 1778 [Ref: J-1146, M-150]. Private, Capt. John Mackall's Co., Calvert County Militia, 15th Bn., June 12, 1778 [Ref: M-146].

HARRISON, Robert. Private, Capt. Thomas Cleland's Co., Calvert County Militia, 1778 [Ref: J-1146, M-147]. One Robert Harrison married Elizabeth Douglas on Feb. 17, 1778, St. Mary's County, by Rev. John Stephen, Rector of All Faith's Parish [Ref: I-536].

HARRISON, Robert Jr. Private, St. Mary's County Militia, 1777 [Ref: M-210].

HARRISON, Samuel. Private, Capt. Thomas Truman Greenfield's Co., Calvert County Militia, 1778 [Ref: J-1146, M-150].

HARRISON, William. Took the Oath of Allegiance in Calvert County in 1778 [Ref: L-37].

HARRISON, William (of Henry). Private, Capt. Thomas Cleland's Co., Calvert County Militia, 1778 [Ref: J-1146, M-147]. Took the Oath of Allegiance in Calvert County in 1778 [Ref: L-37].
HARRISON, William (of James). Private, Capt. Thomas Truman Greenfield's Co., Calvert County Militia, 1778 [Ref: J-1146, M-150].
HARRISON, William (of William). Private, Capt. Thomas Truman Greenfield's Co., Calvert County Militia, 1778 [Ref: J-1146, M-150].
HARTLEY, Catherine. See "Joseph Abell," q.v.
HARVARD, James. See "Joseph Kibley," q.v.
HARVEY, Benjamin. Private, Calvert County, enlisted by Capt. John Brooke on July 26, 1776 [Ref: D-33].
HARVEY, Newman. Took the Oath of Allegiance in Calvert County in 1778 [Ref: L-37].
HARWOOD, Thomas III (c1757-c1805). Resided in both Calvert and Prince George's Counties, alternatively, although his public service was primarily in Calvert County during the end of the war and thereafter. He married Ann Gantt, daughter of George Gantt, by 1779 and had children Thomas and Caroline. Served as a member of the House of Delegates from Calvert County in 1783. Court Justice from 1789-1791 and Judge of the Orphans Court, 1789. He was styled as "Major" at his death [Ref: N-88, N-421, N-422, which latter source noted this: "Identification problem - The distinguishing characteristic that helped to identify the legislator was his signature, "the 3rd." However, in 1792 while serving as a justice of the peace, he signed his name "Jr." [Ref: N-422].
HASKINS, John. See "John Hoskins," q.v.
HASLE, Jeremiah. See "Jeremiah Hazel," q.v.
HASLETINE, Charles. See "Charles Hazeltine," q.v.
HATTER, Lawrence. Took the Oath of Allegiance before the Hon. Jeremiah Jordan in St. Mary's County in 1778 [Ref: J-1146, K-67].
HAYCOCK, Solomon. Private, Maryland Line, 1781, possibly served from St. Mary's County [Ref: D-409].
HAYDEN, Basil. Private, St. Mary's County Militia, 1777 [Ref: M-211]. Supplied provisions (wheat, mutton, or bacon) to the Army in 1780 [Ref: S-158, S-77, which also listed the name as "Bassell Hayden"]. Basil Hayden and William Hayden were among the leaders of the Maryland League of early Catholic settlers who migrated to Nelson County, Kentucky in 1785 [Ref: MK-67].
HAYDEN, Charles. Private, St. Mary's County Militia, 1777 [Ref: M-211]. Supplied corn to the Army in 1780 [Ref: S-158].
HAYDEN, Clement. Took the Oath of Allegiance before the Hon. John Ireland in St. Mary's County in 1778 [Ref: J-1146, K-65]. Supplied provisions (wheat, mutton, or bacon) to the Army in 1780 [Ref: S-77, S-158]. Clement died by April, 1790, leaving orphans Elizabeth and

Clement Hayden, with James Hayden appointed as their guardian [Ref: SO-153, SO-206].

HAYDEN, Elizabeth. See "Clement Hayden," q.v.

HAYDEN, Francis. Took the Oath of Allegiance before the Hon. Henry Reeder in St. Mary's County in 1778 [Ref: J-1146, K-64].

HAYDEN, George. Took the Oath of Allegiance before the Hon. Henry Reeder in St. Mary's County in 1778 [Ref: J-1146, K-64].

HAYDEN, Gerrard. Private, St. Mary's County Militia, 1777 [Ref: M-210].

HAYDEN, James. Private, St. Mary's County Militia, 1777 [Ref: M-210]. Took the Oath of Allegiance before the Hon. Jeremiah Jordan in St. Mary's County in 1778 [Ref: J-1146, K-67].

HAYDEN, William. This name appeared twice as a private, St. Mary's County Militia, 1777 [Ref: M-210, M-212]. One took the Oath of Allegiance before the Hon. John Reeder in St. Mary's County in 1778 [Ref: J-1146, K-69]. One William Hayden died by Jan., 1788 [Ref: SO-118]. See "Basil Hayden," q.v.

HAYDEN, William (of George). Took the Oath of Allegiance before the Hon. John Ireland in St. Mary's County in 1778 [Ref: J-1146, K-65].

HAYS, John Hawkins (Feb. 13, 1759 - Sep. 29, 1838). Private, 3rd Maryland Line, Rawlings Regiment, 1777-1779. Applied for a pension in St. Mary's County on Aug. 14, 1832, stating he was born Feb. 13, 1759 in St. Mary's County, lived in Prince George's County at the time of his enlistment, moved to Virginia after the war, and returned to St. Mary's County after 2 or 3 years. He died there on Sep. 29, 1838, and his widow Teresa applied for and received pension W2544 on Jan. 31, 1853, and bounty land warrant #2433-160-55 on April 3, 1858 [Ref: P-1580, D-128, D-281]. Pension rolls of 1835 lists his age as 74, noting he had been dropped from the rolls under the Act of May 1, 1820 [Ref: U-40]. The Treasurer of Maryland was directed in 1828 to pay John H. Hays, of St. Mary's County, during life, half yearly, half pay of a private, as further remuneration for his services during the Revolutionary War. On March 8, 1850 the Treasurer of Maryland was directed "to pay Theresa Hays, of St. Mary's County, widow of John H. Hays, a private in the war of the American Revolution, half pay of a private for the remainder of her life, commencing Jan. 1, 1850." [Ref: I-352].

HAYWOOD, Thomas. Private, Capt. Uriah Forrest's Co., Flying Camp, St. Mary's County, July 28, 1776 [Ref: D-30]. The Register of St. Andrew's Episcopal Church states that Thomas Haywood and Mary Shermentine were married (by license) Oct. 16, 1781 [Ref: MB-384]. Pensioner in 1818 [Ref: S-158]. On March 10, 1832, Treasurer of Maryland "was directed to pay to Thomas Haywood, of St. Mary's County, a soldier of the Revolutionary War, during life, half pay of a private, for his services during said war." [Ref: I-353].

HAZEL, Bennett. Took the Oath of Allegiance before the Hon. John Reeder in St. Mary's County in 1778 [Ref: J-1146, K-69]. Private, St.

Mary's County Militia, 1777 [Ref: M-213, which listed the name as "Bennit Hazle"].

HAZEL, Edward. Private, St. Mary's County Militia, 1777 [Ref: M-213, which listed the name as "Edward Hazle"]. Took the Oath of Allegiance before the Hon. John Reeder in St. Mary's County in 1778 [Ref: J-1146, K-69]. Private (substitute), St. Mary's County, Continental Army, Aug. 1, 1781 [Ref: D-408, D-384, which listed the name as "Edwd. Hasil"]. Discharged on Dec. 3, 1781 [Ref: S-109, H-11].

HAZEL, Jeremiah. Private, St. Mary's County Militia, 1777 [Ref: M-211, which listed the name as "Jeremiah Hazle"]. Took the Oath of Allegiance before the Hon. Ignatius Fenwick, Jr. in St. Mary's County in 1778 [Ref: J-1146, K-68]. Private, St. Mary's County, drafted July 27, 1781 [Ref: D-384]. Private, Continental Army, 1781 [Ref: D-409, which listed the name as "Jere Hazle"]. "Jeremiah Hazle, farmer" moved from Lower Resurrection to Montgomery County, Maryland, in 1797 [Ref: X-86].

HAZEL, John Jr. Private, St. Mary's County Militia, 1777 [Ref: M-211, which listed the name as "John Hazell, Junr"]. Took the Oath of Allegiance before the Hon. Ignatius Fenwick, Jr. in St. Mary's County in 1778 [Ref: J-1146, K-68].

HAZELTINE (HASLETINE), Charles. Private, St. Mary's County Militia, 1777 [Ref: M-213, which listed the name as "Charles Hazeldine"]. One "Charles Hasletine" died by April, 1779, and Charles Hasletine was granted guardianship of his orphan son James. Another Charles Hasletine died by Feb., 1787, leaving orphans Elizabeth Briscoe Hasletine and Charles Hasletine, with Chloe Hasletine as their guardian. Chloe married William Compton by 1789 [Ref: SO-110, SO-140, SO-246].

HAZELTINE, Chloe and Elizabeth. See "Charles Hazeltine," q.v.

HAZELTINE, John. Private, St. Mary's County Militia, 1777 [Ref: M-211].

HEARD, Ann. See "Joseph Williams," q.v.

HEARD, Cuthbert. Took the Oath of Allegiance before the Hon. Henry G. Sothoron in St. Mary's County in 1778 [Ref: J-1146, K-69].

HEARD, Edmund. Private, St. Mary's County Militia, 1777 [Ref: M-211]. See "Matthew Heard," q.v.

HEARD, Ignatius. (1) Private, St. Mary's County Militia, 1777 [Ref: M-212]. Took the Oath of Allegiance before the Hon. Henry Reeder in St. Mary's County in 1778 [Ref: J-1146, K-64]. (2) Private, St. Mary's County Militia, 1777 [Ref: M-211]. Took the Oath of Allegiance before the Hon. Jeremiah Jordan in St. Mary's County in 1778 [Ref: J-1146, K-67]. One Ignatius Heard died on Feb. 3, 1832, aged 73 [Ref: R-398].

HEARD, James. This name appeared twice as a private, St. Mary's County Militia, 1777 [Ref: M-210, M-211]. One took the Oath of Allegiance before the Hon. Jeremiah Jordan in St. Mary's County in 1778 [Ref: J-1146, K-67]. See "Joseph Williams," q.v.

HEARD, James (of William). Took the Oath of Allegiance before the Hon. Ignatius Fenwick, Jr. in St. Mary's County in 1778 [Ref: J-1146, K-68].
HEARD, Jane. See "Henry Spalding, Jr.," q.v.
HEARD, John. This name appeared twice as a private, St. Mary's County Militia, 1777 [Ref: M-212]. One took the Oath of Allegiance before the Hon. John Ireland in St. Mary's County in 1778 [Ref: J-1146, K-65]. Also see "Jonathan Heard," q.v.
HEARD, John Basil. Took the Oath of Allegiance before the Hon. Henry Reeder in St. Mary's County in 1778 [Ref: J-1146, K-64].
HEARD, John (of Mark). Private, St. Mary's County Militia, 1777 [Ref: M-214]. Took the Oath of Allegiance before the Hon. Robert Watts in St. Mary's County in 1778 [Ref: J-1146, K-62].
HEARD, Jonathan. Ensign, Lower Bn., St. Mary's County, June 22, 1780 [Ref: M-86, F-201, S-158, which latter source listed the name as "Jno. Heard"].
HEARD, Luke. Took the Oath of Allegiance before the Hon. Henry Reeder in St. Mary's County in 1778 [Ref: J-1146, K-64].
HEARD, Matthew. Private, St. Mary's County Militia, 1777 [Ref: M-214]. Took the Oath of Allegiance before the Hon. John Ireland in St. Mary's County in 1778 [Ref: J-1146, K-65]. One Matthew Heard died by Feb., 1798, leaving orphan sons Edmund (aged 14 on March 25, 1795), Walter (above the age of 14 in 1798), and Matthew (aged 16 on Oct. 7, 1799). [Ref: SO-225, SO-267, SO-282].
HEARD, Ralph. Private, St. Mary's County Militia, 1777 [Ref: M-214].
HEARD, Richard. This name appeared twice as a private, St. Mary's County Militia, 1777 [Ref: M-212, M-214].
HEARD, Walter. See "Matthew Heard," q.v.
HEARD, William. Private, St. Mary's County Militia, 1777 [Ref: M-211]. Two men with this name took the Oath of Allegiance in 1778 in St. Mary's County: one before the Hon. John Ireland and one before the Hon. Ignatius Fenwick, Jr. [Ref: J-1146, K-65, K-68]. The Register of St. Francis Xavier Catholic Church states that one William Heard and Susan Abell were married Nov. 27, 1776 [Ref: SC-35].
HEARD, William Jr. Took the Oath of Allegiance before the Hon. John Ireland in St. Mary's County in 1778 [Ref: J-1146, K-65].
HEATH, James. Private, St. Mary's County Militia, 1777 [Ref: M-214, which listed the name as "James Haith"]. Took the Oath of Allegiance before the Hon. Bennett Biscoe in St. Mary's County in 1778 [Ref: J-1146, K-63].
HEATHMAN, Thomas. Private, Capt. Charles Williamson's Co., Calvert County Militia, 1778 [Ref: J-1146, M-147].
HEBB, Anna. See "Vernon Hebb," q.v.
HEBB, Caleb. Paid for making salt in St. Mary's County in 1782 [Ref: S-158].
HEBB, Elizabeth. See "William Somerville," q.v.

HEBB, Jesse. Sergeant, 1st Maryland Line, enlisted March 8, 1777 and discharged July 10, 1777 [Ref: S-117, S-158]. Took the Oath of Allegiance before the Hon. John Shanks in St. Mary's County in 1778 [Ref: J-1146, K-70]. One Jesse Hebb died intestate by Aug., 1791 [Ref: SO-169].

HEBB, John. Took the Oath of Allegiance before the Hon. Vernon Hebb in St. Mary's County in 1778 [Ref: J-1146, K-67]. One John Hebb died intestate by April, 1791 [Ref: SO-166].

HEBB, Joseph (c1745-1782). Private, St. Mary's County Militia, 1777 [Ref: M-214]. Took the Oath of Allegiance before the Hon. Vernon Hebb in St. Mary's County in 1778 [Ref: J-1146, K-67]. He married Mary Cole [Ref: Y-319].

HEBB, Joshua. Took the Oath of Allegiance in St. Mary's County in 1780 [Ref: Q-112]. Private, St. Mary's County, who was discharged some time after Aug. 4, 1781 [Ref: V-420].

HEBB, Thomas. Private, St. Mary's County Militia, 1777 [Ref: M-214]. Took the Oath of Allegiance before the Hon. Vernon Hebb in St. Mary's County in 1778 [Ref: J-1146, K-67]. One Thomas Hebb was buried in St. Mary's County on Jan. 17, 1799 [Ref: R-399].

HEBB, Vernon (1742 - Aug., 1796). Elected to serve on a General Committee in St. Mary's County in accordance with the resolves of the Continental Congress in 1775 [Ref: MR-127]. Capt. Vernon Hebb served on the Committee of Observation in 1776 [Ref: S-16, B-100]. Lieutenant Colonel, Lower Bn., St. Mary's County Militia, on Aug. 26, 1777 [Ref: M-86, C-346, V-145]. He served as a justice who administered the Oath of Allegiance in St. Mary's County in 1778 [Ref: J-1146, K-67]. Vernon Hebb married Ann (Anna) Hopewell [Ref: N-758, Y-319]. He died intestate by Aug., 1796, and Anna Hebb and William Hebb were administrators of his estate [Ref: SO-246]. Vernon Hebb, son of William and Ann, is buried in a private cemetery at Porto Bello in Drayden [Ref: S-129]. See "William Somerville," q.v.

HEBB, William. Private, Capt. Uriah Forrest's Co., Flying Camp, St. Mary's County, July 28, 1776 [Ref: D-30, SM-113]. Took the Oath of Allegiance before the Hon. Vernon Hebb in St. Mary's County in 1778 [Ref: J-1146, K-67]. One William Hebb died testate by Aug., 1789 [Ref: SO-141, SO-144, SO-145]. See "Vernon Hebb," q.v.

HEBB, William Jr. Private, St. Mary's County Militia, 1777 [Ref: M-214]. "William Hebb, Jr., elite" moved from St. George's to Prince George's County, Maryland, in 1811 [Ref: X-86].

HEIGHE, James. Son of Capt. James Heighe (died 1757) and Betty Holdsworth (born 1715). He married Elizabeth Mackall (born 1743). [Ref: N-430]. First Lieutenant, 15th Bn., Calvert County, April 10, 1776 through April 16, 1778 [Ref: M-86, A-320, E-37]. Took the Oath of Allegiance in Calvert County in 1778 [Ref: L-37].

HELLEN (HILLEN), Basil. Drummer, Calvert County, enlisted by Capt. John Brooke on July 25, 1776 [Ref: D-33].
HELLEN (HILLEN), Benjamin. Private, Capt. Richard Parran's Co., Calvert County Militia, 1778 [Ref: J-1146, M-149]. Took the Oath of Allegiance in Calvert County in 1778 [Ref: L-37, which listed the name as "Benjamin Hillen"].
HELLEN (HILLEN), David. This name appeared twice on the list of those who took the Oath of Allegiance in Calvert County in 1778, one as "David Hillen" and the other as "David Hellen" [Ref: L-37].
HELLEN (HILLEN), Dawkins. Private, Capt. Walter Smith's Co., Calvert County Militia, 1778 [Ref: J-1146, M-148]. Took the Oath of Allegiance in Calvert County in 1778 [Ref: L-37, which listed the name as "Dawkins Hillen"].
HELLEN (HILLEN), Edmund. Private, Capt. Walter Smith's Co., Calvert County Militia, 1778 [Ref: J-1146, M-148]. Took the Oath of Allegiance in Calvert County in 1778 [Ref: L-37, which listed the name as "Edmund Hillen"].
HELLEN (HILLEN), Jacob. Took the Oath of Allegiance in Calvert County in 1778 [Ref: L-37, which listed the name as "Jacob Hillen"].
HELLEN (HILLEN), James. Private, Calvert County, enlisted by Capt. John Brooke on July 26, 1776 [Ref: D-33]. Private, Capt. Benjamin Bond's Co., Calvert County Militia, 1778 [Ref: J-1146, M-149]. The Christ Church Register in Calvert County records the birth of "James Hellen," son of Peter Hellen and Penelope Pattison, on Dec. 24, 1747 [Ref: O-15]. "James Hillen, Jr." and "James Hillen, Sr." both took the Oath of Allegiance in Calvert County in 1778 [Ref: L-37]. "James Hillen" and Lydia Blackburn were married on Jan. 5, 1778, by Rev. Francis Lauder, of Christ Church Parish [Ref: K-33].
HELLEN, Jane. See "Alexander Ogg," q.v.
HELLEN, Mary. See "Abraham Hooper," q.v.
HELLEN (HILLEN), Nathan. Took the Oath of Allegiance in Calvert County in 1778 [Ref: L-37, which listed the name as "Nathan Hillen"].
HELLEN (HILLEN), Nathaniel. Took the Oath of Allegiance in Calvert County in 1778 [Ref: L-37, which listed the name as "Nathaniel Hillen"].
HELLEN, Peter Jr. Private, Capt. Walter Smith's Co., Calvert County Militia, 1778 [Ref: J-1146, M-148]. Took the Oath of Allegiance in Calvert County in 1778 [Ref: L-37]. The Christ Church Register in Calvert County records the birth of Peter Hellen, son of Peter Hellen and Penelope Pattison, on March 28, 1752 [Ref: O-15].
HELLEN, Richard. Took the Oath of Allegiance in Calvert County in 1778 [Ref: L-37].
HELLEN, Richard Jr. Took the Oath of Allegiance in Calvert County in 1778 [Ref: L-37].
HELLEN, Scarth. Private, Capt. Richard Parran's Co., Calvert County Militia, 1778 [Ref: J-1146, M-149].

HELLEN (HILLEN), William. "William Hillen" took the Oath of Allegiance in Calvert County in 1778 [Ref: L-37]. The Christ Church Register in Calvert County records the birth of "William Hellen," son of Peter Hellen and Penelope Pattison, on Nov. 20, 1754 [Ref: O-15]. "William Hillen" and Dorcas Johnson were married on Feb. 4, 1779, by Rev. Francis Lauder, of Christ Church Parish [Ref: K-35].

HELLEN, William Allnutt. Took the Oath of Allegiance in Calvert County in 1778 [Ref: L-37]. Private, Capt. Walter Smith's Co., Calvert County Militia, 1778 [Ref: J-1146, M-148, which listed the name as "William A. Hellen"].

HEMINGWAY, James. Private, Capt. Frederick Skinner's Co., Calvert County Militia, 1778 [Ref: J-1146, M-150].

HEMSWORTH, Hugh. Private, Capt. James Patterson's Co., Calvert County Militia, Aug. 10, 1777 [Ref: M-146]. Took the Oath of Allegiance in Calvert County in 1778 [Ref: L-37]. Private, Capt. Frederick Skinner's Co., Calvert County Militia, 1778 [Ref: J-1146, M-150].

HENDLEY, James. Private, Capt. Richard Parran's Co., Calvert County Militia, 1778 [Ref: J-1146, M-149]. Took the Oath of Allegiance in Calvert County in 1780 [Ref: Q-112, which listed the name as "James Henly"].

HENDLEY, John. This name appeared twice as a private, St. Mary's County Militia, 1777 [Ref: M-211, M-214]. One "John Hendly" died testate in 1797 [Ref: SO-264].

HENDLEY, Mary. See "Walter Smith," q.v.

HENDRY, William. Private, Capt. Uriah Forrest's Co., Flying Camp, St. Mary's County, July 28, 1776 [Ref: D-30, SM-113].

HENNING, Anne. See "John Bean," q.v.

HENNING, Bennett. Private, St. Mary's County Militia, 1777 [Ref: M-215]. Took the Oath of Allegiance in St. Mary's County in 1780 [Ref: Q-112]. Property of "Bennett Henny" was destroyed by the British in 1781 [Ref: S-158].

HENNING, Jeremiah. Took the Oath of Allegiance in St. Mary's County in 1780 [Ref: Q-112].

HENNING, John. Private and Drummer & Fifer, St. Mary's County, 2nd Maryland Line, 1779-1781 [Ref: D-118, D-395, D-541, which listed the name as "John Hannon"]. The Register of St. Andrew's Episcopal Church states that "John Henning" and Mary Abell were married (by license) Sep. 5, 1781 [Ref: MB-384].

HENNING, Stephen. Private, St. Mary's County Militia, 1777 [Ref: M-214].

HENRY, Caleb. Property destroyed by the British in St. Mary's County in 1781 [Ref: S-158].

HENRY, Elias. Private, St. Mary's County Militia, 1777 [Ref: M-215, which listed the name as "Elias Henny"]. Private, 3rd Maryland Line, Capt. Armstrong's Co., enlisted on April 4 or May 4, 1778, for 3 years

[Ref: D-299, D-329]. Took the Oath of Allegiance before the Hon. Bennett Biscoe in St. Mary's County in 1778 [Ref: J-1146, K-63]. Sergeant when discharged on Oct. 1, 1780, and re-enlisted on Dec. 21, 1781 [Ref: S-158].

HENRY, Elizabeth. See "Basil Booth," q.v.

HENRY, Martin. Private, St. Mary's County Militia, 1777 [Ref: M-210]. "Martin Henry, farmer" moved to Berkley County, Virginia, in 1793 [Ref: X-86].

HENTON, Thomas Jr. Private, Capt. Charles Williamson's Co., Calvert County Militia, 1778 [Ref: J-1146, M-147].

HERBERT, Barbara. Loaned money in St. Mary's County for the war effort in 1781 [Ref: SM-187]. Barbara Herbert was administratrix of Michael Herbert in 1778, and she died intestate by Oct., 1793 [Ref: SO-15, SO-200]. Property of "Barbary Herbert" was destroyed by the British in 1781 [Ref: S-158].

HERBERT, Charles and Eleanor. See "Jeremiah Herbert," q.v.

HERBERT, Elijah. Took the Oath of Allegiance in St. Mary's County in 1780 [Ref: Q-112].

HERBERT, Elisha. Private, St. Mary's County Militia, 1777 [Ref: M-213, which listed the name as "Elisha Harbert"].

HERBERT, Elizabeth and F. K. See "Jeremiah Herbert," q.v.

HERBERT, Francis. Seaman from St. Mary's County who served aboard the State ship *Defence* in 1776; Boatswain's Mate in 1777 [Ref: S-25, S-158, D-606]. Also see "Jeremiah Herbert," q.v.

HERBERT, Ignatius. Took the Oath of Allegiance before the Hon. Bennett Biscoe in St. Mary's County in 1778 [Ref: J-1146, K-63, which listed the name as "Ignatius Harbert"].

HERBERT, James. "James Harbert" was a private in the St. Mary's County Militia, 1777 [Ref: M-210]. "James Herbert" married Mary Marshall on Jan. 2, 1778, by Rev. John Stephen, Rector of All Faith's Parish [Ref: I-536]. Also see "Jeremiah Herbert," q.v.

HERBERT, Jeremiah (Jan. 26, 1758/63 - July 25, 1833). Private, St. Mary's County, drafted on July 27, 1781 [Ref: D-384]. Private, Continental Army, 1781 [Ref: D-409, which listed the name as "Jere Hubbard, or Herbert"]. Applied for pension on Jan. 28, 1833, in Washington County, Kentucky, aged 70, and died on July 25, 1833. His widow Mary (born Jan. 13, 1766) applied for and received pension W9061 on March 25, 1839, stating they had married in 1786 and had these children: Francis (born Feb. 22, 1788); Rebecca (born March 13, 1790); Elizabeth (born Dec. 21, 1791 or 1792); Eleanor (born Feb. 22, 1794); John T. (born March 17, 1796 or Sep. 17, 1796); James R. (born June 7, 1800); F. K. (born Feb. 14, 1802); Charles (born Jan. 20, 1804); and, Mary Ann (born Dec. 28, 1807). [Ref: P-1610, W-56, MK-70].

HERBERT, Jesse. Private, Capt. Uriah Forrest's Co., Flying Camp, St. Mary's County, July 28, 1776 [Ref: D-30, SM-113].

HERBERT, John. Private, St. Mary's County Militia, 1777 [Ref: M-213, which listed the name as "John Harbert"].
HERBERT, John T. See "Jeremiah Herbert," q.v.
HERBERT, Mary. Loaned money in St. Mary's County for the war effort in 1781 [Ref: SM-187]. Property destroyed by the British in 1781 [Ref: S-158]. Also see "Jeremiah Herbert," q.v.
HERBERT, Michael. See "Barbara Herbert," q.v.
HERBERT, Rebecca. See "Jeremiah Herbert," q.v.
HERBERT, Thomas. Marine on the State ship *Defence* from Jan. 15, 1777 to Nov. 15, 1777 [Ref: D-657, which listed the name as "Thomas Harbest or Harbert"].
HERBERT, William. Private, St. Mary's County Militia, 1777 [Ref: M-213]. Took the Oath of Allegiance before the Hon. Bennett Biscoe in St. Mary's County in 1778 [Ref: J-1146, K-63]. "William Harbert" was a "seaman" aboard the State ship *Defence* in 1776 and a "sailor" in 1777 [Ref: S-25, D-606, D-656]. "William Herbert" was an ensign in the 21st Bn., St. Mary's County Militia, on April 16, 1778 [Ref: M-87, E-37]. The Register of St. Inigoes Catholic Church states that a William Herbert and Anne Milbourne were married on Jan. 10, 1768 [Ref: SC-33].
HERMANS, Mary Sprigg. See "Thomas Gantt, Jr.," q.v.
HIATT, Shadrach. Private, Maryland Line. Applied for and received pension S13361 on Nov. 8, 1832, in Montgomery County, Kentucky, stating he was born on Aug. 15, 1749, near Old Town in St. Mary's County and lived in the Turkey Foot Settlement in the Allegheny Mountains in Maryland at the time of his enlistment. About 1802 he moved to Kentucky for 5 years, then to Indiana for a few years, and then to Montgomery County, Kentucky in 1825 [Ref: P-1620, W-58, MK-70]. "Soldier's wife Phebe signed power of attorney on 4 Sep 1811 Mar 1835 *[sic]* in Montgomery County, Kentucky" [Ref: P-1620].
HICKMAN, Nathaniel. Private, St. Mary's County Militia, 1777 [Ref: M-215]. Took the Oath of Allegiance before the Hon. Bennett Biscoe in St. Mary's County in 1778 [Ref: J-1146, K-63].
HICKS, George. Took the Oath of Allegiance in St. Mary's County in 1780 [Ref: Q-113]. One George Hicks died intestate by Oct., 1785 [Ref: SO-84, SO-210].
HIGDON, John. Took the Oath of Allegiance before the Hon. Jeremiah Jordan in St. Mary's County in 1778 [Ref: J-1146, K-67].
HIGGINS, Samuel. Private, St. Mary's County Militia, 1777 [Ref: M-215].
HIGGS, Samuel. Private, St. Mary's County Militia, 1777 [Ref: M-210].
HIGHFIELD, Jonathan. Private, St. Mary's County Militia, 1777 [Ref: M-210].
HIGHFIELD, Leonard. Private, St. Mary's County Militia, 1777 [Ref: M-210]. "Leonard Highfield, farmer" moved from St. Clements to Pendleton County, Kentucky, in 1796 [Ref: X-86].
HILL, Aloysia. See "Ignatius Clarke," q.v.

HILL, Ann. See "Richard Hill," q.v.
HILL, Edmund. Private, St. Mary's County, enlisted May 29, 1778, for 9 months, Continental Army [Ref: D-329, SM-113].
HILL, Edward. Private, St. Mary's County Militia, 1777 [Ref: M-213].
HILL, Ester. See "David Weems," q.v.
HILL, Ignatius. Private, St. Mary's County Militia, 1777 [Ref: M-212]. Took the Oath of Allegiance in St. Mary's County in 1780 [Ref: Q-113].
HILL, John. Private, St. Mary's County Militia, 1777 [Ref: M-213]. Paid for making salt in 1782 [Ref: S-158].
HILL, John Baptist. Private, St. Mary's County Militia, 1777 [Ref: M-215]. Took the Oath of Allegiance before the Hon. Robert Watts in St. Mary's County in 1778 [Ref: J-1146, K-62].
HILL, Joseph. Private, St. Mary's County Militia, 1777 [Ref: M-212].
HILL, Mary. See "Charles Williams," q.v.
HILL, Richard. Corporal, 2nd Maryland Line, 1777, who served until discharged on Jan. 10, 1780 [Ref: D-119]. On Feb. 10, 1832, the "register of land office issued to Lydia Brown and Ann Hill, of St. Mary's County, legal representatives of Richard Hill, a soldier of the Revolutionary War, a common warrant for 50 acres vacant land in Allegany County and a patent upon survey, without compensation money." [Ref: I-354]. Richard Hill married Sarah King on Jan. 7, 1783, in St. Mary's County, by Rev. John Stephen, Rector of All Faith's Parish [Ref: I-536]. See "Barton King," q.v.
HILL, Thomas. See "Ignatius Clarke," q.v.
HILL, William. Private, St. Mary's County Militia, 1777 [Ref: M-209]. Took the Oath of Allegiance in St. Mary's County in 1780 [Ref: Q-113].
HILL, Zachariah. Private, St. Mary's County Militia, 1777 [Ref: M-212]. Took the Oath of Allegiance in St. Mary's County in 1780 [Ref: Q-113].
HILL, Zachariah Jr. Private, St. Mary's County Militia, 1777 [Ref: M-213, which listed the name as "Zacharia Hills Jun."]. Took the Oath of Allegiance before the Hon. Henry G. Sothoron in St. Mary's County in 1778 [Ref: J-1146, K-69].
HILLEN, Dorcas. See "Benjamin Parran," q.v.
HILLEN, Elizabeth. See "Thomas Hutchins," q.v.
HILLEN, James. See "James Hellen," q.v.
HILLEN, Mary. See "George Young," q.v.
HILLEN, William. See "William Hellen," q.v.
HILLHOUSE, William. Took the Oath of Allegiance in Calvert County in 1778 [Ref: L-37].
HILTON, Francis. Private, St. Mary's County Militia, 1777 [Ref: M-212]. Two men with this name took the Oath of Allegiance in 1778: one before the Hon. Robert Watts and one before the Hon. John Shanks [Ref: J-1146, K-62, K-70].

HILTON, John. Private, St. Mary's County Militia, 1777 [Ref: M-212]. Took the Oath of Allegiance before the Hon. John Shanks in St. Mary's County in 1778 [Ref: J-1146, K-70].
HILTON, Leonard. Private, St. Mary's County Militia, 1777 [Ref: M-210].
HILTON, Matthew. Took the Oath of Allegiance in St. Mary's County in 1780 [Ref: Q-113].
HILTON, Stephen. Private, St. Mary's County Militia, 1777 [Ref: M-212].
HILTON, Thomas. Private, St. Mary's County Militia, 1777 [Ref: M-214]. Took the Oath of Allegiance in St. Mary's County in 1780 [Ref: Q-113].
HILTON, William. Private, St. Mary's County Militia, 1777 [Ref: M-215]. Took the Oath of Allegiance before the Hon. Robert Watts in St. Mary's County in 1778 [Ref: J-1146, K-62].
HILTON, William Jr. Took the Oath of Allegiance in St. Mary's County in 1780 [Ref: Q-112].
HINDMORE, Richard. Private, Capt. Uriah Forrest's Co., Flying Camp, St. Mary's County, July 28, 1776 [Ref: D-30]. Private, 3rd Maryland Line, died Feb. 11, 1777 [Ref: SM-113, R-402, D-281].
HINNEN (HENNEN), Caleb. Took the Oath of Allegiance before the Hon. Bennett Biscoe in St. Mary's County in 1778 [Ref: J-1146, K-63].
HINNEN (HENNEN), Judiah. Took the Oath of Allegiance before the Hon. Bennett Biscoe in St. Mary's County in 1778 [Ref: J-1146, K-63].
HINNEN (HENNEN), Nathan. Took the Oath of Allegiance before the Hon. Bennett Biscoe in St. Mary's County in 1778 [Ref: J-1146, K-63].
HINNEN (HENNEN), Thomas A. Took the Oath of Allegiance before the Hon. Bennett Biscoe in St. Mary's County in 1778 [Ref: J-1146, K-63].
HINTON, Galloway. Took the Oath of Allegiance in Calvert County in 1778 [Ref: L-37].
HINTON, Josias. Took the Oath of Allegiance in Calvert County in 1778 [Ref: L-37].
HINTON, Richard. This name appeared twice as a private, Capt. James Grahame's Co., Calvert County Militia, 1778 [Ref: J-1146, M-148, M-149]. One took the Oath of Allegiance in Calvert County in 1778 [Ref: L-37].
HINTON, Thomas. Private, Capt. Charles Williamson's Co., Calvert County Militia, 1778 [Ref: J-1146, M-147].
HINTON, Thomas Jr. Took the Oath of Allegiance in Calvert County in 1778 [Ref: L-37].
HINTON, Thomas Sr. Took the Oath of Allegiance in Calvert County in 1778 [Ref: L-37].
HOBB, Thomas. Paid for services (unspecified) to the State of Maryland in St. Mary's County in 1776 [Ref: S-159].
HOGAN, Elizabeth. See "Henry Carter," q.v.
HOLDSWORTH, Ann. See "Thomas Mackall," q.v.
HOLDSWORTH, Betty. See "James Heighe," q.v.
HOLLADY, Ephim. Private, St. Mary's County Militia, 1777 [Ref: M-215].

HOLLAND, Frances. See "Edward Reynolds" and "Thomas Reynolds," q.v.
HOLLAND, John. Private, Capt. Uriah Forrest's Co., Flying Camp, St. Mary's County, July 28, 1776 [Ref: D-30, SM-113].
HOLLAND, Thomas. Took the Oath of Allegiance in Calvert County in 1778 [Ref: L-37].
HOLLANDSHEAD, Francis. Private, Capt. Thomas Cleland's Co., Calvert County Militia, 1778 [Ref: J-1146, M-147]. Took the Oath of Allegiance in Calvert County in 1778 [Ref: L-37].
HOLLANDSHEAD, John H. Private, Capt. Edward Wood's Co., Calvert County Militia, 1778 [Ref: J-1146, M-147].
HOLLANDSHEAD, Mary. See "James Scarf (Sacrfe)," q.v.
HOLLANDSHEAD, Richard. Private, Capt. James Patterson's Co., Calvert County Militia, Aug. 10, 1777 [Ref: M-146]. Private, Capt. John Mackall's Co., Calvert County Militia, 15th Bn., June 12, 1778 [Ref: M-146].
HOLLANDSHEAD, Thomas. Took the Oath of Allegiance in Calvert County in 1778 [Ref: L-37].
HOLLANDSHEAD, William. Private, Capt. Thomas Cleland's Co., Calvert County Militia, 1778 [Ref: J-1146, M-147].
HOLLYDAY, Ann. See "Isaac Gardiner," q.v.
HOLLYDAY, Elizabeth. See "Isaac Hooper," q.v.
HOLMES, John. Private, St. Mary's County, 3rd Maryland Line, enlisted on April 30, 1778, for 3 years; missing after the Battle of Camden on Aug. 16, 1780; discharged on April 30, 1781 [Ref: D-298, D-329, S-159].
HOLT, Benjamin. Private, Capt. Frisby Freeland's Co., Calvert County Militia, 1778 [Ref: J-1146, M-148]. Took the Oath of Allegiance in Calvert County in 1778 [Ref: L-37].
HOLT, Francis. Private, Capt. Thomas Cleland's Co., Calvert County Militia, 1778 [Ref: J-1146, M-147]. Took the Oath of Allegiance in Calvert County in 1778 [Ref: L-37].
HOLT, Philip. Private, Capt. Thomas Truman Greenfield's Co., Calvert County Militia, 1778 [Ref: J-1146, M-150].
HOLT, William. Private, St. Mary's County, enlisted April 23, 1778, for 3 years, Smallwood's Regiment, in the Maryland Line; discharged Oct. 14, 1778 [Ref: D-329, S-159].
HOLTON, Catharine. See "William Fenwick," q.v.
HOLTON, William (1750 - April 11, 1812). Private, St. Mary's County Militia, 1777 [Ref: M-215]. Ensign, 21st Bn., April 16, 1778 [Ref: M-88, E-37]. The Register of St. Andrew's Episcopal Church states that William Holton and Elizabeth Craghill were married Dec. 31, 1779 [Ref: MB-383]. "William Holton, Esq." is buried near St. Nicholas Catholic Church in St. Mary's County [Ref: HG-34].
HONE (HON), Henry. Took the Oath of Allegiance before the Hon. John Reeder in St. Mary's County in 1778 [Ref: J-1146, K-69].

HOOKER, Robert Deakins. Took the Oath of Allegiance in Calvert County in 1778 [Ref: L-37].

HOOPER, Abraham. Private, Capt. Walter Smith's Co., Calvert County Militia, 1778 [Ref: J-1146, M-148]. Took the Oath of Allegiance in Calvert County in 1778 [Ref: L-37]. The Christ Church Register in Calvert County records the birth of the children of Abraham Hooper and Mary Hellen (married Jan. 8, 1764) as follows: Jacob (born Sep. 17, 1764); Abraham (born Nov. 6, 1766); Isaac (born June 19, 1769); and, Elizabeth (born Aug. 9, 1773). [Ref: O-16]. Also, Abraham Hooper, son of Jacob and Betty Hooper, was born on Oct. 4, 1742 [Ref: O-17].

HOOPER, Anne and Benjamin. See "Isaac Hooper," q.v.

HOOPER, Elizabeth. See "Abraham Hooper" and "Isaac Hooper," q.v.

HOOPER, Isaac. Private, Capt. Walter Smith's Co., Calvert County Militia, 1778 [Ref: J-1146, M-148]. Took the Oath of Allegiance in Calvert County in 1778 [Ref: L-37]. The Christ Church Register in Calvert County records the birth of the children of Isaac Hooper and Elizabeth Hollyday, who were married on Nov. 10, 1770, as follows: Jane (born Jan. 29, 1772); Priscilla (born Aug. 23, 1774); John (born Jan. 23, 1777); James (born Nov. 25, 1780); Anne (born May 2, 1782); Isaac (born Aug. 23, 1784); William (born June 21, 1787); Benjamin (born March 23, 1790); Abraham (born Dec. 12, 1791); and, Rachel (born March 15, 1794). [Ref: O-16, O-17]. Also see "Abraham Hooper," q.v.

HOOPER, Jacob. See "Abraham Hooper," q.v.

HOOPER, James, Jane, and John. See "Isaac Hooper," q.v.

HOOPER, Mary. See "Abraham Hooper," q.v.

HOOPER, Priscilla and Rachel. See "Isaac Hooper," q.v.

HOOPER, Roger. Second Lieutenant, Capt. Thomas Cleland's Co., Calvert County Militia, April 16, 1778, and First Lieutenant, 15th Bn., May 3, 1780 [Ref: E-37, F-162, J-1146, M-89, M-147]. Took the Oath of Allegiance in Calvert County in 1778 [Ref: L-37].

HOOPER, William. See "Isaac Hooper," q.v.

HOOTON, John. Took the Oath of Allegiance before the Hon. Jeremiah Jordan in St. Mary's County in 1778 [Ref: J-1146, K-67].

HOPEWELL, Ann. See "Vernon Hebb" and "Hugh Hopewell," q.v.

HOPEWELL, Bennett. Took the Oath of Allegiance before the Hon. John Ireland in St. Mary's County in 1778 [Ref: J-1146, K-65]. Private, St. Mary's County Militia, 1777 [Ref: M-210]. Died on Dec. 31, 1823, in St. Mary's County [Ref: R-403].

HOPEWELL, Elizabeth. See "Hugh Hopewell," q.v.

HOPEWELL, George. Private, St. Mary's County Militia, 1777 [Ref: M-215]. Took the Oath of Allegiance before the Hon. Robert Watts in St. Mary's County in 1778 [Ref: J-1146, K-62]. First Lieutenant, Lower Bn., May 7, 1781 [Ref: M-89]. Property destroyed by the British in 1781 [Ref: S-159].

HOPEWELL, Hannah. See "Hugh Hopewell," q.v.

HOPEWELL, Hugh. Elected to serve on a General Committee in St. Mary's County in accordance with the resolves of the Continental Congress, 1774-1775 [Ref: MR-127, S-159]. "Some time in Feb., 1777, Hugh Hopewell from Calvert County wrote his will, but by some unfortunate accident he was prevented from executing it. He died between Feb. and July, 1777, leaving four sons, Hugh, James, Pollard, and Thomas, and two daughters, Ann who married ---- Hebb, and Elizabeth Hopewell who was single at the time of his death" in St. Mary's County [Ref: R-403, SO-11, SO-101, SO-103, SO-104]. See "Hugh Hopewell, Jr.," q.v.

HOPEWELL, Hugh Jr. Quartermaster, 21st Bn., St. Mary's County Militia, on Jan. 12, 1776 [Ref: M-89, M-215]. Captain, Lower Bn., from Aug. 28, 1777 through May 7, 1781 [Ref: M-89, C-346, G-426, S-159]. Took the Oath of Allegiance before the Hon. Jenifer Taylor in St. Mary's County in 1778 [Ref: J-1146, K-64]. Hugh Hopewell died by 1786, leaving orphans Ann, James, Elizabeth and Lucretia Hopewell. It appears that his widow Hannah Hopewell married Dr. Thomas Keemer by 1790 [Ref: SO-151, SO-154, SO-187, SO-193, SO-194, SO-196]. See "Hugh Hopewell" and Thomas Keymer," q.v.

HOPEWELL, James. Private, St. Mary's County Militia, 1777 [Ref: M-213]. Took the Oath of Allegiance before the Hon. Robert Watts in St. Mary's County in 1778 [Ref: J-1146, K-62]. See "Hugh Hopewell," q.v.

HOPEWELL, Lucretia. See "Hugh Hopewell," q.v.

HOPEWELL, Mary. See "William Clarke," q.v.

HOPEWELL, Pollard. Second Lieutenant, Lower Bn., St. Mary's County Militia, May 7, 1781 [Ref: S-95]. See "Hugh Hopewell," q.v.

HOPEWELL, Richard. Private, St. Mary's County Militia, 1777 [Ref: M-210].

HOPEWELL, Thomas. Midshipman on the State ship *Defence* from Feb. 2, 1777 to Dec. 31, 1777 [Ref: D-657]. See "Hugh Hopewell," q.v.

HOPKINS, Basil. Private, St. Mary's County Militia, 1777 [Ref: M-215, which listed the name as "Basil Hoplins"]. Took the Oath of Allegiance before the Hon. Robert Armstrong in St. Mary's County in 1778 [Ref: J-1146, K-62].

HOPKINS, Jacob. Private, St. Mary's County Militia, 1777 [Ref: M-210]. Took the Oath of Allegiance before the Hon. Henry Tubman in St. Mary's County in 1778 [Ref: J-1146, K-70].

HOPWOOD, Edward. Private, St. Mary's County Militia, 1777 [Ref: M-215]. Took the Oath of Allegiance before the Hon. Robert Armstrong in St. Mary's County in 1778 [Ref: J-1146, K-62].

HORNBY, William. Took the Oath of Allegiance in Calvert County in 1778 [Ref: L-37, which listed the name as "William Hornbee"]. Private, Capt. Edward Wood's Co., Calvert County Militia, 1778 [Ref: J-1146, M-147].

HORNER, Gustavus. Private, St. Mary's County Militia, 1777 [Ref: M-213].

HORRELL, Henry. Took the Oath of Allegiance before the Hon. Richard Barnes in St. Mary's County in 1778 [Ref: J-1146, K-66].
HORRELL, John. Took the Oath of Allegiance before the Hon. John Reeder in St. Mary's County in 1778 [Ref: J-1146, K-69]. Supplied provisions (wheat, mutton, or bacon) to the Army in 1780 [Ref: S-77, S-159]. The Register of St. Francis Xavier Catholic Church states that John Horrell and Monica Brown were married Dec. 22, 1772 [Ref: SC-34].
HORRELL, Thomas. Took the Oath of Allegiance before the Hon. John Reeder in St. Mary's County in 1778 [Ref: J-1146, K-69].
HOSKINS, Benjamin. Private, St. Mary's County Militia, 1777 [Ref: M-212, which listed the name as "Benjamin Horskins"]. Took the Oath of Allegiance before the Hon. John Ireland in St. Mary's County in 1778 [Ref: J-1146, K-65, which listed the name as "Benjamin Haskins"].
HOSKINS, John. Private, St. Mary's County Militia, 1777 [Ref: M-212, which listed the name as "John Horskins"]. Two men with this name took the Oath of Allegiance in 1778: one before the Hon. John Ireland and one before the Hon, John Shanks [Ref: J-1146, K-65, K-70, which latter source listed the name as "John Haskins"].
HOSKINS, Randall. Private, St. Mary's County, 1st Maryland Line, from Feb. 2, 1779 to Jan. 8, 1782 [Ref: D-118, D-359]. See "Bennett Dailey," q.v.
HOSKINS, Zepheniah. Private, St. Mary's County Militia, 1777 [Ref: M-213, which listed the name as "Zephaniah Haskins"]. Private, St. Mary's County, enlisted May 30, 1778, for 9 months; discharged on April 14, 1779 [Ref: D-330, S-159].
HOUSE, William. Took the Oath of Allegiance in Calvert County in 1778 [Ref: L-37].
HOWARD, Ann (Anne). See "John Drudge" and "Ignatius Gough," q.v.
HOWARD, Austin (Auston). Private, Capt. Uriah Forrest's Co., Flying Camp, St. Mary's County, July 28, 1776 [Ref: D-30]. Private, St. Mary's County Militia, 1777 [Ref: M-210]. Private, St. Mary's County, enlisted April 30, 1778, for 3 years [Ref: D-329]. Took the Oath of Allegiance before the Hon. Richard Barnes in St. Mary's County in 1778 [Ref: J-1146, K-66]. Private, St. Mary's County, 3rd Maryland Line, Capt. Armstrong's Co., 1778-1780 [Ref: D-298].
HOWARD, Basil. Private, St. Mary's County Militia, 1777 [Ref: M-212].
HOWARD, Charles. Private, St. Mary's County Militia, 1777 [Ref: M-210].
HOWARD, Charles Wallace. Designated by the Council of Maryland to receive the blankets collected for the troops in the southern counties, including St. Mary's County [Ref: C-196, C-197, S-33].
HOWARD, Clement. Private, St. Mary's County Militia, 1777 [Ref: M-214].
HOWARD, Edmond. Private, St. Mary's County Militia, 1777 [Ref: M-213].

HOWARD, Edward. Private, St. Mary's County Militia, 1777 [Ref: M-211]. Took the Oath of Allegiance in St. Mary's County in 1780 [Ref: Q-113].

HOWARD, George. Private, St. Mary's County Militia, 1777 [Ref: M-210]. Took the Oath of Allegiance before the Hon. Richard Barnes in St. Mary's County in 1778 [Ref: J-1146, K-66]. Supplied provisions (wheat, mutton, or bacon) to the Army in 1780 [Ref: S-77]. See "John Howard," q.v.

HOWARD, Henrietta. See "James Fenwick," q.v.

HOWARD, Ignatius. Private, St. Mary's County, drafted July 27, 1781 [Ref: D-384]. Private, Continental Army, 1781 [Ref: D-409]. There was an Ignatius Howard who died by June, 1780, when his son Massey Howard (aged 10 on Sep. 6, 1780) was bound out to learn to be a shoemaker [Ref: SO-33].

HOWARD, James. Private, St. Mary's County Militia, 1777 [Ref: M-212]. "James Howard, Sr." took the Oath of Allegiance before the Hon. John Ireland in St. Mary's County in 1778 [Ref: J-1146, K-65].

HOWARD, John. Private, Capt. Frederick Skinner's Co., Calvert County Militia, 1778 [Ref: J-1146, M-150]. Private, Capt. John Mackall's Co., Calvert County Militia, 15th Bn., June 12, 1778 [Ref: M-146]. Took the Oath of Allegiance in Calvert County in 1778 [Ref: L-37]. The Christ Church Register in Calvert County records the birth of John Howard, son of George and Margaret Howard, on Nov. 18, 1734 [Ref: O-17]. "John Baptist Howard, farmer" moved from St. Michaels to Nelson County, Kentucky, in 1794 [Ref: X-86].

HOWARD, Jonathan. Private, St. Mary's County Militia, 1777 [Ref: M-213]. Took the Oath of Allegiance before the Hon. John Ireland in St. Mary's County in 1778 [Ref: J-1146, K-65].

HOWARD, Joseph. Private, St. Mary's County Militia, 1777 [Ref: M-212]. Took the Oath of Allegiance before the Hon. John Ireland in St. Mary's County in 1778 [Ref: J-1146, K-65].

HOWARD, Joseph (of Benjamin). Private, St. Mary's County Militia, 1777 [Ref: M-213].

HOWARD, Leonard. Private, St. Mary's County Militia, 1777 [Ref: M-210]. Private, St. Mary's County, enlisted May 23, 1778, for 9 months [Ref: D-330]. Took the Oath of Allegiance before the Hon. Richard Barnes in St. Mary's County in 1778 [Ref: J-1146, K-66].

HOWARD, Margaret. See "John Howard," q.v.

HOWARD, Massey. See "Ignatius Howard," q.v

HOWARD, Peregrine. Private, St. Mary's County Militia, 1777 [Ref: M-210]. Private, 3rd Maryland Line, Capt. Armstrong's Co., 1778-1780 [Ref: D-298, which listed the name as "Perrygreen Howard"].

HOWARD, Peter. Private, St. Mary's County Militia, 1777 [Ref: M-213]. Took the Oath of Allegiance before the Hon. John Shanks in St. Mary's County in 1778 [Ref: J-1146, K-70].

HOWARD, Peter ("Neck"). Private, St. Mary's County Militia, 1777 [Ref: M-210].
HOWARD, Peter (of Thomas). Took the Oath of Allegiance before the Hon. John Ireland in St. Mary's County in 1778 [Ref: J-1146, K-65].
HOWARD, Peter (of Thomas, "Bay Side"). Took the Oath of Allegiance before the Hon. John Ireland in St. Mary's County in 1778 [Ref: J-1146, K-65].
HOWARD, Richard. This name appeared twice on the list as a private in Capt. Frederick Skinner's Co., Calvert County Militia, 1778 [Ref: J-1146, M-150].
HOWARD, Roger. Private, Calvert County, enlisted by Ensign James Somervill on July 26, 1776 [Ref: D-34].
HOWARD, Sarah. See "Alexander Somerville," q.v.
HOWARD, Thomas. Private, St. Mary's County Militia, 1777 [Ref: M-214]. Seaman on the State ship *Defence* in 1776 and midshipman from May 15 to Dec. 31, 1777 [Ref: D-607, D-657, S-25]. Took the Oath of Allegiance before the Hon. John Shanks in St. Mary's County in 1778 [Ref: J-1146, K-70].
HOWARD, William. (1) Private, Capt. Henry Skinner's Foot Co. of Hunting Hundred, Calvert County, 1777 [Ref: T-1814, O-125]. (2) Private, Capt. Uriah Forrest's Co., Flying Camp, St. Mary's County, July 28, 1776 [Ref: D-30]. Took the Oath of Allegiance before the Hon. Ignatius Fenwick, Jr. in St. Mary's County in 1778 [Ref: J-1146, K-68]. One William Howard was a Marine and another was a Carpenter's Mate on the State ship *Defence* from 1776 to Dec. 31, 1777 [Ref: D-657]. The Register of St. Francis Xavier Catholic Church states that one William Howard and Eleanor Thompson were married July 11, 1776 [Ref: SC-35].
HOWE, Mary. See "John Mackall," q.v.
HOWE, Sarah. See "Alexander Somerville," q.v.
HOWELL, Henry. Private, St. Mary's County Militia, 1777 [Ref: M-214].
HOWELL, Richard. Private, Capt. Henry Skinner's Foot Co. of Hunting Hundred, Calvert County, 1777 [Ref: T-1814, O-125].
HOWERTON, John. Private, Capt. Henry Skinner's Foot Co. of Hunting Hundred, Calvert County, 1777 [Ref: T-1814, O-125].
HOWES, Leonard. Private, Capt. Thomas Truman Greenfield's Co., Calvert County Militia, 1778 [Ref: J-1146, M-150].
HOWES, William. Private, Capt. Thomas Truman Greenfield's Co., Calvert County Militia, 1778 [Ref: J-1146, M-150].
HOWSE, Keziah. See "Richard Allsop," q.v.
HUBBARD, Jeremiah. See "Jeremiah Herbert," q.v.
HUDSON, John. Private, Capt. Edward Wood's Co., Calvert County Militia, 1778 [Ref: J-1146, M-147]. Took the Oath of Allegiance in Calvert County in 1778 [Ref: L-37].

HUDSON, Jonathan. Property destroyed by the British in St. Mary's County in 1781 [Ref: S-159].

HUDSON, Richard. Private, Calvert County, enlisted by Capt. John Brooke on July 26, 1776 [Ref: D-33]. Private, Capt. Thomas Truman Greenfield's Co., Calvert County Militia, 1778 [Ref: J-1146, M-150]. Richard Hudson and Jane James were married on June 25, 1778, by Rev. Francis Lauder, of Christ Church Parish [Ref: K-34].

HUDSON, William. Private, Capt. Henry Skinner's Foot Co. of Hunting Hundred, Calvert County, 1777 [Ref: T-1814, O-125].

HUGHES, Ann and David. See "William Fitzhugh, Jr.," q.v.

HUGHES, James. First Lieutenant, Capt. Frisby Freeland's Co., Calvert County Militia, 1778 [Ref: J-1146, M-148].

HUGHES, John. Took the Oath of Allegiance before the Hon. Bennett Biscoe in St. Mary's County in 1778 [Ref: J-1146, K-63]. Private, Capt. Uriah Forrest's Co., Flying Camp, St. Mary's County, July 28, 1776 [Ref: D-30, SM-113].

HUGHES, Richard. Private, Capt. Henry Skinner's Foot Co. of Hunting Hundred, Calvert County, 1777 [Ref: T-1814, O-125].

HUNGERFORD, John. Private, Calvert County, enlisted by Capt. John Brooke on July 25, 1776 [Ref: D-33]. Private, Capt. Richard Parran's Co., Calvert County Militia, 1778 [Ref: J-1146, M-149]. Took the Oath of Allegiance in Calvert County in 1778 [Ref: L-37]. The Christ Church Register in Calvert County records the birth of John Hungerford, son of Benjamin and Jane Hungerford, on Feb. 10, 1750 [Ref: O-17]. John Hungerford and Mary Cowen were married on Nov. 24, 1778, by Rev. Francis Lauder, of Christ Church Parish [Ref: K-34].

HUNT, Arthur. Private, Capt. Richard Parran's Co., Calvert County Militia, 1778 [Ref: J-1146, M-149, which listed the name as "Ortor(?) Huntt"].

HUNT, Basil. Private, St. Mary's County Militia, 1777 [Ref: M-210].

HUNT, Henry. Private, Capt. James Patterson's Co., Calvert County Militia, Aug. 10, 1777 [Ref: M-146]. Took the Oath of Allegiance in Calvert County in 1778 [Ref: L-37]. Private, Capt. Frederick Skinner's Co., Calvert County Militia, 1778 [Ref: J-1146, M-150, which listed the name as "Henry Huntt"].

HUNT, Philip. Private, Capt. Frederick Skinner's Co., Calvert County Militia, 1778 [Ref: J-1146, M-150, which listed the name as "Philip Huntt"]. Private, Capt. John Mackall's Co., Calvert County Militia, 15th Bn., June 12, 1778 [Ref: M-146]. Took the Oath of Allegiance in Calvert County in 1780 [Ref: Q-113].

HUNT, William. Private, Capt. Thomas Cleland's Co., Calvert County Militia, 1778 [Ref: J-1146, M-147, which listed the name as "William Huntt"].

HUNTER, David Jr. Private, Capt. Richard Parran's Co., Calvert County Militia, 1778 [Ref: J-1146, M-149]. Took the Oath of Allegiance in Calvert County in 1778 [Ref: L-37].

HUNTER, David Sr. Took the Oath of Allegiance in Calvert County in 1778 [Ref: L-37].

HUNTER, William. (1) Private, Capt. Frisby Freeland's Co., Calvert County Militia, 1778 [Ref: J-1146, M-148]. Took the Oath of Allegiance in Calvert County in 1778 [Ref: L-37]. (2) Private, Capt. Richard Parran's Co., Calvert County Militia, 1778 [Ref: J-1146, M-149]. Took the Oath of Allegiance in Calvert County in 1778 [Ref: L-37].

HURST, Phineas. Private, St. Mary's County Militia, 1777 [Ref: M-211]. Private, St. Mary's County, enlisted June 10, 1778, for 9 months, Continental Army, Smallwood's Regiment [Ref: D-330, SM-113]. Sergeant, St. Mary's County, 3rd Maryland Line, Capt. Armstrong's Co., 1778-1779, and reported "deserted" on Jan. 1, 1780 [Ref: D-298, which listed the name as "Phinchas Hurst"].

HUTCHINS (HUTCHINGS), Ann. See "Richard Pilkinton," q.v.

HUTCHINS, Bennett. Private, St. Mary's County Militia, 1777 [Ref: M-211]. Took the Oath of Allegiance before the Hon. Henry Reeder in St. Mary's County in 1778 [Ref: J-1146, K-64]. The Register of St. Andrew's Episcopal Church states that Bennett Hutchins and Jane Stone were married Nov. 7, 1779 [Ref: MB-383].

HUTCHINS, Catharine. See "Clarke Abell," q.v.

HUTCHINS, Clement. Private, Calvert County, enlisted by Capt. John Brooke on July 26, 1776 [Ref: D-33]. Took the Oath of Allegiance in Calvert County in 1778 [Ref: L-37]. Private, Capt. Edward Wood's Co., Calvert County Militia, 1778 [Ref: J-1146, M-147, which listed the name as "Clement Hutchings"].

HUTCHINS, Dorothy. See "Basil Raley," q.v.

HUTCHINS, Francis. This name appeared twice on the list of those who took the Oath of Allegiance in Calvert County in 1778, one as "Francis Hutchins" and the other as "Francis Hutchings" [Ref: L-37]. (1) Private, Capt. Henry Skinner's Foot Co. of Hunting Hundred, Calvert County, 1777 [Ref: T-1814, O-125, which listed the name as "Francis Hutchens"]. Private, Capt. Edward Wood's Co., Calvert County Militia, 1778 [Ref: J-1146, M-147]. (2) Private, Capt. Walter Smith's Co., Calvert County Militia, 1778 [Ref: J-1146, M-148, which listed the name as "Francis Hutchings"]. One Francis Hutchings died intestate by Sep., 1777, in St. Mary's County, and Susanna Hutchings was his administratrix [Ref: SO-2].

HUTCHINS, Ignatius. Took the Oath of Allegiance in Calvert County in 1778 [Ref: L-37]. Private, Capt. Edward Wood's Co., Calvert County Militia, 1778 [Ref: J-1146, M-147, which listed the name as "Ignatius Hutchings"].

HUTCHINS, John. (1) Private, St. Mary's County Militia, 1777 [Ref: M-211]. Took the Oath of Allegiance before the Hon. Richard Barnes in St. Mary's County in 1778 [Ref: J-1146, K-66]. (2) Took the Oath of Allegiance in Calvert County in 1778 [Ref: L-37]. Private, Capt. Edward Wood's Co., Calvert County Militia, 1778 [Ref: J-1146, M-147]. John Hutchins was among the early Catholic settlers who migrated to Nelson County, Kentucky in 1785 [Ref: MK-78]. Another "John Hutching" died intestate in St. Mary's County by March, 1793, when his orphan son John chose "Thomas Hutching of Calvert County" as his guardian (also spelled "Hutchins"). [Ref: SO-189, SO-246].

HUTCHINS, Joseph. Took the Oath of Allegiance in Calvert County in 1778 [Ref: L-37]. Private, Capt. Edward Wood's Co., Calvert County Militia, 1778 [Ref: J-1146, M-147, which listed the name as "Joseph Hutchings"]. Joseph Hutchins and Mary Hardesty were married on Jan. 5, 1779, by Rev. Francis Lauder, of Christ Church Parish [Ref: K-34].

HUTCHINS, Mary. See "Charles Flower" and Samuel Hance," q.v.

HUTCHINS, Stephen. Private, Calvert County, enlisted by Capt. John Brooke on July 25, 1776 [Ref: D-33, which listed the name as "Stephen Hutchings"]. Took the Oath of Allegiance in Calvert County in 1778 [Ref: L-37]. Private, Capt. Edward Wood's Co., Calvert County Militia, 1778 [Ref: J-1146, M-147].

HUTCHINS, Susanna. See "Francis Hutchins," q.v.

HUTCHINS, Thomas. First Lieutenant, Capt. Edward Wood's Co., Calvert County Militia, 1778 [Ref: M-147, which listed the name as "Thomas Hutchings"]. Took the Oath of Allegiance in Calvert County in 1778 [Ref: L-37]. "Thomas Hutchings" and Elizabeth Hillen were married on Jan. 1, 1778, by Rev. Francis Lauder, of Christ Church Parish [Ref: K-33]. See "John Hutchins," q.v.

HUTCHINS, Thomas Gauslen. Private, Capt. Henry Skinner's Foot Co. of Hunting Hundred, Calvert County, 1777 [Ref: T-1814, O-125, which listed the name as "Thomas Gauslen Hutchens"].

HUTCHINSON, Bennett. Private, St. Mary's County Militia, 1777 [Ref: M-212]. Took the Oath of Allegiance before the Hon. Henry G. Sothoron in St. Mary's County in 1778 [Ref: J-1146, K-69].

HUTCHINSON, Joshua. Private, St. Mary's County Militia, 1777 [Ref: M-211].

HUTCHINSON, Phebe. See "William Glover," q.v.

HUTCHINSON, Thomas. Took the Oath of Allegiance in St. Mary's County in 1780 [Ref: Q-113, which listed the name as "Hutchison"].

HUTCHINSON, Winifred. See "Joseph Stone," q.v.

HUTTON, Asenath. See "Charles Grahame," q.v.

IRELAND, Dicandia. See "John Ireland," q.v.

IRELAND, Elizabeth Wilson. See "Alexander Somerville," q.v.

IRELAND, George. Private, Calvert County, enlisted by Capt. John Brooke on July 26, 1776 [Ref: D-33]. George Ireland and Mary Dare were married on April 11, 1779, by Rev. Francis Lauder, of Christ Church Parish [Ref: K-35].

IRELAND, Gideon. Private, Capt. Richard Parran's Co., Calvert County Militia, 1778 [Ref: J-1146, M-149]. Took the Oath of Allegiance in Calvert County in 1778 [Ref: L-37]. Gave his deposition in 1780 regarding the status and questionable loyalty of some Calvert Countians [Ref: V-257].

IRELAND, Gilbert (c1740-1784). Son of "William Ireland, Sr.," q.v. He married Eleanor ---- who subsequently married Rezin Estep [Ref: N-479]. Ensign, Capt. Richard Lane's Co., Calvert County Militia, 1778. Second Lieutenant, 15th Bn., April 16, 1778 [Ref: J-1146, M-91, M-149, E-37]. Took the Oath of Allegiance in Calvert County in 1778 [Ref: L-37].

IRELAND, John. (1) Doctor and Justice who administered the Oath of Allegiance in St. Mary's County in 1778. He married Susannah Reeder [Ref: J-1146, K-65, N-675, S-159]. "Dr. John Ireland" was elected to a General Committee in St. Mary's County in accordance with the resolves of the Continental Congress in 1775 [Ref: MR-127]. He died by 1788, leaving an orphan daughter Dicandia, and his widow Susanna married Dr. Gustavus Brown by Aug., 1788 [Ref: SO-127]. (2) Private, Capt. Frisby Freeland's Co., Calvert County Militia, 1778 [Ref: J-1146, M-148]. Took the Oath of Allegiance in Calvert County in 1778 [Ref: L-37].

IRELAND, Joseph. Son of "William Ireland, Sr.," q.v. [Ref: N-479]. First Lieutenant, 15th Bn., Capt. Thomas Cleland's Co., Calvert County Militia, April 16, 1778 [Ref: J-1146, M-91, M-147, E-37]. Took the Oath of Allegiance in Calvert County in 1778 [Ref: L-37].

IRELAND, Margaret. See "Charles Somerset Parran," q.v.

IRELAND, Mary. See "Robert Brown," q.v.

IRELAND, Richard. Took the Oath of Allegiance in Calvert County in 1778 [Ref: L-37].

IRELAND, Susanna. See "John Ireland" and "Gustavus Brown," q.v.

IRELAND, Thomas. Private, Capt. James Grahame's Co., Calvert County Militia, 1778 [Ref: J-1146, M-149].

IRELAND, William. Private, Capt. Frisby Freeland's Co., Calvert County Militia, 1778 [Ref: J-1146, M-148]. Took the Oath of Allegiance in Calvert County in 1778 [Ref: L-37].

IRELAND, William Sr. (c1714-1775). Clerk of Calvert County, 1749-1775 [Ref: N-479].

IRELAND, William Jr. (c1742-c1787). Son of "William Ireland, Sr.," q.v. Justice of Calvert County, 1773-1787. Took the Oath of Allegiance in Calvert County in 1778 [Ref: L-37]. Subscription Officer, Continental Loan Office, 1779. Justice of the Orphans Court, 1781. Justice of the Peace, 1781-1782. Member of the House of Delegates in 1783. Judge, Court of Appeals for Tax Assessment, 1786 [Ref: V-472, N-88, N-479].

ISAACK, Richard. Took the Oath of Allegiance in Calvert County in 1778 [Ref: L-37]. Private, Capt. Thomas Cleland's Co., Calvert County Militia, 1778 [Ref: J-1146, M-147, which listed the name as "Richard Isaacks"].
ISAACK, Thomas. Private, Capt. Frederick Skinner's Co., Calvert County Militia, 1778 [Ref: J-1146, M-150, which listed the name as "Thomas Isaac"]. Took the Oath of Allegiance in Calvert County in 1778 [Ref: L-37]. Private, Capt. John Mackall's Co., Calvert County Militia, 15th Bn., June 12, 1778 [Ref: M-146, which listed the name as "Thomas Isacke"].
IVEY, James. Private, Capt. Richard Parran's Co., Calvert County Militia, 1778 [Ref: J-1146, M-149]. Took the Oath of Allegiance in Calvert County in 1780 [Ref: Q-114]. The Christ Church Register in Calvert County records the birth of James Ivey, son of John and Eleanor Ivey, on Sep. 30, 1747 [Ref: O-17].
IVEY, John. Private, Capt. Richard Parran's Co., Calvert County Militia, 1778 [Ref: J-1146, M-149]. Took the Oath of Allegiance in Calvert County in 1780 [Ref: Q-114]. The Christ Church Register in Calvert County records the birth of John Ivey, son of John and Eleanor Ivey, on Aug. 24, 1743 [Ref: O-17]. One "John Ivy" and Elizabeth Powell were married on Nov. 12, 1780, by Rev. Francis Lauder, of Christ Church Parish [Ref: K-36].
JACKSON, Abednigo. Private, St. Mary's County, enlisted May 25, 1778, for 9 months; discharged April 3, 1779 [Ref: D-329, S-159].
JACKSON, Zachariah. Took the Oath of Allegiance in St. Mary's County in 1780 [Ref: Q-114].
JAMES, Jane. See "Richard Hudson," q.v.
JAMES, John. Private, St. Mary's County Militia, 1777 [Ref: M-213].
JANES, Austin and John. See "John Jeans," q.v.
JANNEY, Barbara and George F. See "Thomas Gantt," q.v.
JARBOE, Arnold. See "Henry Jarboe," q.v.
JARBOE, Athanatius. Captain from St. Mary's County who lost his ship at Tangier on April 4, 1779 [Ref: S-159].
JARBOE, Benjamin. See "Henry Jarboe," q.v.
JARBOE, Bennett. Took the Oath of Allegiance before the Hon. Richard Barnes in St. Mary's County in 1778 [Ref: J-1146, K-66].
JARBOE, Charles. Private, St. Mary's County Militia, 1777 [Ref: M-211]. "Charles Jarboe, Jr." took the Oath of Allegiance before the Hon. Ignatius Fenwick, Jr. in St. Mary's County in 1778 [Ref: J-1146, K-68]. The Register of St. Francis Xavier Catholic Church states that a Charles Jarboe and Elizabeth Stone were married Oct. 19, 1772 [Ref: SC-34]. One Charles Jarboe died intestate by Dec., 1793 [Ref: SO-203].
JARBOE, Elizabeth. See "Thomas Griffin," q.v.
JARBOE, Henrietta. See "James Attwood (Atwood)," q.v.
JARBOE, Henry (Jan., 1710 - April, 1795). Took the Oath of Allegiance before the Hon. Bennett Biscoe in St. Mary's County in 1778 [Ref: J-1146, K-63]. He married Elizabeth Stiles in Dec., 1730, and son John

Jarboe (1731-1794) married Elizabeth Grafton Abell in 1751 [Ref: Y-366, and Maryland Society, Sons of the American Revolution, Supplemental Membership Application No. 2907-B, filed by Richard Diederick Beall, and approved in 1988 by the National Society]. Henry Jarboe, Stephen Jarboe, Arnold Jarboe, and Benjamin Jarboe were among the early settlers of Cartwright Creek in now Washington County, Kentucky circa 1785 [Ref: MK-79].

JARBOE, Henry Jr. Took the Oath of Allegiance before the Hon. Bennett Biscoe in St. Mary's County in 1778 [Ref: J-1146, K-63]. Paid for making salt in 1782 [Ref: S-159].

JARBOE, John (1731-1794). Took the Oath of Allegiance before the Hon. Henry G. Sothoron in St. Mary's County in 1778 [Ref: J-1146, K-69]. He married Elizabeth Grafton Abell (1734-1800) in 1751 and had several children including a son Raphael Jarboe (1771-1822) who married Catherine Remond Barnes in 1792 [Refer to "Henry Jarboe," q.v., for source and additional family information].

JARBOE, John Baptist. Took the Oath of Allegiance before the Hon. Bennett Biscoe in St. Mary's County in 1778 [Ref: J-1146, K-63].

JARBOE, Joshua. Private, St. Mary's County Militia, 1777 [Ref: M-211]. Took the Oath of Allegiance before the Hon. Richard Barnes in St. Mary's County in 1778 [Ref: J-1146, K-66].

JARBOE, Mark. Took the Oath of Allegiance before the Hon. Henry G. Sothoron in St. Mary's County in 1778 [Ref: J-1146, K-69].

JARBOE, Matthew. Took the Oath of Allegiance before the Hon. Henry Reeder in St. Mary's County in 1778 [Ref: J-1146, K-64].

JARBOE, Nancy. See "Peter Jarboe," q.v.

JARBOE, Peter. Private, St. Mary's County Militia, 1777 [Ref: M-211]. Took the Oath of Allegiance before the Hon. Henry Reeder in St. Mary's County in 1778 [Ref: J-1146, K-64]. Private (substitute) in Maryland Line on July 31, 1781 [Ref: D-384, D-409, which listed the name as "Peter Jarber"]. Discharged on Dec. 3, 1781 [Ref: S-109, H-11]. The Register of St. Andrew's Episcopal Church states that Peter Jarboe and Nancy Jarboe were married on Jan. 16, 1779 [Ref: MB-382].

JARBOE, Philip. Took the Oath of Allegiance before the Hon. Henry Reeder in St. Mary's County in 1778 [Ref: J-1146, K-64].

JARBOE, Raphael. See "Henry Jarboe," q.v.

JARBOE, Richard. Private, St. Mary's County Militia, 1777 [Ref: M-211]. Took the Oath of Allegiance before the Hon. Richard Barnes in St. Mary's County in 1778 [Ref: J-1146, K-66]. Discharged from the Maryland Line on Dec. 3, 1781 [Ref: S-159]. One Richard Jarboe died intestate by Oct., 1788 [Ref: SO-128]. Another Richard Jarboe settled on Cox's Creek in Kentucky before 1800 [Ref: MK-79].

JARBOE, Robert. Private, St. Mary's County Militia, 1777 [Ref: M-211, M-215]. Ensign, Lower Bn., Aug. 26, 1777 [Ref: M-92, C-346]. Took the

Oath of Allegiance before the Hon. Robert Watts in St. Mary's County in 1778 [Ref: J-1146, K-62].

JARBOE, Robert Jr. (Jan. 3, 1752 - March 21, 1803) Took the Oath of Allegiance before the Hon. Richard Barnes in St. Mary's County in 1778 [Ref: J-1146, K-66]. Private, St. Mary's County Militia, 1777. Private, St. Mary's County, drafted July 27, 1781. Private, Continental Army, 1781 [Ref: M-211, D-384, D-409]. Robert and wife Elizabeth (1750-1810) are buried in St. Nicholas Catholic Church yard at the Patuxent Naval Air Station [Ref: R-407, HG-34, S-129].

JARBOE, Rodolph. "Rodolph Jarboe" took the Oath of Allegiance before the Hon. Bennett Biscoe in St. Mary's County in 1778 [Ref: J-1146, K-63]. The Register of St. Francis Xavier Catholic Church states that "Rodulphus Jarboe" and Monica Williams were married Nov. 17, 1772 [Ref: SC-34].

JARBOE, Stephen. Took the Oath of Allegiance before the Hon. Bennett Biscoe in St. Mary's County in 1778 [Ref: J-1146, K-63]. See "Henry Jarboe," q.v.

JARBOE, Thomas. Private, St. Mary's County Militia, 1777 [Ref: M-214]. Private, St. Mary's County, enlisted May 29, 1778, for 9 months, Continental Army [Ref: D-329, SM-113]. Took the Oath of Allegiance before the Hon. Henry Reeder in St. Mary's County in 1778 [Ref: J-1146, K-64]. The Register of St. Francis Xavier Catholic Church states that Thomas Jarboe and Ann Lucust were married Nov. 22, 1772 [Ref: SC-34].

JEANS, John. Took the Oath of Allegiance before the Hon. John Shanks in St. Mary's County in 1778 [Ref: J-1146, K-70]. Private, St. Mary's County Militia, 1777 [Ref: M-212, which listed the name as "John Geanes"]. "John Janes" and Austin Janes were among the early Catholic settlers who migrated to Cartwright's Creek in now Washington County, Kentucky circa 1785 [Ref: MK-79].

JEANS, Thomas. Took the Oath of Allegiance before the Hon. Bennett Biscoe in St. Mary's County in 1778 [Ref: J-1146, K-63].

JEFFERSON, Basil (Bazil). Took the Oath of Allegiance in Calvert County in 1778 [Ref: L-37]. Private, Capt. Edward Wood's Co., Calvert County Militia, 1778 [Ref: J-1146, M-147].

JEFFERSON, Benjamin. Private, Capt. Edward Wood's Co., Calvert County Militia, 1778 [Ref: J-1146, M-147]. Took the Oath of Allegiance in Calvert County in 1778 [Ref: L-37].

JEFFERSON, Benjamin Jr. Private, Capt. Edward Wood's Co., Calvert County Militia, 1778 [Ref: J-1146, M-147].

JEFFERSON, Henry. Private, Capt. Henry Skinner's Foot Co. of Hunting Hundred, Calvert County, 1777 [Ref: T-1814, O-125]. Private, Capt. Edward Wood's Co., Calvert County Militia, 1778 [Ref: J-1146, M-147]. Took the Oath of Allegiance in Calvert County in 1778 [Ref: L-37].

JEFFERSON, John. Private, Capt. Henry Skinner's Foot Co. of Hunting Hundred, Calvert County, 1777 [Ref: T-1814, O-125]. Took the Oath of Allegiance in Calvert County in 1778 [Ref: L-37]. One John Jefferson and Marcy (Masey?) Gray were married on Jan. 5, 1779, by Rev. Francis Lauder, of Christ Church Parish [Ref: K-34, MM-118].
JEFFERSON, John Jr. Private, Capt. Henry Skinner's Foot Co. of Hunting Hundred, Calvert County, 1777 [Ref: T-1814, O-125].
JEFFERSON, Jestinian (Justinian). Private, Maryland Line, 1781, probably from Calvert County or St. Mary's County [Ref: D-409].
JEFFERSON, Rebecca. See "William Ramsay," q.v.
JEFFERSON, Thomas. See "William Coe," q.v.
JEFFERY, Joseph. Private, St. Mary's County Militia, 1777 [Ref: M-215].
JEFFERY, Whitten. Took the Oath of Allegiance before the Hon. Robert Armstrong in St. Mary's County in 1778 [Ref: J-1146, K-62].
JENIFER, Ann. See "Ignatius Taylor" and "Jenifer Taylor," q.v.
JENIFER, Parker. Private, St. Mary's County Militia, 1777 [Ref: M-215]. Took the Oath of Allegiance before the Hon. Robert Armstrong in St. Mary's County in 1778 [Ref: J-1146, K-62].
JENIFER, Samuel. Elected to serve on a General Committee in St. Mary's County in accordance with the resolves of the Continental Congress in 1775 [Ref: MR-127]. Private, St. Mary's County Militia, 1777 [Ref: M-212]. Captain, Lower Bn., Aug. 26, 1777 [Ref: M-92, C-346]. Took the Oath of Allegiance before the Hon. Robert Watts in St. Mary's County in 1778 [Ref: J-1146, K-62].
JENKINS, Ann. See "James Atwood," q.v.
JENKINS, Augustine (1747 - Feb. 3, 1800). Catholic Priest who took the Oath of Allegiance in St. Mary's County in 1778. He is buried in St. Francis Xavier Catholic Church Cemetery at Newtown [Ref: SM-185, HG-35].
JENKINS, Augustine (of Richard). Took the Oath of Allegiance before the Hon. John Ireland in St. Mary's County in 1778 [Ref: J-1146, K-65].
JENKINS, Edmund. Took the Oath of Allegiance before the Hon. Henry Reeder in St. Mary's County in 1778 [Ref: J-1146, K-64]. The Register of St. Francis Xavier Catholic Church states Edmund Jenkins and Elizabeth Milborn were married May 26, 1773 [Ref: SC-34].
JENKINS, Edward. Private, St. Mary's County Militia, 1777 [Ref: M-214].
JENKINS, Eleanor. See "William Jenkins," q.v.
JENKINS, George. Private, St. Mary's County Militia, 1777 [Ref: M-214]. Took the Oath of Allegiance before the Hon. Bennett Biscoe in St. Mary's County in 1778 [Ref: J-1146, K-63]. The Register of St. Andrew's Episcopal Church states that George Jenkins and Margaret Wise were married (by license) March 31, 1782 [Ref: MB-384]. "George Jenkins, farmer" moved from Lower St. Mary's to Bullitt County, Kentucky, in 1797 [Ref: X-86].

JENKINS, Henry. Took the Oath of Allegiance before the Hon. Robert Watts in St. Mary's County in 1778 [Ref: J-1146, K-62].
JENKINS, Jeremiah. Private, St. Mary's County Militia, 1777 [Ref: M-214]. One Jeremiah Jenkins died by Dec., 1793, leaving a son Lewis Jenkins (under the age of 14 in Feb., 1795) with William Jenkins as his guardian [Ref: SO-204, SO-222].
JENKINS, John. Took the Oath of Allegiance before the Hon. Bennett Biscoe in St. Mary's County in 1778 [Ref: J-1146, K-63].
JENKINS, Lewis. See "Jeremiah Jenkins," q.v.
JENKINS, Mary. See "William Jenkins" and "Ignatius Fenwick, Sr.," q.v.
JENKINS, Richard. See "William Jenkins," q.v.
JENKINS, Thomas. First Lieutenant, Lower Bn., St. Mary's County Militia, Aug. 26, 1777 [Ref: M-92, C-346, SM-113]. Took the Oath of Allegiance before the Hon. Bennett Biscoe in St. Mary's County in 1778 [Ref: J-1146, K-63]. The Register of St. Andrew's Episcopal Church states that Thomas Jenkins and Mary Mackall were married Jan. 13, 1780 [Ref: MB-383]. See "William Jenkins," q.v.
JENKINS, William. "William Jenkins" took the Oath of Allegiance before the Hon. Robert Watts in St. Mary's County in 1778 [Ref: J-1146, K-62]. "William Jenkins, Jr." was elected to a General Committee in St. Mary's County in accordance with the resolves of the Continental Congress in 1775 [Ref: MR-127]. One William Jenkins died testate by Feb., 1780, leaving orphans Thomas Jenkins (above the age of 14 in Aug., 1786), Mary Jenkins, and Richard Jenkins. It appears that his widow was Eleanor Jenkins and she married ---- Lurty between April, 1797 and Feb., 1798 [Ref: SO-29, SO-103, SO-228, SO-260, SO-268]. See "Jeremiah Jenkins," q.v.
JENNINGS, Anne. See "John Grahame," q.v.
JENNINGS, John. Private (substitute), St. Mary's County, July 31, 1781 [Ref: D-384].
JOHNS, Benjamin. Private, Calvert County, enlisted by Lt. Nathaniel Wilson on Aug. 31, 1776 [Ref: D-34]. Took the Oath of Allegiance in Calvert County in 1778 [Ref: L-37].
JOHNS, Benjamin (of John). Private, Capt. Thomas Cleland's Co., Calvert County Militia, 1778 [Ref: J-1146, M-147, which listed the name as "Benjamin Johns, for John"].
JOHNS, Cuthbert. See "Cuthbert Jones," q.v.
JOHNS, David. Private, St. Mary's County Militia, 1777 [Ref: M-214]. Private, St. Mary's County, enlisted May 23, 1778, for 9 months, Continental Army [Ref: D-330, SM-113].
JOHNSON, Barney. Drum & Fife, St. Mary's County, 3rd Maryland Line, Capt. Armstrong's Co., 1778-1780 [Ref: D-298].
JOHNSON, David. Took the Oath of Allegiance before the Hon. John Reeder in St. Mary's County in 1778 [Ref: J-1146, K-69].
JOHNSON, Dorcas. See "William Hellen (Hillen)," q.v.

JOHNSON, Edward (c1737 - Sep. 24, 1797, Baltimore, Maryland). He was in Calvert County by 1763 and married Ann ----, probably a daughter of David Arnold and Rebecca Boyce. Children: Edward and Rebecca. By profession Edward was a physician and surgeon. He took the Oath of Allegiance in Calvert County in 1778 [Ref: L-37, which listed the name as "E. Johnson"]. Served as a Justice of Calvert County, 1773-1782, Member of the House of Delegates, 1780-1781, Committee of Observation, 1774-1776, Justice of the Orphans Court, 1779-1782. He moved to Baltimore Town in 1782 and became President of the Medical Society of Baltimore in 1798 [Ref: N-84, N-492].

JOHNSON, George. Took the Oath of Allegiance in Calvert County in 1778 [Ref: L-37].

JOHNSON, Henry. (1) Private, Capt. Richard Lane's Co., Calvert County Militia, 1778 [Ref: J-1146, M-150]. (2) Private, 3rd Maryland Line, May 24, 1780; from St. Mary's County [Ref: S-160].

JOHNSON, Jery. Took the Oath of Allegiance in Calvert County in 1778 [Ref: L-37].

JOHNSON, John. (1) Private, Capt. Richard Lane's Co., Calvert County Militia, 1778 [Ref: J-1146, M-150]. (2) Supplied provisions (wheat, mutton, or bacon) to the Army in St. Mary's County in Oct., 1780 [Ref: S-77, S-160].

JOHNSON, Joseph. (1) Private, Capt. Benjamin Bond's Co., Calvert County Militia, 1778 [Ref: J-1146, M-149]. (2) This name appeared twice on the list of those who subscribed to the Oath of Allegiance and Fidelity in Calvert County in 1778 [Ref: L-37]. (3) This name also appeared twice as a private in the St. Mary's County Militia in 1777 [Ref: M-213, M-215]. Private, Continental Army, May 23, 1778 [Ref: SM-113].

JOHNSON, Joseph ("Clifts"). Private, Capt. Benjamin Bond's Co., Calvert County Militia, 1778 [Ref: J-1146, M-149].

JOHNSON, Leonard (of David). Private, St. Mary's County Militia, 1777 [Ref: M-213]. The Register of St. Francis Xavier Catholic Church states Leonard Johnson and Mary Molohorn were married Jan. 11, 1774 [Ref: SC-35].

JOHNSON, Philip. Private, St. Mary's County Militia, 1777 [Ref: M-212].

JOHNSON, Rebecca. See "Edward Johnson," q.v.

JOHNSON, Richard. Private, Capt. Charles Williamson's Co., Calvert County Militia, 1778 [Ref: J-1146, M-147].

JOHNSON, Samuel. Private, Capt. Walter Smith's Co., Calvert County Militia, 1778 [Ref: J-1146, M-148]. Took the Oath of Allegiance in Calvert County in 1778 [Ref: L-37].

JOHNSON, Thomas. Ensign, 15th Bn., Capt. Walter Smith's Co., Calvert County Militia, April 10, 1776 through April 16, 1778 [Ref: M-93, A-320, E-37, J-1146, M-148]. See "John Grahame," q.v.

JOHNSON, Thomas ("Clifts"). Granted a bond by the State to erect a saltworks at the Clifts in Calvert County on Aug. 5, 1777 [Ref: V-115]. Took the Oath of Allegiance in Calvert County in 1778 [Ref: L-35, which mistakenly listed the name as "Thomas Johnson Clifts"].

JOHNSON, William. (1) Private, Capt. Richard Parran's Co., Calvert County Militia, 1778 [Ref: J-1146, M-149]. Took the Oath of Allegiance in Calvert County in 1780 [Ref: Q-114]. (2) Private, Capt. Charles Williamson's Co., Calvert County Militia, 1778 [Ref: J-1146, M-147]. (3) Private, Flying Camp, St. Mary's County, July 28, 1778 [Ref: SM-113]. Took the Oath of Allegiance before the Hon. John Ireland in St. Mary's County in 1778 [Ref: J-1146, K-65]. (4) One William Johnson was accounted and paid for driving cattle for the State in Calvert County in 1781 [Ref: V-442].

JOHNSON, William (of Jeremiah). Private, Capt. Richard Lane's Co., Calvert County Militia, 1778 [Ref: J-1146, M-149, which listed the name as "William Johnson, for Jeremiah"]. "William Johnson, of Jery" took the Oath of Allegiance in Calvert County in 1778 [Ref: L-37].

JOHNSON, William (of George). Took the Oath of Allegiance in Calvert County in 1778 [Ref: L-37].

JOHNSON, William Sergeant. Private, Capt. Frisby Freeland's Co., Calvert County Militia, 1778 [Ref: J-1146, M-148]. Took the Oath of Allegiance in Calvert County in 1778 [Ref: L-39, which mistakenly listed the name as "Sergt. Johnson Will"].

JOHNSTON, Joseph. Private, St. Mary's County, enlisted May 31, 1778, for 9 months [Ref: D-330].

JOHNSTONE, Joseph. Private, Capt. Uriah Forrest's Co., Flying Camp, St. Mary's County, July 28, 1776 [Ref: D-30].

JOHNSTONE, William. Private, Capt. Uriah Forrest's Co., Flying Camp, St. Mary's County, July 28, 1776 [Ref: D-30].

JONES, Ann. See "Solomon Jones," q.v.

JONES, Benjamin. Private, Capt. Charles Williamson's Co., Calvert County Militia, 1778 [Ref: J-1146, M-148]. Benjamin Jones and Sarah Gibson were married on Feb. 1, 1778, by Rev. Francis Lauder, of Christ Church Parish [Ref: K-33].

JONES, Caleb. See "Matthias Jones," q.v.

JONES, Charles. Private, Capt. Uriah Forrest's Co., Flying Camp, St. Mary's County, July 28, 1776 [Ref: D-30, SM-113].

JONES, Clare. See "Solomon Jones," q.v.

JONES, Cuthbert. Private, 3rd Maryland Line, enlisted April 4, 1777 [Ref: D-298, which listed the name as "Cuthbert John (or Jones)"]. Private (substitute), St. Mary's County, Aug. 12, 1781 [Ref: D-127, D-384, S-33]. Private, Continental Army, 1781 [Ref: D-409].

JONES, Elizabeth. See "Thomas Thompson," q.v.

JONES, James. Private, Capt. James Grahame's Co., Calvert County Militia, 1778 [Ref: J-1146, M-148]. Took the Oath of Allegiance in Calvert County in 1778 [Ref: L-37].

JONES, John. (1) Private, St. Mary's County Militia, 1777 [Ref: M-213]. Private, enlisted on May 31, 1778, for 9 months, Continental Army [Ref: D-330, SM-113]. Took the Oath of Allegiance before the Hon. Henry G. Sothoron in St. Mary's County in 1778 [Ref: J-1146, K-69]. (2) Private, Capt. Charles Williamson's Co., Calvert County Militia, 1778 [Ref: J-1146, M-147]. This name appeared three times on the list of those who took the Oath of Allegiance in Calvert County in 1778 [Ref: L-37]. See "Matthias Jones," q.v.

JONES, Joseph. Seaman from St. Mary's County who served aboard the State ship *Defence* in 1776 [Ref: S-25, D-606].

JONES, Lewis. Private, Capt. Richard Lane's Co., Calvert County Militia, 1778 [Ref: J-1146, M-149].

JONES, Lewis Jr. Took the Oath of Allegiance in Calvert County in 1778 [Ref: L-37].

JONES, Mary. See "Matthias Jones," q.v.

JONES, Matthew. Property destroyed by the British in St. Mary's County in 1781 [Ref: S-160].

JONES, Matthias. Private, St. Mary's County Militia, 1777 [Ref: M-215]. Took the Oath of Allegiance before the Hon. Robert Armstrong in St. Mary's County in 1778 [Ref: J-1146, K-62]. One Matthias Jones died intestate by Dec., 1799, and Matthias Jones was his administrator. He made distributive shares of the estate to William Jones, Mary Jones, Thomas Ann Griffin, John Jones, Parker Jones, and Caleb Jones in Nov., 1800 [Ref: SO-295, SO-200].

JONES, Mordecai (April 19, 1747 - June 6, 1829). Private in the St. Mary's County Militia in 1777 [Ref: M-215]. Buried at "Cornfield Harbor" near Scotland in St. Mary's County [Ref: R-409, HG-42].

JONES, Morris. Took the Oath of Allegiance before the Hon. Bennett Biscoe in St. Mary's County in 1778 [Ref: J-1146, K-63].

JONES, Moses. Private, Capt. Frisby Freeland's Co., Calvert County Militia, 1778 [Ref: J-1146, M-148]. Took the Oath of Allegiance in Calvert County in 1778 [Ref: L-37].

JONES, Parker. See "Matthias Jones," q.v.

JONES, Roger. Took the Oath of Allegiance in Calvert County in 1778 [Ref: L-37].

JONES, Solomon. Took the Oath of Allegiance before the Hon. Robert Armstrong in St. Mary's County in 1778 [Ref: J-1146, K-62]. One Solomon Jones died by April, 1796, at which time his orphan son Solomon (above the age of 14) chose his mother Ann Jones as his guardian. In Dec., 1799, John Gough was appointed guardian of Clare Jones, orphan of Solomon Jones [Ref: SO-241, SO-296].

JONES, Thomas. Second Lieutenant, Capt. James Grahame's Co., Calvert County Militia, Sep. 24, 1777, and First Lieutenant, April 16, 1778 [Ref: J-1146, M-94, M-148, C-384]. This name also appeared twice on the list of those who took the Oath of Allegiance in Calvert County in 1778 [Ref: L-37].

JONES, Thomas Jr. Private, Capt. Thomas Truman Greenfield's Co., Calvert County Militia, 1778 [Ref: J-1146, M-150].

JONES, Thomas (of James). Took the Oath of Allegiance in Calvert County in 1778 [Ref: L-37].

JONES, William. Private, Capt. Henry Skinner's Foot Co. of Hunting Hundred, Calvert County, 1777 [Ref: T-1814, O-125]. Took the Oath of Allegiance in Calvert County in 1778 [Ref: L-37]. See "Matthias Jones," q.v.

JORDAN, Ann Willson. See "Justinian Jordan," q.v.

JORDAN, Charles. Captain, Upper Bn., St. Mary's County Militia, Aug. 28, 1777, and Captain, 1st Maryland Line, from Oct. 28, 1780 through at least May 9, 1782 [Ref: M-94, SM-150]. Took the Oath of Allegiance before the Hon. Jeremiah Jordan in St. Mary's County in 1778 [Ref: J-1146, K-67]. Appointed Inspector of the Wicomico Warehouse on Oct. 6, 1780 [Ref: SM-150, F-342].

JORDAN, Elinor. See "Jeremiah Jordan," q.v.

JORDAN, Elizabeth. See "Justinian Jordan" and "John Lewellin," q.v.

JORDAN, Henry. See "James Jordan," q.v.

JORDAN, James (c1730-1787). Son of Justinian Jordan and Mary Coode. He married by 1752 to Ann Yates and had a son Henry who died circa 1776. Served as St. Mary's County Surveyor in 1766. Private, Capt. Uriah Forrest's Co., Flying Camp, St. Mary's County, July 28, 1776. Served as a Delegate in the Lower House, 1777-1780; Tax Commissioner, 1778 and 1781; and Judge, Court of Appeals for Tax Assessment, 1786 [Ref: D-30, N-76, N-82, N-499]. Took the Oath of Allegiance before the Hon. Jeremiah Jordan in St. Mary's County in 1778 [Ref: J-1146, K-67]. One James Jordan died by Feb., 1787, and in Feb., 1790, his two grandchildren, James Jordan and William McWilliams Jordan, were mentioned with James Jordan as their guardian [Ref: SO-109, SO-119, SO-132, SO-149].

JORDAN, Jeremiah (c1733 - Jan. 12, 1806). Son of Justinian Jordan and Mary Coode. He married Susannah ---- and had children Richard, Robert, John, Elinor, and Ann. Jeremiah served in many official capacities: Court Justice, St. Mary's County, 1760-1764, 1768-1786; County Sheriff, 1764-1767; Justice of the Court of Oyer and Terminer and Gaol Delivery, 1771-1775; Delegate to the Maryland Convention, 1775-1776; Tax Commissioner at various times between 1777 and 1790; Colonel, St. Mary's County Militia, Jan. 1, 1776 through at least Nov., 1778; Register of Wills, 1777-1806; and, Subscription Loan Officer, Continental Land Office, 1779 [Ref: M-94, C-345, V-193, N-70, N-72, N-

74]. Justice who administered the Oath of Allegiance in St. Mary's County in 1778 [Ref: J-1146, K-67]. There was also a Jeremiah Jordan who was a sailor on the State ship *Defence* from Jan. 23, 1777 to Dec. 31, 1777 [Ref: D-657]. "Jeremiah Jordon" was elected to a General Committee in St. Mary's County in accordance with the resolves of the Continental Congress in 1775, and served on the Committee of Correspondence [Ref: MR-127]. "Colonel Jeremiah Jordan" was named executor of the estate of Justinian Jordan in March, 1794 [Ref: SO-208]. There was also a Jeremiah Jordan who served as a seaman aboard the State ship *Defence* in 1777 [Ref: S-160].

JORDAN, Jesse. Private, Capt. Uriah Forrest's Co., Flying Camp, St. Mary's County, July 28, 1776 [Ref: D-30, SM-113, S-160].

JORDAN, John. Sergeant of Marines aboard the State ship *Defence* from Jan. 23, 1777 to Dec. 31, 1777 [Ref: D-657]. Took the Oath of Allegiance before the Hon. John Ireland in St. Mary's County in 1778 [Ref: J-1146, K-65]. Private, 5th Maryland Line, 1780 [Ref: D-218, S-37]. John Jordan, of St. Inigoes, died on Feb. 5, 1806 [Ref: R-410]. Also see "Jeremiah Jordan," q.v.

JORDAN, Justinian. Private, St. Mary's County, 3rd Maryland Line, Capt. Armstrong's Co., enlisted on April 18, 1777. Sergeant, April 2, 1778, and reduced to private on May 25, 1779 [Ref: SM-113, D-298, D-127, which listed the name as "Justinian Jourdan" and "Justian. Jordon" and "Jestinian Jordon"]. One "Justinean Jordan" died testate by Feb., 1791, and in Oct., 1796, his orphaned children were Ann Willson Jordan, Mary Jordan, and Elizabeth Jordan (all were above the age of 14). [Ref: SO-161, SO-249]. Source S-141 indicates also that Justinian Townshend Jordan (1743-1789), son of Justinian Jordan and Elizabeth Eden, married Elizabeth Bond in 1753. Served in 3rd Maryland Line, Continental Army, from April 8, 1777 to May 25, 1779. See "James Jordan" and "Jeremiah Jordan," q.v.

JORDAN, Margaret. See "Ignatius Taylor," q.v.

JORDAN, Mary. See "Justinian Jordan," q.v.

JORDAN, Richard and Robert. See "Jeremiah Jordan," q.v.

JORDAN, Samuel. Private, Capt. Uriah Forrest's Co., Flying Camp, St. Mary's County, July 28, 1776 [Ref: D-30]. Private, St. Mary's County Militia, 1777 [Ref: M-212]. Corporal of Marines on the State ship *Defence* from Oct. 22 to Dec. 31, 1777 [Ref: D-657]. Took the Oath of Allegiance before the Hon. John Shanks in St. Mary's County in 1778 [Ref: J-1146, K-70].

JORDAN, Susannah. See "Jeremiah Jordan," q.v.

JORDAN, William. Private, St. Mary's County Militia, 1777 [Ref: M-212]. One William Jordan died intestate by Dec., 1796 [Ref: SO-252]. Also see "James Jordan," q.v.

JOSEPH, Clement. Private, St. Mary's County Militia, 1777 [Ref: M-213].

JOSEPH, Ignatius. Took the Oath of Allegiance before the Hon. John Reeder in St. Mary's County in 1778 [Ref: J-1146, K-69].
JOSEPH, Jesse. Private, St. Mary's County Militia, 1777 [Ref: M-212].
JOSEPH, Joseph. Private, St. Mary's County Militia, 1777 [Ref: M-213].
JOSEPH, Justinian. Took the Oath of Allegiance before the Hon. John Reeder in St. Mary's County in 1778 [Ref: J-1146, K-69].
JOSEPH, William. Took the Oath of Allegiance before the Hon. John Reeder in St. Mary's County in 1778 [Ref: J-1146, K-69].
JOURNEY, William. Took the Oath of Allegiance in Calvert County in 1778 [Ref: L-37].
JOWLES, Mary. See "Henry Greenfield Sothoron," q.v.
JOWLES, Rebecca. See "Philip Key," q.v.
JOY, Athanasius (Athenatius). Private, St. Mary's County Militia, 1777 [Ref: M-211, M-212]. Took the Oath of Allegiance before the Hon. John Reeder in St. Mary's County in 1778 [Ref: J-1146, K-69].
JOY, Charles. Private, St. Mary's County Militia, 1777 [Ref: M-213]. Took the Oath of Allegiance before the Hon. Ignatius Fenwick, Jr. in St. Mary's County in 1778 [Ref: J-1146, K-68].
JOY, Enoch. Private, St. Mary's County Militia, 1777 [Ref: M-211].
JOY, Ignatius Jr. Private, St. Mary's County Militia, 1777 [Ref: M-211]. Took the Oath of Allegiance before the Hon. Ignatius Fenwick, Jr. in St. Mary's County in 1778 [Ref: J-1146, K-68]. Ignatius Joy died on March 29, 1827 [Ref: R-410]. One Ignatius Joy, orphan son of Ignatius Joy, was above the age of 14 in Feb., 1781 [Ref: SO-39].
JOY, Ignatius Sr. Took the Oath of Allegiance before the Hon. Ignatius Fenwick, Jr. in St. Mary's County in 1778 [Ref: J-1146, K-68].
JOY, Peter. (1) Private, St. Mary's County Militia, 1777 [Ref: M-211, which listed the name as "Peter Joyh"]. Took the Oath of Allegiance before the Hon. Ignatius Fenwick, Jr. in St. Mary's County in 1778 [Ref: J-1146, K-68]. (2) Private, St. Mary's County Militia, 1777 [Ref: M-212]. Took the Oath of Allegiance before the Hon. John Ireland in St. Mary's County in 1778 [Ref: J-1146, K-65].
JOY, Thomas. Private, St. Mary's County Militia, 1777 [Ref: M-212]. The Register of St. Francis Xavier Catholic Church states Thomas Joy and Sarah Fields were married Feb. 16, 1775 [Ref: SC-35].
KAHILL, Nathaniel. See "Nathaniel Cahill," q.v.
KAIN, Thomas. Private, St. Mary's County Militia, 1777 [Ref: M-215].
KEECH, James (1745-c1790). Private, St. Mary's County Militia, 1777 [Ref: M-213]. Took the Oath of Allegiance before the Hon. Henry Tubman in St. Mary's County in 1778 [Ref: J-1146, K-70]. He married Ann Estep [Ref: Y-378].
KEECH, John. Private, St. Mary's County Militia, 1777 [Ref: M-213]. Took the Oath of Allegiance before the Hon. John Reeder in St. Mary's County in 1778 [Ref: J-1146, K-69].

KEECH, Timothy. Took the Oath of Allegiance before the Hon. Bennett Biscoe in St. Mary's County in 1778 [Ref: J-1146, K-63, which listed the name as "Timothy Keech"]. The Register of St. Andrew's Episcopal Church states that Timothy Keech and Araminta Uldra were married (by publication) Feb. 27, 1783 [Ref: MB-385].
KEEMER, Thomas. See "Thomas Keymer" and "Hugh Hopewell," q.v.
KEIRK (KERRK), Joseph. Took the Oath of Allegiance before the Hon. Robert Armstrong in St. Mary's County in 1778 [Ref: J-1146, K-62].
KELLOW, Edna. See "Leonard Bean," q.v.
KELLOW, William. Private, 1st Maryland Line, enlisted June 1, 1778. Corporal, Aug. 1, 1779. Sergeant, Jan. 1, 1780 [Ref: D-129].
KELLY, Joseph. Private, St. Mary's County, discharged from the Continental Army on Dec. 3, 1781 [Ref: S-161, S-109, H-11].
KELLY, Patrick. Private, St. Mary's County, enlisted on April 20, 1778, for 3 years. Served in the 3rd Maryland Line until reported "deserted" on June 29, 1778 [Ref: D-130, D-329, SM-114, S-161].
KELLY, Vincent. Paid for his services (unspecified) in St. Mary's County to the State of Maryland on July 24, 1782 [Ref: S-161].
KELTY, William. Ensign, Capt. James Grahame's Co., Calvert County Militia, Sep. 24, 1777 [Ref: C-384, J-1146, M-94, M-148]. Took the Oath of Allegiance in Calvert County in 1778 [Ref: L-37].
KENDRICK, Zachariah. Private, St. Mary's County Militia, 1777 [Ref: M-214]. Took the Oath of Allegiance before the Hon. Vernon Hebb in St. Mary's County in 1778 [Ref: J-1146, K-67, which listed the name as "Zacharias Kendruk"].
KENNICK, George. Took the Oath of Allegiance before the Hon. Henry G. Sothoron in St. Mary's County in 1778 [Ref: J-1146, K-69, which source listed the name as "George Hennick"].
KENNICK, Jasper. Took the Oath of Allegiance in St. Mary's County in 1780 [Ref: Q-114].
KENT, Daniel. Ensign, Capt. Charles Williamson's Co., Calvert County Militia, May 10, 1776 through April 16, 1778 [Ref: J-1146, A-320, E-37, M-95, M-147]. Took the Oath of Allegiance in Calvert County in 1778 [Ref: L-37].
KENT, Isaac. Private, Capt. Benjamin Bond's Co., Calvert County Militia, 1778 [Ref: J-1146, M-149]. Took the Oath of Allegiance in Calvert County in 1778 [Ref: L-37]. The Christ Church Register in Calvert County records the birth of Isaac Kent, son of John and Jeannett Kent, on Dec. 21, 1731, and the birth of Isaac Kent, son of John Kent and Elizabeth Dare, on May 19, 1759 [Ref: O-18].
KENT, John, Jeannett, and Elizabeth. See "Isaac Kent," q.v.
KEOUGH, William. Took the Oath of Allegiance before the Hon. Robert Watts in St. Mary's County in 1778 [Ref: J-1146, K-62].
KEY, Anna Heath, Cecelia Brown, Edward Hall, Eliza Maynadier, Henry Greenfield Sothoron, and John Hall. See "Philip Key," q.v.

KEY, John and Mary. See "Philip Key" and "Thomas Bond," q.v.

KEY, Philip (1750 - Jan. 4, 1820). Son of Dr. John Key and Cecelia Brown. He married twice: (1) Rebecca Jowles Sothoron, daughter of "Henry Greenfield Sothoron," q.v., on March 4, 1778; and (2) Sophia Hall (1765-1833), daughter of Col. Aquila Hall (1727-1779), of Baltimore (now Harford) County. Children: Philip Key, Robert Morris Key, John Key, Henry Greenfield Sothoron Key, Edward Hall Key, Upton Scott Key, Thomas White Key, John Hall Key, Mary Key, Cecelia Brown Key, Rebecca Sothoron Key, Eliza Maynadier Key, Clarissa Bond Key, Sophia Hall Key, Susanna Gardiner Key, Anna Heath Key, and Mary Hall Key [Ref: N-509, I-536, Y-384, which latter source listed his year of death as 1840]. Philip served on the Committee of Correspondence in 1774, in the Lower House from St. Mary's County in 1773, 1779-1780, 1783, 1785, 1787-1788, 1790, 1795-1796 (speaker), and in the U. S. Congress, 1791-1793 [Ref: N-82, N-87, N-508, N-509]. He and Uriah Forrest wrote to the Governor on Dec. 26, 1779, regarding the readiness for sailing of the State ship *Union* [Ref: V-253]. Philip Key provided wheat in St. Mary's County for the use of the Army in 1780 and 1781, and loaned money for the war effort in 1781 [Ref: V-408, X-78, H-493, H-494, S-77]. He is buried in the vault at Christ Church Cemetery in Chaptico, which was desecrated by the British during the War of 1812 (no stone). [Ref: S-129]. See "Thomas Bond," q.v.

KEY, Rebecca Jowles, Rebecca Sothoron, Robert Morris, and Sophia Hall. See "Philip Key," q.v.

KEY, Susannah Gardiner. See "Philip Key" and "Thomas Bond," q.v.

KEY, Thomas White and Upton Scott. See "Philip Key," q.v.

KEYMER (KEEMER), Samuel. Private, St. Mary's County Militia, 1777 [Ref: M-213].

KEYMER (KEEMER), Thomas. Took the Oath of Allegiance before the Hon. Vernon Hebb in St. Mary's County in 1778 [Ref: J-1146, K-67, which listed the name as "Thomas Keimer"]. "Dr. Thomas Keemer" died by Dec., 1794 [Ref: SO-238, SO-244]. See "Hugh Hopewell," q.v.

KIDD, John. Private, 4th Maryland Line, enlisted Aug. 25, 1777, probably from Calvert County, and served through 1780 [Ref: D-131].

KIDD, Margerit. See "James Marquess," q.v.

KIBLEY, Joseph. Private, St. Mary's County Militia, 1781, and served as a substitute for James Harvard in the Maryland Line. Applied for pension in 1835 in Union County, Kentucky, stating he was born in St. Mary's County in 1763, enlisted at Leonardtown and moved to Kentucky in 1805, settling in Union County about 1820. His application (R5905) was rejected due to lack of proof [Ref: W-55, MK-84, but not listed in P-1938]. However, Joseph Kibley did serve and was discharged from the Maryland Line in 1781 [Ref: D-409].

KILBURN, William. Took the Oath of Allegiance before the Hon. Bennett Biscoe in St. Mary's County in 1778 [Ref: J-1146, K-63].

KILGOUR, William. (1) Captain, Upper Bn., St. Mary's County, Aug. 26, 1777 [Ref: M-95, C-346]. Provided wheat for the military on Feb. 2, 1780 [Ref: V-267, which listed the name as "William Kilgore"]. Justice of the Peace and Judge of the Orphans Court in St. Mary's County, 1777-1782 [Ref: S-161]. (2) Private, St. Mary's County Militia, 1777 [Ref: M-209]. See "Leonard Bean," q.v.

KILPATRICK, William. Private, St. Mary's County, discharged from the Continental Army on Dec. 3, 1781 [Ref: S-161, H-11].

KING, ----. See "Walter Smith," q.v.

KING, Adam. Private, Calvert County, enlisted by Lt. Nathaniel Wilson on Aug. 23, 1776 [Ref: D-34].

KING, Barton. This name appeared twice as a private, St. Mary's County Militia, 1777 [Ref: M-209, M-215]. One took the Oath of Allegiance before the Hon. Henry G. Sothoron in St. Mary's County in 1778 [Ref: J-1146, K-69]. One Barton King died intestate by June, 1782, leaving orphans James King and Elizabeth King, and his widow Sarah King married Richard Hill in Jan., 1783 [Ref: SO-49, SO-150]. See "Richard Hill," q.v.

KING, Benjamin. (1) Took the Oath of Allegiance in Calvert County in 1778 [Ref: L-37]. (2) Took the Oath of Allegiance in St. Mary's County in 1780 [Ref: Q-114]. One "Benjamin King, farmer" moved to Barren County, Kentucky, in 1793 [Ref: X-86].

KING, Benjamin (of James). Private, Capt. Thomas Truman Greenfield's Co., Calvert County Militia, 1778 [Ref: J-1146, M-150].

KING, Charles Jr. Took the Oath of Allegiance before the Hon. Robert Watts in St. Mary's County in 1778 [Ref: J-1146, K-62]. He died by June, 1782, leaving a son Charles who chose John King, Jr. as his guardian [Ref: SO-52].

KING, Cornelius. Private, St. Mary's County Militia, 1777 [Ref: M-209]. Took the Oath of Allegiance in St. Mary's County in 1780 [Ref: Q-114]. One "Cornelius King, farmer" moved from Upper Resurrection to Nelson County, Kentucky, in 1808 [Ref: X-87].

KING, Dorcas. See "Vernon St. Clair," q.v.

KING, Elizabeth. See "Barton King," q.v.

KING, Francis. (1) Recommended to the Governor on Dec. 27, 1777, that he be appointed the Register of Wills for Calvert County [Ref: V-134]. Private, Capt. Thomas Truman Greenfield's Co., Calvert County Militia, 1778 [Ref: J-1146, M-150]. Took the Oath of Allegiance in Calvert County in 1778 [Ref: L-37]. (2) Took the Oath of Allegiance in St. Mary's County in 1780 [Ref: Q-114].

KING, Francis, "of Harford County." Took the Oath of Allegiance before the Hon. Ignatius Fenwick, Jr. in St. Mary's County in 1778 [Ref: J-1146, K-68].

KING, George (1758-1821). Private, 2nd Maryland Line, enlisted on Jan. 21, 1778 [Ref: D-129]. Took the Oath of Allegiance before the Hon. John

Ireland in St. Mary's County in 1778 [Ref: J-1146, K-65]. "George King, Sr." died in Georgetown, D. C. *[sic]* on Oct. 9, 1821, aged 63 [Ref: R-413].

KING, Henry. (1) Private, Capt. James Patterson's Co., Calvert County Militia, Aug. 10, 1777 [Ref: M-146]. Private, Capt. James Grahame's Co., Calvert County Militia, 1778 [Ref: J-1146, M-149]. (2) Sergeant, 3rd Maryland Line, 1778; from St. Mary's County [Ref: S-161]. See "Henry King, Jr.," q.v.

KING, Henry Jr. Private, St. Mary's County Militia, 1777 [Ref: M-214]. Took the Oath of Allegiance before the Hon. Bennett Biscoe in St. Mary's County in 1778 [Ref: J-1146, K-63]. The Register of St. Andrew's Episcopal Church states that Henry King and Catharine Watts were married (by license) June 17, 1784 [Ref: MB-385].

KING, Henry Sr. Private, St. Mary's County Militia, 1777 [Ref: M-215]. Private, St. Mary's County, enlisted May 25, 1778, for 9 months [Ref: D-330]. Took the Oath of Allegiance before the Hon. Robert Watts in St. Mary's County in 1778 [Ref: J-1146, K-62]. One Henry King owned "Indian Bridge" (Beaverdam Manor) and died testate in 1795 in St. Mary's County, leaving a son Stephen King who was his executor in 1800 [Ref: R-413, SO-309]. See "Henry King," q.v.

KING, James. Private, Capt. Frisby Freeland's Co., Calvert County Militia, 1778 [Ref: J-1146, M-148]. It must also be noted that one "James King, alias James McMullen" of the 3rd Maryland Line (county of residence not stated) was charged with desertion and was given 100 lashes and fined $120, which was the bounty he had received at the time of his enlistment [Ref: *Summer Soldiers: A Survey & Index of Revolutionary War Courts-Martial*, by James C. Neagles (1986), page 175]. See "Barton King," q.v.

KING, James, "of Harford County." Took the Oath of Allegiance before the Hon. Ignatius Fenwick, Jr. in St. Mary's County in 1778 [Ref: J-1146, K-68].

KING, James (of John). Took the Oath of Allegiance before the Hon. John Ireland in St. Mary's County in 1778 [Ref: J-1146, K-65].

KING, Jeremiah. Private, St. Mary's County Militia, 1777 [Ref: M-214]. Private, St. Mary's County, enlisted May 22, 1778, for 9 months [Ref: D-330]. Corporal, 3rd Maryland Line, 1778, until discharged on April 3, 1779 [Ref: S-161].

KING, John. There were several men with this name: (1) Private, Calvert County, enlisted by Lt. Nathaniel Wilson on Aug. 23, 1776 [Ref: D-34]. (2) Private, Capt. James Patterson's Co., Calvert County Militia, Aug. 10, 1777 [Ref: M-146]. (3) Private, Capt. Frederick Skinner's Co., Calvert County Militia, 1778 [Ref: J-1146, M-150]. (4) Private, Capt. Richard Lane's Co., Calvert County Militia, 1778 [Ref: J-1146, M-150]. (5) Private, St. Mary's County Militia, 1777 [Ref: M-211]. (6) Private, St. Mary's County, drafted July 27, 1781 [Ref: D-384]. (7) John King, among others, recommended the appointment of Enoch Fenwick as an Inspector of Tobacco in St. Mary's County on Dec. 22, 1776 [Ref: V-74]. One John King died intestate in St. Mary's County by Aug., 1791, and his son John was aged between 15 and 16 years of age in Feb., 1796 [Ref: SO-168, SO-240].

KING, John Jr. (1) Took the Oath of Allegiance before the Hon. Robert Watts in St. Mary's County in 1778 [Ref: J-1146, K-62]. (2) Private, Capt. James Grahame's Co., Calvert County Militia, 1778 [Ref: J-1146, M-149]. See "Charles King, Jr.," q.v.

KING, John (of Charles Jr.). Private, St. Mary's County Militia, 1777 [Ref: M-213]. See "Charles King, Jr.," q.v.

KING, John (of Thomas). Took the Oath of Allegiance before the Hon. Henry Reeder in St. Mary's County in 1778 [Ref: J-1146, K-64].

KING, Margaret. See "Thomas Wherritt," q.v.

KING, Mary. See "Alexander Parran," q.v.

KING, Peter. Took the Oath of Allegiance in St. Mary's County in 1780 [Ref: Q-114].

KING, Richard. Second Lieutenant, Lower Bn., St. Mary's County Militia, Aug. 26, 1777, and First Lieutenant, May 7, 1781 [Ref: C-3436, G-426, M-95, M-213]. Took the Oath of Allegiance before the Hon. Robert Watts in St. Mary's County in 1778 [Ref: J-1146, K-62]. Richard King and Sarah Rawlings were married on Dec. 17, 1778, by Rev. Francis Lauder, of Christ Church Parish [Ref: K-34].

KING, Robert. Private, St. Mary's County Militia, 1777 [Ref: M-212, which listed the name as "Rob King"]. Took the Oath of Allegiance before the Hon. John Shanks in St. Mary's County in 1778 [Ref: J-1146, K-70].

KING, Sarah. See "Barton King" and "Richard Hill," q.v.

KING, Stephen. See "Henry King, Sr.," q.v.

KING, Thomas. Private, 1st Maryland Line, enlisted in April, 1779 and served through 1780 [Ref: D-129]. Took the Oath of Allegiance before the Hon. Ignatius Fenwick, Jr. in St. Mary's County in 1778 [Ref: J-1146, K-68].

KING, William. There were several men with this name: (1) Private, St. Mary's County Militia, 1777 [Ref: M-211]. (2) Private, Capt. James Grahame's Co., Calvert County Militia, 1778 [Ref: J-1146, M-149]. (3) One took the Oath of Allegiance before the Hon. John Reeder in St. Mary's County in 1778 [Ref: J-1146, K-69]. (4) One took the Oath of Allegiance in St. Mary's County in 1780 [Ref: Q-114]. (5) One was a Seaman in 1776 and an Ordinary Sailor on the State ship *Defence* in 1777 [Ref: D-607, D-657, S-25]. (6) William King, of Francis, took the Oath of Allegiance in St. Mary's County in 1780 [Ref: Q-114].

KINNAMAN, John. Took the Oath of Allegiance before the Hon. Henry G. Sothoron in St. Mary's County in 1778 [Ref: J-1146, K-69].

KIRBY, Charles. Private, St. Mary's County Militia, 1777 [Ref: M-215].

KIRBY, Elizabeth. See "William Leatherland," q.v.
KIRBY, Francis. "Francis Kerbey" was a private, St. Mary's County Militia, 1777 [Ref: M-215]. The Register of St. Andrew's Episcopal Church states that Francis Kirby and Millburn Hagar were married (by license) Jan. 1, 1782 [Ref: MB-384].
KIRBY, Hopewell. Private, St. Mary's County Militia, 1777 [Ref: M-215].
KIRBY, Joseph. Private (substitute), St. Mary's County, July 31, 1781 [Ref: D-384].
KIRBY, Richard. Private, Capt. Uriah Forrest's Co., Flying Camp, St. Mary's County, July 28, 1776 [Ref: D-30, SM-114].
KIRBY (KERBEY), William. This name appeared twice as a private in the St. Mary's County Militia in 1777 [Ref: M-215].
KIRBY, Zachariah. Took the Oath of Allegiance in St. Mary's County in 1780 [Ref: Q-114].
KIRK, Elizabeth. See "Richard Thompson, of Joseph," q.v.
KIRKPATRICK, William. Private (substitute), St. Mary's County, July 26, 1781. Private, Continental Army, 1781 [Ref: D-384, D-409].
KIRSHAW (KERSHAW), Francis. Private, Capt. Henry Skinner's Foot Co. of Hunting Hundred, Calvert County, 1777 [Ref: T-1814, O-125]. The Christ Church Register in Calvert County records the birth of Francis Kirshaw, son of Francis Kirshaw (born June 4, 1727, son of James and Margaret Kirshaw) and Rebecca Brady (married Sep. 12, 1756), on Nov. 18, 1760, and he married Ann P. Duke on July 22, 1784 [Ref: O-19].
KIRSHAW (KERSHAW), James. Sergeant, Foot Co. of Hunting Creek Hundred, Calvert County, 1777 [Ref: T-1814, O-125]. Took the Oath of Allegiance in Calvert County in 1778 [Ref: L-37, which listed the name as "James Kirshaw"]. Also see "Francis Kirshaw," q.v.
KIRSHAW (KERSHAW), James Jr. Private, Capt. Henry Skinner's Foot Co. of Hunting Hundred, Calvert County, 1777 [Ref: T-1814, O-125]. Private, Capt. Benjamin Bond's Co., Calvert County Militia, 1778 [Ref: J-1146, M-149, which listed the name as "James Kirshaw, Jr."].
KIRSHAW, Ann and Margaret. See "Francis Kirshaw," q.v.
KIRSHAW (KERSHAW), Mary. See "John McKinney," q.v.
KIRSHAW, Rebecca. See "Francis Kirshaw," q.v.
KNIGHT, Philip. Paid for services (unspecified) in St. Mary's County to the State of Maryland on Nov. 27, 1781 [Ref: S-161].
KNOTT, Ignatius. Private, Capt. Uriah Forrest's Co., Flying Camp, St. Mary's County, July 28, 1776 [Ref: D-30, SM-114]. There was another Ignatius Knott (1747-1835) who was born in St. Mary's County, moved to Washington County in 1768, enlisted in Hagerstown, Maryland, and in 1799 moved to Clermont County, Ohio. He applied for and received pension S4481 in 1832 [Ref: P-1978, Y-393]. See "James Knott," q.v.
KNOTT, James. This name appeared twice as a private in the St. Mary's County Militia in 1777 [Ref: M-212, M-213]. One took the Oath of

Allegiance before the Hon. Robert Watts in St. Mary's County in 1778 [Ref: J-1146, K-62, which listed the name as "James Nott"]. One received bounty land in Feb., 1790 [Ref: P-1978]. James Knott and Jeremiah Knott both served in the 2nd Maryland Line and were reported to be "dead or deserted" in 1778 [Ref: D-129]. A James Knott was prisoner of war in Jan., 1780, and returned to service from Jan. 1, 1782 to Nov. 15, 1783 [Ref: S-161]. One James Knott was deceased by May, 1799, when Ignatius Knott was appointed guardian to his niece Susanna Knott, orphan daughter of James Knott. There appears to have been other children, although none were named in this particular record [Ref: SO-286, SO-287].

KNOTT, Jeremiah. See "James Knott," q.v.

KNOTT, John. Private, St. Mary's County Militia, 1777 [Ref: M-213]. Took the Oath of Allegiance before the Hon. Henry G. Sothoron in St. Mary's County in 1778 [Ref: J-1146, K-69].

KNOTT, Nathaniel. Private, St. Mary's County Militia, 1777 [Ref: M-213]. Corporal, 3rd Maryland Line, who was taken prisoner at the Battle of Camden in South Carolina on Aug. 16, 1780 [Ref: D-147, which listed the name as "Nathanl. Nott"].

KNOTT, Susannah. See "James Knott," q.v.

LAKE, John. Took the Oath of Allegiance before the Hon. Jenifer Taylor in St. Mary's County in 1778 [Ref: J-1146, K-64].

LAMB, John. Private, St. Mary's County Militia, 1777 [Ref: M-213].

LAMBDEN, Ann. See "Thomas Goldsmith," q.v.

LAMBIRTH (LAMBATH), William. Private, Capt. Richard Lane's Co., Calvert County Militia, 1778 [Ref: J-1146, M-149]. Took the Oath of Allegiance in Calvert County in 1778 [Ref: L-37].

LANCASTER, Jeremiah. Private, St. Mary's County Militia, 1777 [Ref: M-213]. "Jeremiah Lancaster, farmer" moved from Upper Newtown to Washington County, Kentucky, in 1810 [Ref: X-87].

LANCASTER, John. Took the Oath of Allegiance before the Hon. John Ireland in St. Mary's County in 1778 [Ref: J-1146, K-65, Y-399].

LANCASTER, Ralph. Private, St. Mary's County Militia, 1777 [Ref: M-213].

LANCASTER, Raphael. Took the Oath of Allegiance before the Hon. John Shanks in St. Mary's County in 1778 [Ref: J-1146, K-70].

LANE, Benjamin. Took the Oath of Allegiance in Calvert County in 1778 [Ref: L-37].

LANE, Benjamin (of Richard). Private, Capt. Richard Lane's Co., Calvert County Militia, 1778 [Ref: J-1146, M-150, which listed the name as "Benjamin Lane, for Richd."].

LANE, Bennett. Private, St. Mary's County Militia, 1777 [Ref: M-214, which listed the name as "Bennet Lane (Lone?)"].

LANE, Elizabeth. See "David Weems," q.v.

LANE, Richard. Captain, Calvert County Militia, 1778 [Ref: J-1146, M-149].
LANE, Samuel and Sarah. See "John Mackall," q.v.
LANGLEY, Henry. Took the Oath of Allegiance before the Hon. Jeremiah Jordan in St. Mary's County in 1778 [Ref: J-1146, K-67].
LANGLEY, James. Private, St. Mary's County Militia, 1777 [Ref: M-215].
LANGLEY, Joseph. Second Lieutenant, Lower Bn., St. Mary's County Militia, Aug. 26, 1777 [Ref: M-96, C-346, SM-114].
LANGLEY, Josiah (Josias). Took the Oath of Allegiance before the Hon. Vernon Hebb in St. Mary's County in 1778 [Ref: J-1146, K-67]. Private, St. Mary's County Militia, 1777 [Ref: M-214].
LANGLEY, William. Took the Oath of Allegiance before the Hon. Robert Armstrong in St. Mary's County in 1778 [Ref: J-1146, K-62].
LANSDALE, John. Private, Capt. Thomas Truman Greenfield's Co., Calvert County Militia, 1778 [Ref: J-1146, M-150].
LATHAM, Matthew. Took the Oath of Allegiance before the Hon. Richard Barnes in St. Mary's County in 1778 [Ref: J-1146, K-66].
LATTIMORE, James. Private, St. Mary's County Militia, 1777 [Ref: M-210].
LAVENDER, Thomas. Private, St. Mary's County, 3rd Maryland Line, Capt. Armstrong's Co., 1778-1780; sick in hospital at Kimbel's Farm, Dec., 1779 - Jan., 1780 [Ref: D-298, D-299].
LAVIELLE (LAVEILLE), Abraham. Private, Capt. Walter Smith's Co., Calvert County Militia, 1778 [Ref: J-1146, M-148].
LAVIELLE (LAVEILLE), Daniel. Private, Capt. Walter Smith's Co., Calvert County Militia, 1778 [Ref: J-1146, M-148]. Took the Oath of Allegiance in Calvert County in 1778 [Ref: L-37].
LAVIELLE (LAVEILLE), John. Private, Capt. Frisby Freeland's Co., Calvert County Militia, 1778 [Ref: J-1146, M-148]. Took the Oath of Allegiance in Calvert County in 1778 [Ref: L-37].
LAWNEY, Eleanor. See "Philip Read," q.v.
LAWRENCE, James. Private, Calvert County, enlisted by Lt. Frederick Skinner on Aug. 23, 1776 [Ref: D-33]. Private, Capt. Benjamin Bond's Co., Calvert County Militia, 1778 [Ref: J-1146, M-149]. Took the Oath of Allegiance in Calvert County in 1778 [Ref: L-37, which listed the name as "Jamel (James?) Lawrance"].
LAWRENCE, John. Private, Capt. Frisby Freeland's Co., Calvert County Militia, 1778 [Ref: J-1146, M-148]. Took the Oath of Allegiance in Calvert County in 1778 [Ref: L-37].
LAWRENCE, Lorrewell. Private, Capt. Edward Wood's Co., Calvert County Militia, 1778 [Ref: J-1146, M-147]. Took the Oath of Allegiance in Calvert County in 1778 [Ref: L-37, which listed the name as "Lorry Lawrance"].

LEACH, Asahel. Private, Capt. Frisby Freeland's Co., Calvert County Militia, 1778 [Ref: J-1146, M-148]. Took the Oath of Allegiance in Calvert County in 1778 [Ref: L-37].
LEACH, Benjamin. Private, Capt. James Grahame's Co., Calvert County Militia, 1778 [Ref: J-1146, M-149]. Took the Oath of Allegiance in Calvert County in 1778 [Ref: L-37].
LEACH, James. (1) First Lieutenant, Capt. Richard Lane's Co., Calvert County Militia, 1778, and Captain, 15th Bn., April 16, 1778 [Ref: E-37, J-1146, M-97, M-149]. (2) Private, St. Mary's County Militia, 1777 [Ref: M-213]. Private, Capt. Thomas Truman Greenfield's Co., Calvert County Militia, 1778 [Ref: J-1146, M-150].
LEACH, Jeremiah. Private, Capt. Thomas Truman Greenfield's Co., Calvert County Militia, 1778 [Ref: J-1146, M-150]. Took the Oath of Allegiance in Calvert County in 1778 [Ref: L-37].
LEACH, John. Took the Oath of Allegiance in Calvert County in 1778 [Ref: L-37].
LEACH, Joshua. Private, Capt. Frisby Freeland's Co., Calvert County Militia, 1778 [Ref: J-1146, M-148]. Took the Oath of Allegiance in Calvert County in 1778 [Ref: L-37].
LEACH, Joshua Jr. Private, Capt. Thomas Truman Greenfield's Co., Calvert County Militia, 1778 [Ref: J-1146, M-150].
LEACH, Mary. See "Charles Lee," q.v.
LEACH, Nehemiah. Private, St. Mary's County Militia, 1777 [Ref: M-209]. Nehemiah Leach married Elizabeth Lyon on May 1, 1783, St. Mary's County, by Rev. John Stephen, Rector of All Faith's Parish [Ref: I-536].
LEACH, Thomas. (1) Second Lieutenant, 15th Bn., Capt. Edward Wood's Co., Calvert County Militia, April 16, 1778 [Ref: M-97, M-147, E-37]. Took the Oath of Allegiance in Calvert County in 1778 [Ref: L-37]. (2) Took the Oath of Allegiance before the Hon. Ignatius Fenwick, Jr. in St. Mary's County in 1778 [Ref: J-1146, K-68]. The Register of St. Francis Xavier Catholic Church states Thomas Leach and Elizabeth Spalden were married Dec. 1, 1776 [Ref: SC-35].
LEACH, William. Private, St. Mary's County Militia, 1777 [Ref: M-211]. Took the Oath of Allegiance before the Hon. John Ireland in St. Mary's County in 1778 [Ref: J-1146, K-65]. One William Leach died intestate by Oct., 1785 [Ref: SO-84].
LEAK (LEAKE), James. Private, St. Mary's County Militia, 1777 [Ref: M-212]. Took the Oath of Allegiance before the Hon. John Shanks in St. Mary's County in 1778 [Ref: J-1146, K-70]. "Rebel James Leake was possibly born in Scotland, came to Maryland and served in the Revolutionary War in St. Mary's County. He migrated to Woodford and Scott Counties, Kentucky, and died circa 1807." [Ref: MK-87].
LEATHERLAND, William. Private, St. Mary's County Militia, 1777 [Ref: M-215]. The Register of St. Andrew's Episcopal Church states that

William Leatherland and Elizabeth Kirby were married (by license) Jan. 16, 1781 [Ref: MB-383].

LEATON, John. Took the Oath of Allegiance before the Hon. John Ireland in St. Mary's County in 1778 [Ref: J-1146, K-65, which source listed the name as "John Seaton"].

LEE, Alice. See "John Weems," q.v.

LEE, Benjamin. Private, Capt. Thomas Truman Greenfield's Co., Calvert County Militia, 1778 [Ref: J-1146, M-150]. Took the Oath of Allegiance in Calvert County in 1778 [Ref: L-37].

LEE, Charles. Took the Oath of Allegiance before the Hon. Bennett Biscoe in St. Mary's County in 1778 [Ref: J-1146, K-63]. The Register of St. Inigoes Catholic Church states that Charles Lee and Elizabeth Moore were married July 22, 1784 [Ref: SC-36, which noted "either they or their descendants eventually settled at The Barrens in Perry County, Missouri."]. Also, a Charles Lee and Mary Leach were married on July 28, 1777, by Rev. Thomas John Clagett, All Saint's Parish [Ref: K-33].

LEE, Hance. Took the Oath of Allegiance before the Hon. Jeremiah Jordan in St. Mary's County in 1778 [Ref: J-1146, K-67].

LEE, Hannah. See "George Plater," q.v.

LEE, John. Took the Oath of Allegiance before the Hon. John Reeder in St. Mary's County in 1778 [Ref: J-1146, K-69].

LEE, Philip. Took the Oath of Allegiance before the Hon. John Shanks in St. Mary's County in 1778 [Ref: J-1146, K-70].

LEE, Richard. See "Thomas Lee" and "George Plater" and "William Fitzhugh," q.v.

LEE, Robert. Private, Capt. Thomas Truman Greenfield's Co., Calvert County Militia, 1778 [Ref: J-1146, M-150]. Took the Oath of Allegiance in Calvert County in 1778 [Ref: L-37].

LEE, Samuel. Took the Oath of Allegiance before the Hon. Jeremiah Jordan in St. Mary's County in 1778 [Ref: J-1146, K-67].

LEE, Thomas. Took the Oath of Allegiance before the Hon. John Shanks in St. Mary's County in 1778 [Ref: J-1146, K-70]. One Thomas Lee died by Feb., 1779, leaving a son Richard Lee, aged 15 on June 13, 1779 [Ref: SO-18].

LEIGH, Christopher. Marine on the State ship *Defence* from May 20, 1777 to Dec. 31, 1777 [Ref: D-658]. Took the Oath of Allegiance before the Hon. Bennett Biscoe in St. Mary's County in 1778 [Ref: J-1146, K-63].

LEIGH, Frances. See "Ignatius Clarke," q.v.

LEIGH, George. Took the Oath of Allegiance before the Hon. Bennett Biscoe in St. Mary's County in 1778 [Ref: J-1146, K-63]. One George Leigh died on Feb. 21, 1807, in St. Mary's County [Ref: R-417].

LEIGH, George Howell. Ensign, Lower Bn., St. Mary's County Militia, Aug. 26, 1777 [Ref: M-97, C-346, M-214]. Took the Oath of Allegiance before the Hon. Bennett Biscoe in St. Mary's County in 1778 [Ref: J-1146, K-63].

LEIGH, James. Private, St. Mary's County Militia, 1777 [Ref: M-214].

LEIGH (LEE), John. Messenger for the "Express" on Sep. 10, 1781, in St. Mary's County [Ref: S-161]. See "Joseph Leigh," q.v.

LEIGH, Joseph. Took the Oath of Allegiance before the Hon. Robert Armstrong in St. Mary's County in 1778 [Ref: J-1146, K-62]. One Joseph Leigh died by Dec., 1785, when his son John Leigh chose Walter Leigh as his guardian [Ref: SO-90].

LEIGH, Joseph Jr. Took the Oath of Allegiance before the Hon. Robert Armstrong in St. Mary's County in 1778 [Ref: J-1146, K-62].

LEIGH, Massey. Elected to serve on a General Committee in St. Mary's County in accordance with the resolves of the Continental Congress in 1775 [Ref: MR-127]. He died testate by Dec., 1787, with William Leigh named as his executor [Ref: SO-117, SO-126].

LEIGH, Phil. Private, St. Mary's County Militia, 1777 [Ref: M-214].

LEIGH, Walter. See "Joseph Leigh," q.v.

LEIGH, William. Surgeon's Mate on the State ship *Defence* in 1777 [Ref: D-658]. Took the Oath of Allegiance before the Hon. Bennett Biscoe in St. Mary's County in 1778 [Ref: J-1146, K-63]. See "Massey Leigh," q.v.

LEMMON, Garbiner. Private, St. Mary's County, 3rd Maryland Line, Capt. Armstrong's Co., enlisted May 19, 1778, for 9 months and then again on Nov. 10, 1778 for the duration; was on furlough in Dec., 1779 [Ref: SM-114, D-329, D-299, which latter source listed the name as "Gerbiner Lemmon"]. Took the Oath of Allegiance before the Hon. Richard Barnes in St. Mary's County in 1778 [Ref: J-1146, K-66, which listed the name as "Garbiner Simon"].

LEMMON, John. Private from St. Mary's County who served as a marine on the State ship *Defence* in 1776 [Ref: S-25, D-606].

LEWELLIN, Charles. Private, Capt. Uriah Forrest's Co., Flying Camp, St. Mary's County, July 28, 1776 [Ref: D-30]. Took the Oath of Allegiance before the Hon. Jeremiah Jordan in St. Mary's County in 1778 [Ref: J-1146, K-67]. He died by June, 1799 [Ref: SO-287]. "Charles Llewellen" supplied provisions (wheat, mutton, or bacon) to the Army in 1780 [Ref: S-77].

LEWELLIN, John. Took the Oath of Allegiance before the Hon. Jeremiah Jordan in St. Mary's County in 1778 [Ref: J-1146, K-67]. "Mr. John Llewellin" was elected to a General Committee in St. Mary's County in accordance with the resolves of the Continental Congress in 1775 [Ref: MR-126]. Source S-142 states that "John Llewellyn" (1716-1785) married Elizabeth Jordan (died 1811). There was also a John Lewellin who died Nov. 24, 1826 [Ref: R-419].

LEWIN, Samuel. Took the Oath of Allegiance in Calvert County in 1778 [Ref: L-37].

LEWIS, John (Catholic Priest). Took the Oath of Allegiance in St. Mary's County in 1778 [Ref: SM-185].

LEWIS, Joseph. Took the Oath of Allegiance before the Hon. Bennett Biscoe in St. Mary's County in 1778 [Ref: J-1146, K-63].

LEWIS, William Francis. Took the Oath of Allegiance in Calvert County in 1780 [Ref: Q-115].

LILBURN, Walter. Midshipman from St. Mary's County who served aboard the State ship *Defence* in 1777 [Ref: S-161].

LILBURN, William. Factor (merchant) at St. Inigoes in St. Mary's County in 1775 whose property was destroyed by the British in 1781 [Ref: S-161].

LIMAN, Tobosia (Tobias?). Private, St. Mary's County Militia, 1777 [Ref: M-215].

LIPPET, Notley. See "Notley Tippett," q.v.

LISBEY, James. Private, Capt. James Patterson's Co., Calvert County Militia, Aug. 10, 1777 [Ref: M-146].

LISBY, Kilman. Private, Calvert County, enlisted by Lt. Frederick Skinner on Aug. 23, 1776 [Ref: D-33].

LITHGOW, James. Took the Oath of Allegiance before the Hon. Jeremiah Jordan in St. Mary's County in 1778 [Ref: J-1146, K-67].

LIU (LEE?), Philip. Private, St. Mary's County Militia, 1777 [Ref: M-212].

LOCH, Sarah and William. See "Samuel Chew," q.v.

LOCKE (LOCK), Alexander. See "Meveral Lock," q.v.

LOCKE (LOCK), George. Took the Oath of Allegiance before the Hon. Jeremiah Jordan in St. Mary's County in 1778 [Ref: J-1146, K-67].

LOCKE (LOCK), Jesse (1755-1815). Son of Meverel and Elizabeth Locke. He married Sarah Bruce [Ref: S-142]. Private, St. Mary's County Militia, 1777 [Ref: M-213].

LOCKE (LOCK), Mary. See "Meveral Locke (Lock)," q.v.

LOCKE (LOCK), Meveral (Meveril, Meverel, Meveral). Ensign, Upper Bn., St. Mary's County Militia, Aug. 26, 1777, and Second Lieutenant, Nov. 18, 1779 [Ref: M-98, C-345, F-18]. Took the Oath of Allegiance before the Hon. Jeremiah Jordan in St. Mary's County in 1778 [Ref: J-1146, K-67]. "Meveril Lock" was elected to a General Committee in St. Mary's County in accordance with the resolves of the Continental Congress in 1775 [Ref: MR-127]. Mevel (Meveral, Meverell) Lock died by March, 1791. His son "Meveral Lock" chose Isaac Smoot as his guardian and his other children, Alexander, Rebecca, and Mary Lock, chose Reubin Craig as their guardian in Sep., 1791. It also appears that his widow was Rebecca and she married Reubin Craig some time in 1791 [Ref: SO-165, SO-172, SO-173, SO-196, SO-237].

LOCKE (LOCK), Rebecca. See "Meveral Lock," q.v.

LOCKE (LOCK), Thomas. Took the Oath of Allegiance before the Hon. Henry G. Sothoron in St. Mary's County in 1778 [Ref: J-1146, K-69].

LOKER, Thomas (1751-1803). Took the Oath of Allegiance before the Hon. Bennett Biscoe in St. Mary's County in 1778 [Ref: J-1146, K-63]. Property destroyed by the British in 1781 [Ref: S-162]. Thomas Loker married Rebecca Mackall (1757-1824). [Ref: S-142].
LOKER, William. Paid for making salt in St. Mary's County in 1782 [Ref: S-162].
LONG, James. Took the Oath of Allegiance before the Hon. Jeremiah Jordan in St. Mary's County in 1778 [Ref: J-1146, K-67].
LONG, Jeremiah. Private, St. Mary's County Militia, 1777 [Ref: M-213]. Took the Oath of Allegiance before the Hon. Jeremiah Jordan in St. Mary's County in 1778 [Ref: J-1146, K-67].
LONG, John. Took the Oath of Allegiance before the Hon. Jeremiah Jordan in St. Mary's County in 1778 [Ref: J-1146, K-67]. John Lang [Long?] married Dorothy Williams on Feb. 14, 1778, St. Mary's County, by Rev. George Goldie [Ref: I-535]. "John Long, of Jerry" died on Dec. 13, 1828 [Ref: R-420].
LONG, Joseph. Private, Capt. Uriah Forrest's Co., Flying Camp, St. Mary's County, July 28, 1776 [Ref: D-30]. Private, 6th Maryland Line, from April 16, 1777 until Nov. 15, 1783 [Ref: S-33, D-224, D-349, D-358, D-440, S-162].
LONG, Peregrine. Private, St. Mary's County Militia, 1777 [Ref: M-213]. "Perry Long" took the Oath of Allegiance before the Hon. Jeremiah Jordan in St. Mary's County in 1778 [Ref: J-1146, K-67]. Peregrine Long married Rebecca Williams on Nov. 12, 1778, St. Mary's County, by Rev. George Goldie [Ref: I-535].
LONG, Robert. Private, St. Mary's County Militia, 1777 [Ref: M-213]. Took the Oath of Allegiance before the Hon. Jeremiah Jordan in St. Mary's County in 1778 [Ref: J-1146, K-67].
LONG, Samuel. Took the Oath of Allegiance before the Hon. Jeremiah Jordan in St. Mary's County in 1778 [Ref: J-1146, K-67].
LONGSON, John. Took the Oath of Allegiance before the Hon. Jeremiah Jordan in St. Mary's County in 1778 [Ref: J-1146, K-67].
LORD, Joseph W. He wrote to the Governor from Leonardtown in St. Mary's County and requested funds from the State on Oct. 16, 1780. However, his official capacity was not stated [Ref: V-327].
LOVE, Joseph. Private, St. Mary's County Militia, 1777 [Ref: M-211].
LOVELL, William. Took the Oath of Allegiance in Calvert County in 1778 [Ref: L-37].
LOWE, Abraham. Private, Capt. Richard Parran's Co., Calvert County Militia, 1778 [Ref: J-1146, M-149]. Took the Oath of Allegiance in Calvert County in 1778 [Ref: L-37].
LOWE, Baptist. Private, St. Mary's County Militia, 1777 [Ref: M-212].
LOWE, Bennett (1751 - May 15, 1801). Son of Thomas and Ann Lowe. Took the Oath of Allegiance before the Hon. Bennett Biscoe in St. Mary's County in 1778 [Ref: J-1146, K-63, R-420].

LOWE, Ignatius. Private, St. Mary's County Militia, 1777 [Ref: M-214]. Took the Oath of Allegiance before the Hon. John Ireland in St. Mary's County in 1778 [Ref: J-1146, K-65]. The Register of St. Francis Xavier Catholic Church states that "Ignatius Low" and Priscilla Norris were married Nov. 20, 1777 [Ref: SC-36].
LOWE, James. Private, St. Mary's County Militia, 1777 [Ref: M-213].
LOWE, John Baptist. Took the Oath of Allegiance before the Hon. John Shanks in St. Mary's County in 1778 [Ref: J-1146, K-70].
LOWE (LOW), Susan. See "Peter Brown," q.v.
LOWE, Thomas and Ann. See "Bennett Lowe," q.v.
LOWERWELL, William. Private, St. Mary's County Militia, 1777 [Ref: M-214].
LOWRY, Elizabeth. See "John Manley," q.v.
LOWRY, James. Private, St. Mary's County Militia, 1777 [Ref: M-214].
LOWRY, Moses, Nancy, and William. See "Thomas Lowry," q.v.
LOWRY, Thomas (Aug., 1760 - Nov. 21, 1846). Born in St. Mary's County, Maryland in 1760, he "was brought over at the age of 3 years to Stafford County, Virginia" where he served in the Virginia Line in 1781. He married Nancy Dedman or Deadman in Orange County, Virginia on Oct. 16, 1805, and moved to Clark County, Kentucky in 1816. He applied for pension on Sep. 25, 1832, and died on Nov. 21, 1846. His widow Nancy applied for and received pension W2139 on March 16, 1853, and bounty land warrant #13444-160-55 in 1855, aged 74. His brother Moses Lowry lived in Bath County, Kentucky in 1832 and a William Lowry lived in Clark County in 1855, but no relationship was stated [Ref: P-2134, W-27, MK-92].
LOYD, Thomas. Private, Capt. Charles Williamson's Co., Calvert County Militia, 1778 [Ref: J-1146, M-147].
LUCAS (LUCUST), Ann. See "Thomas Jarboe," q.v.
LUCAS, Henry. Private, St. Mary's County Militia, 1777 [Ref: M-211]. One Henry Lucas was among the early Catholic settlers in Nelson County, Kentucky in 1785 [Ref: MK-92].
LUCAS, John. Took the Oath of Allegiance before the Hon. John Reeder in St. Mary's County in 1778 [Ref: J-1146, K-69]. One John Lucas was a sergeant, 4th Maryland Line, 1777-1780, and another was a private, 2nd Maryland Line, 1778-1780 [Ref: D-133, D-135].
LUFF, Thomas. Private, St. Mary's County, 3rd Maryland Line, Capt. Armstrong's Co., 1778-1780 [Ref: D-298].
LURTY, Eleanor. See "William Jenkins," q.v.
LURTY (LERTY), James. Took the Oath of Allegiance in St. Mary's County in 1780 [Ref: Q-115].
LUSBY, Henry. Midshipman from St. Mary's County who served aboard the State ship *Defence* on Oct. 15, 1777 and was Lieutenant of Marines on Dec. 31, 1777 [Ref: S-162].

LUSBY, John. Private, Capt. Richard Parran's Co., Calvert County Militia, 1778 [Ref: J-1146, M-149]. Took the Oath of Allegiance in Calvert County in 1778 [Ref: L-37].
LYLES, Henry. Private, Capt. Charles Williamson's Co., Calvert County Militia, 1778 [Ref: J-1146, M-147]. Took the Oath of Allegiance in Calvert County in 1778 [Ref: L-37].
LYLES, Samuel. Private, Capt. Frederick Skinner's Co., Calvert County Militia, 1778 [Ref: J-1146, M-150]. Private, Capt. John Mackall's Co., Calvert County Militia, 15th Bn., June 12, 1778 [Ref: M-146]. Took the Oath of Allegiance in Calvert County in 1778 [Ref: L-37, which listed the name as "Lyes"].
LYLES, Samuel Jr. Private, Capt. Frederick Skinner's Co., Calvert County Militia, 1778 [Ref: J-1146, M-150]. Private, Capt. John Mackall's Co., Calvert County Militia, 15th Bn., June 12, 1778 [Ref: M-146].
LYLES, Thomas. Private, Capt. John Mackall's Co., Calvert County Militia, 15th Bn., June 12, 1778 [Ref: M-146]. Private, Capt. Frederick Skinner's Co., Calvert County Militia, 1778 [Ref: J-1146, M-150]. Took the Oath of Allegiance in Calvert County in 1778 [Ref: L-37].
LYLES, Thomas Jr. Private, Capt. Frederick Skinner's Co., Calvert County Militia, 1778 [Ref: J-1146, M-150]. Private, Capt. John Mackall's Co., Calvert County Militia, 15th Bn., June 12, 1778 [Ref: M-146].
LYLES, William (died in 1790). Served in the Lower House from Calvert County, 1773-1774, Delegate to the Maryland Convention in 1775, Commissioner of Tax, 1777-1778, Judge of the Court of Appeals appointed under the "Act to Procure Troops" in Calvert County, 1778 [Ref: N-70, N-557, N-558]. Took the Oath of Allegiance in Calvert County in 1778 [Ref: L-37]. There was also a William Lyles who was a private in Capt. Frederick Skinner's Co., Calvert County Militia, 1778, and a private, Capt. John Mackall's Co., Calvert County Militia, 15th Bn., 1778 [Ref: J-1146, M-146, M-150].
LYLES, William Jr. Took the Oath of Allegiance in Calvert County in 1778 [Ref: L-37]. Private, Capt. Richard Lane's Co., Calvert County Militia, 1778 [Ref: J-1146, M-149].
LYNCH, Elizabeth and Hannah. See "Thomas Lynch," q.v.
LYNCH, John. Took the Oath of Allegiance before the Hon. Bennett Biscoe in St. Mary's County in 1778 [Ref: J-1146, K-63].
LYNCH, Joshua and Rebecca. See "Thomas Lynch," q.v.
LYNCH, Richard Jones. Took the Oath of Allegiance before the Hon. Bennett Biscoe in St. Mary's County in 1778 [Ref: J-1146, K-63].
LYNCH, Stephen. Private, St. Mary's County Militia, 1777 [Ref: M-214]. See "Thomas Lynch," q.v.
LYNCH, Thomas (1739 - Nov. 13, 1832). Private, St. Mary's County Militia, 1777 [Ref: M-215]. Applied for and received pension S34969 on April 28, 1818, aged 59, in St. Mary's County, stating he had served in the Maryland Line. In 1820 he had two daughters aged 30 and 25, a son

aged 18 or 19, and a grandson aged 6 or 7, in his family, but no names were given [Ref: P-2152]. The pension rolls of 1835 noted that he had been suspended under the Act of May 1, 1820, and restored commencing on May 9, 1829. He died in 1832, aged 73 [Ref: U-40]. In 1828 the Treasurer of Maryland was directed to pay him during life, half yearly, half pay of a private, as further remuneration for his services during the war. On March 8, 1833, the Treasurer was directed "to pay James M. K. Hammett, administrator of Thomas Lynch, sum due said Lynch, on pension roll of Maryland, Nov. 13, 1832, date of his death." [Ref: I-368]. One Thomas Lynch was appointed guardian to his four children, namely Hannah, Joshua, Rebecca, and Elizabeth, by the St. Mary's County Orphans Court in 1796, and Stephen Lynch was a security [Ref: SO-253].

LYON, Elizabeth. See "Nehemiah Leach," q.v.

LYON, James. Private, Capt. Charles Williamson's Co., Calvert County Militia, 1778 [Ref: J-1146, M-147]. Took the Oath of Allegiance in Calvert County in 1778 [Ref: L-37].

LYON, John. Private, St. Mary's County Militia, 1777 [Ref: M-210]. Private, Capt. Thomas Truman Greenfield's Co., Calvert County Militia, 1778 [Ref: J-1146, M-150]. One John Lyon married Sarah Thompson on Jan. 19, 1783, St. Mary's County, by Rev. John Stephen, Rector of All Faith's Parish [Ref: I-536].

LYON, Leonard. Private, St. Mary's County Militia, 1777 [Ref: M-210].

LYON, Michael. Private, St. Mary's County Militia, 1777 [Ref: M-213]. Took the Oath of Allegiance in St. Mary's County in 1780 [Ref: Q-115].

LYON, Rachel. See "Hezekiah Moran," q.v.

LYON, Richard. Private, St. Mary's County Militia, 1777 [Ref: M-209].

LYON, Thomas. Private, Capt. Frisby Freeland's Co., Calvert County Militia, 1778 [Ref: J-1146, M-148].

MACKALL, Ann. See "John Mackall" and "Thomas Mackall," q.v.

MACKALL, Barbara. See "Benjamin Mackall, Jr.," q.v.

MACKALL, Benjamin. See "John Mackall," q.v.

MACKALL, Benjamin Jr. (Feb. 16, 1723 - April, 1795). Son of Benjamin Mackall and Barbara Smith (widow of Thomas Holdsworth). He married Rebecca Covington, daughter of Leonard Covington of Prince George's County, on April 24, 1756, and had six children: Barbara, Levin, Benjamin, Walter, Richard, and Rebecca. Benjamin Mackall served several official capacities: Maryland Legislature, 1749-1765, Justice of Calvert County, 1766-1773, Member of the Constitutional Convention in 1774, Chairman of the Committee of Safety in 1776, and Lieutenant Commander of Calvert County [Ref: N-560, N-561, *Colonial Families of the United States of America*, Volume I, by George Norbury Mackenzie (1907), pp. 331-333]. See "Levin Covington Mackall," q.v.

MACKALL, Benjamin IV (1745-c1803). Son of James John Mackall and Mary Hance, of Calvert County. Benjamin married Rebecca Potts in

Annapolis in 1769 (no surviving children). He served in the Lower House, 1768-1776; Judge, Court of Appeals, 1778-1803; Colonel, 15th Bn., Calvert County, on Jan. 6, 1776, and reviewed and passed new recruits in July, 1776; Delegate to the Maryland Convention in 1775 and 1776; and, County Lieutenant, 1777-1780 [Ref: M-99, C-303, D-33, D-34, G-272, V-82, V-120, V-125, V-126, N-70, N-72, N-74, N-561, N-562, O-20, O-21]. Took the Oath of Allegiance in Calvert County in 1778 [Ref: L-37]. He also served as Chief Justice of Maryland, and Brigadier General, 8th Brigade, Maryland Militia, 1799-1803 [Ref: N-562, and *Colonial Families of the United States of America*, Volume I, by George Norbury Mackenzie (1907), p. 330].

MACKALL, Benjamin Hance. See "John Mackall," q.v.

MACKALL, Benjamin (of John). Private, Capt. Walter Smith's Co., Calvert County Militia, 1778 [Ref: J-1146, M-148]. Took the Oath of Allegiance in Calvert County in 1778 [Ref: L-37].

MACKALL, Dorcas and Edward. See "John Mackall," q.v.

MACKALL, Elizabeth. See "James Heighe," q.v.

MACKALL, Frances Holland. See "John Mackall," q.v.

MACKALL, James. (1) Ensign, Capt. Thomas Truman Greenfield's Co., 15th Bn., Calvert County Militia, April 10, 1776 through at least April 16, 1778 [Ref: A-320, E-37, J-1146, M-99, M-150]. (2) Private, Capt. Frisby Freeland's Co., Calvert County Militia, 1778 [Ref: J-1146, M-148]. The Christ Church Register in Calvert County records the birth of James Mackall, son of James John Mackall and Mary Hance, on Oct. 21, 1747, and the birth of James Mackall, son of James Mackall and Mary Howe, on Jan. 30, 1734 [Ref: O-20, O-21]. Also see "John Mackall" and "Thomas Mackall," q.v.

MACKALL, James John. See "John Mackall" and "Thomas Mackall" and "Benjamin Mackall IV," q.v.

MACKALL, James (of John). Took the Oath of Allegiance in Calvert County in 1778 [Ref: L-37, which listed the name twice].

MACKALL, Jane. See "John Mackall" and "Thomas Parran," q.v.

MACKALL, John. There were several men with this name: (1) One John Mackall (May 10, 1740 - 1799), son of James John Mackall and Mary Hance, married three times: (1) Mary Reynolds, daughter of Thomas Reynolds, circa 1762; (2) Sarah Lane, daughter of Samuel Lane, of Anne Arundel County, in 1780; and, (3) Jane Magruder, widow of Alexander H. Magruder, in 1788. Children: James John, Benjamin Hance, Edward, Richard, John James, Mary and Frances Holland. John was First Lieutenant, Calvert County Militia, July 5, 1776, later Captain, 15th Bn., and Delegate to the Maryland Convention, 1776-1778. He sold all his land in Maryland after several lawsuits in Anne Arundel County and probably died in Rockingham County, Virginia, in 1799 [Ref: M-99, M-146, N-74, N-78, N-565, N-566, Y-432]. (2) One John Mackall (Oct. 22, 1738 - Aug. 18, 1813), son of James Mackall and Mary Howe, married

Margaret Gough of Calvert County in 1758 and had these children: Thomas Howe, John Jr., James, Benjamin, Mary, Rebecca, Ann, Margaret, Sarah, and Dorcas. Served as Captain, Lower Bn., St. Mary's County, Aug. 26, 1777 to Jan., 1782; Member of the House of Delegates from 1778 to 1781; and, Justice, St. Mary's County, 1779-1784, 1800-1801, 1805-1806 [Ref: M-99, C-346, N-80, N-82, N-84, N-564, O-20, Y-432]. He is buried in the Graveyard Lot on the left hand side of the road leading from Trinity Church to St. Inigoes [Ref: S-129]. (3) Another John Mackall was a private in Capt. Walter Smith's Co., Calvert County Militia, 1778 [Ref: J-1146, M-148]. (4) The name of John Mackall appeared three times on the list of those who took the Oath of Allegiance in Calvert County in 1778, and one took the Oath before the Hon. Bennett Biscoe in St. Mary's County in 1778 [Ref: J-1146, K-63, L-37]. "John Mackall, Jr." was a member of the House of Delegates representing Calvert County in 1777 and "John Mackall IV" was a member of the House of Delegates representing Calvert County in 1778 and 1779 [Ref: N-76, N-81]. The Christ Church Register in Calvert County records these births: John Mackall, son of James and Mary, born Oct. 22, 1738; John Mackall, son of James John and Mary, born May 10, 1740; and John Mackall, son of John Mackall and Margaret Gough, born Aug. 20, 1764 [Ref: O-20, O-21]. Also see "Thomas Mackall," q.v.

MACKALL, John James. See "John Mackall," q.v.

MACKALL, Levin Covington (1760-c1804). Son of "Benjamin Mackall, Jr.," q.v., and Rebecca Covington. He married Margaret Weems in 1784 and had children (names not given). Private, Capt. Edward Wood's Co., Calvert County Militia, 1778 [Ref: J-1146, M-147]. Took the Oath of Allegiance in Calvert County in 1778 [Ref: L-37]. Levin served as a Member of the House of Delegates, 1780-1781, 1783, and 1790, and Calvert County Court Justice and Judge of the Orphans Court, 1783-1794 [Ref: N-84, N-88, N-566].

MACKALL, Margaret. See "John Mackall" and "James Mackall," q.v.

MACKALL, Mary. See "Thomas Jenkins" and "John Mackall" and "Edward Reynolds" and "John Brome (Broome)," q.v.

MACKALL, Rebecca. See "John Mackall" and "Benjamin Mackall" and "Thomas Loker," q.v.

MACKALL, Richard. See "Benjamin Mackall, Jr." and "John Mackall," q.v.

MACKALL, Sarah. See "John Mackall," q.v.

MACKALL, Susanna. See "Thomas Gantt, the 4th, Jr." and "John Brome (Broome)," q.v.

MACKALL, Thomas (Aug. 31, 1751 - Dec., 1799). Son of James John Mackall and Mary Hance, of Calvert County. He married twice: (1) Ann or Asenath Grahame, daughter of "Charles Grahame," q.v., and (2) Ann -----, possibly Holdsworth. Children: John, James, and Ann. Thomas served as Court Justice, 1773, Member of the House of Delegates, 1778-

1779, and Tax Commissioner at times between 1783 and 1798. Private, Capt. Benjamin Bond's Co., Calvert County Militia, 1778 [Ref: J-1146, M-149, N-80, N-566, N-567, O-21]. Took the Oath of Allegiance in Calvert County in 1778 [Ref: L-37].

MACKALL, Thomas Howe. See "John Mackall," q.v.

MACKALL, Walter. See "Benjamin Mackall, Jr.," q.v.

MACKENZIE, ---- [blank]. Took the Oath of Allegiance in Calvert County in 1778 [Ref: L-37].

MACKEY, George. Private, Capt. Frederick Skinner's Co., Calvert County Militia, 1778 [Ref: J-1146, M-150]. Took the Oath of Allegiance in Calvert County in 1778 [Ref: L-37, which listed the name as "George Mackoy"].

MACKEY, John. See "John McKay," q.v.

MACKEY, Robert. Took the Oath of Allegiance in Calvert County in 1778 [Ref: L-37, which listed the name as "Robert Mackay"].

MACKEY, Thomas. Private, 3rd Maryland Line, 1778-1780 [Ref: D-141].

MACKON, George. Private, Capt. James Patterson's Co., Calvert County Militia, Aug. 10, 1777 [Ref: M-146].

MADDOX, Catharine. See "George Carpenter," q.v.

MADDOX, John. Private, Capt. Uriah Forrest's Co., Flying Camp, St. Mary's County, July 28, 1776 [Ref: D-30]. Marine on the State ship *Defence* from June 3 to Oct. 15, 1777 [Ref: D-658]. Took the Oath of Allegiance before the Hon. Jeremiah Jordan in St. Mary's County in 1778 [Ref: J-1146, K-67]. Private (substitute), St. Mary's County, July 28, 1781 [Ref: D-384]. Private, Continental Army, 1781 [Ref: D-410, which listed the name as "John Maddux"].

MADDOX, Samuel (1728-1798). Second Lieutenant, Upper Bn., St. Mary's County Militia, Aug. 26, 1777, and First Lieutenant, Nov. 18, 1779 [Ref: M-100, C-345, F-18, which listed the name as "Samuel Maddux"]. Took the Oath of Allegiance before the Hon. Jeremiah Jordan in St. Mary's County in 1778 [Ref: J-1146, K-67]. Samuel Maddox married Lydia Turner circa 1750 [Ref: S-143]. He is buried at Christ Church Cemetery and his name appears on a stained glass window of the church [Ref: S-129].

MAGEE, Charles. Private, St. Mary's County, 3rd Maryland Line, Capt. Armstrong's Co., 1778-1780 [Ref: D-298].

MAGEE, Raphael. Took the Oath of Allegiance before the Hon. Ignatius Fenwick, Jr. in St. Mary's County in 1778 [Ref: J-1146, K-68].

MAGEE, Sarah. See "William Magee," q.v.

MAGEE, William. Private, St. Mary's County, 3rd Maryland Line, Capt. Armstrong's Co., 1778-1780 [Ref: D-298]. On Feb. 15, 1830, the Treasurer of Maryland was directed "to pay unto Sarah Magee, of St. Mary's County, amount of money due William Magee, her deceased husband, a pensioner of this State." [Ref: I-371].

MAGRUDER, Alexander. See "John Mackall," q.v.

MAGRUDER, Alexander Wilson. Private, Capt. Richard Lane's Co., Calvert County Militia, 1778 [Ref: J-1146, M-150].
MAGRUDER, Eleanor. See "James Marquess," q.v.
MAGRUDER, Jane. See "John Mackall," q.v.
MAGRUDER, John. See "Michel Taney," q.v.
MAHONEY, Basil. (1) Private, St. Mary's County Militia, 1777 [Ref: M-211]. (2) Private, St. Mary's County Militia, 1777 [Ref: M-212]. (3) Took the Oath of Allegiance before the Hon. John Reeder in St. Mary's County in 1778 [Ref: J-1146, K-69].
MAHONEY, John Smith. Private, St. Mary's County Militia, 1777 [Ref: M-213]. Took the Oath of Allegiance before the Hon. John Reeder in St. Mary's County in 1778 [Ref: J-1146, K-69].
MAHONEY, Smith. Private, St. Mary's County, enlisted May 28, 1778, for 9 months, Maryland Line, Continental Army [Ref: D-330, SM-114].
MAITELAND (MAITILAND), James. Took the Oath of Allegiance before the Hon. Bennett Biscoe in St. Mary's County in 1778 [Ref: J-1146, K-63].
MALLEY, Margaret. See "William Barrett," q.v.
MALOHONE (MOLLEHONE, MOLOHORN), Mary. See "Leonard Johnson," q.v.
MALOHONE (MOLLEHONE, MOLLOHORN), William. Private, St. Mary's County Militia, 1777 [Ref: M-212]. It is also curious to note that one "William Mattehannan" was a private in the 3rd Maryland Line in 1780 [Ref: D-141].
MALOHONE (MOLLEHONE, MOLLOHORN), William (of Thomas). Took the Oath of Allegiance before the Hon. John Ireland in St. Mary's County in 1778 [Ref: J-1146, K-65].
MANHALL, Henry. Took the Oath of Allegiance in Calvert County in 1778 [Ref: L-37].
MANLEY, John. Took the Oath of Allegiance before the Hon. Bennett Biscoe in St. Mary's County in 1778 [Ref: J-1146, K-63]. Loaned money to the State of Maryland in Dec., 1783 [Ref: S-162]. The Register of St. Inigoes Catholic Church states that "John Manly" and Elizabeth Lowry were married on July 11, 1784 [Ref: SC-36].
MANLEY, Matthew. Took the Oath of Allegiance before the Hon. Bennett Biscoe in St. Mary's County in 1778 [Ref: J-1146, K-63]. See "Rodolph Manley," q.v.
MANLEY, Rodolph (Rhodolph). Took the Oath of Allegiance before the Hon. Bennett Biscoe in St. Mary's County in 1778 [Ref: J-1146, K-63]. "Rhodolph Manly" died by April, 1790, at which time Matthew Manly petitioned the Court and stated that he had four children of Rhodolph Manly "on his hands and prayed to know how they were to be maintained" (no names given). It appears that "Statia Mandly" was the widow of Rodolph Manley and she had died by Dec., 1794. William Wheatley

was administrator of their estates in 1794 and 1796 [Ref: SO-153, SO-218, SO-251]. See "James Wheatley," q.v.
MANLEY, Statia. See "Rodolph Manley," q.v.
MANNING, Elizabeth. See "Robert Fenwick," q.v.
MANNING, Jane. See "John Smith, Sr.," q.v.
MANNING, John. (1) Private, St. Mary's County Militia, 1777 [Ref: M-214]. Took the Oath of Allegiance before the Hon. Richard Barnes in St. Mary's County in 1778 [Ref: J-1146, K-66]. (2) Private, Capt. Walter Smith's Co., Calvert County Militia, 1778 [Ref: J-1146, M-148]. Took the Oath of Allegiance in Calvert County in 1778 [Ref: L-37]. The Christ Church Register in Calvert County records the birth of John Manning, son of Thomas and Joshann [sic] Manning, on Dec. 7, 1731 [Ref: O-22].
MANNING, Jonathan. Served as a petit juror in Calvert County and gave his deposition on Nov. 26, 1777 [Ref: V-129].
MANNING, Mary. See "Ignatius Combs," q.v.
MAREMAN, Joseph. Private, St. Mary's County Militia, 1777 [Ref: M-210]. Took the Oath of Allegiance before the Hon. John Ireland in St. Mary's County in 1778 [Ref: J-1146, K-65].
MAREMAN, Joshua. Private, St. Mary's County Militia, 1777 [Ref: M-210]. Took the Oath of Allegiance before the Hon. John Ireland in St. Mary's County in 1778 [Ref: J-1146, K-65].
MAREMAN, William. Private, St. Mary's County Militia, 1777 [Ref: M-210]. Took the Oath of Allegiance before the Hon. John Ireland in St. Mary's County in 1778 [Ref: J-1146, K-65].
MAREMAN, Zachariah. Private, St. Mary's County Militia, 1777 [Ref: M-210]. Took the Oath of Allegiance before the Hon. John Ireland in St. Mary's County in 1778 [Ref: J-1146, K-65].
MARGUN, Eleanor. See "William Barefoot (Barford)," q.v.
MARQUESS, James. Private, Capt. Frederick Skinner's Co., Calvert County Militia, 1778 [Ref: J-1146, M-150, which listed the name as "James Marquis"]. Private, Capt. John Mackall's Co., Calvert County Militia, 15th Bn., on June 12, 1778 [Ref: M-146]. The will of Margerit Smith was probated in Calvert County on Feb. 8, 1774, naming her children James Marquess, Ann Turner, William Marquess, Sarah Stevens, Kidd Marquess, and John Marquess, and grandson Wilkonson Marquess [Ref: *Maryland Calendar of Wills, Volume 16, 1774-1777*, p. 17]. Some researchers have indicated that Kidd (or William Kidd) Marquess (1744-1812), son of John Marquess and Margerit Kidd (Marquess) Smith, married Eleanor Magruder (1746-1826), settled in Montgomery County, Maryland, later moved to Hampshire County, Virginia, and eventually settled in Nelson County and Simpson County, Kentucky [Ref: *Revolutionary Patriots of Montgomery County, Maryland, 1776-1783*, by Henry C. Peden, Jr. (1996), pp. 219-220].
MARQUESS, John, Kidd, and Margerit. See "James Marquess," q.v.

MARQUESS, William. Private, Calvert County, enlisted by Capt. John Brooke on July 26, 1776 [Ref: D-33, which listed the name as "William Marques"]. Private, Capt. Henry Skinner's Foot Co. of Hunting Hundred, Calvert County, 1777 [Ref: T-1814, O-125, which listed the name as "William Marquis"]. Took the Oath of Allegiance in Calvert County in 1778 [Ref: L-37, which listed the name as "William Marquies"]. See "James Marquess," q.v.

MARQUESS, Wilkonson. See "James Marquess," q.v.

MARR, Thomas. Private, Capt. Charles Williamson's Co., Calvert County Militia, 1778 [Ref: J-1146, M-147].

MARSHALL, Edward. Private, Capt. Uriah Forrest's Co., Flying Camp, St. Mary's County, July 28, 1776 [Ref: D-30, SM-114].

MARSHALL, Henry. Private, Capt. James Grahame's Co., Calvert County Militia, 1778 [Ref: J-1146, M-148].

MARSHALL, John. Property destroyed by the British in St. Mary's County in 1781 [Ref: S-162].

MARSHALL, John Jr. Captain, 15th Bn., Calvert County Militia, July 4, 1776 [Ref: M-101, A-548].

MARSHALL, Mark. Private, Capt. James Patterson's Co., Calvert County Militia, Aug. 10, 1777 [Ref: M-146].

MARSHALL, Martin. Private, Capt. James Grahame's Co., Calvert County Militia, 1778 [Ref: J-1146, M-148]. Took the Oath of Allegiance in Calvert County in 1778 [Ref: L-37].

MARSHALL, Mary. See "James Herbert," q.v.

MARSHALL, Richard. Private, Calvert County, enlisted by Ensign James Somervill on July 26, 1776 [Ref: D-34]. Private, Capt. James Patterson's Co., Calvert County Militia, Aug. 10, 1777 [Ref: M-146]. Private, Capt. Charles Williamson's Co., Calvert County Militia, 1778 [Ref: J-1146, M-147]. Took the Oath of Allegiance in Calvert County in 1778 [Ref: L-37].

MARSHALL, Thomas. Private, Capt. Frederick Skinner's Co., Calvert County Militia, 1778 [Ref: J-1146, M-150]. Private, Capt. James Patterson's Co., Calvert County Militia, Aug. 10, 1777 [Ref: M-146]. Private, Capt. John Mackall's Co., Calvert County Militia, 15th Bn., June 12, 1778 [Ref: M-146]. Private, Capt. Charles Williamson's Co., Calvert County Militia, 1778 [Ref: J-1146, M-148].

MARSHALL, Thomas Jr. Took the Oath of Allegiance in Calvert County in 1778 [Ref: L-37].

MARSHALL, William. Took the Oath of Allegiance in Calvert County in 1778 [Ref: L-37].

MARSHALL, ---- [blank]. Colonel, Calvert County Militia, July 17, 1776 [Ref: M-101, B-67].

MARTIN, Thomas. Private, Capt. Uriah Forrest's Co., Flying Camp, St. Mary's County, July 28, 1776 [Ref: D-30, SM-114]. Private, St. Mary's County Militia, 1777 [Ref: M-215, which listed the name as "Thos. Marten"].

MARTIN, William. Private, St. Mary's County Militia, 1777 [Ref: M-215]. Took the Oath of Allegiance before the Hon. Vernon Hebb in St. Mary's County in 1778 [Ref: J-1146, K-67]. The Register of St. Andrew's Episcopal Church states that William Martin and Anne Thompson were married Feb. 3, 1780 [Ref: MB-383].

MARTIN, William Jr. Private, St. Mary's County Militia, 1777 [Ref: M-214]. See "William Martin," q.v.

MARTINDALE, John. Private, St. Mary's County Militia, 1777 [Ref: M-213].

MASON, Abell. Seaman from St. Mary's County who served aboard the State ship *Defence* in Sep., 1776 [Ref: S-25, S-162, D-606].

MASON, George and Mary. See "William Fitzhugh," q.v.

MASON, Henry. Took the Oath of Allegiance in St. Mary's County in 1780 [Ref: Q-115].

MASON, Isachar. Private, St. Mary's County Militia, 1777 [Ref: M-212].

MASON, John. Private, St. Mary's County Militia, 1777 [Ref: M-214, which listed the name as "Jno. Masson"]. One John Mason died on Aug. 17, 1806, in St. Mary's County [Ref: R-424].

MASON, Richard. Took the Oath of Allegiance before the Hon. John Ireland in St. Mary's County in 1778 [Ref: J-1146, K-65].

MASSEY, Austin. Paid for making salt in St. Mary's County in 1782 [Ref: S-162].

MASSEY, Henry Lee. Soldier in Capt. John Allen Thomas' Co., St. Mary's County Militia, April, 1777, who became a Midshipman on the State ship *Defence* from May 10 to Dec. 31, 1777 [Ref: D-658, S-162].

MASSEY, William Lee. Private, St. Mary's County Militia, 1777 [Ref: M-212].

MATRECE(?), Joseph. Private, Capt. Thomas Truman Greenfield's Co., Calvert County Militia, 1778 [Ref: J-1146, M-150].

MATTEHANNAN, William. See "William Mallehone," q.v.

MATTHEWS, Ignatius (1730 - May 11, 1790). Catholic Priest who took the Oath of Allegiance in St. Mary's County in 1778. He is buried in St. Francis Xavier Catholic Cemetery at Newtown [Ref: SM-185, HG-35].

MATTIN, Henry. Took the Oath of Allegiance before the Hon. John Ireland in St. Mary's County in 1778 [Ref: J-1146, K-65].

MATTING, Robert. Private, St. Mary's County Militia, 1777 [Ref: M-214].

MATTINGLY, Ann. See "Basil Brown," q.v.

MATTINGLY, Barton. Private, St. Mary's County Militia, 1777 [Ref: M-212].

MATTINGLY, Benjamin. Took the Oath of Allegiance before the Hon. Bennett Biscoe in St. Mary's County in 1778 [Ref: J-1146, K-63]. Also see "William Mattingly," q.v.

MATTINGLY, Bennett. Took the Oath of Allegiance before the Hon. John Ireland in St. Mary's County in 1778 [Ref: J-1146, K-65]. One Bennett Mattingly died on May 18, 1807 [Ref: R-425].

MATTINGLY, Catherine. See "William Mattingly" and "Thomas Forrest, Jr.," q.v.

MATTINGLY, Charles. Private, 3rd Maryland Line, May 24, 1780; from St. Mary's County [Ref: S-162].

MATTINGLY, Clement. Took the Oath of Allegiance before the Hon. Jeremiah Jordan in St. Mary's County in 1778 [Ref: J-1146, K-67]. One Clement Mattingly died on Feb. 19, 1826 [Ref: R-425].

MATTINGLY, Edward (1752 - Sep. 5, 1821). Ensign, Flying Camp, St. Mary's County, on July 12, 1776, and First Lieutenant, Upper Bn., on Aug. 26, 1777, and Captain on Nov. 18, 1779; served throughout the war [Ref: D-30, M-101, C-346, F-18, R-425, SM-148; *The Maryland Gazette*, Sep. 20, 1821; and, *Maryland Genealogical Society Bulletin*, Volume 6, No. 2 (1965), p. 15]. Took the Oath of Allegiance before the Hon. John Ireland in St. Mary's County in 1778 [Ref: J-1146, K-65]. Edward Mattingly married Martha Sym on Sep. 17, 1779, by Rev. John Bolton [Ref: I-535]. Also see "William Mattingly," q.v.

MATTINGLY, Eleanor. See "Richard Wathen," q.v.

MATTINGLY, Elizabeth and Felix. See "William Mattingly," q.v.

MATTINGLY, Francis. Took the Oath of Allegiance before the Hon. John Ireland in St. Mary's County in 1778 [Ref: J-1146, K-65]. Supplied provisions (wheat, mutton, or bacon) to the Army in 1780 [Ref: S-77, S-162].

MATTINGLY, George. See "William Mattingly" and "Robert Wimsatt," q.v.

MATTINGLY, Ignatius. This name appeared twice on the list as a private in the St. Mary's County Militia in 1777; perhaps one was "Ignatius Mattingly, Jr.," q.v. [Ref: M-210, M-212]. Private, St. Mary's County, drafted July 27, 1781. Private, Continental Army, 1781 [Ref: D-384, D-410]. See "William Mattingly," q.v.

MATTINGLY, Ignatius Jr. Took the Oath of Allegiance before the Hon. John Ireland in St. Mary's County in 1778 [Ref: J-1146, K-65]. See "Ignatius Mattingly," q.v.

MATTINGLY, James. See "William Mattingly," q.v.

MATTINGLY, James Barton. Took the Oath of Allegiance before the Hon. John Shanks in St. Mary's County in 1778 [Ref: J-1146, K-70].

MATTINGLY, John. See "Thomas and William Mattingly," q.v.

MATTINGLY, Joseph. Took the Oath of Allegiance in Calvert County in 1778 [Ref: L-37]. A Joseph Mattingly died intestate by Sep., 1778 in St. Mary's County [Ref: SO-14, SO-186, SO-190]. A "Capt. Joseph Mattingly" died at St. Inigoes in St. Mary's County on Dec. 24, 1790, and Mrs. Joseph Mattingly, of Newtown, died in the City of Washington on Oct. 18, 1819. She was buried in St. Mary's County on Oct. 22, 1819 [Ref: R-426].

MATTINGLY, Julia, Leonard, and Lucas. See "William Mattingly," q.v.

MATTINGLY, Luke Sr. Took the Oath of Allegiance before the Hon. John Ireland in St. Mary's County in 1778 [Ref: J-1146, K-65]. Private,

St. Mary's County Militia, 1777, and discharged after Aug. 4, 1781 [Ref: M-213, V-420]. The Register of St. Francis Xavier Catholic Church states that "Luke Mattingly and Eleanor Thompson, related in the second degree" were married Feb. 11, 1772 [Ref: SC-34].
MATTINGLY, Malinda. See "Richard Thompson, of Joseph," q.v.
MATTINGLY, Mary. See "William Fowler" and "Thomas Mattingly" and "Thomas Harris" and "William Mattingly," q.v.
MATTINGLY, Nellie. See "Aaron Spalding," q.v.
MATTINGLY, Philip. Private, St. Mary's County, enlisted May 31, 1778, for 9 months [Ref: D-330]. Private, 2nd Maryland Line, from June 1, 1778 until April 3, 1779, when discharged [Ref: D-139].
MATTINGLY, Richard. See "William Mattingly," q.v.
MATTINGLY, Robert. Private, St. Mary's County Militia, 1777 [Ref: M-210]. Took the Oath of Allegiance before the Hon. John Ireland in St. Mary's County in 1777 or 1778 [Ref: J-1146, K-65]. There was a Robert Mattingly who died by Aug., 1777 [Ref: SO-1, SO-2].
MATTINGLY, Susan. See "William Mattingly," q.v.
MATTINGLY, Thomas. Private, St. Mary's County Militia, 1777 [Ref: M-212]. Private, St. Mary's County, enlisted May 31, 1778, for 9 months [Ref: D-330]. Private, 2nd Maryland Line, from May 31, 1778 until April 3, 1779, when discharged [Ref: D-139]. One Thomas Mattingly died by Aug., 1780, leaving a son John (above the age of 14 in 1786) and daughter Mary [Ref: SO-36].
MATTINGLY, William. Private, St. Mary's County Militia, 1777 [Ref: M-210]. He married twice: (1) Catherine Spalding; (2) Elizabeth Clarke [Ref: Y-444]. William Mattingley, followed by his brothers Leonard and Lucas, migrated to Kentucky with the early Catholics from the Maryland League between 1785 and 1791. William had three sons, James, Edward, and Richard, by his first wife, and ten by his second wife: William, Mary, Benjamin, Felix, Ignatius, Julia, George, Susan, Catherine, and John [Ref: MK-96].
MAULDING, Jeremiah. Private, Capt. Frisby Freeland's Co., Calvert County Militia, 1778 [Ref: J-1146, M-148].
MAYHUE, Richard. Private, Capt. Thomas Truman Greenfield's Co., Calvert County Militia, 1778 [Ref: J-1146, M-150].
MAYNARD, Samuel. Took the Oath of Allegiance in Calvert County in 1778 [Ref: L-37].
McALLISTER, Alex. Took the Oath of Allegiance in Calvert County in 1778 [Ref: L-37].
McATEE, John. Private, St. Mary's County, enlisted April 26, 1778, for 9 months, and reported to be a "vagrant or deserter" in June, 1778 [Ref: D-329].
McATEE, Leonard. Private, St. Mary's County, enlisted April 26, 1778, for 9 months, and was reported to be a "vagrant or deserter" in June,

1778 [Ref: D-329]. However, he later served and was discharged from the 3rd Maryland Line on Feb. 19, 1779 [Ref: D-141].

McATEE, Thomas. Private, 3rd Maryland Line, from April 26, 1778 to Feb. 19, 1779, when discharged [Ref: D-141].

McBEAN, Malcomb. Took the Oath of Allegiance in St. Mary's County in 1780 [Ref: Q-116].

McBRIDE, James. Private, St. Mary's County, enlisted June 10, 1778, for 3 years, Maryland Line, Continental Army [Ref: D-330, SM-114].

McBRIDE, Peggy. See "John Wood," q.v.

McCALL, John. Elected to serve on a General Committee in St. Mary's County in accordance with the resolves of the Continental Congress in 1775 [Ref: MR-127].

McCALLEY, John. Private, St. Mary's County, enlisted May 19, 1778, for 9 months, Continental Army, and discharged April 4, 1779 [Ref: D-329, S-162].

McCLAIN, William. Private, St. Mary's County Militia, 1777 [Ref: M-211].

McCLAYLAND, John. Private, St. Mary's County Militia, 1777 [Ref: M-214]. Paid for making salt in 1782 [Ref: S-163, which listed the name as "John McClaland"].

McCLEAN, John. Took the Oath of Allegiance before the Hon. Henry G. Sothoron in St. Mary's County in 1778 [Ref: J-1146, K-69]. Member of the Committee of Safety and Correspondence on Dec. 23, 1774 [Ref: S-163, which listed the name as "John McLean"].

McCLELAND, Bennett. Private, St. Mary's County, enlisted May 23, 1778, for 9 months, Continental Army [Ref: D-330, SM-114, S-163, which listed the name as "Bennett McLeland"].

McCLELAND, Robert. Private, Capt. Uriah Forrest's Co., Flying Camp, St. Mary's County, July 28, 1776 [Ref: D-30, which listed the name as "Robert McClannon (McClelland)"]. Marine on the State ship *Defence* from June 26, 1777 to Dec. 31, 1777 [Ref: D-658, which listed the name as "Robert McClenan (McCleland)"].

McCLURE, Frank. See "Leonard Bean," q.v.

McCOLEY, John. Private, St. Mary's County Militia, 1777 [Ref: M-214].

McCOY, Jacob. Private, St. Mary's County, 2nd Maryland Line, until discharged April 14, 1779 [Ref: S-162].

McCOY, John. Private, St. Mary's County, 3rd Maryland Line, who was in the service several years and lost a leg on Aug. 15 [or 16?], 1780 [Ref: S-163].

McDANIEL, Edward. Private, Capt. Charles Williamson's Co., Calvert County Militia, 1778 [Ref: J-1146, M-148]. Took the Oath of Allegiance in Calvert County in 1778 [Ref: L-37].

McDANIEL, William. Private, Calvert County, enlisted by Lt. Frederick Skinner on Aug. 23, 1776 [Ref: D-33]. Private, Capt. Frisby Freeland's Co., Calvert County Militia, 1778 [Ref: J-1146, M-148]. Took the Oath of Allegiance in Calvert County in 1778 [Ref: L-37].

McDOWELL, John. Private, Capt. Walter Smith's Co., Calvert County Militia, 1778 [Ref: J-1146, M-148]. Took the Oath of Allegiance in Calvert County in 1778 [Ref: L-37]. John McDowell and Mary Willin were married on April 13, 1779, by Rev. Francis Lauder, of Christ Church Parish [Ref: MM-144, K-35, which latter source listed the name as "John McDonnell"].

McDOWELL, William. Took the Oath of Allegiance in Calvert County in 1778 [Ref: L-37].

McFARLANE, Alexander. Private, 3rd Maryland Line, 1780-1781 [Ref: D-142].

McFARLANE, George. Took the Oath of Allegiance in Calvert County in 1778 [Ref: L-37]. Private, Capt. Frisby Freeland's Co., Calvert County Militia, 1778 [Ref: J-1146, M-148, which listed the name as "George Mackfarland"].

McFLALAND, Bent. Private, St. Mary's County Militia, 1777 [Ref: M-215].

McGEE, Charles (1758-1832). Private, St. Mary's County, enlisted April 28, 1778, for the duration; discharged Nov. 1, 1780; re-enlisted as a private, 3rd Maryland Line, and served to Nov. 15, 1783 [Ref: D-141, D-329, S-163]. Applied for and received pension S34979 on April 24, 1818, aged 60, in St. Mary's County, and in 1820 his wife (unnamed) was aged 60 [Ref: P-2276]. Pension rolls of 1835 stated he died on May 19, 1832 [Ref: U-40]. The Register of St. Andrew's Episcopal Church states that "Charles McGie" and Mary Bradford were married (by license) May 11, 1784 [Ref: MB-385].

McGEE, Hugh. Private, 3rd Maryland Line, 1778 [Ref: D-141].

McGEE, William (1755-1829). Private, St. Mary's County Militia, 1777 [Ref: M-213]. Private, 3rd Maryland Line, enlisted April 20 1778, for 3 years; discharged on Nov. 1, 1780; re-enlisted and served to Nov. 15, 1783 [Ref: D-141, D-329, S-163]. "William McGee or McGhee" applied for and received pension S34980 on April 27, 1818, aged 63, in St. Mary's County, and in 1820 had a wife and 2 children (a boy and a girl) both above age 21, but no names were given. On Aug. 23, 1828, he signed a power of attorney to Thomas Carberry for bounty land warrant #1355-100 in St. Mary's County [Ref: P-2277]. Pension rolls of 1835 stated he died on June 10, 1829, aged 73 [Ref: U-40].

McGILL, Arthur. Private, St. Mary's County Militia, 1777 [Ref: M-211]. The Register of St. Francis Xavier Catholic Church states that Arthur McGill and Ann Stone were married Oct. 12, 1778 [Ref: SC-36].

McGILL, John. See "Zachariah Brewer," q.v.

McGILL, Mary. See "Joseph Hall," q.v.

McINTOSH, Daniel. Took the Oath of Allegiance before the Hon. Bennett Biscoe in St. Mary's County in 1778 [Ref: J-1146, K-63, which listed the name s "Daniel Mackintush"].

McKARTENEY, Edward. Private, St. Mary's County, enlisted May 29, 1778, for 9 months; discharged in June, 1778 [Ref: D-329, S-163].

McKAY, Benjamin. Took the Oath of Allegiance before the Hon. Bennett Biscoe in St. Mary's County in 1778 [Ref: J-1146, K-63].

McKAY, John. Private, Capt. Uriah Forrest's Co., Flying Camp, St. Mary's County, July 28, 1776 [Ref: D-30, which listed the name as John McKoy (McKay)"]. "John Mackay" was a corporal in the 3rd (and possibly 5th) Maryland Line who applied for and received an allowance from the Court in 1785, 1786, 1788, and 1789, for having been "rendered totally incapable of getting his livelihood" due to the injuries from his service [Ref: SO-83, SO-87, SO-130, D-227].

McKAY, Richard. Private, St. Mary's County Militia, 1777 [Ref: M-214]. Took the Oath of Allegiance before the Hon. Vernon Hebb in St. Mary's County in 1778 [Ref: J-1146, K-67].

McKAY, Robert. Private, Capt. James Grahame's Co., Calvert County Militia, 1778 [Ref: J-1146, M-148].

McKEY, Jacob. Private, St. Mary's County, enlisted June 1, 1778, for 9 months, Continental Army [Ref: D-330, SM-114, S-163].

McKINNEY, James. Private, Capt. Benjamin Bond's Co., Calvert County Militia, 1778 [Ref: J-1146, M-149]. Took the Oath of Allegiance in Calvert County in 1778 [Ref: L-37].

McKINNEY, John. Private, Calvert County, enlisted by Capt. John Brooke on July 25, 1776 [Ref: D-33, which listed the name as "John McKenney"]. Private, Capt. Benjamin Bond's Co., Calvert County Militia, 1778 [Ref: J-1146, M-149]. Took the Oath of Allegiance in Calvert County in 1778 [Ref: L-37]. "John Mackinnie" and Mary Kershaw were married on Dec. 28, 1777, by Rev. Francis Lauder, of Christ Church Parish [Ref: K-33].

McKINNEY, John Jr. Took the Oath of Allegiance in Calvert County in 1778 [Ref: L-37].

McKINNEY, Rubin. Private, St. Mary's County Militia, 1777 [Ref: M-214, which listed the name as "Rubin McKenny"].

McKINNOCK, George. Private, St. Mary's County Militia, 1777 [Ref: M-213].

McLEAN, John. Elected to serve on a General Committee in St. Mary's County in accordance with the resolves of the Continental Congress in 1775 [Ref: MR-127]. Took the Oath of Allegiance before the Hon. Richard Barnes in St. Mary's County in 1778 [Ref: J-1146, K-66]. One John McLean was buried on June 2, 1799, in St. Mary's County [Ref: R-427]. Also see "John McClean," q.v.

McLEAN, William. Private, St. Mary's County Militia, 1777 [Ref: M-213].

McLELAND, Bennett. See "Bennett McCleland," q.v.

McLONEY, Andrew. Private, St. Mary's County Militia, 1777 [Ref: M-213].

McMULLEN, James. See "James King," q.v.

McMULLIN, Henry. Took the Oath of Allegiance before the Hon. Jeremiah Jordan in St. Mary's County in 1778 [Ref: J-1146, K-67].

McWILLIAMS, Kenelm. Private, St. Mary's County Militia, 1777 [Ref: M-213, which listed the name as "Kenelin McWilliams"]. Took the Oath of Allegiance before the Hon. Jeremiah Jordan in St. Mary's County in 1778 [Ref: J-1146, K-67]. "Kenelum McWilliams" died by March, 1798, leaving son John as his administrator [Ref: SO-272].

McWILLIAMS, Thomas. Captain of Marines on the State ship *Molly* in 1777 [Ref: SM-187]. Took the Oath of Allegiance before the Hon. Jeremiah Jordan in St. Mary's County in 1778 [Ref: J-1146, K-67]. Thomas McWilliams died on Sep. 30, 1806, and is buried in a private cemetery on his plantation "Broad Neck" at St. Clements Bay [Ref: R-428, S-129].

McWILLIAMS, William. Private, 2nd Maryland Line, enlisted June 1, 1778 and died July 15, 1778; from St. Mary's County [Ref: S-163].

MEDCALF, John. Private, St. Mary's County Militia, 1777 [Ref: M-213]. Private, St. Mary's County, enlisted on June 1, 1778, for 9 months. Private, 2nd Maryland Line, died on July 15, 1778 [Ref: D-330, R-428, D-139, SM-114, which sources listed the name as "John Metcalf" and "Jno. Metcalf"].

MEDCALF, Kenelm. Private, St. Mary's County Militia, 1777 [Ref: M-213, which listed the name as "Kenelin Medcalf"].

MEDCALF, Richard. Private, 1st Maryland Line, 1778 [Ref: D-138, which source listed the name as "Richd. Medcalf"].

MEDCALF, Robert. Private, 1st Maryland Line, 1780 [Ref: D-138, which source listed the name as "Robt. Medcaff"].

MEDCALF, Sarah. See "Sylvester Wheatley," q.v.

MEDLEY, Eleanor. See "Jeremiah Tarlton," q.v.

MEDLEY, Enoch. Private, St. Mary's County Militia, 1777 [Ref: M-214], and seaman on the State ship *Defence* from Oct. 23 to Dec. 31, 1777 [Ref: D-658]. Took the Oath of Allegiance before the Hon. Bennett Biscoe in St. Mary's County in 1778 [Ref: J-1146, K-63]. He was a seaman "blown up in barge" in 1778 [Ref: R-428, SM-114].

MEDLEY, George. Private, St. Mary's County Militia, 1777 [Ref: M-214]. Took the Oath of Allegiance before the Hon. Richard Barnes in St. Mary's County in 1778 [Ref: J-1146, K-66].

MEDLEY, Henry. Private, St. Mary's County Militia, 1777 [Ref: M-211]. Took the Oath of Allegiance before the Hon. Henry Reeder in St. Mary's County in 1778 [Ref: J-1146, K-64]. Supplied provisions (wheat, mutton, or bacon) to the Army in 1780 [Ref: S-77]. The Register of St. Francis Xavier Catholic Church states that Henry Medley and Margaret Ford were married Feb. 7, 1779 [Ref: SC-36].

MEDLEY, Ignatius. See "John Medley," q.v.

MEDLEY, John. Private, St. Mary's County Militia, 1777 [Ref: M-214]. Took the Oath of Allegiance before the Hon. Henry Reeder in St.

Mary's County in 1778 [Ref: J-1146, K-64]. John Medley, Thomas Medley, and Ignatius Medley were among the early Catholic settlers on Hardin's Creek in Washington County, Kentucky in 1786 [Ref: MK-100]. See "Philip Medley," q.v.

MEDLEY, Joseph. Private, St. Mary's County Militia, 1777 [Ref: M-214]. Took the Oath of Allegiance before the Hon. Richard Barnes in St. Mary's County in 1778 [Ref: J-1146, K-66]. Supplied provisions (wheat, mutton, or bacon) to the Army in 1780 [Ref: S-77].

MEDLEY, Mary. See "Ignatius Wimsatt (Winsett)," q.v.

MEDLEY, Philip. Took the Oath of Allegiance before the Hon. Richard Barnes in St. Mary's County in 1778 [Ref: J-1146, K-66]. One Philip Medley died testate by Feb., 1798, leaving a son Philip (above the age of 14) and a son John, who was his executor [Ref: SO-267, SO-268, SO-274]. Another Philip Medley died on Aug. 8, 1836 [Ref: R-428].

MEDLEY, Thomas. Private, 5th Maryland Line, Dec. 10, 1778 to June 17, 1779, when he reportedly "deserted" [Ref: D-228]. See "John Medley," q.v.

MEDLEY, William. Private, St. Mary's County Militia, 1777 [Ref: M-214]. Took the Oath of Allegiance before the Hon. Henry Reeder in St. Mary's County in 1778 [Ref: J-1146, K-64].

MELLEY (MELLY), James. Private, Capt. Benjamin Bond's Co., Calvert County Militia, 1778 [Ref: J-1146, M-149]. Took the Oath of Allegiance in Calvert County in 1778 [Ref: L-37].

MELLEY (MELLY), John. Private, Capt. Benjamin Bond's Co., Calvert County Militia, 1778 [Ref: J-1146, M-149]. Took the Oath of Allegiance in Calvert County in 1778 [Ref: L-37].

MELLEY (MILLEY), Moses. Private, Capt. Walter Smith's Co., Calvert County Militia, 1778 [Ref: J-1146, M-148].

MELTON (MILTON), George. Private, St. Mary's County Militia, 1777 [Ref: M-213].

MELTON (MILTON), James. "James Melton" was a private, Capt. Uriah Forrest's Co., Flying Camp, St. Mary's County, July 28, 1776 [Ref: D-30, SM-114]. "James Milton" was a private, St. Mary's County Militia, 1777 [Ref: M-213].

MELTON (MILTON), Philip. Private, St. Mary's County Militia, 1777 [Ref: M-212].

MELTON, Susan. See "James French," q.v.

MENGER, ---- [blank]. Lieutenant, St. Mary's County Militia, May 21, 1778 [Ref: M-103, E-104].

MERRILL, Joshua. Private, St. Mary's County Militia, 1777 [Ref: M-212].

MERRITT, James. Took the Oath of Allegiance in Calvert County in 1778 [Ref: L-38].

MILBORN, Elizabeth. See "Edmund Jenkins," q.v.

MILBOURNE, Anne. See "William Herbert," q.v.

MILBURN, Austin. Took the Oath of Allegiance before the Hon. Bennett Biscoe in St. Mary's County in 1778 [Ref: J-1146, K-63]. Property destroyed by the British in 1781 [Ref: S-163]. One Austin Milburn died intestate by Oct., 1798 [Ref: SO-278].

MILBURN, Edward. Took the Oath of Allegiance before the Hon. Robert Watts in St. Mary's County in 1778 [Ref: J-1146, K-62]. One Edward Milburn was buried on Dec. 24, 1799 [Ref: R-429].

MILBURN, Jeremiah. Private, St. Mary's County Militia, 1777 [Ref: M-214, which listed the name as "Jeremh. Millburn"]. Took the Oath of Allegiance before the Hon. Richard Barnes in St. Mary's County in 1778 [Ref: J-1146, K-66].

MILBURN, John Horn. Private, St. Mary's County Militia, 1777 [Ref: M-215]. Took the Oath of Allegiance in St. Mary's County in 1780 [Ref: Q-116, which listed the name as "John Horn Milbourn"].

MILBURN, Joseph. Took the Oath of Allegiance before the Hon. Bennett Biscoe in St. Mary's County in 1778 [Ref: J-1146, K-63]. Property destroyed by the British in 1781 [Ref: S-163]. One Joseph Milburn, also referred to as Joseph Milburn, Jr., died intestate by Aug., 1796 [Ref: SO-246, SO-250, SO-251]. Source S-143 states that Joseph Milburn, patriot, was born in 1755 and died in 1818.

MILBURN, Nicholas (1750-1830). Private, St. Mary's County, 6th Maryland Line, 1778, and corporal, 3rd Maryland Line, 1781 [Ref: Y-467, D-228, D-347, D-440, which also listed the name as "Nicholas Milbourne"]. Served until Nov. 15, 1783; pensioner in 1818 [Ref: S-163].

MILBURN, Richard. Took the Oath of Allegiance before the Hon. Robert Watts in St. Mary's County in 1778 [Ref: J-1146, K-62]. Paid for making salt in 1782 [Ref: S-163].

MILBURN, Stephen. Took the Oath of Allegiance before the Hon. Robert Watts in St. Mary's County in 1778 [Ref: J-1146, K-62]. Paid for making salt in 1782 [Ref: S-163]. One Stephen Milburn died and was buried on Sep. 1, 1803 [Ref: R-430].

MILES, Barton. See "Philip Miles," q.v.

MILES, Belinda. See "Robert Fenwick," q.v.

MILES, Henry. Took the Oath of Allegiance before the Hon. John Reeder in St. Mary's County in 1778 [Ref: J-1146, K-69]. One Henry Miles died on March 6, 1817, and another died on Oct. 19, 1835 [Ref: R-430]. See "Philip Miles," q.v.

MILES, Philip. Took the Oath of Allegiance before the Hon. John Reeder in St. Mary's County in 1778 [Ref: J-1146, K-69]. Philip Miles and son Harry (or Henry), Barton Miles, and John S, Miles were among the early Catholic settlers who migrated to Hardin's Creek in Washington County, Kentucky between 1785 and 1789. They migrated with their relatives in the Hill family [Ref: MK-102].

MILES, Richard. Private, St. Mary's County Militia, 1777 [Ref: M-212]. Served in Maryland Line; reported "deserted." [Ref: D-416].

MILES, Robert. Paid for services (unspecified) to the State of Maryland in St. Mary's County on Feb. 16, 1781 [Ref: S-163].
MILES, Tabitha Dorcas. See "Cornelius Wildman," q.v.
MILLARD, Francis. First Lieutenant, Upper Bn., St. Mary's County Militia, Aug. 26, 1777, and Captain, Nov. 18, 1779 [Ref: M-104, C-346, F-18]. Francis Millard was one of the executors of Mary Millard, deceased, in June, 1797 [Ref: SO-169, SO-175].
MILLARD, Joseph. Took the Oath of Allegiance before the Hon. Henry Reeder in St. Mary's County in 1778 [Ref: J-1146, K-64].
MILLARD, Joshua. Private, St. Mary's County Militia, 1777 [Ref: M-212]. Took the Oath of Allegiance before the Hon. Henry Reeder in St. Mary's County in 1778 [Ref: J-1146, K-64]. One Joshua Millard died intestate by April, 1797 [Ref: SO-261, SO-262].
MILLER, David. Took the Oath of Allegiance in Calvert County in 1780 [Ref: Q-116].
MILLER, Elizabeth. See "John Weems," q.v.
MILLER, Isaac. Private, Capt. Frisby Freeland's Co., Calvert County Militia, 1778 [Ref: J-1146, M-148]. Took the Oath of Allegiance in Calvert County in 1778 [Ref: L-38].
MILLER, John. (1) Private, Capt. Frisby Freeland's Co., Calvert County Militia, 1778 [Ref: J-1146, M-148]. (2) Private, Capt. Thomas Truman Greenfield's Co., Calvert County Militia, 1778 [Ref: J-1146, M-150]. (3) Took the Oath of Allegiance in Calvert County in 1778 [Ref: L-38]. Private, Capt. Henry Skinner's Foot Co. of Hunting Hundred, Calvert County, 1777 [Ref: T-1814, O-125].
MILLER, John Jr. Took the Oath of Allegiance in Calvert County in 1778 [Ref: L-38].
MILLER, Sarah. See "Joseph Davis," q.v.
MILLER, Susannah. See "John Yoe," q.v.
MILLER, William. Private, Capt. Benjamin Bond's Co., Calvert County Militia, 1778 [Ref: J-1146, M-149].
MILLS, Bernard. Private, St. Mary's County Militia, 1777 [Ref: M-214]. One Bernard Mills was among the early Catholic settlers on Rolling Creek in Kentucky circa 1786 [Ref: MK-103]. See "Nicholas Mills," q.v.
MILLS, Charles. Private, St. Mary's County Militia, 1777 [Ref: M-210]. Charles Mills died intestate in St. Mary's County, Maryland, by Sep., 1777 [Ref: SO-2]. "Charles Nathaniel Mills" married Elizabeth Ryal (Byal?) on Jan. 17, 1778, St. Mary's County, by Rev. John Stephen, Rector of All Faith's Parish. He was born in 1758 in St. Mary's County and was among the Episcopal families who settled in Rowan County, North Carolina around 1794. He soon after moved to Iredell County and died in 1843 [Ref: I-536, MC-111]. See "William Mills," q.v.
MILLS, Edward and Elizabeth. See "Thomas Goldsmith," q.v.
MILLS, Elizabeth Temperance. See "George Dent," q.v.

MILLS, Francis. Took the Oath of Allegiance before the Hon. John Reeder in St. Mary's County in 1778 [Ref: J-1146, K-69].
MILLS, Ignatius. Took the Oath of Allegiance before the Hon. Richard Barnes in St. Mary's County in 1778 [Ref: J-1146, K-66]. See "Nicholas Mills," q.v.
MILLS, James. (1) c1733 - March 9, 1791. He married Susannah ----, with no known children. Quartermaster, 6th Bn., St. Mary's County, Jan. 12, 1776. Member of the House of Delegates, 1780-1782. Coroner, St. Mary's County, 1765-1791. County Sheriff, 1777-1778 [Ref: M-104, N-84, N-86, N-598, N-599, R-431]. Took the Oath of Allegiance before the Hon. Jeremiah Jordan in St. Mary's County in 1778 [Ref: J-1146, K-67]. (2) Private, Capt. Walter Smith's Co., Calvert County Militia, 1778 [Ref: J-1146, M-148]. Took the Oath of Allegiance in Calvert County in 1778 [Ref: L-38]. (3) This name also appeared twice as a private in the St. Mary's County Militia in 1777 [Ref: M-213, M-214]. One James Mills supplied provisions (wheat, mutton, or bacon) to the Army in St. Mary's County in 1780 [Ref: S-77].
MILLS, James (of John). Took the Oath of Allegiance before the Hon. John Ireland in St. Mary's County in 1778 [Ref: J-1146, K-65].
MILLS, James Andrew. Private, St. Mary's County Militia, 1777 [Ref: M-210].
MILLS, John. (1) Ensign, Capt. Benjamin Bond's Co., Calvert County Militia, April 16, 1778, and Second Lieutenant, Feb. 2, 1779 [Ref: E-37, E-290, J-1146, M-104, M-149]. (2) This name appeared twice as a private, St. Mary's County Militia, 1777 [Ref: M-210, M-211]. (3) Ensign, Lower Bn., St. Mary's County, Aug. 26, 1777, and First Lieutenant, Lower Bn., May 7, 1781 [Ref: M-104, C-346, G-426]. (4) Captain, Upper Bn., St. Mary's County, Aug. 26, 1777 [Ref: M-104, C-346]. One John Mills, of St. Mary's City, wrote to the Governor on Aug. 28, 1781, about prolonged furloughs, draftees, and horse deliveries [Ref: V-429]. One John Mills was among the early Catholic settlers on Hardin's Creek in Kentucky circa 1786 [Ref: MK-103].
MILLS, John 3rd. Took the Oath of Allegiance before the Hon. Jeremiah Jordan in St. Mary's County in 1778 [Ref: J-1146, K-67].
MILLS, John (of Jesse). Took the Oath of Allegiance before the Hon. Richard Barnes in St. Mary's County in 1778 [Ref: J-1146, K-66].
MILLS, Jonathan. Seaman from St. Mary's County who served aboard the State ship *Defence* in May, 1777 [Ref: S-163].
MILLS, Joseph. See "William Mills," q.v.
MILLS, Joshua. Took the Oath of Allegiance before the Hon. John Reeder in St. Mary's County in 1778 [Ref: J-1146, K-69].
MILLS, Justinian. Private, St. Mary's County Militia, 1777 [Ref: M-211]. Took the Oath of Allegiance before the Hon. Jeremiah Jordan in St. Mary's County in 1778 [Ref: J-1146, K-67]. The Register of St. Andrew's

Episcopal Church states that Justinian Mills and Mary Dant were married Oct. 26, 1751 [Ref: MB-382].

MILLS, Leonard. Private, Capt. Benjamin Bond's Co., Calvert County Militia, 1778 [Ref: J-1146, M-149]. Took the Oath of Allegiance in Calvert County in 1778 [Ref: L-38]. Leonard Mills and China Fraser were married on Dec. 4, 1777, by Rev. Francis Lauder, of Christ Church Parish [Ref: K-33].

MILLS, Levin (Leavin). Adjutant, 15th Bn., Calvert County Militia, March 7, 1776 [Ref: M-104, C-24]. Took the Oath of Allegiance in Calvert County in 1778 [Ref: L-38].

MILLS, Margaret. See "Robert Abell" and "Thomas Goldsmith," q.v.

MILLS, Nicholas. Private, St. Mary's County Militia, 1777 [Ref: M-214]. Took the Oath of Allegiance before the Hon. Richard Barnes in St. Mary's County in 1778 [Ref: J-1146, K-66]. One Nicholas Mills died testate by Aug., 1785, and his executors were Bernard Mills, Ignatius Mills, and Winefred Mills [Ref: SO-82, SO-85, SO-114].

MILLS, Susannah. See "Joshua Abell," q.v.

MILLS, Thomas. See "Thomas Goldsmith," q.v.

MILLS, William. Private, St. Mary's County Militia, 1777 [Ref: M-212]. Took the Oath of Allegiance before the Hon. Jeremiah Jordan in St. Mary's County in 1778 [Ref: J-1146, K-67]. One William Mills died by Dec., 1785, leaving orphan sons Joseph, William (aged 16), and Charles [Ref: SO-88, SO-89].

MILLS, Winefred. See "Nicholas Mills," q.v.

MILSAP, Jean. See "John Billingsley," q.v.

MITCHELL, Sarah. See "Thomas Freeman," q.v.

MITCHELL, William. Took the Oath of Allegiance before the Hon. Richard Barnes in St. Mary's County in 1778 [Ref: J-1146, K-66].

MITTS, George. Private, St. Mary's County Militia, 1777 [Ref: M-212].

MOLES (MULES), James. Private, Capt. Frederick Skinner's Co., Calvert County Militia, 1778 [Ref: J-1146, M-150]. Private, Capt. James Patterson's Co., Calvert County Militia, Aug. 10, 1777 [Ref: M-146].

MOLES (MULES), William. Private, Capt. Uriah Forrest's Co., Flying Camp, St. Mary's County, July 28, 1776 [Ref: S-163, D-30, which latter source mistakenly listed the name as "Tom Moles"].

MOLLEHONE, William. See "William Malohone (Mollehone)," q.v.

MONARCH (MONARK, MONACH), Edward. Private, St. Mary's County, drafted July 27, 1781, Maryland Line, Continental Army; discharged in Dec., 1781 [Ref: D-384, D-410, S-163]. "Edward Monach" died intestate by June, 1800 [Ref: SO-304].

MONETT, Isaac. Private, Capt. Walter Smith's Co., Calvert County Militia, 1778 [Ref: J-1146, M-148]. Took the Oath of Allegiance in Calvert County in 1778 [Ref: L-38]. One "Isaac Monnett" (1726-c1798) married Elizabeth Osborne [Ref: Y-474]. The Christ Church Register in

Calvert County records the birth of Isaac Monett, son of Isaac Monett, on Dec. 18, 1748 [Ref: O-22].

MONETT, Thomas. Private, Capt. Henry Skinner's Foot Co. of Hunting Hundred, Calvert County, 1777 [Ref: T-1814, O-125].

MONETT, William. Private, Capt. Henry Skinner's Foot Co. of Hunting Hundred, Calvert County, 1777 [Ref: T-1814, O-125].

MONETT, William Jr. Private, Capt. Henry Skinner's Foot Co. of Hunting Hundred, Calvert County, 1777 [Ref: T-1814, O-125].

MONROE, John. Private, St. Mary's County Militia, 1777 [Ref: M-210]. Took the Oath of Allegiance in St. Mary's County in 1780 [Ref: Q-116, which listed the name as "John Monro"]. It must also be noted that a "John Munroe" of the Maryland Line (county of residence wsa not stated) was charged with desertion and was given 100 lashes some time between Feb., 1778 and June, 1779 [Ref: *Summer Soldiers: A Survey & Index of Revolutionary War Courts-Martial*, by James C. Neagles (1986), page 208].

MONTGOMERY, Susan. See "Ignatius Gough," q.v.

MOORE, Benedict. Took the Oath of Allegiance before the Hon. Bennett Biscoe in St. Mary's County in 1778 [Ref: J-1146, K-63]. The Register of St. Francis Xavier Catholic Church states that "Benedict More and Susan Peacock (NC), both widowed" were married Dec. 14, 1775 [Ref: SC-35, which noted "either they or their descendants eventually settled at The Barrens in Perry County, Missouri." Also, "NC" meant "non-Catholic"].

MOORE, Bennett. Private, St. Mary's County Militia, 1777 [Ref: M-214].

MOORE, Elizabeth. See "Joseph Stone" and "Charles Lee," q.v.

MOORE, George. (1) Private, St. Mary's County Militia, 1777 [Ref: M-210]. Took the Oath of Allegiance before the Hon. Henry Tubman in St. Mary's County in 1778 [Ref: J-1146, K-70]. (2) Private, Capt. Richard Parran's Co., Calvert County Militia, 1778 [Ref: J-1146, M-149].

MOORE, Ignatius. Property destroyed by the British in St. Mary's County in 1781 [Ref: S-163].

MOORE, James. Private, St. Mary's County Militia, 1777 [Ref: M-211]. Took the Oath of Allegiance before the Hon. Ignatius Fenwick, Jr. in St. Mary's County in 1778 [Ref: J-1146, K-68]. The Register of St. Francis Xavier Catholic Church states James Moore and Ann Dorsey were married March 4, 1776 [Ref: SC-35].

MOORE, Jesse. Took the Oath of Allegiance before the Hon. Ignatius Fenwick, Jr. in St. Mary's County in 1778 [Ref: J-1146, K-68].

MOORE, John. (1) Private, St. Mary's County Militia, 1777 [Ref: M-210]. (2) Private, St. Mary's County Militia, 1777 [Ref: M-214]. (3) Private, St. Mary's County Militia, 1777 [Ref: M-211]. (4) Private, Capt. Uriah Forrest's Co., Flying Camp, St. Mary's County, July 28, 1776 [Ref: D-30, SM-114]. (5) One took the Oath of Allegiance before the Hon. Bennett Biscoe in St. Mary's County in 1778 [Ref: J-1146, K-63], and another took the Oath of Allegiance before the Hon. Ignatius Fenwick, Jr. in St. Mary's County in 1778 [Ref: J-1146, K-68].

MOORE, Joseph. Private, St. Mary's County, enlisted June 10, 1778, for 9 months, Continental Army, but was incapable of service and was subsequently discharged on June 22, 1778 [Ref: D-330, S-163].

MOORE, Leonard. (1) Private, Calvert County, enlisted by Lt. Nathaniel Wilson on Aug. 23, 1776 [Ref: D-34]. (2) Private, St. Mary's County Militia, 1777 [Ref: M-211]. Took the Oath of Allegiance before the Hon. Ignatius Fenwick, Jr. in St. Mary's County in 1778 [Ref: J-1146, K-68].

MOORE, Mary. See "John Dean" and "Aaron Spalding," q.v.

MOORE, Matthew. Private, St. Mary's County, 3rd Maryland Line, Capt. Armstrong's Co., 1778-1780 [Ref: D-298].

MOORE, Nicholas. Private, St. Mary's County Militia, 1777 [Ref: M-214, which listed the name as "Nicholas More"]. Property destroyed by the British in 1781 [Ref: S-163].

MOORE, Thomas. Seaman from St. Mary's County who served aboard the State ship *Defence* in 1776 [Ref: S-25, D-606]. See "Thomas More," q.v.

MORAN, Hezekiah. Private, St. Mary's County Militia, 1777 [Ref: M-213]. Took the Oath of Allegiance in St. Mary's County in 1780 [Ref: Q-116]. Hezekiah Moran married Rachel Lyon on Feb. 11, 1778, St. Mary's County, by Rev. John Stephen, Rector of All Faith's Parish [Ref: I-536]. "Hezekiah Moran, blacksmith" moved from Chaptico to Charles County, Maryland, in 1809 [Ref: X-87].

MORAN, Jonathan. Private, St. Mary's County Militia, 1777 [Ref: M-213]. "John Moran, farmer" moved from Upper Resurrection to Gerrard County, Kentucky, in 1797 [Ref: X-87].

MORAN, Joseph. Private, St. Mary's County Militia, 1777 [Ref: M-209].

MORE, Thomas. Private, St. Mary's County, enlisted May 28, 1778, for 9 months [Ref: D-330]. Thomas More married Mary Burroughs on Feb. 23, 1783, St. Mary's County, by Rev. John Stephen, Rector of All Faith's Parish [Ref: I-536]. See "Thomas Moore," q.v.

MORGAN, Benjamin. (1) Second Lieutenant, Lower Bn., St. Mary's County Militia, Aug. 26, 1777, and mentioned as a Brevet Captain by General Smallwood on June 25, 1778. With his name having disappeared from military records thereafter, it has been assumed that he died in the service [Ref: SM-148, M-105, C-346, SM-114]. (2) Private, St. Mary's County, drafted June 10, 1778 [Ref: D-330]. Took the Oath of Allegiance before the Hon. Henry Reeder in St. Mary's County in 1778 [Ref: J-1146, K-64].

MORGAN, Eleanor. See "William Barefoot (Barford)," q.v.

MORGAN, James. Took the Oath of Allegiance before the Hon. John Ireland in St. Mary's County in 1778 [Ref: J-1146, K-65].

MORGAN, Jeremiah. Private, St. Mary's County, enlisted May 26, 1778, for 9 months, Continental Army [Ref: D-329, SM-114].

MORGAN, John (Sep. 22, 1761 - July 1, 1840). Applied for and received pension S1238 on Sep. 21, 1832, in Oldham County, Kentucky, stating he was born in St. Mary's County and when young moved to Dorchester County where he enlisted in the Maryland Line in 1780. John moved to Kentucky in 1794 (age 33) and he had a twin brother Thomas living in 1832 who also served in the Revolutionary War [Ref: P-2417, P-2419, W-61, MK-106].

MORGAN, John Sr. Private, St. Mary's County Militia, 1777 [Ref: M-210]. Took the Oath of Allegiance before the Hon. John Ireland in St. Mary's County in 1778 [Ref: J-1146, K-65].

MORGAN, Mary. See "John Edwards," q.v.

MORGAN, Thomas. Private, Maryland Line, 1781 [Ref: D-410]. Applied for and received pension S2859 in 1828 in Oldham County, Kentucky, and later moved to Trimble County. He had moved to Kentucky in 1806 [Ref: P-2419]. Twin brother of "John Morgan," q.v.

MORGAN, William. (1) Took the Oath of Allegiance in Calvert County in 1778 [Ref: L-38]. (2) Took the Oath of Allegiance before the Hon. John Ireland in St. Mary's County in 1778 [Ref: J-1146, K-65]. Took the Oath of Allegiance in St. Mary's County in 1780 [Ref: Q-116]. One William Morgan died intestate by Aug., 1797 [Ref: SO-264].

MORRIS, Clem. Supplied provisions (wheat, mutton, or bacon) to the Army in St. Mary's County in Oct., 1780 [Ref: S-77, S-164].

MORRIS, James. Private, St. Mary's County Militia, 1777 [Ref: M-210].

MORRIS (MORRISS), John. (1) Private, St. Mary's County Militia, 1777. Private, 3rd Maryland Line, Capt. George Armstrong's Co., enlisted on April 14, 1778. He was wounded (shot through the groin) at the Battle of Cowpens in South Carolina on Jan. 17, 1781, and was discharged as an invalid on June 10, 1781 [Ref: M-214, SM-147, D-142, D-299, D-545, S-164]. (2) Private, Calvert County, enlisted by Capt. John Brooke on July 26, 1776 [Ref: D-33].

MORRIS, Mary. See "John Shanks," q.v.

MORRIS, Peter (1735 - April 19, 1784). Catholic Priest who took the Oath of Allegiance in St. Mary's County in 1778 [Ref: SM-185]. He is buried in St. Francis Xavier Catholic Cemetery at Newtown [Ref: HG-35].

MORRIS, Richard. Private, Capt. Uriah Forrest's Co., Flying Camp, St. Mary's County, July 28, 1776 [Ref: D-30, SM-114].

MORRIS, William. Served from St. Mary's County as Sergeant of Marines aboard the State ship *Defence* in 1776 [Ref: S-25, D-606].

MORSELL, James. Private, Capt. Thomas Truman Greenfield's Co., Calvert County Militia, 1778 [Ref: J-1146, M-150].

MORSELL, James Jr. Took the Oath of Allegiance in Calvert County in 1778 [Ref: L-38].

MORT, Joseph. Private, St. Mary's County Militia, 1777 [Ref: M-210].

MOSELEY, Joseph Rev. S. J. (Catholic Priest). Took the Oath of Allegiance in St. Mary's County in 1778 [Ref: SM-185, S-164].

MOULDS, William. Took the Oath of Allegiance before the Hon. Jeremiah Jordan in St. Mary's County in 1778 [Ref: J-1146, K-67].

MUDD, Joseph. Private, St. Mary's County Militia, 1777 [Ref: M-213]. Took the Oath of Allegiance before the Hon. Henry Tubman in St. Mary's County in 1778 [Ref: J-1146, K-70].

MUDD, Thomas. Private, 1st Maryland Line, from Aug. 14, 1777 to Oct. 18, 1777, when discharged [Ref: D-137]. Took the Oath of Allegiance before the Hon. Richard Barnes in St. Mary's County in 1778 [Ref: J-1146, K-66].

MUGG, John. Private, St. Mary's County Militia, 1777 [Ref: M-210].

MUGG, Walter. Private, St. Mary's County Militia, 1777 [Ref: M-210]. Took the Oath of Allegiance in St. Mary's County in 1780 [Ref: Q-116].

MUIR, James Farlic and Janet. See "William Muir," q.v.

MUIR, William. Took the Oath of Allegiance before the Hon. Jeremiah Jordan in St. Mary's County in 1778 [Ref: J-1146, K-67]. William was appointed guardian of his children Janet Muir and James Farlic Muir in June, 1796 [Ref: SO-243]. "William Muir, farmer" moved from Chaptico to Washington County, Kentucky, in 1808 [Ref: X-87].

MULES, William. See "William Moles (Mules)," q.v.

MURPHY, Hezekiah. Private, Maryland Line, 1781 [Ref: D-410]. Hezekiah Murphy married Mary Robinson on Feb. 13, 1778, St. Mary's County, by Rev. John Stephen, Rector of All Faith's Parish [Ref: I-536].

MURRAIN, Valentine. Took the Oath of Allegiance before the Hon. Jeremiah Jordan in St. Mary's County in 1778 [Ref: J-1146, K-67].

MURRAY, James. Private, St. Mary's County Militia, 1777 [Ref: M-213]. One James Murray died by April, 1789, leaving orphans Jane, James, and Richard Murray [Ref: SO-135].

MURRAY, Valentine. Private, St. Mary's County, 3rd Maryland Line, Capt. Armstrong's Co., enlisted on May 14, 1778, and still in the service in 1780 [Ref: D-298, D-299].

NEALE, Bennett. Took the Oath of Allegiance before the Hon. John Shanks in St. Mary's County in 1778 [Ref: J-1146, K-70].

NEALE, Charles. Private, St. Mary's County Militia, 1777 [Ref: M-212]. Took the Oath of Allegiance before the Hon. Henry G. Sothoron in St. Mary's County in 1778 [Ref: J-1146, K-69]. One Charles Neale died on Dec. 10, 1815 [Ref: R-434]. "Charles Neall" was a private, 3rd Maryland Line, 1778 [Ref: D-146].

NEALE, Francis (Doctor). Commissioned an Assistant Surgeon, Gen. Smallwood's Bn., on Oct. 10, 1776. Ordered to join the bn. in New York and then disappeared from the records. He most likely died in service [Ref: SM-150].

NEALE, Harriet. See "Philip Ford," q.v.

NEALE, Henry. (1) 1740-1815. Third Lieutenant, 5th Independent Maryland Co., St. Mary's County, Jan. 2, 1776, and Second Lieutenant in Aug. 9, 1776. He participated in the Battle of Brooklyn and the New York Campaign in 1776 [Ref: SM-148, D-25]. He married Eleanor Plowden [Ref: Y-491]. Took the Oath of Allegiance before the Hon. Jeremiah Jordan in St. Mary's County in 1778 [Ref: J-1146, K-67]. He was promoted to Lieutenant Colonel of the St. Mary's County Militia in 1794 [Ref: SM-148]. Col. Henry Neale died on Dec. 12, 1815 [Ref: R-435]. (2) Private, St. Mary's County Militia, 1777 [Ref: M-213]. One Henry Neale was appointed guardian of his children Mary Gardiner Neale and Margaret Elizabeth Neale in April, 1789 [Ref: SO-134]. "Henry C. Neale, merchant" moved from Leonardtown to Baltimore, Maryland, in 1808 [Ref: X-87].

NEALE, James. Served as Commissary General during the Revolutionary War. James' eldest son Charles Neale, Esq., died in St. Mary's County on Feb. 9, 1845, in his 85th year [Ref: *Baltimore Sun*, Feb. 17, 1845, *Maryland Genealogical Society Bulletin*, Volume 6, No. 3 (1965), p. 52]. One James Neale died on Jan. 2, 1810 [Ref: R-435]. "James Neale, youngest" took the Oath of Allegiance before the Hon. Jeremiah Jordan in St. Mary's County in 1778 [Ref: J-1146, K-67].

NEALE, Jeremiah. Private, St. Mary's County Militia, 1777 [Ref: M-213]. Took the Oath of Allegiance before the Hon. Jeremiah Jordan in St. Mary's County in 1778 [Ref: J-1146, K-67].

NEALE, Margaret E. and Mary G. See "Henry Neale," q.v.

NEALE, Raphael. Took the Oath of Allegiance before the Hon. Jeremiah Jordan in St. Mary's County in 1778 [Ref: J-1146, K-67]. Ensign, Upper Bn., Nov. 18, 1779 [Ref: SM-114].

NEALE, Raphael Jr. Took the Oath of Allegiance before the Hon. John Ireland in St. Mary's County in 1778 [Ref: J-1146, K-65]. "Raphael Neale, formerly Member of Congress from St. Mary's County, died on Oct. 19, 1833, in St. Mary's County, and leaves a wife and two children." [Ref: R-435].

NEALE, Thomas. Private, 1st Maryland Line, 1778-1780 [Ref: D-146].

NEALE, Wilfred. Took the Oath of Allegiance before the Hon. John Shanks in St. Mary's County in 1778 [Ref: J-1146, K-70]. Elected to serve on a General Committee in St. Mary's County in accordance with the resolves of the Continental Congress in 1775 [Ref: MR-127, which incorrectly listed the name as "Wilfres Neale"]. "Mr. Wilfred Neale" served on the Committee of Observation in 1776 [Ref: S-16, B-100].

NELSON, Elenor, Elizabeth, and George. See "Seneca Nelson," q.v.

NELSON, John. Private, St. Mary's County, 4th Maryland Line, until discharged on May 3, 1780 [Ref: D-147, D-411]. There was also a John Nelson who was an ensign in the 1st Maryland Line on Jan. 26, 1780 [Ref: D-146].

NELSON, Seneca (Senna). Took the Oath of Allegiance before the Hon. John Ireland in St. Mary's County in 1778 [Ref: J-1146, K-65]. One Seneca Nelson died and his widow Elenor married John Railey (Raley or Ryley) by Aug., 1796. His children were Elizabeth, Elenor and George Nelson [Ref: SO-287, SO-290, SO-291, SO-293, SO-301].
NETTLE, Thomas Dutton. Private, St. Mary's County Militia, 1777 [Ref: M-210].
NEVISON, Mary. See "William Bond," q.v.
NEVITT, Charles. Took the Oath of Allegiance before the Hon. Henry G. Sothoron in St. Mary's County in 1778 [Ref: J-1146, K-69].
NEVITT, John. Took the Oath of Allegiance before the Hon. Jeremiah Jordan in St. Mary's County in 1778 [Ref: J-1146, K-67].
NEVITT, John Baptist. Took the Oath of Allegiance before the Hon. Jeremiah Jordan in St. Mary's County in 1778 [Ref: J-1146, K-67].
NEVITT, Joseph. (1) Private, St. Mary's County Militia, 1777 [Ref: M-212]. (2) One took the Oath of Allegiance before the Hon. Jeremiah Jordan in St. Mary's County in 1778 [Ref: J-1146, K-67], and another took the Oath of Allegiance before the Hon. John Shanks in St. Mary's County in 1778 [Ref: J-1146, K-70].
NEWBERN, Mary. See "Thomas Gantt, Jr.," q.v.
NEWCOMB, James. See "Richard Pierceall," q.v.
NEWELL, Baptist. Private, St. Mary's County Militia, 1777 [Ref: M-214].
NEWELL, John. Took the Oath of Allegiance in Calvert County in 1778 [Ref: L-38].
NEWTON, Basil. Private, Calvert County, enlisted by Ensign James Somervill on July 25, 1776 [Ref: D-34]. Private, 6th Maryland Line, from March 17, 1777, to at least Jan. 1, 1780 [Ref: D-235].
NEWTON, Bernard. Private, St. Mary's County Militia, 1777 [Ref: M-214]. Took the Oath of Allegiance before the Hon. Richard Barnes in St. Mary's County in 1778 [Ref: J-1146, K-66]. The Register of St. Francis Xavier Catholic Church states that Bernard Newton and Mary Payne were married Dec. 11, 1769, and Bernard Newton and Mary Pike were married Feb. 8, 1775 [Ref: SC-33, SC-35].
NEWTON, Clement. See "Clement Sewall," q.v.
NEWTON, Delbert. Private, St. Mary's County Militia, 1777 [Ref: M-212]. Took the Oath of Allegiance before the Hon. Henry Reeder in St. Mary's County in 1778 [Ref: J-1146, K-64].
NEWTON, Elizabeth. See "Joshua Greenwell," q.v.
NEWTON, Gabriel. Private, St. Mary's County Militia, 1777 [Ref: M-211]. Took the Oath of Allegiance before the Hon. John Ireland in St. Mary's County in 1778 [Ref: J-1146, K-65]. The Register of St. Francis Xavier Catholic Church states Gabriel Newton and Henrietta Wheatley, widow, were married Oct. 24, 1775 [Ref: SC-35].
NEWTON, Grace. See "Ward Newton," q.v.

NEWTON, Henry. Private, Calvert County, enlisted by Ensign James Somervill on July 25, 1776 [Ref: D-34].
NEWTON, Ignatius. Private, St. Mary's County Militia, 1777 [Ref: M-212]. Two men with this name took the Oath of Allegiance in St. Mary's County in 1778: one before the Hon. John Ireland and one before the Hon. Ignatius Fenwick, Jr. [Ref: J-1146, K-65, K-68]. One "Ignatius Newton, elite" moved from Lower Resurrection in St. Mary's County to Washington County, Kentucky, in 1797 [Ref: X-87].
NEWTON, John. Private, St. Mary's County Militia, 1777 [Ref: M-215].
NEWTON, Joseph. Private, St. Mary's County Militia, 1777 [Ref: M-213]. Private, Maryland Line, drafted July 27, 1781 [Ref: D-384].
NEWTON, Thomas. See "Ward Newton," q.v.
NEWTON, Ward. Private, Capt. Richard Parran's Co., Calvert County Militia, 1778 [Ref: J-1146, M-149, which listed the name as "Ward Nuton"]. Took the Oath of Allegiance in Calvert County in 1778 [Ref: L-38]. The Christ Church Register in Calvert County records the birth of Ward Newton, son of Thomas and Grace Newton, on April 24, 1746/7 [Ref: O-23].
NEWTON, William. Private, St. Mary's County Militia, 1777 [Ref: M-212]. There was also a William Newton who was a private in the 2nd Maryland Line from Dec. 10, 1776 through 1780 [Ref: D-146].
NEWTON, Zachariah. Private, St. Mary's County Militia, 1777 [Ref: M-212]. Took the Oath of Allegiance before the Hon. John Ireland in St. Mary's County in 1778 [Ref: J-1146, K-65]. Private, St. Mary's County, drafted on July 27, 1781 [Ref: D-384]. Private, Continental Army; discharged "not fit for duty" by Dr. Murray on Oct. 18, 1781 [Ref: D-410, S-107, S-164, G-646].
NICHOLLS, Thomas. First Lieutenant, St. Mary's County Militia, Aug. 26, 1777. Appointed as Inspector of Tobacco at Chaptico on Aug. 20, 1780 [Ref: M-210, S-164].
NIVISON (NEVISON), James. Took the Oath of Allegiance before the Hon. Jeremiah Jordan in St. Mary's County in 1778 [Ref: J-1146, K-67].
NOAKES, Richard. Private, St. Mary's County Militia, 1777 [Ref: M-212]. Took the Oath of Allegiance before the Hon. Robert Watts in St. Mary's County in 1778 [Ref: J-1146, K-62, which listed the name as "Richard Nokes"].
NOAKES, Thomas. Took the Oath of Allegiance before the Hon. John Shanks in St. Mary's County in 1778 [Ref: J-1146, K-70].
NOBEL, Joseph. Took the Oath of Allegiance before the Hon. Bennett Biscoe in St. Mary's County in 1778 [Ref: J-1146, K-63].
NOE, George. Took the Oath of Allegiance before the Hon. Henry Tubman in St. Mary's County in 1778 [Ref: J-1146, K-70].
NOE, Joseph. Private, St. Mary's County Militia, 1777 [Ref: M-213].
NOE, Thomas. Private, St. Mary's County Militia, 1777 [Ref: M-210].

NORFOLK, James. Private, Capt. Frisby Freeland's Co., Calvert County Militia, 1778 [Ref: J-1146, M-148].

NORFOLK, John. Two men with this name took the Oath of Allegiance in Calvert County in 1778 [Ref: L-38].

NORFOLK, John (of James). Private, Capt. Thomas Cleland's Co., Calvert County Militia, 1778 [Ref: J-1146, M-147, which listed the name as "John Norfolk, for James"]. "John Norfolk, of James" was a private in Capt. Frisby Freeland's Co., Calvert County Militia, 1778 [Ref: J-1146, M-148].

NORFOLK, John (of John). Private, Capt. Thomas Cleland's Co., Calvert County Militia, 1778 [Ref: J-1146, M-147, which listed the name as "John Norfolk, for John"]. "John Norfolk, Jr." was a private, Capt. Thomas Truman Greenfield's Co., Calvert County Militia, 1778 [Ref: J-1146, M-150]. Took the Oath of Allegiance in Calvert County in 1778 [Ref: L-38].

NORFOLK, Thomas Jr. Private, Capt. Thomas Cleland's Co., Calvert County Militia, 1778 [Ref: J-1146, M-147].

NORFOLK, William. Private, Capt. Thomas Cleland's Co., Calvert County Militia, 1778 [Ref: J-1146, M-147].

NORRIS, Arnold. Private, St. Mary's County, drafted July 27, 1781 [Ref: D-384]. Private, Continental Army, discharged on Dec. 10, 1781 [Ref: D-410, S-164].

NORRIS, Barton. Private, St. Mary's County Militia, 1777 [Ref: M-214].

NORRIS, Bennett. Private, St. Mary's County Militia, 1777 [Ref: M-214, which listed the name as "Bennr(?) Norris"]. Took the Oath of Allegiance before the Hon. Henry Reeder in St. Mary's County in 1778 [Ref: J-1146, K-64].

NORRIS, Clement. Private, St. Mary's County Militia, 1777 [Ref: M-214]. Took the Oath of Allegiance before the Hon. Richard Barnes in St. Mary's County in 1778 [Ref: J-1146, K-66].

NORRIS, Edmund. This name appeared twice on the list as a private in St. Mary's County Militia in 1777 [Ref: M-211, M-214]. One took the Oath of Allegiance in St. Mary's County in 1780 [Ref: Q-117]. See "James Norris, of Norrh (Mark?)," q.v.

NORRIS, Edmund Barton. "Edmund B. Norris" took the Oath of Allegiance before the Hon. Henry Reeder in St. Mary's County in 1778 [Ref: J-1146, K-64]. "Edmund Barton Norris" died intestate by April, 1796 [Ref: SO-242].

NORRIS, Gerrard. Private, St. Mary's County Militia, 1777 [Ref: M-214].

NORRIS, Henry. Took the Oath of Allegiance before the Hon. Richard Barnes in St. Mary's County in 1778 [Ref: J-1146, K-66]. Private, St. Mary's County, drafted July 27, 1781 [Ref: D-384]. Private, Continental Army, 1781; discharged, unfit, in Dec., 1781 [Ref: D-411]. See "Rodolph Norris," q.v.

NORRIS, Ignatius. Private, St. Mary's County Militia, 1777 [Ref: M-214]. Two men with this name took the Oath of Allegiance in St. Mary's County in 1778: one before the Hon. Richard Barnes and one before the Hon. John Ireland [Ref: J-1146, K-65, K-66].

NORRIS, James. Private, St. Mary's County Militia, 1777 [Ref: M-211]. Took the Oath of Allegiance before the Hon. Richard Barnes in St. Mary's County in 1778 [Ref: J-1146, K-66]. Took the Oath of Allegiance again in St. Mary's County in 1780 [Ref: Q-117]. The Register of St. Francis Xavier Catholic Church states that James Norris and Monica Greenwell married on March 6, 1773 [Ref: SC-34].

NORRIS, James, of Norrh (Mark?). Private, St. Mary's County Militia, 1777 [Ref: M-211]. In 1789, the Orphans Court appointed Mark Norris as guardian of Edmund Norris, orphan of James Norris, deceased [Ref: SO-143].

NORRIS, John. There were several men with this name: (1) Private, St. Mary's County Militia, 1777 [Ref: M-214]. (2) Private, St. Mary's County, enlisted May 29, 1778, for 9 months [Ref: D-330]. (3) Name appeared twice as a private in the Continental Army in 1781 [Ref: D-411]. (4) Private (substitute), St. Mary's County, Aug. 2, 1781 [Ref: D-384]. (5) One took the Oath of Allegiance before the Hon. Henry Reeder in St. Mary's County in 1778 [Ref: J-1146, K-64]. (6) One took the Oath of Allegiance before the Hon. Richard Barnes in St. Mary's County in 1778 [Ref: J-1146, K-66]. (7) One took the Oath of Allegiance in St. Mary's County in 1780 [Ref: Q-117]. John Norris (1762-1814) was a private in St. Mary's County [Ref: Maryland Society, Sons of the American Revolution, Approved Membership Application No. 2528-A]. (8) Private, Capt. Frederick Skinner's Co., Calvert County Militia, 1778 [Ref: J-1146, M-150]. (9) Private, Capt. John Mackall's Co., Calvert County Militia, 15th Bn., June 12, 1778 [Ref: M-146]. (10) Private, Capt. James Patterson's Co., Calvert County Militia, Aug. 10, 1777 [Ref: M-146]. One took the Oath of Allegiance in Calvert County in 1778 and another took the Oath of Allegiance in Calvert County in 1780 [Ref: Q-117, L-38].

NORRIS, John Basil. Private, St. Mary's County Militia, 1777 [Ref: M-211]. Took the Oath of Allegiance in St. Mary's County in 1780 [Ref: Q-117].

NORRIS, John Heard. Private, St. Mary's County Militia, 1777 [Ref: M-211].

NORRIS, Mackelva. Took the Oath of Allegiance before the Hon. Vernon Hebb in St. Mary's County in 1778 [Ref: J-1146, K-67].

NORRIS, Mark Jr. Private, St. Mary's County Militia, 1777 [Ref: M-211]. Took the Oath of Allegiance before the Hon. Richard Barnes in St. Mary's County in 1778 [Ref: J-1146, K-66].

NORRIS, Mark Sr. Took the Oath of Allegiance before the Hon. Richard Barnes in St. Mary's County in 1778 [Ref: J-1146, K-66]. See "James Norris, of Norrh (Mark?)," q.v.

NORRIS, Martin. Second Lieutenant, Capt. Richard Lane's Co., Calvert County Militia, 1778, and First Lieutenant, 15th Bn., April 16, 1778 [Ref: J-1146, M-107, M-149, E-37]. Took the Oath of Allegiance in Calvert County in 1778 [Ref: L-38].

NORRIS, Mary. See "Ignatius Shirley," q.v.

NORRIS, Matthew. Took the Oath of Allegiance before the Hon. Robert Watts in St. Mary's County in 1778 [Ref: J-1146, K-62].

NORRIS, Philip. This name appeared twice as a private in St. Mary's County Militia in 1777 [Ref: M-210, M-214]. One took the Oath of Allegiance before the Hon. John Ireland in St. Mary's County in 1778 [Ref: J-1146, K-65].

NORRIS, Philip (of Thomas). Private, St. Mary's County Militia, 1777 [Ref: M-214].

NORRIS, Priscilla. See "Ignatius Lowe," q.v.

NORRIS, Rodolph. "Rode Norris" was a private, St. Mary's County Militia, 1777 [Ref: M-214]. "Rodolph Norris" took the Oath of Allegiance before the Hon. Henry Reeder in St. Mary's County in 1778 [Ref: J-1146, K-64]. "Rudolphus Norris" and Henry Norris were early Catholic settlers on Pottinger Creek in Washington County, Kentucky in 1785 [Ref: MK-110].

NORRIS, Stephen. Private, St. Mary's County Militia, 1777 [Ref: M-211].

NORRIS, Thomas. Private, St. Mary's County Militia, 1777 [Ref: M-214]. Two men with this name took the Oath of Allegiance in St. Mary's County in 1778: one before the Hon. Henry Reeder and one before the Hon. John Ireland [Ref: J-1146, K-64, K-65]. One also took the Oath of Allegiance in 1780 [Ref: Q-117].

NORRIS, Vincent. Private, St. Mary's County Militia, 1777 [Ref: M-214]. Took the Oath of Allegiance in St. Mary's County in 1780 [Ref: Q-117]. "Vincent Norris, farmer" moved from Lower Newtown to Charles County, Maryland, in 1810 [Ref: X-87].

NORRIS, William. Private, St. Mary's County Militia, 1777 [Ref: M-214]. Took the Oath of Allegiance before the Hon. Bennett Biscoe in St. Mary's County in 1778 [Ref: J-1146, K-63]. The Register of St. Andrew's Episcopal Church states that William Norris and Dorothy White were married Nov. 22, 1778 [Ref: MB-382].

NORRIS, William (of Thomas). Private, St. Mary's County Militia, 1777 [Ref: M-211].

NORTHEY, Samuel. Private, Capt. Richard Lane's Co., Calvert County Militia, 1778 [Ref: J-1146, M-150].

NOTTINGHAM, Basil. See "John Basil Nottingham," q.v.

NOTTINGHAM, Benjamin. Took the Oath of Allegiance before the Hon. Henry Reeder in St. Mary's County in 1778 [Ref: J-1146, K-64]. "Bent.

[Benj.?] Nottingham" was a private in St. Mary's County Militia in 1777 [Ref: M-214].
NOTTINGHAM, John Basil. Private, St. Mary's County Militia, 1777 [Ref: M-211]. Took the Oath of Allegiance before the Hon. Ignatius Fenwick, Jr. in St. Mary's County in 1778 [Ref: J-1146, K-68]. The Register of St. Francis Xavier Catholic Church states that "Basil Nottingham and Jane Stone, widow" were married Dec. 31, 1774 [Ref: SC-35].
NOTTINGHAM, Mary. See "Thomas Reswick (Riswick)," q.v.
NOTTINGHAM, Philip. Private, St. Mary's County Militia, 1777 [Ref: M-214]. Took the Oath of Allegiance before the Hon. Henry Reeder in St. Mary's County in 1778 [Ref: J-1146, K-64].
NOWELL, Gilbert. Private, Capt. Charles Williamson's Co., Calvert County Militia, 1778 [Ref: J-1146, M-148]. Took the Oath of Allegiance in Calvert County in 1778 [Ref: L-38].
NOWELL, James. Private, Capt. John Mackall's Co., Calvert County Militia, 15th Bn., June 12, 1778 [Ref: M-146].
NOWELL, Jeremiah. Private, St. Mary's County Militia, 1777 [Ref: M-214].
NOWELL, John Jr. Private, Capt. Thomas Cleland's Co., Calvert County Militia, 1778 [Ref: J-1146, M-147].
NOWELL, William. Private, Capt. Frederick Skinner's Co., Calvert County Militia, 1778 [Ref: J-1146, M-150]. Private, Capt. James Grahame's Co., Calvert County Militia, 1778 [Ref: J-1146, M-148]. Took the Oath of Allegiance in Calvert County in 1778 [Ref: L-38].
NOWLES, James. Took the Oath of Allegiance before the Hon. Richard Barnes in St. Mary's County in 1778 [Ref: J-1146, K-66].
NOWLES, John. Took the Oath of Allegiance in St. Mary's County in 1780 [Ref: Q-117].
NOWRIE, William. Private, Capt. James Patterson's Co., Calvert County Militia, Aug. 10, 1777 [Ref: M-146].
NUGENT, Jere. Private, St. Mary's County Militia, 1777 [Ref: M-214].
NUGENT, Robert. Private, St. Mary's County Militia, 1777 [Ref: M-214]. Paid for his services to the State in 1782 [Ref: S-164].
NUGENT, Willoughby. Private, St. Mary's County Militia, 1777 [Ref: M-214, which listed the name as "Williby Nuigent"].
O'BRIEN, Ellinore. See "Samuel Abell," q.v.
O'NEILL, Bernard. Took the Oath of Allegiance before the Hon. Jeremiah Jordan in St. Mary's County in 1778 [Ref: J-1146, K-67].
O'REILLY, Elizabeth. See "Clement Sewall," q.v.
OGDEN, Aaron. Private, Capt. Thomas Truman Greenfield's Co., Calvert County Militia, 1778 [Ref: J-1146, M-150]. Took the Oath of Allegiance in Calvert County in 1778 [Ref: L-38].

OGDEN, Elisha. Private, Capt. Thomas Truman Greenfield's Co., Calvert County Militia, 1778 [Ref: J-1146, M-150]. Took the Oath of Allegiance in Calvert County in 1778 [Ref: L-38].
OGDEN, James. Private, Capt. Thomas Truman Greenfield's Co., Calvert County Militia, 1778 [Ref: J-1146, M-150]. Took the Oath of Allegiance in Calvert County in 1778 [Ref: L-38].
OGDEN, John. Took the Oath of Allegiance in Calvert County in 1778 [Ref: L-38].
OGDEN, Moses. Private, Capt. Thomas Truman Greenfield's Co., Calvert County Militia, 1778 [Ref: J-1146, M-150]. Took the Oath of Allegiance in Calvert County in 1778 [Ref: L-38].
OGG, Alexander. Private, Capt. Frisby Freeland's Co., Calvert County Militia, 1778 [Ref: J-1146, M-148]. Took the Oath of Allegiance in Calvert County in 1778 [Ref: L-38]. Alexander Ogg married Jane Hellen on June 1, 1782 [Ref: O-23].
OGLEBY, John. Private, Capt. Henry Skinner's Foot Co. of Hunting Hundred, Calvert County, 1777 [Ref: T-1814, O-125].
OLIVER, Lewis. Private, St. Mary's County Militia, 1777 [Ref: M-215].
OLIVER, Lewis Jr. Took the Oath of Allegiance in St. Mary's County in 1780 [Ref: Q-117].
ORD (OARD), Jesse. "Jesse Ord" was a private in St. Mary's County Militia, 1777 [Ref: M-212]. "Jesse Oard" died intestate by Oct., 1789, with Ann Oard as his administratrix [Ref: SO-146, SO-171].
ORD (OARD), William. Private, St. Mary's County Militia, 1777 [Ref: M-213, which listed the name as "William Oard(?)"].
ORMS, Robert. Private, Capt. Henry Skinner's Foot Co. of Hunting Hundred, Calvert County, 1777 [Ref: T-1814, O-125].
ORMS, William. Private, Capt. Henry Skinner's Foot Co. of Hunting Hundred, Calvert County, 1777 [Ref: T-1814, O-125]. One "William Orm" was a corporal in the 2nd Maryland Line in 1780 [Ref: D-148].
OSBORNE, Elizabeth. See "Isaac Monett," q.v.
OWENS, Charles. Private, Capt. Frisby Freeland's Co., Calvert County Militia, 1778 [Ref: J-1146, M-148]. Took the Oath of Allegiance in Calvert County in 1778 [Ref: L-38]. Charles Owens and Betty Barton were married in Oct., 1777, by Rev. Thomas John Clagett, All Saint's Parish [Ref: K-33].
OWENS, James. Private, Capt. Walter Smith's Co., Calvert County Militia, 1778 [Ref: J-1146, M-148]. Took the Oath of Allegiance in Calvert County in 1778 [Ref: L-38].
OWENS, John. Private, 1st Maryland Line, from Dec. 10, 1776 until March 6, 1778, when reported as "deserted" but a John Owens enlisted in the 3rd Maryland Line on March 11, 1778 and served to Dec., 1778 [Ref: D-148, which listed the name once as "John Owings"]. The Register of St. Andrew's Episcopal Church states that John Owens and Sarah Saunders were married Oct. 3, 1779 [Ref: MB-283].

OWENS, Joseph. Private, St. Mary's County Militia, 1777 [Ref: M-210]. Took the Oath of Allegiance before the Hon. Jeremiah Jordan in St. Mary's County in 1778 [Ref: J-1146, K-67]. Private, 1st Maryland Line, from June 5, 1778 until Feb., 1779, when discharged [Ref: D-148, which listed the name as "Joseph Owings"].

OWENS, Samuel. Private, Capt. Thomas Cleland's Co., Calvert County Militia, 1778 [Ref: J-1146, M-147]. One Samuel Owens was a private, 1st Maryland Line, 1780, and another was a corporal, 2nd Maryland Line, 1778-1780 [Ref: D-148, which listed the name as "Samuel Owings"].

PAIN, Francis. See "Francis Payne" and "Raphael Wimsatt," q.v.

PANTER, Christian. Private, Capt. Walter Smith's Co., Calvert County Militia, 1778 [Ref: J-1146, M-148]. Took the Oath of Allegiance in Calvert County in 1778 [Ref: L-38, which listed the name as "Christian Paster"].

PANTER, Francis. Private, Capt. Benjamin Bond's Co., Calvert County Militia, 1778 [Ref: J-1146, M-149]. Took the Oath of Allegiance in Calvert County in 1778 [Ref: L-38, which listed the name as "Francis Paster"].

PANTER, Peter. Took the Oath of Allegiance in Calvert County in 1778 [Ref: L-38, which listed the name as "Peter Paster"].

PANTRY, John. Private, Capt. Benjamin Bond's Co., Calvert County Militia, 1778 [Ref: J-1146, M-149]. Took the Oath of Allegiance in Calvert County in 1778 [Ref: L-38].

PANTRY, William. Private, Capt. Henry Skinner's Foot Co. of Hunting Hundred, Calvert County, 1777 [Ref: T-1814, O-125].

PARDOE, Ann. See "John Pardoe," q.v.

PARDOE, Benjamin. Private, Maryland Line, 1778 [Ref: D-411, which listed the name as "Benjamn Pardo"].

PARDOE, Catherine Haseltine. See "John Pardoe," q.v.

PARDOE, John. Took the Oath of Allegiance in Calvert County in 1778 [Ref: L-38]. Private, Capt. Benjamin Bond's Co., Calvert County Militia, 1778 [Ref: J-1146, M-149, which mistakenly listed the name as "John Pards"]. John Pardoe married Margaret Frazier on Nov. 23, 1769, and their children were Catherine Haseltine Pardoe (born Dec. 5, 1770), John Pardoe (born May 5, 1772), Ann Pardoe (born Feb. 5, 1776), and Peter Pardoe (born June 5, 1778). [Ref: O-23].

PARDOE, Peter. See "John Pardoe," q.v.

PARKER, Fielder. Private, Capt. John Mackall's Co., Calvert County Militia, 15th Bn., June 12, 1778 [Ref: M-146]. Private, Capt. Richard Parran's Co., Calvert County Militia, 1778 [Ref: J-1146, M-149].

PARKER, Fielder Jr. Private, Capt. Frederick Skinner's Co., Calvert County Militia, 1778 [Ref: J-1146, M-150].

PARKER, George. Private, Capt. Thomas Cleland's Co., Calvert County Militia, 1778 [Ref: J-1146, M-147].

PARKER, Jacob. Took the Oath of Allegiance in Calvert County in 1778 [Ref: L-38].

PARKER, Peter. Private, Capt. Edward Wood's Co., Calvert County Militia, 1778 [Ref: J-1146, M-147].

PARKER, William (of George). Private, Capt. Frederick Skinner's Co., Calvert County Militia, 1778 [Ref: J-1146, M-150, which listed the name as "Wm. Parker son George"].

PARKER, William (of William). Private, Capt. John Mackall's Co., Calvert County Militia, 15th Bn., June 12, 1778 [Ref: M-146]. Private, Capt. Frederick Skinner's Co., Calvert County Militia, 1778 [Ref: J-1146, M-150, which listed the name as "Wm. Parker son Wm."].

PARKINS, Jacob. Took the Oath of Allegiance in Calvert County in 1778 [Ref: L-38].

PARRAN, Alexander. Private, Capt. Richard Parran's Co., Calvert County Militia, 1778 [Ref: J-1146, M-149]. Took the Oath of Allegiance in Calvert County in 1778 [Ref: L-38, which listed the name as "Alexander Parron"]. Alexander Parran and Mary King were married on Feb. 10, 1778, by Rev. Francis Lauder, of Christ Church Parish [Ref: K-34].

PARRAN, Benjamin. Private, Calvert County, enlisted by Capt. John Brooke on July 26, 1776 [Ref: D-33]. Private, Capt. Richard Parran's Co., Calvert County Militia, 1778 [Ref: J-1146, M-149]. Took the Oath of Allegiance in Calvert County in 1778 [Ref: L-38, which listed the name as "Benjamin Parron"]. Benjamin Parran and Dorcas Hillen were married on Jan. 15, 1778, by Rev. Francis Lauder, of Christ Church Parish [Ref: K-33].

PARRAN, Bennett. Took the Oath of Allegiance before the Hon. John Ireland in St. Mary's County in 1778 [Ref: J-1146, K-65, which listed the name as "Bennet Perran"].

PARRAN, Charles Somerset. Private, Capt. Richard Parran's Co., Calvert County Militia, 1778 [Ref: J-1146, M-149]. Private, Capt. Richard Parran's Co., Calvert County Militia, 1778 [Ref: J-1146, M-149]. Took the Oath of Allegiance in Calvert County in 1780 [Ref: Q-117].

PARRAN, Charles Somerset Jr. Took the Oath of Allegiance in Calvert County in 1778 [Ref: L-38]. The Register of St. Andrew's Episcopal Church states that "Charles Somersett Parran" and Margaret Ireland were married (by license) Dec. 17, 1782 [Ref: MB-384].

PARRAN, John Jr. Private, Capt. Richard Parran's Co., Calvert County Militia, 1778 [Ref: J-1146, M-149]. Took the Oath of Allegiance in Calvert County in 1778 [Ref: L-38, which listed the name as "John Parron, Jr."].

PARRAN, John Sr. Took the Oath of Allegiance in Calvert County in 1778 [Ref: L-38, which listed the name as "John Parron, Sr."]. Private, Capt. Richard Parran's Co., Calvert County Militia, 1778 [Ref: J-1146, M-149].

PARRAN, Mary. See "Thomas Gantt, 4th" and" John Chesley," q.v.

PARRAN, Nathaniel. See "Ignatius Taylor," q.v.
PARRAN, Richard (died in 1782). Son of Young Parran and Elizabeth Smith Wilkinson, of Calvert County. He married Sarah ---- and had daughters Elizabeth S., Sarah, and Mary. Member of the House of Delegates, 1773-1777, Justice, 1772-1782, Judge of the Orphans Court, 1777-1782, and Commissioner of Tax, 1778. Captain, Calvert County Militia, 1778 [Ref: J-1146, M-149, N-76, N-636]. Took the Oath of Allegiance in Calvert County in 1778 [Ref: L-38, which listed the name as "Richard Parron"].
PARRAN, Robert. Captain, 15th Bn., Calvert County Militia, April 16, 1778 [Ref: M-110, E-37].
PARRAN, Samuel. Took the Oath of Allegiance in Calvert County in 1778 [Ref: L-38, which listed the name as "Samuel Parron"].
PARRAN, Thomas Jr. "Thomas Parran, Jr." took the Oath of Allegiance in Calvert County in 1780 [Ref: Q-117]. The Register of St. Andrew's Episcopal Church states that "Thomas Parran" and Jane Mackall were married (by license) on Feb. 6, 1783, St. Mary's County [Ref: MB-385].
PARRAN, Thomas Sr. "Thomas Parran, Sr." took the Oath of Allegiance in Calvert County in 1778 [Ref: L-38]. "Thomas Parran" was a private, Capt. Richard Parran's Co., Calvert County Militia, 1778 [Ref: J-1146, M-149]. See "Thomas Parran, Jr.," q.v.
PARRAN, Young. See "Richard Parran," q.v.
PARRISH, Pernina. See "Thomas Price," q.v.
PARSONS, Bennit. Private, St. Mary's County Militia, 1777 [Ref: M-212].
PARSONS, Clement. Private, St. Mary's County Militia, 1777 [Ref: M-213]. Took the Oath of Allegiance before the Hon. John Reeder in St. Mary's County in 1778 [Ref: J-1146, K-69]. One Clement Parsons died testate by April, 1793 [Ref: SO-194]. Another Clement Parsons was among the early Catholic settlers on Rolling Fork near Lebanon, Kentucky, prior to 1800 [Ref: MK-113].
PARSONS, James. Private, St. Mary's County Militia, 1777 [Ref: M-211]. Took the Oath of Allegiance before the Hon. Ignatius Fenwick, Jr. in St. Mary's County in 1778 [Ref: J-1146, K-68].
PATTERSON, Basil. Private, St. Mary's County Militia, 1777 [Ref: M-210].
PATTERSON, James. Captain, Calvert County Militia. When relieved as commander of the county militia, it led to a protest and a petition by his men to Gov. Thomas Johnson on Aug. 10, 1777, stating that "his successor was totally obnoxious to the county." [Ref: M-146, V-116]. Took the Oath of Allegiance in Calvert County in 1778 [Ref: L-38].
PATTERSON, John. Private, Capt. Richard Parran's Co., Calvert County Militia, 1778 [Ref: J-1146, M-149].
PATTISON, Elizabeth. See "John Pattison," q.v.
PATTISON, James. First Lieutenant, Capt. Frederick Skinner's Co., Calvert County Militia, 1778 [Ref: J-1146, M-150].

PATTISON, Jeremiah. Private, Capt. Benjamin Bond's Co., Calvert County Militia, 1778 [Ref: J-1146, M-149]. Took the Oath of Allegiance in Calvert County in 1778 [Ref: L-38].
PATTISON, John (1743-1805). Took the Oath of Allegiance in Calvert County in 1778 [Ref: L-38]. He and his wife Elizabeth (1748-1808) are buried on a farm formerly owned by Mr. Hellen (1908) on Mill Creek in Calvert County [Ref: HG-58].
PATTISON, Richard. Private, Capt. Benjamin Bond's Co., Calvert County Militia, 1778 [Ref: J-1146, M-149].
PATTISON, Thomas. Private, Capt. Benjamin Bond's Co., Calvert County Militia, 1778 [Ref: J-1146, M-149]. Took the Oath of Allegiance in Calvert County in 1778 [Ref: L-38].
PATTISON, William. Private, Capt. Walter Smith's Co., Calvert County Militia, 1778 [Ref: J-1146, M-148]. Took the Oath of Allegiance in Calvert County in 1778 [Ref: L-38].
PAYNE, Barnard. Private, St. Mary's County, enlisted on May 29, 1778, for 9 months [Ref: D-329, which listed the name as "Barnard Pane"]. Private (substitute), St. Mary's County, July 31, 1781 [Ref: D-384, which listed the name as "Barnard Pain"]. "Barney Payne" was a private in the Continental Army in 1781, discharged on Dec. 3, 1781 [Ref: D-411, S-109, H-11]. "Barnard Paine" was a private in the 2nd Maryland Line, 1778-1781 [Ref: S-164].
PAYNE, Elizabeth. See "John Bowles," q.v.
PAYNE, Francis. Private, St. Mary's County Militia, 1777 [Ref: M-210]. Took the Oath of Allegiance before the Hon. Richard Barnes in St. Mary's County in 1778 [Ref: J-1146, K-66]. In support of the pension application of "Raphael Wimsatt (Wimsett)," q.v., in 1840, "Francis Pain" (aged 83) stated he was born and raised in St. Mary's County and he was a neighbor of Susannah Cissel when she married Raphael Winsett in 1783. About a year later he moved with them to Nelson County, Kentucky, and has since been their neighbor [Ref: MK-113].
PAYNE, Ignatius. Private (substitute), St. Mary's County, July 28, 1781 [Ref: D-384, which listed the name as "Igns. Pain"]. Private, Maryland Line, Continental Army, discharged on Dec. 3, 1781 [Ref: D-411, S-164, S-109, H-11].
PAYNE, James. Private, St. Mary's County Militia, 1777 [Ref: M-215]. Took the Oath of Allegiance before the Hon. John Ireland in St. Mary's County in 1778 [Ref: J-1146, K-65].
PAYNE, James (of Richard). Took the Oath of Allegiance before the Hon. Richard Barnes in St. Mary's County in 1778 [Ref: J-1146, K-66].
PAYNE, John. Private, St. Mary's County Militia, 1777 [Ref: M-212, which listed the name as "John Pain"]. Took the Oath of Allegiance before the Hon. John Shanks in St. Mary's County in 1778 [Ref: J-1146, K-70].

PAYNE, John Baptist. Private, St. Mary's County Militia, 1777 [Ref: M-214, which listed the name as "Jno. Bapts. Payne"]. Took the Oath of Allegiance before the Hon. Henry Reeder in St. Mary's County in 1778 [Ref: J-1146, K-64].
PAYNE, Leonard. Private, St. Mary's County Militia, 1777 [Ref: M-210].
PAYNE, Mary. See "Bernard Newton," q.v.
PAYNE, Michael. See "Mickal Peign," q.v.
PAYNE, Raphael. Private, St. Mary's County Militia, 1777 [Ref: M-210]. Took the Oath of Allegiance before the Hon. John Ireland in St. Mary's County in 1778 [Ref: J-1146, K-65].
PAYNE, Richard. Took the Oath of Allegiance before the Hon. Richard Barnes in St. Mary's County in 1778 [Ref: J-1146, K-66].
PAYNE, Vincent. Private, St. Mary's County Militia, 1777 [Ref: M-210]. Took the Oath of Allegiance before the Hon. Richard Barnes in St. Mary's County in 1778 [Ref: J-1146, K-66].
PAYNE, William. Private, St. Mary's County Militia, 1777 [Ref: M-212]. Took the Oath of Allegiance before the Hon. John Shanks in St. Mary's County in 1778 [Ref: J-1146, K-70].
PEACE, William. Private, Capt. Richard Lane's Co., Calvert County Militia, 1778 [Ref: J-1146, M-150]. Private, Capt. James Grahame's Co., Calvert County Militia, 1778 [Ref: J-1146, M-148].
PEACOCK, Ignatius. Private, St. Mary's County Militia, 1777 [Ref: M-211]. Took the Oath of Allegiance before the Hon. Ignatius Fenwick, Jr. in St. Mary's County in 1778 [Ref: J-1146, K-68].
PEACOCK, Paul. Took the Oath of Allegiance before the Hon. Henry Reeder in St. Mary's County in 1778 [Ref: J-1146, K-64].
PEACOCK, Samuel. Private, Capt. Henry Skinner's Foot Co. of Hunting Hundred, Calvert County, 1777 [Ref: T-1814, O-125].
PEACOCK, Susan. See "Benedict Moore," q.v.
PEACOCK, William. Private, Capt. James Patterson's Co., Calvert County Militia, Aug. 10, 1777 [Ref: M-146]. Private, Capt. Thomas Cleland's Co., Calvert County Militia, 1778 [Ref: J-1146, M-147]. Took the Oath of Allegiance in Calvert County in 1778 [Ref: L-38].
PEAKE, Augustin. Private, St. Mary's County Militia, 1777 [Ref: M-210]. Took the Oath of Allegiance before the Hon. Richard Barnes in St. Mary's County in 1778 [Ref: J-1146, K-66].
PEAKE, Baptist. Took the Oath of Allegiance before the Hon. Robert Watts in St. Mary's County in 1778 [Ref: J-1146, K-62]. The Register of St. Inigoes Catholic Church states that "John Baptist Peek" and Grace Craghill were married Feb. 16, 1768 [Ref: SC-33].
PEAKE, Ignatius. Private, St. Mary's County Militia, 1777 [Ref: M-214]. Took the Oath of Allegiance before the Hon. Henry Reeder in St. Mary's County in 1778 [Ref: J-1146, K-64]. One Ignatius Peake was buried at St. Johns in May, 1844 [Ref: R-440].
PEAKE, James. Private, St. Mary's County Militia, 1777 [Ref: M-214].

PEAKE, John. Took the Oath of Allegiance before the Hon. Richard Barnes in St. Mary's County in 1778 [Ref: J-1146, K-66]. The Register of St. Francis Xavier Catholic Church states that "John Peak and Susan Yets" were married Dec. 11, 1769 [Ref: SC-33].
PEAKE, Kenelm. Private, St. Mary's County Militia, 1777 [Ref: M-212, which listed the name as "Kenelin Peak"].
PEAKE, Nathan. Private, 1st Maryland Line, "certified by Ensign B. Burgess that his time of service expired 17 Nov 82" [Ref: D-149].
PEAKE, Peter. Private, St. Mary's County Militia, 1777 [Ref: M-214, which listed the name as "Petr. Peak"]. Took the Oath of Allegiance before the Hon. John Ireland in St. Mary's County in 1778 [Ref: J-1146, K-65].
PEAKE, Philip. Took the Oath of Allegiance before the Hon. Robert Watts in St. Mary's County in 1778 [Ref: J-1146, K-62].
PEAKE, Robert. Took the Oath of Allegiance before the Hon. Richard Barnes in St. Mary's County in 1778 [Ref: J-1146, K-66].
PEAKE, Susannah. See "Bennett Shirley," q.v.
PEARCE, Richard. Private, Capt. Henry Skinner's Foot Co. of Hunting Hundred, Calvert County, 1777 [Ref: T-1814, O-125].
PEIGN, Mickal. Private, Capt. Frederick Skinner's Co., Calvert County Militia, 1778 [Ref: J-1146, M-150].
PENN, Marcus Hatton. Private, St. Mary's County Militia, 1777 [Ref: M-210].
PENN, Mark. Private, St. Mary's County Militia, 1777 [Ref: M-214].
PERKINS, Jacob. Private, Capt. Frederick Skinner's Co., Calvert County Militia, 1778 [Ref: J-1146, M-150].
PERKINSON, Thomas. Private, Maryland Line, 1781 [Ref: D-411].
PETERS, Robert. Private, Capt. Frederick Skinner's Co., Calvert County Militia, 1778 [Ref: J-1146, M-150]. Private, Capt. James Patterson's Co., Calvert County Militia, Aug. 10, 1777 [Ref: M-146]. Took the Oath of Allegiance in Calvert County in 1778 [Ref: L-38].
PHERSON (PHEARSON), Samuel. Took the Oath of Allegiance before the Hon. Jeremiah Jordan in St. Mary's County in 1778 [Ref: J-1146, K-67]. Private, St. Mary's County Militia, 1777 [Ref: M-213].
PHILIP, ---- [blank]. Second Lieutenant, 21st Bn., St. Mary's County Militia, Feb. 23, 1776 [Ref: M-111, A-181].
PHILLIPS, Henry. Private, St. Mary's County Militia, 1777 [Ref: M-213]. Took the Oath of Allegiance before the Hon. John Reeder in St. Mary's County in 1778 [Ref: J-1146, K-69]. Private, St. Mary's County, enlisted on May 16, 1778, for 3 years; discharged May 1, 1781 [Ref: D-329, S-164]. Henry Phillips married Elizabeth Walker on Feb. 23, 1784, St. Mary's County, by Rev. John Stephen, Rector of All Faith's Parish [Ref: I-536].
PHILLIPS, Jonathan. Took the Oath of Allegiance before the Hon. John Reeder in St. Mary's County in 1778 [Ref: J-1146, K-69].

PHILPOTT, Tayman. Private, Capt. Frederick Skinner's Co., Calvert County Militia, 1778 [Ref: J-1146, M-150]. Private, Capt. James Patterson's Co., Calvert County Militia, Aug. 10, 1777 [Ref: M-146, which listed the name as "Tayman Philpotts"]. Took the Oath of Allegiance in Calvert County in 1778 [Ref: L-38, which listed the name as "Taymon Philpot"]. Private, Capt. John Mackall's Co., Calvert County Militia, 15th Bn., June 12, 1778 [Ref: M-146].

PHILPOTT, Thomas. Private, Continental Army, 1781 [Ref: D-411].

PIBUS (PYBUS), James. Took the Oath of Allegiance in Calvert County in 1778 [Ref: L-38]. Private, Capt. Richard Lane's Co., Calvert County Militia, 1778 [Ref: J-1146, M-150, which listed the name as "James Pybus"].

PIERCE, Sapphira. See "Thomas Chilton," q.v.

PIERCEALL, Richard (1744-c1841). Private, St. Mary's County, Maryland Line. "Richard Pearcall, farmer" moved from Leonardtown to Washington County, Kentucky, in 1795 [Ref: X-87, which mistakenly listed it as Webb County, Kentucky]. "Richard Pierceall" applied for and received pension S1245 on June 10, 1833, in Green County, Kentucky, stating he was born March 25, 1744 in St. Mary's County, enlisted on Dec. 27, 1776 at Leonardtown in St. Mary's County and served in Capt. John Allen Thomas' 5th Independent Co.. Zachariah Yates stated his brother served with Richard Pierceall and he was acquainted with him for 35 or 40 years. He was living with his son-in-law James Newcomb in 1840 [Ref: MK-117, W-43, Y-522, P-2698, SM-6, SM-7, SM-8, which latter source gives a complete abstract of his pension application].

PIERCY, George. Took the Oath of Allegiance in St. Mary's County on March 31, 1778. Served on the galley *Conqueror* in May, 1778 [Ref: S-164].

PIERCY, Richard. Took the Oath of Allegiance before the Hon. Jeremiah Jordan in St. Mary's County in 1778 [Ref: J-1146, K-67, which listed the name as "Richard Pearcy"].

PIERCY, William. Sailor from St. Mary's County who served as a yeoman on the State ship *Defence* in 1776 [Ref: S-25, D-606].

PIKE (PYKE), Ann. See "Ignatius Goddard (Goddart)," q.v.

PIKE, Archibald. Private, St. Mary's County Militia, 1777 [Ref: M-212]. Took the Oath of Allegiance in St. Mary's County in 1780 [Ref: Q-118].

PIKE, Benedict and Bibiana. See "Henry Pike," q.v.

PIKE, Henry. Private, St. Mary's County Militia, 1777 [Ref: M-214]. Took the Oath of Allegiance before the Hon. Henry Reeder in St. Mary's County in 1778 [Ref: J-1146, K-64]. One Henry Pike died by Nov., 1800, and it appears that his widow was Bibiana Pike who was appointed guardian of her four children at that time, namely, Benedict, Louisa, Ignatius, and Henry Pike [Ref: SO-308, SO-309].

PIKE, John. Marine on the State ship *Defence* from Jan. 21, 1777 to Dec. 31, 1777 [Ref: D-658]. There was also a John Pike who was a fifer, 4th

Maryland Line, Jan. 27, 1778, and private, May 12, 1780, who reportedly "deserted" in July, 1780 [Ref: D-153].
PIKE, Ignatius and Louisa. See "John Pike," q.v.
PIKE, Mary. See "Bernard Newton," q.v.
PIKE, Thomas. Private, 3rd Maryland Line, 1777-1778 [Ref: D-152].
PIKE, William. Private, 3rd Maryland Line, enlisted June 5, 1778 and reported missing at the Battle of Camden in South Carolina on Aug. 16, 1780 [Ref: D-152]. He returned to service as a private (substitute), from St. Mary's County on Aug. 2, 1781, and was discharged on Dec. 3, 1781 [Ref: D-384, D-411, S-109, H-11].
PILES, Leonard. Private, Capt. James Grahame's Co., Calvert County Militia, 1778 [Ref: J-1146, M-149]. Took the Oath of Allegiance in Calvert County in 1778 [Ref: L-38].
PILKINTON (PINKERTON, PILKETON), Michael. Private, 5th Maryland Line, enlisted on June 3, 1778, and was still in service on Jan. 21, 1780; probably from St. Mary's County [Ref: D-237].
PILKINTON (PINKERTON, PILKETON), Richard. The Register of St. Francis Xavier Catholic Church states that "Richard Pilketon" and Elizabeth Siford were married July 18, 1772, and "Richard Pilketon and Ann Hutchings, both widowed" were married Feb. 28, 1775 [Ref: SC-34, SC-35]. "Richard Pinkerton" took the Oath of Allegiance before the Hon. Ignatius Fenwick, Jr. in St. Mary's County in 1778 [Ref: J-1146, K-68].
PINKSTON, Polly and Turner. See "John Wood," q.v.
PITCHER, John. Took the Oath of Allegiance in Calvert County in 1778 [Ref: L-38].
PITCHER, Richard. Private, Capt. Henry Skinner's Foot Co. of Hunting Hundred, Calvert County, 1777 [Ref: T-1814, O-125].
PITCHER, Samuel. Took the Oath of Allegiance in Calvert County in 1778 [Ref: L-38].
PITHINGTON, Richard. Private, St. Mary's County Militia, 1777 [Ref: M-211].
PLATER, Ann and Elizabeth. See "George Plater," q.v.
PLATER, George (Nov. 8, 1735 - Feb. 10, 1792). Son of George Plater and Rebecca Addison, of "Sotterly" in St. Mary's County. He married twice: (1) Hannah Lee, daughter of Richard Lee, of Charles County, in 1762; and (2) Elizabeth Rousby, daughter of John Rousby, married in 1764, died in July, 1802. George Plater's children were: George B. (died 1802), John Rousby (became a judge and died in 1832), Thomas, William, Ann, and Rebecca (married Uriah Forrest). George served in a number of official capacities, including: Colonel, by 1764; Naval Officer at Patuxent, 1767-1777; Justice, Court of Oyer, Terminer, and Gaol Delivery, 1771-1772; Provincial Council, 1771-1774; Delegate from St. Mary's County to the Maryland Convention in 1776; Collector of Gold and Silver, 1776; Member of the Maryland Council of Safety, 1776-1777; Member of the Maryland Senate, 1777-1781; Delegate to the Continen-

tal Congress, 1777-1780; Presidential Elector in 1789; President of the Maryland Senate at various times between 1781 and 1790; Member of the Constitution Ratification Committee, 1788; and, Governor of Maryland, 1791-1792 [Ref: N-76, N-78, N-80, N-86, N-87, N-650, N-651, N-652, SO-174]. He died in Annapolis and his remains were brought to "Sotterly" and interred in the family vault located in the rose garden [Ref: R-442, S-129]. See "Uriah Forrest," q.v.

PLATER, John Rousby. See "George Plater," q.v.

PLATER, Rebecca. See "Uriah Forrest" and "George Plater," q.v.

PLATER, Thomas and William. See "George Plater," q.v.

PLATFORD, David. Private, Capt. Richard Parran's Co., Calvert County Militia, 1778 [Ref: J-1146, M-149]. Took the Oath of Allegiance in Calvert County in 1778 [Ref: L-38]. David Platford and Sarah Cotton were married on April 23, 1778, by Rev. Francis Lauder, of Christ Church Parish [Ref: K-34].

PLOWDEN, Ann H., Anna C., and Charles. See "Edmund Plowden," q.v.

PLOWDEN, Edmund (1751 - April 20, 1804). Son of Edmund Plowden and Henrietta Slye, of St. Mary's County. He married Jane or Janette Hammersly (1759-1804) in 1779 and they had these children: George (1780-1782), Edmund (1796-1814, captain), William Hammersly (1790-1832), Charles, Elizabeth, Mary, Jane, Margaret Brent, Ann Harriet (1796-1798), and Anna Cecelia. He was a Captain, Upper Bn., St. Mary's County, 1776-1777; Member of the House of Delegates, 1777-1784, 1792, and 1797; Maryland Senator, 1786, 1791, 1796, and 1801; Court Justice, 1787-1796; Judge of the Orphans Court, 1791-1804; and, Presidential Elector, 1801 [Ref: M-111, C-346, Y-538, N-78, N-84, N-86, N-652, N-653, R-442, R-443, S-143, and Maryland Society, Sons of the American Revolution, Approved Membership Applications Nos. 2324, 2335, 2342]. Took the Oath of Allegiance before the Hon. Jeremiah Jordan in St. Mary's County in 1778 [Ref: J-1146, K-67]. Loaned money for the war effort in 1781 [Ref: X-78, H-188, H-479]. He was appointed guardian of his children Edmund, Elizabeth, Mary, and Jane in April, 1789 [Ref: SO-133]. "There can be little doubt that Edmond [sic] Plowden lies buried in the old portion of Sacred Heart Church Cemetery near his estate "Bushwood Manor." The stone, if there was one, has disappeared." [Ref: S-129]. It appears that there was also an Edmund Plowden who was a private in the St. Mary's County Militia in 1777 [Ref: M-210].

PLOWDEN, Eleanor. See "Henry Neale," q.v.

PLOWDEN, Elizabeth. See "Edmund Plowden," q.v.

PLOWDEN, Francis. Private, St. Mary's County Militia, 1777 [Ref: M-211]. "Francis G. Plowden" took the Oath of Allegiance before the Hon. Ignatius Fenwick, Jr. in St. Mary's County in 1778 [Ref: J-1146, K-68]. He loaned money to the State in 1783 [Ref: S-164]. Francs Plowden supplied provisions (wheat, mutton, or bacon) to the Army in 1780 [Ref: S-77].

PLOWDEN, George. See "Edmund Plowden," q.v.

PLOWDEN, Henrietta (died 1796). Daughter of Gerard Slye, widow of Edmund Plowden, and mother of "Edmund Plowden," q.v. She loaned money in St. Mary's County for the war effort in 1781 [Ref: X-78, H-414, R-443, SM-187].

PLOWDEN, Jane, Margaret Brent, Mary, and William. See "Edmund Plowden," q.v.

PLUMMER, Eleanor. See "Joseph Booker," q.v.

PLUMMER, James. Took the Oath of Allegiance before the Hon. John Reeder in St. Mary's County in 1778 [Ref: J-1146, K-69].

POOLE, James Jr. Took the Oath of Allegiance in Calvert County in 1778 [Ref: L-38]. Private, Capt. Richard Parran's Co., Calvert County Militia, 1778 [Ref: J-1146, M-149].

POOLE, Peter. Took the Oath of Allegiance in Calvert County in 1778 [Ref: L-38].

POOLE, Richard. Private, Capt. Richard Parran's Co., Calvert County Militia, 1778 [Ref: J-1146, M-149].

POOLE, Thomas. Took the Oath of Allegiance in Calvert County in 1778 [Ref: L-38].

POSTON, Judith. See "Hatch Dent," q.v.

POSTWINE, Thomas. Private, St. Mary's County Militia, 1777 [Ref: M-212, which listed the name as "Thomas Pojtwine"].

POTTS, Rebecca. See "Benjamin Mackall IV," q.v.

POWELL, Elizabeth. See "John Ivey," q.v.

POWELL, William. Private, Capt. Richard Parran's Co., Calvert County Militia, 1778 [Ref: J-1146, M-149]. William Powell and Alice Evans were married on Feb. 12, 1778, by Rev. Francis Lauder, of Christ Church Parish [Ref: K-34].

POWER, Clement. Ensign, Upper Bn., St. Mary's County. Aug. 26, 1777. Second Lieutenant, Nov. 18, 1779 [Ref: M-112, C-346, F-18, SM-114]. One Clement Power died intestate by Dec., 1788, with Sarah Power as his administratrix [Ref: SO-129].

POWER, Edward. Took the Oath of Allegiance in St. Mary's County in 1780 [Ref: Q-118].

POWER, James (1755, Prince William County, Virginia - Sep. 4, 1851, Allegheny County, Pennsylvania). Applied for pension R8406 on May 16, 1848, aged between 92 and 93 years, at Indiana Township in Allegheny County, Pennsylvania, stating he had lived there for 50 years. He was born in Virginia and enlisted about June 7, 1776, while a resident of Old Town at the forks of the Potomac River in Maryland [St. Mary's County]. He stated he was present at the surrender of Fort Washington on York Island and was discharged on Dec. 7, 1776 at Philadelphia. Wife not named, but these sons were: Samuel Power lived in Derry Township, Westmoreland County, Pennsylvania in 1852; Roliter Power lived in Fairview, Houston P. O., Allegheny County, Pennsylvania in 1853, aged 59, and in Clarion County, Pennsylvania in 1862; and, James B. Power lived in Indiana Township, Allegheny County in 1857, aged 50. James Power's pension application was rejected due to failure to prove 6 months service, and he is not listed in *Archives of Maryland, Volume 18* [Ref: P-2751, and *National Genealogical Society Quarterly*, Volume 26, No. 2 (1938), pp. 44-45].

POWER (POWERS), Jesse. Applied for and received pension S35030 on May 12, 1818, aged about 57, in St. Mary's County, stating he had enlisted in Charles County. In 1820 he had a wife (aged 35) and 3 daughters aged 21, 15, and 10, but no names were given [Ref: P-2751]. Pension rolls of 1835 listed his age as then 73 [Ref: U-40].

POWER, Roliter and Samuel. See "James Power," q.v.

POWER, Sarah. See "Clement Power," q.v.

PRATT, John. Private in Capt. John Allen Thomas' Co., 5th Maryland Independent Co., who was invalided (disabled) and discharged on Nov. 22, 1776 [Ref: S-165]. Private, St. Mary's County Militia, 1777 [Ref: M-211].

PRATT, William. Private, St. Mary's County, drafted July 27, 1781, Maryland Line; discharged in Dec., 1781 [Ref: D-384, D-411].

PRATT, Zephaniah. Private, St. Mary's County Militia, 1777 [Ref: M-211].

PRICE, Ann. See "Archibald Price," q.v.

PRICE, Archibald. Private, St. Mary's County Militia, 1777 [Ref: M-215]. One Archibald Price died testate by June, 1794, leaving wife Ann (his executrix) and minor son Archibald [Ref: SO-213, SO-271].

PRICE, Bennett. Took the Oath of Allegiance before the Hon. Bennett Biscoe in St. Mary's County in 1778 [Ref: J-1146, K-63]. "Bent. Price" was a private in the St. Mary's County Militia in 1777 [Ref: M-215]. Supplied provisions (wheat, mutton, or bacon) to the Army in Oct., 1780 [Ref: D-165, D-77, which listed the name as "Bennett Aprice (Bennett A. Price?)"].

PRICE, Brian. Took the Oath of Allegiance in Calvert County in 1778 [Ref: L-38].

PRICE, James. (1) Private, St. Mary's County Militia, 1777 [Ref: M-215]. Took the Oath of Allegiance in St. Mary's County in 1780 [Ref: Q-118]. (2) Private, Capt. Henry Skinner's Foot Co. of Hunting Hundred, Calvert County, 1777 [Ref: T-1814, O-125].

PRICE, John. Took the Oath of Allegiance in St. Mary's County in 1780 [Ref: Q-118]. One John Price died intestate by Oct., 1791 [Ref: SO-172].

PRICE, John Jr. Private, Capt. Uriah Forrest's Co., Flying Camp, St. Mary's County, July 28, 1776 [Ref: D-30, SM-114].

PRICE, Joseph. Private, St. Mary's County Militia, 1777 [Ref: M-215]. Took the Oath of Allegiance in St. Mary's County in 1780 [Ref: Q-118]. "Josseph Price, farmer" move from St. Inigoes to Charles County, Maryland, in 1797 [Ref: X-87].

PRICE, Thomas (March, 1762 - Jan. 10, 1847). Born in St. Mary's County and lived in Johnston County, North Carolina at the time of his enlistment in the Revolutionary War. He applied for a pension in 1832 in Hawkins County, Tennessee, and died there in 1847. His widow, Pernina (nee Parrish), whom he married in 1815, applied for and received pension W10227 in 1855 in Davidson County, Tennessee, aged 65 [Ref: MC-130, P-2771].

PRICE, William. (1) Private, Calvert County, enlisted by Capt. John Brooke on July 25, 1776 [Ref: D-33]. Took the Oath of Allegiance in Calvert County in 1778 [Ref: L-38]. (2) Took the Oath of Allegiance in St. Mary's County in 1780 [Ref: Q-118].

PRIOR, Benjamin. Private, Count Pulaski's Legion, enlisted in July, 1779, while serving with the Maryland Line in Charleston, South Carolina [Ref: D-593, SM-114, S-165]. Corporal, 1783 [Ref: D-551].

PROCTOR, Charles, James, and Walter. See "Joseph Proctor," q.v.

PROCTOR, Joseph. Born in 1762 and lived in St. Mary's County at the time of his enlistment in the Revolutionary War. He applied for a pension (R8497) in 1835 in Granville County, North Carolina and stated he had two brothers (not named) who were killed in the war. His application was rejected for lack of proof. However, he did in fact serve in the 1st Maryland Line until discharged on Nov. 29, 1783, with James Proctor, perhaps another brother [Ref: MC-130, P-2777, D-510, D-551]. It should also be noted that Charles Proctor died on Nov. 3, 1778 while serving in the 1st Maryland Line, as did Walter Proctor who died on March 10, 1779. It appears that these were the unnamed brothers of Joseph Proctor that he had mentioned in his pension application [Ref: D-150].

PROCTOR, William. Supplied provisions (wheat, mutton, or bacon) to the Army in St. Mary's County in Dec., 1780 [Ref: S-165].

PRONSO, Jacob. Private, Maryland Line, 1781 [Ref: D-411].

PROUT, Arthur. Private, Capt. Thomas Cleland's Co., Calvert County Militia, 1778 [Ref: J-1146, M-147].

PROUT, Daniel. Private, Capt. Frederick Skinner's Co., Calvert County Militia, 1778 [Ref: J-1146, M-150]. Private, Capt. John Mackall's Co., Calvert County Militia, 15th Bn., June 12, 1778 [Ref: M-146]. Took the Oath of Allegiance in Calvert County in 1778 [Ref: L-38].

PROUT, John. Private, Calvert County, enlisted by Lt. Frederick Skinner on Aug. 23, 1776 [Ref: D-33].

PURDLE (PURTLE), Robert. Private, St. Mary's County, enlisted May 25, 1778, for 9 months, and served in the 2nd Maryland Line [Ref: SM-114, D-330, which listed the name as "Robert Turtle"]. Pension application W4397 of Catharine Wistel or Whistler, former widow of Robert Purtle, was filed on Aug. 1, 1849, aged 81, at Baltimore, stating that her maiden name was Stitler and she married Robert Purtle in Baltimore in Aug. 4, 1796, and he died in 1797. She married second to

William Wistel who later died (no date given). However, the affidavit of Caroline Stitler, aged 75, of Baltimore, stated that Robert Purtle died on March 12, 1802 in St. Mary's County; no relationship was given. The widow Catherine also applied for bounty land warrant #38340-160-55 on Jan. 8, 1856, aged 92, at Baltimore [Ref: P-2788]. Robert Purdle married Catherine Stitler on Aug. 4, 1796 [Ref: Z-121].

PUSKIM, James. Private, Capt. James Patterson's Co., Calvert County Militia, Aug. 10, 1777 [Ref: M-146].

PUSY, John. Took the Oath of Allegiance before the Hon. Bennett Biscoe in St. Mary's County in 1778 [Ref: J-1146, K-63].

QUAREY, Elisha. Private, Calvert County, enlisted by Ensign James Somervill on July 26, 1776 [Ref: D-34].

RAILEY (RALEY, RYLEY), John. See "Seneca Nelson," q.v.

RALEY (RALEIGH), Basil. Private, St. Mary's County Militia, 1777 [Ref: M-211, which listed the name as "Basil Raily"]. Took the Oath of Allegiance before the Hon. Ignatius Fenwick, Jr. in St. Mary's County in 1778 [Ref: J-1146, K-68]. The Register of St. Andrew's Episcopal Church states that "Basil Railey" and Dorothy Hutchins were married (by license) Dec. 28, 1780 [Ref: MB-383]. "Basil Raleigh, Henry Raleigh and John Raleigh were settlers from Maryland who resided at Rolling Fork in Nelson County, Kentucky, prior to 1800." [Ref: MK-119].

RALEY, Bennett. Took the Oath of Allegiance before the Hon. Robert Watts in St. Mary's County in 1778 [Ref: J-1146, K-62]. Private, St. Mary's County Militia, 1777 [Ref: M-212].

RALEY, Henrietta. See "Zachariah Forrest," q.v.

RALEY (RAILEY), Henry Jr. Private, St. Mary's County Militia, 1777 [Ref: M-211]. "Henry Railey, farmer" moved to Washington County, Kentucky, in 1795 [Ref: X-87]. See "Basil Raley," q.v.

RALEY, Henry Silvester. Took the Oath of Allegiance before the Hon. Ignatius Fenwick, Jr. in St. Mary's County in 1778 [Ref: J-1146, K-68].

RALEY (RAILEY), John. Two men were listed by this name as privates, St. Mary's County Militia, 1777 [Ref: M-211, which listed the name as "John Raily"]. Private, St. Mary's County Militia, 1777 [Ref: M-214, which listed the name as "Jno. Railey"]. "John Raley, Sr." took the Oath of Allegiance before the Hon. Ignatius Fenwick, Jr. in St. Mary's County in 1778 [Ref: J-1146, K-68]. One John Raily died intestate by Feb., 1779 [Ref: SO-17]. See "Basil Raley" and "Seneca Nelson," q.v.

RALEY, John Jr. "Jno. Raily (of Jno.)" was a private in St. Mary's County Militia, 1777 [Ref: M-211]. "John Raley, Jr." took the Oath of Allegiance before the Hon. Ignatius Fenwick, Jr. in St. Mary's County in 1778 [Ref: J-1146, K-68].

RALEY, John (of Henry). Private, St. Mary's County Militia, 1777 [Ref: M-212, which listed the name as "John Raily (of Henry)"]. Took the Oath of Allegiance before the Hon. Ignatius Fenwick, Jr. in St. Mary's County in 1778 [Ref: J-1146, K-68].

RALEY, John Baptist. Private, St. Mary's County, enlisted April 24, 1778, for 3 years [Ref: D-329, which mistakenly listed the name as "John Bapt. Baley"]. Took the Oath of Allegiance before the Hon. Richard Barnes in St. Mary's County in 1778 [Ref: J-1146, K-66].

RALEY, John Michael. Private, St. Mary's County Militia, 1777 [Ref: M-211].

RALEY, John W. Took the Oath of Allegiance before the Hon. Ignatius Fenwick, Jr. in St. Mary's County in 1778 [Ref: J-1146, K-68].

RALPH, Catherine and George. See "John DeButts," q.v.

RALPH, John. Private, Capt. Thomas Truman Greenfield's Co., Calvert County Militia, 1778 [Ref: J-1146, M-150]. Took the Oath of Allegiance in Calvert County in 1778 [Ref: L-38].

RAMSDIN, Joseph. Private, St. Mary's County Militia, 1777 [Ref: M-213].

RAMSEY (RAMSAY), Charles. Private, 7th Maryland Line, enlisted March 17, 1777, and discharged March 17, 1780 [Ref: D-242]. The Register of St. Andrew's Episcopal Church states that Charles Ramsay and Anne Taylor were married (by license) Aug. 1, 1784 [Ref: MB-385].

RAMSEY (RAMSAY), John. Private, Capt. Henry Skinner's Foot Co. of Hunting Hundred, Calvert County, 1777 [Ref: T-1814, O-125]. Took the Oath of Allegiance in Calvert County in 1778 [Ref: L-38]. John Ramsay and Susanna Wood were married on Feb. 1, 1780, by Rev. Francis Lauder, of Christ Church Parish [Ref: K-35].

RAMSEY (RAMSAY), John Jr. Private, Calvert County, enlisted by Lt. Frederick Skinner on Aug. 23, 1776 [Ref: D-33]. Private, Capt. Thomas Truman Greenfield's Co., Calvert County Militia, 1778 [Ref: J-1146, M-150].

RAMSEY (RAMSAY), William. Private, Capt. Edward Wood's Co., Calvert County Militia, 1778 [Ref: J-1146, M-147]. This name appeared twice in the list of those who took the Oath of Allegiance in Calvert County in 1778 [Ref: L-38]. William Ramsay and Rebecca Jefferson were married on Jan. 7, 1779, and William Ramsay and Rebecca Bond were married on Oct. 31, 1780, both marriages by Rev. Francis Lauder, of Christ Church Parish [Ref: K-34, K-35].

RAMSEY, Winmar. Private, Capt. Edward Wood's Co., Calvert County Militia, 1778 [Ref: J-1146, M-147].

RANDALL, Edward. Private, Capt. Thomas Cleland's Co., Calvert County Militia, 1778 [Ref: J-1146, M-147, which listed the name as "Edward Randle"]. Took the Oath of Allegiance in Calvert County in 1778 [Ref: L-38].

RANDALL, John. Took the Oath of Allegiance in Calvert County in 1778 [Ref: L-38].

RAPIER, Charles and James. See "Richard James Rapier," q.v.

RAPIER, Richard. Private, St. Mary's County Militia, 1777 [Ref: M-212].

RAPIER, Richard James (c1740-c1815). Captain, Upper Bn., St. Mary's County Militia, Nov. 18, 1779 [Ref: M-114, F-18, which latter source listed his name as "Robert James Rapier"]. Took the Oath of Allegiance before the Hon. John Ireland in St. Mary's County in 1778 [Ref: J-1146, K-65]. Richard James Rapier married Margaret Thompson [Ref: Y-557]. "Capt. James Rapier and his sons Charles and William left Maryland and settled near Bardstown, Kentucky between 1776 and 1786 in the Poplar Neck Community." [Ref: MK-120].

RAPIER, William. Second Lieutenant, Upper Bn., St. Mary's County Militia, Aug. 26, 1777, and First Lieutenant, Nov. 18, 1779 [Ref: M-114, M-212, C-346, F-18]. Took the Oath of Allegiance before the Hon. Henry Reeder in St. Mary's County in 1778 [Ref: J-1146, K-64].

RAWLINGS, Daniel. (1) First Lieutenant, Capt. Richard Parran's Co., Calvert County Militia, 1778 [Ref: J-1146, M-149]. (2) Private, Capt. Richard Parran's Co., Calvert County Militia, 1778 [Ref: J-1146, M-149]. Took the Oath of Allegiance in Calvert County in 1778 [Ref: L-38].

RAWLINGS, Elizabeth. See "John Sedwick," q.v.

RAWLINGS, John. Private, St. Mary's County Militia, 1777 [Ref: M-210, which listed the name as "John Rawlins"]. Private, Capt. Richard Parran's Co., Calvert County Militia, 1778 [Ref: J-1146, M-149]. Took the Oath of Allegiance in Calvert County in 1778 [Ref: L-38].

RAWLINGS (ROLLINS), Nathan. Private, St. Mary's County Militia, 1777 [Ref: M-213, which listed the name as "Nathan Rollins"].

RAWLINGS, Sarah. See "Richard King," q.v.

READ, Eleanor. See "Philip Read," q.v.

READ, John Hatton (Oct. 16, 1746 - 1781). Son of Philip Read and Ann ----, widow of William Read, of St. Mary's County. Lieutenant Colonel, 21st Bn., St. Mary's County Militia, on Jan. 12, 1776. "Colo. Jno. H. Read" served on the Committee of Observation in 1776, member of the House of Delegates, 1777-1780, and a Court Justice, 1773 and 1778-1780 [Ref: M-114, N-76, N-78, N-82, N-674, S-16, B-100]. "John H. Read" was elected to a General Committee in accordance with the resolves of the Continental Congress in 1775 [Ref: MR-127]. (2) Another John H. Read was a private in the St. Mary's County Militia in 1777 [Ref: M-211].

READ, John Baptist. Took the Oath of Allegiance before the Hon. John Ireland in St. Mary's County in 1778 [Ref: J-1146, K-65].

READ, Philip (1751 - c1793). Son of Philip Read and a brother of "John Hatton Read," q.v. Private, St. Mary's County Militia, 1777 [Ref: M-211]. Took the Oath of Allegiance before the Hon. Richard Barnes in St. Mary's County in 1778 [Ref: J-1146, K-66]. Supplied provisions (wheat, mutton, or bacon) to the Army in 1780 [Ref: S-77]. The Register of St. Andrew's Episcopal Church states that "Philip Read" and Eleanor Lawney were married (by license) Oct. 1, 1781 [Ref: MB-384]. The Register of St. Francis Xavier Catholic Church states that "Philip Reed" and Ann Smith were married July 16, 1776 [Ref: SC-35]. One Philip Read died intestate between Oct., 1792 and June, 1794, with Elenor Walbert Read named as the administratrix [Ref: SO-180, SO-212].

READ, William. See "John Hatton Read," q.v.
REDMAN, Alice. Volunteered as a nurse in St. Mary's County and served (no dates were given) in the hospital in Annapolis during the Revolutionary War [Ref: SM-187].
REDMAN, Benjamin. Private, St. Mary's County Militia, 1777 [Ref: M-214]. Took the Oath of Allegiance in St. Mary's County in 1780 [Ref: Q-118]. One Benjamin Redman was buried on Jan. 27, 1807 [Ref: R-446].
REDMAN, Dorcas and Elizabeth. See "Jonathan Redman," q.v.
REDMAN, Jonathan. Private, St. Mary's County Militia, 1777 [Ref: M-215]. One Jonathan Redman died intestate by Oct., 1790, with Priscilla Redman as his administratrix and leaving orphans William, Dorcas, and Elizabeth Redman [Ref: SO-159, SO-164, SO-166, SO-220].
REDMAN, Joshua. Private, St. Mary's County Militia, 1777 [Ref: M-214]. "Joshuary Redman" took the Oath of Allegiance before the Hon. Bennett Biscoe in St. Mary's County in 1778 [Ref: J-1146, K-63]. See "William Redman," q.v.
REDMAN, Malinda, Mary, and Susanna. See "William Redman," q.v.
REDMAN, Thomas. Private, 4th Maryland Line, 1778-1780 [Ref: D-159].
REDMAN, William. Private, St. Mary's County Militia, 1777 [Ref: M-213]. Took the Oath of Allegiance in St. Mary's County in 1780 [Ref: Q-118]. One William Redman died by Oct., 1796, with John Redman named as administrator and apparently leaving a widow Mary and children Susanna, Malinda, and Joshua [Ref: SO-251, SO-252].
REECE, John. Private, St. Mary's County Militia, 1777 [Ref: M-215]. Took the Oath of Allegiance before the Hon. Bennett Biscoe in St. Mary's County in 1778 [Ref: J-1146, K-63].
REED, Mary Cavey. See "Jesse Floyd," q.v.
REED, Philip. Second Lieutenant, St. Mary's County, Leonardtown Co., 21st Bn.; resigned Feb. 23, 1776 [Ref: S-165].
REEDER, Elizabeth. See "Dr. Henry Reeder," q.v.
REEDER, Henry (Doctor). Private, St. Mary's County Militia, 1777. [Ref: M-214, which listed the name as "Henry Reader"]. Justice who administered the Oath of Allegiance in St. Mary's County in 1778. Died circa 1787, a son of Thomas Reeder (1711-1773) and Susannah Graves(?) who died in 1771 [Ref: J-1146, K-64, N-675, R-447]. "Dr. Henry Reeder" was elected to a General Committee in St. Mary's County in accordance with the resolves of the Continental Congress in 1775, and served on the Committee of Correspondence [Ref: MR-127]. Doctor Henry Reeder died by Aug., 1790, at which time an Elizabeth Reeder, possibly his wife, was appointed guardian of his children, John Reeder and Robert Dugun Reeder, both under the age of 14 [Ref: SO-157, SO-192]. He is buried in a private cemetery at "Ellenborough" near Leonardtown in an unmarked grave beside his wife, Judith Townley Reeder [Ref: S-129].
REEDER, Hezekiah. Lieutenant, 3rd Maryland Line, from March 14, 1777 until Feb. 9, 1778, when he resigned [Ref: D-156].

REEDER, John. Private, St. Mary's County Militia, 1777 [Ref: M-214]. First Lieutenant, 21st Bn., St. Mary's County, April 16, 1778 [Ref: M-114, E-37, SM-114]. Took the Oath of Allegiance before the Hon. Vernon Hebb in St. Mary's County in 1778 [Ref: J-1146, K-67. Source S-165 lists him as "John Reeder, Jr.", not to be confused with Col. John Reeder, Jr.]. See "Henry Reeder," q.v.

REEDER, John Jr. (c1732 - 1780). Son of Thomas Reeder (1711-1773) and Susannah Graves(?) who died in 1771 in St. Mary's County. He married twice: (1) Dicandia Smith, daughter of Charles Somerset Smith; and (2) Catherine ----, who subsequently married Nathaniel Ewing in 1784. His only child Susannah married twice: (1) Dr. John Ireland, and (2) Dr. Gustavus Brown. John Reeder served in the Lower House, 1756-1758, 1773-1776, as Court Justice, 1764-1777, Justice of the Court of Oyer, Terminer, and Gaol Delivery, 1772, Justice of the Orphans Court, 1777-1778, and was a justice who administered the Oath of Allegiance in 1778. Also, on the Committee of Observation, 1775, as a Delegate to the Maryland Convention in 1775 and 1776, and Commissioner of Tax, 1777 [Ref: R-447, J-1146, K-69, N-70, N-72, N-675, I-535]. Lieutenant Colonel, 6th Bn., St. Mary's County Militia, Jan. 12, 1776 [Ref: M-114, which listed the name as "John Reider, Jr."]. "John Reeder, Jun." was elected to a General Committee in St. Mary's County in accordance with the resolves of the Continental Congress in 1775. "Mr. John Reeder, Jr." served on the Committee of Correspondence [Ref: MR-127].

REEDER, Judith Townley and Robert Dugun. See "Henry Reeder," q.v.

REEDER, Thomas and Susannah. See "John Reeder" and "Henry Reeder, Jr." and "Thomas Attaway Reeder," q.v.

REEDER, Thomas Attaway (1740 - Aug. 14, 1806). Son of Thomas Reeder (1711-1773) and Susannah Graves(?) who died in 1771 in St. Mary's County. Thomas Reeder married Catherine Vemere. He served as Captain, Upper Bn., St. Mary's County, from Aug. 26, 1777 through Nov. 18, 1779 [Ref: M-114, C-346, F-18, N-675, R-447]. Took the Oath of Allegiance before the Hon. John Reeder in St. Mary's County in 1778 [Ref: J-1146, K-69]. It appears Thomas Attaway Reeder was a private in the St. Mary's County Militia in 1777 and subsequently became a militia captain in that same year [Ref: M-212, S-143]. Yet, note this interesting quote: "While the State records omit him, the records of the Major William Thomas Chapter, DAR, disclosed that he entered the service [Nov. 18, 1779] in Smallwood's 1st Bn.." [Ref: SM-149, S-143]. "Thomas A. Reeder" was elected to a General Committee in St. Mary's County in accordance with the resolves of the Continental Congress in 1775 [Ref: MR-127]. "Thomas Attaway Reeder" was a Presidential Elector in the 4th Presidential Election in 1801 [Ref: S-143].

REEDER, William. Private, St. Mary's County Militia, 1777 [Ref: M-215]. Took the Oath of Allegiance before the Hon. Bennett Biscoe in St. Mary's County in 1778 [Ref: J-1146, K-63].

REEVES, Elizabeth and Thomas. See "William Thomas," q.v.
RESWICK, Elenor. See "Wilfred Reswick," q.v.
RESWICK (RISWICK), Joseph. Private, St. Mary's County Militia, 1777 [Ref: M-210, which listed the name as "Joseph Reshwick"]. Took the Oath of Allegiance before the Hon. Richard Barnes in St. Mary's County in 1778 [Ref: J-1146, K-66]. Private, St. Mary's County, enlisted May 30, 1778, for 9 months [Ref: D-330]. Private, 2nd Maryland Line, 1778-1779 [Ref: D-156, D-411, D-406, which listed the name as "Joseph Risswick" and "Joseph Beswick" and "Jos. Riswick"]. Private (substitute), July 28, 1781, Maryland Line; discharged in Dec., 1781 [Ref: D-384, S-165].
RESWICK (RISWICK), Thomas. Took the Oath of Allegiance before the Hon. Henry Reeder in St. Mary's County in 1778 [Ref: J-1146, K-64, which listed the name as "Thomas Ryswick"]. Private, St. Mary's County Militia, 1777 [Ref: M-210, which listed the name as "Thomas Reshwick"]. The Register of St. Francis Xavier Catholic Church states that "Thomas Riswick" and Mary Nottingham were married July 27, 1773 [Ref: SC-34].
RESWICK (RISWICK), Wilfred. Took the Oath of Allegiance before the Hon. Richard Barnes in St. Mary's County in 1778 [Ref: J-1146, K-66, which listed the name as "Wilfred Riswick"]. Ensign, St. Mary's County Militia, Aug. 26, 1777 [Ref: M-115, M-210, SM-114, C-346, which listed the name as "Wilford Reshwick" and "Wilfred Reswick"]. Wilfred Reswick died testate by Aug., 1789, with Elenor Reswick as his executrix [Ref: SO-141].
RESWICK (RISWICK), William. Supplied provisions (wheat, mutton, or bacon) to the Army in St. Mary's County in 1780 [Ref: S-77].
REYNOLDS, Ann. See "Edward Reynolds," q.v.
REYNOLDS, Edward (died by 1820). Son of Thomas Reynolds and Frances Holland, of Upper Clifts Hundred, Calvert County. Edward married twice: (1) Mary Mackall, daughter of James John Mackall; and, (2) Ann ----, married by 1780. His children were James John, William, Joseph W., Edward G., and a daughter (name not stated, but she married John Hamilton Chew). Second Lieutenant, Capt. Frisby Freeland's Co., Calvert County Militia, April 10, 1776 to April 16, 1778 [Ref: A-320, E-37, J-1146, M-115, M-148]. Took the Oath of Allegiance in 1778 [Ref: L-38]. Delegate to the Maryland Convention in 1775; Member of the House of Delegates, 1778, 1779, 1783; Member of the Committee of Observation in 1774; Coroner in 1775; and Commissioner of Tax, 1777 to 1782 [Ref: N-70, N-80, N-87, N-677].
REYNOLDS, Ignatius. Private, St. Mary's County Militia, 1777 [Ref: M-211].
REYNOLDS, James John. See "Edward Reynolds," q.v.
REYNOLDS, John. (1) Took the Oath of Allegiance before the Hon. Ignatius Fenwick, Jr. in St. Mary's County in 1778 [Ref: J-1146, K-68]. (2) Took the Oath of Allegiance before the Hon. Henry Reeder in St. Mary's County in 1778 [Ref: J-1146, K-64]. The Register of St. Francis

Xavier Catholic Church states one John Reynolds and Ann French married on Jan. 19, 1778 [Ref: SC-36].

REYNOLDS, Joseph W. See "Edward Reynolds," q.v.

REYNOLDS, Mary. See "John Mackall," q.v.

REYNOLDS, Thomas (died July, 1778). Son of Edward Reynolds. Married Frances Holland and was the father of "Edward Reynolds," q.v. Took the Oath of Allegiance in Calvert County in 1778 [Ref: L-38, N-677]. Also see "John Mackall," q.v.

REYNOLDS, William. See "Edward Reynolds," q.v.

RHODES, Abraham Jr. Took the Oath of Allegiance in Calvert County in 1778 [Ref: L-38].

RHODES, Abraham Sr. Took the Oath of Allegiance in Calvert County in 1778 [Ref: L-38]. Private, Capt. Frisby Freeland's Co., Calvert County Militia, 1778 [Ref: J-1146, M-148].

RHODES, Abram. Took the Oath of Allegiance before the Hon. Robert Watts in St. Mary's County in 1778 [Ref: J-1146, K-62]. The Register of St. Inigoes Catholic Church states that Abram Rhodes and Mary Dant were married June 21, 1784 [Ref: SC-36, which noted "either they or their descendants eventually settled at The Barrens in Perry County, Missouri."]. Abram Rhodes was among the early Catholic settlers in Nelson County, Kentucky circa 1785 [Ref: MK-122].

RHODES, Albert. Property destroyed by the British in St. Mary's County in 1781 [Ref: S-166].

RHODES, Barnaby. Took the Oath of Allegiance before the Hon. Robert Watts in St. Mary's County in 1778 [Ref: J-1146, K-62]. The Register of St. Inigoes Catholic Church states that "Barny Rhodes" and Melinda Smith were married July 6, 1784 [Ref: SC-36].

RHODES, Jeremiah. Private, St. Mary's County Militia, 1777 [Ref: M-215]. Private, St. Mary's County, enlisted on May 31, 1778, for 9 months, 3rd Maryland Line; re-enlisted on April 17, 1779, and was discharged on Feb. 17, 1782 [Ref: S-166, D-330, which latter source listed the name as "Jeremiah Rhoades"].

RHODES, John. Took the Oath of Allegiance before the Hon. Robert Watts in St. Mary's County in 1778 [Ref: J-1146, K-62]. Private, 3rd Maryland Line, enlisted on April 17, 1779, and discharged on Feb. 17, 1782 [Ref: S-166].

RHODES, Susanna. See "Thomas Talbott," q.v.

RHODES, Thomas. Took the Oath of Allegiance in Calvert County in 1778 [Ref: L-38].

RIBBON, Robert. Private, St. Mary's County Militia, 1777 [Ref: M-209]. Took the Oath of Allegiance before the Hon. Henry Tubman in St. Mary's County in 1778 [Ref: J-1146, K-70].

RICE, Thomas. Private, Calvert County, enlisted by Lt. Frederick Skinner on Aug. 23, 1776 [Ref: D-33].

RICH, Henry. Private, St. Mary's County Militia, 1777 [Ref: M-214].

RICHARDSON, Ann, Elenor, and Elizabeth. See "William Richardson," q.v.

RICHARDSON, Isaac. Private, St. Mary's County Militia, 1777 [Ref: M-215].

RICHARDSON, James (1752 - Feb. 27, 1821). Private, St. Mary's County Militia, 1777 [Ref: M-215, R-448]. Paid for making salt in 1782 [Ref: S-166].

RICHARDSON, Jane. See "William Richardson," q.v.

RICHARDSON, Thomas. Private, St. Mary's County Militia, 1777 [Ref: M-215]. Two men with this name took the Oath of Allegiance in 1778: one before the Hon. Bennett Biscoe and one before the Hon. Robert Armstrong in St. Mary's County in 1778 [Ref: J-1146, K-62, K-63]. One Thomas Richardson was buried on Dec. 27, 1799 [Ref: R-448].

RICHARDSON, Thomas Sr. Took the Oath of Allegiance before the Hon. Bennett Biscoe in St. Mary's County in 1778 [Ref: J-1146, K-63].

RICHARDSON, William. Private, St. Mary's County Militia, 1777 [Ref: M-215]. Took the Oath of Allegiance before the Hon. Bennett Biscoe in St. Mary's County in 1778 [Ref: J-1146, K-63]. One William Richardson died by April, 1783, with wife Elenor as administratrix and orphans Ann, Jane, and Elizabeth [Ref: SO-35, SO-59, SO-63].

RICHIE (RITCHIE), James. Took the Oath of Allegiance before the Hon. Bennett Biscoe in St. Mary's County in 1778 [Ref: J-1146, K-63, which listed the name as "James Ritchie"]. Property destroyed by the British in 1781 [Ref: S-166].

RICHIE (RITCHIE), Peter. Private, St. Mary's County Militia, 1777 [Ref: M-213]. Private, St. Mary's County, enlisted May 29, 1778, for 9 months, Continental Army [Ref: D-329, SM-114, S-166].

RICHMOND, John. Took the Oath of Allegiance in Calvert County in 1778 [Ref: L-38].

RIDDING, William. Private, St. Mary's County, 3rd Maryland Line, Capt. Armstrong's Co., 1778-1780 [Ref: D-298].

RIDERWOOD, Charles. Private, St. Mary's County Militia, 1777 [Ref: M-215, which listed the name as "Charles Wriderwood"].

RIDGELY, Thomas. Private, St. Mary's County Militia, 1777 [Ref: M-215].

RIGBY, Ann. See "Thomas Sedwick," q.v.

RIGBY, Henry. Private, Maryland Line. In June, 1779 the Orphans of St. Mary's County "bound Joseph Rigby, son of Henry Rigby who is now in the service of the United States, to George Haden to learn to be a shoemaker" [Ref: SO-22; however, Henry Rigby is not on the lists contained in the *Archives of Maryland, Volume 18*].

RIGBY, James. Took the Oath of Allegiance in Calvert County in 1778 [Ref: L-38].

RIGBY, John. Private, Capt. Benjamin Bond's Co., Calvert County Militia, 1778 [Ref: J-1146, M-149]. Took the Oath of Allegiance in Calvert County in 1778 [Ref: L-38].

RIGBY, Joseph. See "Henry Rigby," q.v.
RILELY, Henry. Took the Oath of Allegiance before the Hon. Henry Reeder in St. Mary's County in 1778 [Ref: J-1146, K-64].
RILEY, Bennett. Private, St. Mary's County Militia, 1777 [Ref: M-214]. Took the Oath of Allegiance before the Hon. Richard Barnes in St. Mary's County in 1778 [Ref: J-1146, K-66]. The Register of St. Inigoes Catholic Church states that "Bennet Reily" and Susanna Drury were married Aug. 16, 1784 [Ref: SC-36].
RINEY, John Jr. Private, St. Mary's County Militia, 1777 [Ref: M-213].
RINEY, Jonathan. Private, St. Mary's County, enlisted May 31, 1778, for 9 months, 2nd Maryland Line; discharged on April 14, 1779 [Ref: D-330, S-166].
RINEY, Thomas (of Jno.). Private, St. Mary's County Militia, 1777 [Ref: M-210].
RIORK, Joseph. Private, St. Mary's County Militia, 1777 [Ref: M-215].
ROACH, Bartholomew. Private, 5th Maryland Line, March 23, 1782; from St. Mary's County [Ref: S-166].
ROACH, James. (1) Captain, Upper Bn., St. Mary's County Militia, on Aug. 26, 1777, having previously refused a commission on May 25, 1777 [Ref: M-116, M-211, C-346, V-107]. Commissioned to collect blankets in Newtown Hundred on April 2, 1777, but declined on May 25, 1777, because "the smallpox rendered him incapable of executing it" [Ref: S-33, S-35]. Took the Oath of Allegiance before the Hon. John Ireland in St. Mary's County in 1778 [Ref: J-1146, K-65]. (2) Private, St. Mary's County Militia, 1777 [Ref: M-212].
ROBERTS, Allen. Second Lieutenant, Capt. Benjamin Bond's Co., Calvert County Militia, April 16, 1778, and First Lieutenant, 15th Bn., Feb. 2, 1779 [Ref: E-37, E-290, J-1146, M-116, M-149, which listed the name as "Allien Roberts"]. Took the Oath of Allegiance in Calvert County in 1778 [Ref: L-38]. Allen Roberts and Ann Wilson were married on Oct. 9, 1777, by Rev. Francis Lauder, of Christ Church Parish [Ref: K-33].
ROBERTS, Anthony. Took the Oath of Allegiance before the Hon. John Ireland in St. Mary's County in 1778 [Ref: J-1146, K-65].
ROBERTS, Araminta. See "James Goldsbury," q.v.
ROBERTS, John. Private, St. Mary's County Militia, 1777 [Ref: M-212]. Took the Oath of Allegiance before the Hon. John Ireland in St. Mary's County in 1778 [Ref: J-1146, K-65]. One John Roberts died intestate by March, 1782 [Ref: SO-46, SO-52, SO-53].
ROBERTSON, George. "George Roberson" took the Oath of Allegiance before the Hon. Bennett Biscoe in St. Mary's County in 1778 [Ref: J-1146, K-63]. The property of "George Robertson" was destroyed by the British in 1781 [Ref: S-166].
ROBERTSON, Jeremiah. Private, St. Mary's County Militia, 1777 [Ref: M-213].

ROBINS, Jeremiah. Took the Oath of Allegiance in St. Mary's County in 1778 [Ref: Q-119].

ROBINSON, John. (1) Private, Capt. James Grahame's Co., Calvert County Militia, 1778 [Ref: J-1146, M-148]. Private, Capt. Edward Wood's Co., Calvert County Militia, 1778 [Ref: J-1146, M-147]. Took the Oath of Allegiance in Calvert County in 1778 [Ref: L-38]. (2) Private, St. Mary's County Militia, 1777 [Ref: M-211].

ROBINSON, Dr. Provided medical service to the military in 1776; from St. Mary's County (no first name was given). [Ref: S-166].

ROBINSON, Mary. See "Hezekiah Murphy," q.v.

ROCK, John. Private, St. Mary's County, 3rd Maryland Line, enlisted on April 20 (or 26), 1778, for 3 years [Ref: D-157, D-298, D-329]. Private, Rawlings Regiment, March 26, 1779; discharged May 2, 1781 [Ref: D-159, S-166].

ROCK, Oliver. Sergeant, 3rd Maryland Line, from Feb. 23, 1777 until Feb. 23, 1780, when discharged [Ref: D-157].

ROCK, Philip. Took the Oath of Allegiance before the Hon. John Ireland in St. Mary's County in 1778 [Ref: J-1146, K-65, which listed the name as "Philip Rocke"].

ROCK, William. Private, Capt. Uriah Forrest's Co., Flying Camp, St. Mary's County, July 28, 1776 [Ref: D-30]. Private, St. Mary's County, 3rd Maryland Line, enlisted on April 26 or May 7, 1778, for 3 years [Ref: D-157, D-298, D-329]. Took the Oath of Allegiance before the Hon. Jeremiah Jordan in St. Mary's County in 1778 [Ref: J-1146, K-67, which listed the name as "William Rocke"]. Discharged May 2, 1781 [Ref: S-166].

RODE (ROOD), John. Private, Capt. James Grahame's Co., Calvert County Militia, 1778 [Ref: J-1146, M-149]. Took the Oath of Allegiance in Calvert County in 1778 [Ref: L-38].

ROFF, Daniel Jr. See "Daniel Ross, Jr.," q.v.

ROGERS, George. Private, St. Mary's County Militia, 1777 [Ref: M-212]. Took the Oath of Allegiance before the Hon. Robert Watts in St. Mary's County in 1778 [Ref: J-1146, K-62]. One George Rogers died intestate by July, 1778, with George Rogers as administrator [Ref: SO-12].

ROGERS, John. Private, St. Mary's County Militia, 1777 [Ref: M-212].

ROGERS, Richard. Private, St. Mary's County Militia, 1777 [Ref: M-212].

ROLLINS, Nathan. See "Nathan Rawlings," q.v.

ROOKE, William. Took the Oath of Allegiance before the Hon. Bennett Biscoe in St. Mary's County in 1778 [Ref: J-1146, K-63].

ROSE, Peregrine. Took the Oath of Allegiance before the Hon. John Shanks in St. Mary's County in 1778 [Ref: J-1146, K-70].

ROSS, Abraham. Private, Capt. Frederick Skinner's Co., Calvert County Militia, 1778 [Ref: J-1146, M-150]. Took the Oath of Allegiance in Calvert County in 1778 [Ref: L-38].

ROSS, Daniel. Took the Oath of Allegiance in Calvert County in 1778 [Ref: L-38].

ROSS, Daniel Jr. Private, Capt. Frederick Skinner's Co., Calvert County Militia, 1778 [Ref: J-1146, M-150]. Took the Oath of Allegiance in Calvert County in 1778 [Ref: L-38]. Private, Capt. James Patterson's Co., Calvert County Militia, Aug. 10, 1777 [Ref: M-146, which listed the name as "Daniel Roff, Jr."].

ROSS, John. Private, St. Mary's County Militia, 1777 [Ref: M-214].

ROSS, Lazerous. Took the Oath of Allegiance before the Hon. Bennett Biscoe in St. Mary's County in 1778 [Ref: J-1146, K-63]. The Register of St. Andrew's Episcopal Church states that Lazarus Ross and Jane Cox were married (by license) Nov. 27, 1780 [Ref: MB-383].

ROUGHTTEN, Jobe. Private, Capt. James Patterson's Co., Calvert County Militia, Aug. 10, 1777 [Ref: M-146].

ROURKE, Philip. Private, St. Mary's County Militia, 1777 [Ref: M-210].

ROUSBY, Elizabeth. See "John Barnes" and "Richard Barnes," q.v.

ROUSBY, John. See "George Plater" and "William Fitzhugh," q.v.

ROWDON, George. Applied for pension S15623 on Feb. 27, 1834, in Graves County, Kentucky, stating he was born on March 25, 1743 in Calvert County, Maryland and at the age of 5 he moved with his father to Frederick County, Virginia. In 1763 they moved to Camden, South Carolina, where he enlisted in May, 1778. After the war he moved to Warren County, Tennessee, and then in 1821 to Madison County, Alabama, and to Graves County, Kentucky in 1830 [Ref: P-2965, W-41, which latter source indicated he served in the Maryland State Militia].

RUFF, James. Private, Capt. Thomas Truman Greenfield's Co., Calvert County Militia, 1778 [Ref: J-1146, M-150]. Took the Oath of Allegiance in Calvert County in 1778 [Ref: L-38, which listed the name as "James Ruffe"].

RUFF, John. Took the Oath of Allegiance in Calvert County in 1778 [Ref: L-38, which listed the name as "John Ruffe"].

RUFF, Sabrett. Private, Capt. Thomas Cleland's Co., Calvert County Militia, 1778 [Ref: J-1146, M-147]. Took the Oath of Allegiance in Calvert County in 1778 [Ref: L-38, which listed the name as "Sabrett Ruffe"].

RUSSELL, Ignatius. Private, St. Mary's County Militia, 1777 [Ref: M-211].

RUSSELL, James. Private, St. Mary's County Militia, 1777 [Ref: M-212]. Took the Oath of Allegiance before the Hon. Ignatius Fenwick, Jr. in St. Mary's County in 1778 [Ref: J-1146, K-68].

RUSSELL, William. Took the Oath of Allegiance before the Hon. Richard Barnes in St. Mary's County in 1778 [Ref: J-1146, K-66]. The Register of St. Francis Xavier Catholic Church states that "William Russell, Jr." and Ann Draden Abell were married May 27, 1774 [Ref: SC-35].

RUSSELL, William Sr. Took the Oath of Allegiance before the Hon. Richard Barnes in St. Mary's County in 1778 [Ref: J-1146, K-66].
RYAL, Elizabeth. See "Charles Mills," q.v.
RYAN, Hugh. Private, Capt. Frisby Freeland's Co., Calvert County Militia, 1778 [Ref: J-1146, M-148]. Took the Oath of Allegiance in Calvert County in 1778 [Ref: L-38, which spelled the name as "Hugh Ryen"].
SALLOMAND, Joseph. Took the Oath of Allegiance in Calvert County in 1778 [Ref: L-38].
SAMPSON, Thomas. Private, St. Mary's County Militia, 1777 [Ref: M-210].
SANDERS, Enoch. Private, Capt. Uriah Forrest's Co., Flying Camp, St. Mary's County, July 28, 1776 [Ref: D-30, SM-114].
SANDERS, John. Private, Calvert County, enlisted by Lt. Frederick Skinner on Aug. 23, 1776 [Ref: D-33]. One "John Sanders, taylor" moved from St. George's in St. Mary's County, Maryland, to Virginia in 1806 [Ref: X-87].
SANDSBERRY, Abraham. Private, Capt. Richard Lane's Co., Calvert County Militia, 1778 [Ref: J-1146, M-150].
SANDSBERRY (SANSBERRY), Richard. Private, 4th Maryland Line, from 1777 or 1778 until discharged on Dec. 14, 1779 [Ref: D-165].
SANNER, Anne. See "Edward Watson," q.v.
SANNER, John Jr. (May 1, 1760 - circa 1842). Private, St. Mary's County Militia, 1777 [Ref: M-215]. Took the Oath of Allegiance before the Hon. Bennett Biscoe in St. Mary's County in 1778 [Ref: J-1146, K-63]. He married Elizabeth Abell (born 1767) on May 1, 1785, and a son John Abell Sanner (1805-1876) married (2nd wife) Serena Ann Sanner (1825-1887) in 1847 [Ref: Y-592, and Maryland Society, Sons of the American Revolution, Membership Application No. 3096, filed by John Edward Drury, and approved in 1991 by the National Society, Sons of the American Revolution]. The Register of St. Andrew's Episcopal Church states that John Sanner and Susannah Goodin were married (by license) on Oct. 17, 1784, and John Sanner and Elizabeth Abell were married (by license) on May 1, 1785 [Ref: MB-386]. Source S-143 states that John Sanner V (1760-1842) was the son of John Sanner IV and his wife Mary, and he married Elizabeth Abell in 1785.
SANNER, John Sr. Private, St. Mary's County Militia, 1777 [Ref: M-211]. Private, St. Mary's County, enlisted on May 29, 1778, for 9 months [Ref: D-329, which listed the name only as "John Senior"]. Private, 2nd Maryland Line, died on Dec. 25, 1778 [Ref: R-451, D-162, D-329, SM-115, which latter sources listed the name as "John Senner" and "John Senior (Sanner?)"]. See "John Sanner, Jr.," q.v.
SANNER, John, Mary, and Serena Ann. See "John Sanner, Jr.," q.v.
SANNER, Thomas. Took an oath of July 27, 1782, concerning the manufacture and sale of salt in St. Mary's County [Ref: V-532]. The

Register of St. Andrew's Episcopal Church states that Thomas Sanner and Mary Collason were married (by license) Dec. 23, 1783 [Ref: MB-385].

SANNER, William. Took the Oath of Allegiance in St. Mary's County in 1780 [Ref: Q-119]. Took an oath on July 24, 1782, concerning the manufacture and sale of salt [Ref: V-531].

SAPP, Jesse. Born in Calvert County on Aug. 19, 1761 and lived in Surry County, North Carolina at the time of his enlistment. Applied for and received pension S1587 in 1833 in Warren County, Tennessee [Ref: MC-138, P-3017].

SAPP, Robert. Private, Capt. Henry Skinner's Foot Co. of Hunting Hundred, Calvert County, 1777 [Ref: T-1814, O-125]. Private, 1st Maryland Line, enlisted April 16, 1777, and reported "deserted" (no date was given). [Ref: D-159].

SAUNDERS, Sarah. See "John Owens," q.v.

SAXE, Elizabeth. See "James Boiquet (Boquet)," q.v.

SAXE (SAX), Henry. Private, Maryland Line, 1780-1781 [Ref: D-411]. The Register of St. Andrew's Episcopal Church states that Henry Saxe and Rennes Denton were married (by license) Jan. 10, 1783 [Ref: MB-384].

SCARF (SCARFE), James. Private, Capt. Thomas Cleland's Co., Calvert County Militia, 1778 [Ref: J-1146, M-147]. James Scarf and Mary Hollandshead were married on April 20, 1780, by Rev. Francis Lauder, of Christ Church Parish [Ref: K-35].

SCOFIELD, Thomas. Private, St. Mary's County Militia, 1777 [Ref: M-215]. Took the Oath of Allegiance in St. Mary's County in 1780 [Ref: Q-119, which listed the name as "Thomas Schoolfield"].

SCOTT, Charles. Private, St. Mary's County Militia, 1777 [Ref: M-213]. "Charles Scott, farmer" moved to Woodford County, Kentucky, in 1793 [Ref: X-87].

SCOTT, James. There were several men with this name who served in the Maryland Line, including one probably from St. Mary's County in the 3rd Regiment in 1781 [Ref: D-396]. One James Scott married Peggy Edwards on Nov. 18, 1783, in St. Mary's County, by Rev. John Stephen, Rector of All Faith's Parish [Ref: I-536].

SCOTT, John. Private, St. Mary's County, 3rd Maryland Line, Capt. Armstrong's Co., 1778-1780 [Ref: D-298].

SCOTT, William. (1) Private, St. Mary's County Militia, 1777 [Ref: M-210]. Took the Oath of Allegiance before the Hon. Henry Tubman in St. Mary's County in 1778 [Ref: J-1146, K-70]. (2) Private, Capt. James Grahame's Co., Calvert County Militia, 1778 [Ref: J-1146, M-148]. Private, Capt. Richard Parran's Co., Calvert County Militia, 1778 [Ref: J-1146, M-149]. One William Scott died intestate in St. Mary's County by Sep., 1778 [Ref: SO-15].

SCRABLER, Jeremiah. Private, St. Mary's County, enlisted April 29, 1778, for 3 years, Continental Army [Ref: D-329, which listed the name as "Jeremiah Scraher"]. Private, 3rd Maryland Line, died on Oct. 14, 1778 [Ref: SM-115, S-166].

SCRIVENER, Richard. Private, Capt. James Grahame's Co., Calvert County Militia, 1778 [Ref: J-1146, M-149].

SEAGER, James. Private, St. Mary's County Militia, 1777 [Ref: M-209]. Took the Oath of Allegiance before the Hon. Henry Tubman in St. Mary's County in 1778 [Ref: J-1146, K-70].

SEAGER, John. Private, St. Mary's County Militia, 1777 [Ref: M-213].

SEAGER, Thomas. Private, St. Mary's County Militia, 1777 [Ref: M-210, which listed the name as "Thomas Seagar"].

SEALE, John. Private, St. Mary's County Militia, 1777 [Ref: M-213].

SEARS, Henry. Private, Capt. Charles Williamson's Co., Calvert County Militia, 1778 [Ref: J-1146, M-148, which listed the name as "Henry Seares"].

SEARS, Mary. See "William Coe," q.v.

SEDWICK, Elisha. Took the Oath of Allegiance in Calvert County in 1778 [Ref: L-38].

SEDWICK, John. Private, Capt. Walter Smith's Co., Calvert County Militia, 1778 [Ref: J-1146, M-148]. "John Sedwick" married Miss Elizabeth Louder Cook on March 1, 1764. "John Sedwick, Jr." married Miss Elizabeth Rawlings on Dec. 1, 1796 [Ref: O-26].

SEDWICK, Thomas. "Thomas Seddwick" was a private in Capt. Benjamin Bond's Co., Calvert County Militia, 1778 [Ref: J-1146, M-149]. "Thomas Sedgwick" and Ann Rigby were married on Dec. 21, 1777, by Rev. Francis Lauder, of Christ Church Parish [Ref: K-33].

SESSON, Caleb. Adjutant, Col. Jeremiah Jordan's Bn., St. Mary's County, April 4, 1777 [Ref: SM-115, S-33, C-199, C-209].

SEWALL (SEWELL), Ann and Charles. See "Nicholas Lewis Sewall," q.v.

SEWALL (SEWELL), Clement (1758 - Jan. 7, 1829). Ensign, Maryland Line. Applied for and received pension S20192 in Dec., 1828, stating that he had lived in St. Mary's County at the time of his enlistment and he had received a disability pension from Jan. 1, 1803. He later reapplied on March 26, 1818, at Georgetown in Washington, D. C., aged 60. He died there Jan. 7, 1829, leaving no widow, but many children and grandchildren, and Jane Sewall was administratrix. He also received a state pension under the Act of Jan. 24, 1823 in Maryland "for the gallant services rendered his country during the struggle for our glorious independence." [Ref: I-39]. In July, 1854, these children were then living: Elizabeth O'Reilly, Clement Sewall, Elenor Fenwick, Nicholas L. Sewall (of Fairfax County, Virginia), Catharine S. Foyles, and Juliana Sewall. Clement Newton, of Georgetown, D. C., *[sic]* stated he knew Clement Sewall during the war [Ref: P-3072]. Took the Oath of Allegiance before the Hon. Richard Barnes in St. Mary's County in 1778 [Ref: J-1146, K-66]. Supplied provisions (wheat, mutton, or bacon) to the Army in 1780 [Ref: S-77]. It also should be noted that there was

another "Clement Sewell" who was very prominent in Queen Anne's County during the revolutionary period [Ref: N-725].
SEWALL (SEWELL), Eleanor. See "Nicholas Lewis Sewall," q.v.
SEWALL (SEWELL), Henry. (1) Took the Oath of Allegiance before the Hon. Jenifer Taylor in St. Mary's County in 1778 [Ref: J-1146, K-64]. (2) Took the Oath of Allegiance before the Hon. Richard Barnes in St. Mary's County in 1778 [Ref: J-1146, K-66]. Private, St. Mary's County Militia, 1777 [Ref: M-215, which listed the name as "Henry Sewell"]. One Henry Sewall (Sewell) died testate by June, 1780, with Mary Sewall, his executrix, having great difficulty administering on his estate between 1780 and 1791 [Ref: SO-32, SO-63, SO-75, SO-107, SO-170]. Also see "Nicholas Lewis Sewall," q.v.
SEWALL (SEWELL), James. Private, Capt. Frisby Freeland's Co., Calvert County Militia, 1778 [Ref: J-1146, M-148, which listed the name as "James Sewell"].
SEWALL (SEWELL), Jane. See "Clement Sewall," q.v.
SEWALL (SEWELL), John. Private, 4th Maryland Line, Jan. 5, 1777 until Jan. 5, 1780, when discharged [Ref: D-166].
SEWALL (SEWELL), Joseph. Seaman from St. Mary's County who was "blown up in barge" in 1778 [Ref: SM-115].
SEWALL (SEWELL), Lettice. See "Nicholas Lewis Sewall," q.v.
SEWALL (SEWELL), Mary. See "Peter Ford" and "Henry Sewall," q.v.
SEWALL (SEWELL), Nicholas. Private, St. Mary's County Militia, 1777 [Ref: M-215]. Took the Oath of Allegiance before the Hon. Jenifer Taylor in St. Mary's County in 1778 [Ref: J-1146, K-64]. "Nicholas Sewall" was elected to a General Committee in St. Mary's County in accordance with the resolves of the Continental Congress in 1775 [Ref: MR-127]. Also see "Clement Sewall," q.v.
SEWALL (SEWELL), Nicholas Lewis (c1721-1800). Son of Henry Sewell and Elizabeth Lawson, of Harvey Hundred in St. Mary's County. He married (wife's name unknown) and had children: Henry, Charles, Nicholas Lewis, Jr., Lettice, Eleanor, and Ann. Served on the Committee of Observation in 1776. Justice of St. Mary's County, 1777-1778. Member of the House of Delegates, 1778-1779. Took the Oath of Allegiance before the Hon. Robert Watts in St. Mary's County in 1778 [Ref: J-1146, K-62, N-80, N-725, N-726, S-16, B-100]. The property of N. Lewis Sewall was destroyed by the British in 1781 [Ref: S-166, which listed the name as "H. Lewis Sewall"]. "Nicholas Levin Sewall" was paid for making salt in 1782 [Ref: S-166].
SEWALL (SEWELL), William. Seaman from St. Mary's County who was "blown up in barge" in 1778 [Ref: SM-115].
SHADNICK, Thomas. Private, St. Mary's County Militia, 1777 [Ref: M-214].
SHADRICK, John. Private, St. Mary's County Militia, 1777 [Ref: M-214]. Took the Oath of Allegiance before the Hon. Vernon Hebb in St. Mary's

County in 1778 [Ref: J-1146, K-68]. First Lieutenant, Lower Bn., May 7, 1781 [Ref: M-119, G-426, which listed the name as "John Shadrack"].

SHAMWELL, Jonathan. Private, St. Mary's County Militia, 1777 [Ref: M-210].

SHAMWELL, Joseph. Private, St. Mary's County Militia, 1777 [Ref: M-211]. Supplied provisions (wheat, mutton, or bacon) to the Army in Oct., 1780 [Ref: S-77, S-166]. Joseph Shamwell married Nancy Billingsley on Nov. 20, 1783, by Rev. John Stephen, Rector of All Faith's Parish [Ref: I-536]. See "William Shamwell," q.v.

SHAMWELL, Priscilla. See "William Shamwell," q.v.

SHAMWELL, William. Private, St. Mary's County Militia, 1777 [Ref: M-211]. One William Shamwell died testate by Sep., 1777, with Priscilla Shamwell and Joseph Shamwell as executors [Ref: SO-3]. See "William Shemwell," q.v.

SHANKS, Alexander. Private, Capt. Uriah Forrest's Co., Flying Camp, St. Mary's County, July 28, 1776 [Ref: D-30].

SHANKS, John (Dec. 25, 1740 - Nov. 22, 1825). Private, St. Mary's County Militia, 1777 [Ref: M-212]. First Lieutenant, Upper Bn., St. Mary's County Militia, Aug. 26, 1777 and Captain, Nov. 18, 1779. John married Mary Morris (1750-1825) in 1764 [Ref: M-119, C-345, F-18, R-453, Y-606, S-166, S-167]. Justice who administered the Oath of Allegiance in St. Mary's County in 1778 [Ref: J-1146, K-69]. Loaned money in St. Mary's County for the war effort in 1781 [Ref: X-78, H-461]. "John Shanks, Sr." took the Oath of Allegiance before the Hon. John Ireland in St. Mary's County in 1778 [Ref: J-1146, K-65]. "John Shanks, Jr." was elected to a General Committee in St. Mary's County in accordance with the resolves of the Continental Congress in 1775 [Ref: MR-127]. "John Shanks" is buried in a private cemetery near River Springs, home of the Blackistone family [Ref: S-129]. Another John Shanks was a private in the 4th Maryland Line from Dec. 14, 1781, until discharged (disabled) on Nov. 15, 1783 [Ref: D-461, D-555].

SHANKS, Joseph. Private, St. Mary's County Militia, 1777 [Ref: M-213]. Took the Oath of Allegiance before the Hon. Jeremiah Jordan in St. Mary's County in 1778 [Ref: J-1146, K-67]. Private, 3rd Maryland line, died Feb. 24, 1779 [Ref: R-453, D-329, D-164, which listed the name as "Joseph Shink"]. The Register of St. Francis Xavier Catholic Church states that Joseph Shanks and Susanna Goldsmith were married Feb. 18, 1772 [Ref: SC-34].

SHANKS, Matthew. Private, Capt. Uriah Forrest's Co., Flying Camp, St. Mary's County, July 28, 1776 [Ref: D-30, SM-115].

SHANKS, Robert. Private, Capt. Uriah Forrest's Co., Flying Camp, St. Mary's County, July 28, 1776 [Ref: D-30, SM-115].

SHANKS, Thomas. Private, St. Mary's County Militia, 1777 [Ref: M-213]. Took the Oath of Allegiance before the Hon. Vernon Hebb in St. Mary's County in 1778 [Ref: J-1146, K-68].

SHAW, William. Private, St. Mary's County Militia, 1777 [Ref: M-212]. Took the Oath of Allegiance before the Hon. John Ireland in St. Mary's County in 1778 [Ref: J-1146, K-65]. Supplied provisions (wheat, mutton, or bacon) to the Army in Oct., 1780 [Ref: S-77, S-167].
SHEAN, John. Private, Capt. James Grahame's Co., Calvert County Militia, 1778 [Ref: J-1146, M-149].
SHEARS, Henry. Took the Oath of Allegiance in Calvert County in 1780 [Ref: Q-120].
SHEARS, John Jr. Took the Oath of Allegiance in Calvert County in 1780 [Ref: Q-120].
SHEMWELL, William (1755-1824). Private, St. Mary's County Militia, 1780. He married Ann Billingsley circa 1787 [Ref: S-143]. Also see "William Shamwell," q.v.
SHEPHERD, Philip. Accounted and paid for collecting cattle for the use of the State in Calvert County in 1781 [Ref: V-442].
SHERCLIFF (SHIRCLIFF), Ann. See "Wilford Thompson," q.v.
SHERCLIFF, John. Took the Oath of Allegiance before the Hon. John Ireland in St. Mary's County in 1778 [Ref: J-1146, K-65]. One "John Sheriliffe" died by 1787, with "Francis Exeverius Shireliffe," the surviving executor, stating that his sister "Henrietta Sheriliffe who is almost an idiot has left him and he is apprehensive she has been enticed away as he apprehends with a view to get the estate ordered by the Court." [Ref: SO-109].
SHERCLIFF, Joseph. Took the Oath of Allegiance before the Hon. Robert Watts in St. Mary's County in 1778 [Ref: J-1146, K-62].
SHERCLIFF, Thomas. Took the Oath of Allegiance before the Hon. John Ireland in St. Mary's County in 1778 [Ref: J-1146, K-65]. Private, Capt. Uriah Forrest's Co., Flying Camp, St. Mary's County, on July 28, 1776 [Ref: SM-115, D-30, which listed the name as "Thoms. Shircliff"].
SHERCLIFF, William. Lieutenant, 4th Maryland Line, from Dec. 6, 1776 until he resigned in Feb., 1778 [Ref: D-166].
SHERILIFFE, Francis and Henrietta. See "John Shercliff," q.v.
SHERMANTINE, Abintl(?). Private, St. Mary's County Militia, 1777 [Ref: M-215].
SHERMANTINE, Anne. See "John Cox," q.v.
SHERMANTINE, Mary. See "Thomas Haywood," q.v.
SHIFFER, John. Private, Maryland Line, 1781 [Ref: D-412].
SHIRLEY, Bennett. Private, St. Mary's County, 1st Maryland Line, 1780-1783, and served in Capt. Benjamin Price's 5th Co. in the Southern Campaign at Camp James Island in 1780 [Ref: D-355, D-442, D-555]. Bennett Shirley married Susannah Peake on May 15, 1793 [Ref: X-122]. "Bennet Shirley or Shurley" died in Baltimore in 1810 and his widow Susanna applied for and received pension W3878 on Aug. 11, 1838, aged 64, at Baltimore, and bounty land warrant #11706-100-1791 was reissued to her on May 27, 1839, "under special act." Surviving children

at that time were Ann Sophia Bennett and Ann Maria Gunby, both of Baltimore [Ref: P-3118].

SHIRLEY, George. Private, St. Mary's County Militia, 1777 [Ref: M-215]. Private, St. Mary's County, enlisted on May 31, 1778, for 9 months, Continental Army [Ref: D-329]. Took the Oath of Allegiance before the Hon. Robert Watts in St. Mary's County in 1778 [Ref: J-1146, K-62, which listed the name as "George Sherley"]. Private, 3rd Maryland Line, died on Aug. 24, 1778 [Ref: SM-115, D-164, R-453, S-167].

SHIRLEY, Ignatius. Private, St. Mary's County Militia, 1777 [Ref: M-214]. The Register of St. Francis Xavier Catholic Church states that "Ignatius Shirly" and Mary Norris were married in Nov., 1775 [Ref: SC-35].

SHIRLEY, Robert. Private, St. Mary's County Militia, 1777 [Ref: M-212].

SHURBENTINE, Joseph. Took the Oath of Allegiance before the Hon. Bennett Biscoe in St. Mary's County in 1778 [Ref: J-1146, K-63].

SIFORD, Elizabeth. See "Richard Pilkinton (Pilketon)," q.v.

SILENCE, John. Private, St. Mary's County Militia, 1777 [Ref: M-212, which listed the name as "John Silance"]. Took the Oath of Allegiance in St. Mary's County in 1780 [Ref: Q-120].

SILENCE, Sabra. See "Abraham Adams," q.v.

SILENCE, Thomas. Private, St. Mary's County Militia, 1777 [Ref: M-213, which listed the name as "Thomas Silences"].

SILENCE, William. Applied for and received pension S35071 on April 9, 1818, in St. Mary's County, aged about 65, stating he served in the Virginia Line and had "but one child, a widowed daughter with 5 helpless children aged 3 to 13 years (no names were given)." He died on Feb. 14, 1831, aged 79 [Ref: P-3132, U-40].

SIM, Barbara. See "Patrick Sim Smith," q.v.

SIM (SYM), Martha. See "Edward Mattingly," q.v.

SIMMONS (SIMMONDS), Elizabeth. See "Robert Daffin," q.v.

SIMMONS, Ignatius. Private, St. Mary's County Militia, 1777 [Ref: M-211, which listed the name as "Ignatius Simons"].

SIMMONS, Isaac. Private, Capt. James Patterson's Co., Calvert County Militia, Aug. 10, 1777 [Ref: M-146]. Private, Capt. Frederick Skinner's Co., Calvert County Militia, 1778 [Ref: J-1146, M-150]. Took the Oath of Allegiance in Calvert County in 1778 [Ref: L-38]. Paid for services (unspecified) to the State and for making salt in St. Mary's County in 1782 [Ref: S-167].

SIMMONS, James. Private, Calvert County, enlisted by Ensign James Somervill on July 26, 1776 [Ref: D-34].

SIMMONS (SIMMONDS), Mary M. See "Cuthbert Abell," q.v.

SIMMONS, Nathaniel. Private, Calvert County, enlisted by Capt. John Brooke on July 26, 1776 [Ref: D-33].

SIMMONS, Thomas. Private, Capt. Richard Parran's Co., Calvert County Militia, 1778 [Ref: J-1146, M-149]. Took the Oath of Allegiance in Calvert County in 1780 [Ref: Q-120].
SIMMS, Anthony. Private, St. Mary's County Militia, 1777 [Ref: M-211]. Took the Oath of Allegiance before the Hon. Ignatius Fenwick, Jr. in St. Mary's County in 1778 [Ref: J-1146, K-68, which listed the name as "Anthony Simmes"]. Supplied provisions (wheat, mutton, or bacon) to the Army in 1780 [Ref: S-77]. "Mr. Simms" was an Assistant Commissary of Purchases for St. Mary's County in 1780 (no first name was given). [Ref: S-167].
SIMMS, Ignatius Jr. Private, Capt. Uriah Forrest's Co., Flying Camp, St. Mary's County, July 28, 1776 [Ref: D-30]. Private, 1st Maryland Line, died on July 17, 1779 [Ref: R-454, SM-115, D-160].
SIMON, Garbiner. See "Garbiner Lemmon," q.v.
SIMPSON, Josias. Took the Oath of Allegiance before the Hon. Jeremiah Jordan in St. Mary's County in 1778 [Ref: J-1146, K-67]. "Josias Simpson, farmer" moved to Washington, D. C. in 1795 [Ref: X-87].
SIMPSON, Thomas. Private, Capt. Richard Lane's Co., Calvert County Militia, 1778 [Ref: J-1146, M-150]. Took the Oath of Allegiance in Calvert County in 1778 [Ref: L-38].
SKINNER, Arthur. Private, Calvert County, enlisted by Lt. Frederick Skinner on Aug. 23, 1776 [Ref: D-33].
SKINNER, Clement. Private, Capt. Thomas Truman Greenfield's Co., Calvert County Militia, 1778 [Ref: J-1146, M-150]. Took the Oath of Allegiance in Calvert County in 1778 [Ref: L-38].
SKINNER, Francis. Prize Master on the State ship *Defence* from Sep. 15, 1777 through Dec. 31, 1777; probably from St. Mary's County [Ref: D-660].
SKINNER, Frederick. First Lieutenant, Calvert County, July, 1776 [Ref: D-33]. Captain, Calvert County Militia, April 16, 1778 [Ref: J-1146, M-121, M-150, E-37]. Took the Oath of Allegiance in Calvert County in 1778 [Ref: L-38].
SKINNER, Henry. Captain, Foot Co. of Hunting Creek Hundred, Calvert County, 1777 [Ref: T-1814, O-125].
SKINNER, James. Private, Capt. Frisby Freeland's Co., Calvert County Militia, 1778 [Ref: J-1146, M-148]. Took the Oath of Allegiance in Calvert County in 1778 [Ref: L-38]. Inspector of tobacco shipments in Calvert County in 1781 [Ref: V-407].
SKINNER, John. Took the Oath of Allegiance in Calvert County in 1778 [Ref: L-38].
SKINNER, Joseph. Took the Oath of Allegiance in Calvert County in 1778 [Ref: L-38].
SKINNER, Katherine. See "John Yoe," q.v.
SKINNER, Leonard. Private, Capt. Thomas Truman Greenfield's Co., Calvert County Militia, 1778 [Ref: J-1146, M-150].

SKINNER, Maryland. Ensign, Foot Co. of Hunting Creek Hundred, Calvert County, 1777 [Ref: T-1814, O-125].
SKINNER, Rebecca. See "James Wilson," q.v.
SKINNER, Richard. Private, Capt. Thomas Cleland's Co., Calvert County Militia, 1778 [Ref: J-1146, M-147]. Took the Oath of Allegiance in Calvert County in 1778 [Ref: L-38].
SKINNER, Robert. Second Lieutenant, 15th Bn., Calvert County Militia, April 10, 1776 [Ref: M-119, A-320]. Lieutenant, Foot Co. of Hunting Creek Hundred, Calvert County, 1777 [Ref: T-1814, O-125]. Second Lieutenant, Capt. Thomas Truman Greenfield's Co., Calvert County Militia, April 16, 1778 [Ref: J-1146, M-150, E-37]. Took the Oath of Allegiance in Calvert County in 1778 [Ref: L-38].
SKINNER, Robert Jr. Private, Capt. Frisby Freeland's Co., Calvert County Militia, 1778 [Ref: J-1146, M-148]. He may have been the "Robt. Skinner" who was a private in the 2nd Maryland Line some time between 1777 and 1780 [Ref: D-161].
SKINNER, Samuel. Private, Capt. Frisby Freeland's Co., Calvert County Militia, 1778 [Ref: J-1146, M-148]. Took the Oath of Allegiance in Calvert County in 1778 [Ref: L-38].
SLATER, Ellis. Private, Capt. Thomas Cleland's Co., Calvert County Militia, 1778 [Ref: J-1146, M-147].
SLYE, Ann. See "William Slye," q.v.
SLYE, Gerard and Henrietta. See "Edmund Plowden" and "Henrietta Plowden," q.v.
SLYE, John. Private, Capt. Edward Wood's Co., Calvert County Militia, 1778 [Ref: J-1146, M-147].
SLYE, Patience (Patient). Private, Capt. Edward Wood's Co., Calvert County Militia, 1778 [Ref: J-1146, M-147]. Took the Oath of Allegiance in Calvert County in 1778 [Ref: L-38].
SLYE, Robert. Private, 4th Maryland Line, from July 7, 1779 until Jan. 17, 1780, when reported as "deserted" [Ref: D-167, S-167].
SLYE, Samuel. Private, Capt. Henry Skinner's Foot Co. of Hunting Hundred, Calvert County, 1777 [Ref: T-1814, O-125]. Private, Capt. Edward Wood's Co., Calvert County Militia, 1778 [Ref: J-1146, M-147]. Took the Oath of Allegiance in Calvert County in 1778 [Ref: L-38]. Samuel Slye married Anne ---- and son John Slye was born in May, 1778 [Ref: O-27].
SLYE, William. Private, Capt. Henry Skinner's Foot Co. of Hunting Hundred, Calvert County, 1777 [Ref: T-1814, O-125]. Private, 7th Maryland Line, enlisted April 30, 1778, and promoted to corporal in July, 1780. He was wounded at the Battle of Camden in South Carolina, was discharged on April 30, 1781, and later returned to service on March 5, 1782 [Ref: SM-147]. He married Ann ---- [Ref: Y-622].
SLYE, Willey. Miss Willey Slye loaned money in St. Mary's County for the war effort in 1781 [Ref: X-78, H-436, SM-187].

SMALLWOOD, William. See "John Truman," q.v.
SMART, Richard. Private, St. Mary's County Militia, 1777 [Ref: M-212]. Private, enlisted May 25, 1778, for 9 months, 3rd Maryland Line; discharged April 4, 1779 [Ref: D-330, S-167].
SMART, William B. Private, St. Mary's County Militia, 1777 [Ref: M-214].
SMITH, Alexander. See "Alexander Hamilton Smith," q.v.
SMITH, Alexander Hamilton (c1748-1784). Physician and son of Major John Smith and Mary Hamilton, of Calvert County. He married Mary Chew, daughter of Richard Chew, in 1767 and had these children: John Thomas, Philemon, Upton Sheredine, Hamilton, Alexander (sea captain), Mary Hamilton Smith, and Sarah Lock Chew Smith. Served in the Maryland House of Delegates from Calvert County, 1779-1780, and Court Justice, 1769, 1773, 1783, and 1784 [Ref: N-82, N-742].
SMITH, Alexander Lawson. See "Patrick Sim Smith," q.v.
SMITH, Ann. See "Philip Read" and "Patrick Sim Smith," q.v.
SMITH, Ann Maria. See "William Smith," q.v.
SMITH, Athanatius. See "John Smith," q.v.
SMITH, Barbara. See "Patrick Sim Smith," q.v.
SMITH, Bartholomew. Took the Oath of Allegiance before the Hon. Bennett Biscoe in St. Mary's County in 1778 [Ref: J-1146, K-63].
SMITH, Basil. (1) Private, St. Mary's County Militia, 1777 [Ref: M-210]. (2) Seaman from St. Mary's County who served aboard the State ship *Defence* in 1776 [Ref: S-25, D-606]. (3) Private, St. Mary's County Militia, 1777 [Ref: M-212]. (3) "Basil C. Smith" took the Oath of Allegiance before the Hon. Ignatius Fenwick, Jr. in St. Mary's County in 1778 [Ref: J-1146, K-68]. One Basil Smith was a supplier of provisions (wheat, mutton, or bacon) in St. Mary's County in 1780 [Ref: S-77].
SMITH, Catherine and Christiana. See "Patrick Sim Smith," q.v.
SMITH, Charles. See "John Reeder, Jr." and "John Smith," q.v.
SMITH, Clement (1718-1792). Captain, Deputy Commissary, and Sheriff of Calvert County. Took the Oath of Allegiance in Calvert County in 1778 [Ref: L-38, N-747]. See "Patrick Sim Smith," q.v.
SMITH, Daniel. Private, Capt. Richard Parran's Co., Calvert County Militia, 1778 [Ref: J-1146, M-149]. Private, Capt. Richard Lane's Co., Calvert County Militia, 1778 [Ref: J-1146, M-150]. Took the Oath of Allegiance in Calvert County in 1778 [Ref: L-38].
SMITH, Dicandia. See "John Reeder, Jr.," q.v.
SMITH, Edward. Private, St. Mary's County Militia, 1777 [Ref: M-210]. Private, enlisted on May 25, 1778, for 9 months, 4th Maryland Line; discharged April 1, 1780 [Ref: D-329, S-69, S-167]. See "John Smith," q.v.
SMITH, Edward Barton. Private, St. Mary's County Militia, 1777 [Ref: M-212]. Took the Oath of Allegiance before the Hon. Ignatius Fenwick, Jr. in St. Mary's County in 1778 [Ref: J-1146, K-68].

SMITH, Elias. Private, St. Mary's County Militia, 1777 [Ref: M-210]. Took the Oath of Allegiance before the Hon. Richard Barnes in St. Mary's County in 1778 [Ref: J-1146, K-66]. Private, enlisted April 28, 1778, 6th Maryland Line, and discharged Jan. 1, 1780 [Ref: S-167]. One Elias Smith died by Aug., 1797, leaving a son Elias Smith [Ref: SO-264].

SMITH, Garin (Gavin) Hamilton. Took the Oath of Allegiance in Calvert County in 1778 [Ref: L-38]. Private, Capt. Charles Williamson's Co., Calvert County Militia, 1778 [Ref: J-1146, M-147].

SMITH, George. Private, Capt. Richard Lane's Co., Calvert County Militia, 1778 [Ref: J-1146, M-149]. Took the Oath of Allegiance in Calvert County in 1778 [Ref: L-38].

SMITH, Hamilton. See "Alexander Hamilton Smith," q.v.

SMITH, Harriet and James. See "Patrick Sim Smith," q.v.

SMITH, James. There were several men with this name: (1) Private, St. Mary's County Militia, 1777 [Ref: M-210]. Took the Oath of Allegiance before the Hon. Robert Armstrong in St. Mary's County in 1778 [Ref: J-1146, K-62]. (2) Private, St. Mary's County Militia, 1777 [Ref: M-215]. Private, Capt. Frederick Skinner's Co., Calvert County Militia, 1778 [Ref: J-1146, M-150]. (3) "James Smith (schoolmaster)" took the Oath of Allegiance before the Hon. Bennett Biscoe in St. Mary's County in 1778 [Ref: J-1146, K-63]. (4) Private, St. Mary's County, who served as a marine aboard the State ship *Defence* in 1776 [Ref: S-25, D-606]. One James Smith died by April, 1779 [Ref: SO-20]. One James Smith married Barbara White on Aug. 2, 1777, by Rev. Thomas John Clagett, All Saint's Parish [Ref: K-33].

SMITH, Jane. See "John Smith," q.v.

SMITH, Jeremiah. Private, Capt. Richard Lane's Co., Calvert County Militia, 1778 [Ref: J-1146, M-150].

SMITH, Jesse. Private, Capt. Richard Lane's Co., Calvert County Militia, 1778 [Ref: J-1146, M-150].

SMITH, John. *There were several men with this name in Calvert and St. Mary's Counties:* (1) Ensign, Lower Bn., St. Mary's County Militia, June 22, 1780, and Captain, Aug. 28, 1777 to June 22, 1780 [Ref: M-122, C-346, F-201, S-167]. "Capt. John Smith" served on the Committee of Observation in 1776 [Ref: S-16, B-100]. (2) Private, St. Mary's County Militia, 1777 [Ref: M-215]. (3) Private, St. Mary's County Militia, 1777 [Ref: M-211]. (4) Private, Capt. Richard Lane's Co., Calvert County Militia, 1778 [Ref: J-1146, M-150]. (5) Three men with this name took the Oath of Allegiance: one before the Hon. Robert Armstrong in St. Mary's County in 1778, one before the Hon. Robert Watts in St. Mary's County in 1778, and one before the Hon. Bennett Biscoe in St. Mary's County in 1778 [Ref: J-1146, K-62, K-63]. (6) Private, Capt. John Mackall's Co., Calvert County Militia, 15th Bn., June 12, 1778 [Ref: M-146]. (7) Private, St. Mary's County Militia, 1777 [Ref: M-215]. (8) One John Smith of the Maryland Line (county of residence not stated) was charged with desertion and was given 100 lashes in 1780 [Ref: *Summer Soldiers: A Survey & Index of Revolutionary War Courts-Martial*, by James C. Neagles (1986), page 246]. (9) "John Smith (Patuxent)" was elected to serve on a General Committee in St. Mary's County in accordance with the resolves of the Continental Congress in 1775 [Ref: MR-127]. The Register of St. Francis Xavier Catholic Church states that John Smith, Sr. and Jane Manning were married Nov. 18, 1773, and John Smith and Elizabeth Ford were married Oct. 1, 1774 [Ref: SC-35]. One John Smith died intestate by Nov., 1799, leaving orphans Edward, Lewis, Jane, Athanatius, and Charles Smith, with John Smith as his administrator [Ref: SO-300]. See "Alexander Hamilton Smith" and "Athanatius Ford," q.v.

SMITH, John Jr. Private, St. Mary's County Militia, 1777 [Ref: M-211]. Took the Oath of Allegiance before the Hon. Richard Barnes in St. Mary's County in 1778 [Ref: J-1146, K-66]. Second Lieutenant, Lower Bn., June 22, 1780 [Ref: M-122, F-201]. See "John Smith" and "John Smith, of John," q.v.

SMITH, John, Sr. Private, St. Mary's County Militia, 1777 [Ref: M-215]. See "John Smith," q.v.

SMITH, John Hamilton. Private, Capt. Charles Williamson's Co., Calvert County Militia, 1778 [Ref: J-1146, M-148]. Took the Oath of Allegiance in Calvert County in 1778 [Ref: L-38].

SMITH, John Sylvester. See "William Smith," q.v.

SMITH, John Thomas. See "Alexander Hamilton Smith," q.v.

SMITH, John (of John). Took the Oath of Allegiance before the Hon. Bennett Biscoe in St. Mary's County in 1778 [Ref: J-1146, K-63]. Also see "John Smith, Jr.," q.v.

SMITH, John (of Joseph). Private, Capt. Richard Lane's Co., Calvert County Militia, 1778 [Ref: J-1146, M-150, which listed the name as "John Smith (son Jos.)"].

SMITH, Joseph. (1) Private, Capt. James Grahame's Co., Calvert County Militia, 1778 [Ref: J-1146, M-149]. (2) Private, St. Mary's County, enlisted May 31, 1778, for 9 months [Ref: D-330]. (3) Private, Count Pulaski's Legion, enlisted in July, 1779, while serving in the Maryland Line in Charleston, South Carolina. On July 26, 1780, he was "taken up as a deserter" before Richard Barnes, Lieutenant of St. Mary's County [Ref: D-593].

SMITH, Joseph ("Crownes"). Private, Capt. Richard Lane's Co., Calvert County Militia, 1778 [Ref: J-1146, M-150].

SMITH, Lewis. See "John Smith," q.v.

SMITH, Mary. See "Thomas Bailey" and "Patrick Sim Smith," q.v.

SMITH, Mary Hamilton. See "Alexander Hamilton Smith," q.v.

SMITH, Melinda. See "Barnaby Rhodes," q.v.

SMITH, Mordecay (Mordecai). Private, Capt. Richard Lane's Co., Calvert County Militia, 1778 [Ref: J-1146, M-150].

SMITH, Nathan. Private, Capt. Richard Lane's Co., Calvert County Militia, 1778 [Ref: J-1146, M-149]. Ensign, Capt. Leach's Co., Calvert County, April 16, 1778 [Ref: M-122, E-37]. Took the Oath of Allegiance in Calvert County in 1778 [Ref: L-38].

SMITH, Patrick Sim (1749-c1793). Son of "Clement Smith," q.v. and Barbara Sim. He married Anne Truman Greenfield, daughter of James Truman Greenfield and granddaughter of Thomas Truman Greenfield (1682-1733), in 1768 and had children: Walter, James, Patrick, Christiana, Catherine, Ann, Barbara, Mary, Susanna, and Harriet. Delegate to the Maryland Convention from Calvert County, 1775-1776; Justice, 1773; Continental Loan Officer, 1778; Purchasing Agent, 1778; Commissary of Purchases, 1780-1782; Commissary for Clothing, 1781; Commissary for Horses, 1781; Clerk, Commissioners of Tax, 1787-1788. Moved to Frederick County in 1784. Justice of the Orphans Court, 1791-1792, and County Court Justice, 1791-1792. Major, Calvert County Militia, 1776, and Lieutenant Colonel, 1778 [Ref: N-72, N-747, N-748]. Wrote to the Governor on June 1, 1780, about raising money for the State in Calvert County [Ref: V-293], and wrote to the Governor on Aug. 24, 1781, about hiring assistants to collect cattle for the use of the State [Ref: V-428]. In 1792 his brother, Alexander Lawson Smith, lived in Harford County [Ref: N-748].

SMITH, Peter Pierre (Pears). Took the Oath of Allegiance before the Hon. Robert Armstrong in St. Mary's County in 1778 [Ref: J-1146, K-62]. "Peter Pierre Smith, merchant" moved from St. Michaels to Culpepper County, Virginia, after 1790 [Ref: X-87]. One Peter Smith died testate in St. Mary's County by Oct., 1785 [Ref: SO-86].

SMITH, Philemon. See "Alexander Hamilton Smith," q.v.

SMITH, Rachel. See "Thomas Gantt, Jr.," q.v.

SMITH, Richard. Private, Capt. Frisby Freeland's Co., Calvert County Militia, 1778 [Ref: J-1146, M-148]. Took the Oath of Allegiance in Calvert County in 1778 [Ref: L-38]. "Richard Smith, schoolmaster" moved from Upper Newtown to Charles County, Maryland, in 1813 [Ref: X-87].

SMITH, Samuel. Took the Oath of Allegiance before the Hon. Bennett Biscoe in St. Mary's County in 1778 [Ref: J-1146, K-63].

SMITH, Sarah and Susanna. See "Alexander Hamilton Smith," q.v.

SMITH, Thomas. (1) Private, Capt. Richard Lane's Co., Calvert County Militia, 1778 [Ref: J-1146, M-149]. Took the Oath of Allegiance in Calvert County in 1778 [Ref: L-38]. (2) Took the Oath of Allegiance in St. Mary's County in 1780 [Ref: Q-120].

SMITH, Upton Sheredine. See "Alexander Hamilton Smith," q.v.

SMITH, Vernon. Private, St. Mary's County Militia, 1777 [Ref: M-215]. Took the Oath of Allegiance before the Hon. Robert Watts in St. Mary's County in 1778 [Ref: J-1146, K-62].

SMITH, Walter. Captain, 15th Bn., Calvert County Militia, April 10, 1776 through April 16, 1778 [Ref: J-1146, M-123, M-148, A-320, E-37]. "W. Smith" took the Oath of Allegiance in Calvert County in 1778 [Ref: L-38]. The Christ Church Register in Calvert County records the birth of Walter Smith, son of Walter Smith of Parker's Creek and his wife Sarah, on Aug. 12, 1747 [Ref: O-27]. The Register of St. Andrew's Episcopal Church in St. Mary's County records Walter Smith and Mary Hendley were married Sep. 19, 1779, and Walter Smith and ---- King were married (by publication) on March 31, 1785 [Ref: MB-383, MB-386]. See "Patrick Smith," q.v.

SMITH, Wat. Took the Oath of Allegiance before the Hon. Robert Watts in St. Mary's County in 1778 [Ref: J-1146, K-62].

SMITH, William. There were several men with this name: (1) Private, St. Mary's County Militia, 1777 [Ref: M-215]. (2) Private, St. Mary's County Militia, 1777 [Ref: M-210]. (3) Private, Capt. Frederick Skinner's Co., Calvert County Militia, 1778 [Ref: J-1146, M-150]. (4) Private, Capt. John Mackall's Co., Calvert County Militia, 15th Bn., June 12, 1778 [Ref: M-146]. (5) Took the Oath of Allegiance in Calvert County in 1778 [Ref: L-38]. William Smith (1757 - Jan. 28, 1829), son of John Smith and Amy Leigh, was a private in the 9th Co. of Light Infantry in St. Mary's County (or Charles County), on Jan. 29, 1776. He married Margaret Williams on Jan. 14, 1796, and had children William Leigh, John Sylvester, and Ann Maria [Ref: D-19, R-456, S-143, S-167]. Another William Smith married Alice Stallings on Aug. 4, 1778, by Rev. Francis Lauder, of Christ Church Parish [Ref: K-34].

SMITH, William Leigh. See "William Smith," q.v.

SMITHERS, Edward. Took the Oath of Allegiance in Calvert County in 1778 [Ref: L-38].

SMITHERS, Gregory. Took the Oath of Allegiance in Calvert County in 1778 [Ref: L-38].

SMOOT, Austin Sanford. Took the Oath of Allegiance before the Hon. Bennett Biscoe in St. Mary's County in 1778 [Ref: J-1146, K-63].

SMOOT, Cuthbert. Private, St. Mary's County Militia, 1777 [Ref: M-215]. Took the Oath of Allegiance before the Hon. Bennett Biscoe in St. Mary's County in 1778 [Ref: J-1146, K-63].

SMOOT, Isaac. See "Meveral Locke (Lock)," q.v.

SMOOT, John. Private, St. Mary's County Militia, 1777 [Ref: M-215]. "John Smoot, Sr." took the Oath of Allegiance before the Hon. Bennett Biscoe in St. Mary's County in 1778 [Ref: J-1146, K-63]. One John Smoot died testate by April, 1790 [Ref: SO-152].

SMOOT, Rachel. See "William Barton Smoot," q.v.

SMOOT, Thomas. Private, St. Mary's County Militia, 1777 [Ref: M-215]. Took the Oath of Allegiance before the Hon. Bennett Biscoe in St. Mary's County in 1778 [Ref: J-1146, K-63].

SMOOT, William. Private, St. Mary's County Militia, 1777 [Ref: M-215]. There was also a William Smoot, sergeant, 1st Maryland Line, from Dec. 10, 1776 to Dec. 27, 1779, when discharged [Ref: D-159]. A William Smoot was also an ensign, 1st Maryland Line, on Jan. 26, 1780 [Ref: D-161]. "William Smoot, farmer" moved to Franklin County, Kentucky in 1793 and "William Smoot, carpenter" moved from St. Inigoes to Washington, D. C. in 1819 [Ref: X-87]. There was also a William Smoot, son of John, who was born circa 1750 in St. Mary's County and migrated to Prince William County, Virginia and Rowan County, North Carolina, where he died in 1815 [Ref: MC-148. For more information on this family see *The Smoots of Maryland and Virginia*, by Harry Wright Newman (1936), pp. 152-159].

SMOOT, William Barton (1750-1794). Captain, Lower Bn., St. Mary's County Militia, Aug. 26, 1777 [Ref: M-123, C-346, S-38]. Took the Oath of Allegiance before the Hon. Vernon Hebb in St. Mary's County in 1778 [Ref: J-1146, K-68]. William Barton Smoot married Rachel Smoot (no date was given). [Ref: Y-630]. "There seems little doubt that he is buried in the family plot at St. George's Episcopal Church in Poplar Hill, but there is no stone." [Ref: S-129].

SOLLERS, James Mackall (c1740-c1810). "James Sollers" was a private in Capt. Benjamin Bond's Co., Calvert County Militia, in 1778 [Ref: J-1146, M-149, and Maryland Society, Sons of the American Revolution, Approved Membership Application No. 2681]. "James M. Sollers" took the Oath of Allegiance in Calvert County in 1778 [Ref: L-38]. "James Sollers" married twice: (1) name unknown; and, (2) Anne Dare [Ref: Y-632]. "James Mackall Sollers" married Rebecca Elt on April 25, 1779, by Rev. Francis Lauder, of Christ Church Parish [Ref: K-35].

SOMERVILLE, Alexander (1734 - March 22, 1783). Son of Dr. James "Somervell" of Scotland, and Sarah Howe, of Calvert County. He married Rebecca Dawkins on Dec. 2, 1759 and had children as follows: Thomas Somerville (born Sep. 24, 1760); Dr. William Dawkins Somerville (born Jan. 30, 1763, and married Elizabeth Wilson Ireland, 1763-1835); and Rebecca Somerville (born March 28, 1765, married James Duke, 1765-1825, and died in 1837). Alexander served in the French and Indian War from 1756 to 1758, and was Lieutenant Colonel in the Calvert County Militia from Jan. 6, 1776 until Jan. 3, 1777, when he resigned [Ref: V-82, M-123, C-13, Y-633, G-426, which listed the name as "Alexander Somervell," and O-27, which listed different last names for the aforementioned wives in the Christ Church Register, i. e., Sarah Howard rather than Sarah Howe, and Rebecca Dare rather than Rebecca Dawkins]. He served in many official capacities: Justice, 1773; Delegate to the Maryland Convention, 1775-1776; Member of the House of Delegates, 1773-1778; County Sheriff, 1769-1772; Collector of Gold and Silver Coin, 1776; and, Commissioner of Tax between 1779 and 1783 [Ref: N-71, N-72, N-76, N-78, N-757, N-758, and information from

Levin W. Wickes, of Philadelphia, Pennsylvania, from a a query in the *Maryland Genealogical Society Bulletin*, Vol. 15, No. 1 (Feb., 1974), p. 19]. "Alexander Sommervill" took the Oath of Allegiance in Calvert County in 1778 [Ref: L-38]. There was an "Alexander Somervell" who was a private in Capt. Richard Parran's Co. in the Calvert County Militia in 1778 [Ref: J-1146, M-149].

SOMERVILLE, Ann Truman. See "James Somerville," q.v.

SOMERVILLE, George Clarke. Surgeon, Continental Army, under Dr. Benjamin Rush, in 1781. Returned to St. Mary's County after the war, lived in Harvey Hundred, and died a bachelor in 1791. He was a brother of "Capt. William Somerville," q.v. [Ref: SM-150, N-758]. There was also a "Dr. George Clarke Somervill" who died by March, 1794, leaving orphaned sons William Clarke Somervill and Henry Vernon Somervill, with William Somervill as guardian in 1796 [Ref: SO-208, SO-252]. Source S-129 indicates "Dr. George Clarke Somerville, Revolutionary patriot" died on Dec. 13, 1800 and is buried at St. George's Episcopal, noting "there are no stones, but he [and William Somerville] appear in the church register."

SOMERVILLE, James (April 19, 1758 - May 4, 1815). Son of James Somerville (Somervell) and Susanna Dare [Ref: O-27]. Ensign, Calvert County, July, 1776; promoted later to captain. He married Anne or Anna Truman. She died on Sep. 1, 1814 [Ref: Y-633, D-33, HG-60, which sources listed the name as both "Somerville" and "Somervell"]. On March 12, 1828, the Treasurer of Maryland was directed "to pay James Somervell, of Prince George's County, a son and one of the heirs of Capt. James Somervell, an officer of the Maryland Line during the Revolutionary War, such sum as may appear to be due to him on the pension list of Maryland at the time of his decease." [Ref: I-395]. See "Alexander Somerville," q.v.

SOMERVILLE, Henry Vernon. See "William Somerville" and "George Clarke Somerville," q.v.

SOMERVILLE, John. (1) 1754-1806. Son of John Somerville (died 1788) and Susannah Clarke. He married Mary Goodloe in 1773. Private, Capt. Frisby Freeland's Co., Calvert County Militia, 1778 [Ref: J-1146, M-148, which listed the name as "John Sumervill"]. Took the Oath of Allegiance in Calvert County in 1778. Eventually migrated to North Carolina [Ref: N-758, L-38, which listed the name as "John Sommervill"]. Another "John Somervell" died on Dec. 24, 1826, aged 70 years, 7 months, and 9 days, and his wife Sarah died on Sep. 1, 1809, aged 48 years, 1 month, and 29 days. They are buried on a farm owned by Mr. Morton (1908) on Hunting Creek in Calvert County [Ref: HG-60]. (2) Took the Oath of Allegiance before the Hon. Henry G. Sothoron in St. Mary's County in 1778. Died in 1788 [Ref: K-69, J-1146, N-758]. See "William Somerville," q.v.

SOMERVILLE, Margaret. See "John DeButts," q.v.

SOMERVILLE, Rebecca. See "Alexander Somerville," q.v.
SOMERVILLE, Sarah. See "John Somerville," q.v.
SOMERVILLE, Thomas. Private, Capt. Walter Smith's Co., Calvert County Militia, 1778 [Ref: J-1146, M-148, which listed the name as "Thomas Somervell"]. Also see "Alexander Somerville," q.v.
SOMERVILLE, William (Dec. 25, 1755 - Dec. 29, 1806). Son of John Somerville (died 1788) and Susannah Clarke. He married twice: (1) Elizabeth Chesley in 1779; and, (2) Elizabeth Hebb, daughter of Col. Vernon Hebb, in 1788. Children: William Clarke, Henry Vernon, and Elizabeth. William was a captain in the St. Mary's County Militia, 1781, and loaned money for the war effort in 1781. Member of the House of Delegates in 1783 and 1785. County Coroner, 1784-1785. Commissioner of Tax, 1785. Justice of the Orphans Court, 1787-1803. Major, 12th Militia Regiment, 1794-1795 [Ref: X-78, H-485, SM-150, N-88, N-758, N-759, R-457]. The Register of St. Andrew's Episcopal Church states "William Somervel and Elizabeth Chisley" were married on Sep. 7, 1779 [Ref: MB-383]. Source S-129 states William Somerville died on Dec. 30, 1806, and is buried in an unmarked grave at St. George's Episcopal Church in Poplar Hill.
SOMERVILLE, William Clarke. See "William Somerville" and "George Clarke Somerville," q.v.
SOMERVILLE, William Dawkins. See "Alexander Somerville," q.v.
SOTHORON, Ann. See "Henry Greenfield Sothoron" and "Hezekiah Burroughs," q.v.
SOTHORON, Eleanor, George Washington, and Henry. See "Henry Greenfield Sothoron," q.v.
SOTHORON, Henry Greenfield (c1732 - Oct., 1793). Son of John Johnson Sothoron (1698-1744) and Mary Jowles. He married twice, both wives named Mary Bond (one was born in 1736 and died in 1763), and he had these children: John, Zachariah, Henry, James Forbes, Thomas, George Washington, Eleanor, Ann, Mary, Rebecca, and another daughter (name not stated). Henry served in the Lower House from St. Mary's County, 1757-1766, Delegate to the Maryland Convention, 1774-1775, Court Justice, 1768-1777, and Captain, 6th Bn., 1776. Justice who administered the Oath of Allegiance in St. Mary's County in 1778 [Ref: J-1146, K-68, N-70, N-759, R-458, SO-202, SO-225]. "Henry G. Sothoron" was elected to a General Committee in St. Mary's County in accordance with the resolves of the Continental Congress in 1775. "Mr. Henry G. Sothoron" served on the Committee of Correspondence in 1775 [Ref: MR-127]. Henry Greenfield Sothoron is buried at The Plains on the Patuxent River in the Charlotte Hall area [Ref: S-130]. See "Philip Key," q.v.
SOTHORON, James F. and John. See "Henry Greenfield Sothoron," q.v.
SOTHORON, John Johnson. Ensign, Upper Bn., St. Mary's County Militia, Aug. 26, 1777 [Ref: M-123, M-209, SM-115, C-346, which listed

the name as "John Johnson Sothern"]. Took the Oath of Allegiance before the Hon. Henry Tubman in St. Mary's County in 1778 [Ref: J-1146, K-70, which mistakenly listed the name as "John I. Sothoron"]. Also see "Henry Greenfield Sothoron," q.v.

SOTHORON, Leven (Levin). Private, St. Mary's County Militia, 1777 [Ref: M-209]. Took the Oath of Allegiance before the Hon. Henry G. Sothoron in St. Mary's County in 1778 [Ref: J-1146, K-69].

SOTHORON, Mary and Rebecca. See "Henry Greenfield Sothoron," q.v.

SOTHORON, Richard Jr. Private, St. Mary's County Militia, 1777 [Ref: M-209]. "Richard Sothoron, of Richard" took the Oath of Allegiance before the Hon. Henry Tubman in St. Mary's County in 1778 [Ref: J-1146, K-70].

SOTHORON, Richard Sr. Private, St. Mary's County Militia, 1777 [Ref: M-209]. Took the Oath of Allegiance before the Hon. Henry Tubman in St. Mary's County in 1778 [Ref: J-1146, K-70]. Supplied provisions (wheat, mutton, or bacon) to the Army in Oct., 1780 [Ref: S-77,S-168]. One Richard Sothoron died testate by Feb., 1784 [Ref: SO-69, SO-74, SO-262].

SOTHORON, Richard (of Samuel). Took the Oath of Allegiance before the Hon. Henry Tubman in St. Mary's County in 1778 [Ref: J-1146, K-70].

SOTHORON, Samuel. Private, St. Mary's County Militia, 1777 [Ref: M-209]. Took the Oath of Allegiance before the Hon. Henry Tubman in St. Mary's County in 1778 [Ref: J-1146, K-70]. One "Samuel Sothon" married Henrietta Bruce on Jan. 9, 1783, St. Mary's County, by Rev. John Stephen, Rector of All Faith's Parish [Ref: I-536], and another Samuel Sothoron died by March, 1782 [Ref: SO-46].

SOTHORON, Thomas and Zachariah. See "Henry Greenfield Sothoron," q.v.

SPALDING, Aaron (1751 - March, 1843). Private, St. Mary's County, who served in a matross co. (artillery) in 1777 [Ref: SM-115]. Private, enlisted Jan. 1, 1777, and mustered as a Sergeant, 2nd Maryland Line, in May, 1780 [Ref: D-161]. In Dec., 1815, the Treasurer of Maryland was directed to pay him, during life, half pay of a sergeant [Ref: I-395, MK-136]. Applied for and received pension S37441 on Aug. 10, 1819, in Washington County, Kentucky, aged 67, stating that he had enlisted in St. Mary's County in the Maryland Line. Aaron married twice: (1) Nellie Mattingly; and, (2) Mary Moore [Ref: Y-634, P-3255]. It should be noted, however, that according to Anderson C. Quisenberry's *Revolutionary Soldiers in Kentucky* (page 164) Aaron Spalding died on June 29, 1825, aged 81. It appears there were two men with this name: one was a private in the 2nd Maryland Line, enlisted on Jan. 1, 1777 and served to Nov. 15, 1783, and another was a private who enlisted as a matross on Feb. 23, 1777 [Ref: S-168].

SPALDING, Alethia. See "Benedict Spalding," q.v.

SPALDING, Alex. (Elexius). "Alex. Spalding" took the Oath of Allegiance before the Hon. John Reeder in St. Mary's County in 1778 [Ref: J-1146, K-69]. "Elezius [sic] Spalding" was a private in St. Mary's County Militia, 1777 [Ref: M-211]. "Elexius Spalding" died testate by April, 1783 [Ref: SO-61].

SPALDING, Ann. See "Raphael Ford" and "Benedict Spalding," q.v.

SPALDING, Benedict. Private, St. Mary's County Militia, 1777 [Ref: M-211]. Took the Oath of Allegiance before the Hon. Henry Reeder in St. Mary's County in 1778 [Ref: J-1146, K-64]. Benedict married Alethia Abell and later followed his brother-in-law Robert Abell to Kentucky in 1790, settling on Rolling Fork in Nelson County. They were devout Catholics. His children were Richard, Thomas, Joseph, William, Ignatius A., Benedict, Ann, Ellen, Elizabeth, Catherine, Mary, and Alethia [Ref: MK-136]. The Register of St. Francis Xavier Catholic Church states "Benedict Spalden and Ann Stone, both widowed" were married Dec. 21, 1779 [Ref: SC-36].

SPALDING, Bennett. Private, St. Mary's County Militia, 1777 [Ref: M-211]. Took the Oath of Allegiance before the Hon. Richard Barnes in St. Mary's County in 1778 [Ref: J-1146, K-66]. He was appointed guardian of his children Edward, Mary, Monica, Lewis, and Bennett, in Feb., 1797 [Ref: SO-256]. "Bennett Spalding, farmer" moved from Lower Resurrection to Washington County, Kentucky, in 1797 [Ref: X-87].

SPALDING, Catherine. See "Benedict Spalding" and "William Mattingly," q.v.

SPALDING, Clark (Clarke). Private, St. Mary's County Militia, 1777 [Ref: M-211]. Discharged circa Aug. 4, 1781 [Ref: V-420, S-168, which latter source listed the name as "Clerk Spalding"].

SPALDING, Edward. Private, Capt. Uriah Forrest's Co., Flying Camp, St. Mary's County, on July 28, 1776 [Ref: D-30, SM-115]. Private, St. Mary's County Militia, 1777 [Ref: M-212]. Took the Oath of Allegiance before the Hon. Ignatius Fenwick, Jr. in St. Mary's County in 1778 [Ref: J-1146, K-68]. One Edward Spalding died by Sep., 1778 [Ref: SO-14]. See "Bennett Spalding," q.v.

SPALDING, Elexius. See "Alex. Spalding," q.v.

SPALDING, Elizabeth. See "Thomas Leach" and "Philip Ford," q.v.

SPALDING, Enoch. Private, St. Mary's County Militia, 1777 [Ref: M-213].

SPALDING, George. Private, St. Mary's County Militia, 1777 [Ref: M-213]. Private, 3rd Maryland Line, enlisted on May 1, 1778, for 9 months; discharged on Feb. 19, 1779 [Ref: D-164, D-329, S-168].

SPALDING, Henry. Took the Oath of Allegiance before the Hon. John Reeder in St. Mary's County in 1778 [Ref: J-1146, K-69]. Supplied provisions (wheat, mutton, or bacon) to the Army in 1780 [Ref: S-77].

SPALDING, Henry Jr. (1758 - Nov. 1, 1829). Private, St. Mary's County Militia, 1777 [Ref: M-211]. Took the Oath of Allegiance before the Hon. John Reeder in St. Mary's County in 1778 [Ref: J-1146, K-69]. Applied for and received pension S35082 on April 24, 1818, in St. Mary's County, aged about 62. In 1825 he had living with him Mrs. Jane Heard and her daughter Jane aged about 11 (no relationship stated). Private, 2nd Maryland Line, Jan. 10, 1777 until discharged on Jan. 10, 1780 [Ref: P-3256, D-162]. Pension rolls of 1835 noted he had been suspended under the Act of May 1, 1820, was restored commencing March 14, 1828, and died on Nov. 1, 1829, aged 71 [Ref: U-40]. In 1811, the Treasurer of Maryland was directed to pay him "the half pay of a private as a provision to him in his indigent situation and advanced life." [Ref: I-395].

SPALDING, John Baptist Sr. Took the Oath of Allegiance before the Hon. John Reeder in St. Mary's County in 1778 [Ref: J-1146, K-69].

SPALDING, Joseph. Took the Oath of Allegiance before the Hon. John Ireland in St. Mary's County in 1778 [Ref: J-1146, K-65]. Joseph Spalding and John Spalding were among the early Catholic settlers in Nelson County, Kentucky, in 1785 [Ref: MK-136].

SPALDING, Lewis and Mary. See "Bennett Spalding," q.v.

SPALDING, Michael. Took the Oath of Allegiance before the Hon. Ignatius Fenwick, Jr. in St. Mary's County in 1778 [Ref: J-1146, K-68]. One Michael Spalding died by June, 1778 [Ref: SO-10].

SPALDING, Michael Jr. "Michael Spalding, Jr." was a private in St. Mary's County Militia, 1777 [Ref: M-212]. "Michael Spalding" wrote to the Governor in Aug., 1781, and requested the return of his confiscated horse [Ref: V-419].

SPALDING, Monica. See "Bennett Spalding," q.v.

SPALDING, Moses C. Took the Oath of Allegiance before the Hon. Ignatius Fenwick, Jr. in St. Mary's County in 1778 [Ref: J-1146, K-68].

SPALDING, Peter. Took the Oath of Allegiance before the Hon. Ignatius Fenwick, Jr. in St. Mary's County in 1778 [Ref: J-1146, K-68].

SPALDING, Philip. (1) Private, St. Mary's County Militia, 1777 [Ref: M-211]. Took the Oath of Allegiance before the Hon. John Reeder in St. Mary's County in 1778 [Ref: J-1146, K-69]. (2) Private, St. Mary's County Militia, 1777 [Ref: M-215]. Took the Oath of Allegiance before the Hon. Bennett Biscoe in St. Mary's County in 1778 [Ref: J-1146, K-63].

SPALDING, Ralph. Private, St. Mary's County Militia, 1777 [Ref: M-214].

SPALDING, Raphael. Took the Oath of Allegiance before the Hon. Henry Reeder in St. Mary's County in 1778 [Ref: J-1146, K-64].

SPALDING, Richard. Private, St. Mary's County Militia, 1777 [Ref: M-213].

SPALDING, Richard Jr. Took the Oath of Allegiance before the Hon. John Reeder in St. Mary's County in 1778 [Ref: J-1146, K-69].

SPALDING, Thomas. Supplied provisions (wheat, mutton, or bacon) to the Army in St. Mary's County in 1780 [Ref: S-77, S-168].

SPALDING, Thomas Jr. Private, St. Mary's County Militia, 1777 [Ref: M-211]. Took the Oath of Allegiance before the Hon. John Reeder in St. Mary's County in 1778 [Ref: J-1146, K-69].

SPALDING, William. Private, St. Mary's County, drafted on June 10, 1778. Private, 1st Maryland Line, died on Nov. 26, 1778 [Ref: D-161, D-330, R-459, SM-115, SO-24, SO-31, S-168]. There were two men with this name who took the Oath of Allegiance in St. Mary's County in 1778: one before the Hon. Bennett Biscoe and one before the Hon. John Reeder [Ref: J-1146, K-63, K-69].

SPALDING, William (of James). Private, St. Mary's County, enlisted on March 30, or April 20, or April 30, 1778 [three different dates given in the records], for 9 months; served in 3rd Maryland Line; discharged in Feb., 1779 [Ref: D-164, D-329, S-168].

SPARKS, Nimrod. Private, Maryland Line, 1781 [Ref: D-412].

SPENCER, Francis. Private, Capt. Benjamin Bond's Co., Calvert County Militia, 1778 [Ref: J-1146, M-149]. Took the Oath of Allegiance in Calvert County in 1778 [Ref: L-38].

SPICER, Roger. Took the Oath of Allegiance in Calvert County in 1778 [Ref: L-38].

SPICKNALL, Basil. Took the Oath of Allegiance in Calvert County in 1778 [Ref: L-38]. Private, Capt. Charles Williamson's Co., Calvert County Militia, 1778 [Ref: J-1146, M-147, which listed the name as "Bazil Specknall"].

SPICKNALL, John. First Lieutenant, 15th Bn., Capt. Charles Williamson's Co., Calvert County Militia, April 10, 1776 through April 16, 1778 [Ref: J-1146, M-124, M-147, A-320, E-37, which listed the name as "John Specknall" and "John Spickernall"]. Took the Oath of Allegiance in Calvert County in 1778 [Ref: L-38].

SPICKNALL, Leonard (1752-1834). Took the Oath of Allegiance in Calvert County in 1778 [Ref: L-38, Y-637]. Private, Capt. Charles Williamson's Co., Calvert County Militia, 1778 [Ref: J-1146, M-147, which listed the name as "Leonard Specknall"].

SPICKNALL, Matthew. On Aug. 26, 1777, Lieut. Davidson reported that "Mathew Spicknoll has not received his pay." [Ref: V-118]. Sergeant, 2nd Maryland Line, discharged on Jan. 10, 1780 [Ref: D-161].

SPICKNALL, Robert. Private, Capt. Henry Skinner's Foot Co. of Hunting Hundred, Calvert County, 1777 [Ref: T-1814, O-125, which listed the name as "Robert Spickernaile"]. Private, Capt. Charles Williamson's Co., Calvert County Militia, 1778 [Ref: J-1146, M-148, which listed the name as "Robert Specknall"]. Took the Oath of Allegiance in Calvert County in 1778 [Ref: L-38]. He was listed as a private in the Maryland Line from Charles County in 1776 [Ref: D-33].

SPINK, Dorothy. See "Joseph Stone," q.v.

SPINK, Edward. Took the Oath of Allegiance before the Hon. Henry Reeder in St. Mary's County in 1778 [Ref: J-1146, K-64].

SPINK, Henrietta. See "Joseph Ford," q.v.
SPINK, William. First Lieutenant, Upper Bn., St. Mary's County Militia, Aug. 26, 1777 [Ref: M-124, M-210. C-346]. Took the Oath of Allegiance before the Hon. Richard Barnes in St. Mary's County in 1778 [Ref: J-1146, K-66]. Members of the Spink family migrated to Washington County, Kentucky by 1788 [Ref: MK-137].
SPRADLIN, Jesse, Ruth, and Sally. See "Cudbeth Stone," q.v.
SPRAGUE, John. Private, St. Mary's County, enlisted April 28, 1778, for 3 years, 3rd Maryland Line; died on March 6, 1779 [Ref: R-460, SM-115, S-168, and D-329 which listed the name as "John Spragu"].
ST. CLAIR, Vernon. "Vernon St. Clair" was a private, St. Mary's County Militia, 1777 [Ref: M-210]. A "Bernard St. Clare" married Dorcas King on Dec. 24, 1778, St. Mary's County, by Rev. John Stephen, Rector of All Faith's Parish [Ref: I-536].
STALL, Edward. Private, Capt. Henry Skinner's Foot Co. of Hunting Hundred, Calvert County, 1777 [Ref: T-1814, O-125].
STALLINGS, Absolom. Private, Capt. Charles Williamson's Co., Calvert County Militia, 1778 [Ref: J-1146, M-147].
STALLINGS, Alice. See "William Smith," q.v.
STALLINGS, Benjamin. (1) Private, Capt. Edward Wood's Co., Calvert County Militia, 1778 [Ref: J-1146, M-147]. (2) Private, Capt. James Grahame's Co., Calvert County Militia, 1778 [Ref: J-1146, M-148]. (3) Private, Capt. Thomas Truman Greenfield's Co., Calvert County Militia, 1778 [Ref: J-1146, M-150]. One took the Oath of Allegiance in Calvert County in 1778 [Ref: L-38].
STALLINGS, Henry. Private, Capt. Richard Parran's Co., Calvert County Militia, 1778 [Ref: J-1146, M-149]. "Henry Stallings, of Calvert County" took the Oath of Allegiance in Calvert County in 1780 [Ref: Q-120].
STALLINGS, Isaac. Private, Capt. James Patterson's Co., Calvert County Militia, Aug. 10, 1777 [Ref: M-146, which listed the name as "Isak Stalling"]. Private, Capt. Frederick Skinner's Co., Calvert County Militia, 1778 [Ref: J-1146, M-150].
STALLINGS, James. Private, Capt. Richard Parran's Co., Calvert County Militia, 1778 [Ref: J-1146, M-149].
STALLINGS, John. Private, Capt. James Grahame's Co., Calvert County Militia, 1778 [Ref: J-1146, M-149]. Took the Oath of Allegiance in Calvert County in 1778 [Ref: L-38].
STALLINGS, Joseph. Took the Oath of Allegiance in Calvert County in 1780 [Ref: Q-120].
STALLINGS, Newman. Private, Capt. Charles Williamson's Co., Calvert County Militia, 1778 [Ref: J-1146, M-147].
STALLINGS, Phenehas (Phineas, Phenus). Took the Oath of Allegiance in Calvert County in 1778 [Ref: L-38]. Private, Capt. Thomas Truman Greenfield's Co., Calvert County Militia, 1778 [Ref: J-1146, M-150].

STALLINGS, Richard. (1) Private, Capt. Charles Williamson's Co., Calvert County Militia, 1778 [Ref: J-1146, M-147]. (2) Private, Capt. James Grahame's Co., Calvert County Militia, 1778 [Ref: J-1146, M-148]. One took the Oath of Allegiance in Calvert County in 1778 [Ref: L-38].

STALLINGS, Thomas. Took the Oath of Allegiance in Calvert County in 1778 [Ref: L-38].

STALLINGS, William. (1) Private, Capt. Richard Parran's Co., Calvert County Militia, 1778 [Ref: J-1146, M-149]. Took the Oath of Allegiance in Calvert County in 1778 [Ref: L-38]. (2) Private, Capt. James Grahame's Co., Calvert County Militia, 1778 [Ref: J-1146, M-148]. Took the Oath of Allegiance in Calvert County in 1778 [Ref: L-38].

STALLIONS, Susanna. See "Joseph Breeden," q.v.

STAMP, Steven. Took the Oath of Allegiance in Calvert County in 1778 [Ref: L-38].

STAMP, Steven Jr. Took the Oath of Allegiance in Calvert County in 1778 [Ref: L-38].

STAMP, Thomas. Private, Capt. Charles Williamson's Co., Calvert County Militia, 1778 [Ref: J-1146, M-147]. Took the Oath of Allegiance in Calvert County in 1778 [Ref: L-38].

STANFORTH, James. Private, Capt. Thomas Truman Greenfield's Co., Calvert County Militia, 1778 [Ref: J-1146, M-150].

STANFORTH, John. Private, Capt. Frisby Freeland's Co., Calvert County Militia, 1778 [Ref: J-1146, M-148]. Took the Oath of Allegiance in Calvert County in 1778 [Ref: L-38, which listed the name as "John Standforth"].

STANFORTH, John Jr. Private, Capt. Thomas Cleland's Co., Calvert County Militia, 1778 [Ref: J-1146, M-147]. Took the Oath of Allegiance in Calvert County in 1778 [Ref: L-38, which listed the name as "John Standforth, Jr."].

STANFORTH, Richard. Private, Capt. Thomas Truman Greenfield's Co., Calvert County Militia, 1778 [Ref: J-1146, M-150]. Took the Oath of Allegiance in Calvert County in 1778 [Ref: L-38, which listed the name as "Richard Standforth"].

STENNETT, Benjamin. Private, Capt. Thomas Truman Greenfield's Co., Calvert County Militia, 1778 [Ref: J-1146, M-150]. Took the Oath of Allegiance in Calvert County in 1778 [Ref: L-38, which listed the name as "Benjamin Stinnet"].

STENNETT, John. Private, Capt. Henry Skinner's Foot Co. of Hunting Hundred, Calvert County, 1777 [Ref: T-1814, O-125]. Took the Oath of Allegiance in Calvert County in 1778 [Ref: L-38, which listed the name as "John Stinnet"].

STENNETT, John Jr. Private, Capt. Edward Wood's Co., Calvert County Militia, 1778 [Ref: J-1146, M-147].

STENNETT, William. Private, Capt. Henry Skinner's Foot Co. of Hunting Hundred, Calvert County, 1777 [Ref: T-1814, O-125].

STEPHEN, John (Reverend). Took the Oath of Allegiance in St. Mary's County, All Faith's Parish, in 1778 [Ref: SM-186]. He died by 1788, leaving orphans Mary, John, and Thomas Reeder Stephen (above the age of 14 in 1792), with Thomas Attaway Stephen as their guardian in 1792 [Ref: SO-118, SO-180 to SO-184, SO-187, SO-191, SO-192, SO-196, SO-197, SO-206, SO-208, SO-219, SO-232].

STEPHENS, Joseph. Supplied provisions (wheat, mutton, or bacon) to the Army in St. Mary's County in 1780 [Ref: S-77, S-168]. See "Joseph Stevens," q.v.

STEVENS, James. This name appeared twice as a private, St. Mary's County Militia, 1777 [Ref: M-213]. James Stevens migrated with the early Catholic settlers to Nelson County, Kentucky, in 1785 [Ref: MK-138].

STEVENS, John. Private, Calvert County, enlisted by Lt. Frederick Skinner on Aug. 23, 1776 [Ref: D-33]. One John Stevens migrated to Ohio County, Kentucky circa 1809 and another John Stevens was an elder in Bardstown, Kentucky, in 1820 [Ref: MK-138].

STEVENS, Joseph. "Joseph Stevens" was a private, St. Mary's County Militia, 1777 [Ref: M-213]. One "Joseph Stephens" died testate by Sep., 1777 [Ref: SO-2]. Also see "Joseph Stephens," q.v.

STEVENS, Richard. Private, Capt. Henry Skinner's Foot Co. of Hunting Hundred, Calvert County, 1777 [Ref: T-1814, O-125].

STEVENS, Richard Jr. Private, Capt. Thomas Cleland's Co., Calvert County Militia, 1778 [Ref: J-1146, M-147].

STEVENS, Sarah. See "James Marquess," q.v.

STEVENS, William. Took the Oath of Allegiance in Calvert County in 1778 [Ref: L-38]. Private, Capt. James Grahame's Co., Calvert County Militia, 1778 [Ref: J-1146, M-148, which listed the name as "William Stephens"].

STEWARD, Edward. Private, Capt. Thomas Truman Greenfield's Co., Calvert County Militia, 1778 [Ref: J-1146, M-150].

STEWARD, James. Private, Calvert County, enlisted by Lt. Nathaniel Wilson on Aug. 23, 1776 [Ref: D-34, which listed the name as "James Stewad"].

STEWARD, John. First Lieutenant, 5th Independent Maryland Co., St. Mary's County, Jan. 2, 1776 [Ref: D-25]. On Aug. 7, 1776, he received a commission from the U. S. Congress to serve in the Marine Service. He probably served for a time in Capt. Fulford's Matross Co. in Annapolis. On June 1, 1779 he was in command of the State ship *Plater* which served as a look-out or patrol boat on the Chesapeake Bay and its tributaries. On June 27, 1780 he was issued Letters of Marque and Reprisal as Commander of the Maryland schooner *Molly* and on Dec. 30, 1780, the sloop *Porpoise* and State ship *Dolphin* were placed under his command (at which time he was addressed as Major). He was still in the service on Dec. 4, 1781 [Ref: SM-148, A-284, A-304, B-436, B-465, B-484, F-206, F-294, G-45, G-102, G-110, G-163, G-243, G-258, G-478; *Archives of Maryland, Volume 47*, p. 562].

STEWART, James. Private, Capt. Benjamin Bond's Co., Calvert County Militia, 1778 [Ref: J-1146, M-149]. Took the Oath of Allegiance in Calvert County in 1778 [Ref: L-38].

STILES, Elizabeth. See "Henry Jarboe," q.v.

STILES, Stephen. Private, St. Mary's County Militia, 1777 [Ref: M-213]. Took the Oath of Allegiance in 1780 [Ref: Q-120, which had listed the name as "Stephen Stilas, of St. Mary's"].

STIRLING, Teresia. See "William Bowling," q.v.

STITLER, Caroline and Catherine. See "Robert Purdle (Purtle)," q.v.

STODDERT, Sarah Parker. See "John Weems," q.v.

STONE, Ann. See "Benedict Spalding" and "Arthur McGill," q.v.

STONE, Cuthbert (Cudbeth, Cutbeth). Private, 7th Maryland Line, from April 18, 1780 to Nov. 1, 1780. He applied for pension on Oct. 21, 1818, in Floyd County, Kentucky, aged about 60, stating that he had enlisted in St. Mary's County on March 29, 1780, for 3 years. He died testate on June 24, 1844, mentioning in his will his daughter Sally Spradlin and son-in-law Jesse Spradlin who lived on the farm lying on the left fork of Abbott Creek, being the same purchased of William Stone and deeded to Cudbeth *[sic]* Stone by John Stone and he now bequeathed to them, and to his son Enoch Stone, a legacy. His widow Sally applied for and received pension W3050 on Sep. 6, 1844, aged 89, stating that they were married on March 17, 1784, in South Carolina. Solomon Stone and Micajah Spradlin were also mentioned in 1844 (no relationships were given). [Ref: W-40, MK-139, P-3353, which latter source stated Sally Stone married Jerry of Jesse Spradlin and in 1844 she was a resident of Floyd County, Kentucky, and they had a daughter Ruth Spradlin].

STONE, Elizabeth. See "Charles Jarboe," q.v.

STONE, Enoch. Private, St. Mary's County Militia, 1777 [Ref: M-211]. Took the Oath of Allegiance before the Hon. Ignatius Fenwick, Jr. in St. Mary's County in 1778 [Ref: J-1146, K-68]. The Register of St. Francis Xavier Catholic Church states Enoch Stone and Monica Goldsberry were married Nov. 11, 1773 [Ref: SC-35]. See "Cudbeth Stone," q.v.

STONE, Hatton. Private, St. Mary's County Militia, 1777 [Ref: M-211].

STONE, Ignatius. "Ignatius Stone" was a private, St. Mary's County Militia, 1777 [Ref: M-211]. "Ignatius F. Stone" took the Oath of Allegiance before the Hon. Ignatius Fenwick, Jr. in St. Mary's County in 1778 [Ref: J-1146, K-68].

STONE, James. Took the Oath of Allegiance in Calvert County in 1778 [Ref: L-38].

STONE, Jane. See "Basil Nottingham" and "Bennett Hutchins," q.v.

STONE, John. Private, St. Mary's County Militia, 1777 [Ref: M-211]. Private, St. Mary's County, enlisted May 25, 1778, for 9 months [Ref: D-329]. Took the Oath of Allegiance before the Hon. Ignatius Fenwick, Jr. in St. Mary's County in 1778 [Ref: J-1146, K-68]. See "Cudbeth Stone," q.v.

STONE, Joseph. (1) Second Lieutenant, Upper Bn., St. Mary's County Militia, Aug. 26, 1777 [Ref: M-126, M-211, C-346]. Took the Oath of Allegiance before the Hon. Richard Barnes in St. Mary's County in 1778 [Ref: J-1146, K-66]. (2) Private, St. Mary's County Militia, 1777 [Ref: M-210]. Private, Maryland Line, enlisted May 29, 1778, for 9 months [Ref: D-329]. Took the Oath of Allegiance before the Hon. Richard Barnes in St. Mary's County in 1778 [Ref: J-1146, K-66]. One Joseph Stone supplied provisions (wheat, mutton, or bacon) to the Army in 1780 [Ref: S-77]. The Register of St. Andrew's Episcopal Church states that one Joseph Stone and Winifred Hutchinson were married (by license) Nov. 28, 1780 [Ref: MB-383]. The Register of St. Francis Xavier Catholic Church states that a Joseph Stone and Dorothy Spink were married Dec. 29, 1772, and Joseph Stone and Elizabeth More were married Feb. 21, 1779 [Ref: SC-34, SC-36].

STONE, Joseph Jr. Took the Oath of Allegiance before the Hon. Ignatius Fenwick, Jr. in St. Mary's County in 1778 [Ref: J-1146, K-68]. See "Joseph Stone," q.v.

STONE, Lydia. See "Hugh Williams," q.v.

STONE, Marshall. Private, Capt. Richard Lane's Co., Calvert County Militia, 1778 [Ref: J-1146, M-150]. Took the Oath of Allegiance in Calvert County in 1778 [Ref: L-38].

STONE, Solomon. See "Cudbeth Stone," q.v.

STONE, Thomas. Private, Calvert County, enlisted by Lt. Nathaniel Wilson on Aug. 31, 1776 [Ref: D-34]. Private, Capt. Charles Williamson's Co., Calvert County Militia, 1778 [Ref: J-1146, M-147]. Took the Oath of Allegiance in Calvert County in 1778 [Ref: L-38].

STONE, Thomas Jr. Private, Capt. James Patterson's Co., Calvert County Militia, Aug. 10, 1777 [Ref: M-146]. Took the Oath of Allegiance in Calvert County in 1778 [Ref: L-38].

STONE, William. (1) Private, Capt. James Patterson's Co., Calvert County Militia, Aug. 10, 1777 [Ref: M-146, M-211]. Private, Capt. James Grahame's Co., Calvert County Militia, 1778 [Ref: J-1146, M-148]. (2) Private, St. Mary's County Militia, 1777 [Ref: M-215]. Took the Oath of Allegiance before the Hon. Ignatius Fenwick, Jr. in St. Mary's County in 1778 [Ref: J-1146, K-68]. See "Cudbeth Stone," q.v.

STONE, William H. Took the Oath of Allegiance before the Hon. Richard Barnes in St. Mary's County in 1778 [Ref: J-1146, K-66].

STORR, William. Took the Oath of Allegiance before the Hon. Bennett Biscoe in St. Mary's County in 1778 [Ref: J-1146, K-63].

STRANGE, Silvester. Private, St. Mary's County Militia, 1777 [Ref: M-214].
STRICKLAND, John. Private, Capt. Frisby Freeland's Co., Calvert County Militia, 1778 [Ref: J-1146, M-148].
STRICKLAND, John Jr. Private, Capt. Thomas Cleland's Co., Calvert County Militia, 1778 [Ref: J-1146, M-147].
STRICKLAND, Joseph. Private, Capt. Thomas Cleland's Co., Calvert County Militia, 1778 [Ref: J-1146, M-147]. Private, Capt. Richard Lane's Co., Calvert County Militia, 1778 [Ref: J-1146, M-150, which listed the name as "Joseph Stricklin"]. Took the Oath of Allegiance in Calvert County in 1778 [Ref: L-38].
STRICKLAND, William. Private, Capt. Thomas Cleland's Co., Calvert County Militia, 1778 [Ref: J-1146, M-147]. Took the Oath of Allegiance in Calvert County in 1778 [Ref: L-38].
STRONG, Mary. See "Zachariah Abell," q.v.
SUIT, Benjamin. Private, St. Mary's County Militia, 1777 [Ref: M-209]. Took the Oath of Allegiance before the Hon. Henry Tubman in St. Mary's County in 1778 [Ref: J-1146, K-70].
SUIT, Dent. Private, St. Mary's County Militia, 1777 [Ref: M-209]. "Dent Suit, Sr." took the Oath of Allegiance before the Hon. Henry G. Sothoron in St. Mary's County in 1778 [Ref: J-1146, K-69].
SUIT, James. Private, St. Mary's County Militia, 1777 [Ref: M-213].
SUIT, John. Private, Continental Army, 1781 [Ref: D-412, which listed the name as "John Sute"].
SUIT, John Dent. Private, St. Mary's County Militia, 1777 [Ref: M-210]. Took the Oath of Allegiance before the Hon. Henry G. Sothoron in St. Mary's County in 1778 [Ref: J-1146, K-69]. Private, Maryland Line (served as a substitute), July 28, 1781 [Ref: D-384]. John Dent Suit died testate by May, 1795, having not signed his will, but Thomas Dent Suit testified to its authenticity [Ref: SO-227].
SUIT, Samuel. Private, St. Mary's County Militia, 1777 [Ref: M-209].
SUIT, Thomas. Private, St. Mary's County Militia, 1777 [Ref: M-209]. See "John Dent Suit," q.v.
SUIT, William. Took the Oath of Allegiance in St. Mary's County in 1780 [Ref: Q-121]. "William Suet" also took the Oath of Allegiance in St. Mary's County in 1780 [Ref: Q-121].
SULLIVAN, Daniel. Took the Oath of Allegiance before the Hon. Bennett Biscoe in St. Mary's County in 1778 [Ref: J-1146, K-63]. He died by June, 1779, leaving an orphan son "Denniss" [Ref: SO-22].
SULLIVAN (SULIVANT), Dennis. Private, Capt. James Grahame's Co., Calvert County Militia, 1778 [Ref: J-1146, M-149]. See "Daniel Sullivan," q.v.
SULLIVAN (SULIVANT), Jeremiah. Took the Oath of Allegiance in Calvert County in 1780 [Ref: Q-121].

SULLIVAN, Philip. Private, Capt. Thomas Truman Greenfield's Co., Calvert County Militia, 1778 [Ref: J-1146, M-150].
SULLIVAN (SULIVANT), Thomas. Private, Capt. Frederick Skinner's Co., Calvert County Militia, 1778 [Ref: J-1146, M-150]. Private, Capt. John Mackall's Co., Calvert County Militia, 15th Bn., June 12, 1778 [Ref: M-146]. Took the Oath of Allegiance in Calvert County in 1780 [Ref: Q-121].
SULLIVAN (SULIVANT), William. Private, Capt. Frederick Skinner's Co., Calvert County Militia, 1778 [Ref: J-1146, M-150]. Private, Capt. John Mackall's Co., Calvert County Militia, 15th Bn., June 12, 1778 [Ref: M-146]. Took the Oath of Allegiance in Calvert County in 1780 [Ref: Q-121].
SUMERHILL, Charles. Private, St. Mary's County Militia, 1777 [Ref: M-212].
SUMERHILL, James. Private, St. Mary's County Militia, 1777 [Ref: M-210].
SUMERHILL, Philip. Private, St. Mary's County Militia, 1777 [Ref: M-211].
SUMERHILL, William. Private, St. Mary's County Militia, 1777 [Ref: M-210]. Took the Oath of Allegiance in St. Mary's County in 1780 [Ref: Q-120, which listed the name as "William Somerhill"].
SUNDERLAND, Benjamin. Private, Capt. James Patterson's Co., Calvert County Militia, Aug. 10, 1777 [Ref: M-146]. Took the Oath of Allegiance in Calvert County in 1778 [Ref: L-38, which listed the name as "Benjamin Sanderland"]. See "John Wood," q.v.
SUNDERLAND, John. Private, Capt. Frederick Skinner's Co., Calvert County Militia, 1778 [Ref: J-1146, M-150]. Private, Capt. James Patterson's Co., Calvert County Militia, Aug. 10, 1777 [Ref: M-146]. Private, Capt. John Mackall's Co., Calvert County Militia, 15th Bn., June 12, 1778 [Ref: M-146].
SUNDERLAND, Joseph. Private, Capt. John Mackall's Co., Calvert County Militia, 15th Bn., June 12, 1778 [Ref: M-146].
SUNDERLAND, Josiah. Private, Capt. Frederick Skinner's Co., Calvert County Militia, 1778 [Ref: J-1146, M-150]. Private, Capt. James Patterson's Co., Calvert County Militia, Aug. 10, 1777 [Ref: M-146, which listed the name as "Josias Sunderlane"].
SUNDERLAND, Lydia. See "Humphrey Beckett," q.v.
SUNDERLAND, Rezin. Private, Capt. John Mackall's Co., Calvert County Militia, 15th Bn., June 12, 1778 [Ref: M-146].
SUNDERLAND, Thomas. (1) Private, Capt. James Patterson's Co., Calvert County Militia, Aug. 10, 1777 [Ref: M-146, which listed the name as "Thomas Sunderland"]. (2) Private, Capt. James Patterson's Co., Calvert County Militia, Aug. 10, 1777 [Ref: M-146, which listed the name as "Thomas Sunderlane"]. (3) Private, Capt. James Patterson's Co., Calvert County Militia, Aug. 10, 1777 [Ref: M-146, which listed the

name as "Thomas Sunderling"]. Private, Capt. Frederick Skinner's Co., Calvert County Militia, 1778 [Ref: J-1146, M-150]. Private, Capt. John Mackall's Co., Calvert County Militia, 15th Bn., June 12, 1778 [Ref: M-146].

SUTTON, John. Private, St. Mary's County Militia, 1777 [Ref: M-214].

SWALES, Elizabeth. See "Jesse Floyd," q.v.

SWALES, Francis. Private, St. Mary's County Militia, 1777 [Ref: M-211, which listed the name as "Francis Swaits"]. Took the Oath of Allegiance before the Hon. Ignatius Fenwick, Jr. in St. Mary's County in 1778 [Ref: J-1146, K-68].

SWALES, John (1742 - Oct. 30, 1788). Private, 5th Maryland Line, Sep. 28, 1782 to Nov. 15, 1783 [Ref: D-427, D-465, D-501, S-168]. "John Swails" married Eleanor ---- [Ref: Y-661].

SWALES, Robert. Private, St. Mary's County Militia, 1777 [Ref: M-211, which mistakenly listed the name as "Robert Swaits"]. Marine on the State ship *Defence* from Oct. 23, 1777 to Dec. 31, 1777 [Ref: D-660, which listed the name as "Robert Swailes"]. Private, enlisted May 25, 1778, for 9 months, 3rd Maryland Line; discharged in Feb., 1779 [Ref: D-329, S-168]. Took the Oath of Allegiance before the Hon. Ignatius Fenwick, Jr. in St. Mary's County in 1778 [Ref: J-1146, K-68].

SWANN (SWAN), Edward. Private, St. Mary's County Militia, 1777 [Ref: M-212]. Took the Oath of Allegiance before the Hon. Henry Reeder in St. Mary's County in 1778 [Ref: J-1146, K-64]. Ensign, Lower Bn., May 7, 1781 [Ref: M-127, G-426].

SWANN (SWAN), Elkanah. "Elkanah Swan" was a private in St. Mary's County Militia, 1777 [Ref: M-210]. "Alhaner [Alkaner] Swann" died intestate by Aug., 1788 [Ref: SO-126].

SWANN (SWAN), Henry. Ensign, Upper Bn., St. Mary's County Militia, Aug. 26, 1777 [Ref: M-127, M-210, C-346, SM-115]. "Henry Swan" married Ann Dyson on Dec. 29, 1777, St. Mary's County, by Rev. John Stephen, Rector of All Faith's Parish [Ref: I-536].

SWANN (SWAN), Ignatius. Private, St. Mary's County Militia, 1777 [Ref: M-214].

SWANN (SWAN), Jesse. Private, St. Mary's County Militia, 1777 [Ref: M-211].

SWANN (SWAN), Zachariah. Supplied provisions (wheat, mutton, or bacon) to the Army in St. Mary's County in 1780 [Ref: S-168].

SWERINGEN, Joseph. This name appeared twice on the list of those who took the Oath of Allegiance in Calvert County in 1778, one time as "Joseph Sweringen" and another time as "Joseph Sweringer" [Ref: L-38]. Also, "Joseph V. Sweringen" took the Oath of Allegiance in Calvert County in 1778 [Ref: L-38].

SWORD, Ignatius. Took the Oath of Allegiance before the Hon. Bennett Biscoe in St. Mary's County in 1778 [Ref: J-1146, K-63].

SYM, Martha. See "Edward Mattingly," q.v.

TABBS, Abigal Hunter. See "Rev. Moses Tabbs," q.v.
TABBS, Barton (1737 - Oct. 30, 1818). Doctor and Assistant Surgeon to Dr. John Hanson Briscoe (who was the Surgeon to the Seven Maryland Independent Companies in 1776). Surgeon of the 7th Maryland Line, 1777, resigned in 1779, and returned in 1780. After the war he founded a medical school at his home at White Plains and was Surgeon to the St. Mary's County Militia in 1794. Son of "Rev. Moses Tabbs," q.v. [Ref: SM-186, S-33, D-252, D-291]. "There is a tradition that because Dr. Tabbs was renowned for his treatment of quinsy he was called upon to treat Gen. George Washington in his last illness, but failed to arrive at Mt. Vernon prior to the General's death." [Ref: SM-150]. Barton Tabbs married Elizabeth Bond on June 20, 1779, by Rev. Francis Lauder, of Christ Church Parish [Ref: K-35]. He served a long time as Associate Judge of the Courts of the County [Ref: R-463, Y-664]. See "Moses Tabbs," q.v.
TABBS, Elizabeth, George, and Mary. See "Moses Tabbs," q.v.
TABBS, Moses (Reverend). Took the Oath of Allegiance before the Hon. Vernon Hebb in St. Mary's County in 1778 [Ref: J-1146, K-68]. Rev. Moses Tabbs, A. M., officiated at both St. Andrew's and St. George's. Three of his sons served in the Revolution: "Dr. Barton Tabbs," q.v., "Ensign Theophilus Tabbs," q.v., and "Lieut. Moses Tabbs," q.v. [Ref: SM-186]. It should be noted that one source states that Rev. Moses Tabbs, Rector of William & Mary Parish, at Poplar Hill, died in Dec., 1776 [Ref: R-463]. See information under "Moses Tabbs, Jr.," q.v., which states his will was written in 1777. An obvious discrepancy exists unless there were two Rev. Moses Tabbs (?). The Orphans Court of St. Mary's County indicates that Dr. Barton Tabbs appeared in Court in Feb., 1780, with the orphaned children of Rev. Moses Tabbs, to wit: Abigal Hunter Tabbs, George Clarke Tabbs, Elizabeth Tabbs, Thomas Tabbs (above the age of 14 in 1786), and Mary Tabbs [Ref: SO-28, SO-29, SO-93]. Moses Tabbs also had sons "Moses Tabbs, Jr.," "Theophilus Tabbs," and "Dr. Barton Tabbs," q.v.
TABBS, Moses Jr. Second Lieutenant, Flying Camp, St. Mary's County, July 12, 1776, and saw action during the Dunmore invasion and the New York campaign of 1776. He apparently was killed or captured as his name disappears from military records and he is not mentioned in the will of his father, "Rev. Moses Tabbs," q.v., which was written in Nov., 1777 [Ref: D-30, SM-115, SM-148, SM-149].
TABBS, Theophilus. Ensign, 1st Maryland Line, Jan. 26, 1780. Son of the "Rev. Moses Tabbs," q.v. [Ref: SM-187, S-168].
TABBS, Thomas. See "Rev. Moses Tabbs," q.v.
TALBOTT, Benjamin. Private, Capt. Thomas Cleland's Co., Calvert County Militia, 1778 [Ref: J-1146, M-147].
TALBOTT, Daniel. Private, Capt. Thomas Cleland's Co., Calvert County Militia, 1778 [Ref: J-1146, M-147].

TALBOTT, Edward. Private, Capt. Thomas Truman Greenfield's Co., Calvert County Militia, 1778 [Ref: J-1146, M-150].
TALBOTT, John (of Joseph). Private, Capt. Thomas Cleland's Co., Calvert County Militia, 1778 [Ref: J-1146, M-147, which listed the name as "John Talbott, for Jos."].
TALBOTT, Mary. See "William Allnutt," q.v.
TALBOTT, Philip. Private, Capt. Frisby Freeland's Co., Calvert County Militia, 1778 [Ref: J-1146, M-148]. Took the Oath of Allegiance in Calvert County in 1778 [Ref: L-38].
TALBOTT, Richard. Private, Capt. Frisby Freeland's Co., Calvert County Militia, 1778 [Ref: J-1146, M-148]. Took the Oath of Allegiance in Calvert County in 1778 [Ref: L-38].
TALBOTT, Thomas. Private, Capt. Thomas Cleland's Co., Calvert County Militia, 1778 [Ref: J-1146, M-147]. Took the Oath of Allegiance in Calvert County in 1778 [Ref: L-38]. Thomas Talbot and Susanna Rhodes were married on April 15, 1780, by Rev. Francis Lauder, of Christ Church Parish [Ref: K-35].
TANEY, Alice and Augustus. See "Michael Taney," q.v.
TANEY, Charles. (1) Private, St. Mary's County Militia, 1777 [Ref: M-212]. Private, St. Mary's County, drafted on July 27, 1781 [Ref: D-412, D-384, which listed the name as "Charles Tawney"]. Private, Maryland Line, Continental Army, 1781 [Ref: D-412]. (2) Took the Oath of Allegiance in Calvert County in 1778 [Ref: L-38].
TANEY, Dorothy. See "Michael Taney," q.v.
TANEY, John F. Took the Oath of Allegiance before the Hon. Ignatius Fenwick, Jr. in St. Mary's County in 1778 [Ref: J-1146, K-68].
TANEY, Joseph. Private, Capt. Benjamin Bond's Co., Calvert County Militia, 1778 [Ref: J-1146, M-149, which listed the name as "Joseph Tawney"]. Ensign, Feb. 2, 1779 [Ref: M-127, E-290].
TANEY, Michael (1750-1820). Son of Michael Taney and Jane Doyne. At St. Francis Xavier Catholic Church in St. Mary's County on June 25, 1771, Michael married Monica Brooke, daughter of Roger Brooke, and had these children: Michael Taney (moved to Missouri), Roger Brooke Taney (Chief Justice of the U. S. Supreme Court), Augustus Taney (attorney), Octavius C. Taney (physician), Dorothy Taney, Sophia Y. Taney, and Alice Taney. Michael Taney served as First Lieutenant, 15th Bn., in Capt. Thomas Truman Greenfield's Co., Calvert County Militia, April 16, 1778. He was a member of the House of Delegates between 1781 and 1798, and Coroner in 1777 and 1785. He killed John Magruder in a duel on July 15, 1819, and fled to Loudoun County, Virginia, where he died in July, 1820 [Ref: N-86, N-798, N-799, E-37, SC-34, J-1146, M-127, M-128, M-150, which listed the name as "Michael Tawney"]. There was also a Michael Tawney in Frederick County who was a second lieutenant in 1778 [Ref: M-128]. See "Ignatius Fenwick, Jr.," q.v.
TANEY, Octavius C. See "Michael Taney," q.v.

TANEY, Raphael. Private, St. Mary's County Militia, 1777 [Ref: M-211]. Took the Oath of Allegiance before the Hon. Ignatius Fenwick, Jr. in St. Mary's County in 1778 [Ref: J-1146, K-68].
TANEY, Roger Brooke. See "Michael Taney," q.v.
TANEY, Sarah. See "Ignatius Fenwick, Jr.," q.v.
TANEY. Sophia Y. See "Michael Taney," q.v.
TANEY, Thomas (1758 - Nov. 8, 1828). Private, Capt. Benjamin Bond's Co., Calvert County Militia, 1778 [Ref: J-1146, M-149, which listed the name as "Thomas Tawney"]. Took the Oath of Allegiance in Calvert County in 1778 [Ref: L-38]. He died at Drum Cliffs on the Patuxent River [Ref: R-463].
TANNER, Henry. Private, Capt. Walter Smith's Co., Calvert County Militia, 1778 [Ref: J-1146, M-148]. Took the Oath of Allegiance in Calvert County in 1778 [Ref: L-38]. Henry Tanner and Mary Games were married on Dec. 10, 1778, by Rev. Francis Lauder, of Christ Church Parish [Ref: K-34].
TARLTON, Ann. See "James Tarlton," q.v.
TARLTON, Bennett. Second Lieutenant, St. Mary's County Militia, 1776-1777 [Ref: M-215, S-168]. Took the Oath of Allegiance before the Hon. Bennett Biscoe in St. Mary's County in 1778 [Ref: J-1146, K-63]. Property destroyed by the British in 1781 [Ref: S-168].
TARLTON, Ann Sevilla, Cecelia, Chloe, Eleanor, and Eliza. See "Jeremiah Tarlton," q.v.
TARLTON, Elizabeth. See "John Taylor" and "Jeremiah Tarlton," q.v.
TARLTON, George and George W. See "Jeremiah Tarlton," q.v.
TARLTON, James. Private, St. Mary's County Militia, 1777 [Ref: M-214]. Took the Oath of Allegiance before the Hon. Vernon Hebb in St. Mary's County in 1778 [Ref: J-1146, K-68]. One James Tarlton died by June, 1780, leaving orphans John and Ann (both under the age of 14). [Ref: SO-32]. See "Jeremiah Tarlton," q.v.
TARLTON, Jeremiah. Private, St. Mary's County, 2nd Maryland Line, on Jan. 10, 1777, corporal on June 1, 1778, and discharged or transferred to the invalids corps on Jan. 10, 1780 [Ref: S-168, D-169, which latter source listed the name as "Jeremha Tarleton"]. He died on July 6, 1826, and his widow applied for and received pension W603 on March 18, 1839, in Scott County, Kentucky, aged 75, stating that Jeremiah had enlisted at Leonardtown in St. Mary's County, Maryland. They married on Jan. 20, 1782, and had these children: Ann (born Nov. 24, 1782); Elizabeth (born June 25, 1785); James 1st (born Aug. 9, 1788); James 2nd (born Aug. 4, 1789); Chloe (born May 31, 1792); Leo (born Aug. 5, 1794); Cecelia (born in March, 1797); Ann Sevilla (born Aug. 2, 1798 or 1799); George (born Feb. 28, 1801?); Matilda (born Sep. 1, 1804); Lando (born Feb. 20, 1808); and, George W. (born in Feb., 1809). It appears that Eleanor Tarlton died by Sep. 4, 1844, as final payment was made to her estate on Nov. 28, 1845 and paying through the earlier 1844 date.

In 1839 an Eliza A. (or H.) Tarlton was a neighbor of the widow Eleanor Tarlton, but no relationship was stated in the record [Ref: P-3421, X-124].

TARLTON, John. Private, St. Mary's County Militia, 1777 [Ref: M-214]. Took the Oath of Allegiance in St. Mary's County in 1780 [Ref: Q-121, which listed the name as "John Talton"]. See "James Tarlton," q.v.

TARLTON, Joshua. Ensign, Lower Bn., St. Mary's County Militia, Aug. 26, 1777 [Ref: M-127, M-214, C-346, SM-115]. Took the Oath of Allegiance before the Hon. Vernon Hebb in St. Mary's County in 1778 [Ref: J-1146, K-68].

TARLTON, Lando, Leo, and Matilda. See "Jeremiah Tarlton," q.v.

TARLTON, Stephen. Coroner of St. Mary's County on April 21, 1777 [Ref: S-33]. Ensign, Upper Bn., St. Mary's County Militia, Aug. 26, 1777 [Ref: M-127, M-212, C-345, SM-115]. See "Gerard Cheseldine," q.v.

TARLTON, Thomas. Took the Oath of Allegiance before the Hon. Bennett Biscoe in St. Mary's County in 1778 [Ref: J-1146, K-63].

TARLTON, William. Took the Oath of Allegiance before the Hon. Bennett Biscoe in St. Mary's County in 1778 [Ref: J-1146, K-63].

TARR, John. Private, St. Mary's County Militia, 1777 [Ref: M-210].

TAWNEYHILL, James. Private, Capt. Richard Lane's Co., Calvert County Militia, 1778 [Ref: J-1146, M-150]. Took the Oath of Allegiance in Calvert County in 1778 [Ref: L-38, which listed the name as "James Tawnihill"].

TAWNEYHILL, John. Private, Capt. Charles Williamson's Co., Calvert County Militia, 1778 [Ref: J-1146, M-147]. Took the Oath of Allegiance in Calvert County in 1778 [Ref: L-38, which listed the name as "John Tawnihill"].

TAWNEYHILL, Leonard. Private, Capt. Richard Lane's Co., Calvert County Militia, 1778 [Ref: J-1146, M-149]. Took the Oath of Allegiance in Calvert County in 1778 [Ref: L-38, which listed the name as "Leonard Tawnihill"].

TAYLOR, Ann. See "Robert Taylor" and "William Taylor" and "Charles Ramsey" and "Ignatius Taylor" and "Jenifer Taylor," q.v.

TAYLOR, Archibald. Private, St. Mary's County Militia, 1777 [Ref: M-214].

TAYLOR, Austin. Private, St. Mary's County Militia, 1777 [Ref: M-215].

TAYLOR, Brian (Bryan). Took the Oath of Allegiance in Calvert County in 1778 [Ref: L-38]. Private, Capt. Walter Smith's Co., Calvert County Militia, 1778 [Ref: J-1146, M-148]. The Christ Church Register in Calvert County records the birth of a Brian Taylor, son of Everard and Sarah Taylor, on May 11, 1741/2 [Ref: O-28]. "William Brian Taylor" married Barbara Dawkins on May 7, 1772, and their children were: Sarah (born Feb. 24, 1773); William (born April 22, 1774); Everard (born Nov. 10, 1775); and, James Mackall (born Aug. 26, 1778). [Ref: O-29].

TAYLOR, Delah (Dilah). Private, Capt. Thomas Truman Greenfield's Co., Calvert County Militia, 1778 [Ref: J-1146, M-150]. Took the Oath of Allegiance in Calvert County in 1778 [Ref: L-39].
TAYLOR, Dryden Ann. See "Robert Taylor," q.v.
TAYLOR, Elizabeth. See "Jesse Floyd" and "John Wood," q.v.
TAYLOR, Everard. See "Brian Taylor," q.v.
TAYLOR, Francis. See "Ignatius Taylor," q.v.
TAYLOR, George. Private, St. Mary's County Militia, 1777 [Ref: M-214].
TAYLOR, Grace. See "William Taylor," q.v.
TAYLOR, Hannah. See "Ignatius Taylor," q.v.
TAYLOR, Henry. (1) Private, St. Mary's County Militia, 1777 [Ref: M-210]. (2) Private, St. Mary's County Militia, 1777 [Ref: M-215]. Took the Oath of Allegiance before the Hon. Richard Barnes in St. Mary's County in 1778 [Ref: J-1146, K-66].
TAYLOR, Ignatius (Sep. 11, 1742 - Sep. 21, 1807). Eldest son of Ignatius Taylor (1708-1761) and Ann Jenifer, of St. Mary's County. He married twice: first circa 1764 to Ann Wilkinson, widow of Nathaniel Parran; and, second to Barbara Bowie, widow of Thomas Henry Hall, in 1790. He may have married a third time because the Register of St. Andrew's Episcopal Church states that one Ignatius Taylor and Margaret Jordan were married May 13, 1780 [Ref: MB-383]. He had a son Francis (1769, Maryland - 1850, Brown County, Ohio) and although records disagree as to the daughters, it appears he had Ann, Margaret, Hannah, Jane, and Lucretia. Ignatius also had a brother "Jenifer Taylor," q.v. (although another source listed the name as "Juniper") and a sister Ann (who died unmarried in 1775). Ignatius was a captain in the Lower Bn. of St. Mary's County Militia in 1776 and a major on Aug. 26, 1777 [Ref: M-128, C-3346], and he took the Oath of Allegiance before the Hon. Richard Barnes in St. Mary's County in 1778 [Ref: J-1146, K-66]. He had also been elected to a General Committee in St. Mary's County in accordance with the resolves of the Continental Congress in 1775 [Ref: MR-127]. He served as a Justice of St. Mary's County (1773, 1777-1780, 1782), Justice of Washington County (1789, 1791-1795, 1797, 1799-1800), Commissioner of the Tax in St. Mary's County in 1782, and Justice of the Orphans Court in Washington County between 1789 and 1800 (Chief Justice, 1801). In 1787 and 1788 he served in the Lower House of the Maryland Legislature [Ref: N-803, plus data collected by Miss Barbara Marvin, of Washington, D. C. (1987), and the Christopher Johnston Genealogical Collection in the Library of the Maryland Historical Society]. (2) Another Ignatius Taylor was a private in the St. Mary's County Militia in 1777 [Ref: M-210].
TAYLOR, James. This name appeared three times as a private in the St. Mary's County Militia in 1777 [Ref: M-210, M-214, M-215]. One took the Oath of Allegiance before the Hon. Richard Barnes in St. Mary's County

in 1778 [Ref: J-1146, K-66]. One James Taylor died by June, 1800, with Rebecca Taylor as administratrix [Ref: SO-304].

TAYLOR, James Mackall. See "Brian Taylor," q.v.

TAYLOR, Jane. See "Ignatius Taylor," q.v.

TAYLOR, Jenifer. Son of Ignatius Taylor and Ann Jenifer, and brother of "Ignatius Taylor," q.v. Served as the High Sheriff of St. Mary's County from 1770 to 1773 [Ref: S-168, and Christopher Johnston Genealogical Collection in the Library of the Maryland Historical Society]. Elected to serve on a General Committee in St. Mary's County in accordance with the resolves of the Continental Congress in 1775 [Ref: MR-127]. Justice who administered the Oath of Allegiance in St. Mary's County in 1778 [Ref: J-1146, K-64].

TAYLOR, Jeremiah. See "Robert Taylor," q.v.

TAYLOR, John. Private, Capt. Thomas Cleland's Co., Calvert County Militia, 1778 [Ref: J-1146, M-147]. Took the Oath of Allegiance before the Hon. Bennett Biscoe in St. Mary's County in 1778 [Ref: J-1146, K-63]. "John Taylor, of St. Mary's County" was given a bond for good behavior on June 15, 1781 [Ref: V-404]. The Register of St. Andrew's Episcopal Church states that John Taylor and Elizabeth Tarlton were married (by license) May 13, 1783 [Ref: MB-385]. One John Taylor died by April, 1798 [Ref: SO-230]. See "Joseph Taylor" and "William Taylor," q.v.

TAYLOR, John Jr. Private, St. Mary's County Militia, 1777 [Ref: M-214]. See "John Taylor," q.v.

TAYLOR, John Sr. Private, St. Mary's County Militia, 1777 [Ref: M-214]. Took the Oath of Allegiance before the Hon. Richard Barnes in St. Mary's County in 1778 [Ref: J-1146, K-66].

TAYLOR, Joseph. Private, St. Mary's County Militia, 1777 [Ref: M-215]. One Joseph Taylor died by July, 1795, with John Taylor as his administrator [Ref: SO-228, SO-232, SO-244].

TAYLOR, Lucretia and Margaret. See "Ignatius Taylor," q.v.

TAYLOR, Matthias. See "William Taylor," q.v.

TAYLOR, Rebecca. See "James Taylor," q.v.

TAYLOR, Richard. Private, St. Mary's County Militia, 1777 [Ref: M-215]. Took the Oath of Allegiance before the Hon. Robert Armstrong in St. Mary's County in 1778 [Ref: J-1146, K-62]. One Richard Taylor was buried on Aug. 31, 1804 [Ref: R-464].

TAYLOR, Robert. Private, St. Mary's County Militia, 1777 [Ref: M-215]. One Robert Taylor died by Feb., 1789, leaving an orphan son Jeremiah Taylor (above the age of 14). The records stated in Oct., 1792, that Jeremiah also died and his mother Dryden Ann [Ann Dryden?] died before the said Jeremiah [Ref: SO-131, SO-179].

TAYLOR, Sarah. See "Brian Taylor," q.v.

TAYLOR, Statia. See "Edward Abell," q.v.

TAYLOR, Thomas. (1) Took the Oath of Allegiance before the Hon. Jeremiah Jordan in St. Mary's County in 1778 [Ref: J-1146, K-67]. (2) Took the Oath of Allegiance in St. Mary's County in 1780 [Ref: Q-121].
TAYLOR, William. (1) Private, Capt. Henry Skinner's Foot Co. of Hunting Hundred, Calvert County, 1777 [Ref: T-1814, O-125]. (2) Private, St. Mary's County Militia, 1777 [Ref: M-215]. Took the Oath of Allegiance before the Hon. Bennett Biscoe in St. Mary's County in 1778 [Ref: J-1146, K-63]. William Taylor (1753-1822) and wife Lavinia Clarke (1768-1827), of St. Mary's County, Maryland, moved to Lexington County, South Carolina after the war. Their son Matthias Taylor (1788-1860) lived in Calhoun County, South Carolina and died in Barbour County, Alabama [Ref: MC-155]. One William Taylor was elected to a General Committee in St. Mary's County in accordance with the resolves of the Continental Congress in 1775, and served on the Committee of Observation in 1776 [Ref: MR-127, S-16, B-100]. One William Taylor died prior to Jan., 1801, when Richard Watts was the administrator of the estates of Grace Taylor, William Taylor, and John Taylor, all deceased [Ref: SO-313]. One William Taylor died by June, 1782, leaving an orphan daughter Ann [Ref: SO-53]. Also see "Brian Taylor," q.v.
TAYLOR, William Jr. Private, St. Mary's County Militia, 1777 [Ref: M-215].
TAYLOW, Thomas Win. Took the Oath of Allegiance in St. Mary's County in 1780 [Ref: Q-121].
TAYMAN, Joseph. Private, Capt. Richard Lane's Co., Calvert County Militia, 1778 [Ref: J-1146, M-150].
TAYMAN, William. Private, Capt. Richard Lane's Co., Calvert County Militia, 1778 [Ref: J-1146, M-150].
TEAR, James. Private, Capt. Uriah Forrest's Co., Flying Camp, St. Mary's County, July 28, 1776 [Ref: D-30, SM-115].
TENNISON, Jesse. Private, Capt. Uriah Forrest's Co., Flying Camp, St. Mary's County, July 28, 1776 [Ref: D-30, SM-115]. Private, St. Mary's County Militia, 1777 [Ref: M-213]. "Jesse Tennison" took the Oath of Allegiance before the Hon. John Ireland in St. Mary's County in 1778 [Ref: J-1146, K-65], and "Jessey Tennison" took the Oath of Allegiance before the Hon. Bennett Biscoe in St. Mary's County in 1778 [Ref: J-1146, K-63].
TENNISON, John. Private, St. Mary's County Militia, 1777 [Ref: M-210]. Took the Oath of Allegiance before the Hon. John Ireland in St. Mary's County in 1778 [Ref: J-1146, K-65]. One John Tennison died by Aug., 1787, leaving an orphan son "Absalom Tenneson" (above the age of 14). [Ref: SO-114].
TENNISON, Matthew. Took the Oath of Allegiance before the Hon. John Shanks in St. Mary's County in 1778 [Ref: J-1146, K-70]. One Matthew Tennison died testate by March, 1795 [Ref: SO-223].

TENNISON, Samuel. Private, St. Mary's County Militia, 1777 [Ref: M-212]. Took the Oath of Allegiance before the Hon. John Shanks in St. Mary's County in 1778 [Ref: J-1146, K-70]. Ensign, Upper Bn., Nov. 18, 1779 [Ref: M-128, F-18, SM-115]. One Samuel Tennison died intestate by May, 1800 [Ref: SO-141].
TENNISON, William. Private, St. Mary's County Militia, 1777 [Ref: M-212]. Took the Oath of Allegiance before the Hon. John Shanks in St. Mary's County in 1778 [Ref: J-1146, K-70].
THEOBALDS (THEOBALD), James. Took the Oath of Allegiance before the Hon. Bennett Biscoe in St. Mary's County in 1778 [Ref: J-1146, K-63].
THEOBALDS (THEOBALD), Samuel. Took the Oath of Allegiance before the Hon. Robert Armstrong in St. Mary's County in 1778 [Ref: J-1146, K-62]. Paid for making salt in July, 1782 [Ref: S-169].
THOMAS, Ann. See "Philip Thomas," q.v.
THOMAS, Elizabeth. See "Thomas Fenwick," q.v.
THOMAS, George (Esquire). Son of William Thomas (1714-1795) and Elizabeth Reeves, of Chaptico, St. Mary's County. Never married. Served in the Lower House, 1787-1788. He died by Sep., 1789, with William Thomas named as his executor [Ref: N-808, SO-141].
THOMAS, Harbert. Took the Oath of Allegiance before the Hon. Bennett Biscoe in St. Mary's County in 1778 [Ref: J-1146, K-63].
THOMAS, Ignatius. See "Philip Thomas," q.v.
THOMAS, Isabella. See "John Allen Thomas," q.v.
THOMAS, J. W. See "William Thomas," q.v.
THOMAS, James. Private, St. Mary's County, 3rd Maryland Line, enlisted on May 1, 1778, for 3 years [Ref: D-298, D-329]. Ensign, Upper Bn., St. Mary's County Militia, Nov. 18, 1779 [Ref: M-128, F-18]. Captured by the enemy prior to Aug. 9, 1781, and died of wounds in Sep., 1781. However, other sources indicate that Ensign James Thomas, son of "Major William Thomas, Sr.," q.v., was wounded at Long Island and died at home on April 21, 1781. James is buried beside his parents in the "Deep Falls" graveyard near Chaptico in St. Mary's County [Ref: SM-115, V-422, R-465, HG-47, S-130, S-169, S-144, and references cited therein].
THOMAS, John. Private, St. Mary's County Militia, 1777 [Ref: M-215]. See "Philip Thomas" and "William Thomas," q.v.
THOMAS, John Allen (Aug. 17, 1734 - c1796/7). Son of William Thomas and Elizabeth Allen, of Talbot county. Moved to St. Mary's County by 1771. He married twice: (1) Sarah ---- by 1783 (died in 1786), and (2) Isabella ----; and probably had no children who reached adulthood [Ref: N-808, SO-259]. Served in many official capacities: Clerk of the Lower House, 1761-1762; Justice of the Court of Oyer, Terminer, and Gaol Delivery, 1771 (clerk and cryer, 1772); Deputy Commissary, St. Mary's County, 1771-1776; Member of the St. Mary's Committee of Safety and

Correspondence in 1774; Delegate to the Maryland Convention of July 26, 1775, and the Provincial Convention of Sep. 12, 1775 and 1776; Member of the House of Delegates in 1778, 1779 and 1782 [Ref: N-70, N-72, N-80, N-86, N-809]. Captain, 5th Independent Maryland Co., St. Mary's County, on Jan. 2, 1776. At the Battle of Brooklyn on Aug. 27, 1776, he was sent by Gen. George Washington to the relief of the beleaguered "Maryland 400" and served throughout the New York campaign of 1776. Commissioned Major, Upper Bn., Aug. 26, 1777, and Lieutenant Colonel, from Nov. 18, 1779 through at least April 24, 1781 [Ref: D-25, M-128, C-345, C-346, F-18, SM-148, S-169, V-165, V-178, V-301]. Took the Oath of Allegiance before the Hon. Henry Reeder in St. Mary's County in 1778 [Ref: J-1146, K-64]. "John A. Thomas" was elected to a General Committee in St. Mary's County in accordance with the resolves of the Continental Congress in 1775, and "Mr. John A. Thomas" served on the Committee of Correspondence in 1775 [Ref: MR-127].

THOMAS, Leven. Private, St. Mary's County Militia, 1777 [Ref: M-215]. "Levy Thomas" took the Oath of Allegiance before the Hon. Bennett Biscoe in St. Mary's County in 1778 [Ref: J-1146, K-64].

THOMAS, Nathan (1758-1822). Private, Capt. Allen Thomas' Co., St. Mary's County, 1776. He married Margaret ---- in 1782 or 1785 and they had six children (no names were given). In 1818, aged 60, he applied for pension (R10507) in Mason County, Kentucky. In 1821 he was in Fleming County and again stated he was aged 60, his wife was between 40 and 50, and his oldest child was aged 15. He died on July 24, 1822 and his wife died in April, 1841 [Ref: P-3467, MK-144]. There was also a "Nath. Thomas" who was a sergeant in the 3rd Co. of Matrosses, Capt. Furnival's Co. of Artillery, 1777 [Ref: D-572]. "Nathaniel Thomas" took the Oath of Allegiance in Calvert County in 1778 [Ref: L-39].

THOMAS, Philip. Took the Oath of Allegiance before the Hon. Bennett Biscoe in St. Mary's County in 1778 [Ref: J-1146, K-64]. In 1792 Philip Thomas was appointed guardian of his children John, Ann, and Ignatius [Ref: SO-181].

THOMAS, Rachel. See "Tyler Thomas," q.v.

THOMAS, Raphael. Supplied provisions (wheat, mutton, or bacon) to the Army in St. Mary's County in 1780 [Ref: S-77, S-169].

THOMAS, Robert. Private, St. Mary's County Militia, 1777 [Ref: M-214]. Took the Oath of Allegiance before the Hon. Henry Reeder in St. Mary's County in 1778 [Ref: J-1146, K-64].

THOMAS, Susannah. See "John Allen Thomas," q.v.

THOMAS, Thomas. Private, 3rd Maryland Line, 1778-1780 [Ref: D-170, D-171]. The Register of St. Andrew's Episcopal Church states that Thomas Thomas and Jane Abell were married (by license) April 27, 1781 [Ref: MB-384].

THOMAS, Tyler (Tylor). Private, St. Mary's County Militia, 1777 [Ref: M-215]. Took the Oath of Allegiance before the Hon. Robert Armstrong in St. Mary's County in 1778 [Ref: J-1146, K-62]. The Register of St. Andrew's Episcopal Church states that Tyler Thomas and Rachel Thomas were married May 9, 1779 [Ref: MB-382].

THOMAS, William. There were several men named William Thomas and two held the rank of major during the Revolutionary War: (1) 1714-1795. Son of John Thomas, of Charles County. He married Elizabeth Reeves, daughter of Thomas Reeves, of St. Mary's County, and had these children: Major William (of St. Mary's County), Colonel John (of Charles County), George (of St. Mary's County), James (died 1781), and Elizabeth (married William Courts). Major, St. Mary's County Militia, by 1754. Served in Lower House, 1760-1761, 1768-1771, and 1777. Adjutant, 25th Bn., 1776. "Major William Thomas, Sr. died March 25, 1795, a soldier of the Revolution. Elizabeth, wife of Major William Thomas, Sr. died Aug. 15, 1808, aged 94 years." [Ref: N-76, N-814, HG-47]. (2) 1758-1813. Son of "William Thomas," q.v. and Elizabeth Reeves. Private, St. Mary's County Militia, 1777 [Ref: M-214]. Second Lieutenant, Upper Bn., Aug. 26, 1777, First Lieutenant, Nov. 18, 1779, and promoted to Major (no date given). He married Catherine Boarman in 1782 and served in the Lower House, 1791-1797, and Senate, 1804-1813. Major William Thomas, Jr. died Aug. 1, 1813 and is buried in the graveyard at "Deep Falls" in St. Mary's County near Major William Thomas, Sr. [Ref: M-214, M-128, C-346, F-18, N-814, HG-47, S-130, S-169]. (3) Another William Thomas was a private in the St. Mary's County Militia in 1777 [Ref: M-215]. A William Thomas moved to what is now Washington County, Kentucky before 1800 and his son J. W. Thomas died in Marion County in 1827 [Ref: MK-144]. The Register of St. Andrew's Episcopal Church states that a William Thomas and Henrietta Briscoe were married April 14, 1779, and a William Thomas and Anne Allen were married May 2, 1780 [Ref: MB-382]. "Mr. William Thomas" was elected to a General Committee in St. Mary's County in accordance with the resolves of the Continental Congress in 1775 [Ref: MR-126, S-144, and references cited therein]. See "James Thomas" and "John Allen Thomas" and "George Thomas," q.v.

THOMAS, William A. Private, St. Mary's County Militia, 1777 [Ref: M-215]. See "William Thomas," q.v.

THOMAS, Zachariah. Private, St. Mary's County Militia, 1777 [Ref: M-210]. Supplied provisions (wheat, mutton, or bacon) to the Army in Oct., 1780 [Ref: S-169].

THOMPSON, Aaron. Private, St. Mary's County Militia, 1777 [Ref: M-212]. Took the Oath of Allegiance before the Hon. John Shanks in St. Mary's County in 1778 [Ref: J-1146, K-70]. "Aaron Thompson, farmer" moved from St. Clements to Fayette County, Pennsylvania, in 1797 [Ref: X-87].

THOMPSON, Alexander. Took the Oath of Allegiance before the Hon. Henry Tubman in St. Mary's County in 1778 [Ref: J-1146, K-70, which listed the name as "Alexander Thomson"].
THOMPSON, Ann. See "Raphael Thompson" and "William Martin," q.v.
THOMPSON, Arthur. Private, St. Mary's County Militia, 1777 [Ref: M-210]. Took the Oath of Allegiance before the Hon. John Ireland in St. Mary's County in 1778 [Ref: J-1146, K-65]. One Arthur Thompson died intestate by Feb., 1778, with Teresia Thompson as his administratrix [Ref: SO-8].
THOMPSON, Athanasius (Athanatius). Private, St. Mary's County Militia, 1777 [Ref: M-210]. Took the Oath of Allegiance before the Hon. John Ireland in St. Mary's County in 1778 [Ref: J-1146, K-65]. "Athas. Thomson" was a private in the 3rd Maryland Line, enlisted on May 12 or June 13, 1778, for 3 years; corporal, Aug. 14, 1778; sergeant, Jan. 1, 1780; Quartermaster Sergeant, March 1, 1780; discharged Dec. 21, 1781 [Ref: S-170, D-170, D-329, D-298, which sources listed the name as "Athantius Thomson," "Athans Thompson," and "Ignats. or Athanatus Thompson"].
THOMPSON, Basil. This name appeared twice as a private, St. Mary's County Militia, 1777 [Ref: M-210, M-213]. "Bazil Thomson" took the Oath of Allegiance before the Hon. John Reeder in St. Mary's County in 1778 [Ref: J-1146, K-69]. The Register of St. Francis Xavier Catholic Church states that Basil Thompson and Cloe Brown were married March 5, 1780 [Ref: SC-36].
THOMPSON, Benjamin. Private, St. Mary's County Militia, 1777 [Ref: M-215]. Private, St. Mary's County, reported as a "deserter from the Continental Army" in June, 1778 [Ref: D-330, which listed the name as "Benjamin Thomson"]. However, a Benjamin Thompson served in the 2nd Maryland Line from Jan. 10, 1777, until discharged on Jan. 10, 1780 [Ref: D-169]. Also, this or another Benjamin Thompson was a seaman aboard the State ship *Defence* in 1776 [Ref: S-25, D-606]. One Benjamin Thompson died by Dec., 1780, leaving sons Benjamin and Bennett [Ref: SO-38, SO-219, SO-225, SO-226].
THOMPSON, Bennett. See "Benjamin Thompson," q.v.
THOMPSON, Catherine. See "John Hardesty," q.v.
THOMPSON, Charles. Private, 1st Maryland Line, June 5, 1778 to April 5, 1779 [Ref: D-168, which listed his name as "Charles Thomson"]. In Dec., 1816, the Treasurer of Maryland was directed "to pay to Chas. Thompson, of St. Mary's County, late a soldier in the Revolutionary War, quarterly, during his life, the half pay of a private, as an additional compensation to him for those services by which his country has been benefitted." [Ref: I-399]. One Charles Thompson was appointed guardian of his son John in Feb., 1796 [Ref: SO-237]. See "Raphael Thompson," q.v.
THOMPSON, Clarissa. See "Peter Thompson," q.v.

THOMPSON, Daniel B. See "Richard Thompson, of Joseph," q.v.

THOMPSON, Eleanor. See "Luke Mattingly" and "William Howard," q.v.

THOMPSON, Electious (1755 - Dec. 30, 1840). Born in Prince George's County, he lived in St. Mary's County at the time of his enlistment in the Revolutionary War. After the war he moved to Loudoun County, Virginia, and then on to North Carolina and Floyd County, Kentucky and Morgan County, Alabama, where he applied for and received pension S32017 in 1832; wife Martha [Ref: MC-156, P-1681, P-3473, which sources both contain more family information].

THOMPSON, George. Seaman from St. Mary's County who served aboard the State ship *Defence* in 1777 [Ref: S-170].

THOMPSON, Henry. Took the Oath of Allegiance before the Hon. John Shanks in St. Mary's County in 1778 [Ref: J-1146, K-70].

THOMPSON, James. (1) Private, St. Mary's County Militia, 1777 [Ref: M-212]. Took the Oath of Allegiance before the Hon. John Shanks in St. Mary's County in 1778 [Ref: J-1146, K-70]. (2) Private, St. Mary's County Militia, 1777 [Ref: M-210]. Took the Oath of Allegiance before the Hon. Richard Barnes in St. Mary's County in 1778 [Ref: J-1146, K-66]. One James Thompson was buried on Oct. 18, 1801 [Ref: R-467].

THOMPSON, James (of Mark). Private, St. Mary's County Militia, 1777 [Ref: M-210].

THOMPSON, Jarret. See "Thomas Thompson," q.v.

THOMPSON, Jesse. Sergeant, Maryland Line. Applied for and received pension S35097 on May 12, 1818, aged 62, in St. Mary's County. In 1820 he had a wife (aged 60) and 5 children of which the oldest was 35 and the youngest was 22 with families (but no names were given). He was dropped from the pension rolls under the Act of May 1, 1820, but restored on July 29, 1828. The 1835 rolls gave his age as 78 [Ref: U-40, U-54].

THOMPSON, John. Took the Oath of Allegiance before the Hon. Richard Barnes in St. Mary's County in 1778 [Ref: J-1146, K-66]. Supplied provisions (wheat, mutton, or bacon) to the Army in Oct., 1780 [Ref: S-170]. One John Thompson was buried on Feb. 14, 1805 [Ref: R-468]. See "Charles Thompson," q.v.

THOMPSON, John Jr. Private, St. Mary's County Militia, 1777 [Ref: M-214, which listed the name as "John Thomson, Jr."].

THOMPSON, John (of Thomas). Private, St. Mary's County Militia, 1777 [Ref: M-210].

THOMPSON, John B. Private, St. Mary's County Militia, 1777 [Ref: M-211]. Took the Oath of Allegiance before the Hon. Richard Barnes in St. Mary's County in 1778 [Ref: J-1146, K-66]. "John B. Thompson, Sr." and John B. Thompson, Jr." were both privates in the St. Mary's County Militia in 1777 [Ref: M-210].

THOMPSON, John Baptist. Took the Oath of Allegiance before the Hon. Ignatius Fenwick, Jr. in St. Mary's County in 1778 [Ref: J-1146, K-68]. Also see "John B. Thompson," q.v.
THOMPSON, John Barton. See "Raphael Thompson," q.v.
THOMPSON, John Basil. Took the Oath of Allegiance before the Hon. John Ireland in St. Mary's County in 1778 [Ref: J-1146, K-65]. Private, St. Mary's County Militia, 1777 [Ref: M-211].
THOMPSON, John Gerard. Took the Oath of Allegiance before the Hon. Richard Barnes in St. Mary's County in 1778 [Ref: J-1146, K-66].
THOMPSON, Joseph. Took the Oath of Allegiance before the Hon. John Reeder in St. Mary's County in 1778 [Ref: J-1146, K-69, which listed the name as "Joseph Thomson"]. This name appeared twice as a private in the St. Mary's County Militia in 1777 [Ref: M-212, M-213]. One Joseph Thompson died by Feb., 1796 [Ref: SO-237]. See "Richard Thompson, of Joseph," q.v.
THOMPSON, Margaret. See "Richard James Rapier," q.v.
THOMPSON, Mary. See "John Fenwick" and "Joshua Clarke" and "Philip Ford," q.v.
THOMPSON, Oswell. Private, St. Mary's County Militia, 1777 [Ref: M-213].
THOMPSON, Peter. Took the Oath of Allegiance before the Hon. Bennett Biscoe in St. Mary's County in 1778 [Ref: J-1146, K-64]. One Peter Thompson died intestate by May, 1799, with Clarissa Thompson as his administratrix [Ref: SO-286].
THOMPSON, Raphael Sr. Private, St. Mary's County Militia, 1777 [Ref: M-210]. Took the Oath of Allegiance before the Hon. Richard Barnes in St. Mary's County in 1778 [Ref: J-1146, K-66]. "Raphael Thompson, farmer" moved from St. Clements to Breckinridge County, Kentucky, in 1797 [Ref: X-87]. "Raphael Thompson, of Mark" died in St. Mary's County by Dec., 1794, leaving orphans Charles, Ann, and John Barton Thompson [Ref: SO-62].
THOMPSON, Raphael (of Arthur). Private, St. Mary's County Militia, 1777 [Ref: M-210].
THOMPSON, Richard. Private, St. Mary's County Militia, 1777 [Ref: M-212]. Took the Oath of Allegiance before the Hon. Bennett Biscoe in St. Mary's County in 1778 [Ref: J-1146, K-64]. Private, 1st Maryland Line, June 1, 1778 until Oct. 21, 1778, when reported dead [Ref: D-168].
THOMPSON, Richard (of Edward). Took the Oath of Allegiance before the Hon. John Reeder in St. Mary's County in 1778 [Ref: J-1146, K-69, which listed the name as "Richard Thomson, of Edward"].
THOMPSON, Richard (of Joseph). Born in St. Mary's County circa 1766, he went to sea when only 10 years old and afterwards became captain of his own ship. He married Elizabeth Kirk in 1801 and they moved to Kentucky in 1803, settling near Raywick. Their son, Daniel B. Thompson, married Malinda Mattingly [Ref: MK-145].

THOMPSON, Robert. Took the Oath of Allegiance before the Hon. Richard Barnes in St. Mary's County in 1778 [Ref: J-1146, K-66]. Paid for services (unspecified) to the State on April 13, 1782 [Ref: S-170].
THOMPSON, Samuel. Paid for services (unspecified) to the State in St. Mary's County on April 13, 1782 [Ref: S-170].
THOMPSON, Sarah. See "John Lyon," q.v.
THOMPSON, Teresia. See "Arthur Thompson," q.v.
THOMPSON, Thomas. Private, St. Mary's County Militia, 1777 [Ref: M-211]. Three men with this name took the Oath of Allegiance: one before the Hon. Henry Reeder in St. Mary's County in 1778 [Ref: J-1146, K-64], and one before the Hon. Richard Barnes in St. Mary's County in 1778 [Ref: J-1146, K-66], and "Thomas Thompson, Sr." before the Hon. John Ireland in St. Mary's County in 1778 [Ref: J-1146, K-65]. The Register of St. Francis Xavier Catholic Church states that one Thomas Thompson and Henrietta Abell were married on Feb. 23, 1772 [Ref: SC-34]. Another Thomas Thompson and Elizabeth Jones were married on Nov. 2, 1780, by Rev. Francis Lauder, of Christ Church Parish [Ref: K-36]. One Thomas Thompson died by Aug., 1797, leaving orphan sons Thomas and Jarret [Ref: SO-218, SO-263]. See "Joshua Clarke," q.v.
THOMPSON, Thomas (of Thomas). Took the Oath of Allegiance before the Hon. John Ireland in St. Mary's County in 1778 [Ref: J-1146, K-65].
THOMPSON, Wilford. "Willifred Thompson" took the Oath of Allegiance before the Hon. John Ireland in St. Mary's County in 1778 [Ref: J-1146, K-65]. The Register of St. Francis Xavier Catholic Church states that "Wilford Thompson" and Ann Shircliff were married Oct. 11, 1774 [Ref: SC-35].
THOMPSON, William. Private, St. Mary's County Militia, 1777 [Ref: M-212]. Took the Oath of Allegiance before the Hon. John Reeder in St. Mary's County in 1778 [Ref: J-1146, K-69, which listed the name as "William Thomson"]. A William Thompson applied for and received pension S30735 on Oct. 16, 1833, in Nelson County, Kentucky, stating he was born in St. Mary's County (date not given) and lived about 16 miles from Fort Frederick, Maryland, when he enlisted in a Rifle Co. at Hagerstown. He moved to Kentucky about 35 years ago (circa 1798). [Ref: P-3483, W-59, MK-145]. It is interesting to note that there was a William Thompson who was born in St. Mary's County on Feb. 1, 1719, lived most of his life in Frederick County, moved to Baltimore County in 1829 and died there on July 22, 1830, at the very advanced age of 111 years [Ref: R-468].
THORNTON, Jessea (Jerrea?). Private, St. Mary's County Militia, 1777 [Ref: M-213].
THORNTON, Vincent. Private, St. Mary's County Militia, 1777 [Ref: M-212]. Took the Oath of Allegiance before the Hon. Henry Reeder in St. Mary's County in 1778 [Ref: J-1146, K-64]. In Oct., 1795, the Orphans

Court appointed Vincent Thornton as guardian to his son William Thornton (who was under the age of 14). [Ref: SO-231].

THORP, Jonathan. Paid for making salt in St. Mary's County in Aug., 1782 [Ref: S-170].

TILLISKEY, Jacob. Took the Oath of Allegiance in Calvert County in 1778 [Ref: L-39].

TIMMONS, Thomas. (1) Private, St. Mary's County Militia, 1777 [Ref: M-215]. (2) Took the Oath of Allegiance in Calvert County in 1780 [Ref: Q-121].

TIMMS, Joseph. Private, 1st Maryland Line, enlisted on Oct. 25, 1777, and was a corporal when discharged on Sep. 14, 1780 [Ref: D-168].

TIMMS, Robert. Took the Oath of Allegiance before the Hon. Bennett Biscoe in St. Mary's County in 1778 [Ref: J-1146, K-64].

TIPPETT, John. Took the Oath of Allegiance before the Hon. Henry G. Sothoron in St. Mary's County in 1778 [Ref: J-1146, K-69].

TIPPETT, John Jr. Took the Oath of Allegiance before the Hon. Jeremiah Jordan in St. Mary's County in 1778 [Ref: J-1146, K-67].

TIPPETT, Jonathan. Private, St. Mary's County Militia, 1777 [Ref: M-213, which listed the name as "Jonathan Tippit"].

TIPPETT, Notley. Private, St. Mary's County Militia, 1777 [Ref: M-210]. Private, St. Mary's County, enlisted on May 26, 1778, for 9 months [Ref: D-329]. Private, Count Pulaski's Legion, enlisted in July, 1779, while serving in the 1st Maryland Line in Charleston, South Carolina [Ref: D-168, D-593]. Discharged on Nov. 1, 1780, re-enlisted, and served to the end of the war on Nov. 15, 1783 [Ref: S-170]. "Notley Lippet" married Ann Wood on Dec. 2, 1783 (banns published), St. Mary's County, by Rev. John Stephen, Rector of All Faith's Parish [Ref: I-536].

TIPPETT, Peter. Private, 3rd Maryland Line, 1777-1780 [Ref: D-170, which listed the name as "Peter Tippits"].

TIPPETT, Philip. Took the Oath of Allegiance in St. Mary's County in 1780 [Ref: Q-122].

TIPPETT, Zachariah. Took the Oath of Allegiance before the Hon. Henry G. Sothoron in St. Mary's County in 1778 [Ref: J-1146, K-69].

TOLLE, Joseph. See "Leonard Bean," q.v.

TOMPKINS, John. Private, St. Mary's County Militia, 1777 [Ref: M-210]. Took the Oath of Allegiance before the Hon. Henry Reeder in St. Mary's County in 1778 [Ref: J-1146, K-64, which listed the name as "John Thomkins"]. The Register of St. Inigoes Catholic Church states that "John Tomkins" and Mary Brewer were married Jan. 21, 1768 [Ref: Sc-33].

TOON, Bennit. Private, St. Mary's County Militia, 1777 [Ref: M-210].

TOON, Henry. Private, Maryland Line, 1779. Migrated to Owen County, Kentucky, probably from St. Mary's County. Henry applied for and received pension S14711 on April 1, 1833 [Ref: MK-145, P-3517, but he is not listed in the *Archives of Maryland, Volume 18*].

TOON, John Baptist. Private, St. Mary's County Militia, 1777 [Ref: M-213, which listed the name as "Jno. Bapts. Toon"].

TOPPIN, Francis. Took the Oath of Allegiance in Calvert County in 1778 [Ref: L-39].

TOPPIN, Peter. Private, 4th Maryland Line, 1777-1780 [Ref: D-171, which listed the name as "Peter Topping"].

TRAGASSKISS (TREGASHES)), Jacob. "Jacob Tregashes" was an Armourer on the State ship *Defence* in 1777. "Jacob Tragasskiss" was a private, St. Mary's County, 3rd Maryland Line, Capt. Armstrong's Co., from 1778 until reported missing at the Battle of Camden in South Carolina on Aug. 16, 1780 [Ref: D-170, D-298].

TRAIL (TRALE), Leonard. Took the Oath of Allegiance before the Hon. Henry G. Sothoron in St. Mary's County in 1778 [Ref: J-1146, K-69].

TRASH, Henry. Took the Oath of Allegiance in St. Mary's County in 1780 [Ref: Q-122].

TROTT, John. Private, Capt. Henry Skinner's Foot Co. of Hunting Hundred, Calvert County, 1777 [Ref: T-1814, O-125].

TROTT, Samuel. Private, Capt. James Grahame's Co., Calvert County Militia, 1778 [Ref: J-1146, M-148].

TROTT, Samuel (of James). Took the Oath of Allegiance in Calvert County in 1778 [Ref: L-37, which mistakenly listed the name as "Samuel Trottson James"].

TROTT, Samuel (of Thomas). Private, Capt. James Grahame's Co., Calvert County Militia, 1778 [Ref: J-1146, M-149]. Took the Oath of Allegiance in Calvert County in 1778 [Ref: L-39, which mistakenly listed the name as "Samuel Trottson of Thomas"].

TROTT, Thomas. Took the Oath of Allegiance in Calvert County in 1778 [Ref: L-39, which listed the name as "Thomas Trottson"].

TROTT, William. Ordinary Sailor on the State ship *Defence* in 1777; probably from Calvert County or St. Mary's County [Ref: D-660].

TRUE, John. Took the Oath of Allegiance before the Hon. Henry Tubman in St. Mary's County in 1778 [Ref: J-1146, K-70].

TRUE, John Bladen. Private, St. Mary's County Militia, 1777 [Ref: M-209].

TRUMAN, Anne or Anna. See "James Somerville," q.v.

TRUMAN, Edward. Private, Capt. Benjamin Bond's Co., Calvert County Militia, 1778 [Ref: J-1146, M-149]. Took the Oath of Allegiance in Calvert County in 1778 [Ref: L-39, which listed the name as "Edward Trueman"].

TRUMAN, John. Private, St. Mary's County Militia, 1777 [Ref: M-214]. Private, St. Mary's County, enlisted on April 30, 1778 [Ref: D-329]. Sergeant, Capt. George Armstrong's Co., 3rd Maryland Line, Dec. 12, 1778; Ensign, 3rd Maryland Line, Jan. 26, 1780; and First Lieutenant, 1st Maryland Line, July, 1781. Maimed and disabled at the Battle of Camden, South Carolina, in March, 1781, and taken prisoner. When released in 1783, he retired from service and received half pay of a lieutenant, which was renewed in 1784 and 1790 [Ref: SM-149, D-170, D-298, D-363, D-478, D-627, H-521, S-170]. "Lieut. John Truman of the Maryland Line was captured in the second action of Camden on April 25, 1781 after having been dangerously wounded and he remained a prisoner until May 1, 1783, during which interval he suffered extremely from his wounds and the want of proper relief, which his present appearance and situation still indicates, and requires attention so far as may be necessary for the attainment of a speedy settlement and payment of what may be due him as pledged by Congress and the State of Maryland to disabled soldiers. Signed: William Smallwood, late Major General, United States Army, Dec. 28, 1783." [Ref: Pension Record S153, Maryland State Archives, Annapolis, Maryland]

TRUMAN, Kenzey Jr. Took the Oath of Allegiance in Calvert County in 1778 [Ref: L-39].

TRUMAN, Margaret. See "John DeButts," q.v.

TUBMAN, Henry. Elected to serve on a General Committee in St. Mary's County in accordance with the resolves of the Continental Congress in 1775, and on the Committee of Observation in 1776 [Ref: MR-127, S-16, B-100]. He was a Justice who administered the Oath of Allegiance in St. Mary's County in 1778 [Ref: J-1146, K-70]. Judge of Elections, 1776. Justice of the Peace, 1777-1778 [Ref: S-170].

TUCKER, Benjamin. Private, Capt. Benjamin Bond's Co., Calvert County Militia, 1778 [Ref: J-1146, M-149]. Took the Oath of Allegiance in Calvert County in 1778 [Ref: L-39].

TUCKER, James. See "John Tucker," q.v.

TUCKER, John. There were several men with this name: (1) Private, Capt. Frisby Freeland's Co., Calvert County Militia, 1778 [Ref: J-1146, M-148]. (2) Private, Capt. Benjamin Bond's Co., Calvert County Militia, 1778 [Ref: J-1146, M-149]. (3) Private, Calvert County, enlisted by Capt. John Brooke on July 25, 1776 [Ref: D-33]. (4) Private, Capt. Edward Wood's Co., Calvert County Militia, 1778 [Ref: J-1146, M-147]. (5) Private, Capt. Henry Skinner's Foot Co. of Hunting Hundred, Calvert County, 1777 [Ref: T-1814, O-125]. (6) Took the Oath of Allegiance in Calvert County in 1778 [Ref: L-39]. The Christ Church Register in Calvert County records the birth of John Tucker, son of James and Sarah Tucker, on July 17, 1735 [Ref: O-29]. One John Tucker and Rebecca Williams were married on July 27, 1780, by Rev. Francis Lauder, of Christ Church Parish [Ref: K-35].

TUCKER, John Jr. Took the Oath of Allegiance in Calvert County in 1778 [Ref: L-39].

TUCKER, John (of William). Took the Oath of Allegiance in Calvert County in 1778 [Ref: L-39].

TUCKER, Joseph. (1) Private, Capt. Henry Skinner's Foot Co. of Hunting Hundred, Calvert County, 1777 [Ref: T-1814, O-125]. (2) Took the Oath of Allegiance before the Hon. Bennett Biscoe in St. Mary's County in 1778 [Ref: J-1146, K-63, which source mistakenly listed the name as "Joseph Tewkes"].

TUCKER, Mitchel. Private, Capt. Henry Skinner's Foot Co. of Hunting Hundred, Calvert County, 1777 [Ref: T-1814, O-125].

TUCKER, Sarah. See "John Tucker," q.v.

TUCKER, Thomas. Private, Capt. Frisby Freeland's Co., Calvert County Militia, 1778 [Ref: J-1146, M-148]. Born on Oct. 14, 1750 and lived in Calvert County during the war, after which he moved to Stokes County, North Carolina for about 14 years. He next lived in Morgan County, Georgia for 2 years and then moved to Warren County, Tennessee, where he applied for and received pension S3835 in 1833 [Ref: MC-159, P-3551]. One Thomas Tucker was a private in the 3rd Maryland Line who enlisted on Sep. 2, 1778, was transferred to the invalids corps, and reported "deserted" on Feb. 11, 1780 [Ref: D-170].

TUCKER, Thomas (of Derrimple). Private, Capt. Benjamin Bond's Co., Calvert County Militia, 1778 [Ref: J-1146, M-149, which listed the name as "Thomas Tucker, for Derrimple"]. See "Thomas Tucker," q.v.

TUCKER, Thomas (of John). Private, Capt. Benjamin Bond's Co., Calvert County Militia, 1778 [Ref: J-1146, M-149, which listed the name as "Thomas Tucker, for John"]. "Thomas Tucker, of John" took the Oath of Allegiance in Calvert County in 1778 [Ref: L-39]. See "Thomas Tucker," q.v.

TUCKER, Thomas III. Took the Oath of Allegiance in Calvert County in 1778 [Ref: L-39].

TUCKER, William. Took the Oath of Allegiance in Calvert County in 1778 [Ref: L-39].

TURBERVILLE, George. See "William Fitzhugh," q.v.

TURNER, Abraham. Took the Oath of Allegiance in Calvert County in 1778 [Ref: L-39].

TURNER, Abraham (of William). Took the Oath of Allegiance in Calvert County in 1778 [Ref: L-39].

TURNER, Alexander. Private, Capt. Richard Lane's Co., Calvert County Militia, 1778 [Ref: J-1146, M-150]. Took the Oath of Allegiance in Calvert County in 1778 [Ref: L-39].

TURNER, Ann. See "James Marquess," q.v.

TURNER, Charles (1745-1796). Son of Edward and Susanna Turner. He married Mary ---- [Ref: S-144]. Private, 5th Independent Co., St. Mary's County, 1776 [Ref: SM-115]. Took the Oath of Allegiance before the Hon. Jeremiah Jordan in St. Mary's County in 1778 [Ref: J-1146, K-67]. In April, 1800, his orphaned children were listed as Mary, Harriot, Samuel, Joseph, and Jesse [Ref: SO-298, SO-302].

TURNER, Edward. See "Charles Turner" and James Carpenter," q.v.

TURNER, Elizabeth. See "Seneca Cheseldine" and "John Gray," q.v.

TURNER, Esther. See "Norman Burroughs," q.v.

TURNER, Harriot and Jesse. See "Charles Turner," q.v.
TURNER, John. (1) First Lieutenant, Capt. Walter Smith's Co., Calvert County Militia, April 10, 1776 through April 10, 1778 [Ref: J-1146, M-131, M-148, A-320, E-37]. Took the Oath of Allegiance in Calvert County in 1778 [Ref: L-39]. (2) Private, St. Mary's County Militia, 1777 [Ref: M-212]. Private, Capt. Charles Williamson's Co., Calvert County Militia, 1778 [Ref: J-1146, M-147]. (3) Private, St. Mary's County, enlisted on May 23, 1778, for 9 months, and served in the 3rd Maryland Line; re-enlisted on Jan. 15, 1779 [Ref: D-170, D-329]. Took the Oath of Allegiance before the Hon. John Shanks in St. Mary's County in 1778 [Ref: J-1146, K-70].
TURNER, Joseph. Private, St. Mary's County Militia, 1777 [Ref: M-210]. See "Charles Turner," q.v.
TURNER, Joshua. Private, St. Mary's County Militia, 1777 [Ref: M-212]. Took the Oath of Allegiance before the Hon. John Shanks in St. Mary's County in 1778 [Ref: J-1146, K-70].
TURNER, Lydia. See "Samuel Maddox," q.v.
TURNER, Richard. (1) Private, Capt. Thomas Cleland's Co., Calvert County Militia, 1778 [Ref: J-1146, M-147]. (2) Private, Capt. Charles Williamson's Co., Calvert County Militia, 1778 [Ref: J-1146, M-148]. One took the Oath of Allegiance in Calvert County in 1778 [Ref: L-39]. (2) Sergeant, St. Mary's County, 3rd Maryland Line, Capt. Armstrong's Co., 1778-1780 [Ref: D-298].
TURNER, Samuel. See "Charles Turner," q.v.
TURNER, Susannah. See "James Carpenter" and "Charles Turner," q.v.
TURNER, Thomas. Private, Capt. Henry Skinner's Foot Co. of Hunting Hundred, Calvert County, 1777 [Ref: T-1814, O-125].
TURNER, William. Private, Capt. Charles Williamson's Co., Calvert County Militia, 1778 [Ref: J-1146, M-147]. Took the Oath of Allegiance in Calvert County in 1778 [Ref: L-39].
TURNER, William Jr. Private, Capt. James Grahame's Co., Calvert County Militia, 1778 [Ref: J-1146, M-148]. Took the Oath of Allegiance in Calvert County in 1778 [Ref: L-39].
TURNER, William Sr. Took the Oath of Allegiance in Calvert County in 1778 [Ref: L-39].
TURNER, William (of Abraham). Took the Oath of Allegiance in Calvert County in 1778 [Ref: L-39].
TURNER, Zachariah. Private, Capt. Richard Lane's Co., Calvert County Militia, 1778 [Ref: J-1146, M-150]. Took the Oath of Allegiance in Calvert County in 1778 [Ref: L-39].
TURTLE, Robert. See "Robert Purdle (Purtle)," q.v.
TYLER, Robert. Private, Capt. Charles Williamson's Co., Calvert County Militia, 1778 [Ref: J-1146, M-147].

TYSOR (TYCER), Robert Clarke. Private, St. Mary's County Militia, 1777 [Ref: M-212]. Took the Oath of Allegiance in St. Mary's County in 1780 [Ref: Q-122].

TYSOR (TYCER), William. Private, St. Mary's County Militia, 1777 [Ref: M-209]. Took the Oath of Allegiance in St. Mary's County in 1780 [Ref: Q-122].

ULDRA, Araminta. See "Timothy Keech," q.v.

URQUHART, Peter. Elected to serve on a General Committee in St. Mary's County in accordance with the resolves of the Continental Congress in 1775 [Ref: MR-127]. Took the Oath of Allegiance before the Hon. Robert Watts in St. Mary's County in 1778 [Ref: J-1146, K-62]. "Peter Urquaant" died testate by Aug., 1790 [Ref: SO-156].

UZZEL, Thomas. Took the Oath of Allegiance before the Hon. Robert Watts in St. Mary's County in 1778 [Ref: J-1146, K-62].

VANSWERINGEN, Joseph Jr. Private, Capt. Walter Smith's Co., Calvert County Militia, 1778 [Ref: J-1146, M-148]. The Christ Church Register in Calvert County records the birth of Joseph Vansweringgin *[sic]*, son of Joseph Vansweringgin and Eleanor Byrn, on Jan. 11, 1759 [Ref: O-29].

VAUGHAN, Thomas. Took the Oath of Allegiance before the Hon. Robert Armstrong in St. Mary's County in 1778 [Ref: J-1146, K-62].

VAUGHAN, William. Took the Oath of Allegiance in Calvert County in 1778 [Ref: L-39].

VEMERE, Catherine. See "Thomas Reeder," q.v.

VEMERE, John. Private, St. Mary's County Militia, 1777 [Ref: M-213, which listed the name as "John Virmier"]. Took the Oath of Allegiance before the Hon. John Reeder in St. Mary's County in 1778 [Ref: J-1146, K-69, which listed the name as "John Vyrmier"].

VENNUMS, Nathan. Took the Oath of Allegiance in Calvert County in 1778 [Ref: L-39].

VERMILLION, James. See "Jesse Vermillion," q.v.

VERMILLION, Jesse (Oct. 25, 1753 - Nov. 2, 1840). Born in Calvert County, he lived in Caswell County, North Carolina at the time of his enlistment in the Revolutionary War. He had married Mary ---- (born March 20, 1766) on Oct. 23, 1783, in the part of Washington County that later became Russell County, Virginia. Their children were: Nancy (born July 28, 1784), Rebecca (born Dec. 28, 1785), James (born Sep. 13, 1787), Wilson (born Nov. 5, 1789), William (born April 30, 1792), Jesse (born May 2, 1795), and Mary (born Dec. 25, 1801). Jesse died in 1840 and his widow applied for and received pension W6362 on Aug. 6, 1844, in Virginia [Ref: MC-163, P-3614, P-3621].

VERMILLION, Mary, Nancy, and Rebecca. See "Jesse Vermillion," q.v.

VERMILLION, Saul. Private, 1st Maryland Line, Dec. 10, 1776 to March 12, 1777 [Ref: D-172].

VERMILLION, William and Wilson. See "Jesse Vermillion," q.v.

VESSELS, Elijah. Private, St. Mary's County Militia, 1777 [Ref: M-215, which listed the name as "Eliger Vessels"]. The Register of St. Andrew's Episcopal Church states that Elijah Vessels and Ann Charam were married (by license) Jan. 5, 1784 [Ref: MB-385].
VESSELS, Ephraim. Private, St. Mary's County Militia, 1777 [Ref: M-213].
VESSELS, James. Private, St. Mary's County Militia, 1777 [Ref: M-212].
VINEYARD, James. Express rider from St. Mary's County to the House of Delegates in 1778 [Ref: V-151]. See "Athanasius Ford," q.v.
VIRMIER, John. See "John Vemere," q.v.
VOWLES, Cyrus. Elected to serve on a General Committee in St. Mary's County in accordance with the resolves of the Continental Congress in 1775 [Ref: MR-127]. Private, St. Mary's County Militia, 1777 [Ref: M-210]. One Cyrus Vowles died testate by Aug., 1785, with Victoria Vowles and John Vowles as his executors [Ref: SO-80].
VOWLES, John. Private, St. Mary's County Militia, 1777 [Ref: M-212, which listed the name as "John Vowls"]. See "Cyrus Vowles," q.v.
VOWLES, Victoria. See "Cyrus Vowles," q.v.
WAINWRIGHT, Elizabeth. See "Elias Barber," q.v.
WAINWRIGHT, Richard. Private, St. Mary's County Militia, 1777 [Ref: M-211].
WAKELIN, Enoch. See "Thomas Wakelin," q.v.
WAKELIN, John. Private, St. Mary's County Militia, 1777 [Ref: M-213]. Took the Oath of Allegiance before the Hon. Henry G. Sothoron in St. Mary's County in 1778 [Ref: J-1146, K-69].
WAKELIN, Thomas. Private, St. Mary's County Militia, 1777 [Ref: M-213]. Took the Oath of Allegiance in St. Mary's County in 1780 [Ref: Q-122, which listed the name as "Thomas Wacklin"]. "Thomas Wakelen" died intestate by Oct., 1794, with "Enoch Wakelen" as his administrator [Ref: SO-216].
WAKELIN, William. Private, St. Mary's County Militia, 1777 [Ref: M-213, S-170, which latter source listed the name "William Wakely"].
WALKER, Elizabeth. See "Henry Phillips," q.v.
WALKER, Henry. Took the Oath of Allegiance before the Hon. John Ireland in St. Mary's County in 1778 [Ref: J-1146, K-65].
WALKER, James. (1) Private, St. Mary's County Militia, 1777 [Ref: M-213]. Took the Oath of Allegiance before the Hon. John Reeder in St. Mary's County in 1778 [Ref: J-1146, K-69]. (2) Private, Capt. Richard Parran's Co., Calvert County Militia, 1778 [Ref: J-1146, M-149].
WALKER, Joseph. Private, St. Mary's County Militia, 1777 [Ref: M-213]. Took the Oath of Allegiance before the Hon. John Reeder in St. Mary's County in 1778 [Ref: J-1146, K-69].
WALKER, Joseph (of Thomas). Took the Oath of Allegiance before the Hon. John Ireland in St. Mary's County in 1778 [Ref: J-1146, K-65].

WALKER, Roger. Private, St. Mary's County Militia, 1777 [Ref: M-211]. Took the Oath of Allegiance in St. Mary's County in 1780 [Ref: Q-122].
WALKER, Stephen. Private, St. Mary's County Militia, 1777 [Ref: M-213].
WALKER, William. Private, St. Mary's County Militia, 1777 [Ref: M-211]. Took the Oath of Allegiance in St. Mary's County in 1780 [Ref: Q-122].
WALLS, George. Private, Maryland Line, 1781 [Ref: D-412].
WALLS, Thomas. Took the Oath of Allegiance before the Hon. Richard Barnes in St. Mary's County in 1778 [Ref: J-1146, K-66].
WALTER, William. Private, St. Mary's County Militia, 1777 [Ref: M-210].
WALTERS, Joseph. Took the Oath of Allegiance before the Hon. John Reeder in St. Mary's County in 1778 [Ref: J-1146, K-69].
WALTON, James, Rev. S. J. (1715, England - Feb. 19, 1803, MD). Catholic Priest who took the Oath of Allegiance before the Hon. John Shanks in St. Mary's County in 1778 [Ref: J-1146, K-70, SM-185]. He was robbed by the British on April 24, 1781 [Ref: S-170]. He served in St. Mary's County for 36 years, 8 months, and 17 days, and is buried in St. Inigoes Cemetery [Ref: R-473, HG-28].
WALTON, William. Second Lieutenant, Upper Bn., St. Mary's County Militia, Aug. 26, 1777 [Ref: SM-115].
WARD, Benjamin. Private, Capt. Frederick Skinner's Co., Calvert County Militia, 1778 [Ref: J-1146, M-150].
WARD, Hannah. See "Jesse Wood," q.v.
WARD, James. (1) Private, Capt. Frederick Skinner's Co., Calvert County Militia, 1778 [Ref: J-1146, M-150]. (2) Private, Capt. Richard Parran's Co., Calvert County Militia, 1778 [Ref: J-1146, M-149]. One James Ward took the Oath of Allegiance in Calvert County in 1780 [Ref: Q-122]. There was also a James Ward who was buried in St. Mary's County on July 11, 1802 [Ref: R-473].
WARD, Richard. Took the Oath of Allegiance in Calvert County in 1778 [Ref: L-39].
WARD, Richard Jr. Private, Capt. Frederick Skinner's Co., Calvert County Militia, 1778 [Ref: J-1146, M-150].
WARE, Benjamin. Private, Capt. John Mackall's Co., Calvert County Militia, 15th Bn., June 12, 1778 [Ref: M-146].
WARE, James. Private, Capt. John Mackall's Co., Calvert County Militia, 15th Bn., June 12, 1778 [Ref: M-146].
WARNER, Hugh. Private, Capt. James Grahame's Co., Calvert County Militia, 1778 [Ref: J-1146, M-149].
WARREN, Edward. Private, St. Mary's County Militia, 1777 [Ref: M-214]. Took the Oath of Allegiance in St. Mary's County in 1780 [Ref: Q-122].
WARREN, William. Private, St. Mary's County Militia, 1777 [Ref: M-214].
WASH, Daniel. Took the Oath of Allegiance in Calvert County in 1778 [Ref: L-39]. Private, Capt. Richard Lane's Co., Calvert County Militia, 1778 [Ref: J-1146, M-150].

WATERS, Joseph. Private, St. Mary's County Militia, 1777 [Ref: M-213].
WATHEN, Edward. Private, St. Mary's County Militia, 1777 [Ref: M-213]. Took the Oath of Allegiance in St. Mary's County in 1780 [Ref: Q-122]. Edward Wathen, Henry H. Wathen, and John Wathen lived on Rolling Fork in Nelson County, Kentucky, prior to 1800 [Ref: MK-151].
WATHEN (WATKIN?), Francis. Private, Capt. Uriah Forrest's Co., Flying Camp, St. Mary's County, July 28, 1776 [Ref: D-30, SM-116]. One "Francis Hudson Wathen" was administrator of the estate of his father Henry Hudson Wathen in St. Mary's County in 1791. Francis Hudson Wathen died by March, 1793 [Ref: SO-168, SO-171, SO-190].
WATHEN, Henry H. See "Edward Wathen" and "Francis Wathen," q.v.
WATHEN (WATKIN?), Ignatius. Private, Capt. Uriah Forrest's Co., Flying Camp, St. Mary's County, July 28, 1776 [Ref: D-30, SM-116, which latter source mistakenly listed the name as "Kgn. Wathen"].
WATHEN, James. Private, St. Mary's County Militia, 1777 [Ref: M-212].
WATHEN, James Warren. Private, St. Mary's County Militia, 1777 [Ref: M-213].
WATHEN, John. Private, St. Mary's County Militia, 1777 [Ref: M-213]. See "Edward Wathen," q.v.
WATHEN (WATKIN?), John C. Private, Capt. Uriah Forrest's Co., Flying Camp, St. Mary's County, July 28, 1776 [Ref: D-30, SM-116].
WATHEN, Joseph. Private, St. Mary's County Militia, 1777 [Ref: M-213].
WATHEN, Leonard. Private, St. Mary's County Militia, 1777 [Ref: M-212].
WATHEN, Richard. Private, St. Mary's County Militia, 1777 [Ref: M-210]. The Register of St. Francis Xavier Catholic Church states that "Richard Wathan, widower" and Eleanor Mattingly were married Sep. 28, 1773 [Ref: SC-35].
WATKINS, John. Took the Oath of Allegiance before the Hon. John Ireland in St. Mary's County in 1778 [Ref: J-1146, K-65].
WATKINS, Nicholas. Corporal, St. Mary's County, 1st Maryland Line, enlisted on Dec. 10, 1776, and discharged on Dec. 27, 1779 [Ref: S-170].
WATSON, Azariah. Private, St. Mary's County Militia, 1777 [Ref: M-210, which listed the name as "Azariah Wattson"].
WATSON, David. Private, Capt. Richard Lane's Co., Calvert County Militia, 1778 [Ref: J-1146, M-150].
WATSON, Edward. Private, St. Mary's County Militia, 1777 [Ref: M-215]. The Register of St. Andrew's Episcopal Church states that Edward Watson and Anne Sanner were married Nov. 26, 1779 [Ref: MB-383].
WATSON, George. Private, Capt. Frisby Freeland's Co., Calvert County Militia, 1778 [Ref: J-1146, M-148]. Took the Oath of Allegiance in Calvert County in 1778 [Ref: L-39].
WATSON, Henry. (1) Private, Capt. Frederick Skinner's Co., Calvert County Militia, 1778 [Ref: J-1146, M-150]. (2) Private, Capt. Thomas Cleland's Co., Calvert County Militia, 1778 [Ref: J-1146, M-147]. (3)

Private, Capt. James Patterson's Co., Calvert County Militia, Aug. 10, 1777 [Ref: M-146, which listed the name as "Henry Wattson"].

WATSON, Henry Jr. Took the Oath of Allegiance in Calvert County in 1778 [Ref: L-39].

WATSON, James Jr. Private, St. Mary's County Militia, 1777 [Ref: M-210, which listed the name as "James Wattson, Jr."].

WATSON, John. Private, Capt. Richard Lane's Co., Calvert County Militia, 1778 [Ref: J-1146, M-150]. Took the Oath of Allegiance in Calvert County in 1778 [Ref: L-39].

WATSON, John Jr. Private, St. Mary's County Militia, 1777 [Ref: M-210, which listed the name as "John Wattson, Jr."].

WATSON, Walter Sr. Took the Oath of Allegiance in Calvert County in 1778 [Ref: L-39].

WATSON, William. Private, Capt. James Patterson's Co., Calvert County Militia, Aug. 10, 1777 [Ref: M-146]. Private, Capt. John Mackall's Co., Calvert County Militia, 15th Bn., June 12, 1778 [Ref: M-146]. Took the Oath of Allegiance in Calvert County in 1778 [Ref: L-39].

WATTS, Alexander. Private, St. Mary's County Militia, 1777 [Ref: M-214].

WATTS, Alexander Hawkins. First Lieutenant, Lower Bn., St. Mary's County Militia, Aug. 26, 1777; Captain, 21st Bn., from April 16, 1778 through May 7, 1781 [Ref: M-134, C-346, E-37, G-426, S-170].

WATTS, Alexander Smith Thomas. "Alexander S. T. Watts" took the Oath of Allegiance before the Hon. Robert Watts in St. Mary's County in 1778 [Ref: J-1146, K-62]. "Alexander Smith Thomas Watts" died testate by March, 1791, with Sarah Watts as his executrix (and she had been appointed guardian to her daughter Sarah Smith Watts in Aug., 1786). [Ref: SO-102, SO-164].

WATTS, Catharine. See "Henry King," q.v.

WATTS, Doctor. See "William Fitzhugh," q.v.

WATTS, Edward. See "William Watts," q.v.

WATTS, Henry. Private, St. Mary's County Militia, 1777 [Ref: M-214]. The Register of St. Andrew's Episcopal Church states that Henry Watts and Susannah Watts were married (by license) April 7, 1785 [Ref: MB-386].

WATTS, John. See "William Watts," q.v.

WATTS, Kenelm Bolt. Private, St. Mary's County Militia, 1777 [Ref: M-212, which listed the name as "Kenelon B. Watts"]. Took the Oath of Allegiance before the Hon. Robert Watts in St. Mary's County in 1778 [Ref: J-1146, K-62]. Paid for making salt in June, 1782 [Ref: S-170].

WATTS, Richard. Private, 4th Maryland Line, Jan. 3, 1776; 1st Maryland Line, Dec. 10, 1777; and, 3rd Maryland Line, 1778. Property destroyed by the British in St. Mary's County in 1781 [Ref: D-11, D-173, D-291, S-170]. See "William Taylor," q.v.

WATTS, Robert. Elected to serve on a General Committee in St. Mary's County in accordance with the resolves of the Continental Congress, 1774-1775 [Ref: MR-127]. Justice who administered the Oath of Allegiance in St. Mary's County in 1778 [Ref: J-1146, K-62]. Justice of the Peace, 1777-1782 [Ref: S-170].

WATTS, Sarah. Loaned money in St. Mary's County for the war effort in 1781 [Ref: SM-187]. Property destroyed by the British in 1781 [Ref: S-170].

WATTS, Susannah. See "Henry Watts," q.v.

WATTS, Thomas. Private, St. Mary's County Militia, 1777 [Ref: M-214]. Two men with this name took the Oath of Allegiance in 1778: one before the Hon. Robert Watts and one before the Hon. Bennett Biscoe [Ref: J-1146, K-62, K-64].

WATTS, William. (1) Private, Capt. Benjamin Bond's Co., Calvert County Militia, 1778 [Ref: J-1146, M-149]. Took the Oath of Allegiance in Calvert County in 1778 [Ref: L-39]. (2) Elected to serve on a General Committee in St. Mary's County in accordance with the resolves of the Continental Congress, 1774-1775 [Ref: MR-127]. Took the Oath of Allegiance before the Hon. Vernon Hebb in St. Mary's County in 1778 [Ref: J-1146, K-68]. Surgeon's Mate, 2nd Maryland Line, Aug., 1781, and 3rd Maryland Line, 1783 [Ref: S-170]. One William Watts died in St. Mary's County by Feb., 1784, leaving orphans Edward and John Watts [Ref: SO-68, SO-69].

WATTS, Willoughby. Private, St. Mary's County Militia, 1777 [Ref: M-212]. Took the Oath of Allegiance in St. Mary's County in 1780 [Ref: Q-123].

WAUGHOP, Henry. See "James Waughop," q.v.

WAUGHOP, James. Private, St. Mary's County Militia, 1777 [Ref: M-214, which listed the name as "Jams. Waughop"]. Took the Oath of Allegiance before the Hon. Vernon Hebb in St. Mary's County in 1778 [Ref: J-1146, K-68]. James Waughop died by April, 1785, leaving orphan sons James and Henry Waughop [Ref: SO-73, SO-76]. Also see "Thomas Palmer Waughop," q.v.

WAUGHOP, Thomas Palmer. Took the Oath of Allegiance before the Hon. Vernon Hebb in St. Mary's County in 1778 [Ref: J-1146, K-68]. Paid for making salt in July, 1782 [Ref: S-170]. Still living in June, 1785, at which time he was charged with "cutting and making waste on the lands of James Waughop's orphans" [Ref: SO-73, SO-76].

WAUGHOP, William C. Took the Oath of Allegiance before the Hon. Vernon Hebb in St. Mary's County in 1778 [Ref: J-1146, K-68].

WEAKLEY (WEAKLIN), Richard. Private, Capt. Uriah Forrest's Co., Flying Camp, St. Mary's County, July 28, 1776 [Ref: D-30, SM-116].

WEDGE, Jonathan. Private, Calvert County, enlisted by Lt. Nathaniel Wilson on Aug. 23, 1776 [Ref: D-34, which listed the name as "Jono. Wedge"]. Private, Capt. Benjamin Bond's Co., Calvert County Militia,

1778 [Ref: J-1146, M-149]. Took the Oath of Allegiance in Calvert County in 1778 [Ref: L-39].

WEEDEN (WHEEDEN), Justinian. Private, Capt. Uriah Forrest's Co., Flying Camp, St. Mary's County, July 28, 1776 [Ref: D-30, SM-116].

WEEMS, David (1706 - May 5, 1779). Private, Capt. James Grahame's Co., Calvert County Militia, 1778 [Ref: J-1146, M-148]. Took the Oath of Allegiance in Calvert County in 1778 [Ref: L-39]. He married twice: (1) Elizabeth Lane; (2) Ester Hill [Ref: Y-726].

WEEMS, George Washington. See "John Weems," q.v.

WEEMS, James. Took the Oath of Allegiance in Calvert County in 1778 [Ref: L-39]. Loaned money to the Continental Congress on March 23, 1778 [Ref: V-153]. Also see "John Weems" and "Samuel Chew," q.v.

WEEMS, James Jr. Private, Capt. Frisby Freeland's Co., Calvert County Militia, 1778 [Ref: J-1146, M-148]. Took the Oath of Allegiance in Calvert County in 1778 [Ref: L-39]. "James Weems, of James" was a private, Capt. Charles Williamson's Co., Calvert County Militia, 1778 [Ref: J-1146, M-147].

WEEMS, James (of David). Private, Capt. James Grahame's Co., Calvert County Militia, 1778 [Ref: J-1146, M-148]. Took the Oath of Allegiance in Calvert County in 1778 [Ref: L-39].

WEEMS, James (of John). Took the Oath of Allegiance in Calvert County in 1778 [Ref: L-39].

WEEMS, John (1737 - Sep. 7, 1813). Son of James Weems and Sarah Parker Stoddert. He married four times: (1) possibly Ann Compton; (2) Elizabeth Miller; (3) Alice Lee; and (4) Mary ----. Children: James, William Lock, John Compton, George Washington, Mary, Sarah Margaret, and probably several more (names not known). Sheriff of Calvert County, 1766-1769. Served in Lower House, 1771-1774, 1778-1784. Delegate to the Maryland Convention in 1775 [Ref: N-70]. Took the Oath of Allegiance in Calvert County in 1778 [Ref: L-39]. Lived in Anne Arundel County by 1796 and was in Louisville, Kentucky by 1812 [Ref: N-876].

WEEMS, John Jr. Took the Oath of Allegiance in Calvert County in 1778 [Ref: L-39]. Private, Capt. Thomas Cleland's Co., Calvert County Militia, 1778 [Ref: J-1146, M-147]. Member of the House of Delegates in 1783 [Ref: N-87].

WEEMS, John Compton. See "John Weems," q.v.

WEEMS, Margaret. See "Levin Covington Mackall," q.v.

WEEMS, Mary. See "John Weems," q.v.

WEEMS, Roger. See "William Allein," q.v.

WEEMS, Sarah. See "Samuel Chew" and "William Allein," q.v.

WEEMS. Sarah Margaret. See "John Weems," q.v.

WEEMS, William. Private, Capt. James Patterson's Co., Calvert County Militia, Aug. 10, 1777 [Ref: M-146]. Private, Capt. James Grahame's Co., Calvert County Militia, 1778 [Ref: J-1146, M-148].

WEEMS, William Lock. See "John Weems," q.v.
WELLS, Henry. Took the Oath of Allegiance in Calvert County in 1778 [Ref: L-39].
WELLS, John. Private, Calvert County, enlisted by Ensign James Somervill on July 26, 1776 [Ref: D-34].
WELLS, Martin. Private, Capt. Charles Williamson's Co., Calvert County Militia, 1778 [Ref: J-1146, M-147]. Took the Oath of Allegiance in Calvert County in 1778 [Ref: L-39].
WELLS, Martin (of Martin). Took the Oath of Allegiance in Calvert County in 1778 [Ref: L-39].
WELLS, Martin (of Thomas). Private, Capt. Charles Williamson's Co., Calvert County Militia, 1778 [Ref: J-1146, M-147, which listed the name as "Martin Wells, for Thom."]. Took the Oath of Allegiance in Calvert County in 1778 [Ref: L-39].
WELLS, Thomas. Took the Oath of Allegiance in Calvert County in 1778 [Ref: L-39].
WELLS, William. Took the Oath of Allegiance in Calvert County in 1778 [Ref: L-39].
WELSH (WELCH), Roger. "Roger Welch" was a private in St. Mary's County Militia in 1777 [Ref: M-215]. "Roger Welsh" died intestate by Sep., 1789 [Ref: SO-143].
WENNER, Daniel Jr. Private, Capt. James Patterson's Co., Calvert County Militia, Aug. 10, 1777 [Ref: M-146].
WEST, Thomas. Took the Oath of Allegiance before the Hon. John Shanks in St. Mary's County in 1778 [Ref: J-1146, K-70].
WHARTON, Jesse. Supplied provisions (wheat, mutton, or bacon) to the Army in St. Mary's County in 1780 [Ref: S-77].
WHARTON, Justinian. Took the Oath of Allegiance before the Hon. Jeremiah Jordan in St. Mary's County in 1778 [Ref: J-1146, K-67].
WHARTON, Revel. Seaman from St. Mary's County who served aboard the State ship *Defence* in 1777 [Ref: S-171].
WHEATLEY, Ann. See "James Fish," q.v.
WHEATLEY, Francis. Private, St. Mary's County Militia, 1777 [Ref: M-211]. Took the Oath of Allegiance before the Hon. John Ireland in St. Mary's County in 1778 [Ref: J-1146, K-65]. The Register of St. Francis Xavier Catholic Church states that Francis Wheatley and Anastatia Cecil were married June 17, 1771 [Ref: Sc-34].
WHEATLEY, Henrietta. See "Gabriel Newton," q.v.
WHEATLEY, Henry. Private, St. Mary's County, 2nd Maryland Line, March 15, 1777 to March 15, 1780, when discharged [Ref: D-174].
WHEATLEY, James. Took the Oath of Allegiance before the Hon. Henry Reeder in St. Mary's County in 1778 [Ref: J-1146, K-64]. One James Wheatley died by Aug., 1779, leaving a son William Wheatley who chose Rhodolph Manley as his guardian at that time [Ref: SO-24].

WHEATLEY, John. Private, St. Mary's County Militia, 1777 [Ref: M-214]. Private, 2nd Maryland Line, enlisted on May 29, 1778, for 9 months, and discharged on April 3, 1779 [Ref: D-175, D-329]. This name is listed twice among those who took the Oath of Allegiance in St. Mary's County in 1778: one before the Hon. Henry Tubman and one before the Hon. Richard Barnes [Ref: J-1146, K-66. K-70].

WHEATLEY, Richard. Two men with this name took the Oath of Allegiance before the Hon. Henry Tubman in St. Mary's County in 1778 [Ref: J-1146, K-70].

WHEATLEY, Samuel. Corporal, 2nd Maryland Line, probably from St. Mary's County; enlisted on Dec. 10, 1776 and was reported to be a prisoner of war on Aug. 22, 1777 [Ref: D-173].

WHEATLEY, Silvester. Private, St. Mary's County, enlisted May 14 or 16, 1778, for 3 years, 2nd Maryland Line; listed among the missing after the Battle of Camden in South Carolina on Aug. 16, 1780; served until discharged on July 1, 1781 [Ref: D-175, D-329, S-170]. The Register of St. Francis Xavier Catholic Church states that "Sylvester Wheatley and Sarah Medcalf, widow" were married March 21, 1768, and "Sylvester Wheatley and Elizabeth Fraiser (NC)" were married on Sep. 7, 1773 [Ref: SC-33, SC-34, which noted that "NC" meant "non-Catholic"].

WHEATLEY, Thomas. Took the Oath of Allegiance before the Hon. Henry Tubman in St. Mary's County in 1778 [Ref: J-1146, K-70].

WHEATLEY, William. Private, St. Mary's County Militia, 1777 [Ref: M-213]. Private, 2nd Maryland Line, from April 20, 1778, through at least Nov. 1, 1780 [Ref: D-174]. There was a William Wheatley, corporal, 1st Maryland Line, who enlisted on Dec. 10, 1776 and was killed on June 28, 1778 [Ref: D-173]. See "Rodolph Manley" and "William Whiteley" and "James Wheatley," q.v.

WHEELER, Elizabeth. See "Edward Gantt," q.v.

WHEELER, Francis. Private, St. Mary's County Militia, 1777 [Ref: M-210]. Took the Oath of Allegiance before the Hon. Richard Barnes in St. Mary's County in 1778 [Ref: J-1146, K-66]. The Register of St. Francis Xavier Catholic Church states Francis Wheeler and Ann Birchmore were married Dec. 19, 1775 [Ref: SC-35].

WHEELER, George. Private, Capt. Richard Parran's Co., Calvert County Militia, 1778 [Ref: J-1146, M-149]. Took the Oath of Allegiance in Calvert County in 1778 [Ref: L-39].

WHEELER, Ignatius. Took the Oath of Allegiance before the Hon. Jeremiah Jordan in St. Mary's County in 1778 [Ref: J-1146, K-67].

WHEELER, Justinian. Private, St. Mary's County Militia, 1777 [Ref: M-210]. Took the Oath of Allegiance before the Hon. John Ireland in St. Mary's County in 1778 [Ref: J-1146, K-65].

WHEELER, Robert. See "Edward Gantt," q.v.

WHERRITT, Abner. Private, St. Mary's County Militia, 1777 [Ref: M-214]. Took the Oath of Allegiance before the Hon. Bennett Biscoe in St. Mary's County in 1778 [Ref: J-1146, K-64].
WHERRITT, Britania. See "Thomas Wherritt," q.v.
WHERRITT, John. Private, St. Mary's County Militia, 1777 [Ref: M-214]. Took the Oath of Allegiance before the Hon. Bennett Biscoe in St. Mary's County in 1778 [Ref: J-1146, K-64].
WHERRITT, Nancy (Nance). See "Thomas Wherritt," q.v.
WHERRITT, Nicholas. Took the Oath of Allegiance before the Hon. Vernon Hebb in St. Mary's County in 1778 [Ref: J-1146, K-68].
WHERRITT, Samuel. See "Thomas Wherritt," q.v.
WHERRITT, Thomas (Jr.?). Private, St. Mary's County Militia, 1777 [Ref: M-214]. Took the Oath of Allegiance before the Hon. Vernon Hebb in St. Mary's County in 1778 [Ref: J-1146, K-68]. It appears that he was married twice (first wife's name unknown) and he had a daughter Nancy Ann, born March 8, 1778. Thomas married secondly to Margaret King in 1792 and moved to Kentucky, where daughter Nancy married John Foutch in 1796 [Ref: Information from Mrs. W. Kennedy W. Cox, of Santa Barbara, California, in a query in the *Maryland Genealogical Society Bulletin*, Vol. 15, No. 1 (Feb., 1974), page 18]. It should be noted, however, that in Thomas W. Westerfield's *Kentucky Genealogy and Biography, Volume 5*, page 298, it states that Thomas P. Wherritt (born 1839, Madison County, Kentucky) was a son of Samuel Wherritt (born 1799, Scott County, Kentucky, and died in 1877 in Richmond, Kentucky) and grandson of William Wherritt (born in St. Mary's County, Maryland). William had married twice: by his first wife he had five children, and his second wife was a Miss King to whom five sons and two daughters were born. He migrated to Scott County, Kentucky in 1796 and to Jessamine County in 1800. His ancestors had come to America from Wales and settled in Maryland during Lord Baltimore's time. It is curious that both Thomas and William Wherritt had married twice, both first wives' names were not known, and both married a King the second time.
WHERRITT, Thomas (Sr.?). Took the Oath of Allegiance before the Hon. Vernon Hebb in St. Mary's County in 1778 [Ref: J-1146, K-68]. One Thomas Wherritt died by Dec., 1787, when another Thomas Wherritt was appointed guardian of his children, namely Britania, Nance (or Nancy), and Thomas [Ref: SO-117, SO-200, SO-211, SO-214, SO-215]. See "Thomas Wherritt, Jr.," q.v.
WHERRITT, William. See "Thomas Wherritt," q.v.
WHILEY, George. Private, Capt. Richard Lane's Co., Calvert County Militia, 1778 [Ref: J-1146, M-150]. Took the Oath of Allegiance in Calvert County in 1778 [Ref: L-39, which listed the name as "George Whyley"].

WHILEY, Henry. Private, Capt. Richard Lane's Co., Calvert County Militia, 1778 [Ref: J-1146, M-150]. Took the Oath of Allegiance in Calvert County in 1778 [Ref: L-39, which listed the name as "Henry Whyley"].
WHILEY, James. Private, Capt. Thomas Cleland's Co., Calvert County Militia, 1778 [Ref: J-1146, M-147].
WHISTLER (WISTEL), Catherine. See "Robert Purdle (Purtle)," q.v.
WHITE, Barbara. See "James Smith," q.v.
WHITE, Dorothy. See "William Norris," q.v.
WHITE, Edward. Private, Capt. Uriah Forrest's Co., Flying Camp, St. Mary's County, July 28, 1776. Enlisted March 18, 1778, in the 2nd Maryland Line; corporal, July, 1780; discharged on Nov. 1, 1780 [Ref: D-30, S-171].
WHITE, James. Private, St. Mary's County Militia, 1777 [Ref: M-215]. Took the Oath of Allegiance before the Hon. Bennett Biscoe in St. Mary's County in 1778 [Ref: J-1146, K-64].
WHITE, Richard. Took the Oath of Allegiance in Calvert County in 1780 [Ref: Q-122].
WHITE, William. Private, Capt. Walter Smith's Co., Calvert County Militia, 1778 [Ref: J-1146, M-148]. Took the Oath of Allegiance in Calvert County in 1778 [Ref: L-39]. One William White was among the early Catholic settlers who went to Nelson County, Kentucky and settled on Cartwright's Creek in 1785 [Ref: MK-154].
WHITELEY, William. Private, St. Mary's County, 3rd Maryland Line, enlisted March 27, 1777, and discharged May 1, 1780 [Ref: D-177]. Also see "William Wheatley," q.v.
WHITTINGTON, Francis Jr. Private, Capt. Richard Lane's Co., Calvert County Militia, 1778 [Ref: J-1146, M-150]. Took the Oath of Allegiance in Calvert County in 1778 [Ref: L-39].
WHITTINGTON, Francis Sr. Took the Oath of Allegiance in Calvert County in 1778 [Ref: L-39].
WHITTINGTON, James. Private, Capt. Richard Lane's Co., Calvert County Militia, 1778 [Ref: J-1146, M-149].
WHITTINGTON, John. Private, Capt. James Grahame's Co., Calvert County Militia, 1778 [Ref: J-1146, M-149].
WHITTINGTON, Samuel. Private, Capt. James Grahame's Co., Calvert County Militia, 1778 [Ref: J-1146, M-148]. Took the Oath of Allegiance in Calvert County in 1778 [Ref: L-39].
WHITTINGTON, William. Private, Capt. Richard Lane's Co., Calvert County Militia, 1778 [Ref: J-1146, M-150]. Took the Oath of Allegiance in Calvert County in 1778 [Ref: L-39]. One William Whittington, of Maryland, moved to Montgomery County, Kentucky and a son H. Whittington was born there on April 13, 1814. By 1833 they were in Clay County, Missouri [Ref: MK-154].

WILDMAN, Cornelius (April, 1742 - Jan. 18, 1812). Private, St. Mary's County Militia, 1777 [Ref: M-211]. He married Tabitha Dorcas Miles (1742 - Oct. 28, 1811) and had at least one son Cornelius, Jr. (1776-1820). Took the Oath of Allegiance before the Hon. John Reeder in St. Mary's County in 1778 [Ref: J-1146, K-69]. Brother of "John Wildman," q.v. [Ref: R-477].

WILDMAN, John (1735 - Feb. 19, 1813). Private, St. Mary's County Militia, 1777 [Ref: M-211]. Took the Oath of Allegiance before the Hon. John Reeder in St. Mary's County in 1778 [Ref: J-1146, K-69]. Brother of "Cornelius Wildman," q.v. [Ref: R-477].

WILEY, John Jr. Private, Capt. Thomas Truman Greenfield's Co., Calvert County Militia, 1778 [Ref: J-1146, M-150].

WILKINSON, Ann. See "Ignatius Taylor," q.v.

WILKINSON, David. Private, Capt. Walter Smith's Co., Calvert County Militia, 1778 [Ref: J-1146, M-148].

WILKINSON, Elizabeth Smith. See "Richard Parran," q.v.

WILKINSON, James. Took the Oath of Allegiance before the Hon. Ignatius Fenwick, Jr. in St. Mary's County in 1778 [Ref: J-1146, K-68].

WILKINSON, Jane. See "John Wilkinson," q.v.

WILKINSON, John. (1) Private, Capt. James Patterson's Co., Calvert County Militia, Aug. 10, 1777 [Ref: M-146]. Private, Capt. Walter Smith's Co., Calvert County Militia, 1778 [Ref: J-1146, M-148]. (2) Second Lieutenant, Capt. Frederick Skinner's Co., Calvert County Militia, 1778 [Ref: J-1146, M-150]. One took the Oath of Allegiance in Calvert County in 1778 [Ref: L-39, which listed the name as "John Wilkerson"]. One John Wilkinson died intestate in St. Mary's County by Aug., 1777, at which time Jane Wilkinson petitioned the Court for her distributive share of the estate from Philip Evans, the administrator [Ref: SO-1, SO-3].

WILKINSON, Joseph. (1) First Major, Calvert County Militia, Jan. 6, 1776, and Colonel, 15th Bn., Calvert County Militia, April 16, 1778 [Ref: M-137, M-146, E-37]. County Lieutenant, Jan. 12, 1781 [Ref: M-137, G-272]. Took the Oath of Allegiance in Calvert County in 1778 [Ref: L-39]. (2) Private, Capt. Richard Lane's Co., Calvert County Militia, 1778 [Ref: J-1146, M-150]. Took the Oath of Allegiance in Calvert County in 1778 [Ref: L-39].

WILKINSON, Philip. Took the Oath of Allegiance in Calvert County in 1778 [Ref: L-39, which listed the name as "Phillip Wilkerson"].

WILKINSON, Richard. Private, Capt. Benjamin Bond's Co., Calvert County Militia, 1778 [Ref: J-1146, M-149]. Took the Oath of Allegiance in Calvert County in 1778 [Ref: L-39]. Richard Wilkinson and Mary Askey were married on Feb. 19, 1778, by Rev. Francis Lauder, of Christ Church Parish [Ref: K-34].

WILKINSON, William. Took the Oath of Allegiance before the Hon. Ignatius Fenwick, Jr. in St. Mary's County in 1778 [Ref: J-1146, K-68].

Private, St. Mary's County Militia, 1777 [Ref: M-211, which listed the name as "William Wilkerson"].

WILKINSON, Young. Took the Oath of Allegiance in Calvert County in 1778 [Ref: L-39].

WILL, Johnson. See "Sergt. Will Johnson," q.v.

WILLARD, John. Private, Maryland Line, 1781 [Ref: D-412].

WILLEN, Edward. Private, Capt. Walter Smith's Co., Calvert County Militia, 1778 [Ref: J-1146, M-148].

WILLEN, Thomas. Private, Capt. Walter Smith's Co., Calvert County Militia, 1778 [Ref: J-1146, M-148].

WILLIAMS, Aaron. Took the Oath of Allegiance in Calvert County in 1778 [Ref: L-39].

WILLIAMS, Aaron Jr. Private, Capt. Thomas Truman Greenfield's Co., Calvert County Militia, 1778 [Ref: J-1146, M-150]. Took the Oath of Allegiance in Calvert County in 1778 [Ref: L-39].

WILLIAMS, B. Private, St. Mary's County Militia, 1777 [Ref: M-215].

WILLIAMS, Benjamin (1738 - July 15, 1821). Ensign, Lower Bn., St. Mary's County Militia, Aug. 26, 1777, and Second Lieutenant, 21st Bn., April 16, 1778 [Ref: M-137, C-346, E-37]. Took the Oath of Allegiance before the Hon. Robert Armstrong in St. Mary's County in 1778 [Ref: J-1146, K-62]. "Capt. Benjamin Williams" is probably buried beside his wife Mary (1758-1814) in St. Inigoes Roman Catholic Cemetery (no stone). [Ref: R-478, HG-28, S-130].

WILLIAMS, Bennett. Born in 1754 in St. Mary's County, he lived in Granville County, North Carolina at the time of his enlistment in the Revolutionary War. He moved to Caswell County, North Carolina and also enlisted there. The area he lived in later became Person County and there he applied for and received pension S7956 in 1832 [Ref: MC-171, P-3849].

WILLIAMS, Charles. Private, 3rd Maryland Line. Applied for and received pension S35122 on May 5, 1818, aged 57, in St. Mary's County, stating he enlisted on March 27, 1780, and participated in the Battles of Camden, Guilford [Court House], Ninety-Six, and Eutaw Springs. Two weeks prior to the expiration of his term of enlistment he went as a guard to prisoners from Annapolis to Frederick and was there discharged in April, 1783. In 1820 he stated he had 6 children between the ages of 10 and 25 (4 sons and 3 daughters), but no names were given. A son James was mentioned in 1833. Charles died on Feb. 16, 1839, leaving two children of which Mary Hill was the only one named [Ref: D-178, U-40, P-3850, and *National Genealogical Society Quarterly*, Volume 34, No. 2 (1946), page 70]. This latter source stated "This pensioner is the only one of the name in the Maryland troops as found in the Revolutionary War records of the Pension Bureau." It should be noted, however, that there was a Charles Williams who served as a private from Harford County and another who was a private from Anne

Arundel County, even though they apparently were not pensioners [Ref: D-59]. There was also a Charles Williams in Calvert County who made a request to the Governor of Maryland for bounty money on June 1, 1779, but the nature of his request was not specified [Ref: V-226].

WILLIAMS, Colmore. Third Lieutenant, 1st Independent Maryland Co., Charles and Calvert Counties, 1776 [Ref: D-20].

WILLIAMS, Dorothy. See "John Long," q.v.

WILLIAMS, Dunbar. Private, Capt. Frisby Freeland's Co., Calvert County Militia, 1778 [Ref: J-1146, M-148]. Took the Oath of Allegiance in Calvert County in 1778 [Ref: L-39].

WILLIAMS, Elizabeth. See "Nathan Wood," q.v.

WILLIAMS, Frances. Miss Frances Williams, of Calvert County, loaned money to the Continental Congress on June 4, 1778 [Ref: V-173].

WILLIAMS, Francis. Private, Capt. Frisby Freeland's Co., Calvert County Militia, 1778 [Ref: J-1146, M-148]. See "William Williams," q.v.

WILLIAMS, Francis Jr. Private, Capt. Thomas Truman Greenfield's Co., Calvert County Militia, 1778 [Ref: J-1146, M-150].

WILLIAMS, Frazier. Took the Oath of Allegiance in Calvert County in 1778 [Ref: L-39].

WILLIAMS, Gabriel. Private, Capt. Uriah Forrest's Co., Flying Camp, St. Mary's County, July 28, 1776 [Ref: D-30]. Private, St. Mary's County Militia, 1777 [Ref: M-211]. Took the Oath of Allegiance before the Hon. Ignatius Fenwick, Jr. in St. Mary's County in 1778 [Ref: J-1146, K-68]. Discharged from the Army on June 18, 1778, but apparently re-enlisted as he was a sergeant in the 7th Maryland Line on Feb. 6, 1780, and in the recruiting service until July, 1780. Reduced to private on March 10, 1781 (no reason given), but returned to rank of sergeant on Aug. 28, 1781. Served in the 2nd Maryland Line until discharged on Feb. 6, 1783 [Ref: S-171].

WILLIAMS, George. Took the Oath of Allegiance before the Hon. Jeremiah Jordan in St. Mary's County in 1778 [Ref: J-1146, K-67].

WILLIAMS, Henry. Took the Oath of Allegiance before the Hon. Jeremiah Jordan in St. Mary's County in 1778 [Ref: J-1146, K-67].

WILLIAMS, Hugh. Private, St. Mary's County Militia, 1777 [Ref: M-211]. Took the Oath of Allegiance before the Hon. Ignatius Fenwick, Jr. in St. Mary's County in 1778 [Ref: J-1146, K-68]. The Register of St. Francis Xavier Catholic Church states that "Hugo Williams" and Lydia Stone were married March 21, 1773 [Ref: SC-34].

WILLIAMS, James. (1) Ensign, Lower Bn., St. Mary's County Militia, Aug. 26, 1777, and First Lieutenant, June 22, 1780 [Ref: M-137, A-205, C-346, F-201, M-213, S-171]. (2) Private, St. Mary's County Militia, 1777 [Ref: M-214]. One took the Oath of Allegiance before the Hon. Richard Barnes in St. Mary's County in 1778 [Ref: J-1146, K-66]. See "Charles Williams" and "William Williams," q.v.

WILLIAMS, John. There were several men with this name: (1) Private, Capt. Edward Wood's Co., Calvert County Militia, 1778 [Ref: J-1146, M-147]. (2) Private, Capt. Benjamin Bond's Co., Calvert County Militia, 1778 [Ref: J-1146, M-149]. (3) One took the Oath of Allegiance in Calvert County in 1778 [Ref: L-39]. (4) One John Williams applied for and received pension S35120 on April 21, 1818 (aged 63), in St. Mary's County, stating that he had served in the Maryland Line. In 1820 he received $44 annually from the State of Maryland [Ref: P-3858]. (5) There were several John Williams' in the Maryland Line, including two in the 1st and 2nd Regiments, 1778-1780 [Ref: D-173, D-175]. The 1835 pension rolls listed "John Williams 2d" in St. Mary's County and he died on Feb. 9, 1825, aged 70 [Ref: U-40]. The Treasurer of Maryland was directed in 1825 "to pay John Williams, St. Mary's County, a late meritorious soldier in the Revolutionary War, the half pay of a corporal as a provision to him in his indigent situation now advanced in life, and as a further remuneration for those services by which his country has been so essentially benefitted." [Ref: I-408].

WILLIAMS, Joseph. Elected to serve on a General Committee in St. Mary's County in accordance with the resolves of the Continental Congress in 1775 [Ref: MR-127]. Took the Oath of Allegiance before the Hon. Jeremiah Jordan in St. Mary's County in 1778 [Ref: J-1146, K-67]. The Register of St. Francis Xavier Catholic Church states that Joseph Williams and "Ann Heard, daughter of James Heard's widow" were married Feb. 5, 1771 [Ref: SC-34].

WILLIAMS, Margaret. See "William Smith," q.v.

WILLIAMS, Mary. See "Benjamin Williams," q.v.

WILLIAMS, Monica. See "Rodolph Jarboe," q.v.

WILLIAMS, Rebecca. See "Peregrine Long" and "John Tucker," q.v.

WILLIAMS, Simpson. Private, St. Mary's County Militia, 1777 [Ref: M-214]. Took the Oath of Allegiance before the Hon. Bennett Biscoe in St. Mary's County in 1778 [Ref: J-1146, K-64].

WILLIAMS, Talbott. Private, Capt. Edward Wood's Co., Calvert County Militia, 1778 [Ref: J-1146, M-147].

WILLIAMS, William. This name appeared twice as a private in Capt. Henry Skinner's Foot Co. of Hunting Hundred, Calvert County, 1777 [Ref: T-1814, O-125]. Also, a William Williams was elected to a General Committee in St. Mary's County in accordance with the resolves of the Continental Congress in 1775 [Ref: MR-127]. One William Williams died testate in St. Mary's County by July, 1778, with Francis and James Williams as his executors [Ref: SO-11].

WILLIAMS, Zephaniah (Zaphaniah). Private, St. Mary's County, enlisted May 2, 1778, for the duration of the war [Ref: D-329]. Private, 3rd Maryland Line, killed on Aug. 16, 1780, at the Battle of Camden in South Carolina [Ref: R-478, SM-116, D-175].

WILLIAMSON, Alexander. Private, Capt. Charles Williamson's Co., Calvert County Militia, 1778 [Ref: J-1146, M-147]. Private, 2nd Maryland Line, from May 24, 1778 to Sep., 1778 [Ref: D-175]. Applied for and received pension S7954 on May 5, 1834, in Iredell County, North Carolina, stating he was born on Nov. 24, 1762 in St. Mary's County, Maryland, and served in the Maryland Line. He moved to Richmond County, North Carolina, in 1804 [Ref: MC-173, P-3872].
WILLIAMSON, Basil. Private, Capt. Charles Williamson's Co., Calvert County Militia, 1778 [Ref: J-1146, M-147]. Took the Oath of Allegiance in Calvert County in 1778 [Ref: L-39].
WILLIAMSON, Charles (c1749 - Jan. 25, 1807). Son of Rev. James Williamson, Rector of All Saints' Parish, Calvert County. Charles married Sarah ---- and had 10 children (in 1800 census; names not given). Member of the House of Delegates, 1779-1781. Captain, 15th Bn., Calvert County Militia, April 10, 1776 through April 16, 1778. Recruiting Officer, 1777. County Sheriff, 1794. Court Justice in 1803 and 1805 [Ref: J-1146, E-37, A-329, M-138, M-147, N-82, N-84, N-893]. Took the Oath of Allegiance in Calvert County in 1778 [Ref: L-39].
WILLIAMSON, Henry. Private, Capt. Charles Williamson's Co., Calvert County Militia, 1778 [Ref: J-1146, M-147]. Took the Oath of Allegiance in Calvert County in 1778 [Ref: L-39].
WILLIAMSON, James. Private, Capt. Charles Williamson's Co., Calvert County Militia, 1778 [Ref: J-1146, M-147]. Took the Oath of Allegiance in Calvert County in 1778 [Ref: L-39]. See "Charles Williamson," q.v.
WILLIAMSON, Sarah. See "Charles Williamson," q.v.
WILLIN, Edward. Took the Oath of Allegiance in Calvert County in 1778 [Ref: L-39].
WILLIN, Keziah. See "William Gardiner," q.v.
WILLIN, Mary. See "John McDowell," q.v.
WILLINGHAM, John Baptist. Private, St. Mary's County, enlisted May 13, 1778, for 9 months, 3rd Maryland Line; discharged in Feb., 1779 [Ref: D-329, S-171].
WILLS, Thomas Jr. Private, Capt. Richard Lane's Co., Calvert County Militia, 1778 [Ref: J-1146, M-150].
WILMAN, Rhode. Private, St. Mary's County Militia, 1777 [Ref: M-213].
WILSON, Ann. See "Allen Roberts" and "John Brome (Broome)," q.v.
WILSON, Barbara. See "Richard Burroughs," q.v.
WILSON, Benjamin. (1) Private, Capt. James Patterson's Co., Calvert County Militia, Aug. 10, 1777 [Ref: M-146]. Private, Capt. John Mackall's Co., Calvert County Militia, 15th Bn., June 12, 1778 [Ref: M-146]. (2) Private, Capt. Frederick Skinner's Co., Calvert County Militia, 1778 [Ref: J-1146, M-150]. One took the Oath of Allegiance in Calvert County in 1778 [Ref: L-39].

WILSON, Hillery (Helarey). Private, Capt. Frederick Skinner's Co., Calvert County Militia, 1778 [Ref: J-1146, M-150]. Took the Oath of Allegiance in Calvert County in 1778 [Ref: L-39].

WILSON, James. Private, Capt. Thomas Cleland's Co., Calvert County Militia, 1778 [Ref: J-1146, M-147]. Took the Oath of Allegiance in Calvert County in 1778 [Ref: L-39]. James Wilson and Rebecca Skinner were married on Nov. 25, 1779, by Rev. Francis Lauder, of Christ Church Parish [Ref: K-35].

WILSON, John. Private, Capt. Benjamin Bond's Co., Calvert County Militia, 1778 [Ref: J-1146, M-149]. Took the Oath of Allegiance in Calvert County in 1778 [Ref: L-39].

WILSON, John Jr. Took the Oath of Allegiance in Calvert County in 1778 [Ref: L-39]. Private, Capt. Thomas Cleland's Co., Calvert County Militia, 1778 [Ref: J-1146, M-147].

WILSON, Nathaniel. Second Lieutenant, Calvert County, July, 1776, First Lieutenant, Capt. Benjamin Bond's Co., Calvert County Militia, April 16, 1778, and Captain, Feb. 2, 1779 [Ref: D-33, E-37, E-290, J-1146, M-138, M-149, which latter source listed the name as "Nathan Willson"]. Took the Oath of Allegiance in Calvert County in 1778 [Ref: L-39]. Nathaniel Wilson and Anne Brome were married on Dec. 3, 1778, by Rev. Francis Lauder, of Christ Church Parish [Ref: K-34].

WILSON, Thomas. Private, Capt. Frederick Skinner's Co., Calvert County Militia, 1778 [Ref: J-1146, M-150]. Private, Capt. John Mackall's Co., Calvert County Militia, 15th Bn., June 12, 1778 [Ref: M-146]. Took the Oath of Allegiance in Calvert County in 1778 [Ref: L-39].

WILSON, William. Private, Calvert County, enlisted by Lt. Frederick Skinner on Aug. 23, 1776 [Ref: D-33].

WIMSATT, Ann. See "Richard Wimsatt," q.v.

WIMSATT, Baptist. See "John Baptist Wimsatt," q.v.

WIMSATT, Cloe, Dorothy, and Gerrard. See "Robert Wimsatt," q.v.

WIMSATT (WINSETT), Henry. Private, St. Mary's County Militia, 1777 [Ref: M-214].

WIMSATT (WINSETT), Ignatius. Private, St. Mary's County Militia, 1777 [Ref: M-214]. Took the Oath of Allegiance before the Hon. Richard Barnes in St. Mary's County in 1778 [Ref: J-1146, K-66]. The Register of St. Francis Xavier Catholic Church states that Ignatius Wimsatt and Mary Medley were married Dec. 31, 1772 [Ref: SC-34].

WIMSATT (WINSETT), James. Private, St. Mary's County Militia, 1777 [Ref: M-211]. Private, 2nd Maryland Line, enlisted May 29, 1778, for 9 months; discharged April 14, 1779 [Ref: S-171, D-329, which listed the name as "James Wimseld," and D-175 which listed the name as "James Winsett"]. Took the Oath of Allegiance before the Hon. Richard Barnes in St. Mary's County in 1778 [Ref: J-1146, K-66]. Supplied provisions (wheat, mutton, or bacon) to the Army in 1780 [Ref: S-77].

WIMSATT (WINSETT), Jemima. See "Joseph Davis," q.v.

WIMSATT (WINSETT), John. Private, St. Mary's County Militia, 1777 [Ref: M-211]. Two men with this name took the Oath of Allegiance in St. Mary's County in 1778: one before the Hon. Richard Barnes and one before the Hon. Henry Reeder [Ref: J-1146, K-64, K-66]. The Register of St. Francis Xavier Catholic Church states that one John Wimsatt and Sarah Howard were married on March 23, 1778 [Ref: SC-36]. See "Richard Wimsatt," q.v.

WIMSATT (WINSETT), John Baptist. "Baptist Wimsatt" was a private, St. Mary's County Militia, 1777 [Ref: M-212]. "John Baptist Wimsatt" took the Oath of Allegiance before the Hon. John Ireland in St. Mary's County in 1778 [Ref: J-1146, K-65].

WIMSATT (WINSETT), Joseph. Private, St. Mary's County Militia, July 27, 1777 [Ref: M-212]. Private, Continental Army, until discharged on Dec. 3, 1781 [Ref: S-171, H-11, D-412, which latter source listed the name as "Joseph Winsett"]. See "Robert Wimsatt," q.v.

WIMSATT (WINSETT), Raphael (Oct., 1753, St. Mary's County, Maryland - May 25, 1828, Nelson County, Kentucky). Private, 1st Maryland Line, 1776, and 2nd Maryland Line, discharged on Jan. 10, 1780 [Ref: D-174]. Raphael Winsett married Susannah Cissell in 1783 and about a year later they moved to Kentucky in co. with Francis Pain, a neighbor (aged 83 in 1840). Raphael Wimsatt (or Winsett) applied for a pension on May 27, 1818, in Nelson County, and died in 1828. Stephen Wimsett was mentioned in 1823, but no relationship was stated. Raphael's widow Susannah applied for and received pension W621 on Oct. 12, 1840, aged 81. A grandson, Silvester Winsett, aged 29, was living in Nelson County in 1840 and was appointed "to take charge of the widow Susannah Winsett." Also, in 1840, a Susannah Cissell, aged 64, was living in Nelson County. She had moved to Kentucky with them in 1784, but no relationship was stated [Ref: P-3908, X-126, MK-157, M-158, W-59, which latter source mistakenly stated that Susannah had died on May 25, 1828].

WIMSATT (WINSETT), Richard. Private, St. Mary's County Militia, 1777 [Ref: M-211]. Took the Oath of Allegiance before the Hon. Richard Barnes in St. Mary's County in 1778 [Ref: J-1146, K-66]. One Richard Wimsatt died by Feb., 1794, leaving orphans Ann (above the age of 14 in 1798) and John [Ref: SO-206, SO-272].

WIMSATT (WINSETT), Robert (1742-1796). Private, St. Mary's County Militia, 1777 [Ref: M-211]. Took the Oath of Allegiance before the Hon. Richard Barnes in St. Mary's County in 1778 [Ref: J-1146, K-66]. Robert Wimsatt married Dorothy Abell [Ref: Y-752]. He died by Feb., 1796, at which time his son Joseph (aged 15 in Dec., 1795) was bound to George Mattingly to learn to be a bricklayer. His son Gerrard (above the age of 14) chose Samuel Wimsatt as his guardian in Dec., 1796. Dorothy Wimsatt was appointed guardian of her two daughters Susanna and Cloe in Oct., 1796 [Ref: SO-238, SO-251, SO-254].

WIMSATT, Silvester and Susannah. See "Raphael Wimsatt," q.v.
WIMSATT (WINSETT), Stephen. Private, St. Mary's County Militia, 1777 [Ref: M-210]. Took the Oath of Allegiance before the Hon. Richard Barnes in St. Mary's County in 1778 [Ref: J-1146, K-66]. See "Raphael Wimsatt (Winsett)," q.v.
WIMSATT (WINSETT), Thomas. Private (substitute), St. Mary's County, July 27, 1781 [Ref: D-384, which listed the name "Thos. Wimsott"].
WIMSATT (WINSETT), William (1759 - Feb. 22, 1820). Private, St. Mary's County Militia, 1777 [Ref: M-210]. Took the Oath of Allegiance before the Hon. Richard Barnes in St. Mary's County in 1778 [Ref: J-1146, K-66]. "William Wimsatt, of Newtown" died at Key's Mill in 1820 [Ref: R-479].
WINFIELD, John. Took the Oath of Allegiance in Calvert County in 1778 [Ref: L-39].
WINFIELD, Jona. Private, Capt. Edward Wood's Co., Calvert County Militia, 1778 [Ref: J-1146, M-147]. Took the Oath of Allegiance in Calvert County in 1778 [Ref: L-39, which listed the name as "Jonah Wenfield"].
WINFIELD, Richard. Private, Capt. Charles Williamson's Co., Calvert County Militia, 1778 [Ref: J-1146, M-147]. Took the Oath of Allegiance in Calvert County in 1778 [Ref: L-39].
WINGATE, Henry. Private, St. Mary's County Militia, 1777 [Ref: M-210].
WINNALL, William. Took the Oath of Allegiance in Calvert County in 1778 [Ref: L-39]. Private, Capt. Edward Wood's Co., Calvert County Militia, 1778 [Ref: J-1146, M-147, which listed the name as "William Winnel"].
WINNERT, Violette. See "John Dent," q.v.
WINSETT, Raphael. See "Raphael Wimsatt," q.v.
WISE, Adam Sr. Took the Oath of Allegiance in St. Mary's County in 1780 [Ref: Q-123]. The Register of St. Andrew's Episcopal Church states that one Adam Wise and Susannah Bryan were married Nov. 2, 1779 [Ref: MB-383].
WISE, Adam (of Adam). Private, St. Mary's County Militia, 1777 [Ref: M-212]. Took the Oath of Allegiance before the Hon. Robert Watts in St. Mary's County in 1778 [Ref: J-1146, K-62]. See "Adam Wise, Sr.," q.v.
WISE, Adam (of Richard). Private, St. Mary's County Militia, 1777 [Ref: M-212]. Took the Oath of Allegiance in St. Mary's County in 1780 [Ref: Q-123]. See "Adam Wise, Sr.," q.v.
WISE, Caleb. Private, St. Mary's County Militia, 1777 [Ref: M-212]. The Register of St. Andrew's Episcopal Church states that Caleb Wise and Catharine Wise were married (by license) Nov. 13, 1783 [Ref: MB-385].
WISE, Caleb (of Richard). Took the Oath of Allegiance in St. Mary's County in 1780 [Ref: Q-124].
WISE, Catherine. See "Caleb Wise," q.v.

WISE, Elijah. Private, St. Mary's County Militia, 1777 [Ref: M-213]. Took the Oath of Allegiance in St. Mary's County in 1780 [Ref: Q-124].
WISE, Elisha. Private, St. Mary's County Militia, 1777 [Ref: M-211].
WISE, Henrietta. See "Stephen Greenwell," q.v.
WISE, Margaret. See "George Jenkins," q.v.
WISE, Mary. See "Matthew Wise, of Matthew," q.v.
WISE, Matthew. Private, St. Mary's County Militia, 1777 [Ref: M-215]. Took the Oath of Allegiance in St. Mary's County in 1780 [Ref: Q-124]. See "Matthew Wise, of Matthew," q.v.
WISE, Matthew Sr. Took the Oath of Allegiance before the Hon. Robert Watts in St. Mary's County in 1778 [Ref: J-1146, K-62].
WISE, Matthew (of Matthew). Took the Oath of Allegiance before the Hon. Robert Watts in St. Mary's County in 1778 [Ref: J-1146, K-62]. Private, St. Mary's County Militia, 1777 [Ref: M-212, which listed the name as "Matthews Wise"]. One Matthew Wise died by Feb., 1797, at which time his daughter Mary (above the age of 14) chose Richard Wise, son of Matthew Wise, as her guardian [Ref: SO-255].
WISE, Miel. Took the Oath of Allegiance in St. Mary's County in 1780 [Ref: Q-124]. Myre or Myel (?) Wise was a private, St. Mary's County Militia, 1777 [Ref: M-213].
WISE, Richard. Took the Oath of Allegiance in St. Mary's County in 1780 [Ref: Q-124]. See "Matthew Wise, of Matthew," q.v.
WISE, Robert. Private, St. Mary's County Militia, 1777 [Ref: M-215].
WISE, Thomas. Private, St. Mary's County Militia, 1777 [Ref: M-212]. Private, St. Mary's County, enlisted May 25, 1778, for 9 months [Ref: D-330]. Took the Oath of Allegiance before the Hon. Robert Watts in St. Mary's County in 1778 [Ref: J-1146, K-62]. Private (substitute), St. Mary's County, Aug. 5, 1781 [Ref: D-384]. Private, Maryland Line, Continental Army, discharged on Dec. 3, 1781 [Ref: D-412, S-109, H-11]. Thomas Wise also took the Oath of Allegiance in St. Mary's County in 1780 [Ref: Q-124].
WISE, William. Private, St. Mary's County Militia, 1777 [Ref: M-212]. Took the Oath of Allegiance before the Hon. Robert Watts in St. Mary's County in 1778 [Ref: J-1146, K-62]. The Register of St. Andrew's Episcopal Church states that William Wise and Elizabeth Clocker were married Nov. 19, 1778 [Ref: MB-382].
WISEMAN, George. Property destroyed by the British in St. Mary's County in 1781 [Ref: S-171].
WISEMAN, Richard. Private, St. Mary's County Militia, 1777 [Ref: M-215]. Took the Oath of Allegiance before the Hon. Robert Watts in St. Mary's County in 1778 [Ref: J-1146, K-62].
WISEMAN, Thomas. Private, 4th Maryland Line, enlisted Dec. 10, 1776 and reported missing at the Battle of Camden in South Carolina on Aug. 16, 1780 [Ref: D-173].
WISTEL, Catherine and William. See "Robert Purdle (Purtle)," q.v.

WITHERINGTON, James. Private, St. Mary's County Militia, 1777 [Ref: M-210]. Took the Oath of Allegiance in St. Mary's County in 1780 [Ref: Q-124].
WITHERINGTON, John. Private, St. Mary's County Militia, 1777 [Ref: M-210].
WOENS(?), Joseph. Private, St. Mary's County Militia, 1777 [Ref: M-213].
WOLFE, Elias. Took the Oath of Allegiance in Calvert County in 1778 [Ref: L-39, which listed the name as "Elias Woolf"]. Private, Capt. Thomas Truman Greenfield's Co., Calvert County Militia, 1778 [Ref: J-1146, M-150, which listed the name as "Elias Woolf"].
WOLFE, Francis. Took the Oath of Allegiance in Calvert County in 1778 [Ref: L-39, which listed the name as "Francis Woolf"].
WOLFE, Francis Jr. Took the Oath of Allegiance in Calvert County in 1778 [Ref: L-39].
WOLFE, John. Took the Oath of Allegiance in Calvert County in 1778 [Ref: L-39, which listed the name as "John Woolf"]. Private, Capt. Frisby Freeland's Co., Calvert County Militia, 1778 [Ref: J-1146, M-148, which listed the name as "John Wolfe"].
WOLSTENHOLME, Daniel. Member of the committee that passed the "Remonstrances to Parliament" in 1765. Collector of Customs in 1776. County Clerk of St. Mary's County in 1777 [Ref: S-171].
WOOD, Alexander. See "John Wood," q.v.
WOOD, Ann. See "Notley Tippett," q.v.
WOOD, Benjamin. Private, Capt. Frisby Freeland's Co., Calvert County Militia, 1778 [Ref: J-1146, M-148]. Took the Oath of Allegiance in Calvert County in 1778 [Ref: L-39]. Also see "John Wood" and "John Wood, Jr." and "Edward Wood," q.v.
WOOD, Dorsey. Private, 3rd Maryland Line, 1778 [Ref: D-177].
WOOD, Edward. Captain, 15th Bn., Calvert County Militia, from April 10, 1776 through at least April 17, 1778 [Ref: M-139, M-147, A-320, E-37]. There was an Edward Wood who was a son of Benjamin Wood who died testate in Calvert County and his will was probated on Jan. 10, 1760, naming Edward as his executor [Ref: *Maryland Calendar of Wills, Volume 11, 1753-1760*, page 254]. One Edward Wood married Rebecca Gray on Sep. 15, 1778, by Rev. Francis Lauder, of Christ Church Parish [Ref: K-34].
WOOD, Edward Jr. Took the Oath of Allegiance in Calvert County in 1778 [Ref: L-39].
WOOD, Eleanor and Elizabeth. See "John Wood," q.v.
WOOD, Henry. Private, Calvert County, enlisted by Lt. Frederick Skinner on Aug. 23, 1776 [Ref: D-33].
WOOD, Isaac. See "John Wood," q.v.
WOOD, Jacob. Private, 4th Maryland Line, 1778-1780 [Ref: D-179].
WOOD, James. Private, Capt. Edward Wood's Co., Calvert County Militia, 1778 [Ref: J-1146, M-147]. Took the Oath of Allegiance in Calvert

County in 1778 [Ref: L-39]. Private, 4th Maryland Line, enlisted Feb. 3, 1780 [Ref: D-179]. See "John Wood," q.v.

WOOD, Jeremiah. Private, Capt. Benjamin Bond's Co., Calvert County Militia, 1778 [Ref: J-1146, M-149]. Took the Oath of Allegiance in Calvert County in 1778 [Ref: L-39].

WOOD, Jesse. Private, Capt. Richard Parran's Co., Calvert County Militia, 1778 [Ref: J-1146, M-149]. Took the Oath of Allegiance in Calvert County in 1778 [Ref: L-39]. Jesse Wood and Hannah Ward were married on Jan. 20, 1778, by Rev. Francis Lauder, of Christ Church Parish [Ref: K-33]. See "John Wood," q.v.

WOOD, John. (1) Ensign, Capt. Edward Wood's Co., Calvert County Militia, from April 10, 1776 through at least April 16, 1778 [Ref: M-139, M-147, A-320, E-37]. Took the Oath of Allegiance in Calvert County in 1778 [Ref: L-39]. (2) Private, Capt. Henry Skinner's Foot Co. of Hunting Hundred, Calvert County, 1777 [Ref: T-1814, O-125]. Took the Oath of Allegiance in Calvert County in 1778 [Ref: L-39]. There were two men named John Wood who were privates in the 3rd Maryland Line: one enlisted on April 28, 1777, was captured, exchanged, rejoined on July 22, 1778, and then was discharged on April 28, 1780; the other enlisted on Jan. 26, 1777 and was still in service on Nov. 1, 1780 [Ref: D-176, D-177]. John Wood, of St. Mary's County, was on the payroll of Capt. Sothoron's Co., 6th Militia Bn., when called out for the alarm for Dunmore's fleet on Aug. 3, 1776 [Ref: Maryland State Papers, Series D, Revolutionary War, Box 6, folder 1]. One John Wood died intestate in St. Mary's County by Aug., 1785, and Sarah Wood was his administratrix. Land records indicate they lived on the tract "Wood's Pleasure" which was situated in Upper Resurrection Hundred in St. Mary's County on the Charles County line. By 1794 Sarah had moved to Rowan County, North Carolina, and by 1811 to Williamson County, Tennessee, where she died in 1829. The children of John and Sarah Wood were Richard, Nancy, John, Jonathan (died in 1843 or 1844 in Bedford County, Tennessee), Leonard (who moved to Christian County, Kentucky), Alexander (born 1781, married twice: first to Polly Pinkston in 1813, secondly to Catharine Bringle in 1846, and died in 1858 in Tipton County, Tennessee), Eleanor or Nelly (married Turner Pinkston in 1797 in Rowan County, North Carolina), Peggy (married a McBride), and James Wood [Ref: SO-79, and the research files of Oliver C. Wood, of Antlers, Oklahoma, and Jo White Linn, of Salisbury, North Carolina, and Henry C. Peden, Jr., of Bel Air, Maryland]. There was also a John Wood (1763-1843) who was from Anne Arundel County or Calvert County and married Elizabeth Sunderland, daughter of Benjamin Sunderland and Elizabeth Taylor (All Saint's Parish in Calvert County) on April 22, 1783. Their children were Obediah, Eleanor, Robert, Levi, John, Elizabeth, Benjamin, William, Sarah, Willis, Isaac, and Jesse. John served in the Maryland Line during the war and was captain of a news boat that sailed between Herring Bay and Baltimore Town at the end of the war. He died in Albemarle County, Virginia on July 28, 1843, and his wife Elizabeth died in 1857 [Ref: Research files of Stewart Estes Wood, of Glen Allen, Virginia (1991), and Maryland State Papers, Revolutionary War, Series D, Box 15, folder 11, and Box 11, folder 19, and Box 2, folder 5, at the Maryland State Archives, Annapolis, Maryland].

WOOD, John Jr. (1) Private, St. Mary's County Militia, 1777 [Ref: M-210]. (2) Private, Capt. Edward Wood's Co., Calvert County Militia, 1778 [Ref: J-1146, M-147]. One John Wood, son of John, was a grandson of Benjamin Wood who died in Calvert County. His will was probated on Jan. 10, 1760 [Ref: *Maryland Calendar of Wills, Volume 11, 1753-1760*, page 254; Wills Liber 30, f. 784].

WOOD, John Sr. Private, St. Mary's County Militia, 1777 [Ref: M-209]. Took the Oath of Allegiance before the Hon. Henry Tubman in St. Mary's County in 1778 [Ref: J-1146, K-70].

WOOD, Jonathan. (1) Private, Capt. Frisby Freeland's Co., Calvert County Militia, 1778 [Ref: J-1146, M-148]. Took the Oath of Allegiance in Calvert County in 1778 [Ref: L-39]. (2) Private, St. Mary's County Militia, 1777 [Ref: M-213]. See "John Wood," q.v.

WOOD, Joseph. Private, Capt. Frisby Freeland's Co., Calvert County Militia, 1778 [Ref: J-1146, M-148]. This name appeared twice in the list of those who took the Oath of Allegiance in Calvert County in 1778 [Ref: L-39].

WOOD, Leonard. (1) Private, Capt. Frisby Freeland's Co., Calvert County Militia, 1778 [Ref: J-1146, M-148]. Took the Oath of Allegiance in Calvert County in 1778 [Ref: L-39]. (2) Private, Capt. Edward Wood's Co., Calvert County Militia, 1778 [Ref: J-1146, M-147, which listed the name as "Lunard Wood"]. (3) Private, St. Mary's County Militia, 1777 [Ref: M-209]. Took the Oath of Allegiance before the Hon. Henry Tubman in St. Mary's County in 1778 [Ref: J-1146, K-70]. See "John Wood," q.v.

WOOD, Leonard Jr. Took the Oath of Allegiance in Calvert County in 1778 [Ref: L-39].

WOOD, Levi. See "John Wood," q.v.

WOOD, Misael. Private, St. Mary's County Militia, 1777 [Ref: M-210]. Supplied provisions (wheat, mutton, or bacon) to the Army in 1780 and 1781 [Ref: S-77, S-171]. There was a "Masael Wood" who was the son of James Wood who died testate in St. Mary's County by Dec. 3, 1777, and left all his property to his son Masael [Ref: Wills Liber JJ #1, ff. 30-31]. Another "Misael Wood" applied for and received pension S32079 in Washington County, Georgia, on Nov. 5, 1832, stating he was born Feb. 28, 1761 in St. Mary's County and moved with his parents (names not given) to Halifax County, North Carolina, where he enlisted and served in the North Carolina Line. After the war he moved to Georgia [Ref: MC-175, P-3934].

WOOD, Nancy. See "John Wood," q.v.

WOOD, Nathan. Private, St. Mary's County Militia, 1777 [Ref: M-210]. Nathan Wood married Elizabeth Williams on Feb. 23, 1783 (banns published), St. Mary's County, by Rev. John Stephen, Rector of All Faith's Parish [Ref: I-536].

WOOD, Obediah, Peggy, Richard, and Robert. See "John Wood," q.v.

WOOD, Robert Slye. Private, St. Mary's County Militia, 1777 [Ref: M-211].

WOOD, Sabret. Private, Capt. Edward Wood's Co., Calvert County Militia, 1778 [Ref: J-1146, M-147]. Took the Oath of Allegiance in Calvert County in 1778 [Ref: L-39].

WOOD, Samuel. Private, Capt. Richard Lane's Co., Calvert County Militia, 1778 [Ref: J-1146, M-149].

WOOD, Sarah. See "John Wood," q.v.

WOOD, Thomas. Private, Capt. Uriah Forrest's Co., Flying Camp, St. Mary's County, July 28, 1776 [Ref: D-30, SM-116]. One Thomas Wood was a private, 4th Maryland Line, 1777-1780, and another Thomas Wood was a private, 3rd Maryland Line, enlisted July 10, 1777 and was reported dead on April 3, 1778 [Ref: D-176, D-178].

WOOD, William. (1) Ensign, 15th Bn., Jan. 3, 1776 [Ref: M-139]. (2) Private, Capt. Henry Skinner's Foot Co. of Hunting Hundred, Calvert County, 1777 [Ref: T-1814, O-125]. Private, Capt. Frisby Freeland's Co., Calvert County Militia, 1778 [Ref: J-1146, M-148]. One William Wood took the Oath of Allegiance in Calvert County in 1778 [Ref: L-39]. One William Wood was a private, 4th Maryland Line, enlisted Dec. 20, 1776, and discharged Dec. 20, 1779 [Ref: D-179]. See "John Wood," q.v.

WOOD, William H. Took the Oath of Allegiance in Calvert County in 1778 [Ref: L-39].

WOOD, William (of Edward). Private, Capt. Charles Williamson's Co., Calvert County Militia, 1778 [Ref: J-1146, M-148].

WOOD, William (of Leonard). Private, Capt. Thomas Truman Greenfield's Co., Calvert County Militia, 1778 [Ref: J-1146, M-150].

WOOD, Willis. See "John Wood," q.v.

WOODARD, John. Took the Oath of Allegiance before the Hon. Henry Reeder in St. Mary's County in 1778 [Ref: J-1146, K-64].

WOODBURN, Daniel. Private, St. Mary's County Militia, 1777 [Ref: M-209]. Took the Oath of Allegiance before the Hon. Henry G. Sothoron in St. Mary's County in 1778 [Ref: J-1146, K-69]. See "Jonathan Woodburn," q.v.

WOODBURN, Esbert and Hezekiah. See "Jonathan Woodburn," q.v.

WOODBURN, John. Private, St. Mary's County Militia, 1777 [Ref: M-209]. Took the Oath of Allegiance before the Hon. Henry Tubman in St. Mary's County in 1778 [Ref: J-1146, K-70]. John Woodburn was the administrator of William Woodburn in Dec., 1777, and Samuel Tennison was administrator of a William Woodburn in Nov., 1793 [Ref: SO-6, SO-14, SO-202].

WOODBURN, Jonathan. Private, St. Mary's County Militia, 1777 [Ref: M-209]. Private, 2nd Maryland Line, enlisted June 1, 1778, for 9 months, and discharged on April 3, 1779 [Ref: D-329, D-175, which listed the name as "Jona. Woodbarn"]. Took the Oath of Allegiance before the Hon. Henry G. Sothoron in St. Mary's County in 1778 [Ref: J-1146, K-69]. Applied for and received pension S35144 on April 21, 1818, aged 59, in St. Mary's County. In 1820 he had the following people living with him, all were named Woodburn, but no relationships were stated: Lydia, aged 35; Leonard, aged 25; Daniel, aged 20; Michael, aged 18; Esbert, aged 16; and Hezekiah, aged about 21 months [Ref: P-3940]. Jonathan Woodburn was still on the pension rolls in 1835 [Ref: U-40].

WOODBURN, Leonard, Lydia and Michael. See "Jonathan Woodburn," q.v.

WOODBURN, William. See "John Woodburn," q.v.

WOODFIELD, Thomas. Private, Capt. Richard Lane's Co., Calvert County Militia, 1778 [Ref: J-1146, M-150]. Took the Oath of Allegiance in Calvert County in 1778 [Ref: L-39].

WOODS, Sarah. See "Thomas Gantt, Jr.," q.v.

WOODWARD, Dorcas. See "William Brown," q.v.

WOODWARD, Joseph. Ensign, Upper Bn., St. Mary's County Militia, Aug. 26, 1777, and Second Lieutenant, Nov. 18, 1779 [Ref: M-139, M-212, C-346, F-18, SM-116, S-171].

WOODWARD, Monica. See "William Clarke," q.v.

WOODWARD, William. Private, St. Mary's County Militia, 1777 [Ref: M-212]. Took the Oath of Allegiance before the Hon. John Shanks in St. Mary's County in 1778 [Ref: J-1146, K-70].

WOOTEN, Ignatius. Private, St. Mary's County Militia, 1777 [Ref: M-214]. Property destroyed by the British in 1781 [Ref: S-171].

WOOTEN, John. Private, St. Mary's County Militia, 1777 [Ref: M-214].

WOOTON, Thomas. Private, St. Mary's County Militia, 1777 [Ref: M-212]. The Register of St. Andrew's Episcopal Church states that "Thomas Wotton" and Nancy Bentley were married (by publication) June 5, 1781 [Ref: MB-384]. "Thomas Wooton, farmer" moved from Upper Newtown to Charles County, Maryland, after 1810 [Ref: X-87].

WORTHINGTON, Charles (of Nicholas). Took the Oath of Allegiance in Calvert County in 1778 [Ref: L-39].

WORTHINGTON, Nicholas. Took the Oath of Allegiance in Calvert County in 1778 [Ref: L-39].

WRIGHT, Randall. Took the Oath of Allegiance in Calvert County in 1778 [Ref: L-39].

YATES, Ann. See "James Jordan," q.v.

YATES, Bennett (Bennit). Private, St. Mary's County Militia, 1777 [Ref: M-212].
YATES, Edward. Took the Oath of Allegiance before the Hon. John Ireland in St. Mary's County in 1778 [Ref: J-1146, K-65].
YATES, Henry. Private, St. Mary's County Militia, 1777 [Ref: M-210].
YATES, James. Private, St. Mary's County Militia, 1777 [Ref: M-212, which mistakenly listed the name as "James Gates"]. Private, 2nd Maryland Line, enlisted on March 29 or May 30, 1778, for 9 months, and discharged on April 3, 1779 [Ref: D-180, D-330, S-171]. Took the Oath of Allegiance before the Hon. Richard Barnes in St. Mary's County in 1778 [Ref: J-1146, K-66]. The Register of St. Francis Xavier Catholic Church states that "James Yets" and Ann Thompson were married in Oct., 1779 [Ref: SC-36].
YATES, John. Took the Oath of Allegiance before the Hon. Ignatius Fenwick, Jr. in St. Mary's County in 1778 [Ref: J-1146, K-68].
YATES, Joseph. Private, Capt. Thomas Cleland's Co., Calvert County Militia, 1778 [Ref: J-1146, M-147].
YATES, Martin. Private, St. Mary's County Militia, 1777 [Ref: M-211]. Took the Oath of Allegiance before the Hon. Richard Barnes in St. Mary's County in 1778 [Ref: J-1146, K-66].
YATES, Mary. See "James Brewer," q.v.
YATES, Richard. Boatswain's Mate on the State ship *Defence* from April 28 to Dec. 8, 1777 [Ref: D-661]. Private, St. Mary's County, 2nd Maryland Line, enlisted March 17, 1778, and died on Sep. 15, 1778. While serving as a boatswain he was "blown up on barge" in 1778 [Ref: R-481, SM-116, D-180, S-171].
YATES, Vachel. Private, St. Mary's County, who served aboard the State ship *Defence* in 1776. Sergeant of Marines, 1777. Lieutenant of Marines, Feb. 15, 1777 to Oct. 15, 1777, and Captain of Marines to Dec. 15, 1777 [Ref: D-606, D-661, S-25]. Reported "blown up on barge" in 1778 [Ref: R-481, SM-116, S-171].
YATES, William. Private, St. Mary's County, who served in the 2nd Maryland Line and died on Sep. 15, 1778 [Ref: SM-116, S-171].
YATES, Zachariah. See "Richard Pierceall," q.v.
YOE, Ann. See "Benjamin Dasheal (Dasheel)," q.v.
YOE, Anna, Benjamin, Harriet, and James. See "John Yoe," q.v.
YOE, John. Private, Capt. Benjamin Bond's Co., Calvert County Militia, 1778 [Ref: J-1146, M-149]. Took the Oath of Allegiance in Calvert County in 1778 [Ref: L-39]. John Yoe, son of Robert and Mary Yoe, was born on July 29, 1750. He married Katherine Skinner on March 19, 1781, and a son Benjamin was born Sep. 4, 1782. Katherine died on Sep. 17, 1782, aged 25. John Yoe married Miss Susanna Miller of Rousby on Jan. 9, 1785, and had these children: John (born Oct. 5, 1785); Robert (born July 12, 1787); Mary (born June 21, 1789); Anna (born Aug. 27,

1791); James (born Aug. 28, 1793); William (born Jan. 28, 1795); Harriet (born Jan. 28, 1799); and, Walter (born Nov. 16, 1800). [Ref: O-31].

YOE, Joseph or Robert [sic]. Private, 5th Maryland Line, enlisted on June 8, 1778; sergeant on July 1, 1778; reduced to private on May 1, 1779; reported "deserted" on Oct. 1, 1779 [Ref: D-259].

YOE, Katherine, Mary, Robert, and Susanna. See "John Yoe," q.v.

YOE, Thomas. Private, 5th Maryland Line, from June 4, 1778 until March 19, 1779, when discharged [Ref: D-259]. There was also a Thomas Yoe, drummer, 7th Maryland Line, from Aug. 15, 1777 to at least Nov., 1780 [Ref: D-259].

YOE, Walter. See "John Yoe," q.v.

YOE, William. Private, Capt. Benjamin Bond's Co., Calvert County Militia, 1778 [Ref: J-1146, M-149]. Took the Oath of Allegiance in Calvert County in 1778 [Ref: L-39].

YOUNG, Anne. See "Philemon Young," q.v.

YOUNG, Benjamin. "Benjamin H. Young" was a private, Capt. Edward Wood's Co., Calvert County Militia, 1778 [Ref: J-1146, M-147]. "Benjamin Young" was a private, 4th Maryland Line, until discharged on Dec. 8, 1779 [Ref: D-180].

YOUNG, Daniel. Private, Capt. Benjamin Bond's Co., Calvert County Militia, 1778 [Ref: J-1146, M-149]. Took the Oath of Allegiance in Calvert County in 1778 [Ref: L-39].

YOUNG, David. Private, Capt. Edward Wood's Co., Calvert County Militia, 1778 [Ref: J-1146, M-147].

YOUNG, Francis. See "Parker Young," q.v.

YOUNG, George. Private, Calvert County, enlisted by Lt. Nathaniel Wilson on Aug. 23, 1776 [Ref: D-34]. Private, Capt. Walter Smith's Co., Calvert County Militia, 1778 [Ref: J-1146, M-148]. Took the Oath of Allegiance in Calvert County in 1778 [Ref: L-39]. George Young and Mary Hillen were married on Dec. 16, 1777, by Rev. Francis Lauder, of Christ Church Parish [Ref: K-33]. Also see "Parker Young," q.v.

YOUNG, Henry. See "Philemon Young," q.v.

YOUNG, Jane. See "Parker Young," q.v.

YOUNG, John Abell. Private, St. Mary's County Militia, 1777 [Ref: M-212].

YOUNG, Joseph. Private, Capt. Henry Skinner's Foot Co. of Hunting Hundred, Calvert County, 1777 [Ref: T-1814, O-125].

YOUNG, Mary and Miles. See "Parker Young," q.v.

YOUNG, Parker. Took the Oath of Allegiance in Calvert County in 1778 [Ref: L-39]. Parker Young was born On Feb. 19, 1714/5, married Sarah ----, and had these children: Francis (born July 26, 1749); Jane (born March 27, 1753); George Parker (born March 26, 1755); Mary (born Sep. 4, 1757); William Miles (born Dec. 4, 1760); Thomas (born March 14, 1765); and, Miles (born May 22, 1771). [Ref: O-32].

YOUNG, Philemon. Took the Oath of Allegiance in Calvert County in 1778 [Ref: L-39]. Philemon Young, son of Henry and Anne Young, was born on Aug. 1, 1712 [Ref: O-31].

YOUNG, Robert. Private, St. Mary's County Militia, 1777 [Ref: M-212]. Took the Oath of Allegiance before the Hon. Robert Watts in St. Mary's County in 1778 [Ref: J-1146, K-62].

YOUNG, Sarah and Thomas. See "Parker Young," q.v.

YOUNG, William. Private, St. Mary's County Militia, 1777 [Ref: M-210].

YOUNG, William Miles. See "Parker Young," q.v.

YOUNGER, Benjamin. Private, Capt. Benjamin Bond's Co., Calvert County Militia, 1778 [Ref: J-1146, M-149]. Took the Oath of Allegiance in Calvert County in 1778 [Ref: L-39].

YOUNGER, David (of John). Private, Capt. Edward Wood's Co., Calvert County Militia, 1778 [Ref: J-1146, M-147, which listed the name as "David Younger, for John"].

YOUNGER, George. Private, Capt. Edward Wood's Co., Calvert County Militia, 1778 [Ref: J-1146, M-147]. Took the Oath of Allegiance in Calvert County in 1778 [Ref: L-39].

YOUNGER, John. Private, Calvert County, enlisted by Lt. Frederick Skinner on Aug. 23, 1776 [Ref: D-33]. Took the Oath of Allegiance in Calvert County in 1778 [Ref: L-39].

YOUNGER, John Jr. Private, Capt. Edward Wood's Co., Calvert County Militia, 1778 [Ref: J-1146, M-147]. Took the Oath of Allegiance in Calvert County in 1778 [Ref: L-37, which listed the name as "John Jounger, Jr."].

YOUNGER, John (of Margarett). Private, Capt. Edward Wood's Co., Calvert County Militia, 1778 [Ref: J-1146, M-147, which listed the name as "John Younger, for Margarett"].

YOUNGER, Joseph. Private, Capt. Edward Wood's Co., Calvert County Militia, 1778 [Ref: J-1146, M-147]. Took the Oath of Allegiance in Calvert County in 1778 [Ref: L-39]. Joseph Younger and Jean Charlton were married on April 15, 1779, by Rev. Francis Lauder, of Christ Church Parish [Ref: K-35].

YOUNGER, William. Private, Capt. Edward Wood's Co., Calvert County Militia, 1778 [Ref: J-1146, M-147]. Took the Oath of Allegiance in Calvert County in 1778 [Ref: L-39].

Other books by the author:

A Closer Look at St. John's Parish Registers [Baltimore County, Maryland], 1701-1801
A Collection of Maryland Church Records
A Guide to Genealogical Research in Maryland: 5th Edition, Revised and Enlarged
Abstracts of the Ledgers and Accounts of the Bush Store and Rock Run Store, 1759-1771
Abstracts of the Orphans Court Proceedings of Harford County, 1778-1800
Abstracts of Wills, Harford County, Maryland, 1800-1805
Baltimore City [Maryland] Deaths and Burials, 1834-1840
Baltimore County, Maryland, Overseers of Roads, 1693-1793
Bastardy Cases in Baltimore County, Maryland, 1673-1783
Bastardy Cases in Harford County, Maryland, 1774-1844
Bible and Family Records of Harford County, Maryland Families: Volume V
Children of Harford County: Indentures and Guardianships, 1801-1830
Colonial Delaware Soldiers and Sailors, 1638-1776
*Colonial Families of the Eastern Shore of Maryland
Volumes 5, 6, 7, 8, 9, 11, 12, 13, 14, and 16*
Colonial Maryland Soldiers and Sailors, 1634-1734
Dr. John Archer's First Medical Ledger, 1767-1769, Annotated Abstracts
Early Anglican Records of Cecil County
*Early Harford Countians, Individuals Living in Harford County, Maryland in Its Formative Years
Volume 1: A to K, Volume 2: L to Z, and Volume 3: Supplement*
Harford County Taxpayers in 1870, 1872 and 1883
Harford County, Maryland Divorce Cases, 1827-1912: An Annotated Index
Heirs and Legatees of Harford County, Maryland, 1774-1802
Heirs and Legatees of Harford County, Maryland, 1802-1846
Inhabitants of Baltimore County, Maryland, 1763-1774
Inhabitants of Cecil County, Maryland, 1649-1774
Inhabitants of Harford County, Maryland, 1791-1800
Inhabitants of Kent County, Maryland, 1637-1787
*Joseph A. Pennington & Co., Havre De Grace, Maryland Funeral Home Records:
Volume II, 1877-1882, 1893-1900*
Maryland Bible Records, Volume 1: Baltimore and Harford Counties
Maryland Bible Records, Volume 2: Baltimore and Harford Counties
Maryland Bible Records, Volume 3: Carroll County
Maryland Bible Records, Volume 4: Eastern Shore
Maryland Deponents, 1634-1799
Maryland Deponents: Volume 3, 1634-1776
*Maryland Public Service Records, 1775-1783: A Compendium of Men and Women of
Maryland Who Rendered Aid in Support of the American Cause against
Great Britain during the Revolutionary War*
*Marylanders to Carolina: Migration of Marylanders to
North Carolina and South Carolina prior to 1800*

Marylanders to Kentucky, 1775-1825

Methodist Records of Baltimore City, Maryland: Volume 1, 1799-1829

Methodist Records of Baltimore City, Maryland: Volume 2, 1830-1839

Methodist Records of Baltimore City, Maryland: Volume 3, 1840-1850 (East City Station)

More Maryland Deponents, 1716-1799

More Marylanders to Carolina: Migration of Marylanders to North Carolina and South Carolina prior to 1800

More Marylanders to Kentucky, 1778-1828

Outpensioners of Harford County, Maryland, 1856-1896

Presbyterian Records of Baltimore City, Maryland, 1765-1840

Quaker Records of Baltimore and Harford Counties, Maryland, 1801-1825

Quaker Records of Northern Maryland, 1716-1800

Quaker Records of Southern Maryland, 1658-1800

Revolutionary Patriots of Anne Arundel County, Maryland

Revolutionary Patriots of Baltimore Town and Baltimore County, 1775-1783

Revolutionary Patriots of Calvert and St. Mary's Counties, Maryland, 1775-1783

Revolutionary Patriots of Caroline County, Maryland, 1775-1783

Revolutionary Patriots of Cecil County, Maryland

Revolutionary Patriots of Delaware, 1775-1783

Revolutionary Patriots of Dorchester County, Maryland, 1775-1783

Revolutionary Patriots of Frederick County, Maryland, 1775-1783

Revolutionary Patriots of Harford County, Maryland, 1775-1783

Revolutionary Patriots of Kent and Queen Anne's Counties

Revolutionary Patriots of Lancaster County, Pennsylvania

Revolutionary Patriots of Maryland, 1775-1783: A Supplement

Revolutionary Patriots of Maryland, 1775-1783: Second Supplement

Revolutionary Patriots of Montgomery County, Maryland, 1776-1783

Revolutionary Patriots of Prince George's County, Maryland, 1775-1783

Revolutionary Patriots of Talbot County, Maryland, 1775-1783

Revolutionary Patriots of Worcester and Somerset Counties, Maryland, 1775-1783

Revolutionary Patriots of Washington County, Maryland, 1776-1783

St. George's (Old Spesutia) Parish, Harford County, Maryland: Church and Cemetery Records, 1820-1920

St. John's and St. George's Parish Registers, 1696-1851

Survey Field Book of David and William Clark in Harford County, Maryland, 1770-1812

The Crenshaws of Kentucky, 1800-1995

The Delaware Militia in the War of 1812

Union Chapel United Methodist Church Cemetery Tombstone Inscriptions, Wilna, Harford County, Maryland

www.ingramcontent.com/pod-product-compliance
Lightning Source LLC
Chambersburg PA
CBHW060554230426
43670CB00011B/1813